NOVELS
for Students

Advisors

Jayne M. Burton is a teacher of English, a member of the Delta Kappa Gamma International Society for Key Women Educators, and currently a master's degree candidate in the Interdisciplinary Study of Curriculum and Instruction and English at Angelo State University.

Mary Beth Maggio teaches seventh grade language arts in Schaumburg, Illinois.

Tom Shilts is the youth librarian at the Okemos branch of Capital Area District Library in Okemos, Michigan. He holds an MSLS degree from Clarion University of Pennsylvania and an MA in U.S. History from the University of North Dakota.

Amy Spade Silverman has taught at independent schools in California, Texas, Michigan, and New York. She holds a bachelor of arts degree from the University of Michigan and a master of fine arts degree from the University of Houston. She is a member of the National Council of Teachers of English and Teachers and Writers. She is an exam reader for Advanced Placement Literature and Composition. She is also a poet, published in *North American Review*, *Nimrod*, and *Michigan Quarterly Review*, among others.

Mary Turner holds a BS in Secondary Education from East Texas State University and a Master of Education from Western Kentucky University. She teaches English 7 and AP English 12 literature and composition at SBEC in Southaven, Mississippi.

Brian Woerner teaches English at Troy High School in Troy, Ohio. He is also a Program Associate of the Ohio Writing Project at Miami University.

NOVELS
for Students

Presenting Analysis, Context, and Criticism on Commonly Studied Novels

VOLUME 39

Sara Constantakis, Project Editor

Foreword by Anne Devereaux Jordan

GALE
CENGAGE Learning

Detroit • New York • San Francisco • New Haven, Conn • Waterville, Maine • London

Novels for Students, Volume 39

Project Editor: Sara Constantakis

Rights Acquisition and Management: Margaret Chamberlain-Gaston, Jacqueline Flowers

Composition: Evi Abou-El-Seoud

Manufacturing: Rhonda Dover

Imaging: John Watkins

Product Design: Pamela A. E. Galbreath, Jennifer Wahi

Content Conversion: Katrina Coach

Product Manager: Meggin Condino

For product information and technology assistance, contact us at **Gale Customer Support, 1-800-877-4253.**
For permission to use material from this text or product, submit all requests online at **www.cengage.com/permissions.**
Further permissions questions can be emailed to **permissionrequest@cengage.com**

While every effort has been made to ensure the reliability of the information presented in this publication, Gale, a part of Cengage Learning, does not guarantee the accuracy of the data contained herein. Gale accepts no payment for listing; and inclusion in the publication of any organization, agency, institution, publication, service, or individual does not imply endorsement of the editors or publisher. Errors brought to the attention of the publisher and verified to the satisfaction of the publisher will be corrected in future editions.

Gale
27500 Drake Rd.
Farmington Hills, MI, 48331-3535

ISBN-13: 978-1-4144-6702-3
ISBN-10: 1-4144-6702-8

ISSN 1094-3552

This title is also available as an e-book.
ISBN-13: 978-1-4144-7368-0
ISBN-10: 1-4144-7368-0
Contact your Gale, a part of Cengage Learning sales representative for ordering information.

Printed in Mexico
1 2 3 4 5 6 7 16 15 14 13 12

Table of Contents

The Informed Dialogue: Interacting with Literature

When we pick up a book, we usually do so with the anticipation of pleasure. We hope that by entering the time and place of the novel and sharing the thoughts and actions of the characters, we will find enjoyment. Unfortunately, this is often not the case; we are disappointed. But we should ask, has the author failed us, or have we failed the author?

We establish a dialogue with the author, the book, and with ourselves when we read. Consciously and unconsciously, we ask questions: "Why did the author write this book?" "Why did the author choose that time, place, or character?" "How did the author achieve that effect?" "Why did the character act that way?" "Would I act in the same way?" The answers we receive depend upon how much information about literature in general and about that book specifically we ourselves bring to our reading.

Young children have limited life and literary experiences. Being young, children frequently do not know how to go about exploring a book, nor sometimes, even know the questions to ask of a book. The books they read help them answer questions, the author often coming right out and *telling* young readers the things they are learning or are expected to learn. The perennial classic, *The Little Engine That Could, tells* its readers that, among other things, it is good to help others and brings happiness:

"Hurray, hurray," cried the funny little clown and all the dolls and toys. "The good little boys and girls in the city will be happy because you helped us, kind, Little Blue Engine."

In picture books, messages are often blatant and simple, the dialogue between the author and reader one-sided. Young children are concerned with the end result of a book—the enjoyment gained, the lesson learned—rather than with how that result was obtained. As we grow older and read further, however, we question more. We come to expect that the world within the book will closely mirror the concerns of our world, and that the author will *show* these through the events, descriptions, and conversations within the story, rather than *telling* of them. We are now expected to do the interpreting, carry on our share of the dialogue with the book and author, and glean not only the author's message, but comprehend how that message and the overall affect of the book were achieved. Sometimes, however, we need help to do these things. *Novels for Students* provides that help.

A novel is made up of many parts interacting to create a coherent whole. In reading a novel, the more obvious features can be easily spotted—theme, characters, plot—but we may overlook the more subtle elements that greatly influence how the novel is perceived by the reader: viewpoint, mood and tone, symbolism, or the use of humor. By focusing on both the obvious and more subtle literary elements within a novel, *Novels for Students* aids readers in both analyzing for message and in determining how and why that message is communicated. In the discussion on Harper Lee's *To Kill a Mockingbird* (Vol. 2), for example, the mockingbird as a symbol of innocence is dealt with, among other things, as is the importance of Lee's use of humor which "enlivens a serious plot, adds depth to the characterization, and creates a sense of familiarity and universality." The reader comes to understand the internal elements of each novel discussed—as well as the external influences that help shape it.

"The desire to write greatly," Harold Bloom of Yale University says, "is the desire to be elsewhere, in a time and place of one's own, in an originality that must compound with inheritance, with an anxiety of influence." A writer seeks to create a unique world within a story, but although it is unique, it is not disconnected from our own world. It speaks to us *because* of what the writer brings to the writing from our world: how he or she was raised and educated; his or her likes and dislikes; the events occurring in the real world at the time of the writing, and while the author was growing up. When we know what an author has brought to his or her work, we gain a greater insight into both the "originality" (the world of the book), and the things that "compound" it. This insight enables us to question that created world and find answers more readily. By informing ourselves, we are able to establish a more effective dialogue with both book and author.

Novels for Students, in addition to providing a plot summary and descriptive list of characters—to remind readers of what they have read—also explores the external influences that shaped each book. Each entry includes a discussion of the author's background, and the historical context in which the novel was written. It is vital to know, for instance, that when Ray Bradbury was writing *Fahrenheit 451* (Vol. 1), the threat of Nazi domination had recently ended in Europe, and the McCarthy hearings were taking place in Washington, D.C. This information goes far in answering the question, "Why did he write a story of oppressive government control and book burning?" Similarly, it is important to know that Harper Lee, author of *To Kill a Mockingbird,* was

born and raised in Monroeville, Alabama, and that her father was a lawyer. Readers can now see why she chose the south as a setting for her novel—it is the place with which she was most familiar—and start to comprehend her characters and their actions.

Novels for Students helps readers find the answers they seek when they establish a dialogue with a particular novel. It also aids in the posing of questions by providing the opinions and interpretations of various critics and reviewers, broadening that dialogue. Some reviewers of *To Kill A Mockingbird,* for example, "faulted the novel's climax as melodramatic." This statement leads readers to ask, "Is it, indeed, melodramatic?" "If not, why did some reviewers see it as such?" "If it is, why did Lee choose to make it melodramatic?" "Is melodrama ever justified?" By being spurred to ask these questions, readers not only learn more about the book and its writer, but about the nature of writing itself.

The literature included for discussion in *Novels for Students* has been chosen because it has something vital to say to us. *Of Mice and Men, Catch-22, The Joy Luck Club, My Antonia, A Separate Peace* and the other novels here speak of life and modern sensibility. In addition to their individual, specific messages of prejudice, power, love or hate, living and dying, however, they and all great literature also share a common intent. They force us to *think*—about life, literature, and about others, not just about ourselves. They pry us from the narrow confines of our minds and thrust us outward to confront the world of books and the larger, real world we all share. *Novels for Students* helps us in this confrontation by providing the means of enriching our conversation with literature and the world, by creating an *informed* dialogue, one that brings true pleasure to the personal act of reading.

Sources

Harold Bloom, *The Western Canon, The Books and School of the Ages,* Riverhead Books, 1994.

Watty Piper, *The Little Engine That Could,* Platt & Munk, 1930.

Anne Devereaux Jordan
Senior Editor, TALL (Teaching and Learning Literature)

Introduction

Purpose of the Book

The purpose of *Novels for Students* (*NfS*) is to provide readers with a guide to understanding, enjoying, and studying novels by giving them easy access to information about the work. Part of Gale's "For Students" Literature line, *NfS* is specifically designed to meet the curricular needs of high school and undergraduate college students and their teachers, as well as the interests of general readers and researchers considering specific novels. While each volume contains entries on "classic" novels frequently studied in classrooms, there are also entries containing hard-to-find information on contemporary novels, including works by multicultural, international, and women novelists. Entries profiling film versions of novels not only diversify the study of novels but support alternate learning styles, media literacy, and film studies curricula as well.

The information covered in each entry includes an introduction to the novel and the novel's author; a plot summary, to help readers unravel and understand the events in a novel; descriptions of important characters, including explanation of a given character's role in the novel as well as discussion about that character's relationship to other characters in the novel; analysis of important themes in the novel; and an explanation of important literary techniques and movements as they are demonstrated in the novel.

In addition to this material, which helps the readers analyze the novel itself, students are also provided with important information on the literary and historical background informing each work. This includes a historical context essay, a box comparing the time or place the novel was written to modern Western culture, a critical essay, and excerpts from critical essays on the novel. A unique feature of *NfS* is a specially commissioned critical essay on each novel, targeted toward the student reader.

The "literature to film" entries on novels vary slightly in form, providing background on film technique and comparison to the original, literary version of the work. These entries open with an introduction to the film, which leads directly into the plot summary. The summary highlights plot changes from the novel, key cinematic moments, and/or examples of key film techniques. As in standard entries, there are character profiles (noting omissions or additions, and identifying the actors), analysis of themes and how they are illustrated in the film, and an explanation of the cinematic style and structure of the film. A cultural context section notes any time period or setting differences from that of the original work, as well as cultural differences between the time in which the original work was written and the time in which the film adaptation was made. A film entry concludes with a critical overview and critical essays on the film.

To further help today's student in studying and enjoying each novel or film, information on media adaptations is provided (if available), as well as suggestions for works of fiction, nonfiction, or film on similar themes and topics. Classroom aids include ideas for research papers and lists of critical and reference sources that provide additional material on the novel. Film entries also highlight signature film techniques demonstrated, and suggest media literacy activities and prompts to use during or after viewing a film.

Selection Criteria

The titles for each volume of *NfS* are selected by surveying numerous sources on notable literary works and analyzing course curricula for various schools, school districts, and states. Some of the sources surveyed include: high school and undergraduate literature anthologies and textbooks; lists of award-winners, and recommended titles, including the Young Adult Library Services Association (YALSA) list of best books for young adults. Films are selected both for the literary importance of the original work and the merits of the adaptation (including official awards and widespread public recognition).

Input solicited from our expert advisory board—consisting of educators and librarians—guides us to maintain a mix of "classic" and contemporary literary works, a mix of challenging and engaging works (including genre titles that are commonly studied) appropriate for different age levels, and a mix of international, multicultural and women authors. These advisors also consult on each volume's entry list, advising on which titles are most studied, most appropriate, and meet the broadest interests across secondary (grades 7–12) curricula and undergraduate literature studies.

How Each Entry Is Organized

Each entry, or chapter, in *NfS* focuses on one novel. Each entry heading lists the full name of the novel, the author's name, and the date of the novel's publication. The following elements are contained in each entry:

Introduction: a brief overview of the novel which provides information about its first appearance, its literary standing, any controversies surrounding the work, and major conflicts or themes within the work. Film entries identify the original novel and provide understanding of the film's reception and reputation, along with that of the director.

Author Biography: in novel entries, this section includes basic facts about the author's life,

and focuses on events and times in the author's life that inspired the novel in question.

Plot Summary: a factual description of the major events in the novel. Lengthy summaries are broken down with subheads. Plot summaries of films are used to uncover plot differences from the original novel, and to note the use of certain film angles or other techniques.

Characters: an alphabetical listing of major characters in the novel. Each character name is followed by a brief to an extensive description of the character's role in the novel, as well as discussion of the character's actions, relationships, and possible motivation. In film entries, omissions or changes to the cast of characters of the film adaptation are mentioned here, and the actors' names—and any awards they may have received—are also included.

Characters are listed alphabetically by last name. If a character is unnamed—for instance, the narrator in *Invisible Man*—the character is listed as "The Narrator" and alphabetized as "Narrator." If a character's first name is the only one given, the name will appear alphabetically by that name.

Variant names are also included for each character. Thus, the full name "Jean Louise Finch" would head the listing for the narrator of *To Kill a Mockingbird*, but listed in a separate cross-reference would be the nickname "Scout Finch."

Themes: a thorough overview of how the major topics, themes, and issues are addressed within the novel. Each theme discussed appears in a separate subhead. While the key themes often remain the same or similar when a novel is adapted into a film, film entries demonstrate how the themes are conveyed cinematically, along with any changes in the portrayal of the themes.

Style: this section addresses important style elements of the novel, such as setting, point of view, and narration; important literary devices used, such as imagery, foreshadowing, symbolism; and, if applicable, genres to which the work might have belonged, such as Gothicism or Romanticism. Literary terms are explained within the entry but can also be found in the Glossary. Film entries cover how the director conveyed the meaning, message, and mood of the work using film in comparison to the author's use of language, literary device, etc., in the original work.

Historical Context: in novel entries, this section outlines the social, political, and cultural climate in which the author lived and the novel was created. This section may include descriptions of related historical events, pertinent aspects of daily life in the culture, and the artistic and literary sensibilities of the time in which the work was written. If the novel is a historical work, information regarding the time in which the novel is set is also included. Each section is broken down with helpful subheads. Film entries contain a similar Cultural Context section because the film adaptation might explore an entirely different time period or culture than the original work, and may also be influenced by the traditions and views of a time period much different than that of the original author.

Critical Overview: this section provides background on the critical reputation of the novel or film, including bannings or any other public controversies surrounding the work. For older works, this section includes a history of how the novel or film was first received and how perceptions of it may have changed over the years; for more recent novels, direct quotes from early reviews may also be included.

Criticism: an essay commissioned by *NfS* which specifically deals with the novel or film and is written specifically for the student audience, as well as excerpts from previously published criticism on the work (if available).

Sources: an alphabetical list of critical material used in compiling the entry, with full bibliographical information.

Further Reading: an alphabetical list of other critical sources which may prove useful for the student. It includes full bibliographical information and a brief annotation.

Suggested Search Terms: a list of search terms and phrases to jumpstart students' further information seeking. Terms include not just titles and author names but also terms and topics related to the historical and literary context of the works.

In addition, each novel entry contains the following highlighted sections, set apart from the main text as sidebars:

Media Adaptations: if available, a list of audiobooks and important film and television adaptations of the novel, including source information. The list also includes stage adaptations, musical adaptations, etc.

Topics for Further Study: a list of potential study questions or research topics dealing with the novel. This section includes questions related to other disciplines the student may be studying, such as American history, world history, science, math, government, business, geography, economics, psychology, etc.

Compare and Contrast: an "at-a-glance" comparison of the cultural and historical differences between the author's time and culture and late twentieth century or early twenty-first century Western culture. This box includes pertinent parallels between the major scientific, political, and cultural movements of the time or place the novel was written, the time or place the novel was set (if a historical work), and modern Western culture. Works written after the mid-1970s may not have this box.

What Do I Read Next?: a list of works that might give a reader points of entry into a classic work (e.g., YA or multicultural titles) and/or complement the featured novel or serve as a contrast to it. This includes works by the same author and others, works from various genres, YA works, and works from various cultures and eras.

The film entries provide sidebars more targeted to the study of film, including:

Film Technique: a listing and explanation of four to six key techniques used in the film, including shot styles, use of transitions, lighting, sound or music, etc.

Read, Watch, Write: media literacy prompts and/or suggestions for viewing log prompts.

What Do I See Next?: a list of films based on the same or similar works or of films similar in directing style, technique, etc.

Other Features

NfS includes "The Informed Dialogue: Interacting with Literature," a foreword by Anne Devereaux Jordan, Senior Editor for *Teaching and Learning Literature (TALL)*, and a founder of the Children's Literature Association. This essay provides an enlightening look at how readers interact with literature and how *Novels for Students* can help teachers show students how to enrich their own reading experiences.

A Cumulative Author/Title Index lists the authors and titles covered in each volume of the *NfS* series.

A Cumulative Nationality/Ethnicity Index breaks down the authors and titles covered in each volume of the *NfS* series by nationality and ethnicity.

A Subject/Theme Index, specific to each volume, provides easy reference for users who may be studying a particular subject or theme rather than a single work. Significant subjects, from events to broad themes, are included.

Each entry may include illustrations, including photo of the author, stills from film adaptations, maps, and/or photos of key historical events, if available.

Citing Novels for Students

When writing papers, students who quote directly from any volume of *NfS* may use the following general forms. These examples are based on MLA style; teachers may request that students adhere to a different style, so the following examples may be adapted as needed.

When citing text from *NfS* that is not attributed to a particular author (i.e., the Themes, Style, Historical Context sections, etc.), the following format should be used in the bibliography section:

"*Night.*" *Novels for Students.* Ed. Marie Rose Napierkowski. Vol. 4. Detroit: Gale, 1998. 234–35.

When quoting the specially commissioned essay from *NfS* (usually the first piece under the "Criticism" subhead), the following format should be used:

Miller, Tyrus. Critical Essay on "*Winesburg, Ohio.*" *Novels for Students.* Ed. Marie Rose Napierkowski. Vol. 4. Detroit: Gale, 1998. 335–39.

When quoting a journal or newspaper essay that is reprinted in a volume of *NfS,* the following form may be used:

Malak, Amin. "Margaret Atwood's *The Handmaid's Tale* and the Dystopian Tradition." *Canadian Literature* 112 (Spring 1987): 9–16. Excerpted and reprinted in *Novels for Students.* Vol. 4. Ed. Marie Rose Napierkowski. Detroit: Gale, 1998. 133–36.

When quoting material reprinted from a book that appears in a volume of *NfS,* the following form may be used:

Adams, Timothy Dow. "Richard Wright: 'Wearing the Mask.'" In *Telling Lies in Modern American Autobiography.* University of North Carolina Press, 1990. 69–83. Excerpted and reprinted in *Novels for Students.* Vol. 1. Ed. Diane Telgen. Detroit: Gale, 1997. 59–61.

We Welcome Your Suggestions

The editorial staff of *Novels for Students* welcomes your comments and ideas. Readers who wish to suggest novels to appear in future volumes, or who have other suggestions, are cordially invited to contact the editor. You may contact the editor via e-mail at: **ForStudentsEditors@cengage.com.** Or write to the editor at:

Editor, *Novels for Students*
Gale
27500 Drake Road
Farmington Hills, MI 48331-3535

Literary Chronology

1824: Wilkie Collins is born on January 8 in London, England.

1868: Wilkie Collin's *The Moonstone* is published.

1889: Wilkie Collins dies of complications from a stroke and bronchitis on September 23 in London, England.

1902: John Steinbeck is born on February 7 in Salinas, California.

1908: William Saroyan is born on August 31 in Fresno, California.

1910: Nicholas Monsarrat is born on March 22 in Liverpool, England.

1932: V. S. Naipaul is born on August 17 in Chaguanas, Trinidad and Tobago.

1937: Lois Lowry is born March 20 in Honolulu, Hawaii.

1939: John Steinbeck's *The Grapes of Wrath* is published.

1939: Margaret Atwood is born on November 18 in Ottawa, Canada

1940: John Steinbeck is awarded the Nobel Prize for Literature for his lifetime's work.

1940: John Steinbeck's novel *The Grapes of Wrath* is awarded the Pulitzer Prize for Fiction.

1940: The film *The Grapes of Wrath* is released.

1940: William Saroyan is awarded the Pulitzer Prize for drama for *The Time of Your Life.*

1941: The film *The Grapes of Wrath* is awarded Academy Awards for Best Director and Best Actress in a Supporting Role.

1943: Marilynne Robinson is born on November 26 in Sandpoint, Idaho.

1943: William Saroyan's The Human Comedy is published.

1947: Larry Watson is born on September 13 in Rugby, North Dakota.

1951: Nicholas Monsarrat's *The Cruel Sea* is published.

1954: Dai Sijie is born on March 2 in Putian, China.

1954: Kazuo Ishiguro is born on November 8 in Nagasaki, Japan.

1956: Elizabeth Strout is born on January 6 in Portland, Maine.

1968: John Steinbeck dies of congestive heart failure on December 20 in New York, New York.

1969: Kathryn Stockett is born in Jackson, Mississippi.

1971: V. S. Naipaul is awarded the Booker Prize for *In a Free State.*

1974: Gene Yang is born in Alameda, California.

1979: Nicholas Monsarrat dies of cancer on August 8 in London, England.

1980: Marilynne Robinson's *Housekeeping* is published.

1981: William Saroyan dies of prostate cancer on May 18 in Fresno, California.

1989: Kazuo Ishiguro's *The Remains of the Day* is published.

1989: Kazuo Ishiguro is awarded the Booker Prize for *The Remains of the Day*.

1989: Lois Lowry's *Number the Stars* is published.

1993: Larry Watson's *Montana 1948* is published.

1993: The film *The Remains of the Day* is released.

2000: Dai Sijie's *Balzac and the Little Chinese Seamstress* is published in French as *Balzac et la Petite Tailleuse chinoise*. It is published in English in 2001.

2000: Margaret Atwood is awarded the Man Booker Prize for *The Blind Assassin*.

2001: V. S. Naipaul is awarded the Pulitzer Prize for Literature.

2001: V. S. Naipaul's *Half a Life* is published.

2003: Margaret Atwood's *Oryx and Crake* is published.

2005: Marilynne Robinson is awarded the Pulitzer Prize for Fiction for *Gilead*.

2006: Gene Yang' *American Born Chinese* is published.

2008: Elizabeth Strout's *Olive Kitteridge* is published.

2009: Elizabeth Strout is awarded the Pulitzer Prize for Fiction for *Olive Kitteridge*.

2009: Kathryn Stockett's *The Help* is published.

Acknowledgements

The editors wish to thank the copyright holders of the excerpted criticism included in this volume and the permissions managers of many book and magazine publishing companies for assisting us in securing reproduction rights. We are also grateful to the staffs of the Detroit Public Library, the Library of Congress, the University of Detroit Mercy Library, Wayne State University Purdy/Kresge Library Complex, and the University of Michigan Libraries for making their resources available to us. Following is a list of the copyright holders who have granted us permission to reproduce material in this volume of *NfS*. Every effort has been made to trace copyright, but if omissions have been made, please let us know.

COPYRIGHTED EXCERPTS IN *NfS*, VOLUME 39, WERE REPRODUCED FROM THE FOLLOWING PERIODICALS:

Athenaeum, July 25, 1868.—*Booklist*, September 15, 2001; January 1, 2008. Copyright © 20001, 2008 by the American Library Association. Both reproduced by permission.—*Chicago Sun Times*, March 31, 2002. Reprinted with permission of *The Chicago Sun-Times*.—*Cineaste*, Winter, 2004. Reproduced by permission.—*College English*, March, 1955.—*Commonweal*, March 25, 2011. Reproduced by permission of Commonweal Foundation.—*English Journal*, April, 1956.—*Essays in Literature*, Spring, 1989. Copyright 1989 by Western Illinois University. Reproduced by permission.—*Fresno Bee*, January 1, 2009.

Reproduced by permission.—*Horn Book*, 1990. Reproduced by permission.—*Journal of Adolescent and Adult Literacy*, March, 2010. Reproduced by permission of the International Reading Association.—*Kirkus Reviews*, February 1, 2008; January 1, 2009. Copyright © 2008, 2009 Kirkus Media. All rights reserved. Both reproduced by permission—*KLIATT*, March, 2003. Copyright © 2003 by *KLIATT*. Reproduced by permission.—*Library Journal*, September 15, 2001; February 1, 2008; January 1, 2009. Copyright © 2001, 2008, 2009 Library Journals LLC, a wholly owned subsidiary of Media Source, Inc. No redistribution permitted. Reproduced by permission.—*Lion and the Unicorn*, January, 2002. Copyright © 2002 by The Johns Hopkins University Press. Reproduced by permission of The Johns Hopkins University Press.—*Lippincott's Magazine of Literature, Science and Education*, December, 1868.—*Literature/Film Quarterly*, 1989; 2007. Copyright © 1989, 2007 Salisbury State College. Reproduced by permission—*London Times*, October 3, 1868.—*MBR Bookwatch*, March, 2008. Reproduced by permission.—*MELUS*, Fall, 2007. Reproduced by permission.—*Mosaic*, March, 2010. Copyright © *Mosaic* 2010. Acknowledgment of previous publication is herewith made.—*Nation*, September 17, 1868.—*National Review*, December 13, 1993. Reproduced by permission.—*New Statesman*, October 1, 2001; May 19, 2003. Copyright © 2001, 2003 New Statesman, Ltd. Reproduced by permission.—*Newsweek*,

November 8, 1993. Copyright © 1993 Newsweek, Inc. All rights reserved. Reprinted by permission.—*Papers on Language & Literature*, Spring, 2005. Reproduced by permission.—*Publishers Weekly*, January 23, 1995. Reproduced from *Publishers Weekly*, published by the PWxyz, LLC, by permission.—*Reading Teacher*, October, 1990. Reproduced by permission of the International Reading Association.—*Rocky Mountain Review of Language and Literature*, Spring, 2007. Reproduced by permission.—*School Library Journal*, September, 2006. Copyright © 2006 Reed Business Information, Inc. Reproduced by permission.—*South Atlantic Review*, January, 1991. Reproduced by permission.—*Spectator*, June 30, 2001; October 6, 2001; April 26, 2003. Copyright © 2001, 2003 by *The Spectator*. All reproduced by permission of *The Spectator*.—**Studies in the Humanities**, June/December, 2001. Reproduced by permission.—*World Literature Today*, April/June, 2003. Reproduced by permission of the publisher.

Contributors

Susan K. Andersen: Andersen holds a Ph.D. in literature. Entry on *The Human Comedy*. Original essay on *The Human Comedy*.

Catherine Dominic: Dominic is a novelist and a freelance writer and editor. Entries on *The Help* and *Number the Stars*. Original essays on *The Help* and *Number the Stars*.

Charlotte M. Freeman: Freeman is a writer, editor, and former academic living in small-town Montana. Entry on *Housekeeping*. Original essay on *Housekeeping*.

Diane Andrews Henningfeld: Henningfeld is a professor of English at Adrian College who writes widely on literature and current events for educational publishers. Entry on *Oryx and Crake*. Original essay on *Oryx and Crake*.

Michael Allen Holmes: Holmes is a writer and editor. Entries on *Balzac and the Little Chinese Seamstress* and *Olive Kitteridge*. Original essays on *Balzac and the Little Chinese Seamstress* and *Olive Kitteridge*.

David Kelly: Kelly is an instructor of literature and creative writing. Entries on *The Remains of the Day* and *The Grapes of Wrath*. Original essays on *The Remains of the Day* and *The Grapes of Wrath*.

Michael J. O'Neal: O'Neal holds a Ph.D. in English. Entries on *The Cruel Sea* and *The Moonstone*. Original essays on *The Cruel Sea* and *The Moonstone*.

April Dawn Paris: Paris is a freelance writer who has an extensive background working with literature and educational materials. Entry on *American Born Chinese*. Original essay on *American Born Chinese*.

Laura Beth Pryor: Pryor is a professional writer with over twenty-five years of experience, with a special interest in fiction. Entry on *Montana 1948*. Original essay on *Montana 1948*.

Bradley A. Skeen: Skeen is a classicist. Entry on *Half a Life*. Original essay on *Half a Life*.

American Born Chinese

GENE LUEN YANG

2006

Gene Luen Yang's graphic novel, *American Born Chinese*, was originally serialized online on *Modern Tales.com*. First Second Books published the complete story in print in 2006. *American Born Chinese* has the distinction of being the first graphic novel to receive the Michael L. Printz Award and was the first graphic novel to be nominated for the National Book Award. The full text is no longer available online. Yang, however, does provide a preview on his home page (http://geneyang.com/american-born-chinese).

American Born Chinese contains three seemingly unrelated narratives that are creatively linked together in the end. The book begins with an account of the Monkey King, a traditional Chinese folktale. It then details the life of Jin Wang, a Chinese American boy who moves to a predominately Caucasian suburb. The final story concerns the Caucasian American Danny and his cousin Chin-Kee. Chin-Kee is a negative Asian stereotype who makes life difficult for his cousin. Each thread of the graphic novel is drawn into an exciting conclusion that explores themes of self-identity and self-acceptance.

AUTHOR BIOGRAPHY

Yang was born in Alameda, California, in 1973. Yang describes his childhood in the California suburb of Saratoga as complex in his *Kartika*

Review interview with Sunny Woan. He saw Saratoga gradually shift from a predominately Caucasian population into a diverse neighborhood that came to include people and cultures from around the globe. The child of Asian immigrants, Yang grew up listening to traditional stories from China such as the Monkey King, which he later included in his graphic novel. He graduated from the University of California at Berkeley with a degree in computer science and a minor in creative writing.

Yang began drawing comics while he was in elementary school. Yang created Humble Comics in 1996 as a vehicle to publish his work. In 1997, he won a Xeric grant to create *Gordon Yamamoto and the King of the Geeks*. Yang has created comics with different themes over the years, including *The Rosary Comic Book*, which incorporates religious themes that reflect the artist's personal beliefs. Many of his other comics are more fantasy-based. Yang self-published some of his early work and serialized other stories, including *American Born Chinese*, online.

The print publication of *American Born Chinese* in its entirety in 2006 brought the author mainstream popularity as he addressed the issues of multiculturalism, assimilation, and identity. He followed this success with a 2009 collaboration with Derek Kirk Kim, *The Eternal Smile*. Yang published *Prime Baby* in 2010 and worked with Thien Pham on the 2011 comic *Level Up*. Several of Yang's comic tales have received the Eisner Award, which is considered the Academy Award for American comic writers.

As of 2011, Yang lived in Fremont, California, with his wife and children. When he was not creating comics, Yang teaches computer science at the Catholic high school Bishop O'Dowd in Oakland, California. He is also a strong supporter of using comics in education.

PLOT SUMMARY

American Born Chinese is a multi-narrative work that develops the three distinct stories of the Monkey King, Jin Wang, and Danny and Chin-Kee. Yang unites these stories at the conclusion. The three narratives are broken into different sections of the book that resemble chapters. As a graphic novel, *American Born Chinese* tells the stories using sequential art.

MEDIA ADAPTATIONS

- Yang explains the concepts behind *American Born Chinese* in a YouTube video posted by the *America.gov* Web site on June 4, 2009.
- Yang discusses his work in a lecture at the University of California Berkley at the Story Hour in the Library Web site (http://wn.com/Story_Hour_in_the_Library __Gene_Yang).

Individual pictures or panels are created to depict moments. The panels are placed in sequence to drive the action of the story, and the text supports the graphics. The square boxes hold narrative text, and the balloons have dialogue or thoughts. The text is written in capital letters so that it is easier to read. A page featuring a character's picture introduces his chapter of the book.

Monkey King

This multi-narrative story begins with the modern retelling of the Monkey King, a centuries-old Chinese fable. The first scene is told by an omniscient narrator and describes a banquet of the gods in heaven. The Monkey King smells the food and becomes hungry. Born out of a rock, he is a "Deity in his own right" and rules the monkeys on Flower-Fruit Mountain. He has also mastered Kung-Fu and the four heavenly disciplines to become immortal. The Monkey King decides he should attend the banquet of the gods in heaven because he is a deity. The gods, however, refuse to associate with him because he is a monkey and does not wear shoes. The Monkey King is insulted and forced to leave. In retaliation, he attacks the guests at the party. When he returns to Flower-Fruit Mountain, however, he feels ashamed of being a monkey. The anger and shame he feels as a result of the rejection of the other gods will affect his future actions.

Jin

Jin Wang begins the story of his life in his first section of the graphic novel. The story begins with Jin's mother telling him a Chinese parable as the family drives to their new home. Jin plays with a Transformer toy as he learns about a boy who moved several times with mother and how each place he lived influenced his life. The Transformer symbolizes the themes of change and transformation that are prevalent throughout the book. Jin explains his background after the panel shows the family arriving at their new home.

Jin was born in Chinatown but moved to a suburb when he is nine. He was happy in Chinatown and fit in with easily with his peers. He went to the herbalist with his mother every week. One day, he tells the herbalist's wife that he wants to become a Transformer. She replies, "It's easy to become anything you wish . . . so long as you are willing to forfeit your soul." This statement is a warning that foreshadows future events.

After the move, Jin attends his new school, where there is only one other Asian student, Suzy Nakamura. He faces racial prejudice from his classmates, and his first friend, Peter, is really a bully who abuses Jin. When Jin is in fifth grade, Wei-Chen arrives from Taiwan. Jin initially dislikes Wei-Chen because he is too Asian. Wei-Chen's English is broken, and he does not understand American culture. Jin refers to him as an F.O.B., which stands for *fresh off the boat*. Jin does not want to associate with someone who is a constant reminder of what makes him different from the other students. At first, Jin refuses to be friends with Wei-Chen. The boys soon bond, however, when Wei-Chen offers to let Jin see his robot that turns into a monkey. This scene is a reminder of Jin's love of Transformers and all that they represent. By the end of this section, Jin reveals that Wei-Chen is his best friend.

Danny and Chin-Kee

The next section of the book is called "Everyone Ruvs Chin-Kee." This is the only section of *American Born Chinese* with a title. It also has a laugh track and clapping at the bottom of different panels. There is no narrator; dialogue and pictures move the story forward. This comical farce is the story of Danny, a blonde, American teenager who is visited by his cousin Chin-Kee.

Danny is studying with a girl he likes, Melanie, when his cousin arrives. She quickly leaves after Chin-Kee makes several insulting comments. Chin-Kee embodies every negative Chinese stereotype. Yang draws him differently from other Asian characters. His features are exaggerated and his clothing is nineteenth-century Chinese dress. He speaks with a severe accent and behaves inappropriately, embarrassing his cousin. On the surface, Chin-Kee is offensive, but Binbin Fu explains, in his review, that the character is an "effective way to dispel the century-old image of the 'Heathen Chinee.'"

Monkey King

Monkey King's second appearance shows how the rejection of the gods has affected him. Humiliated, he is determined to transform himself and the other monkeys. He begins by ordering all monkeys to wear shoes. The shoes make life more difficult for his subjects, who spend much of their time in trees. The Monkey King then locks himself away to study other Kung-Fu disciplines. He masters the four major disciplines of invulnerability and the four major disciplines of bodily form. Mastering these disciplines allows the Monkey King to change his size, clone himself, shape shift, and become invulnerable to injury and death. After attaining these powers, the Monkey King decides that he will no longer be a monkey and changes his name to the Great Sage, Equal of Heaven. He makes himself taller and appears more human.

When he returns to his subjects, the Monkey King learns that he has been sentenced to execution because of his attack in heaven. Monkey King goes to the Dragon King of the Eastern Sea, who is ordered to execute him. The Dragon King finds it impossible to execute the Monkey King because of his invulnerability. The Monkey King takes on a larger form and attacks the Dragon King to convince him that he is no longer a monkey. In his defeat, the Dragon King gives the Monkey King a magic cudgel.

The Monkey King goes on to visit the sage Lao-Tzu, Yama of the Underworld, and the Jade Emperor of the Celestials. Each one laughs at the Monkey King, and each one is defeated by him. Afraid of the Monkey King's transformation, the deities and spirits beg the emissaries of Tze-Yo-Tzuh to ask him to save them from the Monkey King.

Tze-Yo-Tzuh, whose name means *He Who Is*, is a supreme being. He finds the Monkey King beating a human and asks why he is so angry. Tze-Yo-Tzuh reveals that he made the Monkey King, and he fully intended the monkey deity to be a monkey. He also explains that he is always with the Monkey King and knows everything he does. The Monkey King refuses to accept his own identity or Tze-Yo-Tzuh's. He tries to escape Tze-Yo-Tzuh and flies beyond the universe. There, he finds five gold pillars and marks one. He returns to tell Tze-Yo-Tzuh how he escaped his grasp, but Tze-Yo-Tzuh shows him a mark on his hand. The five gold pillars were Tze-Yo-Tzuh's fingers. Stubbornly determined to change his identity, the Monkey King attempts to fight Tze-Yo-Tzuh and is imprisoned under a pile of rocks for five hundred years. A seal on the rocks prevents the Monkey King from using Kung-Fu.

Jin

The next section of the novel returns to Jin's story. Now in middle school, he develops a crush on his Caucasian classmate Amelia Harris. Jin confides his feelings to Wei-Chen, who laughs at him for falling in love so young. Jin reminds him that they are in America and that it is normal to date girls. Wei-Chen takes his advice and begins dating the other Asian American student, Suzy Nakamura. Jin finds it impossible to talk with the girl of his dreams and convinces himself that she likes another boy, Greg. Jin copies Greg's hairstyle to make himself more appealing. The curly hairstyle does not suit Jin just as the shoes do not suit the monkeys. As Jin and his friends handle typical teenage problems, they suffer racial slurs from other students.

Wei-Chen and Amelia take care of animals for science class, and they accidentally lock themselves in a supply closet one day. While they are alone together, Wei-Chen tells Amelia what a good friend Jin is to him. Amelia is impressed by Wei-Chen's story, and asks him if Jin likes her. When Jin lets them out of the closet, Wei-Chen tells him to ask Amelia out. Jin finally has the courage to make his feelings known, and Amelia agrees to go out with him.

Danny and Chin-Kee

The second installment of Danny and Chin-Kee takes place in Danny's high school. Again, Chin-Kee exhibits the worst Asian stereotypes. He obnoxiously answers all of the questions in class. He talks about eating cat. He quotes proverbs and talks about finding an American wife. He even plays a disgusting joke on Danny's friend Steve, explaining that he does it because he is Chinese. By the end of the day, the other students are mocking Chin-Kee and avoiding Danny. Danny confides in Steve that he is forced to change schools every year after Chin-Kee visits because, "by the time he leaves, no one thinks of me as Danny anymore. I'm Chin-Kee's cousin." Danny's anger is visible by the end of this section.

Monkey King

The story of the Monkey King continues after a five-hundred–year break. It begins with the history of Wong Lai-Tsao, who is one of the four monks to achieve legendary status. He is only impressive in one way: he spends every day feeding and helping the vagrants outside town. He does this faithfully even though the vagrants do not appreciate him. One day, a vagrant asks Wong Lai-Tsao why he helps them. The monk replies that Tze-Yo-Tzuh loves him and he must share that love. The vagrants transform into the emissaries of Tze-Yo-Tzuh after Wong-Lai-Tsao answers. The emissaries tell Wong Lai-Tsao that Tze-Yo-Tzuh wishes him to travel to the West with three gifts. If he accepts the mission, he will be in danger from demons who believe eating a monk will make them immortal. He will also have three disciples, and one of his disciples will be the Monkey King.

The monk accepts the mission and travels to find the Monkey King under the mountain of rock. Wong Lai-Tsao tells the Monkey King that Tze-Yo-Tzuh wants him to be his disciple, and he must free himself from the rock. The Monkey King still refuses to be a monkey, insisting that he is the Great Sage, Equal of Heaven. He reminds Wong Lai-Tsao that he cannot free himself because Tze-Yo-Tzuh placed a seal on the rock preventing the Monkey King from using Kung-Fu. Wong Lai-Tsao explains that if he releases his Kung-Fu and takes his true form, the Monkey King will be small enough to free himself.

The panels show demons following the monk. The Monkey King refuses to return to his true form, and he tells Wong Lai-Tsao that he will watch the demons eat him. As the demons attack, the monk tells the Monkey King that this is his last chance for freedom. At the final moment, the Monkey King takes his true form and escapes. He saves Wong Lai-Tsao from the demons using Kung-Fu. He accepts his role as the monk's disciple and agrees to help him on the journey to the West. Wong Lai-Tsao makes one final demand of the Monkey King. He must give up his shoes before starting the mission. The Monkey King leaves his shoes behind and begins his journey to the West. By leaving his shoes, he is fully relinquishing his identity as the Great Sage, Equal of Heaven.

Jin

Jin is excited about his date with Amelia, but he has a problem. He is not allowed to date because his parents want him to focus on his schoolwork. Jin plans to tell his mother that he is studying at Wei-Chen's house and convinces Wei-Chen to lie if his mother calls looking for him. Wei-Chen is not comfortable with lying and only agrees out of his loyalty to Jin. Readers later learn that lying goes against his oath to Tze-Yo-Tzuh.

On his date with Amelia, Jin recalls dating instructions from his older cousin, Charlie. He takes Amelia to the movies on his bike and is sweating when they arrive. His parents do not buy deodorant, and he remembers his cousin's advice to use restroom soap under his arms when out with a girl. Jin follows this advice, but is horrified when he realizes that he left soap bubbles on Amelia's shoulder after putting his arm around her. As they leave the movie, Greg is watching them in the picture.

The next day, Jin is worried that Amelia did not enjoy their date. Wei-Chen attempts to help Jin by asking Amelia if she had a good time. She does not mention noticing the soap bubbles, and she tells Wei-Chen that she had fun. Jin is happy and dreams about his future with Amelia until Greg talks to him. Greg asks Jin not to go out with Amelia again because "she has to start paying attention to who she hangs out with." Flustered by the request, Jin reluctantly agrees, but he fantasizes about telling Greg *no* and hitting him. When he does run into Greg and Amelia, he does not say anything.

Angry and humiliated, Jin finds Suzy crying alone on the street. She tells him about being ignored by an old friend at a party and a boy, Timmy, calling her a racial slur. She admits that she feels like a foreigner all the time. Jin kisses Suzy when she is vulnerable. She becomes angry and hits him before running away.

Jin has an ice pack on his face when Wei-Chen comes over. He asks Jin why he would betray him and kiss his girlfriend. Wei-Chen tells Jin that they are brothers because they are alike, but this reminds Jin of what makes him different. Jin lashes out at Wei-Chen instead of the people who discriminated against him. He calls Wei-Chen a F.O.B. and tells him that he is not good enough for Suzy. Wei-Chen punches Jin before leaving.

That night, Jin dreams of the herbalist's wife. She asks him what he would like to become, and he transforms into Danny. Jin wakes up to see Danny's face in the mirror. Jin is happy, but the figure of the herbalist's wife indicates that the transformation has cost Jin his soul.

Danny and Chin-Kee

Danny finds Chin-Kee dancing and singing on a table in the library, in the final installment of their story. Some students comment that he is spitting and that they need to be tested for the SARS virus. Danny drags his cousin out of the library and tells him to go back to China. Chin-Kee refuses, and Danny begins to hit him. Chin-Kee warns Danny to stop, but Danny refuses. The boys fight, and Chin-Kee beats up Danny, telling him that he will stay in America forever. Danny then hits Chin-Kee so hard that his head falls off, revealing the Monkey King.

The Monkey King tells Danny that they should both take their true forms, and Danny turns back into Jin. The Monkey King reveals that Wei-Chen was really his son sent by Tze-Yo-Tzuh as an emissary. Wei-Chen initially valued his friendship with Jin, but later decided that humans are "petty, soulless creatures." This comment reminds readers that Jin had to lose his soul to transform into Danny. After Jin's betrayal, Wei-Chen chooses to spend his time on earth living for pleasure.

Jin believes that the Monkey King used Chin-Kee to punish him for Wei-Chen's disobedience, but the Monkey King explains that he was only acting as Jin's conscience. He wants Jin to accept himself for who he is. Jin retains his true form after encountering the Monkey King. By seeing himself clearly, Jin regains his soul and begins an internal transformation. The Monkey King leaves Jin, and a card for a bakery falls into Jin's hand. Jin returns home and tells his mother and father that Chin-Kee is gone. Each parent has assumed that Chin-Kee was the other's nephew.

Jin goes to the bakery on the card every day for a month. Finally, a transformed Wei-Chen drives up to the bakery. He looks more Americanized. He is smoking and no longer speaks broken English, but his language is coarse. Initially, he is rude and angry with Jin. Jin, however, tells Wei-Chen that he saw his father and wants to talk to him. They order pearl milk tea, and Jin apologizes to Wei-Chen. Wei-Chen does not immediately accept his apology, but he offers to take Jin to a place that serves better pearl milk tea.

The final picture in the book appears after the end of the story. It is one of Jin and Wei-Chen as the Back Dorm Boys, according to Yang's interview with Sunny Woan. This is a pop-culture reference to the popular online video. The Back Dorm Boys are two Chinese students in a dorm who lip-synch American pop songs.

CHARACTERS

Charlie

Jin's older cousin, Charlie, is a minor character. He only appears in Jin's memory. Jin remembers all of Charlie's advice about dating. Charlie is the one who tells Jin about using the soap in public restrooms as deodorant.

Chin-Kee

Chin-Kee is introduced to readers as Danny's cousin from China. He is a negative Chinese stereotype whose offensive behavior humiliates Danny and alienates him from his friends. At the climax, Chin-Kee is revealed as the Monkey King in disguise. He masquerades as Chin-Kee to be Danny's, or Jin's, conscience.

Danny

Danny is a blond, all-American high school student who is embarrassed each year when his cousin Chin-Kee comes to visit. Every year Danny changes schools because of his cousin. At the climax of the story, the readers learns that Danny is really Jin transformed.

Demons

Wong Lai-Tsao is attacked by nameless demons when he first meets the Monkey King. The demons believe that eating a monk will make them live forever. The Monkey King escapes from the mountain of rocks and uses his Kung-Fu skills to save Wong Lai-Tsao from the demons.

Dragon King of the Eastern Sea

The Dragon King of the Eastern Sea is a Chinese deity. He is instructed to execute the Monkey King for his assault on heaven. The Dragon King of the Eastern Sea, however, cannot kill the Monkey King because of his invulnerability. After being defeated by the Monkey King, the Dragon King of the Eastern Sea gives him a magic cudgel.

Emissaries of Tze-Yo-Tzuh

The original servants of Tze-Yo-Tzuh are the ox, the eagle, the lion, and the human. They communicate messages to and from Tze-Yo-Tzuh. They give Tze-Yo-Tzuh the message from the gods and tell Wong Lai-Tsao about his mission to the West. The Monkey King later calls himself an emissary of Tze-Yo-Tzuh. Wei-Chen briefly serves as an emissary of Tze-Yo-Tzuh, but he abandons his mission.

Greg

Greg is a blond student with curly hair in the same class as Jin and Wei-Chen Sun. He is a friend of Timmy's, but he does not call Jin and his friends racial slurs. He will not, however, do anything to stop Timmy and another boy from insulting Jin, Suzy, and Wei-Chen Sun. Jin is jealous of Greg's friendship with Amelia and copies Greg's hairstyle to impress her. Greg asks Jin to stay away from Amelia because being seen out with Jin is not good for her reputation.

Amelia Harris

Amelia is a pretty, blonde classmate of Jin's and his eighth grade crush. She does not share the prejudices of some of the other students and even goes on a date with Jin. She likes Jin, but Jin allows her friend, Greg, to come between them.

Herbalist's Wife

A name is never given for the herbalist's wife in Chinatown, but she is important to the story. She tells Jin that he can become anything if he will sacrifice his soul. She appears in Jin's dream before he transforms into Danny.

Jade Emperor

The Jade Emperor of the Celestials does not believe that the Monkey King is a threat until he faces the Monkey King's magic cudgel. After being defeated by the Monkey King, the Jade Emperor and other deities complain to the emissaries of Tze-Yo-Tzuh and ask for help.

Wong Lai-Tsao

As one of the four legendary monks, Wong Lai-Tsao has only one attribute that makes him legendary: he can share the love of his creator. Wong Lai-Tsao consistently loves and cares for vagrants who are not kind to him. The vagrants transform into the emissaries of Tze-Yo-Tzuh after testing him. They inform him that Tze-Yo-Tzuh has a mission for him to travel West with three disciples. The first disciple Wong Lai-Tsao finds is the Monkey King trapped under the rock mountain. Wong Lai-Tsao teaches the Monkey King how to accept his true identity and free himself from the mountain of rocks.

Lao-Tzu

Lao-Tzu is a sage and patron of immortality. He laughs at the Monkey King for saying that he is no longer a monkey. Lao-Tzu grows afraid of the Monkey King after he uses his shape-shifting ability.

Melanie

Melanie is a girl Danny likes. He is studying with her when Chin-Kee arrives. After meeting Chin-Kee, she tells Danny that she only wants to be friends and says that he has buck teeth.

Monkey King

The Monkey King is a popular character from Chinese folktales. The story of the Monkey King has been in print since the sixteenth-century book *Journey to the West*. Yang borrows elements from the traditional story for his graphic novel but alters a few details. In this story, the Monkey King is born from a rock and becomes the ruler and deity of the monkeys on Flower-Fruit Mountain. He masters Kung-Fu disciplines, including the four heavenly disciplines that make him immortal. The Monkey King is happy until he attempts to enter a banquet of the gods. He is not allowed inside because he is a monkey and because he has no shoes. He grows ashamed of being a monkey.

The Monkey King transforms himself by mastering the major disciplines of invulnerability and the four major disciplines of bodily form. The disciplines of invulnerability make him impervious to harm, and the disciplines of bodily form allow him to change his shape and size and clone himself. Having mastered all of the Kung-Fu disciplines, the Monkey King calls himself the Great Sage, Equal of Heaven and makes himself physically larger and more intimidating. He is sentenced to death for attacking the other gods, but he cannot be killed. The Monkey King attacks the deities who laughed at him to prove that he is no longer a monkey.

The Monkey King refuses to listen to Tze-Yo-Tzuh, his creator, and insists that he is the Great Sage, Equal of Heaven. He is trapped under a mountain of rocks for five hundred years after trying to fight Tze-Yo-Tzuh, who places a seal on the rocks to prevent the Monkey King from practicing Kung-Fu. The Monkey King becomes the disciple of the monk Wong Lai-Tsao and escapes the mountain when he learns to accept himself as a monkey. The Monkey King later becomes the emissary of Tze-Yo-Tzuh and the father of Wei-Chen Sun. He also masquerades as Danny's cousin, Chin-Kee.

Suzy Nakamura

Suzy is a Japanese American student in the same class as Jin and Wei-Chen. She dates Wei-Chen Sun, and she punches Jin after he kisses her.

Peter

Peter is Jin's first friend at school. Peter is a bully who demands that Jin be his friend. He is abusive and plays cruel games with Jin. He leaves one summer and does not return.

Steve

Steve is Danny's friend. They are on the basketball team together. Chin-Kee plays a joke on Steve that eventually drives them apart.

Wei-Chen Sun

Wei-Chen Sun emigrates from Taiwan and joins Jin's class in the fifth grade. Jin initially rejects Wei-Chen's friendship. Wei-Chen speaks broken English at first. He has a robot that transforms into a monkey, and Jin bonds with Wei-Chen Sun over the robot. Wei-Chen soon becomes Jin's most loyal friend. He dates Suzy Nakamura and ends his friendship with Jin after Jin kisses her.

At the end of the story, he is revealed to be the son of the Monkey King sent as an ambassador by Tze-Yo-Tzuh. He refuses to follow his mission after Jin betrays him, and he seeks to please only himself. His appearance and manner of speaking change to illustrate how his anger and selfish behavior have negatively affected him. Jin eventually finds Wei-Chen Sun and apologizes to him at the end of the story.

Timmy

Timmy is a boy whom Jin encounters on his first day at his new school. He is quick to make racist comments about Jin. He continues his abuse over the years. In middle school, he calls Suzy a racial slur that makes her cry.

Tze-Yo-Tzuh

Tze-Yo-Tzuh is a supreme being and creator of all things, including the gods. When the Monkey King becomes too powerful, the gods turn to Tze-Yo-Tzuh's emissaries and ask for his help. Tze-Yo-Tzuh tries to reason with the Monkey King but has to trap him under a mountain of rocks when the Monkey King attacks him. He later sends Wei-Chen as an emissary to humanity.

Jin Wang

Jin is a young Chinese American boy who moves from San Francisco's Chinatown to the suburbs. He plays with Transformers as a young child in Chinatown, and he wishes to become one. As one of only three Asian American students in a suburban school, he faces racial prejudice and stereotyping. He tries to fit in with his Caucasian peers, but he is not fully accepted by most of them.

Jin initially dislikes Wei-Chen Sun because he is new to America, but they soon bond over transforming robots and become best friends. In the eighth grade, Jin develops a crush on Amelia Harris and changes his hair to look more American. He goes on one date with Amelia thanks to the help of Wei-Chen. The date goes well, but another student, Greg, asks Jin to stay away from Amelia for the sake of her reputation.

Jin is frustrated by the prejudice he faces and kisses Suzy, Wei-Chen Sun's girlfriend, in an emotional moment. He lashes out at Wei-Chen when confronted and ends their friendship. Jin eventually transforms into Danny, who is tormented by his Chinese cousin Chin-Kee. Jin returns to his true form after encountering the Monkey King.

Mrs. Wang

Jin's mother tells him stories of the Monkey King.

Yama

As the caretaker of the underworld, Yama is an important deity. Monkey King uses his ability to turn his hair into clones to convince Yama that he is no longer a monkey but the Great Sage Equal of Heaven.

THEMES

Self Identity

The two main characters in *American Born Chinese* have trouble accepting their personal identities. In a sense, the characters feel trapped between two worlds. Both Jin and the Monkey King suffer rejection because they are different. In an attempt to conform and be accepted, each one rejects a part of himself. The Monkey King is both a monkey and a deity, but he refuses to be identified as a monkey. He wishes to be only the Great Sage, Equal of Heaven. He changes his form and wears shoes to become someone else. Jin is a Chinese American who rejects his Chinese heritage to transform into the Caucasian American, Danny.

Both Jin and the Monkey King face their greatest struggles by rejecting their personal identities. They only find peace by accepting who and what they truly are. The Monkey King is released from his prison of rock by reverting into his true form as a monkey. Danny ends his humiliation at the hands of Chin-Kee when he confronts his fear of being stereotyped as Asian and again becomes Jin.

Stereotypes

Stereotypes are commonly used in comics and graphic novels because "everything in comic books, including character, is reduced to two-dimensional images," as Randy Duncan and Matthew J. Smith point out in *The Power of Comics: History, Form, and Culture*. Early comics often featured unflattering stereotypes of minority characters. The character Chin-Kee is an extreme stereotype who reflects the early Western caricatures of Chinese people. His name is also a play on a negative term for Chinese individuals. At first glance, Chin-Kee is

TOPICS FOR FURTHER STUDY

- Read *The Absolutely True Diary of a Part-Time Indian*, Sherman Alexie's young-adult novel about a Native American teenager, Arnold Spirit, who faces the challenges of being Native American, poor, and mentally challenged. This 2007 National Book Award winner is a narrative mixed with cartoons that the main character draws to explore his feelings. Compare and contrast this book with *American Born Chinese* in an essay. How are the themes, characters, and use of graphics similar? How are they different?

- Research the history of comics and graphic novels from the 1960s to the present. Create a video or multimedia presentation that shows the changes in form, subject matter, and critical reception. Include Yang's work in this presentation, and point out the specific techniques used in *American Born Chinese* and his other comic art. Complete your presentation by speculating on the future of the medium.

- In "Origins of American Born Chinese—part 1" (available at http://firstsecondbooks.typepad.com/mainblog/2006/08/gene_yang_origi.html), Yang wrote, "The Monkey King is universal." Read the book *Monkey: A Folk Novel of China*, and study the different representations of the Monkey King over the centuries. Create an original story involving the Monkey King and include illustrations. You may write a narrative, draw a comic, or create a Web comic.

- Explore the history of Asian American art. Create a Web page providing an overview of Asian American art and artists that includes different genres. Provide a brief biography for each artist and incorporate links to examples of his or her art. Be sure to include Yang in your Web page.

offensive, but Yang uses the character to turn the stereotype on its head.

Chin-Kee's extreme behavior is so stereotypical that he becomes unbelievable. He represents Danny's, or Jin's, greatest fears about being Chinese in America. The author explains the purpose of Chin-Kee in the "Origins of ABC— part 3" when he notes that "in order for us to defeat our enemy, he must first be made visible." By exposing the stereotype as ludicrous, Yang reveals it for the farce that it is and removes its power.

Transformation

Transformation is an underlying theme throughout *American Born Chinese*, as Fu and other critics point out. In this story, transformation is not always positive. The different characters learn how to transform themselves both inside and out. Physical transformation, however, does not lead to maturity, enlightenment, or peace. The Monkey King masters the disciplines of bodily form as part of an effort to change himself from the Monkey King to the Great Sage, Equal of Heaven. He is able to change physically but inside he remains the same. The true transformation of the Monkey King occurs when he learns to accept himself and return to his true physical form.

Transformation is a concept essentially linked to Jin's character. As a child, Jin's favorite toy is a Transformer, and he bonds with Wei-Chen over a transforming robot. These toys are images of his desire to change. Jin loves Transformers so much that he wants to be one when he grows up. The herbalist's wife gives Jin the secret of becoming a transformer before he moves to the suburbs: "It's easy to become anything you wish . . . so long as you are willing to forfeit your soul." After betraying Wei-Chen, Jin physically transforms into Danny. Danny, however, has the same anger and fear that Jin had before the transformation. Danny confronts his feelings of fear and anger at the climax of the story, and the Monkey King returns Jin to his true physical form. Jin begins a journey toward self-acceptance, which leads to an internal transformation.

Wei Chen's transformation is more complex than the transformations of the other characters. He is physically transformed by Tze-Yo-Tzuh to serve as an emissary on earth. This transformation from a monkey to a human does not

The first part of the novel is the story of the Asian Monkey King, depicted here as a character in a Chinese opera performance. *(shupian | Shutterstock.com)*

negatively affect Wei-Chen. He is a positive character until Jin betrays their friendship. Wei-Chen remains human after the betrayal, but he takes on a negative transformation after ending his friendship with Jin. He abandons his mission, speaks coarsely, dresses differently, and smokes.

STYLE

Graphic Novel

American Born Chinese is considered a graphic novel. Graphic novel is a term used to describe literary works drawn in the same style as comic books. The main difference between comic books and graphic novels is their length. Both comic books and graphic novels employ sequential art. In sequential art, pictures of specific moments are called panels, as Duncan and Smith explain. The panels are placed in a specific order to illustrate a sequence of events. Most

comics add text in the form of narration or dialogue to the assist with the plot.

Comic books are usually serialized, meaning that each comic book tells a portion of the story. Terms for longer or complete comic stories were discussed as early as the 1960s; however, Will Eisner made the term graphic novel popular with his 1978 book *Contract with God and other Tenement Stories*, according to Stephen Weiner in "Pioneer and Storyteller: The Graphic Novels of Will Eisner." Eisner is considered by experts such as Weiner to be the father of the graphic novel.

Yang's *American Born Chinese* has all of the attributes of a graphic novel. It uses the style of a comic book to complete this multi-narrative story. The book was originally serialized online at *Modern Tales.com*, but it is now published in the graphic-novel format.

Multi-narrative

American Born Chinese is a complex, multi-narrative text that explores different stories as well as different points of view within each narrative. Each story is unique. Jin's story is told in the first person, while the Monkey King has an omniscient narrator. Danny and Chin-Kee are not narrated. Their story relies on dialogue and resembles a sitcom script with laughing and clapping at the bottom of some panels. The separate stories effectively come together at the climax of the book to give the readers a clear understanding of all the events.

Intertextuality

A Handbook to Literature notes that Julia Kristeva (an influential modern-day French literary critic and philosopher) coined the term intertextuality. The term applies when one text echoes another in any way. This can occur when someone borrows a story, quotes a line, creates a parody, or alludes to another text. For example, poets sometimes quote other authors or allude to classical stories in their work. Intertextuality appears on different scales. They can be a few words or permeate the entire narrative. *American Born Chinese* applies intertextuality on a large scale by adopting the traditional tale of the Monkey King. Yang, however, alters the details and focus of the character from the *Journey to the West* to fit his narrative and worldview. For example, he removes the elements of political satire found in the novel.

HISTORICAL CONTEXT

Asian American History

Asian Americans are Americans of Asian descent. The term technically applies to families from all parts of Asia. Most Americans, however, associate the term with people whose ancestors are from East Asia, such as China and Japan, because Yuji Ichioka developed the term in the 1960s as an alternative to the word Oriental, according to K. Connie Kang's obituary for Ichioka in the *Los Angeles Times*.

Asian Americans are an integral part of American culture. According to the "Timeline of Asian American History" on the *Digital History* Web site, there was a Filipino settlement in Louisiana before the American Revolution, and Chinese and Japanese sailors landed in Hawaii in the early nineteenth century. Unfortunately, the rights of Asians have been limited in American history. For example, the Naturalization

Act of 1790 restricted citizenship to Caucasian Americans.

A significant number of Chinese and Japanese immigrants began arriving in the United States in the 1840s in response to the Gold Rush. Hikozo Hamada was the first Japanese man to be naturalized as an American citizen in 1850, but many Americans feared granting citizenship to Asians. Citizenship and rights for Asians were limited even after the Fourteenth Amendment granted citizenship to former slaves. The Naturalization Act of 1870, for example, denied citizenship to Chinese laborers and did not allow their wives to join them. The Chinese Exclusion Act of 1882 essentially prevented the entry of new Chinese laborers and repealed any state laws that would naturalize individuals from China.

Fear of an unknown culture created stereotypes of Chinese Americans in the nineteenth century that Fu, in a *MELUS* article, calls the *Heathen Chinee*. Different states within the United States created anti-miscegenation laws, which prohibited marriage between Chinese and other Asians with Americans. Deenesh Sohoni points out in *Law & Society Review* that these laws persisted into the early twentieth century.

To counter the fear of Asians in America, social scientists between 1910 and 1960 focused on the assimilation of Asians into Western society, as Sucheng Chan explains in "The Writing of Asian American History." Despite these efforts, many Americans considered all Asians to be foreigners. World War II saw the relocation of Japanese Americans to internment camps. Despite this discrimination, the Japanese 442nd Regimental Combat Team was the most decorated American unit during the war.

The 1960s saw the rise of civil rights support. The civil rights movement affected different minorities in America and signaled a turning point for Asian American rights. The term Asian American, as we know it, was coined, and colleges began including ethnic studies programs. Asian Americans were elected to office and served as judges, and laws protecting the rights of immigrants were created.

Chan considers the 1980s to be the decade when "Asian American historiography is finally coming of age." The Civil Liberties Act of 1988 made reparations for Japanese Americans interred during World War II. The rights of Asian American are now guaranteed. Centuries

The second story in the novel is that of Jin Wang, a second-generation immigrant. (*Apollofoto / Shutterstock.com*)

of stereotyping Asian cultures, however, have left an impression on American perception. In his graphic novel, Yang addresses these stereotypes and the challenges Asian Americans still face.

Comics and Graphic Novel History

Sequential art, or a series of pictures that tell a story, has been used for centuries. Experts such as Duncan and Smith, however, consider Rodolphe Tölpffer to be the father of the comic book because of the picture stories he created between 1827 and 1844. Soon after, popular comic strips mirroring Tölpffer's technique began to appear in the newspapers. The *Yellow Kid*, for example, was released in 1863, and the comics were later reprinted into books.

The modern form of the comic book was seen in 1929 with *The Funnies*. Comic books became a popular form of entertainment in the United States in the 1930s and 1940s. Comic books developed into different genres beyond humor to include adventure, detective fiction, and superhero fiction. The 1950s saw a decline in the demand for comic books. As American

households acquired televisions, fewer comic books were sold. There was also a backlash against comic books with explicit subject matter after *The Seduction of the Innocent: The Influence of Comic Books on Today's Youth* was released in 1954. A Senate subcommittee investigated the effect of comics on delinquent behavior the same year. In response to public concern, the Code of the Comics Magazine Association was created. The Association's seal indicated that comic books were suitable for children.

The 1960s and 1970s saw a move away from commercialism in the comic book industry. Comics developed as an art form that focused on literary themes. The appeal of underground and independent publishers grew during this time. The term *graphic novel* was created to describe book-length comics and was applied to Eisner's 1978 text, *Contract with God and other Tenement Stories*.

Graphic novels and comics became appreciated as literature in the 1980s and 1990s. *Maus*, *The Watchmen*, and *The Dark Knight Returns* were published in 1986 and "won attention in the popular press," as Duncan and Smith point out. Critical appreciation for graphic novels developed in the 1990s, and *Maus II* won a special Pulitzer Prize in 1992. Respect for graphic novels and comics continues to grow in the twenty-first century. They are embraced in classrooms and still draw critical acclaim; *American Born Chinese*, for example, is the first graphic novel to be nominated for the National Book Award.

CRITICAL OVERVIEW

American Born Chinese was physically published in 2006 and became Yang's first profitable work as a comic writer and artist. The reviews have been overwhelmingly positive. Most critics quickly noticed the importance of the book's subject matter in modern American society. Jesse Karp, in *Booklist*, notes that "the stories have a simple, engaging sweep to them, but their weighty subjects—shame, racism, and friendship—receive thoughtful, powerful examination." In the *Journal of Adolescent & Adult Literacy*, Michael D. Boatright praises the relevance of *American Born Chinese* and how it relates to "immigrant identity issues."

Some critics immediately applauded Yang's strong narrative ability, while others found the multi-narrative approach unappealing. In his review of *American Born Chinese* for *MELUS*, Fu opines that "what makes it especially appealing to both young and mature readers is its narrative depth." He calls the climax "cleverly woven together." Ned Vizzini, in the *New York Times*, however, argues that the book is "hampered by a confusing ending that stretches to resolve the three tales."

In a graphic novel, the quality of the drawing and color choices is important. Critics have predominantly united over the visual appeal of *American Born Chinese*, praising its simplicity and use of color. A contributor to the *Bulletin of the Center for Children's Books* comments that "the palette is softly muted, so that even the strongest colors in the action scenes never reach the intensity of a visual assault." Fu also calls it "mature in artistic design and visually engaging."

CRITICISM

April Dawn Paris

Paris is a freelance writer who specializes in literature. In the following essay, she argues that American Born Chinese *illustrates how attempts to assimilate lead to negative, harmful transformations.*

The concepts of transformation and personal identity are pivotal in all three narratives of *American Born Chinese*. Transformations can be positive or negative, depending upon the factors that motivate them. *American Born Chinese* offers examples of both positive and negative transformations. Negative transformations in this book are associated with feelings of anger or shame. They are attempts to assimilate, and as the herbalist's wife explains to Jin, they require you to "forfeit your soul." The positive transformations, on the other hand, are related to acts of kindness and selflessness. Unlike efforts to integrate, a positive transformation leaves a person's soul intact and helps guide others on their journey.

Michael Boatright notes in the *Journal of Adolescent & Adult Literacy* that the main characters of the story reflect the immigrant experience by "living in two often contradictory cultural worlds." The Monkey King, Jin, Wei-Chen Sun, Danny, and Chin-Kee all have divided identities, and they all undergo their own transformations. The initial transformations of Jin and the Monkey King are attempts at assimilation and reflect "the impact of the American dream on those outside the dominant culture," according to a review in *School Library Journal* that appears on the First Second Web site. Yang explains this innate desire to assimilate in a *Kartika Review* interview with Sunny Woan: "There's definitely a temptation to become fully assimilated, fully a part of America, but as Asian Americans, we have to constantly struggle against that."

Jin and the Monkey King transform themselves for the wrong reasons. They are willing to tear apart their personal identities so that they will fit in with societies that reject them. When transformations are made out of shame or an effort to assimilate, they cause more harm than good. Both Jin and the Monkey King wound themselves and others in their quests to change themselves. In reality, all that they need to change is their point of view.

WHAT DO I READ NEXT?

- Tanuja Desai Hidier's work of young-adult fiction, *Born Confused*, was published in 2002. This is the story of Dimple Lala, an American teenager who, like Yang's characters, struggles between two worlds. Dimple is an Indian American who attempts to fit in with both her family and American peers as she discovers who she is.

- *The Chinese in America: A Narrative History* (2006) by Iris Chang is a historical account of Chinese immigration to America in the nineteenth and twentieth centuries, as well as the resistance immigrants faced. By employing a narrative style, Chang makes it easier for the readers to understand the historical events that led to the cultural setting of *American Born Chinese*.

- Yang followed *American Born Chinese* by collaborating with Derek Kirk Kim in the 2009 young-adult graphic novel *The Eternal Smile: Three Stories*. The stories in this book differ from Yang's previous work by exploring the connection between fantasy and reality.

- Stephen Weiner's *Faster Than a Speeding Bullet: The Rise of the Graphic Novel* (2003) provides a historic look at the rise of popular comics and graphic novels. The nonfiction account looks at graphic novels as part of the general publishing industry.

- Art Spiegelman first published *Maus I: A Survivor's Tale: My Father Bleeds History* in 1986. This novel-length work of sequential art, based on the events of the Holocaust, was one of the first graphic novels accepted as mainstream literature. The second installment, *Maus II: A Survivor's Tale: And Here My Troubles Began*, won a special Pulitzer Prize in 1992 and helped pave the way for other comic artists and writers to be taken seriously. This dark story contrasts with *American Born Chinese* and shows the versatility of the comic medium.

- Edited by Keith Lawrence and Floyd Cheung, *Recovered Legacies: Authority and Identity in Early Asian American Literature* (2005) is a collection of essays that examine early Asian American literature and its influence on culture and identity. The essays address little-known Asian American stories that, like *American Born Chinese*, reflect the experiences of Asian Americans throughout history.

The Monkey King has three identities at the beginning of the story. He is simultaneously a monkey, a king, and a deity. He is a fair ruler who is loved and appreciated by his subjects. He is content with his life until he is thrown out of a banquet for the gods. Although he is a deity, the other gods will not accept him as an equal and laugh at him. Humiliated, the Monkey King immediately lashes out in anger, but he inwardly agrees with the gods' belief that monkeys are inferior. He leaves the banquet and notices the smell of monkey fur for the first time and "stayed awake for the rest of the night thinking of ways to get rid of it." By accepting the gods' perception of him, the Monkey King loses his self-respect and turns his back on his identity as a monkey.

Filled with anger and shame, he masters the disciplines of bodily form, which enable him to change his size and shape. The Monkey King makes himself physically intimidating, begins wearing shoes, and changes his name to the Great Sage, Equal of Heaven. All of this work is done in an effort to be accepted by the same deities who humiliated him. This physical transformation, however, does not end the Monkey King's feelings of anger or self-loathing; neither does it change the way that others see him.

" WHEN TRANSFORMATIONS ARE MADE OUT OF SHAME OR AN EFFORT TO ASSIMILATE, THEY CAUSE MORE HARM THAN GOOD. BOTH JIN AND THE MONKEY KING WOUND THEMSELVES AND OTHERS IN THEIR QUESTS TO CHANGE THEMSELVES. IN REALITY, ALL THAT THEY NEED TO CHANGE IS THEIR POINT OF VIEW."

The gods still mock the Monkey King after he changes form. His anger remains, and he uses violence to convince others to accept his chosen identity.

The anger and shame that the Monkey King feels interferes with his duty as a king. He transfers his feelings of inferiority onto the other monkeys and decrees that his subjects too must wear shoes. The panel of this decree shows the monkeys falling off tree branches because of their slippery shoes. This is the Monkey King's final decree before he distances himself from his subjects. They are a reminder of an identity he is afraid of embracing. The Monkey King abandons the monkeys he is meant to care for in order "to announce my new name to all of Heaven." With this action, he chooses to seek the respect of individuals who do not care for him by deserting those who do.

The Monkey King's desire to be someone other than himself is dangerous. He cannot release the anger and embarrassment that he feels, and he takes it out on others. He becomes violent when anyone calls him a monkey. Tze-Yo-Tzuh asks the Monkey King why he so angry, but by calling him a "little monkey," the creator of all deities only incites the Monkey King's fury. The Monkey King refuses to believe that Tze-Yo-Tzuh made him to be a monkey because, in his mind, this makes him inferior. Because he stubbornly holds onto his anger and refuses to embrace his complete identity, the Monkey King is trapped under a mountain of rocks for five hundred years. He is only released from his prison when he embraces his personal identity and reverts to his original form. In a conversation with his fellow transformer, Jin, he explains that he could have spared himself this tribulation "had I only realized how good it is to be a monkey."

Jin is focused on transforming himself throughout his narrative. Jin is both Chinese and an American. Even as a young boy in Chinatown, Jin wants to be a Transformer. When he arrives at a predominately Caucasian school in the suburbs, Jin experiences prejudice and rejection. People in Jin's new school make assumptions about him based on his ancestry, and he becomes a target for individuals who make racial slurs. His encounters at school echo the Monkey King's conflict with the gods. Jin attempts to disassociate himself from his Chinese heritage in order to fit in and reduce his visibility as a target. For example, Jin perms his hair. This effort to assimilate, however, is as ridiculous as a monkey wearing shoes.

Like the Monkey King, Jin finds any reminder of what makes him different from the other students distasteful, despite the fact that other Asian Americans become his closest friends. He initially dislikes Wei-Chen Sun and refuses to become friends with the new student from Taiwan. Later, Jin calls Wei-Chen his best friend, but he is also ashamed of Wei-Chen because he is a first-generation immigrant who does not fit into American society. Wei-Chen is a constant reminder of Jin's family origins. Jin may not realize how obvious his embarrassment is, but Wei-Chen understands. He admits to Jin's crush, Amelia, "I think sometimes my accent embarrass him." Wei-Chen, however, is able to accept himself in a way that Jin cannot.

Jin further imitates the Monkey King by turning his back on both his friend and his heritage. He betrays Wei-Chen by kissing his girlfriend and then flies into a rage when Wei-Chen says that they are the same. His anger mirrors the Monkey King's, but Jin does not have the same Kung-Fu skills as the mythical character. Both Wei-Chen and Suzy hit Jin when he behaves inappropriately. After his final betrayal of Wei-Chen, Jin "forfeits his soul" and transforms into the Caucasian American Danny. This leads him to an even greater identity crisis. Danny has to cope with looking Caucasian but being Chinese. This crisis reaches its high point every year when his cousin Chin-Kee comes to visit.

Binbin Fu calls Chin-Kee the "epitome of transformation and subversion" in his *MELUS* article. As a stereotype, Chin-Kee is offensive. This two-dimensional caricature, however, conceals the Monkey King. Fu goes on to explain that Chin-Kee and the Monkey King are "two sides of the same coin." The Monkey King is a beloved myth and Chin-Kee is a reminder of racism. Together they represent the positive and negative history of Asian Americans. The Monkey King uses a negative stereotype as a tool to help Danny, or Jin, face his feelings. By forcing Danny to confront his fear of being Asian, he acts as Jin's conscience. Chin-Kee's antics help Jin find his soul again and embrace his dual identity. The Monkey King's transformation into Chin-Kee is a generous and selfless act that mirrors the transformation of Wei-Chen into a human child.

Wei-Chen undergoes a complex transformation in the book. Before he appears in the story, Wei-Chen is transformed from a monkey to a Taiwanese boy and sent to America by Tze-Yo-Tzuh. This necessary transformation enables Wei-Chen to complete his task as an emissary to humans. The initial transformation is helpful because it is merely physical. Wei-Chen remains true to himself and ignores the taunts of his classmates because his friendship with Jin gives him hope and strength. Unfortunately, his world changes after Jin verbally assaults him.

Like the Monkey King and Jin, Wei-Chen undergoes an inward transformation after experiencing rejection. He retains the human form that Tze-Yo-Tzuh gives him, but he abandons his mission and identity as an emissary. The same anger and self-loathing that Jin and the Monkey King experience are mirrored in his behavior. He becomes aggressive and casts off all that he is by choosing a life of pleasure. The Monkey King and Jin both return to their true form and learn the importance of embracing who they are in the book. Wei-Chen, however, does not accept who he is or renounce his life of pleasure at the end the story. There is hope, however, that a renewed friendship with Jin will help Wei-Chen release his anger and find himself again.

Source: April Dawn Paris, Critical Essay on *American Born Chinese*, in *Novels for Students*, Gale, Cengage Learning, 2012.

Michael D. Boatright

In the following excerpt, Boatright presents Wang's novel as representative of immigration literature through its themes of identity conflict.

. . . Yang's (2006) contemporary *American Born Chinese* offers yet another immigrant experience as represented in a graphic novel. Yang's novel, illustrated using the full color palette, recounts the fictional story of Jin Wang, a second-generation, American-born Chinese boy dealing with issues of identity and acceptance while growing up in San Francisco. Concurrent with Jin Wang's coming-of-age story line are two other connected narratives interwoven throughout the graphic novel: One is the mythological tale of the Monkey King, and the other revolves around the antics of Chin-Kee, a hyperbolic representation of negative Chinese stereotypes. Yang complements and complicates Jin Wang's narrative by interpolating these two story lines.

In the course of the narrative, Yang's young adolescent protagonist, Jin Wang, finds himself attracted to a European American girl named Amelia Harris. Jin's skin color is depicted with a paler hue than Amelia's, whose blonde hair and peach-toned skin grab Jin's attention one day while in class. From that moment onward, Jin convinces himself that the only way for a girl like Amelia to notice him is to reimage himself after a fellow classmate who happens to be white. The author's accentuation of skin color plays a prominent role in his protagonist's development of an immigrant identity (Tummala-Narra, 2001). Jin Wang perceives that his only route to securing a date with Amelia rests in somehow altering his physical appearance. Because he cannot control his skin color, a self-perceived roadblock to achieving his ambitions, he instead curls his straight hair to mirror the hairstyles of his white high school peers. From a critical literacy perspective, English language arts teachers could draw connections with and interrogate Jin Wang's desire to transform his physical appearance to the hegemony of whiteness as a socially constructed preferred skin color in the United States (Segura-Mora, 2009).

Another instance of identity conflict issuing from Yang's graphic novel is brought into sharp relief in the parallel story line involving Chin-Kee, who represents an overblown Chinese teenager saturated in negative stereotypes with slanted eyes, two protruding front teeth, traditional Chinese attire, the phonetic intermingling of the *r* and the *l* sounds, and pale-yellow skin that easily distinguishes him from the rest of the European American community. Although Chin-Kee means well, he represents an embarrassment to Danny, his unassuming and insecure European American teenage cousin, who attempts to disassociate himself from his Chinese heritage. By using a caricature like Chin-Kee, whose European American cousin desperately attempts to avoid, and through Jin Wang's desire to look more acceptable by refashioning his hairstyle after his European American male peers, Yang arrives at the heart of the immigrant identity issues at work in his graphic novel. In both instances, characters confront what it means to be Asian American. English language arts teachers may critique such immigrant identity issues with their students by engaging in dialogues that trouble the unstable identity construct of a second-generation immigrant that, in turn, question privileged as well as marginalized second-generation immigrant identity constructs.

In an interview about the impact of *American Born Chinese*, Yang was asked about the assimilation issues central to his graphic novel:

> I'm still trying to figure out what it means to be Asian American. I think I've progressively gotten away from shame in my own culture, although it's still there.... There's definitely a temptation to become fully assimilated, fully a part of America, but as Asian Americans, we have to constantly struggle against that. (Woan, 2007, p. 78)

The tension Yang cites in resisting absolute assimilation into American culture while at the same time maintaining his Asian identity articulates a desire to reside in both Asian and American cultures. This hybrid identity (Suárez-Orozco & Suárez-Orozco, 2001) that Yang spoke of represents a complex balancing act between acculturation and assimilation that second-generation immigrants may experience. Even though Jin Wang, the graphic novel's teenage protagonist, eventually comes to terms with his Asian American identity, his journey toward this hybrid identity gestures toward a problematic and complex reality for second-generation immigrants in the United States living in two often contradictory cultural worlds. Because identity formation constitutes a central concept for many adolescents, Yang's work offers a provocative conduit for investigating this theme with students. . . .

Source: Michael D. Boatright, "Graphic Journeys: Graphic Novels' Representations of Immigrant Experiences," in *Journal of Adolescent & Adult Literacy*, Vol. 53, No. 6, March 2010, pp. 468–76.

> ❝ WHAT IS PARTICULARLY WORTH EMPHASIZING IS THAT THE ORIGINS OF THIS OSTENTATIOUS DISPLAY OF CONSUMERIST SELF-REINVENTION, OF WHICH WEI-CHEN BECOMES A PART, IS A RACIAL ONE, A WAY OF FORCIBLY ASSERTING VALUE TO WHAT WAS WIDELY SEEN AS VALUELESS, NAMELY ASIAN AMERICAN MASCULINITY."

Min Hyoung Song

In the following excerpt, Song analyzes the character of Chin-Kee in American Born Chinese.

. . . *American Born Chinese* is divided into three distinct but interwoven parts that artfully fuse into a single narrative by the book's end. The first, a fanciful retelling of the classic sixteenth-century Ming epic *Journey to the West* by Ch'eng-en Wu, focuses on the difficulties of the Monkey King. The second is about a Chinese American boy named Jin Wang who was born in San Francisco's Chinatown but whose family has relocated to a predominantly white, suburban town. His only friend is a recently arrived Taiwanese immigrant named Wei-Chen. This second part thus fits easily into the well-worn grooves of the ethnic bildungsroman. The third part is perhaps the most interesting. In it a white high-school student named Danny is revealed to have a Chinese cousin named Chin-Kee. (Yes, as in "chinky"!) Chin-Kee, we are later told, visits Danny every time he moves to a new school and begins to make friends, and is so unpopular his unpopularity rubs off on Danny, forcing him to start over somewhere else.

At this point, it is easy to see why comics are ideal for the story *American Born Chinese* wishes to tell. Chin-Kee is exactly what his name calls forth. He is a grotesque stereotype of the Chinese as racially alien, a stereotype first cast in the nineteenth century as Western imperial countries chipped away at China's sovereignty and Chinese workers began to populate California and the rest of the American West in visibly large numbers. In a volume of carefully selected artwork and cartoon drawings entitled

The Coming Man: 19th Century American Perceptions of the Chinese, Philip Choy, Lorraine Dong, and Marlon Hom graphically demonstrate that popular racial exaggerations had the effect of creating a consistent, powerful visual vocabulary for imagining the Chinese as from elsewhere and as therefore not belonging in the United States. In almost all of the images they provide, the Chinese are depicted in strikingly similar ways. For example, in the San Francisco illustrated weekly magazine *The Wasp*, edited during its heyday by Ambrose Bierce, the Chinese figure as the embodiment of unfair competition who, in league with the big manufacturers, are the enemy of struggling white labour in California. In the illustration, the classic topos of the caricatured coolie is in evidence in this figure's slant-eyes, short stature, sallow skin, predictably Chinese clothing, claw-like fingertips, and long menacing queue. One quotation from this volume of *The Wasp* stands out: "The unsophisticated Mongol, imitating, ape-like, his fellow of this country, attains a monopoly of the cigar and laundry business, and smiles a cunning smile of triumph at his discomfited rivals" (qtd. in Choy et al. 91 . . .).

The visual vocabulary developed in such early caricatures of the Chinese and buttressed by this kind of commentary is what causes Chin-Kee to remain such a complex, and troubling, figure in *American Born Chinese*. The very first time readers meet him, he appears in a full-page panel arranged to look like the opening title of an old television show. In big yellow lettering, the reader is told in heavily accented English, "Everyone Ruvs Chin-Kee." And immediately under and to the right of this lettering, Chin-Kee's head appears with a big grin, pronounced buckteeth, eyes so small they are never seen except as a bold black line, sickly pale yellow skin, and a queue. To emphasize further that this is an image originally formalized in newspapers and popular entertainment and later largely disseminated through the growth of popular mass media, the words "clap clap clap" line the entire bottom of the panel. This, and the words "ha ha ha," are likewise repeated in other panels, replicating the canned laughter and applause of television sit-coms. Within the narrative itself, Chin-Kee soon arrives at Danny's house, dressed in an outfit meant to be traditionally Chinese, shouts "Harro Amellica!," and leaves his luggage, made of over-sized Chinese-food take-out cartons, for Danny's father to

handle. Finally, just in case we do not get what is being mocked, Chin-Kee immediately proceeds to hit on Melanie, the girl that Danny has been flirting with before his arrival. Chin-Kee says, "Such pletty Amellican girl wiff bountiful Amellican bosom! Must bind feet and bear Chin-Kee's children!" As he says these words, he is depicted in best Fu Manchu manner, as hunched forward, arms stretched outward, hands claw-like, and drool spitting from his mouth.

Chin-Kee's presence, however, refuses to remain merely a satirical reference to long-dead racial conventions. The next time Yang introduces Chin-Kee, he begins to embody not only nineteenth-century stereotypes about the Chinese coolie but also late twentieth-century ideas about Asian American youths as stellar students. The day after his arrival, Chin-Kee follows Danny to each of his classes and raises his hands immediately whenever a teacher poses a question. It turns out that he knows more than any of the students at Danny's school about the three branches of the United States government, Columbus's first voyage to the New World, the names of different bones in the human arm, algebraic equations, the meaning of a story written in Spanish, chemical formulas, and lines from Shakespeare's *Romeo and Juliet*. During lunch, other students are depicted in the background pointing at him, whispering to one another, and casting furtive glances in his direction. Two students look as if they are about to throw up when they see Chin-Kee eating something with a cat's head poking out of a take-out carton. Even still, as disgusting as this is, it is not clear what upsets the students more: Chin-Kee's questionable food choices, outlandish clothing, and "r"-deficient accent or the fact that Chin-Kee consistently outshines them all in their subjects. In the very first class period, the teacher exhorts his students, "You know people—it would behoove you all to be a little more like Chin-Kee." No wonder, then, that despite his invocation as irony, Chin-Kee's presence in *American Born Chinese* is just as likely to elicit a groan as a laugh, or perhaps both at the same time. As Binbin Fu observes, Chin-Kee "is provocatively repulsive and hilariously funny at the same time. An intruder into the American classroom, he sings 'She Bang, She Bang' (a la well-known *American Idol* contestant William Hung) while dancing grotesquely in a traditional Chinese dress on a desk."

In addition to pitting nineteenth- and twentieth-century racial assumptions about Asian Americans against each other in this way, Chin-Kee's presence in this narrative thread also enlivens the question of how exactly Chin-Kee is related to Danny. This is resolved when it is revealed that the other two parts of this work—the retelling of the Monkey King's fantastic epic and Jin Wang's realist bildungsroman—meet in the story of Danny and Chin-Kee. In the first part, the Monkey King is shown being denied entry to a party comprised of other immortals. The guard tells him he cannot let him in because he is not wearing any shoes. Later, when pushed, the guard admits, "You may be a king—you may even be a deity—but you are still a monkey." This insult leads the Monkey King to murder all the guests (a bloodletting that is meant to be satisfying), which in turn sets him on a violent path that lasts for several pages. In a sequence of extraordinary drawings, the Monkey King confronts several deities who can barely consider him a threat. Each of the deities and their flunkies laugh when the Monkey King insists that he is not a monkey but their equals, and are then thoroughly punished by the Monkey King for their laughter.

At the end of *American Born Chinese*, the Monkey King is revealed to be none other than Chin-Kee himself, a disguise he puts on to become Danny's "conscience [. . .] a signpost to your soul." As such, he imparts the lesson the Monkey King himself has learned the hard way: "how good it is to be a monkey." At this moment in the book, Danny is also revealed to be a disguise. In fact, Danny is Jin Wang (from the second narrative thread), who is so full of self-hatred as a result of the ways in which he has been slighted by everyone at his school that he has turned on his only friend, Wei-Chen, first by making an impulsive pass at Suzy Nakamura, a Japanese American girl Wei-Chen is dating, and then by calling Wei-Chen an "F.O.B." The next morning, Jin wakes up to discover that he has magically turned into Danny. These dizzying revelations emphasize the ways in which *American Born Chinese* is interested in what is hidden from view. Outward identities lead inexorably to secret identities, and bodies are always capable of transforming themselves—much like the transformer robots that Jin and Wei-Chen liked to play with when they first met. As the Hasbro marketing motto puts it, there is "more than meets the eye."

One way to interpret these transformations, which would follow Walter Benn Michaels's lead, is to say that Danny is the person Jin could become, someone who could be socially accepted as if he were white if he so chooses. That Yang explicitly treats such a willed act of racial belonging as a lack of conscience reveals an abiding, and possibly unreasonable, attachment to the concept of race. Danny is followed by Chin-Kee only because the latter believes that what the former is doing, finding social acceptance, is somehow a betrayal of who he really is. And such race pride, in turn, feeds into a more general culture of reified-diversity talk that allows one to focus, as Michaels has argued, on "differences we can love, like those between Asian Americans and Caucasians[,] rather than differences (like the ones between smart people and stupid people or, more to the point, rich people and poor people) that are not so obviously appealing" (Trouble 84). In short, the contemporary desire to insist on racial difference is a transparent form of deliberately fake consciousness that allows one to avoid talking about the more disturbing reality of economic inequality.

This reasoning seems to make a marginal amount of sense in explaining the dynamics of *American Born Chinese*'s end, where Jin learns a lesson that might appear preoccupied with race pride. But Michaels's insistence that one can only choose between focusing on race or inequality lacks explanatory power in thinking about the transformations that Wei-Chen also undergoes. For most of the narrative, he is presented as a nerdy but fearless recent immigrant from Taiwan, but after his break with Jin he becomes an angry and despondent Asian American hipster. He is also figured ultimately as a monkey in disguise, like his father, who is revealed to be the Monkey King. More interesting still, his rage at being rejected by Jin is channeled into a specific, and highly visible, form of Asian American cultural activity: the Japanese import car scene. This scene's sensational mix of tricked-out automobiles, dangerous street racing, and objectified female models is easily one of the most salient examples of an organic Asian American pop-cultural innovation.

The import car scene, before it became popularized for mass consumption in more racially familiar ways, was originally created by disaffected Asian American youths in Southern

California who felt actively unwelcome at white car-racing events involving Detroit muscle cars. These youths also took inspiration from the intentional oppositionality of Mexican American low-rider car culture. As a sign of defiance, then, these youths began to modify and race smaller, lighter Japanese imports, which at the time were perceived to be poorly made and cheap. By fitting the most generic imports they could find with more efficient and powerful engines and flashy exteriors that emphasized speed and a hyper-modern aesthetic, these youths helped fashion the Japanese import into a synonym for an agile East Asian capitalist style capable of outperforming the more weighted down and brutish Detroit muscle car (Rodriguez and Gonzalez 254; Kwon 3–5). What is particularly worth emphasizing is that the origins of this ostentatious display of consumerist self-reinvention, of which Wei-Chen becomes a part, is a racial one, a way of forcibly asserting value to what was widely seen as valueless, namely Asian American masculinity.

Hence, if Wei-Chen's apparent middle-class status in *American Born Chinese* signals the very kind of "economic success" that Michaels tells us is "a measure of success in America" (Shape 130), it seems important to wonder what it might mean for Asian Americans to be visibly perceived as economically successful and yet to remain racially different from those who are normatively thought to be American. This is a question that has grown more difficult to answer since 1965, as the majority of Asian Americans became foreign-born rather than native-born; as laws favoured Asian immigrants of professional background who have, in turn, taken much of the spotlight from the many Asian immigrants who have entered through family reunification, as refugees, or without documentation and who make up a kind of other Asian America; and as the number of ethnicities represented in the overall Asian American population has become much larger. Still, despite these often repeated caveats about the role of the state and the exercise of biopolitics in the current configuration of a heterogeneous, hybrid, and multiple Asian America (Lowe 66), it remains clear that many commentators often fail to convey any of these nuances. Michaels in particular demonstrates a culpable lack of historical understanding. (At one point in his writings,

Michaels approvingly quotes Henry Ford as saying "history is bunk" [Trouble 18].) This willful ignorance has allowed him to blame people of colour—and Asian Americans in particular—for being overly attached to the concept of race, without acknowledging the legacy of a white supremacy that has continually made the topic of race unforgettable, and that has facilitated the creation of alternative spheres of cultural expression like the Japanese import car scene. . . .

Source: Min Hyoung Song, "'How Good It Is To Be a Monkey': Comics, Racial Formation, and *American Born Chinese*," in *Winnipeg Mosaic*, Vol. 43, No. 1, March 2010, pp. 73–92.

Binbin Fu

In the following review, Fu proposes that American Born Chinese *might turn the tide of opinion toward accepting Asian American graphic literature into the mainstream of literature in the United States.*

Asian America has not had a great many opportunities to enjoy graphic literature in the mainstream media in the United States. Historically, this particular genre has been more damaging than uplifting to the Asian American communities. The predominant image of the slit-eyed, pig-tailed, and buck-toothed "Heathen Chinee" that originated from the nineteenth-century cartoon culture has apparently left a lasting imprint on the popular American imagination. Even in the supposedly more mature and more realistic medium, film, Asian and Asian American characters have oftentimes been cartoonized into racial stereotypes. The insidious Dr. Fu Manchu, the effeminate Detective Charlie Chan, the Dragon Lady, and any number of cinematic reincarnations of these characters provide ample evidence that there exists a racially biased, dehumanizing comic gallery of Asian Americans. Even subversive revisioning, an element presumably inherent in cartoons and comic alike, has yet to liberate Asian Americans from racial degradation.

In this light, Gene Luen Yang's new graphic novel might have just changed the tide in a significant way. Nominated for the 2006 National Book Award in the Young People's Literature category, *American Born Chinese* is mature in artistic design and visually engaging.

Yet what makes it especially appealing to both young and mature readers is its narrative depth. Juxtaposing three seemingly unrelated story lines, the novel opens with a retelling of the story of the Monkey King, the renowned mythic hero in Chinese folklore. The second tale, a Bildungsroman, illustrates how Jin Wang (later becoming Danny), a Chinese American boy, struggles to survive exclusion and racist bullying in his search for an identity in a predominantly white suburban school. In the third narrative thread, Chin-Kee, a deluxe combo of the worst racial stereotypes involving Asian Americans, pays an annual visit to his cousin Danny in America, turning the latter's school life into a nightmare. By the end of the novel, however, the three separate tales are cleverly woven together in a dramatic climax, highlighting the work's focus on ethnic self-acceptance and empowerment.

Yang uses the idea of transformation to give the novel thematic and structural unity, although transformative acts are not always in the right direction for Yang's characters. Jin Wang's favorite toy, for instance, is a robotic "transformer," but when his wish to transform himself is granted in a moment of "oriental magic," he finds himself displaced from his familiar Chinatown milieu and facing the ridicules of some white students in the American suburbia. Later in the narrative, dreaming of escaping the humiliation his cousin, Chin-kee, has brought him, Danny becomes Caucasian overnight, only to find out quickly that this self-willed racial makeover leads him further into an identity crisis. However, the most fascinating transformer in the novel is none other than the Monkey King himself. The author's evocation of the mythic Chinese hero should not be a surprise to those familiar with the history of Chinese American literature. The legendary trickster figure has been repeatedly re-imagined by Chinese American writers as a source of cultural strength, a symbol of subversion and resistance, and a metaphor for cross-cultural and interracial negotiation. Yang's new rendition, by transforming the proverbial monkey's tale into one of self-search and self-acceptance, provides an illuminating parallel to Jin Wang's/Danny's coming-of-age narrative. While the author's transcultural adaptation might undermine the

theme of rebellion in the original myth, the superhero-like Monkey King figure introduces a powerful alternative image to the likes of Superman, Batman, and Spider-Man, who dominate the comic world.

If the Monkey King serves as a source of cultural empowerment in Jin Wang's personal development, Chin-Kee's character appears to be the monkey's evil double. He is provocatively repulsive and hilariously funny at the same time. An intruder into the American classroom, he sings "She Bang, She Bang" (a la the well-known American Idol contestant William Hung) while dancing grotesquely in a traditional Chinese dress on a desk. His spittle—which is rumored to have spread SARS around the school—and his home-made "Clispy Flied Cat Gizzards wiff Noodle" make him an ultimate spectacle of racial degradation. Yet he is also wickedly smart and subversive, reminding the reader of the Monkey King himself. The blatant racial stereotype that Chin-Kee stands for has long denied Asians a place in American culture. Yet, in Yang's novel, when Chin-Kee finally reveals his true identity, he emerges as the epitome of transformation and subversion. Some readers may find his character offensive or at least strange, but Yang's reinvention of such a figure is an effective way to dispel the century-old image of the "Heathen Chinee."

Both the Monkey King and Chin-Kee, functioning as two sides of the same coin, add significant depth to Jin Wang's search for acceptance. The three story lines give the novel an extraordinary energy and psychological realism. In contrast, Jin Wang's white schoolmates, displaying a myriad of blatant or subtle racial biases and racist attitudes, deserve more attention in the story. While we might not want a graphic novel to be completely didactic, we do want to see a more in-depth exploration of the roots of racism. If change is possible for the young Asian American protagonist, is it also possible for those harboring racist ideas? Nevertheless, just as Yang's heroes transform themselves from self-negation to self-acceptance, his work may perhaps transform Asian Americans' view of the graphic novel as a medium that can liberate more than it restrains.

Source: Binbin Fu, Review of *American Born Chinese*, in *MELUS*, Vol. 32, No. 3, Fall 2007, pp. 274–76.

Rick Margolis

In the following interview, Margolis asks Yang about how he deals with racial prejudice in American Born Chinese.

American Born Chinese *features three story lines—one about the Monkey King, a traditional Chinese folk hero; another about Jin Wang, an Asian-American boy who attends an all-white school; and the third about Chin-Kee, the embodiment of negative Chinese stereotypes. How did you come up with the idea?*

Originally, I was going to do it as three separate books, and I was trying to decide which one I wanted to tackle first. Eventually, I saw that there were a lot of common thematic elements across the three stories: there's one about transformation, another about what it means to be an Asian American, and another theme about prejudice and acceptance.

When you were growing up, was your experience of racism as disturbing as Jin Wang's?

I spent most of my childhood in a small town next to San Jose, CA, called Saratoga. In elementary school, I was one of a handful of Asian-American students in my classes. A lot of the more virulent racism, the more outright racism, I experienced in junior high. There was a group—we called them stoners, back then—that were particularly virulent. A lot of the words that come out of [the character] Timmy's mouth were from that group of kids. I wasn't good at sports, and I was pretty geeky. When I got into high school, it became really unclear to me whether things were happening to me because I was just kind of a geek or things were happening to me because I was Asian.

When did you start drawing comics?

I had a fifth-grade friend named Jeremy Kuniyohi, who brought me to my first comics shop, and we started drawing comics together. Now he's a doctor, but I kept drawing comics. What attracted me to the form was, originally, when I was in third or fourth grade, I read all these books on Walt Disney. I decided I wanted to be an animator when I grew up because I liked to draw, and I really liked to tell stories. But I found with a comic book, one person can have control over the entire thing.

How did you develop such a clean, expressive style of drawing?

I was heavily influenced by Disney cartoons and animation, in general. *Batman*, the animated

series, also influenced me. Bruce Timm's designs on that series were really brilliant. I also have a day job, so I need to be able to draw pretty quickly.

What's your day job?

I've been at Bishop O'Dowd High School in Oakland, CA, for nine and a half years. I started as a math and computer science teacher. Later on, I worked for three or four years as an educational technologist, which is just a fancy way of saying that I help other teachers develop tech-based instructional units. And then just this year, I'm moving into another position with an even fancier title. I am now the director of information services.

What's been the reaction of Asian Americans to American Born Chinese*?*

Most of the Asian Americans that I've shown it to—they're my friends, so I don't know how honest they're being—seem to like it. They say it does resonate with them, which makes me happy. I have heard through my publisher that some Asian Americans have been offended by the third story line.

Why? Chin-Kee seems like a caricature of all the negative Chinese stereotypes rolled into one.

That's exactly what he's supposed to be. Some people feel like just having that character there perpetuates those stereotypes. But I wanted to show that even though in modern-day society that stereotype is inexplicit, it's still around. A lot of things that happen today, in 2006, really point to that.

Source: Rick Margolis, "*American Born Chinese,*" in *School Library Journal*, Vol. 52, No. 9, September 2006, p. 41.

SOURCES

"American Born Chinese—Reviews," in *First Second Books.com,* http://www.firstsecondbooks.com/reviews/reviewsABC.html (accessed July 15, 2011); originally published in *Bulletin of the Center for Children's Books,* November 2006.

"American Born Chinese—Reviews," in *First Second Books.com,* http://www.firstsecondbooks.com/reviews/reviewsABC.html (accessed July 15, 2011); originally published in *School Library Journal,* September 2006.

Boatright, Michael D., "Graphic Journeys: Graphic Novels' Representations of Immigrant Experiences," in *Journal of Adolescent & Adult Literacy*, Vol. 53, No. 6, March 2010, pp. 468–76.

Chan, Sucheng, "The Writing of Asian American History," in *OAH Magazine of History*, Vol. 10, No. 4, Summer 1996, pp. 8–17.

Duncan, Randy, and Matthew J. Smith, *The Power of Comics: History Form and Culture*, Continuum International Publishing, 2009, pp. 25–26, 71, 135.

Fu, Binbin, Review of *American Born Chinese*, in *MELUS*, Vol. 32, No. 3, Fall 2007, pp. 274–76.

Garrity, Shaenon, "The History of Webcomics," in *Comics Journal*, http://www.tcj.com/the-history-of-webcomics/ (accessed July 15, 2011).

"Gene Yang Biography," in *Gene Yang Home Page*, http://wn.com/Gene_Yang (accessed on July 15, 2011).

"Intertextuality," in *A Handbook to Literature*, 9th ed., edited by William Harmon and Hugh Holman, Prentice Hall, 2003, p. 268.

Kang, K., Connie, "Yuji Ichioka, 66; Led Way in Studying Lives of Asian Americans," in *UCLA Asian American Studies Center*, http://www.aasc.ucla.edu/archives/yuji 66latimes.asp (accessed July 20, 2011); originally published in *Los Angeles Times*, September 7, 2002.

Karp, Jesse, Review of *American Born Chinese*, in *Booklist Online*, http://www.booklistonline.com/American-Born-Chinese-Gene-Luen-Yang/pid = 1735514 (accessed July 14, 2011).

Review of *American Born Chinese*, in *First Second Books. com*, http://www.firstsecondbooks.com/reviews/reviews ABC.html (accessed July 15, 2011); originally published in *Bulletin of the Center for Children's Books*, November 2006.

Sohoni, Deenesh, "Unsuitable Suitors: Anti-Miscegenation Laws, Naturalization Laws, and the Construction of Asian Identities," in *Law and Society Review*, Vol. 41, No. 3, September 2007, pp. 587–618.

"Timeline of Asian American History," in *Digital History*, http://www.digitalhistory.uh.edu/asian_voices/asian _timeline.cfm (accessed July 25, 2011).

Vizzini, Ned, "High Anxiety," in *New York Times Sunday Book Review*, May 13, 2007, http://www.nytimes.com/ 2007/05/13/books/review/Vizzini-t.html?sq = Gene%20 Yang%20and%20American%20Born%20Chinese&st = nyt&adxnnl = 1&scp = 1&adxnnlx = 1312154208-5lmbfCp9/ IlsX3/x8f2ODg (accessed July 13, 2011).

Weiner, Stephen, "Pioneer and Storyteller: The Graphic Novels of Will Eisner," in *The Will Eisner Companion: The Pioneering Spirit of the Father of the Graphic Novel*, D. C. Comics, 2004, pp. 107–110.

Woan, Sunny, "Interview with Gene Yang: Author of American Born Chinese," in *Kartika Review*, http://www.kartikareview.com/issue1/1gene.html (accessed July 12, 2011).

Yang, Gene, "About Gene Yang," in *Humble Comics. com*, http://geneyang.com/about (accessed on July 12, 2011).

———, *American Born Chinese*, colored by Lark Pien, First Second, 2006.

———, "Origins of American Born Chinese—part 1," in *First Second Weblog*, http://firstsecondbooks.typepad. com/mainblog/2006/08/gene_yang_origi.html (accessed July 15, 2011).

———, "Origins of American Born Chinese—part 3," in *First Second Weblog*, http://firstsecondbooks.typepad. com/mainblog/2006/08/gene_yang_origi_2.html (accessed July 15, 2011).

FURTHER READING

Lee, Jennifer, and Min Zhou, eds., *Asian American Youth: Culture, Identity and Ethnicity*, Routledge Press, 2004.

> This book is a collection of essays that study the effects of immigration and assimilation on young people from Asia in America. The concepts of ethnicity, multiculturalism, and personal identity reflect Yang's themes.

McCloud, Scott, *Making Comics: Storytelling Secrets of Comics, Manga and Graphic Novels*, Harper Paperbacks, 2006.

> McCloud uses the comic book format to describe how comics are made. This book is useful for anyone who wants a better understanding of the comic genre or who is interested in attempting sequential art.

Okihiro, Gary, *The Columbia Guide to Asian American History*, Columbia University Press, 2001.

> Professor Okihiro examines more than two hundred years of Asian American history and culture. A useful introduction to Asian American studies, this book includes narratives that explore the Asian American experience.

Wright, Bradford W., *Comic Book Nation: The Transformation of Youth Culture in America*, Johns Hopkins University Press, 2001.

> This nonfiction book explores how the comic genre reflects American history and society. Wright also touches on the influence comic books have on American culture.

Yang, Gene and Thiem Pham, *Level Up*, First Second, 2011.

> Yang's young-adult graphic novel collaboration with Pham examines the idea of national identity, personal identity, and rebellion. While this book shares the theme of personal identity with *American Born Chinese*, it expands on the conflict between parental expectations and personal choice.

SUGGESTED SEARCH TERMS

Gene Yang

American Born Chinese

Asian American history

Gene Yang AND American Born Chinese

graphic novel AND history

comics AND graphic novels

The Monkey King

Asian American culture

American Born Chinese AND criticism

Gene Yang AND criticism

Gene Yang AND graphic novel

Balzac and the Little Chinese Seamstress

DAI SIJIE

2000

The Chinese émigré filmmaker and author Dai Sijie earned resounding praise among French-speaking audiences, as well as five literary prizes, with the publication of his first novel, *Balzac et la Petite Tailleuse chinoise* (2000), translated into English by Ina Rilke in 2001 as *Balzac and the Little Chinese Seamstress*. Dai directed the film version of the novel, which was released in 2002 and brought him further global exposure.

The tale revolves around two urban youths who, during Chinese Communist dictator Mao Zedong's infamous Cultural Revolution, find themselves condemned to indefinite "reeducation" in a rural village near the peak of a mountain dubbed Phoenix of the Sky, where manual labor is intended to reorient the youths away from suspicious bourgeois interests. But the youths happen upon a friend's stash of forbidden books. The works of Honoré de Balzac (1799–1850), one of the most treasured figures in French literature, and other Western authors play revolutionary roles in the lives of the two young men and a mutual friend, the strikingly beautiful Little Seamstress. Offering meditations on the trappings of rural life, the value of literature, and the nature of love—with occasional discreet references to physical romance—the book is an enlightening read for younger and older adults alike.

Dai Sijie *(Ulf Andersen / Getty Images)*

AUTHOR BIOGRAPHY

Dai Sijie was born in the city of Putian, Fujian Province—on the southeastern coast of China, opposite the island of Taiwan—on March 2, 1954. Both of his parents were doctors, and in 1971, during Mao Zedong's Cultural Revolution, he was sent along with three other teenage boys to a rural village for reeducation, a stay that would last three years. His circumstances and experiences under reeducation in many respects mirror those of the narrator of *Balzac and the Little Chinese Seamstress* (2000), his first novel, which is acknowledged to be autobiographical in foundation. As Dai told Yu Sen-lun in the *Taipei Times*, "There was a real love story, but not as romantic. The stealing books part is true and the experience of reading stories to farmers is also true." The Cultural Revolution effectively ended with Mao's death in 1978. In 1984, Dai won a scholarship to attend France's École des Beaux-Arts and left China to study Western art and then cinema. He would become a permanent resident of Paris.

Dai began his artistic career as a filmmaker, earning critical recognition for such films as *Chine, ma douleur* (1989), *Le mangeur de lune* (1993), and *L'onzieme* (1998), for which he wrote the screenplay. Looking for more substantial audiences, he turned to writing fiction, and *Balzac et la Petite Tailleuse chinoise* (*Balzac and the Little Chinese Seamstress*) became an immediate success and would be translated into some thirty other languages. He was permitted by Chinese authorities to film his novel in China, but both the book and the film have been banned there, as censors refused to allow that the seamstress would be so profoundly changed by Western literature. At one point, Dai hoped to be able to return to China and write and direct films in his native language, but Chinese censors have continued to ban his works—including a film focusing on a love story between two women—and he has become resigned to filming his stories set in China in other locations, such as Vietnam.

Dai has also published *Mr. Muo's Travelling Couch* (2005) and *Once on a Moonless Night* (2010), a love story revolving around a lost Buddhist scroll.

PLOT SUMMARY

Part I

When the narrator and his friend Luo arrive in a mountain village for their reeducation, the narrator's violin is inspected with curiosity, and he plays a sonata. His parents are doctors who have been labeled state enemies. Luo's father, a dentist, once suffered a public humiliation for being a reactionary.

The village that is their destination is the poorest on the mountain called Phoenix of the Sky and is situated at the mountain's summit. Their home is set on stilts over a pigsty. In the mornings before their grueling manual labor, they manipulate the headman by resetting their alarm clock. He likes their retellings of films they have seen, so he gives them several days off to walk to the nearest town, Yong Jing, watch a film, and report back.

The two young men meet the region's tailor, who is carried on a chair by porters, on their way to the abode of their old friend Four-Eyes. The tailor comments enthusiastically on the narrator's violin. Weeks later, they visit the tailor's

MEDIA ADAPTATIONS

- Dai, already an accomplished filmmaker by the time his novel was published in 2000, directed a film version of *Balzac and the Little Chinese Seamstress* (2002), with dialogue in the Sichuan dialect of Mandarin. The film stars the Chinese actors Liu Ye, Chen Kun, and Zhou Xun. Dai altered the storyline somewhat for the film, lending enhanced modern relevance by situating the villages in the vast area flooded by the construction of the Three Gorges Dam—370 miles of the Yangtze River—and adding scenes in which the narrator, Ma, attempts to find the Little Seamstress later in life, before the mass flooding.

shop and meet his famously beautiful daughter, the Little Seamstress, who is charmed by Luo.

Luo and the narrator must spend two months working in the perilous coal mine, which leaves both young men fearing death. Luo becomes stricken with malaria, and the miners use a folk remedy: they whip Luo's back with branches, to drive away the sickness, until he is incapacitated. The narrator then finds a letter from the Little Seamstress, who has gotten permission for them to take two days off to come and tell her village a film story.

Along the way, Luo begins to suffer a bout of malaria, and when they arrive, the Little Seamstress applies a natural poultice to his wrist. She also invites four old sorceresses to drive out the evil spirits responsible. When they begin nodding off, the narrator starts telling the story of a North Korean melodrama, with the ailing Luo interjecting a voiceover with exquisite timing. Luo and the Little Seamstress share a kiss.

Part II

Feeling better, Luo walks with the narrator back toward their village, meeting Four-Eyes on the way. His buffalo knocks off his glasses, which the narrator helps him find. Looking for warm clothes, the narrator finds a peculiar locked suitcase, which Four-Eyes refuses to acknowledge at all. The two young men later speculate that Four-Eyes's literary parents had sent him away with books. When Four-Eyes breaks his glasses and is unable to safely transport his rice tax to the district station, the narrator and Luo help in exchange for the loan of a book—one by Balzac.

Luo spends all night reading the entire novel, *Ursule Mirouët*, and then embarks for the Little Seamstress's house. The narrator in turn reads and then, inspired, copies his favorite passages onto the inside of his coat. Luo comes back with evidence of making love to the seamstress.

In the summer, Luo and the narrator find Four-Eyes boiling his clothes to kill lice; he had become infested when visiting, in vain, an old miller rumored to know rustic ballads that Four-Eyes could submit to a literary journal. Luo offers a deal: the two will obtain the ballads if he will lend them more books. The narrator and Luo visit the miller acting as government official and translator, respectively. They earn his trust by sharing his dish of saltwater pebbles and are rewarded with a tune, a bawdy lyric, and a stomach that the miller ripples at will. Four-Eyes finds the material unusable but adapts it to his purpose, offending the narrator, who clobbers him.

Luo, the narrator, and the Little Seamstress visit Yong Jing to watch a movie, which mesmerizes the seamstress. They hear of a city woman come to save her son from reeducation. On the walk home, they stop at a cemetery, where the woman's porter overtakes them. Disarmed by the narrator's city accent, the woman chats with him in a friendly way; the narrator learns that she is Four-Eyes's mother and is a poetess. The narrator poses as Luo and learns that Four-Eyes disapproves of him for coveting the suitcase. When the woman leaves, the Little Seamstress suggests they steal the books.

Together, they fashion a skeleton key (one that can open a variety of locks). The day before a planned departure feast to celebrate Four-Eyes's departure, a buffalo conspicuously falls into a ravine; Four-Eyes drinks some of its blood to ward off cowardice. A stew is begun, and the four sorceresses, plus a fifth, arrive to perform a ritual. As the banquet begins, Luo and the narrator dash to Four-Eyes's hut, pick the lock, and lock themselves inside. They find the suitcase and open it to see the many books—but Four-Eyes is ill and returns with his mother for medicine, so they hide under the beds. Four-Eyes suddenly needs to defecate and rushes outside, trailed by his mother. The two thieves flee with the suitcase.

Part III

With the headman gone to a Communist conference, Luo and the narrator abscond from work to read constantly, with Luo often visiting the seamstress. Torrential rain narrows a stretch of the path to a perilous ridge, and joining Luo one day, the narrator cannot make the crossing, where a raven likes to circle. Luo goes on alone. The narrator soon dreams of the Little Seamstress plummeting to her death at the perilous ridge.

The headman asks Luo to help cure his toothache, as a doctor pulled out the wrong tooth, but Luo declines. Days later, the tailor arrives, to the delight of the villagers, especially the women. He stays with the two friends and at night demands a story, which the narrator provides, telling of *The Count of Monte Cristo*, a nineteenth-century novel by the French author Alexandre Dumas, père (Senior). The story lasts not only all that night but for the next eight nights as well. One night, the headman eavesdrops, grows suspicious, and insists that either Luo attend to his tooth or the narrator will be interrogated. During the improvised surgery, the narrator slackens the speed of the sewing-machine drill to torture the headman.

The three following sections, narrated by the miller, Luo, and the seamstress, respectively, read as if spoken to and recorded by the narrator. The old miller reports that he saw the Little Seamstress and Luo—whom he recognized as the translator—being romantic together at a secluded waterfall. Luo relates how the seamstress dives from great heights at the waterfall and boldly retrieves his keys from the pool's bottom as a game—until one day they lose the keys. Luo has received word that he is to visit his ailing mother for a month. The seamstress relates that she enjoys her and Luo's acting sessions and that the key ring was lost because she was bitten underwater by a snake.

With Luo gone, the narrator becomes the seamstress's protective domestic companion,

reading to her and helping with chores. One day upon leaving her, he is taunted by jealous locals, led by the village cripple, and a scuffle results in him dropping a book. When he grabs the book and flees, someone throws a stone that wounds his ear. That night, the pain leaves the narrator with delirious visions of abuse that transition to fantasies of the seamstress.

When the seamstress realizes she is pregnant, the narrator heads to Yong Jing to seek assistance with an abortion. He identifies a gynecologist and, in trying to visit an old preacher on his deathbed—one whose sons hope to record a last revolutionary slogan but get only muttered Latin phrases—happens to see the doctor; the narrator catches up with him in the emergency room and offers him a book by Balzac for his help. The next week, the doctor gives the seamstress an abortion, and afterward, she and the narrator pay their respects at the preacher's grave.

Three months later, Luo and the narrator are drunkenly burning the books. Recently, the seamstress has been fashioning stylish modern garments for herself, and she has cut her hair. One morning, the tailor arrives, crestfallen, and reports that she has left for good. They race down the mountain after her, catching up with her near the cemetery hours later. Luo collapses on the ground, and she sits in silence. They speak, and then she starts to leave, running off when the narrator shouts after her. Luo tells the narrator that Balzac has taught her the pricelessness of a woman's beauty.

CHARACTERS

Doctor

When the narrator realizes that the doctor, a gynecologist, is not a foe but an ally of his father's, he risks offering a book in exchange for medical assistance. Proving sympathetic, the doctor accepts the deal.

Four-Eyes

Possessive of his books—especially since their discovery could doom his chances of ending his reeducation—Four-Eyes evidently derives a sense of superiority from his enhanced knowledge. Though his friends succeed in obtaining ballads from the old miller, Four-Eyes disparages their efforts because he is not satisfied with the results. Fear of reprisal from the authorities prevents Four-Eyes from reporting the theft of his books.

Headman

The headman of Luo and the narrator's village is a domineering, impetuous man who dictates the daily activities of the two young men. His ignorance of how their alarm clock actually works signifies the average peasant farmer's disconnect from modern civilization and leaves him susceptible to manipulation through their resetting it. This disconnect accounts for his fascination with stories from films that he does not have the time to attend, but to which he can send the two young men. (Another headman, that of Four-Eyes's village, also appears in the story.)

Little Seamstress

The epitome of a rural beauty—physically flawless, genuine in behavior, and wild at heart—the Little Seamstress inspires Luo to journey to her village frequently, and when he brings the first Balzac volume, their romance begins. Luo intends to refine and civilize the seamstress by reading to her. After her abortion—which marks her rejection of the traditional village woman's roles of wife and mother—she begins making a set of modern-style clothes for herself. What she learns about love and romance from Balzac in fact leads her to become so civilized that she abandons her new friends, condemned as they are to their rural reeducation, to move to the city.

Luo

Between Luo and the narrator, Luo, a year older, is the quicker thinker, as evidenced by his off-the-cuff defense of the patriotic value of the narrator's violin in the opening pages. The narrator at first considers Luo, who brings the sorceresses to tears with a perfectly timed voice-over, the better storyteller. Instantly smitten with the Little Seamstress upon meeting her, Luo charms and befriends her, and with literary inspiration, their romance blossoms. He proves so devoted that even the terrifying experience of clambering across a dangerous ridge cannot prevent him from visiting her. However, his month-long absence leaves the seamstress to decide alone what to do with the unborn child that might tie her to Luo for the rest of her life. After running down the mountain for hours to

catch up with the seamstress only to have her reject him, Luo can only despair at the fate she has chosen.

Narrator

The narrator has a fascinating relationship with Luo, whom he admires and supports and at times seems jealous of. The narrator certainly envies Luo's relationship with the seamstress, whom they both recognize as an unsurpassed beauty. But after Luo uses a charming line about similar toes to snare her attention, the match is practically preordained, and the narrator must resign himself to a background role in their collective relationship. Left in his solitude, his dreams become ever more gripping—especially when they involve the seamstress's tragic death—and he clings to the novels' stories to cope with the grind of potentially endless reeducation.

Luo's absence gives the narrator a chance to bask in the seamstress's beauty, even as he remains loyal to Luo in neglecting to make any romantic advances. He becomes her domestic companion, a sort of servant. In this role, he can ward off the advances of any stray suitors, and he finds a sort of peace in accessing his feminine side and carrying out his tasks with unswaying devotion. He also evolves as a storyteller, learning to adapt his tale to better interest and entertain his audience, the Little Seamstress. In the course of the two young men's flight down the mountain, the narrator recognizes the ambiguity of his role, wondering what is keeping him running: "Was it friendship? Was it my affection for his girlfriend? Or was I merely an onlooker anxious not to miss the ending of a drama?" The likely answer is all three, but the narrator's crucial role as onlooker is attested to by the novel itself, written by the narrator's hand.

Old Miller

The old miller invites the disguised protagonists into his lice-ridden lair to suck salty pebbles and hear bawdy old songs. His role suggests that where some seek rustic romanticism in looking to the past, they may instead find merely crudity, a state of existence less refined than the modern civilized state. Accordingly, the old miller does not shy away from voyeuristic appreciation of Luo and the beautiful seamstress sharing love, though he does feel ashamed.

Old Preacher

When his Bible was discovered, the preacher was sentenced to indefinite forced labor, sweeping the central street of Yong Jing every day. Twenty years into his sentence, he grows deathly ill, and though his sons try to record a last-minute affirmation of Maoist sensibilities, he only mutters Latin phrases, signaling his sustained adherence to Christianity.

Poetess

Four-Eyes's mother is a regionally famous poetess (a female poet; the somewhat old-fashioned feminine form of the word is used in the novel) whose status allows her to arrange for her son's rescue from reeducation—provided he can gather and write down some admirable romantic ballads from the villagers. The poetess has a natural affinity for city folk, chatting amiably with the narrator, but she is careful to deny any knowledge of her son's books.

Sorceresses

Four sorceresses are summoned by the seamstress to help rid Luo of his malaria by warding off the spirits responsible. A fifth joins them for Four-Eyes's departure feast, where they all wield bows and arrows to ward off malevolent spirits. Their acceptance of payment from the poetess betrays the capitalist nature of their supposedly spiritual activities.

Tailor

Respected in all the mountain villages for the joy he brings through his beautiful clothing, the tailor lives like a king. He proves so spellbound by the narrator's storytelling that he gives up sleep to hear the story of *The Count of Monte Cristo*.

THEMES

Storytelling

Dai has explicitly referred to *Balzac and the Little Chinese Seamstress* as an homage (an expression of respect) to literature, and it follows that a primary theme in the novel is the power of storytelling. This power is first demonstrated in the purest possible context, through oral communication between people who are present together, when the narrator and Luo gain admiration and privilege for their ability to relate the stories of films they have seen, in what are dubbed "oral cinema"

shows. Luo's method of acting out each of the characters in turn proves especially riveting. A second storytelling context, that of the written word, comes into play when Luo and the narrator gain access to Four-Eyes's Western novels. Having only ever been exposed to a narrow range of Communist-approved literature, the narrator was "still slumbering in the limbo of adolescence," but Balzac's work has him "falling headlong into a story of awakening desire, passion, impulsive action, love, of all the subjects that had, until then, been hidden from [him]." Luo and the Little Seamstress are likewise infused with visions of love and are inspired to begin a romance together. Luo goes so far as to proclaim, "This fellow Balzac is a wizard. He touched the head of this mountain girl with an invisible finger, and she was transformed, carried away in a dream." The tailor is so riveted by the retelling of Alexandre Dumas' *The Count of Monte Cristo* that he apparently functions on only a few hours' sleep a night for nine days straight. The reader becomes most familiar with the literary inspiration found by the narrator in Romain Rolland's musician title character Jean-Christophe, who, "with his fierce individualism utterly untainted by malice, was a salutary revelation." "Without him," the narrator says, he "would never have understood the splendour of taking free and independent action as an individual." This passage highlights how many individualist notions would be shielded from citizens of Communist China, who would instead be indoctrinated with social theories prioritizing collective needs. Dai may be suggesting that Communist propaganda instills citizens with a sense that all individualist acts, in giving a lower priority to the community, are by definition malicious.

The enlightening qualities of the French novels are often foregrounded in considerations of the thematic significance of Dai's novel, but the potentially deeper significance of the young men's storytelling success among the villagers is revealed in the Little Seamstress's later comments on the joys of acting: "It was a totally new experience for me. Before, I had no idea that you could take on the role of a completely different person, actually become that person . . . and still be your own self." That is, if the seamstress's perspective can be taken as representative of the villagers', they live their lives without any conscious acting; they have only ever behaved precisely as they are naturally inclined to behave. Exposure to Luo's convincing impersonations is revolutionary, then, in providing

TOPICS FOR FURTHER STUDY

- Write an essay about a novel you have read that altered your outlook on life, suggested a path to follow, inspired a transformation, or changed your life in any other way. In your essay, after an introduction, provide a brief summary of the novel's plot, discussions of how and why you relate to various characters and plot incidents, a brief biography of the author, a comparison with your own life, an analysis of what the author intended to communicate through the novel, how the novel affected you personally, and other reflections.

- Think of an activity or a collection of activities that you performed over some period of time that left you feeling more physiologically balanced, both mentally and physically in a holistic way. This could be several days of camping out, a sports practice, a dance performance, a simple walk across town, or anything at all. Write a short story, narrated in the first person, in which the narrator experiences some distress but gains balance through the activity you have identified. This equilibrium may or may not represent the resolution of the story.

- Watch the film *Balzac and the Little Chinese Seamstress* and write a review in which you first consider the film as an independent creation and then consider it as an adaptation of the book. Address whether the film met your expectations after you read the book, how the book and movie differ, and the relevance of changes that were made. Post your review to your Web page or blog site and invite others to add to the review.

- Read Ji-li Jiang's young-adult novel *Red Scarf Girl: A Memoir of the Cultural Revolution* (1998), which details the author's experiences in and around Shanghai beginning when she was twelve. Imagine that the narrator of Dai's novel and Ji-li had access to the Internet and could have met online. Create online profiles of the two characters, as might be found on Facebook, Twitter, or another social media site, and compose a dialogue between the two representing an online chat, in which they get to know each other by relating their respective situations and asking each other for insight and advice.

- Research traditional Chinese medicine and write a paper about the practice of traditional Chinese medicine and its influences in the United States today.

---

a model for intentional self-transformation. Whether such a transformation will be genuine if undertaken by an ordinary person, however, not by an actor, is an open question. It is surely no coincidence that the role of the Count of Monte Cristo's former fiancée (Mercedes), which the seamstress inhabits with such confidence, foreshadows the essence of the last meeting between the seamstress and Luo: "She pretends not to recognise him, and she does so with such conviction that you'd swear she had truly forgotten her past. Oh, it was heart-breaking!" Thus, casting ambiguous light on the Little Seamstress's integrity, the novel echoes Gustave Flaubert's *Madame Bovary*—one of the titles among Four-Eyes's stash—in suggesting that exposure to stories that function as fantasy can lead the discontented soul to fashion an artificial life in search of fantastic, ultimately shallow goals.

Love

Intertwined with the theme of the power of storytelling is a thematic glorification of love and beauty. The repressive Communist regime is shown to allow its young citizens literary access to "nothing but revolutionary blather about patriotism, Communism, ideology and propaganda." The novel suggests, though, that life is lived not only in the rational mind but

Luo and Ma are sent to a reeducation center after their parents are declared enemies of the people in the Chinese Cultural Revolution. *(Apollofoto | Shutterstock.com)*

also in the sentimental heart and feeling body, and this full life is experienced most intensely through love. Surely many readers will envy Luo and the seamstress's perfect romantic interludes in the sort of lush waterfall setting that few city dwellers have access to. It is Luo's intentional education and civilization of the seamstress through literature that makes this romance blossom. But the pregnancy reveals a hitch: such a civilized relationship has serious consequences if undertaken by people without the means to raise a child and without contraception. Maoist society made such romances triply problematic, as Dai reports, by forbidding marriage by people under twenty-five, labor assistance for unmarried women, and abortions. When it turns out that the Little Seamstress is able to get an abortion without too much difficulty, however, it is as if she has passed through the gateway to "civilized" love. No longer willing to abide by the romantic limitations inherent in village life—where people's first romantic encounters, under the watchful eyes of tight-knit communities, are likely to quickly lead to marriage and family—the seamstress is compelled to head to the city, presumably

to dabble in modern, casual romance. The closing lines of the novel pinpoint precisely what, in terms of romance, Balzac has instilled in the Little Seamstress: a heightened self-consciousness of her own beauty, as well as a conviction that to give herself to one man—Luo—would be to restrict the appreciation of her beauty and thereby assign a value to it. That is, if she were to commit to an attachment to Luo, her beauty would become worth all that Luo, and Luo alone, could give her in appreciation. In going to the city, for as long as she avoids pregnancy and marriage, she can consider her beauty potentially available for appreciation by anyone—and thus of untold value, beyond any price. The novel leaves the reader to assess the moral worth of the lesson the Little Seamstress has learned.

STYLE

First-Person Narration
Balzac and the Little Chinese Seamstress is narrated primarily in the first person by a young

man sent to a rural mountain area for reeducation. There are also three chapters giving the first-person perspectives of the Old Miller, Luo, and the Little Seamstress, as related to the narrator (whose questions and comments are occasionally implied). It is noteworthy that the narrator goes unnamed for the length of the novel. One passage does specify the Chinese characters of the narrator's name as representing a galloping horse, an ornate sword, and a bell, and the horse character is recognized as being pronounced "Ma"—the name given the narrator in Dai's film based on his book. Despite this clue, for the average reader, the narrator remains nameless. This strategy was used perhaps most famously by Ralph Ellison in his notable 1952 novel on the contemporary African American experience, *Invisible Man*. One result of this strategy is that the narrator's personality is free to float around in the reader's mind. Where a name is provided, all of a character's thoughts, actions, and words become attached to the name, producing a collective impression of the character that is embodied in that name. In the course of Dai's novel, for example, the reader develops an impression of Luo that before long is attached to and evoked by the name *Luo*. But where the narrator has no name, there is no word to attach the character's behavior to, such that he is thought of as more changeable and more affected by his circumstances. This novel's thematic focus is on the power of literature, and the narrator indeed undergoes a transformation, spurred not only by his exposure to Western literature but also by his solitude and his devotion to the seamstress, which motivates him to evolve as a storyteller as well as to perform domestic tasks that seem to bring him a measure of inner peace. Another effect of the narrator's namelessness is that, without a name to identify the narrator as an other, the reader may more readily identify with the narrator, subconsciously placing him- or herself in the narrator's shoes. This heightens the reader's vicarious involvement in and appreciation of the setting and workings of the novel.

French Literature

Though this novel is set in China, it is a work of French literature, written by Dai in the language of his adopted homeland. Accordingly, while Four-Eyes's cache of books is representative of various Western nations, the French authors—Balzac, Romain Rolland, and Flaubert—are emphasized. Those three authors might be understood as the main influences on Luo, the narrator, and the Little Seamstress, respectively, with the seamstress recognizable as a literary descendant of Flaubert's wayward romantic Madame Bovary. Given that the closing pages of *Madame Bovary* record the tragic ending earned by the title character through her questionable choices, she should not necessarily be understood as a positive role model for the seamstress. However, the works of Balzac and Rolland are praised for blessing Luo and the narrator with insight into love, romance, and personal independence, and Dai's novel is typically characterized as an ode to the power of literature. However, as Ian McCall notes in an essay in *Romance Studies*, Dai seems to have cleverly skewed the connotations of the French works, in particular Balzac's. In having the young Chinese men first awakened by *Ursule Minuët*, Dai chose one of Balzac's lesser-known works, allowing the average reader to remain ignorant of the fact that the novel actually describes many unsavory aspects of modern society, with an emphasis on ambition, envy, hate, greed, betrayal, and vengeance—all ignored in the narrator's commentary on the novel. Whether Dai intended more to glorify France or subjugate China, his selective portrayals of the French works, as McCall notes, "allow a French readership to bask in the satisfaction that culturally France has the upper hand and that it is fully justified for [its] influence to make itself felt."

HISTORICAL CONTEXT

Mao's Cultural Revolution

By beginning his novel with the arrival of the two protagonists in the village they have been assigned to for reeducation, Dai effectively avoids almost all discussion of the actual politics behind their fate. He does provide a clarifying passage on reeducation during the Cultural Revolution (1966–1976) following the opening scene, but the narrator notes that the reasons behind Mao's directives were not entirely clear to them. The factors causing the punishment are seen to be "Mao's hatred of intellectuals" and their parents' status as medical professionals and so-called "enemies of the people." The circumstances were indeed convoluted and unfavorable

COMPARE
&
CONTRAST

- **1970s:** Under Mao Zedong, chairman of the Chinese Communist Party until his death in 1976, the nation orients policy around the notion of continuous revolution, marked by attempts to favor and uplift the proletariat (the ordinary working people) and also instill the bourgeoisie (the middle class, wealthier than the proletariat) with proletarian values.

  Today: With leaders since Mao focusing more on the nation's economic advancement than on adhering to strict Communist ideology—as with the free-market reforms implemented in 1978—President Hu Jintao now leads the nation that is widely recognized as the most significant global economy of the early twenty-first century.

- **1970s:** In the early 1970s, following the educational chaos of the onset of the Cultural Revolution, urban students widely expect to be sentenced to the countryside regardless of academic efforts, and morale and

  exam performance in secondary schools plummet.

  Today: With the education system reformed by Mao's successors, China stuns international educational experts in 2010 with high test scores. Fifteen-year-old students in Shanghai rank first in the world in science, reading, and math (while U.S. students rank between seventeenth and thirty-first in those subjects).

- **1970s:** With a rapidly expanding population, climbing from 830 million to nearly 1 billion over the course of the decade, in 1979 China institutes a one-child policy that applies to most urban families. Minorities and rural residents can apply for authorization to have additional children.

  Today: With an estimated 300 million to 400 million births avoided since 1980, birth laws are proving effective in curbing the growth of China's population, which nonetheless reaches 1.34 billion in 2010.

during this time period for many middle-class families labeled as among the bourgeoisie or intelligentsia (the intellectual class).

Mao Zedong, born in 1893, had been a central figure in the Chinese Revolution of 1949, which brought the People's Republic of China under Communist control, as shaped by Marxist-Leninist theory on mandatory roles for state and citizens and the constrained movement of capital. By the 1960s, the revolutionary impetus had faded somewhat. Although the nation's youth had been successfully indoctrinated with Maoist concepts, which valued the working classes and political loyalty, the upper ranks of the Communist Party had grown unstable; while Mao was largely adhering to the original revolutionary directives, rivals within the party leadership were leaning toward revisionist efforts that would modernize the nation's outlook and

governance. For example, where Mao had instituted the Great Leap Forward in 1958–1959, bringing poor and lower-middle-class students into higher levels of education and emphasizing involvement in political activities—leveling the playing field, so to speak—the foreign minister later asserted that in general, devotion to research and intellectual advancement should not be sacrificed for the sake of politics. Thus, the poorer students found themselves welcomed into higher education only to be set up for failure in comparison with bourgeois students with better resources.

In this context, Mao—a visionary idealist who still believed that great transformations could be made under his leadership, especially with the involvement of youth—realized that students, especially the disillusioned peasantry, could be a valuable resource in his efforts to

The boys hide and steal Western classic books to use to educate the little seamstress. (*Mark Graves /* *Shutterstock.com*)

undermine his political rivals. When, in 1966, a group of teachers at Peking University displayed a poster criticizing the bourgeois administration, Mao, being specifically concerned about academic circles that were questioning his policies, lent support by broadcasting the revolutionary poster nationwide. What followed was a campaign led by proletarian students, who organized as Red Guards and were encouraged by Mao, denouncing the elitist professors, academics, and scholars who essentially favored a merit-based system of advancement rather than more politically oriented educational mandates. Over the next two years, some teachers were subjected by revolutionary students to physical abuse and public humiliation, and the chaos and violence necessitated extensive closures of schools.

As order was gradually restored, educational reforms involved Communist Party selection of students who would proceed to higher education, and specific job assignments for all others. In

agreement with proletarian ideals and a directive issued by Mao in December 1968, most bourgeois, or middle-class, urban high-school graduates were assigned to rural labor intended to assimilate them into the peasant classes. These rusticated students (that is, those who were sent to the country) were not always welcomed by communities in the often crowded countryside, since the peasants were obliged to instruct the newcomers and share their limited harvests with them. Between 1968 and the spring of 1970, some six million youths were relocated to the countryside. This rustication program continued through the early 1970s, but it was reversed in some provinces even before Mao's death in 1976. By 1978, the government acknowledged that rustication had not been successful, and great numbers of youths were recalled to the cities. By mid-1979, out of the eighteen million youths who had been rusticated since the beginning of the Cultural Revolution, about six or seven million remained in the countryside. The reader of Dai's novel does not discover whether or not Luo and the narrator ultimately gain release from their rural reeducation.

CRITICAL OVERVIEW

Most reviewers have had warm compliments for *Balzac and the Little Chinese Seamstress*. In the *New Statesman*, Lisa Allardice calls it a "charming book" that manages to illuminate a difficult period in Chinese history with "simplicity" and "playfulness." Allardice concludes that "like his young heroes, Sijie is a captivating, amusing storyteller, his writing as seductive and unaffected as the little seamstress herself." In *Kliatt*, Janice Bees calls the novel "a little jewel of a book, with images both dainty and coarse, and a thoroughly entertaining read." Similarly, Elsa Gaztambide writes in *Booklist* that "this little gem of a book spins magic thread out of broken dreams"; it is "truly enchanting." In *Library Journal*, Barbara Hoffert states that Dai "wonderfully communicates the awesome power of literature—of which his novel is proof." A *Publishers Weekly* contributor concludes that "the warmth and humor of Sijie's prose and the clarity of Rilke's translation distinguish this slim first novel, a wonderfully human tale." In the *Spectator*, Paul Tebbs asserts that Dai's tale is "a jewel of world literature."

Considering Dai's nuanced use of the Western texts found in Four-Eyes's suitcase, Ian McCall concludes, in a *Romance Studies* essay, that the author might be seen as catering to Western audiences. McCall states that "Dai Sijie does not subject his intertexts [the books that appear in this novel] to any real critical scrutiny" and thereby "conveys an image of Western superiority and consolidates received Western opinion about" China. On the other hand, the reader should keep in mind that the versions of the Western works heard by the Little Seamstress, for one, have been altered by the narrator for the sake of entertainment value. McCall points out that Dai thus "seems to be highlighting how easily texts can be manipulated and distorted" and also "shows how works of art can be 'realized' differently by individual readers." Also focusing on the role of translation in the enlightenment of Dai's characters, Karen L. Thornber concludes in a *Contemporary French and Francophone Studies* essay that the novel draws "attention to the deep intertwining of French and Chinese rhetoric, intertwining that both depends on and springs from translation: distinctions among languages are shown not as solidifying but rather as undermining differences among literatures."

CRITICISM

Michael Allen Holmes

Holmes is a writer and editor. In the following essay, he reflects on the complex message conveyed in Balzac and the Little Chinese Seamstress *regarding the values of civilization versus rural ways.*

The typical modern assessment of Mao Zedong's village-level reeducation of urban high-school graduates—indeed, the official Chinese Communist Party perspective—is that it was a backwards-minded mistake. Dai has noted the absurdity of having the illiterate educate the literate, and a majority of rusticants were returned to urban locations by the end of the 1970s. On the surface, *Balzac and the Little Chinese Seamstress* seems to affirm such a critical assessment, as Dai occasionally highlights the comic irony of folk beliefs, approaching them from a modern perspective. For example, the narrator belittles the four sorceresses who come to aid the malaria-stricken Luo

WHAT DO I READ NEXT?

- One of Dai's novels is *Mr. Muo's Travelling Couch* (2005), in which a French-trained Chinese psychiatrist returns to China in the hopes of gaining his college sweetheart's release from prison.

- In *Colors of the Mountain* (2001), a nonfiction work, Da Chen tells of his youth in China during the Cultural Revolution, when he allied with juvenile delinquents, and after, when he set his sights on higher education.

- Elizabeth Foreman Lewis tells of a young man whose experiences are the inverse of Dai's narrator—he leaves his rural village at thirteen to experience life in the city—in the young-adult novel *Young Fu of the Upper Yangtze* (1932), which won the Newbery Medal.

- The Chinese author Gao Xingjian, who moved to France not long after Dai in 1987, won the Nobel Prize in Literature in 2000. His challenging novel *Soul Mountain* (1990) uses an unusual narrative structure to tell the story of a man's escape from city life to search through the Chinese countryside for the fabled mountain of Lingshan.

- The well-known Chinese American author Amy Tan portrays the modern, Westernized perspective of a Chinese American girl and the spiritual beliefs of her older, Chinese-born sister in *The Hundred Secret Senses* (1995).

- The Russian author Leo Tolstoy provides one of literature's most insightful explorations into the spiritual relevance of rural values through the character of Levin in his masterpiece on tangled love, *Anna Karenina* (1877).

- Though he is mentioned only once, Herman Melville is one of the authors Dai's narrator falls in love with. He may have read Melville's *Typee* (1846), based on Melville's own experiences in Polynesia, in which an American sailor is captured by natives, whose nobility is highly praised, and enjoys a brief love affair with one young woman.

> THROUGH THE NARRATOR'S PERSONAL EVOLUTION, DAI SIGNALS THAT A CIVILIZED YOUNG MAN CAN INDEED BENEFIT SPIRITUALLY FROM A RURAL REEDUCATION."

in commenting, "It was hard to say which of them was the most ugly and likely to frighten off evil spirits"—as if their mere appearances actually outweigh their supposed powers. Dai heightens the comedic value of the sorceresses when he has the poor old ladies falling asleep during their vigil against spirits. Luo and the narrator may be presumed to have modern knowledge that malaria is best cured by actual medicine; this is reflected in Luo's request that the narrator continue flogging him, with the peach and willow branches identified as necessary by the miners, not as a true remedy but only because "it'll warm me up." Beyond the novel's clear division between civilized and folk understandings, however, Dai subtly supports the notion that urban youths may indeed learn valuable lessons from living a village-level life, while also suggesting that urban life is not without its psychological perils.

The ethical significance of the division between civilization and countryside is suggested in the novel's opening paragraph. There, among the possessions the two young men have brought with them, the narrator's violin is described as "the sole item that exuded an air of foreignness, of civilisation, and therefore aroused suspicion." That is, modern city life is so fundamentally different from village life that, to the villagers, the city amounts to a foreign country, and such a broad gap separates their customs that the villagers cannot be certain that urban customs are safe, wise, or beneficial. On the other hand, the narrator's impression of this mountain region comes in part from the record of the French missionary who passed through in the 1940s, who wrote of fearsome opium growers and described a "wild and lonely place, so thickly screened by giant trees, tangled creepers and lush vegetation as to make one expect to see a bandit leaping from the shadows at any

moment." Ending the Jesuit's account on this note highlights his association of the natural growth of the countryside with the danger of the hidden unknown and an instinctive response of fear. Thus, the city boys and the villagers are both set up as wary of the others' motives and ways.

The significance of being civilized is made central to the plot when the Little Seamstress's character comes into consideration. When asked by the narrator whether he is romantically interested in the Little Seamstress, Luo replies, "She's not civilised, at least not enough for me!" Yet the narrator has described her uncivilized aspects admiringly: "When she laughed I noticed an untamed quality about her eyes, which reminded me of the wild girls on our side of the mountain. Her eyes had the gleam of uncut gems, of unpolished metal." The metaphorical suggestion is that her very rawness, her lack of refinement—her remaining in a natural, uneducated, genuine state—is what defines her particular allure. Luo would surely second this notion, since their romantic meetings at the waterfall are made possible by the fact that the Little Seamstress is a self-proclaimed "mountain girl" who enjoys the pure movement and exercise of, for example, diving to the bottom of a pool to retrieve something. Nonetheless, the narrator describes her as "the lovely mountain girl in need of culture," and Luo is driven by "his ambition to endow the lovely Little Seamstress with culture." That is, they imagine that civilizing her can only be an improvement to her character.

But civilization is not universally hailed as preferable in the course of the novel. Dai communicates a genuine lament when the narrator states, after hailing Luo's tale-telling abilities, "Modern man has moved beyond the age of the Thousand-and-One-Nights, and modern societies everywhere, whether socialist and capitalist, have done away with the old storytellers— more's the pity." While the urban boys are accustomed to life being governed by the passage of time as tracked by a clock—whereby one may find oneself ever wondering how many more hours or minutes are to pass before the current activity ends or the next begins—their manipulation of the clock hands leaves them with "no idea what the time really was"; this statement closes a section, connoting that there was something profound about their not knowing the true time. He later connects a sense of timelessness to mindful absorption in a task and the art of the storyteller when he remarks, in the course of mesmerizing listeners with his retelling of *The Count of Monte Cristo*: "I lost all sense of time." Moments later, Luo offers him singular praise for his narrative skill. The narrator also hints at the tranquility of a clock-free life when he observes how the water-wheels at the mill move "at an appropriately measured, rural sort of pace"—a comment implying that an urban pace is likely to be poorly measured, sped up too much. The narrator again aligns positive terms with village-level life when he notes that the banquet scene "made a pastoral, good-natured impression."

An interesting development occurs when, following Luo's departure to visit his ailing mother for a month, the narrator becomes more of a confidant of the seamstress's. Until this point, the narrator has proven partly at odds with his solitude in the mountain village. Various comments make clear his affection for the Little Seamstress, which he has been unable to act upon, and although playing his violin brings some consolation, he experiences disturbing nightmares. After reading *Ursule Minuët*, he experiences jealousy for the first time, as if encouraged to envy others by the goings-on of the novel, and also feels an original desire to copy out passages from the novel word for word. He charts those passages onto the inside of his jacket, and thus figuratively onto his skin, imprinting the patterns of the text onto his consciousness through the act. This can be seen as reflecting the impulse to mimic the lives of others that is inspired by romantic or sensational tales. The Little Seamstress, too, feels this impulse, as evidenced by her enjoyment of playing acting games with Luo. When the narrator becomes better friends with the seamstress, however, rather than indulging in any desire to, say, mimic the life of his friend Luo by hitting on the seamstress, he hones his storytelling craft with creative additions, and he adopts a domestic routine that involves near-constant labor and that seems to bring him inner peace. He remarks, "I took great pleasure in these humble tasks," which include chopping wood, tending a fire, cooking, and doing laundry by hand in a stream. This peaceful presence of mind in daily acts aligns well with the sort of idealized existence practiced by Zen Buddhists and Taoists. The narrator further notes, "This voluntary domestication on my part not only softened my temperament but also gave me more intimate access

to the female realm." The narrator thus drifts into the role of a rural young woman, which seems to agree with his inner nature. Through the narrator's personal evolution, Dai signals that a civilized young man can indeed benefit spiritually from a rural reeducation.

Meanwhile, the seamstress undergoes a countertransformation. Her fashioning a brassiere for herself reflects sustained femininity, but the white tennis shoes are gender-neutral, and the Mao-style jacket she adapts is marked by "mannish details"—such as shiny brass buttons that are precisely the opposite of the "unpolished metal" of her eyes. She trims her long pigtail in favor of a "short bob." In sum, "The lovely, unsophisticated mountain girl had vanished without a trace." Luo and the narrator rejoice at the time, but they later realize that her transformation foreshadows her departure for the city. After the seamstress's last interaction with Luo—which allows her to mimic the forlorn circumstances from *The Count of Monte Cristo* that they had acted out together—her fate is left to the reader's imagination. As such, the narrator's recurring nightmare, in which the seamstress plummets from the perilous ridge to a grisly death, should perhaps be understood to metaphorically refer to her fate. The path itself falls away steeply on either side, and at the bottom, "the trees were swathed in mist." Mist is given symbolic significance early on, in the episode of Luo's father's public confession, when he remarks regarding the nurse he is accused of sleeping with: "As soon as I touched her, I fell . . . into mist and clouds." Mist might thus suggest the treacherousness of romance, wherein one has difficulty seeing beyond one's immediate surroundings to assess the security of the area. When Luo is inspired to cross the perilous, mist-surrounded ridge by his love for the seamstress—while the narrator, denied such mutual love, is unable to cross at all—crossing the ridge at the risk of falling into the mist can be understood as analogous to embracing the risky pursuit of love. In the narrator's dream as in reality, Luo does this carefully, on all fours. But in the dream, the Little Seamstress "wasn't walking across the ridge, she was prancing," and "her hair floated out over her shoulders like wings." Presumably, her carelessness is what leads to her dreamed death. In reality later on, the young men's flight down the mountain after the seamstress evokes an explicit comparison: "The scene was like one of the bad dreams that had been troubling me lately,

从来也没有看见人民群
众象现在这样精神振奋，斗
志昂扬，意气风发。

毛泽东

Communist Party Chairman and dictator Mao Zedong was responsible for the Cultural Revolution in China. (John Lock | Shutterstock.com)

with the Little Seamstress losing her footing and falling into the void." In the end—with avian imagery reminding readers of the dream—the seamstress "took off like a bird, growing smaller and smaller until she vanished." The parallels between the dream and the final turn of events suggest that the seamstress's carefree descent to the city, enabled by her abandonment of the simple but genuine rural life in search of the sort of modern urban love defined by appreciation of beauty rather than emotion, is like a fall from a cliff into shrouds of mist and a spiritual death.

Source: Michael Allen Holmes, Critical Essay on *Balzac and the Little Chinese Seamstress*, in *Novels for Students*, Gale, Cengage Learning, 2012.

Janice Bees

In the following review, Bees is impressed with the translation, saying that it preserves the beauty of the novel.

Sijie's tale takes place during the Cultural Revolution in Communist China of the '60s and '70s. The teenaged protagonist (the reader never

learns his name) is the son of doctors, and his friend, Luo, is the son of a famous dentist. Because of this, the protagonist and Luo are labeled as intellectuals, and sent to a mountain village to be "re-educated."

Hopelessly out of place in the mountain's peasant culture, both young men find clever ways to bend the rules made against Western influences. In one particularly funny moment at the beginning of the book, the protagonist entertains the locals with a violin piece by the forbidden Mozart, because Luo convinces the audience the piece is entitled Mozart is Thinking of Chairman Mao. When not doing hard labor, the two also entertain the people of the village with storytelling. One of their most ardent listeners is the little seamstress in the town, a lovely young countrywoman.

The two teenagers come to learn that another intellectual young man, Four-Eyes, has a suitcase filled with forbidden books. They manage to borrow Four-Eyes' copy of Balzac's *Ursule Mirouet*, and find an enchanting new tale to use to attempt to woo the little seamstress. When Four-Eyes won't lend them any more books, they resolve to steal the suitcase.

Balzac and the Little Chinese Seamstress was originally written in French, and then translated "into English for this edition. I have not read the original, but am quite impressed with the poetic language that appears to have been retained through translation. This is a little jewel of a book, with images both dainty and coarse, and a thoroughly entertaining read. There are some mature themes, but they are handled in a subtle manner.

Source: Janice Bees, Review of *Balzac and the Little Chinese Seamstress*, in *Kliatt*, Vol. 37, No. 2, March 2003, p. 22.

Barbara Hoffert

In the following review, Hoffert comments that Sijie "wonderfully communicates the awesome power of literature."

This deceptively small novel has the power to bring down governments. In Mao's China, the Cultural Revolution rages, and two friends caught in the flames find themselves shuttled off to the remote countryside for reeducation. The stolid narrator occasionally comforts himself by playing the violin, and both he and more outgoing friend Luo find that they have a talent for entertaining others with their recreations of films they have seen. A little light comes their way when they meet the stunning daughter of the tailor in the town nearby, with whom Luo launches an affair. But the real coup is discovering a cache of forbidden Western literature—including, of course, Balzac—that forces open their world like a thousand flowers blooming. The literature proves their undoing, however, finally losing them the one thing that has sustained them. Dai Sijie, who was himself reeducated in early 1970s China before fleeing to France, wonderfully communicates the awesome power of literature—of which his novel is proof. Highly recommended.

Source: Barbara Hoffert, Review of *Balzac and the Little Chinese Seamstress*, in *Library Journal*, Vol. 126, No. 15, September 15, 2001, p. 110.

Elsa Gaztambide

In the following review, Gaztambide describes Balzac and the Little Chinese Seamstress *as an enchanting fable.*

Stories set in China during the Cultural Revolution usually follow a trail of human struggle and tragedy, but this little gem of a book spins magic thread out of broken dreams. Already a best-seller in France and slated for release in 19 countries, this novel is the story of two whimsical young men ordered to the countryside for reeducation as a result of their parents' political designation as "class enemies." Assigned the revolting task of carrying buckets of excrement up a hillside for the peasant farmers, the boys design a venue of storytelling sessions and quickly earn the headman's leniency in return. When they meet the local tailor's beautiful daughter, the luminescent Little Seamstress, and discover a wealth of forbidden Western books, life on the hillside takes a brighter turn. His book is truly enchanting, written with the rhythm of a fable. Dai Sijie is himself a survivor of that fateful time in China's history, yet he incorporates delightful humor into sketching his innovative cast of characters.

Source: Elsa Gaztambide, Review of *Balzac and the Little Chinese Seamstress*, in *Booklist*, Vol. 98, No. 2, September 15, 2001, p. 196.

Paul Tebbs

In the following excerpt, Tebbs expresses a belief that the novel has a "universal significance."

. . . Set at the height of Chairman Mao's Cultural Revolution in 1971, *Balzac and the Little Chinese Seamstress* is an enchanting tale about the power of story-telling and its capacity to liberate. The 17-year-old narrator and his best friend, Luo, are enemies of the state because their fathers are doctors. Sent to a remote mountain village to be 're-educated' by peasants, they fear their banishment is permanent. Possessing only a violin to remind them of their past, they convince the village headman not to destroy their 'bourgeois toy' by performing a pleasing sonata quickly named 'Mozart is Thinking of Chairman Mao'.

Cultural rehabilitation consists of carrying buckets of dripping excrement up and down craggy mountain passes. Relief comes when the village headman, seduced by the boys' stories about films, sends them to the local cinema. On their return, they must perform the narratives they have witnessed. Their masterful renditions beguile the whole village and the roles of educator and educated subtly shift.

Their own education takes an unexpected and dangerous turn, when the boys steal a stash of forbidden Western literature from a fellow cultural outcast. Intellectually and emotionally awakened, they attempt to educate a beautiful seamstress through the writings of Balzac. But she has just as much to teach them.

Dai Sijie was himself separated from his family and 're-educated' in the 1970s. But this novel transcends personal tragedy and aspires to a universal significance. From a pernicious period in Chinese history Sijie has written a jewel of world literature....

Source: Paul Tebbs, Review of *Balzac and the Little Chinese Seamstress*, in *Spectator*, Vol. 286, No. 9021, June 30, 2001, p. 43.

SOURCES

Allardice, Lisa, Review of *Balzac and the Little Chinese Seamstress*, in *New Statesman*, Vol. 131, No. 4583, April 15, 2002, p. 56.

Bees, Janice, Review of *Balzac and the Little Chinese Seamstress*, in *Kliatt*, Vol. 37, No. 2, March 2003, p. 22.

"China's Population, 1969–2006," in *Chinability*, http://www.chinability.com/Population.htm (accessed June 26, 2011).

Dai Sijie, *Balzac and the Little Chinese Seamstress*, translated by Ina Rilke, Anchor Books, 2002.

Dillon, Sam, "Top Test Scores from Shanghai Stun Educators," in *New York Times*, December 7, 2010, http://www.nytimes.com/2010/12/07/education/07education.html?_r = 1 (accessed June 26, 2011).

Flambard-Weisbart, Véronique, "'Ba-er-za-ke' ou imaginaire chinois en français," in *Contemporary French and Francophone Studies*, Vol. 11, No. 3, August 2007, pp. 427–34.

Gaztambide, Elsa, Review of *Balzac and the Little Chinese Seamstress*, in *Booklist*, Vol. 98, No. 2, September 15, 2001, p. 196.

Guan Xiaofeng, "Most People Free to Have More Child," in *China Daily*, http://www2.chinadaily.com.cn/china/2007-07/11/content_5432238.htm (accessed June 26, 2011).

Hoffert, Barbara, Review of *Balzac and the Little Chinese Seamstress*, in *Library Journal*, Vol. 126, No. 15, September 15, 2001, p. 110.

McCall, Ian, "French Literature and Film in the USSR and Mao's China: Intertexts in Makine's *Au temps du fleuve Amour* and Dai Sijie's *Balzac et la Petite Tailleuse chinoise*," in *Romance Studies*, Vol. 24, No. 2, July 2006, pp. 159–70.

Review of *Balzac and the Little Chinese Seamstress*, in *Kirkus Reviews*, Vol. 69, No. 15, August 1, 2001, p. 1046.

Review of *Balzac and the Little Chinese Seamstress*, in *Publishers Weekly*, Vol. 248, No. 35, August 27, 2001, p. 51.

Riding, Alan, "Artistic Odyssey: Film to Fiction to Film," in *New York Times*, July 27, 2005, http://www.nytimes.com/2005/07/27/movies/MoviesFeatures/27balz.html (accessed June 25, 2011).

Singer, Martin, *Educated Youth and the Cultural Revolution in China*, Center for Chinese Studies, University of Michigan, 1971, pp. 1–16, 65–67.

Tebbs, Paul, Review of *Balzac and the Little Chinese Seamstress*, in *Spectator*, Vol. 286, No. 9021, June 30, 2001, p. 43.

Thornber, Karen L., "French Discourse in Chinese, in Chinese Discourse in French—Paradoxes of Chinese Francophone Émigré Writing," in *Contemporary French and Francophone Studies*, Vol. 13, No. 2, March 2009, pp. 223–32.

Unger, Jonathan, *Education under Mao: Class and Competition in Canton Schools, 1960–1980*, Columbia University Press, 1982, pp. 110–38, 160–70.

Yu Sen-lun, "Romantic Boyhood Memories of a Chinese Filmmaker," in *Taipei Times*, May 20, 2002, http://www.taipeitimes.com/News/feat/archives/2002/05/20/136866 (accessed June 25, 2011).

FURTHER READING

Guldin, Gregory Eliyu, *Farewell to Peasant China: Rural Urbanization and Social Change in the Late Twentieth Century*, M. E. Sharpe, 1997.

> Guldin investigates the directions and destinies of rural regions undergoing transformation throughout China.

McDougall, Bonnie S., and Kam Louie, *The Literature of China in the Twentieth Century*, Columbia University Press, 1999.

> This volume provides a comprehensive survey of the impact of historical events on the development of Chinese literature in the twentieth century.

Weinbaum, Alys Eve, ed., *The Modern Girl around the World: Consumption, Modernity, and Globalization*, Duke University Press, 2008.

> This collection addresses the curious development of modern and/or feminist values among women worldwide since the 1920s.

Yihong Pan, *Tempered in the Revolutionary Furnace: China's Youth in the Rustication Movement*, Lexington Books, 2009.

> Along with a number of her peers, Yihong was sent to the countryside after graduating from middle school, and in this volume she draws on her own and many other people's experiences in assessing the effects of the rustication policy.

SUGGESTED SEARCH TERMS

Dai Sijie AND Balzac and The Little Chinese Seamstress

Dai Sijie AND filmography

Dai Sijie AND Gao Xingjian

Balzac AND French literature

Mao Zedong AND Chinese Cultural Revolution

China AND Cultural Revolution AND rustication OR reeducation

China AND France AND relations

China AND countryside OR rural AND life OR culture

Dai Sijie

Dai Sijie AND Chinese Cultural Revolution

The Cruel Sea

NICHOLAS MONSARRAT
1951

The Cruel Sea is a novel written in 1951 by British author Nicholas Monsarrat. The novel is set during World War II and depicts the six-year-long Battle of the Atlantic from the point of view of sailors in Great Britain's navy, who faced constant threats from German submarines. In particular, Monsarrat, who based the novel on his own wartime experience, wanted to convey the point of view of sailors on "small ships" such as corvettes (small, fast, lightly armed warships of less than a thousand tons) and frigates (generally larger than corvettes but less than two thousand tons) that were used primarily as escorts for convoys of supply ships and in antisubmarine warfare. (These figures for the size of the ships refer to the amount of water the ship displaces.) These sailors faced as much danger from the "cruel sea" as they did from German submarines.

Monsarrat was a prolific author who wrote more than three dozen books over his career. *The Cruel Sea*, though, was perhaps his most popular novel and the one book from the author's body of work that is still widely read. The popularity of *The Cruel Sea* and the reputation of Monsarrat were enhanced by a 1953 film adaptation of the novel, which brought the story to a wider audience. While many novels written during the war were patriotic novels intended to boost morale and support for the war among citizens, *The Cruel Sea* was a major work during the postwar period when many writers were giving greater emphasis to the cruelty and horror of war.

Nicholas Monsarrat *(Evening Standard / Getty Images)*

The Cruel Sea is available in a 1969 edition published by Alfred A. Knopf.

AUTHOR BIOGRAPHY

Monsarrat was born on March 22, 1910, in Liverpool, England, where he grew up in comfortable circumstances. His father was an eminent surgeon; his mother ran the household with a strictness that Monsarrat came to resent. In his early years, he was sent to boarding school, where he was mercilessly bullied. During his youth, he took up sailing as a form of escape from what he saw as a repressive home life, and his sailing skills would prepare him for his later career in the British navy. Indeed, during World War II, the British navy actively recruited people with yachting or boating experience. He attended Trinity College at Cambridge University, earning a bachelor's degree in law in 1931. He worked for two years in a lawyer's office, but he quickly concluded that he was more interested in being a writer. He published his first novel,

Think of Tomorrow, in 1934. Two more novels quickly followed in the mid-1930s. He also wrote a play, *The Visitor*, which provided him with some measure of fame. Although the play met with a lukewarm critical reception, it starred the famous actress Greer Garson.

Monsarrat described himself as a pacifist, but when England entered World War II, he joined the Royal Navy and served until after the end of the war, rising to the rank of lieutenant commander. During most of the war, he served on a ship that escorted supply convoys across the Atlantic. He also wrote *H. M. Corvette* (1942), *East Coast Corvette* (1943), and *Corvette Command* (1944)— all based on his personal experiences at sea and mined from the notebooks and journals he kept. (H. M. stands for "his majesty's," referring to the king of England.) Although he faced considerable danger at sea, he seems to have thrived on that danger, and in his many sea stories, he depicted a kind of lost world of honor, duty, pride, and decency that, in his view, was under assault by the cruelties and evils of the modern world.

After leaving the navy, Monsarrat became something of an exile from England. He served with the British Information Services as chief in South Africa until 1952, then in Canada until 1956. He spent his final years living on a Mediterranean island with his third wife. Meanwhile, in 1951, he published *The Cruel Sea*, which won the Heinemann Foundation Prize for Literature. His work ethic as a writer was extraordinary, as he published a book almost each year until his death, although some of these books were collections of earlier, shorter works. In the 1960s, he took a break from novel writing to write a two-volume autobiography, *Life Is a Four Letter Word*; the first volume, *Breaking In*, was published in 1966 and the second, *Breaking Out*, in 1970. Other novels that attracted international attention were *The Story of Esther Costello* (1953), *The Tribe That Lost Its Head* (1956), and *Richer than All His Tribe* (1968). Monsarrat was at work on a three-volume work titled *The Master Mariner* when he died of cancer in a London hospital on August 8, 1979. The first volume, *Running Proud*, was published in 1978 and quickly became a best seller in England. The second volume was published the same year, although it was unfinished. The Royal Navy honored his request to have his ashes scattered at sea.

PLOT SUMMARY

Part One—1939: Learning

The Cruel Sea consists of seven parts, each part corresponding with one year of World War II. In Part One, Lieutenant-Commander George Ericson has just been called out of retirement from the navy and given command of the corvette *Compass Rose* after the outbreak of World War II. His first lieutenant is James Bennett, an Australian. Lieutenants Keith Lockhart and Gordon Ferraby report for duty on the ship. It is clear that most of the ship's crew is inexperienced. In the period of calm before the ship puts to sea, Chief E.R.A. Jim Watts (E.R.A. stands for engine-room artificer) spends time ashore getting drunk. Lockhart and Ferraby check on the ships stores, Bennett picks up a prostitute at a hotel, and Ericson spends time with his wife in a hotel.

In the weeks that follow, the ship is readied for service at sea, and discipline is imposed on the inexperienced crew. Ericson travels to Glasgow, Scotland, to receive sailing orders. The ship travels downriver to take on additional supplies and arrives at the naval anchorage off Greenock, joining a large fleet of ships of various types. Over a two-week period, the men undergo training exercises involving the firing of guns and the use of antisubmarine depth charges. When the ship leaves harbor, Ericson is troubled by its handling, which is not of the best quality. The ship then proceeds to the naval base at Ardnacraish, where it is taken out to sea for the first time. Vice-Admiral Sir Vincent Murray-Forbes, now regarded as too old for a command at sea, is placed in charge of training exercises at Ardnacraish. The training is rigorous, with all the ship's crew cross trained in different functions. Lockhart tries to shield Ferraby from Bennett, and it is clear that Lockhart and Bennett will never get along. The *Compass Rose* wraps up training with a firing exercise at night. Murray-Forbes writes his final report on the ship and its officers, pointing out both strengths and weaknesses. Ericson receives the report, along with orders to join a convoy at sea.

Part Two—1940: Skirmishing

Part Two opens by describing conditions in the Atlantic with the outbreak of World War II. German U-boats (submarines) are on the offensive. The *Compass Rose* is assigned to convoy duty, meaning that its role will be to accompany supply ships across the Atlantic. Initially, heavy

MEDIA ADAPTATIONS

- *The Cruel Sea* was adapted for film in 1953. The movie was directed by Charles Frend and starred Jack Hawkins, Donald Sinden, Denholm Elliott, Virginia McKenna, and Stanley Baker. The movie was released on DVD by Starz/Anchor Bay in 2006. Running time is 126 minutes.

- An audiocassette version of *The Cruel Sea* was released by Caedmon Audio Cassette in 1983.

- Another audio version of *The Cruel Sea*, with narration by actors Donald Sinden, Philip Madoc, Paul Rhys, Michael Maloney, Helen Baxendale, Emma Cunniffe, Jack Davenport, and Joe Dunlop, was produced by BBC Radio and released by BBC Audiobooks in 1998.

weather impedes the ship's operations, making many of the crew seasick—but it also has the advantage of preventing the U-boats from attacking. The ship returns to port at Liverpool. Ericson requests that another officer be appointed to the ship. Accordingly, Lieutenant John Morell arrives.

The ship takes part in further convoys, following the lead of the battleship *Viperous*. The crew's nerves are strained as the ship zigzags through the ocean; nights, when the U-boats are more likely to attack, are especially stressful. Again the ship returns to port, and Ericson, Morell, and Ferraby are able to spend several days with their wives, while Bennett spends time in a hotel with a prostitute; Lockhart has to remain on duty aboard the ship. Bennett returns to the ship with an ulcer, which means that he must be relieved of duty and stay on shore; Lockhart takes his place as "Number One," or second in command. Morale aboard the ship improves with Bennett's absence.

The U-boats are more active after the evacuation of Dunkirk and after France and Norway fall to the Germans. The *Compass Rose* has its first engagement with a German U-boat, losing one of the ships it is escorting. Ferraby conducts himself well in an operation to rescue the survivors of the torpedoed ship. Ultimately, the *Compass Rose* sails on eleven convoy missions during 1940, traveling to Iceland, Gibraltar, and the mid-Atlantic. At the end of the year, the crew witnesses the sinking of an iron-ore ship, which breaks in half and goes down in less than a minute.

Part Three—1941: Grappling

Part Three begins with a domestic matter. Able Seaman Thomas Gregg did not return to the ship after shore leave and was missing for seventeen days. At first, he refuses to defend himself, but eventually he confesses that he returned home to his wife because he had received a letter from a friend suggesting that she was being unfaithful to him. The seaman discovers that his wife is pregnant by another man. Ericson is sympathetic, especially since Gregg always did his duty well.

The *Compass Rose* begins a six-week cruise as U-boat activity in the Atlantic increases. Ericson is injured when he is thrown out of his bunk as the ship rolls, and Lockhart assumes command as the convoy passes through dense fog. At Gladstone Dock, where the escort ships berth, the men and ships of numerous navies—Dutch, Norwegian, and French, but no American ships yet—rub elbows. Ireland has remained neutral, allowing the Germans to maintain an espionage center in Dublin. The sister of one of the crew is killed when Gladstone Dock is attacked from the air by German bombers. The *Compass Rose* goes on four more escort missions before putting into port for maintenance and refitting. Ferraby returns home, where he is able to play with his six-month-old baby girl. Morell is disappointed when his wife, an actress, chooses to go to a theater party rather than meet with him. Lockhart spends his leave in London, where he meets with a former employer, then gets drunk.

The *Compass Rose*, now refitted, puts to sea again and is spotted by a German reconnaissance plane. Tension builds as the crew learns that the area is infested with U-boats. Over the following days, several of the ships in the convoy are lost, and the *Compass Rose* picks up survivors. As the ship is steaming back to port, a mechanical problem develops, and the crew, led by Watts, has to make repairs. Tension continues to build because the ship has to slow down, making it an easier target for U-boats. Finally the ship is repaired, but as it gets under way, a U-boat is picked up on

radar trailing a convoy, and the *Compass Rose* spots it on the surface. The ship attacks, firing its guns, and although the U-boat fires back, it is severely damaged. Several Germans are taken captive, including the U-boat's captain. Ericson treats the German captain with contempt and is repulsed by his thought that his men should have just shot the German survivors in the water.

Part Four—1942: Fighting

Part Four opens by summarizing the historical situation: Britain lost two major ships in a bombing attack, and the United States lost half its fleet at Pearl Harbor in Hawaii, bringing America into the war. The Battle of the Atlantic is reaching a climax, with major losses of Allied shipping. The *Compass Rose* comes across a dead sailor in a lifeboat. The *Compass Rose* is sent on a rescue mission to find a ship, and they do find it, bombed and derelict. Morell leads a detachment that boards the ship and discovers numerous bodies. The ship receives word of heavy losses on a Gibraltar convoy. Lockhart tends to the wounds of a badly burned survivor the ship has picked up. They come across a torpedoed ship and find numerous corpses still floating in the water. The "most hideous hour of the whole war" for the men is watching a torpedoed oil tanker burn, for the flames and burning oil on the water make it impossible to approach the tanker and help its crew.

It is time for the crew to have a long leave. Seaman Gregg returns home to his wife, who has given birth to a baby that is not his. Lockhart spends time in London, including a visit to a publisher regarding an article about corvettes that he wrote. Ericson spends time with his wife, who is living with her mother. Ferraby goes home to spend time with his wife and baby, and Morell quarrels with his wife.

After leave is ended, a new convoy is assembled, and the *Compass Rose* is escorting it to a location near Iceland when it is struck by a torpedo. In a scene of confusion and amid the death of numerous crew members, including Gregg, Watts, and Morell, the survivors have to abandon the ship. Some leap into the icy North Atlantic waters. Only eleven of the crew survive in lifeboats. Eventually, the ship *Viperous* finds them and rescues them.

Part Five—1943: The Moment of Balance

Part Four begins on shore. Lockhart and Ericson meet to celebrate Ericson's promotion to captain. Ericson says that he met with Morell's wife, only to discover that she had already taken up with a new man. He also explains that he will assume command of the frigate *Saltash*, one of a new class of ship, and that he wants Lockhart to serve as second in command as a first lieutenant. Compared with a corvette, the *Saltash* is bigger and faster, has a greater range, and is able to carry and drop more depth charges. Lockhart, though, has doubts about joining Ericson because he is still shaken by the sinking of the *Compass Rose*. Later, Ericson and Lockhart join the crew of the nearly completed *Saltash* at the Clyde shipyard in Scotland. Gunnery Officer Allingham arrives, along with a ship's doctor and other officers and crew. In the weeks that follow, the *Saltash* is readied for sea.

The *Saltash* puts to sea in the middle of the year. The situation in the Atlantic has been improving somewhat during the year, and Allied escort ships have been sinking about as many U-boats as they have lost to U-boats. New techniques and new technology are changing the tide of the war in the Atlantic. After a first mission, the *Saltash* returns to port, where Lockhart meets with a love interest, Julie Hallam, a Wren (the colloquial name for members of the Women's Reserve Naval Service). On its next mission, the *Saltash* encounters a different kind of enemy, the sea, as it battles a major storm. Afterward, it takes the *Saltash* two full days to round up the scattered ships in the convoy. The convoy's wing escort, the *Pergola* engages in a hunt for a U-boat, with the *Saltash* taking part by dropping depth charges. After the two ships play cat and mouse with the U-boat, the *Pergola* finally destroys it. The ship returns to port, where Lockhart meets Julie Hallam, and the two stay in a cottage in Scotland.

Part Six—1944: Winning

After working for several months of the new year, the *Saltash* receives word that it is being refitted. The crew will get two months' leave while the ship docks at the Brooklyn Navy Yard in New York City. Lockhart has a discussion with a radio producer, who wants to air an interview with him. He also receives a letter from Julie telling him she is pregnant. Later, he receives a letter from a friend informing him that Julie has been killed in a boating mishap. Ericson is invited to tour an American destroyer and is impressed by what he sees as the kindness of Americans. After the *Saltash* returns to action, it is clear that the tide is turning, with large numbers of U-boats being sunk by Allied

ships. On D-day, June 6, 1944 (the date of a massive Allied invasion of Europe at Normandy, France), the *Saltash* is on patrol in a support role in the English Channel. Christmas arrives, and the ship is back home at Clyde.

Part Seven—1945: The Prize

The end of the war is in sight, and discussion centers on what will happen to postwar Germany. Early in the year, the *Saltash* continues to perform convoy duty, but U-boat attacks have sharply diminished. Then in April, U-boat activity intensifies. May arrives, and the *Saltash* is ordered to separate itself from convoys and remain on patrol in the vicinity of Rockall, a tiny island in the Atlantic. There the crew receives word that Germany has surrendered and that all U-boats have been ordered to surrender. All over the Atlantic and around the British Isles, U-boats surface, displaying a black surrender flag. The *Saltash* accompanies two U-boats to Scotland, but before arriving, the ship encounters one last U-boat, which surfaces but does not appear willing to surrender. The *Saltash* fires on the U-boat, which then raises its surrender flag. The war in the Atlantic is over.

CHARACTERS

The Cruel Sea contains a large number of named characters, many of them in minor roles. This character list includes only the more significant characters.

Gunnery Officer Allingham

Allingham, an Australian, is described as "lanky" and "fresh-faced." He is a popular and efficient officer, "so obviously efficient, and so obviously ready to jump in and do the job himself, any time of the day, that he carried his men along with him without a hitch."

Lieutenant James Bennett

Bennett, an Australian, is the first lieutenant of the *Compass Rose*. A stern disciplinarian, he is described as a man who "looked tough, and knew it, and liked it: everything about him—his red face, the stocky figure, the cap worn at an unusual angle—all proclaimed the homespun sailorman with no frills and no nonsense." Bennett is an unlikable man, and under his discipline, morale on the ship is poor. Midway through the novel, he develops an ulcer and has to go ashore for treatment. In his absence, morale on the ship improves.

Lieutenant-Commander George Eastwood Ericson

Ericson is described on the opening page as "a big man, broad and tough: a man to depend on, a man to remember: about forty-two or –three, fair hair going grey, blue eyes as level as a foot rule." Ericson is the commander of the corvette *Compass Rose*, although at one point he is injured from the rolling of the ship and has to relinquish command to Lieutenant Lockhart. Later, after he is promoted to captain, he assumes command of the *Saltash*.

Lieutenant Gordon Ferraby

Ferraby is described as "short, fair, immature—a very young man in a proud uniform, and not yet sure that he deserved the distinction." He is proud and excited to join the navy, but he is disappointed, particularly because of the vulgarity and poor manners of Bennett. He is regarded as the most vulnerable officer, the "weak link that betrayed the rest of the chain."

Able Seaman Thomas Gregg

Gregg does not return to the ship after shore leave and is missing for seventeen days. At first, he refuses to defend himself, but eventually he confesses that he returned home to his wife because he had received a letter suggesting that she was being unfaithful to him. The seaman discovers that his wife is pregnant by another man. Later, while he is on leave, he returns home to find his wife and the baby in a tawdry domestic situation. Gregg dies when the *Compass Rose* is torpedoed in 1942 near Iceland.

Julie Hallam

Hallam is a member of the Wrens, the informal name for women in the Women's Reserve Naval Services. She meets with Lockhart in 1943, after the *Saltash* puts into port. She is described as pretty and elegant looking, and she and Lockhart have an affectionate and playful intimate relationship. In a letter, she informs Lockhart that she is pregnant. She is later killed in a boating accident.

Lieutenant Keith Lockhart

Lockhart, age twenty-seven, is described as "tall, black-haired, thin-faced: he had a watchful air, as though feeling his way in a situation." Lockhart has to take command of the ship after Lieutenant-Commander Ericson is injured. Lockhart survives the sinking of the *Compass Rose*, but he is badly shaken by the ordeal. He is promoted to first lieutenant and joins Ericson on the *Saltash* in 1943. He has a romantic relationship with Julie Hallam.

Lieutenant John Morell

Morell is assigned to the *Compass Rose* after its first mission. He is described as "a very proper young man, so correct and so assured that it appeared fantastic for him to grace anything as crude as a corvette." Later, he is said to be "grave, slow-moving, and exceedingly courteous." Morell plays a major role in 1942 in a mission to rescue a bombed and derelict ship. He is horrified by what he sees on the ship. Morell is killed when the *Compass Rose* is torpedoed in 1942 near Iceland.

Vice-Admiral Sir Vincent Murray-Forbes

Murray-Forbes is a veteran naval officer who served with distinction in World War I but is now considered too old for a command at sea. He is placed in charge of training at the naval base at Ardnacraish.

Chief E.R.A. Jim Watts

Watts is the senior engine-room rating (enlisted man) on the *Compass Rose*. He is described as "small, with a quick decisive manner and an air of competence." He plays a major role in repairing the ship after a mechanical problem develops. Watts is killed when the *Compass Rose* is torpedoed in 1942 near Iceland.

THEMES

Seafaring

The sea plays a prominent role in *The Cruel Sea*. The very title of the novel makes clear that the sea is as much an enemy as the German U-boats are. At one point, in 1943, the *Compass Rose* faces a particularly virulent storm at sea. Ironically, someone plays the song "Someone's Rocking My Dream-Boat" over the ship's loudspeakers.

TOPICS FOR FURTHER STUDY

- Conduct research into the contributions of Britain's North American allies in the fight against Nazi Germany in the early stages of World War II, particularly in the Battle of the Atlantic. What specific aid did the United States supply before its entry into the war in late 1941? What contributions did Canada make? How effective were these contributions? Write a feature article that you imagine might have appeared in a British magazine of the time, summarizing the results of your research.

- Imagine that you have been given the job of finding images for an illustrated edition of *The Cruel Sea*. Using the Internet, find images of the vessels referred to in the novel: corvettes, frigates, battleships, and German U-boats. Prepare a PowerPoint presentation that includes the technical specifications of these vessels and share your images with your classmates orally or through a Web page.

- In 1973, German author Lothar-Günther Buchheim published a novel titled *Das Boot* ("The Boat"; the German word *Boot* is pronounced like the English word *boat*). The novel was turned into a successful 1981 movie directed by Wolfgang Petersen. It tells the story of the Battle of the Atlantic from the point of view of a German U-boat crew. Watch the film (which is available on DVD and Blu-Ray) and then prepare a chart outlining the similarities and differences between Buchheim's story and Monsarrat's story in *The Cruel Sea*.

- The name Captain Georg von Trapp is famous as that of a leading character in *The Sound of Music*. Von Trapp was a historical person who commanded a German U-boat during World War I. His memoirs, *To the Last Salute: Memories of an Austrian U-Boat Commander*, were translated and published in English in 2007. Locate and read selections from these memoirs and then write a script in which you imagine von Trapp and Lieutenant Commander George Ericson, now both retired, reflecting on their wartime experiences. Share your script with your classmates on a blog or social networking site, or enlist the help of a classmate and perform your script for your classmates.

- Codes and coded messages played a key role in World War II. The Allies were finally able to prevail in the Atlantic by breaking the German naval code, called Enigma. In the war in the Pacific, the United States used codes as well. Specifically, commanders found that the Navajo language was a "code" the Japanese were unable to break. The story of Navajo marine Code Talkers is told in Joseph Bruchac's *Code Talker: A Novel about the Navajo Marines of World War II*. Imagine that the novel's major character, Ned Begay, is coming to your school to talk. Capture the essence of his message in a poster advertising the event.

- *Soldier Boys* by Dean Hughes is a young-adult novel that tells the story of two teenage boys, one American, one German, who join their respective armies in World War II and fight in the 1944–1945 Battle of the Bulge on the European front. Read the novel and write a report comparing and contrasting the situation of soldiers in land battles with that of sailors in sea battles.

- Research the history of the Women's Royal Naval Service. When was it created? What role did it play in World War II? What other military organizations for women existed during World War II in England? Prepare a chart that outlines your findings. Supplement your chart using Jing (http://www.techsmith.com/jing/) to create a visual presentation of your findings.

(Monsarrat probably has in mind a 1941 recording of the song by the Four Tones, but the song has been recorded by the Ink Spots, Vera Lynn, Natalie Cole, and even Bugs Bunny in a Disney cartoon.) In chapter 6 of Part Five can be found passages such as this:

> It was more than a full gale at sea, it was nearer to a great roaring battlefield.... The convoy no longer had the shape of a convoy, and indeed a ship was scarcely a ship, trapped and hounded in this howling wilderness." The description of the storm goes on: "Huge waves, a mile from crest to crest, roared down upon the pigmies that were to be their prey.

The *Compass Rose* labors to stay afloat. The men are seasick, and a number of them are injured from the rolling of the ship in the waves. The suggestion of these and other passages is that the men aboard the ship are victims of an environment they are unable to control.

Community

It is commonplace for authors to see ships at sea as a microcosm, that is, a "little world" (from the Greek roots *micro-*, meaning "small," and *cosmos*, meaning "world"). A ship at sea is isolated from the surrounding world. The men on the ship form a community that lives, works, eats, jokes, plays, and—during wartime—fights together. Authors commonly ensure that the little world they create includes a diversity of character types. Monsarrat does so in *The Cruel Sea*. Some of the men are courageous; others are more timid. Some are cruel; others are more kindly. The men come from different backgrounds, such as journalism and the law. Some are veterans; others are raw recruits. The ship, then, becomes a crucible for examining human behavior during times of danger and stress. Implicitly, then, the microcosm of the ship becomes a commentary on the macrocosm of the world—in this novel's case, the world at war.

Wars

Clearly, *The Cruel Sea* is a war novel. It examines the way a diverse group of men behaves under the stress of war. At various points, characters comment on the nature of war. For example, in a conversation with Julie Hallam, Lockhart says, "War has to be a matter of dedication: anything else gets in the way. You have to be single-minded, free of distraction, tough, un-tender—all the words that don't go with marriage." Late in the novel, Allingham is asked whether he believes it is right to "dress the war up a bit, make it a matter of conviction" so that the men believe in the causes for which they fight. He responds, "I used to. I started the war like that, anyway. Now I'm not so sure. We've got to win the bloody thing, whatever material we use—willing or not.... Perhaps it doesn't make a hell of a lot of difference, either way, when it comes to action." In his view, the only issue is success or failure; a warrior either destroys his enemy or is destroyed himself.

The novel makes clear that war changes men. Late in the novel, Lockhart reflects on how the war has changed him:

> 'The best years of my life have vanished. . . .' But that was not really true, Lockhart knew well enough: for him, they were not lost years, in spite of the futility and wastefulness of war. He had grown up fast in the meantime, he was a different person from the twenty-seven-year-old, goal-less, motive-less, not very good journalist who had joined up in 1939. War had given him something, and the personal cost was not a whit too high.... [H]e had gained in every other way—in self-discipline, in responsibility, in simple confidence and the rout of fear.

Death

The prospect of death hangs over the crew of the ships, and many of the men who serve on the *Compass Rose* lose their lives when the ship is torpedoed in 1942. Monsarrat handles the issue of their deaths in an interesting way. Rather than focusing on the individuals, he focuses on classes of men and *how* they die. He begins his catalog of death with the simple statement, "Presently, men began to die." He writes that "some men died well" and lists several names. One man dies while making lists. Others die badly, including Watts and Gregg. One man dies while treacherously taking another's place in a lifeboat. Monsarrat concludes the catalog with the bald statement: "Some men just died." Most of the men die as they have lived, and their deaths reflect their heroism, nobility, cowardice, treachery, and other human triumphs and failings. But death at sea is treated in an almost matter-of-fact way. It is inevitable that some men will die. Their deaths represent not the climax of the novel but rather part of the inescapable reality of war.

Commander Ericson is the main character in The Cruel Sea. *(Joe Gough / Shutterstock.com)*

STYLE

Narrative and Dialogue

The Cruel Sea consists of a mixture of narration and dialogue. In this respect, it is no different from most other novels. What is noteworthy, though, is the nature of both the narration and the dialogue. Much of the narration takes a broad perspective. It summarizes the events of the war, including geopolitical events (U.S. entry into the war, for example), the events surrounding the Battle of the Atlantic (including precise figures on, for example, the number of ships lost during a given time span), and the technology of conducting antisubmarine warfare. This narration is not filtered through the mind of the characters but rather comes from the "outside." In a similar vein, the passages of dialogue tend not to emphasize character and character development. Rather, the dialogue is much like what the reader would expect to hear from seamen fighting a war. They comment on their duties, on the Germans, on the progress of the war, and on their own chances for success or failure, for living or dying. Thus, the style of the novel deliberately avoids psychological analysis, satire, political commentary, or philosophy. The war is accepted as a given, and some of the men called to it will die. The novel is one about men doing a job under difficult conditions and doing it to the best of their abilities, such as they are.

Point of View

Closely related to the narrative style is the novel's point of view. *The Cruel Sea* takes very much an omniscient third-person point of view. *Omniscient* means that the narrative voice is all knowing. *Third-person* means that the characters are referred to as "he," "she," and "they": the story is told *about* the characters, not *by* any one of the characters. This style of narration allows the narrative voice to summarize historical events, comment on what characters are thinking and feeling, and move about in time and space. The narrator consistently knows more than any of the characters do.

Consider, for example, this passage, which describes the death of Morell when the *Compass Rose* is torpedoed:

He thought a great deal about Elaine [his wife]: his thoughts of her lasted, as he himself did, till nearly daylight. But there came a time, toward five o'clock, when his cold body and his tired brain seemed to compass a full circle and meet at the same point of futility and exhaustion. He saw now that he had been utterly foolish, where Elaine was concerned: foolish, and ineffective.

The passage goes on in this vein. Notice that the narrative point of view allows the reader access not only to external events (for example, Morell reaches a conclusion at a particular time, around five o'clock, something only the narrator could know) but also to comment on Morell's state of mind. The words, though, remain the narrator's, not Morell's; it is the narrator who comes up with an expression like "compass a full circle and meet at the same point." The point of view is not filtered through Morell's mind and consciousness but rather remains outside. This point of view is consistent with Monsarrat's apparent aim of presenting not a probing psychological analysis but rather a historical account grounded in fact and observation.

HISTORICAL CONTEXT

World War II began on September 1, 1939, when Nazi Germany, in the iron grip of dictator Adolf Hitler, invaded Poland. After issuing an ultimatum to Germany—an ultimatum that was ignored—Great Britain declared war on Germany on September 3, 1939.

As an island nation, Great Britain was dependent on its allies for food, raw materials, military supplies, and later troops. These were all supplied by other British Commonwealth nations, particularly Canada, and by the United States and other allies in Central and South America. In an effort to starve England (part of Great Britain) into submission, Germany tried to cut it off from these lifelines by controlling the Atlantic Ocean. The chief threat to shipping across the Atlantic was the German *Unterseeboot,* or U-boat—that is, the submarine. Throughout the early stages of the war, German submarines routinely sank ships from Allied countries, prompting British Prime Minister Winston Churchill to call the sustained conflict the Battle of the Atlantic. This "battle" can be said to have begun on September 3, 1939, the day England declared war on Germany, when the British liner *Athenia* was torpedoed and sunk by a German U-boat.

The threat of German submarines grew after Germany invaded Norway and France and after Allied troops (the Allies were the countries that opposed Germany) had to be evacuated from the beaches harbor of Dunkirk, France, in late May and early June of 1940. Massive submarine pens in such places as Bordeaux, France, gave the Germans forward bases from which to launch U-boats, increasing their range. Additionally, the Germans developed long-range aircraft that enabled them to patrol the Atlantic and carry out reconnaissance for the U-boats.

To meet the threat, the British had to provide naval escorts for convoys of supply ships, but at the war's beginning, Britain was critically short of escort vessels. During the first year, German U-boats, attacking at night in "wolf packs," sank three million tons of Allied shipping. Matters improved, at least somewhat, with the building of swift corvettes to serve as escorts. Also helping was the Allied occupation of Iceland (giving the Allies a mid-Atlantic base of operations) and the rapid growth of the Royal Canadian Navy. Beginning in May 1941, the U.S. Navy began to provide escort service in the Atlantic. The development of longer-range aircraft would eventually allow the Allies to patrol the mid-Atlantic, where shipping was most vulnerable. The Allies also gained ground after cracking the German Enigma code, which German military commanders used to communicate with submarines.

The threat of German submarine warfare reached a crisis point in 1943. England was running out of oil and other supplies. Germany had more than two hundred operational U-boats. Allied shipyards could not keep pace with losses, although the United States was stepping up production of "Liberty Ships" that would help turn the tide. More aggressive antisubmarine tactics, along with new technologies such as better radar, were also making a difference. In April and May of 1943, the Allies were able to sink forty-five U-boats. By 1945, the German U-boats were having far less of an impact.

The Battle of the Atlantic was a costly one. Some 75,000 to 85,000 Allied sailors lost their lives, along with 28,000 German U-boat crewmen. Additionally, massive numbers of Allied ships were lost, most from U-boat attacks: 222 in 1939, 1,059 in 1940, 1,328 in 1941, 1,661 in 1942, 597 in 1943, 247 in 1944, and 105 in 1945.

COMPARE & CONTRAST

- **1939:** World War II begins with the German invasion of Poland on September 1. In response, Great Britain declares war on Germany on September 3. On that day, the British liner *Athenia* is torpedoed and sunk, launching the Battle of the Atlantic.

  1951: World War II has been over for six years. Germany is divided into democratic West Germany and communist East Germany. West Germany joins with some of Nazi Germany's former enemies in the formation of the European Coal and Steel Community, one of the precursors of the European Union.

  Today: Most of the nations of Europe are military allies through the North Atlantic Treaty Organization (NATO) and are members of the European Union, an economic and political union designed to break down trade barriers and integrate the European economies. East and West Germany reunified in 1990.

- **1939:** Submarines are powered by diesel fuel and electricity. They can remain submerged for only a few days before having to surface and refuel.

  1951: In July, the U.S. Congress authorizes the construction of the first nuclear-powered submarine, the USS *Nautilus*, which will be commissioned in 1954. Nuclear-powered submarines can remain submerged for months at a time and never need refueling during their life spans.

  Today: Because of their high cost, only the United States, Russia, the People's Republic of China, France, the United Kingdom, and India have nuclear-powered submarines.

- **1939:** The Women's Royal Naval Service (the "Wrens"), first created in World War I, is revived with the onset of World War II.

  1951: Unlike after World War I, the Wrens remain active, serving a vital auxiliary function for the British Royal Navy.

  Today: The Women's Royal Naval Service was disbanded in 1993. Women are allowed to serve alongside men in Britain's Royal Navy.

CRITICAL OVERVIEW

The Cruel Sea met with a mixed critical reception. Many reviewers praised the book highly. A *Time* magazine contributor, for example, calls attention to characterization, noting that "Ericson and Lockhart stand out as sharp, deeply drawn characters." So, too, does the reviewer for the *New Republic*, reporting that Monsarrat's "people are separate and completely convincing human beings." This reviewer writes that "the greatest merit of *The Cruel Sea* is Monsarrat's unification of externals and internals; the passages dealing with battle and storm have enormous impact, but the individuals who are both subject and cause of so much pain make themselves felt as known and sentient personalities."

Some commentators regarded the novel as a classic. Michael Rogers, writing in *Library Journal* in 2000 on the issuance of a paperback edition of the novel, calls it "one of the classic naval adventure stories of World War II" and notes that "the book was a smash when released in 1951." Indeed, according to J. Jaffe's entry on Monsarrat in the *Oxford Dictionary of National Biography*, the British publisher sold more than 1.3 million copies in hardback by 1981, and other sources estimate up to four million copies worldwide since the book's publication.

Not all reviewers were as kind. George Miles, writing in *Commonweal* when *The Cruel Sea* was first published, says that "this book does not succeed in being a realistic war story, or a convincing creation of human stress and endurance

Ericson and Lockhart are lucky to be rescued when a torpedo sinks their ship. *(Snaprender | Shutterstock.com)*

in time of war." He calls attention to what he regards as "hackneyed ways of phrasing" and "sentimentality"; the deaths at sea, seen as extensions of the characters' natures, are "artificial" and fall short of the author's goals. The love stories in the book, Miles feels, "are abrupt, unbalanced and unreal." The reviewer for the *New Yorker* was even harsher, calling the book a "dismal tale" and writing that "at his best, Mr. Monsarrat is a dull, often sentimental writer. At his worst—that is to say, when women enter the picture—he becomes possessed by a gamy, winking coyness that clogs his pen even when he tries to deal with a serious love scene."

CRITICISM

Michael J. O'Neal

O'Neal holds a Ph.D. in English. In the following essay, he examines The Cruel Sea *in the context of novels about war.*

Fictionalized accounts of war occupy an honored place in the history of literature. In antiquity, Homer recreated the events surrounding the Trojan War in his great epic poems *The Iliad* and *The Odyssey*. In the Middle Ages, the legends of King Arthur depicted heroism on the battlefield, and in the Renaissance, Shakespeare, in such plays as *Henry V*, combined historical events with reflections on the ethics of warfare in drama. Many of these early treatments of warfare—not just in the English and European traditions but throughout the world—were intended to memorialize key events in the formation and development of a culture.

The depiction of war in fiction became more commonplace in the nineteenth century. In *The Charterhouse of Parma*, for example, French author Stendhal depicted the Battle of Waterloo in the Napoleonic Wars. These wars were also at the center of Leo Tolstoy's monumental *War and Peace*. In the American tradition, Stephen Crane's *The Red Badge of Courage* is set in the

WHAT DO I READ NEXT?

- Monsarrat's *The Story of Esther Costello*, first published in 1953, is available in a 2009 edition. It tells the story of a young girl in an Irish village who, after being rendered deaf and blind by an accident, is taken to America for care by a tourist who then exploits her condition for monetary gain. Ultimately, this controversial novel is a satirical examination of the charity industry.

- Readers interested in Monsarrat's shorter fiction could start with the collection *HMS Marlborough Will Enter Harbour and Other Short Stories*, available in a 2008 edition. The lead story is about a ship that is torpedoed and a captain who refuses to submit to what appears to be his fate.

- *Escort Commander* (1979) by Terence Robertson is a biography of Captain Frederic John Walker of the Royal Navy. (The book was originally titled *Walker R. N.*) Walker was a World War II–era pioneer in antisubmarine warfare.

- *Japanese Destroyer Captain: Pearl Harbor, Guadalcanal, Midway—the Great Naval Battles as Seen through Japanese Eyes* by Tameichi Hara was originally published in the 1960s and was reprinted in 2011. As the title suggests, it is a memoir written from the viewpoint of the captain of a Japanese destroyer.

- *Iron Coffins: A Personal Account of the German U-Boat Battles of World War II* (2002) by Herbert A. Werner is an autobiographical account of the Battle of the Atlantic by a former German U-boat commander.

- John Mannock's similarly titled *Iron Coffin* (2004) is a novel about a German U-boat that is damaged by patrol bombers off Cuba. It finds refuge in the bayous of coastal Louisiana, where an isolated clan of Cajun trappers renders aid.

- *Nick of Time* is a young-adult novel written by Ted Bell (2008). It tells the story of a twelve-year-old boy, Nick McIver, the son of a lighthouse owner, who, in 1939, finds a sea chest containing a time-travel device that allows him to bounce around in time to fight pirates, serve with Napoleon's navy, and battle Nazi spies patrolling the coast of Great Britain in an experimental U-boat.

- *Mare's War* by Tanita S. Davis (2009) is a young-adult novel narrated from the perspective of a grandmother who tells her granddaughters about her experiences in Europe during World War II as a member of the African American regiment of the Women's Army Corps, an American counterpart to the British Women's Royal Naval Services.

- *The Cruel Sea Retold: The Truth Behind Monsarrat's Epic Convoy Drama*, by naval historian Bernard Edwards (2008), examines the specific operations in the Battle of the Atlantic that form the backbone of Monsarrat's novel.

Civil War. World War I gave rise to a number of important war novels. Perhaps the most famous ones are *All Quiet on the Western Front* by German author Erich Maria Remarque and *A Farewell to Arms* by Ernest Hemingway. It was after World War II, though, that war novels flooded the literary marketplace: Hemingway's *For Whom the Bell Tolls*, Joseph Heller's *Catch-22*, Kurt Vonnegut's *Slaughterhouse Five*, James Jones's *From Here to Eternity*, Thomas Pynchon's *Gravity's Rainbow*, and of course many of the stories of Nicholas Monsarrat, including *The Cruel Sea*.

Why has warfare emerged as a popular subject for fiction writers? The answers seem obvious. Warfare holds out the possibility for dramatic action. It provides a cauldron in which character can form and be examined. It intensifies emotions

WAR IS PART OF THE COLLECTIVE MEMORY
OF A PEOPLE, AND FICTION ABOUT WAR HELPS
TO SHAPE AND PRESERVE THAT MEMORY."

and motivations, for death is always imminent. It focuses the mind, not only of soldiers on the front and sailors at sea but also of people on the home front, who suffer the hardships if not the dangers of war. War and the way it is conducted are a reflection of the cultural values of the nation that wages it. War is part of the collective memory of a people, and fiction about war helps to shape and preserve that memory.

The central question, then, concerns the specific way in which a particular novel shapes and preserves the memory of a culture. Consider, for example, a war novel such as *My Brother Sam Is Dead* by James Lincoln Collier and Christopher Collier. The novel is set during the American Revolution, a war preserved in American memory as a noble war fought by idealistic patriots who threw off tyranny and established an independent nation. Cultural symbols, from Fourth of July celebrations to songs such as "Yankee Doodle," contribute to American mythology about the Revolution. Yet *My Brother Sam Is Dead* paints a very different picture. It depicts the war as a confusing, destructive, muddled affair, one that makes little sense, that sweeps up the innocent as well as the guilty, and that ultimately resolves nothing.

Or consider a novel such as Heller's fiercely satirical *Catch-22*, set during the later stages of World War II. The title of the novel continues to be widely used to refer to a conundrum with no solution. The "catch" of the novel is that, according to military regulations, a pilot does not have to fly combat missions if he is mentally unfit. However, fear and avoidance are rational responses to danger, so a pilot who requests a mental evaluation to get out of combat duty thereby proves his sanity and must fly. Ultimately, the novel turns on its head conventional notions of patriotism, pride, heroism, duty, justice, and integrity, underlining the absurdity of warfare.

Still other novels place emphasis on the psychology of the individual soldier. *All Quiet on the Western Front* is perhaps the classic novel in this vein. The novel's emphasis is not on heroic action during battle. Rather, the novel emphasizes the mental stresses and hardships that individual soldiers at the Western Front in World War I endured. The author said that his purpose was to show that even those who survived the bullets and shells of trench warfare were destroyed by the war, for psychologically they could never be the same as they were before experiencing the war's horrors.

World War II survives in British and American memory as a "good war," a "just war." Death and destruction were widespread, but the war had to be fought to combat European fascism and Nazism and the expansionist aims of the militaristic Japanese empire in the Pacific. During the war itself, American and British popular culture overwhelmingly supported the war and the aims of the Allied governments. After all, who could oppose a war against Hitler? Movies depicted the heroic struggles of sailors and combat soldiers, as well as of European civilians who faced the barbarity of Nazi Germany and its allies. Great Britain endured years of hardship, first with German aerial bombardment of London and other cities, then the threatened starvation of the nation through the efforts of German U-boats. Through sheer force of will, British Prime Minister Winston Churchill led Britain to victory in the war. Allied soldiers carried out heroic missions; they made daring escapes from prisoner-of-war camps; they embarked on dangerous missions to knock out German gun emplacements; they stormed beaches and rooted out enemy units. Newspapers and radio broadcasts traced the progress of the war as Allied armies swept across the continent. Justice and right faced grave threats but were ultimately triumphant.

It was in the postwar context that Monsarrat wrote *The Cruel Sea*, based on his experiences in the British Royal Navy. The novel was published in 1951, and by that time, new perspectives on the war were developing. The war was over, so it was no longer necessary for writers and journalists to function as cheerleaders for the Allied cause. Men and women who had taken part in the war or had suffered the war's hardships at home were now in a position to examine the war, and warfare generally, often in the hope that, in the cold war age of nuclear weapons, such a war would never have to be fought again.

In this climate, *The Cruel Sea* places less emphasis on the psychology of the characters and more emphasis on the hardships of combat at sea. The novel's omniscient narrator takes a largely objective view of the war, frequently commenting on the war and its progress in passages such as this one, from the opening of Part Four (1942):

> The old year, triumphant only at its close, had achieved a level of violence and disaster that set the tone for the new. Just before Christmas, two Allied countries had sustained naval losses of shocking dimensions: Britain had lost two great ships—*Prince of Wales* and *Repulse*—in a single bombing attack, and America, at Pearl Harbor, had suffered a crippling blow that robbed her of half her effective fleet at one stroke.... The attack brought America into the war, an ally coming to the rescue at a most crucial moment.... For now the battle was in spate, now the wild and vicious blows of both sides were storming toward a climax.

The narration here is strictly from the outside; one could almost be reading a history book rather than a novel. The point of view adopted here is not that of one of the characters. The author does not allow the reader to arrive at these conclusions through the depiction of action. Some readers might fault Monsarrat here and elsewhere in the novel for placing too much emphasis on telling the reader about the war rather than showing the war's effects through dramatic action, but telling is part of the novel's strategy. Above all else, Monsarrat wanted his novel to be accurate and truthful, a mirror for the reality of warfare at sea. He wanted to set the actions of his characters within a firm historical context, making those actions and the viewpoints the characters express, credible and rooted in fact. The characters exist not as sharply drawn individuals but rather as types, each one filling an appropriate role in the parade of historical events that passes—a parade emphasized by the structure of the novel, with its division into seven parts, each part representing a year of the war.

Thus, *The Cruel Sea* is neither pro-war nor anti-war, and it avoids satire almost entirely. Men may grumble about the decisions of their superiors, but those decisions invariably reflect the realities of the war, and the orders of superiors are issued with good reason. The combat scenes are rendered dispassionately, with an eye to historical and technical accuracy. While some emphasis is given to the psychology of characters, the key word is *some*, for the novel is less about the minds and hearts of the characters and more about the historical events and personal tragedies that shaped, and in many cases ended, their lives.

THERE ARE OTHER SCENES THAT EVINCE MORE ACTION THAN THIS ONE, BUT IN ALL OF THEM, HE IS A SUPERB REPORTER. HE MAKES YOU SEE, HEAR, AND FEEL."

Very often, the essence of a novel can be found in its first words and its last words. The first words of *The Cruel Sea* set the novel's tone: "Lieutenant-Commander George Eastwood Ericson, R.N.R., sat in a stone cold, draughty, corrugated-iron hut beside the fitting-out dock of Fleming's Shipyard on the River Clyde." This sentence makes a promise: that the novel is to be grounded entirely in reality, in the details of military life, its discomforts, its ugliness, its emphasis on rank and place. The novel closes with Ericson's words, spoken sixty-eight months later: "I must say I'm damned tired." Ericson does not make a speech; he does not comment on the war. Like his nation, he is tired and just wants to rest.

Source: Michael J. O'Neal, Critical Essay on *The Cruel Sea*, in *Novels for Students*, Gale, Cengage Learning, 2012.

Thomas D. Jarrett

In the following excerpt, Jarrett praises Monsarrat's "novelistic reportage" in The Cruel Sea *but faults the work for lack of character development.*

Five years ago Nicholas Monsarrat wrote a 200,000-word novel, *The Cruel Sea*. It was an immediate success. The publishers sold 130,000 copies, exclusive of the 175,000 copies issued by the Book-of-the-Month Club. It was serialized in eighteen newspapers in the United States and Canada, and it appeared in at least fifteen languages. Recently it was re-issued in a "Pocket Book" edition, and it became a successful movie. Prior to the publication of *The Cruel Sea* (1951) Monsarrat had written eleven books—five of them novels. Since then two other novels have appeared, the latest, *Castle Garac*, a Literary Guild selection for November 1955. Yet it is safe to say that, aside from book reviews, little attempt has been made to appraise his talent as a novelist. Probably this is the first magazine article to discuss his work as a whole.

Convoys of ships were used to protect against attack by German U-boats. (Kevin Norris / Shutterstock.com)

Monsarrat, the son of a brilliant surgeon, was born in Liverpool in 1910, educated at Winchester and Trinity College, Cambridge, where he received his honors degree in 1931, and practiced for two years in Liverpool before he decided to leave the business of law "with its calculated rake-off on human misfortune" and move into a London slum area, where he wrote three novels that had only a moderate success. Momentarily he turned to drama, wrote and saw *The Visitor* presented in London's West End, with Greer Garson as the leading lady, and then joined the Royal Navy in 1939, eventually serving as lieutenant commander of convoy escorts during the most turbulent days of World War II. After demobilization he was appointed director of the United Kingdom Information Office in Johannesburg, South Africa. He now holds a similar position in Ottawa, Canada.

. . . Internationally, Monsarrat is best known for *The Cruel Sea*, a work that has been referred to as a novel of contemporary history. The author draws heavily on materials employed in earlier works (there is considerable resemblance between the "Corvette Series" and parts of *The Cruel Sea*), arranging the historical events to suit his story, giving a more detailed account of some action previously described, and adding characters and dialogue. Emphasis is placed on incident, on "the strength and fury of that ocean [the Atlantic], its moods, its violence, its gentle balm, its treachery: what men can do with it, and what it can do with them." Although type-characters, such as the sagacious captain, the cruel officer, the strong-hearted enlisted man, and the woman who waits for her man to return, are in evidence, emphasis seems to be primarily on naval incidents. Captain Ericson, Lieutenant Lockhart, and Julie Hallam, among others, are presented interestingly; however, they seem to exist primarily for the purpose of moving along the story. Monsarrat swings his spotlight to and fro on all of the characters, pauses momentarily, and then introduces to the reader a new scene, often with new characters. He wants the reader to grasp the scope of action, to get the feel of sea warfare as experienced by those who man the *H. M. S. Compass Rose* and the *Saltash*.

The Cruel Sea is a good example of novelistic reportage. Monsarrat is interested in the *what* and *how* of things. By means of description we know how the seamen are fitted for the voyage, taken out to sea, pitted against the weather and the relentless enemy, brought back for refitting, and given a leave, only to return to severe trials, often previously experienced. The reader becomes aware of "the pride and comradeship which nothing could surpass," or he is informed that the men know "how to die without wasting any one's time," or he is given a frightening view of a direct bomb hit. In episode after episode, covering the period of the Battle of the North Atlantic, Monsarrat describes vividly the actions of daring, courageous men. He has at his command the right words, rhythmical sentences, and massive details. And he knows how to keep the reader in suspense.

In one of the chapters entitled "1942: Fighting," it is reported that an aircraft is down at sea. *The Compass Rose* checks its swift forward course in search of the wreckage. Specks are sighted far away on the surface of the water, and Captain Ericson exclaims, "Survivors, by God!" Men crowd to the ship's rail to view the survivors ahead of them. All wait anxiously as the ship nears the scene. Ericson peers through his long-range glasses. Then he sees that the floating objects are not parts of the wrecked aircraft, but

> ... riding high out of the water, held up-right by their life-jackets, were featureless bony images—skeletons now for many a day and night.

> There was something infinitely obscene in the collection of lolling corpses, with bleached faces and white hairless heads, clustered together like men waiting for a bus that had gone by twenty years before. There were nine of them in that close corporation; they rode the water not more than four or five yards from each other: here and there a couple had come together as if embracing. *Compass Rose* circled, starting a wash that set the dead men bobbing and bowing to each other, like performers in some infernal dance.

Now all the seamen note that the dead men are roped together. *The Compass Rose* continues to circle around them.

> There was not an ounce of flesh under the yellow skins, not a single reminder of warmth or manhood. They had perished and they had gone on perishing, beyond the grave, beyond the moment when the last man alive found rest. . . .

> 'But why roped together?' asked Morell, puzzled, as the ship completed her last circle, and drew away, and left the men behind. 'It doesn't make sense.'

> Ericson had been thinking. 'It might,' he said, in a voice infinitely subdued. 'If they were in a lifeboat, and the boat had been swamped, they might tie themselves together so as not to lose touch during the night. It would give them a better chance of being picked up.'

> He was wondering how long it had taken the nine men to die: and what it was like for the others when the first man died: and what it was like when half of them had gone: and what it was like for the last man left alive, roped to his tail of eight dead shipmates, still hopeful, but surely feeling himself doomed by his company.

I have quoted Monsarrat at length to show how vividly and compellingly he presents a scene; how effectively he describes the actions and reactions of the seamen; how pointedly and meaningfully he employs descriptive terms like "something infinitely obscene," "close corporation," "bobbing and bowing," and "not a single reminder of warmth and manhood"; and how carefully he blends the conversation of the men with the description of the scene in such a way as to capture the horror of the experience. There are other scenes that evince more action than this one, but in all of them, he is a superb reporter. He makes you see, hear, and feel.

But while Monsarrat tells with considerable verve "the long and true story of one ocean, two ships, and about a hundred and fifty men," he is not as successful in the portrayal of character. As the story develops, one wants to know more about the characters than one is told. It is not enough to watch them, to be *told* of their anxieties and fears and that compassion holds them together and keeps them fighting, or that they developed "a professional inhumanity which was the best guarantee of efficiency." One also wants to know how the trials of Captain Ericson and his men affect their personalities, how and in what way they change their attitudes toward life. One wants to view their inner struggles, to see the change in them. But there seems to be little concern for character development. The characters do not alter events, and the events evoke no change in the characters.

I believe, then, that *The Cruel Sea* falls short of being a great novel because it is too discursive and because too little attention is given to character development. It is true that the good novelist should make you see, hear, and feel; but in the dictum of Conrad, who also wrote about the sea, he must employ his imagination to do more than "create events that are properly speaking, *accidents only*." There must be some unifying principle beyond the passage of time. Even though the writer is dealing with facts that are true, he must do more than present a series of scenes that are related to a specific phase of life.

Actually *The Cruel Sea* poses the recurring question of where journalism ends and fiction begins, of what should be the relation between the two. It is a remarkable feat in itself to give the layman a comprehensible account of naval action, to include in one book such an enormous amount of action and detail; yet apart from the problem of integration, one other that Monsarrat must have encountered was that of deciding when and how what happens in the story was to be subordinated and related to what the happenings mean to the characters in terms of change and growth. Nevertheless, in spite of the writer's belief that this problem was not solved, it cannot be denied that some of the episodes which appear in *The Cruel Sea* are as compelling as any to be found in novels that treat World War II.

On reviewing the fictional output of Monsarrat from 1940, when his first novel of importance appeared, to 1951, the year which marked the appearance of *The Cruel Sea*, two features seem particularly noticeable: first, all of his novels, with the possible exception of *Leave Cancelled*, seem to be largely autobiographical or to deal with phases of his life; second, all indicate the tremendous impact of World War II on him. In them he has given especial prominence to the disrupting yet maturing effect of war (*This Is The Schoolroom*), the tragedy of the separation of families (*Leave Cancelled*), and man's capacity for devotion as well as his patriotism and courage in times of crises (*Depends What You Mean By Love* and *The Cruel Sea*). Only in his last two novels has he departed from the war scene. . . .

Source: Thomas D. Jarrett, "The Talent of Nicholas Monsarrat," in *English Journal*, Vol. 45, No. 4, April 1956, pp. 173–80.

SOURCES

"Battle of the Atlantic," in *History Learning Site*, http://www.historylearningsite.co.uk/atlantic.htm (accessed June 16, 2011).

Cook, Bernard A., "Great Britain, Women's Royal Naval Service (WRNS), Reorganization Before World War II," in *Women and War: A Historical Encyclopedia from Antiquity to the Present*, Vol. 1, edited by Bernard A. Cook, ABC-CLIO, 2006, pp. 248–49.

Flower, Desmond, and Clare L. Taylor, "Monsarrat, Nicholas John Turney," in *Oxford Dictionary of National Biography*, Vol. 38, edited by H. C. G. Matthew and Brian Harrison, Oxford University Press, 2004, pp. 666–68.

Jaffe, J., "Nicholas Monsarrat," in *Dictionary of Literary Biography*, Vol. 15, *British Novelists, 1930–1959*, edited by Bernard Oldsey, Bruccoli Clark Layman, 1983, pp. 369–75.

Miles, George, Review of *The Cruel Sea*, in *Commonweal*, August 24, 1951, pp. 485–86.

Monsarrat, Nicholas, *The Cruel Sea*, Knopf, 1969.

Review of *The Cruel Sea*, in *New Republic*, December 31, 1951, p. 20.

Review of *The Cruel Sea*, in *New Yorker*, August 18, 1951, p. 85.

Review of *The Cruel Sea*, in *Time*, August 6, 1951, pp. 84–85.

Rogers, Michael, Review of *The Cruel Sea*, in *Library Journal*, June 1, 2000, p. 212.

Sheffield, Gary, "The Battle of the Atlantic: The U-Boat Peril," in *BBC History*, http://www.bbc.co.uk/history/worldwars/wwtwo/battle_atlantic_01.shtml (accessed June 16, 2011).

"Submarine Chronology," in *Office of the Chief of Naval Operations, Submarine Warfare Division*, http://www.navy.mil/navydata/cno/n87/history/chrono.html (accessed June 17, 2011).

FURTHER READING

Ambrose, Stephen E. *The Good Fight: How World War II Was Won*, Atheneum, 2001.

This illustrated volume, written by a veteran historian, is primarily for middle-school readers. It succinctly tells the story of American involvement in World War II, beginning with the Japanese bombing of Pearl Harbor and ending with the atomic bombing of Japan.

Dunmore, Spencer, *In Great Waters: The Epic Story of the Battle of the Atlantic*, McClelland & Stewart, 1999.

This volume is a nonfiction account of the Battle of the Atlantic. Dunmore is a Canadian historian, so he gives particular attention to the previously neglected contributions of the Canadian Royal Navy in prosecuting the Battle of the Atlantic.

Jefferson, David, *Coastal Forces at War*, 2nd ed., Haynes Publishing, 2009.

This volume tells the story of Great Britain's coastal fleet, which patrolled the English

Channel and the North Sea. These gunboats and torpedo boats fought close-quarter battles with the German navy, striking quickly at night and then withdrawing into the cover of darkness, often after brief but deadly firefights.

Monsarrat, Nicholas, *Life Is a Four Letter Word*, William Morrow, 1971.
This book contains both volumes of Monsarrat's two-volume autobiography, *Breaking In*, first published in 1966, and *Breaking Out*, first published in 1970. The first volume describes his upbringing in Edwardian England. The second volume deals with his later life.

Parrish, Tom, *The Submarine: A History*, Penguin, 2005.
This volume spans the history of submarine warfare, including the use of submarines during World War II. Readers interested in submarine warfare will appreciate the emphasis on the technological developments that made submarine warfare possible.

Paterson, Michael, *The Secret War: The Inside Story of the Codemakers and Codebreakers of World War II*, 2nd ed., David & Charles, 2007.
This volume provides a comprehensive look at the efforts of both the Allies and the Axis powers to create, and to break, codes used by military commands. Among these codes was the Enigma code that German military commanders used to communicate with U-boats.

SUGGESTED SEARCH TERMS

antisubmarine warfare

Battle of the Atlantic

British Royal Navy

corvette ships

Enigma code

Nicholas Monsarrat

Nicholas Monsarrat AND Cruel Sea

submarine warfare

submarines

U-boats

World War II AND Europe

World War II AND Nicholas Monsarrat

war literature AND Nicholas Monsarrat

The Grapes of Wrath

1940   John Steinbeck's novel *The Grapes of Wrath*, published in 1939, is a searing social commentary about the plight of poor farmers who have lost their homes and are struggling to survive during the Great Depression. The story follows the Joads, an extended family from Oklahoma, who travel in their makeshift truck to California hoping to find menial jobs picking fruit, only to find themselves unable to fight off starvation. It is an angry, politically powerful book, often considered Steinbeck's best.

When the rights to film the book were bought months after its publication, observers were surprised to find that it was to be produced by Darryl F. Zanuck and directed by John Ford. Both men held staunchly conservative views, in direct opposition to the elements of socialism that ground Steinbeck's story. In addition, the Motion Picture Production Code, in charge of approving the moral content of films before they could be released, frowned seriously on the kind of plainspoken language that is common in Steinbeck's book, and stories that could be seen as promoting Communism were strictly forbidden.

The film version of *The Grapes of Wrath*, released in 1940, is markedly different from the novel. Characters and scenes are omitted, as happens when adapting any movie, but the entire focus of the story is shifted as well. While Steinbeck struggled to show how good, honest,

© *AF archive | Alamy*

hardworking people can be slowly crushed by the competitive capitalist system, Ford and screenwriter Nunnally Johnson used the story of the Joads to show a group of eternal optimists who keep believing that their day will come, no matter how many setbacks they are forced to endure. Henry Fonda, playing angry ex-convict Tom Joad, was nominated for an Academy Award for his performance, but he did not win. Jane Darwell, providing the story's moral center with her performance as Ma Joad, who believes that the poor will survive and eventually triumph, did win. Ford also won for best director.

The Grapes of Wrath is available on DVD from Twentieth Century Fox.

PLOT SUMMARY

The credits for *The Grapes of Wrath* play over an orchestra and banjo playing the song "Red River Valley," a traditional Western ballad that is played in variations throughout the film, usually by a single accordion.

The film begins with a lone man, Tom Joad, approaching a desolate crossroads in flat farm lands. As he comes to a gas station, a truck parked to the side bears the name "Oklahoma City Transport Company," indicating where this takes place. He approaches the driver of the truck and asks for a ride. The driver points out a posted sign that says that passengers are not allowed, but Tom convinces him that a good man would not follow such a rule.

In the truck, Tom explains that he is going home to his parents, who are sharecroppers. The driver shows little interest, but Tom turns angry about his "nosiness" and admits that he has been in prison for four years. As he leaves the truck, Tom explains, before slamming the door, that he was in for homicide.

Walking through the field to his family home, Tom comes across a man sitting under a tree. The man, Casy, recognizes Tom and announces that he baptized him. Casy is no longer a preacher, though, having lost the spirit. Tom shares a bottle of whiskey with him, and Casy talks about being uncertain about the Holy Spirit and being unable to quell the lust he had for the women in the congregation. Tom describes having killed a man in a fight at a dance, when they were both drunk. Casy says he has no reason to go any particular direction, so he joins Tom. As they walk, the wind kicks up, in a visual reference to the dust storms that destroyed the farming conditions in Oklahoma; the film makes no other mention of this historical fact.

In a powerful wind storm, Tom and Casy find the Joad cabin darkened and empty. Tom fears that his family is "gone or dead," especially when he finds his mother's good shoe on the floor. By candlelight, they find Muley Graves, a neighbor, in a darkened corner of the cabin. Muley explains that Tom's family has moved to his uncle John's home, but soon they all will have to leave. When Tom asks, "Who done it?" Muley recalls, in a flashback, how a representative of the Shawnee Land and Cattle Company came one day to evict him. The irate farmers with him asked who was responsible, but the man, smoking a fat cigar, admitted that he did not know and then drove away.

Muley then tells Tom and Casy about the coming of "the Cats," or Caterpillar tractors, that moved into the land, tilling the soil and tearing down houses. As they came to his cabin, he and his family stood in front with

FILM TECHNIQUE

- In film, diegetic sounds are the sounds that can be heard by the characters. Nondiegetic sound often includes voice-overs and soundtrack music. This film uses mostly natural, diegetic sound, such as dialogue and car noises and train whistles in the distance, there is little background music used. Much of the music provided is diegetic as well, starting with the song "A-Tisket, A-Tasket" at the truck stop in the first scene and continuing to the songs that are sung by Connie and Tom over the course of the movie. The little soundtrack music used often repeats a song that is already familiar ("Red River Valley"), drawing particular attention to the nostalgic implications of the few scenes where nondiegetic music is added.

- Filming in black and white allows for a wide range of different shades, as many as recording on color film does. Few things in a black-and-white film are absolutely black or absolutely white, but instead are some shade of gray. Films that light sets evenly and are shot in black and white show little variation in their scenes. This effect is used in the daytime, outdoor scenes of *The Grapes of Wrath*, in which the entire screen seems to be of one uniform color. With outdoor filming, the director has little control over the lighting, much of which is provided by the sun. The filmmakers here used high-contrast lighting to its best effect in the indoor scenes (including those in the truck cab) and the many night scenes. Lights often come from identifiable sources off to the side, which makes faces clear but backgrounds fade into blackness. Shadows are prominent, giving richness to the visual scheme. The overall effect is to help viewers clearly distinguish different objects on the screen, giving the director a greater range of choices.

- When television started to become popular, motion pictures began framing characters in tight shots; directors knew that when their films eventually played on the small screen, the background details would be cropped out and the central focus—the characters' faces—would be expanded to fill the screen. The close-up and the two-shot (in which two characters face each other) became the most common shots. Ford almost never uses close-ups. When the camera shows only one person, that person is usually filmed in a medium shot, from approximately the waist up, and is usually off-center, so that the frame shows the surrounding details. More often, two or three people are in a shot, and their faces are not the only thing on the screen. Ford often shoots people at an angle, with one person behind the other, to remind viewers of the three-dimensional depth of the world on the screen.

- The technique of multiple exposure has been around as long as film has. It is the method of exposing a piece of film to one image and then exposing it to one or more other images so that they overlap, creating the impression that everything in the photograph existed in the same space. Ford did not use postproduction editing to achieve this effect. Instead, he used reflective glass in the windshield of the Joad truck to show two scenes at once. As the family drives across the desert, the barren land is reflected on the glass in front of Tom, Al, and Pa's faces, capturing their grim expressions as they worry about the dangerous journey and, at the same time showing the sights that are troubling them.

---

rifles. Muley recognized the driver, a local boy, who explained that he was turning against his own people for the good salary he was making, to support his family. He ignored Muley's threats and ran his tractor through the home. The scene ends with a shot of Muley, his wife, and his son casting their shadows across the tractor's wide tracks.

As a car approaches, Muley leads Tom and Casy to a field behind the Joad cabin, so that they will not be arrested for trespassing.

Early in the morning, Tom and Casy approach Uncle John's cabin. The film introduces the Joads. Ma and Pa Joad are there, as well as Grandma and Grandpa, Uncle John, Ruthie, and Winfield. They discuss a handbill that announces that there is plenty of work to be had in California, picking fruit. Grandpa Joad, shaking with excitement, explains his plan to pick so many grapes that he can rub them all over his body.

As he fantasizes about the opulent life in California, Ma Joad glances out the window and sees Tom in the yard. Her excitement is tempered by her cautious question of whether he escaped from jail, but he assures her he has been paroled. Ma worries about whether he has been hurt and whether his pain has made him a mean man, but he assures her that he has not. The rest of the family runs out, excited and assuming that he has broken out. His brother Al drives up in a truck as Grandpa Joad chants, "The jailbird's back!" In the back of the truck is his pregnant sister Rosasharn and her husband, Connie. Their joyous reunion is interrupted by a man from the land company who shouts to them, reminding Uncle John that they must leave by sunup.

At night, the Joads prepare for their trip. They have accumulated money by selling their possessions, and they think that should be enough for the trip. Alone, Ma sorts through letters and souvenirs, deciding which to give up.

As they prepare to leave, Grandpa Joad refuses to go. They knock him out with "soothing syrup" disguised as coffee and load him into the truck when he is asleep. Casy says goodbye, but they invite him to join them on their journey, and he accepts.

A montage of scenes shows the loaded truck driving down Route 66 through cities in Oklahoma. When they stop at the side of the road, Grandpa, feebly complaining, dies before their eyes. They bury him there after sundown, with a note giving his name and the conditions under which he died, in case someone should think he was murdered. The family implores Casy to say a eulogy, though he is not a preacher anymore.

The truck stops at a camp. Connie sings a traditional folk song, "Going Down the Road Feeling Bad." Pa Joad enters into a discussion with others at the camp, including a man from Arkansas who gave up his store and is going to California to find work, and a bemused man coming back from California who could not make any money there. The man returning explains how unlikely it is that anyone could make the kind of money promised on the handbills that have been distributed across the Midwest until another man accuses him of being a troublemaker and a "labor fink," which he vehemently denies. His two children and his wife starved to death in California, he explains, in tears. As he leaves, the Joads discuss how what was true for that man might be the truth for them.

The truck pulls into a truck stop in New Mexico with its engine overheating. The proprietor treats the Joads with suspicion, asking whether they have money and intend to buy anything. Pa enters the stop's diner to buy a loaf of bread. At first, the waitress is hostile, saying that they only sell fifteen-cent loaves, though Pa only has a dime. The gruff cook insists she sell him loaf for a dime, lying and saying that it is old bread. Seeing Ruthie and Winfield staring at some candy sticks, the formerly gruff waitress sell them to Pa at a rate of two for a penny. The truck drivers at the counter, witnessing this, note when the Joads leave that those candies are a nickel apiece. To reward her kindness, they each leave a half-dollar tip for the waitress.

As they enter Arizona, an inspection official gruffly tells the Joads to keep on moving through to California. They drive past Native American villages, drawing the link between the migrants who have been driven from their land and those who have been limited to living on reservations.

Stopping at the Arizona side of the Colorado River, they look across to California, seeing it, as Pa puts it, as "the land of milk and honey" (a biblical phrase describing a fertile, rich land). On the California side of the bridge, the men of the Joad family take time to swim in the water. The film clearly shows Noah Joad in this scene, though it does not show, as Steinbeck's novel does, that this is where Noah splits apart from the family to start a new life for himself.

As they try to prepare the truck for the coming trip across the desert, Ma Joad dribbles cool water on Grandma, who is feverish and delirious.

The truck pulls away from a truck stop, and the station attendants, in crisp white uniforms, share a stick of chewing gum while they discuss how the "Oakies" are less than human.

They cross the desert cautiously, with the children wide-eyed at seeing sights they have never imagined. Grandma, on Ma's lap, reaches to the sky and calls out to Grandpa. Connie tells Rosasharn that he regrets not studying radio repair instead of embarking on a journey like this.

At a state inspection stop, officials tell the Joads to unload the truck. Ma explains that they need to get Grandma to a doctor and swears that there is nothing on the truck needing inspection. Later, they stop to marvel at the lush Salinas Valley, and Ma admits that Grandma was already dead when the inspector stopped them.

Pushing the truck into a town, they encounter a policeman who says he has seen thousands of handbills like the one that brought the Joads to California. He is from Oklahoma himself. There is a moment of kinship between the policeman and the Joads, but he remembers his official duties and threatens to arrest them if they are not out of town by nightfall.

The car pulls into a campground for migrant workers called a Hooverville—a makeshift collection of shacks for the homeless, named for President Hoover, who was blamed for deepening the economic depression. This is where the film starts making major structural departures from Steinbeck's novel: in the book, there was a descent downward into poverty, with the Joads' work at the peach farm (which is where Tom gets into trouble and has to leave) coming well before their stops at the Wheat Patch camp or the Hooverville settlement.

In the Hooverville camp, the Joads encounter the poverty that is their fate, as the camera scans across the blank faces of desolate men, women, and children. As Ma prepares dinner, the children from the camp gather around her cooking pot. Ma offers to give the children anything left after her family is fed, and they all scurry to the trash heap for sticks to eat with. The Joads hide in their tent, hanging their heads with guilt.

A well-dressed man, accompanied by a policeman, drives into the camp and offers work. Someone asks him to write what he is paying into a contract, and when he refuses to do so, the questioner then becomes angry. The well-dressed man asks the policeman with him about

the angry man in the crowd, and the policeman replies that he recognizes him as a suspect in a robbery. When the policeman tries to arrest the man, he runs; the policeman shoots, hitting a woman in the hand. He tries to shoot again, but Tom tackles him and Casy knocks him out. Casy takes the sheriff's gun and empties it of bullets and then sends Tom into hiding. A carload of policemen arrives, and Casy is arrested.

Tom sneaks back that night with the warning that a crowd of local vigilantes is coming to burn the camp down. Ma tells him that Connie has left the family.

As the Joads drive toward town, an armed mob stops them. A man in the mob orders them to turn around and head north.

While the Joads are stopped to change a flat tire the next day, a man pulls up in a car and offers them work at the Keene ranch, picking peaches. When they arrive, they find the entrance to the ranch surrounded by policemen and picketers. The Joads are confused about the chaotic scene. A guard questions Tom and allows him to drive through the picketers, who are kept out with gates and guns. Truckloads of families in trucks pull into the ranch's campground and register with an agent, who assigns each family a one-room cabin. Everywhere the Joads go, men wearing badges and carrying rifles watch them.

At dinner, they complain about the high cost of food at the company store. Tom goes out into the night to explore the camp, even though a policeman tells him to go to his cabin. Passing out of the camp, he runs into Casy, who is with some other men. They plan to hold a strike against the deceptive pay rates Keene offers laborers. Tom says he cannot get his family to walk away from what little they are getting, and Casy admits that he does not know what is right, but that he is trying to learn.

Lawmen break up the meeting and chase the labor organizers, going straight for Casy. One strikes Casy down, and Tom takes the club from him and strikes him. Tom is hit across the face. Casy is dead, and Tom's cheek is broken, making him easily identifiable.

The next morning, Ma returns to the cabin with the news that the police are after Tom. He wants to leave, but Ma remembers the time when they were a family tied to the land and implores him to stay with them. "We're cracking up, Tom," she says. "We ain't no family no more."

That night, the Joads load their truck, hiding Tom between mattresses. Policemen look the truck over and ask about the missing man, whom Al identifies as a hitchhiker who left them in the morning.

The truck breaks down about a mile from the Wheat Patch camp. They are greeted by a man identified in the credits as the caretaker, a kind man who assigns them to their tent site in "Number 4 Sanitary Unit," explaining that the camp is run by its own internal rules, with no police interference. The Joads are suspicious, but Tom agrees to go into the office and fill out a registration card. When he finds out that the government runs the camp, Tom asks why there are not more like it. Spencer admits that he does not know.

Passing a water spigot that someone has left running, Tom stops and turns it off, showing that he is becoming conscious of his role in policing his new community.

When Ruthie shows Winfield the toilet facilities, he pulls the chain that flushes the toilet. Having never seen anything like it, they think they have broken it, and run away.

Tom and other men working on a ditch to lay pipe are approached by their boss, Mr. Thomas. He knows that they live at the government camp, so he gives them a tip: agitators plan on infiltrating the camp's dance on Saturday night, giving the sheriff and his men an excuse to invade the camp.

At the dance, the citizens of Wheat Patch are having a happy, peaceful gathering. The men are ready for trouble, checking the people who enter the camp. When they see a group of men they suspect are there to create trouble, they keep an eye on them.

A scout returns to report that there are armed deputies parked outside of the camp. The suspected agitators are followed. At an appointed time, they try to start fights, but men from the camp surround them and subdue them. The sheriffs try to enter the camp and are kept out because the violence they anticipated has not occurred.

In the middle of the night, the caretaker leads officers to the Joad truck, and they take down the license number. Tom, seeing this, knows that they are after him and that he must leave before they can come back with a warrant to arrest him. Before he can leave, Ma wakes up and talks to

him; they go outside and, as a train whistle sounds in the distance, Tom gives one of the most often quoted speeches in American literature. He says they are a part of one universal soul and tells his mother that wherever she goes, he will be there. A long shot shows him walking off across the flat landscape into the sunrise.

In the morning, the Joads load up their truck, along with the weak and listless Rosasharn, and leave Wheat Patch to follow a promise of twenty days' work in the north. Al is enthusiastic, and Ma explains that she will be no longer be afraid because she has gotten through the most difficult times. Pa mentions that they have taken a beating, but Ma explains that people like the Joads are "the people that live," and they will not be defeated.

The Joad truck joins a procession of similar trucks, driving in the sunrise with the hope of a better tomorrow.

CHARACTERS

Caretaker

When the Joads arrive at the Wheat Patch camp, they are greeted by a man who is so kindly and soft-spoken that he almost seems angelic. This man, played by Grant Mitchell, is not identified by name and is only called "Caretaker" in the film's credits. He is by far the kindest person in the film, a representative of the goodwill that human beings can have for one another if they try.

Casy

Casy is a former preacher who has known the Joad family for years: as he mentions when Tom Joad runs into him in a barren field, he baptized Tom. He is played by John Carradine, who was actually a year younger than the actor who played Tom, indicating that Tom was baptized late in life and that Casy was a young preacher. In the novel, he is identified as Jim Casy, but his first name is never given in the film.

From the start of the film, Casy raises theological questions with his adamant denial that he is a preacher. He tells Tom that he has lost the calling, and when asked to say a prayer over Grandpa Joad's grave, he makes it clear that he is not a preacher, though he is willing to speak a few words in an unofficial capacity.

When Tom is in danger of being arrested for hitting a sheriff, Casy confesses to the crime. He uses his demeanor of mental instability to his advantage, confessing cheerfully to a crime that another man would deny.

Later in the Joads' journey, Tom and he cross paths when Casy is part of a team that plans to hold a strike for workers' wages. The local police have him identified as a labor organizer and target him, out of everyone in the crowd, for arrest. He puts up only the slightest resistance before a deputy bashes his head in with a club and kills him.

Driver

The truck driver in the first scene refuses to give Tom Joad a ride, initially, but he soon agrees, once Tom convinces him that it is what "a good guy" would do. He tries to make conversation and is surprised when Tom turns angry and defensive.

Muley Graves

Muley is an old neighbor of the Joad family who has been driven crazy by the events that destroyed Oklahoma agriculture. When Tom and Casy find him, he is hiding out in the abandoned Joad house, evading the guards who work for the land company. He recalls in a flashback how he resisted being thrown from the land he had farmed for years, but his armed resistance was ignored. His wife and son, shown in the flashback scene, have apparently moved on, but Muley stays with his land, living like an animal to survive. Ford uses this character in the film to provide a small amount of background information about the way the Oklahoma agricultural industry was ravaged in the 1930s.

Al Joad

Al is Tom Joad's sixteen-year-old brother. Steinbeck's novel spends much more time with him than the film does, developing him as a young man with two interests, women and cars. His skill with automobile maintenance is what keeps the Joads' truck on the road, but his interest in women almost takes him away from the family at the end of the novel, as he plans to leave with the family of a young woman he has met. In the film version, Al is a friendly young man with no particular personality. He is played with bright-eyed enthusiasm by O. Z. Whitehead.

Grandma Joad

Grandma Joad is the matriarch, or female leader, of the Joad family. She becomes ill while the family is on the road, calling out to Grandpa, who died soon after their journey began. Grandma dies just before they enter the fertile land of the Salinas Valley. As Ma Joad, who kept her death a secret from the family, notes, she will at least be buried in a beautiful place.

Grandpa Joad

Grandpa is played by veteran character actor Charley Grapewin. In Steinbeck's novel, he represents the tradition of working the land that the Joads had followed until they were evicted, shortly before the beginning of the story. In the film, however, Grandpa is usually used to provide comic relief, as he complains humorously about the indignities that have the others feeling angry or ashamed. The family tricks him when he refuses to board the truck, slipping a strong alcoholic or narcotic syrup into his coffee to make him fall asleep. The first time the truck stops after taking off on the road, Grandpa, still complaining, dies before the eyes of his family members.

Uncle John Joad

Uncle John is Pa Joad's widowed older brother. In the novel, he is conspicuous for his constant struggle against alcoholism. The film version of the story has him mentioning his desire for a drink, but his character remains obscure.

Ma Joad

Jane Darwell won the Academy Award for Best Actress in a Supporting Role for her performance as Ma Joad, the spiritual center of the Joad family and of the movie. Ford gives her several poignant moments in the film. The first, soon after she is introduced, is a quiet moment while she sorts through her belongings, choosing which letters and souvenirs she can take with her as the family leaves its home. Later, she shows herself to be cunning when she needs to be: she staves off a state agricultural inspector who wants to look through the family's truck, telling him that Grandma Joad is ill and not telling her own family that Grandma is actually dead until the danger of inspection has passed.

The film gives Ma Joad a final speech as they travel down the road in search of what seems to be the best financial opportunity they have seen in a long time. She reflects that women are better made for getting through difficulties than men are after her husband notes that she is "the only one keeping [them] going." She ends the film with the philosophical reflection that poor people will always keep rising and will never be wiped out. This speech is taken from a much earlier part of Steinbeck's novel, and it is put at the end of the film to leave audiences with an elevated feeling as the final credits roll.

Noah Joad

Noah is one of the Joad boys. He is significant in the book because he walks away from the family when they are swimming in the Colorado River, wandering off with no particular plan. In the film, however, Noah's disappearance is never explained.

Pa Joad

As the nominal head of the Joad family, Pa is increasingly disillusioned about the prospects he sees before him. In the film's last scene, he admits to Ma that he has been thinking more and more about how their lives are worse than they once were.

Ruth Joad

Ruth is the youngest Joad girl. She is called "Ruthie" consistently throughout the novel.

Tom Joad

Tom is played by Henry Fonda, in a role that gained him an Academy Award nomination. He comes into the film as a cynic. He was in prison for four years for killing a man in self defense, but he is immediately faced with the frightening prospect that he may never see his family again after he finds their home gone. When he is reunited with them at his Uncle John's house, which they are on the verge of leaving, he is happy, and he assures his mother that prison has not made a hardened man of him.

Throughout the trip west, as one indignity after another is heaped on his family, Tom's anger slowly grows. He is not afraid to question authority, and he breaks rules when he wants to, as when he attacks the guard who shoots an uninvolved bystander in the Hooverville camp or when he leaves the guarded Keene ranch at night after being ordered not to. His temper against the injustices his people have to suffer grows until he ends up killing the man who strikes his friend Casy dead. Marked with a scar on his cheek, Tom offers to leave the family, and in

Steinbeck's novel, this is when he leaves. In the film, however, his mother begs him to stay and keep the family together. He does stay until he finds out that the law has followed him into the Wheat Patch settlement, at which point he admits that he would only be a burden to the family.

As he takes leave of his mother, Tom explains that he is searching for something that he cannot describe. He has learned from Casy a vague sense that all people are connected to one united soul, though Tom is not able to explain what it is or where it is leading him. Tom takes off on the road to find truth, leaving his family behind.

Winfield Joad

Winfield is the youngest Joad boy. He always appears with his sister, Ruth.

Connie Rivers

Connie is the new husband of Rosasharn. He has misgivings about going to California, thinking that he could have done well for himself if he had stayed in Oklahoma and trained to be a radio repairman. He disappears abruptly from the story when the family is leaving Hooverville, and Ma announces that Connie has left them.

Connie is conspicuous only in one scene when, at a campground on the road, the director gives Eddie Quillan, the actor playing Connie, a long solo singing "Going Down the Road Feeling Bad."

Rosasharn Joad Rivers

Rosasharn is the older daughter of Ma and Pa. She has recently married Connie and is expecting a baby.

The name Rosasharn is a phonetic pronunciation of "Rose of Sharon." Steinbeck's book uses the formal spelling for the narrative voice and "Rosasharn" when other characters speak of her.

Throughout the film, Rosasharn is relegated to the background. When her husband leaves the family, she deludes herself into thinking that he will be back, though no one else is convinced. At the dance at the Wheat Patch camp, she is buoyant and happy.

Though the miscarriage of Rosasharn's baby is critical to the ending of the novel, Ford's film does not even touch on it. The last that is seen of Rosasharn in the film, she is weak and is being lifted up onto the truck, indicating that she is still expecting her child.

Rose of Sharon Joad Rivers
See Rosasharn Joad Rivers

Spencer
When the Joad truck has broken down at the side of a road, a man drives up and offers them work. This man directs them to the Keene ranch and instructs them to tell the guard at the gate that Spencer sent them; the guard is prepared to turn the truck away until he hears Spencer's name.

Mr. Thomas
Thomas is the man who hires Tom, Pa, Al, and Uncle John to dig ditches. He gives the Joads and other occupants of the Wheat Patch camp a warning that local thugs intend to invade the upcoming dance. Though warning them is not in his interest, he is one of the few employers who can see the humanity in the transient workers.

THEMES

Survival
Ford's film of this story is not as brutal as the novel, but both stories concern what people will do to survive. The poor are chased from one place to another by bulldozers, angry mobs, and policemen acting on behalf of the rich, but the film does not show their lives threatened by nature. Steinbeck's book documents the diminishing quantities of food available to the Joads—not just, as Tom explains to Casy when a strike is proposed, the presence or absence of meat, but the presence of the barest sustenance, such as a few potatoes or biscuits.

In the film, as in the novel, death takes on a symbolic tinge. Grandpa Joad dies soon after he is unwillingly taken on the journey, as if he cannot live when his roots are cut from the land he tended for so long. Ma Joad dies, like Moses in the Bible, before being able to enter the Promised Land.

The film looks at death as a way of strengthening the poor people: Ma Joad's speech at the end, a vindication of those persecuted for the sake of righteousness (a biblical phrase supporting people who suffer in a good cause), is a variation of the Beatitude of Jesus that says the poor shall inherit the earth: both imply that the rich will be left weaker eventually because of the comfort they now enjoy. The novel does not promise the survival of the Joad line. Instead of nursing a healthy new member of the family, Rosasharn ends up, perversely, nursing a shriveled, undernourished skeleton of a man. In the film, survival is assured, while the book tells readers that survival is possible but not likely.

Law and Order
The Joads are honest, law-abiding people, generally, but they live outside of the legal system. This is shown from the very start, when Tom arrives home and the entire family assumes, with glee, that he is home early because he broke out of prison.

Throughout the film, the Joads are victimized by police, who are clearly there to protect the interests of those with money. When a man comes to the Hooverville camp to exploit the unemployed workers, he actually brings an armed, uniformed policeman in his car with him. One man tries to assert his legal rights for a written contract, and the officer makes up a charge for which to arrest him. When he flees, the policeman fires, putting a bullet through the hand of a woman standing nearby, ruining her capability for manual labor. After Tom and Casy knock the officer out, a carload of policemen shows up immediately, ready to quell any uprising.

Later, the Joad family find themselves virtual prisoners at the Keene ranch. When policemen break up a meeting of men discussing the possibility of striking for more wages, an officer clubs Casy to death.

In contrast to the violent, brutish ways of the official legal system, the impoverished people of the Wheat Patch camp run an orderly society. They vote for their representatives and obey what they say, and the results are clear in the cleanliness and order of the camp. The dance is a happy occasion, and when outside agitators try to incite violence, they are not met with equal violence but are instead quietly ushered away. The film's point is that poor people do not need to be controlled by force; they are intelligent people who will behave civilly for their own sake.

Social Class
When they are among their own people, there is a degree of sympathy for the Joads. The young man who runs a bulldozer through Muley's home addresses him by name and apologizes

READ,
WATCH,
WRITE

- Read *Studs Terkel's Hard Times: An Oral History of the Great Depression*, a collection of interviews with people who tell their stories about living through the rough economy of the 1930s. Adapt one of the interviews to a ten-minute play and perform it for your class. Have the audience evaluate you on how well your script brought attention to the main points made in the interview.

- Many countries around the world experienced the Depression at the same time that America did. Study how the economic collapse affected one other country during the 1930s, and prepare a slide show presentation that compares the economic situations and political results in the countries you choose. Choose at least one country from each continent.

- James D. Sexton's novel *Campesino: The Diary of a Guatemalan Indian* did not gain the international attention when it was published in 1985 that Steinbeck's book did in 1939, but it does a similar job in revealing the world of an impoverished people, the Indians of Central America. After reading Sexton's book, devise a list of ten truths that you feel he and Steinbeck would agree are universal about poverty. Use Glogster to create a post representing those truths.

- Ford chose to present this film, like many of his films, with little background music. Choose a scene that is not scored and record

a musical background that you think will enhance viewers' understanding of the significance of the action. Present your altered version of the scene to your class.

- In both the novel and the film, Tom Joad leaves the story after a speech to his mother about his budding awareness of social responsibilities. Write a short story that shows Tom twenty years later, during the Red Scare, when people suspected of being involved in labor movements were investigated by the American government for communist leanings. Include a bibliography of sources that you used to show that your story is historically accurate, as well as a brief journal of your research procedure.

- Popular songs today deal with growing up in poverty more explicitly than music of the 1930s did. Create a rap song for the Joad children, Ruth and Winfield, in which they testify about their life in California.

- Read *Dark Water*, Laurie McNeal's acclaimed novel for young adults about a fifteen-year-old girl who becomes infatuated with an illegal migrant worker in southern California during the famous 2007 wildfires. Use the book to lead a discussion in your class about how the same economic forces used against the Joad family in this film are still used to lure illegal immigrants over the border to a place where they are exploited and resented.

---

for what must be done, though his sorrow does not hinder his actions. The waitress at the diner begins by being gruff with Pa and his youngest children, but by the time their scene is over, she is lying about the price of candy to preserve Pa's pride. When they reach California, they talk with a policeman who momentarily bonds with them, as a former Oklahoman himself. When he remembers his duty to protect his town from the presumed threat posed by the waves of poor arriving

every day, a wall goes up between them, and for the rest of the film that wall remains in place.

The Joads are repeatedly hired for work by men in cars and watched carefully by armed guards, with no access to anyone from outside their class. When their truck is stopped on the road outside of the Hooverville camp, the cause of social division is made clear. "We don't want no more Oakies in this town," an armed man tells Tom. "There ain't enough work for them

© *United Archives GmbH | Alamy*

that's already here." The poor are seen as a threat to property by the rich and as competition by the other poor.

Family

Ford shows the corrosive effects of poverty during the Depression by cutting the Joad family down throughout the film. As their truck pulls away from the Joad home in the beginning of the film, there are eleven Joads, plus Connie Rivers and Casy. By the end of the film, Grandpa, Grandma, Casy, Connie, Noah, and Tom are gone. The deaths of Grandma and Grandpa are explained as results of the hardship of the rigorous trip; Connie has left without saying goodbye, apparently bitter about finding out how difficult life is in California; Casy has been killed by a policeman; and Tom has gone into hiding for having assaulted the policeman who killed him. Noah's disappearance is never explained.

In the book, the family's hopes ride on Rosasharn's baby, which will start a new generation of Joads. When the baby is stillborn at birth, they are sad, but Ma Joad speaks encouragingly about the possibility for her young daughter to have more children. The film never mentions what happens to Rosasharn's baby. Instead of focusing on the future of the Joad family, Ford focuses on the future of America's underclass.

STYLE

Soundtrack

Alfred Newman is credited as the musical director of this film. For most of the film, however, John Ford uses no background music. When he does use music, it is usually the traditional folk song "Red River Valley," a song that is more evocative of the settlers who drove west across the continent in the late 1800s, which is a time frame that was covered in many of Ford's most popular movies. There are several versions of "Red River Valley" used in the film, but the most common one is that of Danny Borzage playing the song on the accordion without accompaniment.

There are a few songs here that appear as part of the story. After the opening credits, for instance, Tom Joad walks toward a diner where the song "A-Tisket, A-Tasket" is playing from a jukebox or radio. The swing band orchestration of this tune tells audiences that this is the 1930s. Later, around a campfire, Connie Rivers plays the guitar and sings the song "Going Down the Road Feeling Bad," and the other characters listen to and comment upon the song. Later still, at the Wheat Patch camp dance, Tom sings "Red River Valley" to his mother as the band plays. Aside from variations on "Red River Valley," this film has just a few minutes of soundtrack music, while other films use music from beginning to end to control the audience's emotions.

Landscapes

Modern viewers often associate landscapes with color photography, especially when the subject is the desert, because of the many hues and various shades associated with the sand and hills and skies. Ford photographs the Joads' journey from outside their truck, for the most part, with a wide-angle lens. The film shows its viewers wide ranges of Oklahoma, New Mexico, Arizona, and California, stretching out to the horizon on both sides of the truck.

Presenting such wide vistas of the land in the picture frame keeps viewers in mind. The style of filming the road part of their adventure gives viewers a sense that they are bound for places of grandeur. This sense builds while they are on the road, so that, when Pa Joad sees the rich, fertile Salinas Valley and calls for his wife and mother to come and look, viewers are well prepared for a breathtaking sight.

Visual Clutter

In the second hour of the film, after the Joads have reached California, Ford shows how their circumstances go downhill by setting scenes in increasingly cramped, compact spaces, such as small shacks and tents. For outdoor scenes, the wide open plains are no longer visible trailing off to the horizon, as the main characters are often surrounded by shacks or by crowds of other people. This technique varies according to the tension of the scene. For instance, their approach to the Keene peach ranch is crowded with hundreds of potential workers and policemen, conveying the chaos of the situation, while the scenes at the Wheat Patch camp are generally empty at the beginning, later to become more filled but never chaotic.

CULTURAL CONTEXT

The Great Depression

This film is set during the Great Depression, a time when countries all over the world fell into a downward economic spiral that lasted for the entire decade of the 1930s.

There is a great deal of disagreement among economists regarding what might have caused the Great Depression. After World War I ended in 1918, most of the countries that had been affected by it climbed back to economic stability and growth. By 1925, most of the world's economy had regained the financial standing that they had held before the war. However, Germany, Italy, and other European countries, devastated by the war, struggled to regain economic stability by printing more money, resulting in inflation. In countries that fully recovered, particularly the United States, installment buying by consumers led to high consumer debt, overspeculation in business investment led to overpriced stocks, and margin buying allowed investors to borrow the money needed to invest in the stock market.

There were signs that the world's economy was ready to shrink after such massive growth by the late 1920s. Countries around the world, from South America to the Pacific, were already noticeably slowing when a massive sell-off on the United States stock market began on Thursday, October 25th, and continued its nose-dive until Black Tuesday, October 29, 1929. That was the worst day in U.S. financial history, when stock prices dropped 18 percent. From 1922 to 1929, the market had gained 218.7 percent in value. From 1929 to the depth of the Depression in 1932, it lost 73 percent of its worth.

The collapse in the stock market was felt throughout the country. Savings were wiped out when investments lost their value. People withdrew their money from bank accounts so swiftly that the banks found it hard to cover deposits, leaving many who had put money aside to find out that they would not get it back as banks failed.

© *Pictorial Press Ltd* | *Alamy*

Businesses were unable to borrow and had to close. At the worst of the Depression, unemployment reached at least 25 percent, a level that has never been matched since then.

The economy gradually recovered after 1933 but then hit another snag with a steep recession in 1937–1938. In 1939, World War II began, and countries across Europe began massive spending on their militaries. The United States, which was across the Atlantic from the fighting and did not join the war until the attack on Pearl Harbor by the Japanese at the end of 1941, found economic growth from providing weapons, ships, and airplanes to the Allied Forces.

The Dust Bowl

At the same time that the Depression hit the country's economic structure, much of its agricultural structure was suffering from a prolonged environmental catastrophe. It started in the beginning of the decade, in 1930; when rainfall totals across the southern states east of the Mississippi River were lower than average. Three years earlier, there had been record rainfall, causing the wide Mississippi to overflow its banks, affecting dozens of towns up and down the center of the country, but 1930 saw record shortages of rain. In the coming years, the drought shifted westward to the southern plains states, particularly Kansas, Colorado, New Mexico, Texas, and Oklahoma, where the Joads of the film had lived for generations.

The lack of moisture in the air led to record-breaking temperatures across the Great Plains. Iowa saw temperatures of 115 degrees in 1934, while Nebraska hit 118 degrees. The heat wave brought deaths in the hundreds, topping 4,500 in the year 1936 alone. Crops shriveled and died or were eaten by swarms of locusts that descended like dark clouds in farm areas in search of food.

Farming soil dried and turned to dust, to be borne away by the wind. The early 1930s saw a series of dust storms blowing across the Plains in proportions that had never been seen before. In 1933, as many as 179 dust storms were reported by weather stations throughout the southern plains states. The most notable of these storms crossed the country in May of 1934, raising dry brown earth from Wyoming and Montana and moving east, hitting Dubuque, Iowa; Chicago, Illinois; Buffalo, New York; Boston, Massachusetts; New York City; and Washington D.C., before blowing out into the Atlantic Ocean. For much of the nation, the May 9th storm was the worst of it, but the southern plains continued to see dust storms for years to come. Agriculture was, of course, ruined, and families like the Joads, who had farmed rented land for generations, found no way to pay the corporations they rented from. At the same time, the corporations found that tractors and bulldozers provided more efficient ways to farm the land than having sharecroppers pay what little they could, so they used the opportunity to foreclose on the sharecroppers, adding to the country's overall unemployment problem.

CRITICAL OVERVIEW

In general, Steinbeck's novel was a critical success upon its release, as can be seen by the fact that it was awarded the Pulitzer Prize for fiction at the end of the year. There were, however, detractors who objected to the book's social stance. In 1939, the book's tale of workers who learn to question a system that exploits them and lean toward organizing for their rights was considered to be an affirmation of communism. In the early years after the book's publication, then, as Robert Con Davis states in his survey of critical interpretations of the novel, *"The Grapes of Wrath": A Collection of Critical Essays*, "Many readers tended to classify *The Grapes of Wrath* as a social document with only marginal literary status."

The book's political implications were toned down for John Ford's film adaptation, but that change further complicated critical reactions. *Time* magazine's movie reviewer, for instance, began with references to "the exaggerations, propaganda and phony pathos of John Steinbeck's best-selling novel," saying that "pinkos who did not bat an eye when the Soviet Government exterminated 3,000,000 peasants by famine" would enjoy it, before declaring that *"The Grapes of Wrath* is possibly the best picture ever made from a so-so book." Though the film only won two of the seven Academy Awards for which it was nominated, they were significant ones, recognizing Ford's directing and the performance of Jane Darwell as Ma Joad, who was arguably the film's main character but was nominated as a supporting actress. That year, *The Grapes of Wrath* was chosen by the National Board of Review of Motion Pictures as the best film of 1940 on the basis of artistic merit and importance.

Time has dimmed the film's social significance, and therefore the heat of critical responses. As Leslie Gossage explained in "The Artful Propaganda of Ford's *The Grapes of Wrath*," "It has been belittled by critics since the emergence of scholarly interest in American films in the 1960s." Gossage cites critics who have looked back on the film as propaganda that has not aged well.

Pauline Kael, often considered one of the greatest film critics of the twentieth century, explained in an essay on the film in *5001 Nights at the Movies: A Guide from A to Z,* "This famous film, high on most lists of the great films of all time, seems all wrong—phony when it should ring true." Kael goes on, though, to begrudgingly note its ability to connect with viewers' emotions: "Yet, because of the material, it is often moving in spite of the acting, the directing, and the pseudo-Biblical pore-people talk."

In 2002, *Chicago Sun-Times* reviewer Roger Ebert included *The Grapes of Wrath* in his compendium of the great movies, identifying it as

> a left-wing parable, directed by a right-wing American director.... The message is boldly displayed, but told with characters of such sympathy and images of such beauty that audiences leave the theater feeling more pity than anger or resolve.

It is in these elements that the film has continuing relevance, regardless of one's opinions of its political views.

CRITICISM

David Kelly

Kelly is an instructor of literature and creative writing. In the following essay, he discusses how the lack of a true central character helps make The Grapes of Wrath *a difficult film for the modern viewer to appreciate.*

In spite of its many interesting and important aspects, John Ford's film *The Grapes of Wrath* is not something that stirs the imagination of the modern viewer. Forget the fact that it is photographed, acted, and edited with pinpoint precision. Ignore the fact that the story is timely for the economic realities of twenty-first century America, concerning a family losing their home to a faceless corporation, a story that has always been relevant since, as the New Testament says, the poor shall always be with us. This is not a film that looks and sounds like the sort of experience modern viewers are accustomed to when they watch a movie, but that should not matter; open-minded viewers know how to get over a little unfamiliarity. More important, though, is the fact that the film has no narrative center, leaving viewers at a loss about where they should be looking.

There will always be a certain number of people who make a distinction between films shot in black and white and films shot in color, refusing to even consider watching the former. For people with such a prejudice, nothing can make a film of this type likable. Still, the visual motif of *The Grapes of Wrath*, so engaging to an experienced viewer, is not easy to appreciate. Ford and Greg Toland, his cinematographer, filmed many scenes at night, with characters gathering around one light source and wandering off into the dark, or they filmed at sunset or sunrise, putting the light behind the action. The result is that the film does not focus viewers' attention for them. Viewers must sort out what is important from what is trivial, though they have been trained by generation after generation of film-school graduates to sit back and have their feelings dictated to them. Similarly, modern films seldom have a quiet moment, filled wall-to-wall with soundtrack music, but such constant musical cues are missing from *The Grapes of Wrath*. To make matters even more confusing, the most common music is the refrain of "Red River Valley," a song more frequently associated with cowboys and Indians, horses

> IN GENERAL, FORD SHOWS THE JOADS AS ONE GROUP, CRAMMED TOGETHER IN AND ON THEIR TRUCK OR TENT, WORKING IN THE FIELDS. IT IS THEIR STORY, REALLY, NOT THE STORY OF ANY PARTICULAR INDIVIDUAL."

and carriages, than with this film's trucks and motorcycles. The first version of the song, over the opening credits, establishes the link between the main characters and the settlers who pushed across the continent a generation or two before them, but repeating it does little beyond telling viewers not to expect any help about what they should be thinking.

But the greatest difficulty in getting modern audiences engaged in this film is that it lacks a clear central character. It is about the Joad family, undeniably, and of them, Tom Joad seems to be the most prominent character, but he is also a background character for most of the film, and he leaves the screen early. In some sense, the arc of the story can be interpreted as being the maturation of Tom Joad from a tough but sentimental ex-convict who only thinks of himself and his family to a social individual who identifies himself as a working man.

When the film was released in 1940, audiences knew that Tom was the character to watch. He is played by Henry Fonda, the only star in the film—just the year before, Fonda had starred in *Jesse James*, *The Story of Alexander Graham Bell*, *Drums along the Mohawk*, and as Abraham Lincoln in *Young Mr. Lincoln*, the latter two directed by Ford. Supporting actors such as John Carradine, Charley Grapewin, Jane Darwell, and Grant Mitchell would have been familiar, but it is Fonda's name that appears first and largest in the credits. Audiences today know to watch Fonda too. If they are not familiar with his long career (he won the Academy Award for Best Actor in 1982 for his work in *On Golden Pond*), they might have heard of his daughter, Jane, his son, Peter, or his granddaughter, Bridget. Additionally, most VHS and DVD versions of the film feature Fonda's face on their covers.

WHAT DO I SEE NEXT?

- The 1930s were a time when the government was treated with suspicion, and criminals, such as John Dillinger and Pretty Boy Floyd, were sometimes cheered as heroes of the working class. Arthur Penn captured this sense of individuals fighting against the law in his ground-breaking 1967 film *Bonnie and Clyde*, starring Warren Beatty, Faye Dunaway, Gene Hackman, and Estelle Parsons.

- In contrast to American poverty of the 1930s, Mira Nair's 1988 film *Salaam Bombay* explores poverty in contemporary India, focusing on the life of one eleven-year-old boy who moves to the city and has to survive by his wits. This internationally acclaimed film won the Caméra d'Or at the Cannes Film Festival and was nominated for the Best Foreign Language Film Academy Award.

- The year before *The Grapes of Wrath* was released, John Steinbeck's novel *Of Mice and Men* was adapted to the screen, with Burgess Meredith and Lon Chaney, Jr., in the lead roles. Stalwart Hollywood director Lewis Milestone directed it. The novel and the film are often used in secondary classrooms.

- John Ford is best remembered as a director of western films. In 1939, he directed *Stagecoach*, which broke new ground for psychological realism in westerns and has come to be considered one of his masterpieces, along with *The Searchers* and *Cheyenne Autumn*. *Stagecoach* concerns a group of strangers thrown together in dangerous circumstances as they cross New Mexico Indian country. It stars John Wayne, Claire Trevor, and John Carradine. It was released as part of the prestigious Criterion Collection in 2010.

- During the Great Depression, few films focused on the country's economic condition, instead offering audiences escapist comedies and musicals. One exception is the 1934 movie *Our Daily Bread*, directed by King Vidor. It is the story of a couple (played by Karen Morley and Tom Keene) who inherits a farm and struggle to make it work during a drought. This story provides a much more uplifting view of agricultural self-sufficiency than *The Grapes of Wrath* does.

- A fictionalized account of the life of folk singer Woody Guthrie, his travels across the country, and his efforts to help organize workers is the subject of *Bound for Glory*, a 1976 biopic (short for "biographical picture") by Hal Ashby. Guthrie is played by David Carradine, the son of the actor who plays Casy in *The Grapes of Wrath*.

The opening minutes of the film certainly make it look like Tom's story. He is the first character on-screen, and immediately he reveals personality quirks, a temper and a suspicious nature; these traits can be tragic flaws that lead to a character's downfall. He also reveals the story's central philosophy when he tells the truck driver that "a good guy don't pay no attention to what some heel makes him stick on his truck." John Steinbeck's novel is a tragedy about how America's have-nots are doomed in tight economic times, but the story that Ford (or, more specifically, the producer, Darryl F. Zanuck) serves to audiences is a morality play about the distinction between good guys and heels.

Tom's story is bracketed by two meetings with Casy, the preacher who, tellingly, once baptized him. Their first meeting takes place out in the middle of an Oklahoma field, while Tom is on his way home after four years in prison for homicide. Casy talks about losing his calling, leaving him with nothing to focus on in this world. Tom is amused by Casy's antics, impatient to get back home to his family, and annoyed by how much of Tom's liquor the former preacher drinks. Any implications about spirituality are lost on him. By contrast, late in the film, he is reunited with Casy, whom he last saw dragged off by abusive policemen, and Casy explains his new social consciousness as a labor organizer. His words barely sink in at first, since Tom resists them, but when Casy is struck dead by a brutal policeman, Tom takes up his cause.

Tom's farewell to his mother is the kind of thing that tells audiences that a character has been changed by the events that have played out before their eyes. Tom, his own eyes hollow and haunted, bracketed by the scar a club-wielding policeman gave him, says that Casy's life and death have made him think. He does not have a plan, but the intention to "scrounge around and find out what it is that is wrong, and see if something can be done about it" is enough to show that all that the Joads have been through has affected him, just as it presumably has affected the viewing audience. He walks away down the center of the screen, the same way he walked into the movie up the center of the screen toward the audience.

All of this makes Tom the focus of the movie, but there is much more than this presented on-screen. Between the beginning and the end, Tom Joad does little to distinguish himself from his father, his uncle John, his brothers Al and Winfield, or any of the other Joads. He has a few individual scenes, but then, so do the others. In general, Ford shows the Joads as one group, crammed together in and on their truck or tent, working in the fields. It is their story, really, not the story of any particular individual. A few of the ways Tom is featured here actually serve to draw attention to this fact. The film often puts him in the cab of the truck with Ma and either Pa or Rosasharn, so that scenes on the road can show Tom in the frame, even though Steinbeck's novel is clear that Al is the mechanic and driver in the family. Ford even adds a song for Fonda to sing ("Red River Valley," of course). The filmmakers seemed to go out of their way to put Fonda, their one recognizable name, onscreen, an admission that the story does not naturally spring from him. They even extended his screen time, having him return to the family after killing a policeman and moving with them to the government camp. Still, as in the novel, Tom is gone off into the unknown before the story is finished.

The structure of *The Grapes of Wrath* is effective. Steinbeck's novel shows the Joad family losing members, reduced to its weakest members, who are then faced with a flood of biblical proportions in the final chapters, and Ford's version of the tale shows Ma Joad as a country philosopher. Tom's insight is that the poor have to fight to survive, while Ma's is that the poor will survive in any case. The novel climaxes with Tom going off to fight the class war while those he left behind continued to sink into despair, a message that Ford could not put across in a studio film in 1940. The film is right for its message, just as the novel is.

Modern audiences, though, are not prepared to watch a movie as the story of a collective people. They want a protagonist, someone whom they, as individuals, can inhabit as they enter the story. *The Grapes of Wrath* seems to have such a person in Tom Joad, but his is only one part of the story; giving him too much attention makes audiences feel hollow when he is not on the screen, and it distracts them from truly seeing the movie's accomplishments.

Source: David Kelly, Critical Essay on *The Grapes of Wrath*, in *Novels for Students*, Gale, Cengage Learning, 2012.

John R. Smith

In the following excerpt, Smith discusses Ford's documentary style in the editing and direction of the film.

. . . Collaboration between image and text in *The Grapes of Wrath* emphasizes conflicting points of view. The first image of the film—Tom at a crossroads—is followed by the image of a store named "Cross Roads," a name that stubbornly remains visible (and readable) in the upper left corner of the frame, through the truck's window, as Tom tries to convince the wary driver to give him a lift. The visual and linguistic hints that Tom has arrived at a juncture in his life give way to the suggestion that Tom and the driver are at cross-purposes, each looking at the other from a particular social perspective. The opening sequence, with the image of the crossroad and the text *cross road*, is thematically significant in pointing to the kind of resistance the Joads will encounter as they travel. Intersections between the Joads and

© *Moviestore collection Ltd | Alamy*

others are sites of confrontation and suspicion. In the language of documentary work, the crossroads reveal the difficulties of moving forward, of collaborating with people who come from opposite directions.

The cuts Ford makes typify viewers' experience of being at the crossroads, too: how to approach the Joads, or people like them? When the Joads pull up at a gas station in New Mexico, their truck enters the frame, and then Ford cuts to a closer shot of Ma and Granny getting out. At the Joads's arrival in Keene Ranch, there is a shot of a group of people looking through a fence; the camera then cuts to a close-up of the children in the group. At the end of the film, there is a cut from Ma, Pa, and Hal in the front seat of the truck, to a closer take of just Ma and Pa. The unfolding narrative, in which we become involved with the Joads, relies on the sequencing and cropping effected by the cuts. In their conspicuousness, the cuts reveal meaning we do not necessarily recognize in the larger frame. Striking in the

documentary work Ford does are the sociological clues the "cropped photos" retain. In a departure from Lange's work, the smaller frame imposed by most any cut manages to include those objects that typify migrant lives. When Ma and Granny get out of the truck in New Mexico, the truck dominates the background, nearly swallowing them up even as it spits them out. The features of the children at the fence are obscured by the wire mesh their fingers clasp and through which their eyes stare. In the medium close-up of Ma and Pa, Hal's hand is prominent on the steering wheel at the edge of the screen.

No matter how involved we become with the Joads and the other migrants, we continue to see particulars—the truck, the fence, the steering wheel—which have the potential to keep us distanced from the migrant world. Once the cut has been made, the possibilities for involvement and alienation are incorporated in the same frame, so that in seeing both person and type, we recognize that there *exists a split* between person and type.

> THE FILM MAY TAKE US INSIDE THE JOADS'S WORLD—IT MAY EVEN LET US LOOK THROUGH THEIR EYES—BUT EVEN THERE, THERE IS AN 'INSIDE' THAT IS NEVER ACCESSIBLE. FORD'S INVITATION TO VIEWERS TO REFLECT ON THIS INACCESSIBILITY IS A SIGNIFICANT PART OF THE DOCUMENTARY WORK HIS FILM DOES."

Consider the scene in which Ma Joad goes through her box of letters and trinkets before leaving home. Stam says that the scene is a good example of the "automatic difference" between a film and a novel: Steinbeck writes that Ma looks at photographs, Ford chooses the photos; Steinbeck mentions the earrings in Ma's box, Ford has her try them on; and so on. In effect, the novel has no impact on how the scene is filmed:

> Nothing in the novel prepares us for the idea that Ma Joad will look at the memorabilia by the light of a fire or that the fire's reflection will flicker over her face. Nothing dictates the point-of-view cutting that alternates close shots of Ma Joad's face with what she is looking at, the contemplative rhythm of shot and reverse shot, or the interplay of on-screen and off-screen space, all of which is arguably in the spirit of the novel but not literally in the written text.

The cuts in this sequence invite us to reflect on Ma's inner life. A shot of Ma's face is followed by a reverse-shot of an object, giving us to understand that this is the object she studies. The cycle of shot/reverse-shot continues throughout the sequence. The principle of suture is at work, "covering up" the disruption between the two shots, helping us make sense of the offscreen space that contains some of the particulars of Ma's life. Yet a split persists between what we see in that space and what those objects may be said to represent. We see the letter Ma unfolds, refolds, kisses, and, at the end of the sequence, burns. But we do not know who sent it. We see the postcard from Willy Mae, "Greetings from New York" and the Statue of Liberty pictured on the front; we see the porcelain dog, the words "Souvenir of Louisiana Purchase Exposition, St. Louis 1904" painted on it; we see the

newspaper clipping and read the headline "Joad Gets Seven Years." But we do not recognize the specific memories that visibly move Ma as she looks at these things. We see the image of Ma in the dirty mirror holding the earrings to her ears. But we cannot be sure that we are seeing exactly what she sees.

The cuts Ford makes in this sequence invite us to reflect on an inner life that cannot be known. We know it is "there," but we remain unable to see it. This does not mean that we are barred from introspection. The objects keep certain aspects of Ma's life hidden, but they also point to particular problems in, to use Coles's words, a troubled nation gone badly awry. Invoking the delights of travel and the American embrace of the world's displaced and dispossessed, the postcard comments ironically on the Joads as emigrants/immigrants in their own country. The souvenir strikes a harsh note, cast as it is against the kinds of government foreclosures and purchases that sent the Joads away from the land they had known and worked. The headline in the paper and Ma's face in the mirror conjure up images of the criminal migrant, the impoverished migrant that much of the country continued to see as defining. Although these things have personal meaning to Ma, they also have *political* meaning; that is, they work to reveal a criticism of government policies for the various impacts they have on people like the Joads. But the film is able to take a position without turning people like the Joads into political advertisements. Ma's inner thoughts are hers alone; the film does not presume to speak for her. The memorabilia resists the suturing effected by the sequence in that a split remains between what we see and what we do not. The effect on viewers is remarkably similar to that of Lange's cropped photograph: our introspection is altogether different from Ma's, but we are invited nevertheless to reflect on the social and moral problems represented here, and throughout *The Grapes of Wrath*.

The gap between our introspection and the Joads' persists throughout the film. Consider Ford's use of the subjective point of view when the family drives into Keene Ranch, eager to work. In one of the earliest moments in the sequence, a thwarted worker jumps into the frame and cries: "No!—turn back!" His warning is for the Joads, but he looks directly at us, which has the effect of locating us in the truck with the

Joads. What is perhaps most telling in the sequence, however, is that the effect is not lasting. When the subjective point of view ends, and the Joads have arrived at their shelter, there is a shot of Tom in the cab of the truck, left hand restless on top of the steering wheel. On the left side of the screen is one of the Keene Ranch authorities, who holds a clipboard in one hand and a pencil in the other. He checks off the names of the workers on his list, and Tom is compelled again to give his name. All hands at work: each person here has been reduced to a type, the authority with his official list, Tom with the mechanism that steers him and his family to uncertain futures. The reduction continues in the shots that follow. A pencil or clipboard is always in view when we see the authority. We do not have full visual access to Tom because the truck's side mirror is in front of him, suggesting that the person is obscured by one of the objects with which he has come to be associated.

The moment evokes Lange: Ford does not edit out defining icons—the clipboard, the pencil, the steering wheel, the truck mirror—as much as he edits them *in*. In the process, he challenges us, like Lange, to reflect on the barriers that keep people and locations apart. "Joad," says the authority during the sequence, looking at his clipboard; "Not here." There is a truth in these words. Joad *is not* there, in the sense that he is distanced by the various things that influence how he is seen.

One of those things is "Henry Fonda." As Stam writes, "the performer [. . .] brings along a kind of baggage, a thespian intertext formed by the totality of antecedent roles." *Grapes* oscillates between undercutting Fonda's star quality so that the character he plays will appear more realistic, and relying on the casting history that contributes to that quality so the character will appear less threatening. It thus becomes difficult to see Tom Joad for who he "really" is. Whether he generates sympathy in viewers for the people he represents, or whether he persists in his look of a threatening stranger, viewers cannot, finally, escape the fact that they are looking at a complex, multifaceted *representation* that keeps them outside of the real lives of real people. The film may take us inside the Joads's world—it may even let us look through their eyes—but even there, there is an "inside" that is never accessible. Ford's invitation to viewers to reflect on this inaccessibility is a significant part of the documentary work his film does.

According to Mitchell, James Agee and Walker Evans come to the conclusion in *Let Us Now Praise Famous Men* that it is impossible to see the people who are captured in image and word. There is what Mitchell calls a "blockage" between photo and text: the two remain separate and independent from one another, literally located in different sections of the book. The photos and text work together to resist the notion that people's images and stories can be taken away from them and used for other purposes, particularly political ones. Mitchell writes: "When all the 'proper' names and places are identified, we are reminded that these are fictional names: the Gudgers, Rickettses, and Woodses do not exist by those names. We may feel we 'know' them through Evans's images, through Agee's intimate meditations on their lives, but we never do, and we never will" (532).

Ford's *Grapes of Wrath* is effective in creating the sense that in knowing the Joads, we come closer to knowing the people the Joads represent. The film is equally effective in undermining that sense. Even as Ford brings us closer to the Joads, he insists that we are still far away: the cropped images become crowded with many of the particulars keeping us distanced. The film thus raises questions about how difference is perceived, and about how it is represented—questions also raised by documentarians such as Agee and Evans. Mitchell calls *Let Us Now Praise Famous Men* a "hybrid discourse" (556), a photographic essay whose hybrid form continually challenges viewers/readers to reflect on their own approach to the people represented. As an adaptation, Ford's *Grapes* works in a similar way, opening itself to the influence of other forms in addition to Steinbeck's novel.

Source: John R. Smith, "Making the Cut: Documentary Work in John Ford's *The Grapes of Wrath*," in *Literature Film Quarterly*, Vol. 35, No. 4, 2007, pp. 323–29.

John Calhoun

In the following review, Calhoun examines the new digital restoration of the original film.

The Grapes of Wrath is one of those classic American movies that seem to capture the temper of an exact moment in time: in this case, a moment of weariness yet resolve at the close of a decade of Depression, and a moment just before the country's attention turned to the larger problems of the world. John Steinbeck's novel was published in 1939, and the film was released in January 1940, which even in the studio era represented an extremely quick transit time from page to screen. Whatever the movie's faults, its sense of immediacy remains. It's there in the faces of the extras in the migrant camps, in the Route 66 signs guiding the Joad family on their journey from Oklahoma to California, and in the parched earth that sends them on their quest for this land of promise.

In terms of image, it's difficult to imagine a better homevideo presentation of *The Grapes of Wrath* than that found in 20th Century Fox Studio Classics' new DVD edition. The digital restoration does full justice to director John Ford's visual lyricism, which perhaps found its most eloquent expression in the hands of director of photography Gregg Toland. The DVD's excellent contrast range allows one to fully appreciate Toland's rich, deep blacks, the silhouetted figures against the landscape, and the pinpoint of eye light that makes the characters seem to burn with an inner fire of anger and strength. Though the reputation of hardly anyone associated with *The Grapes of Wrath* needs burnishing, this DVD should at least remind viewers that Toland did a lot of miraculous work in his career besides *Citizen Kane*.

The outlines of Steinbeck's story are well known to most high-school English students. Driven off the land they've sharecropped for generations by the forces of Dust Bowl drought and 1930s economics, the Joads load all of their possessions onto a rickety truck—which, not coincidentally, calls to mind a pioneer wagon—and head west, to seek advertised work in the fertile fields of California's agricultural belt. But once there, the family encounters dehumanizing hostility and derision, and blatant wage-slashing by the big farm bosses looking for ever-cheaper labor. (Giving *Grapes of Wrath* contemporary relevance is one's awareness of how this process has continued, largely with undocumented alien workers rather than Steinbeck's Okies.) Outraged by the injustice around him, eldest son Tom (indelibly played in the film by Henry Fonda) determines to take up the banner of the oppressed, while Ma Joad (Jane Darwell) mainly strives to keep what remains of her disintegrating family together.

However naively elucidated, Steinbeck's message was undeniably socialistic, and it is remarkably undiluted in the film version. This may be surprising coming from the studio of an antilabor executive like Darryl F. Zanuck, but the producer also longed for the prestige afforded by social protest films. And while *The Grapes of Wrath* wasn't the only movie articulating sentiments that got a lot of people into trouble ten years down the road, it put forward its arguments with an intriguing blend of despair and hope. The film was meant by Ford and Johnson to end with Tom's famous scene of leave-taking from Ma, a bittersweet moment if there ever was one. Zanuck imposed a slightly more upbeat ending, in which Ma delivers her "We keep a comin'; we're the people that live" speech, but still, the conclusion is fraught with uncertainty and no little amount of fear. If there is any doubt of this, one glance at actor Russell Simpson's face as Pa Joad listens to his hardier wife declaim will put it to rest.

Of course, Steinbeck's considerably grimmer ending, which is nonetheless powered by the conviction that, as Tom puts it, "A fellow ain't got a soul of his own, just a little piece of one big soul," could not be filmed. In the novel, the Joads suffer flood, starvation, and the stillborn delivery of daughter Rosasharn's baby. Coming upon a dying man, Rosasharn, who remains an undefined character in the movie, offers him her full breasts to nurse. The filmmakers also reordered the author's narrative somewhat, so that the humane government-run Wheat Patch Camp (an actual site, used in the movie) comes at a later point to establish a more optimistic trajectory. But despite such changes, says DVD commentator and Steinbeck scholar Susan Shillingaw, the author was gratified by how closely the movie adhered to the book's spirit.

Shillingaw shares the commentary with critic Joseph McBride, and the pair are a good match from a historical standpoint, with one filling in information where the other's expertise leaves off. Shillingaw is excellent on the California agricultural context, while McBride, who has written two books about Ford, picks up on recurring themes and obsessions in the director's films, from the loss of home to the indignation over injustice. He says that the Joads' plight carried strong echoes for Ford of his ancestors' suffering during the nineteenth-century Irish potato famine, and of their subsequent immigration to America. Though it is good to hear Shillingaw and McBride discuss their subjects' complicated political evolutions (Steinbeck was a lifelong liberal who later denounced communism, while Ford seems to have become far more conservative over the years), things get a little out of hand when they start bickering over whether Steinbeck supported the Vietnam War. For five minutes or more they argue, while on screen the death of an important character, John Carradine's firebrand preacher-turned-organizer Casey, goes by without comment.

Such is the scattershot nature of DVD commentaries, which only rarely seem to strike a perfect balance between historical context, esthetic analysis, and gossip. I could have done with more of McBride's canny observations about Ford's art—about the way in which the director withheld close-ups and camera movement, for instance, so that when he finally employed such techniques, they packed a punch. One of the elements that make the Joads' entrance into the first migrant camp so strong, he points out, is the uncharacteristic use of subjective camera tracking. McBride is also great on providing information about the often-unbilled bit players—like D.W. Griffith heroine Mae Marsh, who shows up in the migrant camp scene—that are such an unforgettable part of the film's fabric.

Watching with Shillingaw and McBride's nonstop commentary does offer one the experience of viewing *The Grapes of Wrath* almost as a silent film. Concentrating on the images tends to increase the movie's power. Jane Darwell's Oscar-winning performance is marred by her cloying line readings, and while it's somewhat toned down here, Ford's penchant for knockabout rural humor is another element that hasn't worn well. Neither is as bothersome with the sound turned low. And sound isn't needed to respond to, say, the half-crazed anguish of John Qualen as a dispossessed farmer, or the shot of hungry children scrambling on a garbage dump, looking for a stick to hold a scrap from Ma Joad's stew pot.

So potent are such sequences that they put to shame the posed and jauntily scored Fox Movietone newsreels about the Dust Bowl that are offered up as extras. (The other major special feature is a ho-hum *A&E Biography* profile of Zanuck.) Though it suffers from moments of phoniness—for example, the studio sets really stick out amidst the film's location scenes, and the New Deal idealization of the Wheat Patch Camp is a bit much—*The Grapes of Wrath* is an authentic American classic, as enduring as the working people it celebrates. This great-looking DVD allows one to appreciate it all over again.

Source: John Calhoun, Review of *The Grapes of Wrath*, in *Cineaste*, Vol. 30, No. 1, Winter 2004, pp. 51–52.

Roger Ebert

In the following review, Ebert proclaims The Grapes of Wrath *to be a "message movie, but not a recruiting poster."*

John Ford's *The Grapes of Wrath* is a left-wing parable, directed by a right-wing American director, about how a sharecropper's son, a barroom brawler, is converted into a union organizer. The message is boldly displayed, but told with characters of such sympathy and images of such beauty that audiences leave the theater feeling more pity than anger or resolve. It's a message movie, but not a recruiting poster.

The ideological journey of the hero, Tom Joad, can be seen by the two killings he is responsible for. The first one takes place in a saloon before the action begins, and Tom describes it to a former preacher: "We was drunk. He got a knife in me and I laid him out with a shovel. Knocked his head plum to squash." After serving four years, Tom is paroled and returns to his family farm in Oklahoma, only to learn the Joads have been "tractored off the land" and are joining the desperate migration to California. Near the end of the film, after seeing deputies and thugs beat and shoot at strikers, he is once again attacked, this time by a "tin badge" with a club. He snatches away the club, and kills him. The lesson is clear: Tom has learned who his real enemies are, and is working now with more deserving targets.

The movie was based on John Steinbeck's novel, arguably the most effective social document of the 1930s, and it was directed by a filmmaker who had done more than any other to document the Westward movement of American settlement. John Ford was the director of *The Iron Horse* (1924), about the dream of a railroad to the West, and made many other films about the white migration into Indian lands, including his Cavalry trilogy (*Fort Apache, She Wore a Yellow Ribbon, Rio Grande*). *The Grapes of Wrath* tells the sad end of the dream. The small shareholders who staked their claims 50 years earlier are forced off their land by bankers and big landholders. "Who's the Shawnee Land and Cattle Company?" asks Muley, a neighbor of the Joads who refuses to sell. "It ain't anybody," says a land agent. "It's a company."

The movie finds a larger socialist lesson in this, when Tom tells Ma: "One guy with a million acres and a hundred thousand farmers starvin'." Of course Tom didn't know the end of the story, about how the Okies would go to work in war industries and their children would prosper more in California than they would have in Oklahoma, and their grandchildren would star in Beach Boys songs. It is easy to forget that for many, *The Grapes of Wrath* had a happy, unwritten, fourth act.

When Steinbeck published his novel in 1939, it was acclaimed as a masterpiece, won the Pulitzer Prize, was snatched up by Darryl F. Zanuck of 20th Century-Fox and assigned to his top director, John Ford. It expressed the nation's rage about the Depression in poetic, Biblical terms, and its dialogue does a delicate little dance around words like "agitators" and "Reds"—who are, we are intended to understand, what the fat cats call anyone who stands up for the little man. With Hitler rising in Europe, Communism would enjoy a brief respite from the American demonology.

The movie won Oscars for best director and best actress (Jane Darwell as Ma Joad) and was nominated for five others, including best actor (Henry Fonda) and best picture (it lost to Hitchcock's *Rebecca*). In a year when there were 10 best film nominees Ford had even another entry, *The Long Voyage Home. The Grapes of Wrath* was often named the greatest American film, until it was dethroned by the re-release of *Citizen Kane* in 1958, and in the recent American Film Institute poll it finished in the top 10. But do many people watch it anymore? It's not even on DVD.

When the DVD restoration does finally arrive, viewers will discover a film that uses realistic black-and-white cinematography to temper its sentiment and provide a documentary quality to scenes like the entry into the Okie transient camp near the California border. Even though the Joad farm is a studio set, Ford liked to shoot on location, and records a journey down Route 66 from the Dust Bowl through New Mexico and Arizona, past shabby gas stations and roadside diners. The dialogue sometimes grows a little too preachy to fit within the simple vernacular of farmers, and Tom Joad's famous farewell to Ma ("Wherever there's a fight so hungry people can eat, I'll be there. Wherever there's a cop beatin' up a guy, I'll be there . . .") always sounds to me like writing, not spontaneous expression.

But it is dialogue spoken by Henry Fonda, whose Tom Joad is one of the great American movie characters, so pure and simple and simply *there* in the role that he puts it over. Fonda was an actor with the rare ability to exist on the screen without seeming to reach or try, and he makes it clear even in his silences how he has been pondering Preacher's conversion from religion to union politics. We're not surprised when he tells Ma, "Maybe it's like Casy says. A fella ain't got a soul of his own, just a little piece of a big soul. The one big soul that belongs to everybody." Just as, in the dream of *One Big Union*, transcendentalism meets Marxism.

The photography is by the great innovator Gregg Toland, who also shot *The Long Voyage Home* and after those two Ford pictures and William Wyler's *The Westerner* moved on directly to his masterpiece, Orson Welles' *Citizen Kane*. In *Voyage* he experimented with the deep-focus photography that would be crucial to *Kane*. In *Grapes* he worked with astonishingly low levels of light; consider the many night scenes and the shots in the deserted Joad homestead, where Tom and the preacher seem illuminated by a single candle, Tom silhouetted, Casy side-lit.

The power of Ford (1884–1973) was rooted in strong stories, classical technique and direct expression. Years of apprenticeship in low-budget silent films, many of them quickies shot on location, had steeled him against unnecessary set-ups and fancy camera work. There is a rigorous purity in his visual style that serves the subject well. *The Grapes of Wrath* contains not a single shot that seems careless or routine.

Fonda and Jane Darwell are the actors everyone remembers, although John Carradine's Casy is also instrumental. Darwell worked in the movies for 50 years, never more memorably than here, where she has the final word ("We'll go on forever, Pa. 'Cause . . . we're the people!"). The novel of course ends with a famous scene that stunned its readers, as Rose of Sharon, having lost her baby, offers her milk-filled breast to a starving man in a railroad car. Hollywood, which stretched itself in allowing Clark Gable to say "damn" a year earlier in *Gone With the Wind*, was not ready for that scene, even by implication, in 1940. Since the original audiences would have known it was left out, the film ended with safe sentiment instead of Steinbeck's bold melodramatic masterstroke.

I wonder if American audiences will ever again be able to understand the original impact of this material, on the page and on the screen. The centenary of Steinbeck's birth is now being observed with articles sniffing that he was not, after all, all that good, that his Nobel was undeserved, that he was of his time and has dated. But one would not want *The Grapes of Wrath* written differently; irony, stylistic experimentation and "modernism" would weaken it.

The novel and movie do last, I think, because they are founded in real experience and feeling. My parents were scarred by the Depression, it was a remembered devastation I sensed in their very tones of voice, and *The Grapes of Wrath* shows half a nation with the economic rug pulled out from under it. The story, which seems to be about the resiliency and courage of "the people," is built on a foundation of fear: Fear of losing jobs, land, self-respect. To those who had felt that fear, who had gone hungry or been homeless, it would never become dated. And its sense of injustice, I believe, is still relevant. The banks and land agents of the 1930s have been replaced by financial pyramids so huge and so chummy with the government that Enron, for example, had to tractor itself off its own land.

Source: Roger Ebert, Review of *The Grapes of Wrath*, in *Chicago Sun Times*, March 31, 2002.

Jim Sanderson

In the following excerpt, Sanderson illustrates how Ford uses vertical and horizontal imagery as referents in The Grapes of Wrath.

In John Ford's films, one or two protagonists try to maintain their sometimes perverse individuality while helping some nuclear, professional, social, or makeshift family. Oftentimes, the family or society may incorporate the individual into its mythology and thus guarantee cultural continuity: "The most basic tension is between the individual and the community, which is perhaps the basic dichotomy expressed

> **THIS IS A STARK IMAGE (AND AN ABSTRACTING ONE), BUT FORD'S IMAGERY SUGGESTS THAT, WHILE THE FAMILY THAT CLINGS TO A VERTICAL HOUSE FOR DEFINITION CAN BE UPROOTED AND DESTROYED, A SHADOW LIKE FAMILY, WHICH DOESN'T OWN HOUSES OR DEFINE BOUNDARIES, CAN ENDURE BY BECOMING HORIZONTAL LIKE THE LAND."**

in art of all forms. In Ford's films, characters often feel a great need to serve the community, to become one with it, yet to hold their individuality somewhat apart from it" (Place, *The Western Films of John Ford*, p. 5). This battle between an individual and his place in his society is typical of American Romanticism. Ford, like most American Romantics, examines the usually doomed individual who attempts to bend his environment to his personality or who tries to maintain his identity against antagonistic cultural, historical, or societal forces beyond his control.

But with the "isms" of the late nineteenth and early twentieth century, the individual's back nearly always breaks from the cultural, artistic, and psychological baggage heaped on him. A Realist like Steinbeck examines the individual who believes in his own power but is mostly a construct of his environment. To artists who are fascinated with personality, the social indignation of a Realist writer like Steinbeck offers no real resolution for their heroes. To a twentieth century artist with a Romantic sensibility, an individual may yearn for psychological or spiritual autonomy but will ultimately confront his own impotence. Transcendence must be some means to combat materialistic impotence. As Ford's eyes failed, his cinematic vision focused on this type of transcendence: "A person's innerself is often at odds with his actions and social manifestations; similarly, the chaotic, determining manifestations of the world beyond the individual (society, the cosmos) are often at odds with the ordering principles whose existence one posits. Thus, the "transcendent" is both beyond and within, both God and the inner ego. And Ford's vision may be interpreted either as Catholic or materialist or both" (Gallagher, p. 384). *The Grapes of Wrath* is the high point of Ford's optimism and romanticism, and it marks the growth of his complexity and ambiguity about the individual. The film begins Ford's personal and cinematic introspection. It is the film "that was to single-handedly transform him from a storyteller of the screen to America's cinematic poet laureate" (Sarris, p. 30).

. . . This imagery and reference in *The Grapes of Wrath* may not entirely be Ford's credit, but the way in which they work together throughout most of the film confirms Ford's control. Darryl F. Zanuck, the Hollywood golden boy of that era, knew which parts of the novel would alienate American viewers and more important which would alienate the Hays Commission. So, as is the case with an art form, which, in America, is also a business, we cannot ever fully dismiss commercial aspirations. Nunnally Johnson, Zanuck's screenwriter and associate producer, understood what elements in Steinbeck's novel could and could not be cinematically manipulated. Johnson was responsible for who was in a scene at what time and what was said. Thus, his "blueprint" suggests nuances that Ford could visually develop. He had, no doubt, the same general ideas of what the cinematic story should be as Ford. In fact, Johnson boasted in his interview with Froug that what was on the screen was also in his script (p. 239.) However, Frank S. Nugent says that the finished film "is always Ford's, never the scriptwriter's" (Nugent, p. 33). Gallagher is probably closest to Ford's method when he says that Ford used the screenwriter's words to free him from the word (the duplicity and amorality of words, which aid Anglo imperialism, is a theme that Gallagher consistently finds in Ford's films) so that he might concentrate on visual narration (p. 464).

Similarly, a movie viewer can see in *The Grapes of Wrath* and in Ford's *The Long Voyage Home*, Gregg Toland developing his use of shadow, perspective, and lightning that will stagger the film industry in *Citizen Kane*. Ford had used chiaroscuro lightning before *The Grapes of Wrath*, most notably in *The Informer*. And, while Toland had the expertise, Ford probably had the finished product in mind. The way the lightning, framing, imagery produces archetypal characters removed from their setting and environment is evident in *The Informer* and *Young Mr. Lincoln*. And, Ford will return to it again for a different effect in one of his "darkest" films, *The Man Who Shot Liberty Valance*. And as Gallagher and others report and as Ford always claimed, he used very little film in order to edit with the camera. In this manner, Ford forced editors to use what he filmed and to piece the film together as he had done in filming. So, despite the collaborative nature of film, this cagey Irishman is responsible for most of what appears in his movies.

The opening scene establishes the horizontal and vertical imagery. We see a horizontal road lined by vertical telephone poles. A barely visible vertical figure walks down the road. Though he is lean and long-legged, he is indistinct. He will be an archetypal moral guide, our avatar, as Faulkner might say. He will guide us to the proper understanding of Ford's imagery. He will become Henry Fonda with his specific features, and then, as he learns, he will again become metaphorically indistinct and walk into the darkness that surrounds us all. From our first glimpse of Tom on the road, to his working on the pipeline where he is surrounded by ditches and pipes, to the truck doors rear view mirrors that trap his face, to the flash light beams thrust into his face, to his exit into darkness. Tom is surrounded by vertical imagery that gradually surrenders to the horizontal imagery.

This road in the very first film image is vital to many of Ford's films. Sarris says that Grandpa's and Ma's argument about going or staying is not just a rural family squabble but "the transformation from a patriarchy rooted in the earth to a matriarchy uprooted on the road" (Sarris, p. 98). As Ford said in his interview with Peter Bogdanovich, he was first attracted to the project because he associated it with his family's migration from Ireland (p. 76). Not surprisingly, still fascinated with visual metaphors for movement, which may teach but will lead to a break up of some family, Ford next used the sea as a road in *The Long Voyage Home*. Traveling down a road causes the destruction of the Joads, the sailor's shipboard family in *The Long Voyage Home*, and the Bundrens.

Even though tragic consequences force the family on the road, the first scene of the Joads on the road and the subsequent montages of Route 66 have an optimistic tone. After Ma has thrown away the mementos of her past and the Joads leave for California in their teetering old truck, we see the truck headed down a dark road and hear a bittersweet "Red River Valley." Then, Ford shifts to a more upbeat tune for a montage of Oklahoma highway, then cuts to Grandpa's death and the bittersweet "Red River Valley." Later, in montages at the Pecos River bridge and at the Navajo reservation, the truck is pointed toward a setting sun and the promise of California. We hear no background music or a sprightly "Red River Valley." It is not so much what is at the end of the road but the horizontal road itself that offers promise. An upbeat version of the song is played once the Joads arrive at the idyllic Government camp. And, at the end of the film, Tom sings the song to Ma as he dances with her; then he walks into darkness to spread his newly learned values. Unlike Ford's use of other folk songs, most typically "Shall We Gather At The River," in which he suggests loss or sacrifice for the community, "The Red River Valley," played sprightly by Dan Borzage on his accordion throughout most of this film, becomes associated not only with familial loss but also with the promise of the road, the government camp, and Tom's quest.

Throughout the film, the exterior montages of the truck going down the road give a sense of hope that is missing in the dark, framed medium or close shots that surround them. These scenes, even with stock footage quality, are more full of detail than Ford's few other exterior shots. Sobchack explains that "through there are some brief long shots of authentic locations in some of the montage sequences, their open quality primarily serves as a striking reminder of the film's overwhelmingly closed visual construction" (p. 75). But, with Ford's serenading, with their placement, though they hasten the break up of the family, these exterior shots remind us of a goal. And, shot with long shots so that we don't distinctly recognize any Joads, these montages remind us of an Emersonian quality where the self can leave self behind to become a part of universal and natural forces. There is no room for the individual or the ego on this transcending road. But, like Emersonian transcendence or Mailer's working backward psychopathy, the individual must learn to give up self or become healthy through embracing his own impulses and instincts; he must use self to get beyond self. He must battle the vertical forces around him. So, these long shot exteriors serve as this

idea. They are the result of Tom's negation of self and family by working through self in the claustrophobic, expressionistic close ups and medium shots in the film.

Early in the film, Ford hints at the way to survive vertical forces and get on the horizontal road. In a flashback of the destruction of Muley's farm, members of Muley's family helplessly watch as a bulldozer plows down their house. Ford cuts to the long shadows of the people across the ground and pans to follow those shadows. Then, he cuts back to the crushed house, then to tracks left by the bulldozer, then to the people, then to the shadows of the people, which now cut across the bulldozer tracks. This is a stark image (and an abstracting one), but Ford's imagery suggests that, while the family that clings to a vertical house for definition can be uprooted and destroyed, a shadow like family, which doesn't own houses or define boundaries, can endure by becoming horizontal like the land.

In fact, though these are farmers, Ford shows very little land: "Those compositions which occur in 'open space' are also chafingly contained and limited by their cardboard and set-like quality and by the relative lack of internal movement of both the camera and the character. . .The visual effect is that there is no field outside the limits of the camera's vision, no land—rather, there is non-space, or a studio set covered with false and aestheticized earth" (Sobchack, p. 77). Ford chooses to make the cultivated land less lasting than the road or the metaphoric land: like "California" where Grandpa can rub grapes on his face, where peaches grow big, where Grandma can die. Horizontal imagery represents a feeling or a Platonic comfort that is beyond reality and specificity. Vertical people, who think in terms of boundaries rather than a flow, perish. Grandpa is too attached to the land to move down the road. Grandma is too old and only slightly less attached to the land than Grandpa. They die. Muley stays on his farm and goes mad. In another sense, in madness, Muley finds a certain freedom and naturalness. He is like a ghost, and the lawmen, with their vertical force, can't catch him. He can not have *his* land, but he can be like the land. . . .

Source: Jim Sanderson, "American Romanticism in John Ford's *The Grapes of Wrath*: Horizontalness, Darkness, Christ, and F.D.R.," in *Literature Film Quarterly*, Vol. 17, No. 4, 1989, pp. 231–44.

SOURCES

Bierman, Harold, "The 1929 Stock Market Crash," in *EH.net Encyclopedia*, edited by Robert Whaples, 2008, http://eh.net/encyclopedia/article/Bierman.Crash (accessed August 10, 2011).

"Cinema: The New Pictures: Feb. 12, 1940," in *Time*, February 12, 1940, http://www.time.com/time/magazine/article/0,9171,884004,00.html#ixzz1UqM6ZFof (accessed August 12, 2011).

Davis, Robert Con, *"The Grapes of Wrath": A Collection of Critical Essays*, Prentice-Hall, 1982, p. 2.

Ebert, Roger, Review of *The Grapes of Wrath*, in *rogerebert.com*, March 31, 2002, http://rogerebert.suntimes.com/apps/pbcs.dll/article?AID=/20020331/REVIEWS08/203310301/1023 (accessed August 12, 2011).

Garraty, John A., *The Great Depression*, Harcourt Brace Jovanovich, 1986, pp. 2–6.

Gossage, Leslie, "The Artful Propaganda of Ford's *The Grapes of Wrath*," in *New Essays on "The Grapes of Wrath"*; edited by David Wyatt, Cambridge University Press, 1990, p. 101.

The Grapes of Wrath, DVD, Twentieth Century Fox, 2004.

Kael, Pauline, "*The Grapes of Wrath*," in *5001 Nights at the Movies: A Guide from A to Z*, Holt, Rinehart and Winston, 1982, p. 227.

Smiley, Gene, "Great Depression," in *The Concise Encyclopedia of Economics*, Library of Economics and Liberty Web site, 2008, http://www.econlib.org/library/Enc/GreatDepression.html (accessed August 10, 2011).

Steinbeck, John, *The Grapes of Wrath*, Penguin Books, 1992.

Worster, Donald, *Dust Bowl: The Southern Plains in the 1930s*, Oxford University Press, 1979, pp. 4–16.

FURTHER READING

Bogdanovich, Peter, *John Ford*, University of California Press, 1978.

This book is more striking than other books about Ford's career because Bogdanovich, an esteemed film director himself (*The Last Picture Show, Paper Moon*), discussed almost every one of Ford's films with him and includes his reflections on each, giving readers a cumulative effect of the man's working style and sensibilities.

Rollins, Peter C., *Hollywood as Historian: American Film in a Cultural Context*, 2nd ed., University Press of Kentucky, 1998.

This study, updated from the influential 1983 edition, looks at *The Grapes of Wrath* in particular and also at the general phenomenon of films bringing social issues to the public consciousness. The book includes detailed analyses of more than a dozen films that have been instrumental in helping moviegoers understand history.

Shindo, Charles J., "The Perfectibility of Man: John Steinbeck and *The Grapes of Wrath*," in *Dust Bowl Migrants in the American Imagination*, University Press of Kansas, 1997, pp. 55–74.

The title of this essay comes from an often-quoted phrase Steinbeck used in his Nobel Prize acceptance speech in 1962, though many critics would argue that it is the film, more than Steinbeck's novel, that presents a view of the world that is hopeful for the future.

Smith, John R., "Making the Cut: Documentary Work in John Ford's *The Grapes of Wrath*," in *Literature Film Quarterly*, Vol. 35, No. 4, pp. 323–29.

In this essay, Smith attempts to connect Ford's film with the stylistic techniques used in documentary films, viewing it as existing primarily to introduce the world of migrant workers to movie-going society.

Steinbeck, John, *Working Days: The Journals of "The Grapes of Wrath,"* Penguin, 1990.

Audiences can tell much about this story by studying the process Steinbeck went through to develop it, including the research he did to authenticate the experience of the Okies and the grueling pace he followed, writing dozens of pages each day.

SUGGESTED SEARCH TERMS

John Steinbeck AND John Ford

John Steinbeck AND Hollywood

The Grapes of Wrath AND film

The Grapes of Wrath AND John Ford

John Ford AND Nunnally Johnson

Okies AND film

Dust Bowl AND film

Great Depression AND migration

The Grapes of Wrath AND socialism

John Ford AND message film

Darryl F. Zanuck AND censorship

Half a Life

V. S. NAIPAUL
2001

Vidiadhar Surajprasad (V. S.) Naipaul is one of the most prominent living writers and the winner of the 2001 Nobel Prize for Literature. Naipaul's 2001 novel *Half a Life* is based on a historical event during the 1930s, when the English novelist Somerset Maugham visited an Indian holy man (*sadhu*), an incident he turned into fiction in *The Razor's Edge*. Naipaul uses this event as a springboard for a study of the aftermath of the British colonial empire that unraveled after World War II. Naipaul courts controversy by eschewing any form of political correctness, and approaches the problem of imperialism from a position that he considers neither conservative nor liberal, but practical. Naipaul recognizes that there has been imperialism in other parts of the world as well, and finds no use in dwelling on recrimination over past events. He realizes that the world has to move forward on the basis of cooperation between nations. The main characters of *Half a Life* are unable to live satisfactorily or to achieve anything useful because they prefer to feel wounded and to offer imperialism as an excuse for their insufficiency. The title suggests that their lives are devalued because they refuse to live fully. The novel is autobiographical to the extent that its main character, Willie Somerset Chandran, lives a life similar to that of Naipaul up to a crucial point, but then chooses a different course than Naipaul did by actively refusing his opportunities in London, rather allowing himself to fall into the colonial morass.

V. S. Naipaul (Indranil Mukherjee | AFP | Getty Images)

AUTHOR BIOGRAPHY

In India, Naipaul's family was of the high Brahmin caste, but fell into extreme poverty. His ancestors accepted indentured servitude in exchange for the chance of immigrating to Trinidad. Naipaul's father, Seepersad, managed, through a socially advantageous marriage, to become a newspaper reporter in Trinidad and published a collection of short stories locally but still could not raise his family out of poverty.

Naipaul was born on August 17, 1932, in Chaguanas, Trinidad. He won an academic scholarship to Oxford University and, after graduation, struggled to establish himself as a writer, writing fiction and working as a journalist, including for the British Broadcasting Corporation Overseas Service. He published several novels before *A House for Mr. Biswas* (1961) established his critical reputation and his financial security. Throughout the 1960s, Naipaul gained increasing recognition and won a series of prestigious British literary awards, including the Somerset Maugham Award in 1960, culminating in the Booker Prize in 1971 for his collection *In a Free State*. He was knighted in 1990.

Naipaul's brother Shiva followed him to Britain and followed a nearly identical career path, though without attaining the elder Naipaul's level of success. Shiva died of a heart attack in 1985. Naipaul became a famous world traveler, and has produced as much travel writing as he has fiction. Naipaul was married to Patricia Hale, who helped financially support him early in their marriage and later acted as his editor, for more than forty years before she died of cancer in 1996.

Half a Life was published in 2001. It was Naipaul's first novel since *A Bend in the River* in 1979. The intervening decades were filled with nonfiction, especially the travel books, an old genre, which, for Naipaul, became a prop for political reflection as he toured the crumbling ruins of the European colonial empires in the third world. Naipaul won the Nobel Prize for Literature in the same year. This certainly boosted his public profile, but even before that, Naipaul had become increasingly reported on in the popular press, as if he were a celebrity. His public feuds with other literary figures, including Paul Theroux and Derek Walcott, seemed to cultivate this attention, as do the provocative statements Naipaul regularly makes to the press (such as claiming that women are inherently incapable of writing as well as men). Naipaul has never made any secret of the fact that he has had a series of mistresses.

Naipaul is often considered the greatest living British novelist. As of 2011, Naipaul lived in a London suburb with his second wife, the Pakistani journalist Nadira Khannum Alvi.

PLOT SUMMARY

1. A Visit from Somerset Maugham

Half a Life is told by a third person narrative voice. The novel begins with Willie Chandran asking his father why his middle name is Somerset, since some of his classmates have found it out and teased him about it. This is followed by a lengthy narrative spoken in the first person by the boy's father (like most of the Indian characters, his first name is never given in the text). The elder Chandran not only answers his son's question but tells the whole story of his family and his own life up to that point.

The Chandran family is of the Brahmin caste and originally served as priests in a temple. But the Islamic and British conquests of India decreased the prestige of the temple and, hence, also its revenues. By the 1890s, Chandran's grandfather was starving, so he went to a nearby city (never named). On the journey, he was surprised to find that people took pity on his wretched condition and gave him alms like he was a beggar. Once he reached the city, a priest from the temple there set him up as a letter writer, writing and reading correspondence for the largely illiterate population for a fee. Eventually he became a clerk for the local maharajah. His son became a more important official, and the elder Chandran himself was sent to college by the maharajah, with the understanding that he would marry the daughter of the headmistress (in India, marriages were usually arranged by parents) and become a very important person indeed in the little world of the maharajah's court.

But the elder Chandran has different ideas. In answer to some inner call, he sets out to sabotage his own life. He tells himself at each step that he is answering Gandhi's call for self-sacrifice (Gandhi was a civil rights leader largely responsible for ending British rule in India through flamboyant acts of civil disobedience in the 1930s and 1940s). But the things Chandran calls sacrifices are ways of limiting and undermining his life. He protests against English learning by burning his textbooks and ceasing to study. No one notices the bonfire of his books and, when the time comes to take his final examinations, he lets himself be talked into taking them. It doesn't matter how badly he does on them because the maharajah wants him to pass. After graduation, he goes to work as an official in the maharajah's tax office and decides to strike against the oppressive tax structure by falsifying the records he deals with. In the bureaucratic muddle, no one notices, and since the maharajah and the college principal act as his patrons, he is promoted. He decides to marry a "backward" girl of low caste as a self-sacrifice and as a blow against the caste system, which is being criticized by Gandhi. He virtually kidnaps her and keeps her in a small apartment (although he does not marry her). When the time comes to plan his wedding with the college principal's daughter, he announces his marriage to the low caste girl. Now his patrons desert him and he finds himself about to be arrested for the irregularities in his tax work that finally come to light. He flees to a temple, which traditionally offers

sanctuary, and begins to live as a begging holy man. He is about to be arrested anyway, when the girl's uncle, a local labor leader known as the firebrand, leads a demonstration in Chandran's favor, saving him against his will. Chandran takes a vow of silence. He represents this as self-sacrifice, but he simply does not want to talk. His cause becomes one of caste rights in connection with his supposed marriage. Chandran feels humiliated because he wanted to protest British oppression of India, not the oppression of one group of Indians against another (oppression and discrimination he actually agrees with).

One day, Chandran is visited by the famous English novelist Somerset Maugham, with the college principal acting as his tour guide. The principal is too infuriated to tell Maugham the truth about Chandran, so he tells Maugham that Chandran is a Brahmin who has returned to the priestly ways of his family and become a holy man who has vowed silence to mitigate the burden of sin that all human beings carry with them according to traditional Indian religion. Maugham is impressed and publicizes the story. After that, Chandran is safe from further official harassment because of his fame in India, and even Britain, and the principal's lie becomes the truth.

Because it was assumed Chandran had already married his low caste girl, no ceremony actually takes place, but they begin living together as husband and wife, and despite Chandran's attempt to vow chastity and his palpable disgust, they have two children: William Somerset and Sarojini. Chandran is horrified by his own children because of their low-caste birth, particularly his daughter, who has dark skin and resembles her mother.

The text briefly returns to the main narrative of the novel and reveals that the story above was constructed from fragments and retellings and transformations over the ten years of Willie's life. At the end of it, Willie naturally has no response but to tell his father he despises him. Chandran attributes this disrespect to the boy's mother's low caste.

2. The First Chapter

The narrative now switches to Willie's attendance at the same Christian school run by Canadian missionaries where his mother was educated. The missionaries easily persuade Willie, disgusted with his own heritage, that he should become a Christian and a missionary, and even a Canadian. When the elder Chandran reads a literary composition to that effect written by his son, he dismisses it as lies (unable to imagine the concept of fiction), and attributes it to the bad influence of the boy's mother. In another composition, Willie turns the life of his family into a fairy tale, in which the young prince grows up to slay his ogre of a father for oppressing his mother. The elder Chandran reads it but is only able to see in it the mother's unworthiness.

Eventually the elder Chandran finds a third story in the composition book. In this fairy tale, a starving Brahmin is on the verge on dying in a cave when a spirit living there says it will make him rich in exchange for the sacrifice of a child once a year. The Brahmin agrees and finds the head of a wealthy temple. Each year, he buys a child from a dark, low-caste tribal people and carries out the sacrifice. After a few years, the tribe becomes rich from this income and no longer feels desperate enough to sell one of its children. But the Brahmin completely reinterprets the story and compels them to give him a child. In fact, they give him two children who, he realizes only after sacrificing them, are not from the tribe but are his own. On reading this, Chandran's only reaction is to blame Willie's mother for inculcating self-hatred in her son.

At school, Willie sees a missionary magazine on whose cover is a photograph of a missionary gloating over having desecrated a statue of the Buddha. When he realizes how destructive missionary work is of Indian tradition, Willie is cured of any wish to become one. His son's depression finally moves the elder Chandran to something like pity, and he writes to Maugham and other prominent Englishmen who visited him to ask if they could help find a place for Willie in an English school. Maugham writes back politely, maintaining the fiction that no request has been made. But another old acquaintance in the House of Lords manages to get a place for him in a college in London.

Willie gets to London at the time of the Suez crisis (in which France, Britain, and Israel unsuccessfully tried to topple the Egyptian government after the country's president seized the Suez Canal and aligned himself with the Soviet Union), a major failure of the colonial powers to control their former colonies. Once he is settled in, Willie befriends Percy Cato, a fellow student who comes from Jamaica. Percy's girlfriend June initiates Willie into sex, not very successfully.

Percy introduces Willie into the cosmopolitan life of Notting Hill, composed of the elite of the immigrant communities coming into England from the former colonies and more adventurous English youths. It was in connection with Percy's parties given for this community that Willie gets a job writing for the BBC overseas service. He is asked by Roger, a producer he meets, to write a brief script about the ancient Christian community in India, since he has broadly put about the lie that his mother came from this group, rather than a low caste. This leads to a series of articles, which might be the beginning of a career. Spurred by Roger's criticism of his work, Willie begins to write more seriously, turning his old school exercise fairy tales and bits of Hollywood movies he had seen into Hemingwayesque short stories. As he continues to write, he discovers deeper insights about himself and his family, but the very act of discovery paralyzes him and he stops writing. Nevertheless, his friend Roger helps him to get the stories published. Willie is at Roger's house on the night the Notting Hill race riots break out. In this disturbance, gangs of young white men, dressed in the mock-Edwardian suits they consider fashionable, invade the Notting Hill neighborhood and beat any blacks that they see, killing some. The BBC wants Willie to cover the disturbance, but he refuses, pretending his academic work is too demanding.

At the same time, Willie reads in a letter from home that his sister, Sarojini, has become engaged to a visitor to his father's temple, a German filmmaker who produces documentaries about revolutionary movements.

3. A Second Translation

Willie misses his friend Percy and learns that he has returned to Panama. Sarojini visits Willie on her way from Germany to Cuba with her new husband. She dismisses Willie's book and predicts he is going to become worthless like their father. Willie is plunged into an agony of self-doubt. Eventually the book is published and indifferently reviewed. But Willie receives a letter from a reader. She comes from a Portuguese colony in Africa (the place is never named, but is clearly Mozambique). She appreciates Willie's book because it is written from a non-Western perspective to which she can relate her own life. Her name is Ana. They meet and quickly become lovers. Willie receives another letter from Sarojini, this time from Cuba; she has met Percy Cato, who has joined Che

Guevara's band of communist guerillas. In the same letter, she dismisses Willie's book as vanity and causes him to consider his own position (he is about to graduate) as hopeless and meaningless. So he goes with Ana back to her plantation in Africa. This move is the second translation (which literally means *crossing over*) of the chapter's title.

The narrative skips ahead eighteen years to 1989, when Willie leaves Ana and goes to his sister in West Berlin. Willie muses that his life, now half over, has been utterly wasted. He learns from Sarojini that Percy was driven out of the communist movement because of his radical idea that the ultimate extension of revolution is that every imperialist has to be killed. He set up a bar in Jamaica. Willie then tells the story of his life in Africa to Sarojini. The remainder of the novel is Willie's first-person narrative.

Willie did not marry Ana, and in Africa, he depends on her more like a child on its mother than as a husband. Willie learns Ana's life story. Her grandfather had been given the estate by the Portuguese government, and during the years of work needed to develop it, had taken an African wife. He sent his daughters to Lisbon to be educated and to marry Portuguese husbands. Ana's mother returned with her husband, but he languished, unable to enter into the work of running the plantation, and disappeared, stealing a great deal of money from the family as he left. Ana's mother had taken a new husband, and her stepfather had tried to molest her. Ana had gone to London to study English because she felt her grandfather's view of the world was limited by his knowing only Portuguese. On learning this, Percy reflects that he is holding on to his own passport and a small supply of money, because somewhere inside, he knows that one day he would run away too.

Willie slowly comes to understand that, though he is in a world of wealth and privilege compared to anything he has known, Ana and her friends—nearby plantation owners—all consider themselves second-class people because they have African ancestry. Willie considers this analogous to his own position with his mixed high- and low-caste background. This mixed condition is one meaning of the title, *Half a Life*.

Eventually, in the 1960s, peasant uprisings begin in Angola (the other large Portuguese colony in Africa) and inevitably spread to Willie's sheltered world in Mozambique. There is no

fighting in Willie's part of Mozambique, and the government is handed over to the guerrillas when the military dictator in Lisbon, Marcelo Gaetano, is peacefully deposed by a socialist revolution. The new government is happy to let go of the colonial empire.

The new native-run government is incompetent, allowing the infrastructure of the country to break down, and faces a new guerilla war with insurgents backed by South Africa. Willie slips on the front steps of Ana's house and has to be hospitalized for concussion. When she visits him there, he tells her he wants to leave. His life is half over and he has never lived on his own account.

CHARACTERS

Ana

Ana is the heiress of a plantation in a Portuguese colony in East Africa. She is enchanted with Willie's book and seeks him out. She approaches Willie as a man, a figure who has gained intellectual and moral autonomy through his book, and also as a non-African, in other words, in the same category as Westerners. These two fictional constructions (which she believes) about himself delight Willie.

Ana's Father

Like many characters in the book, he is never named. He was happy, during the Great Depression, to marry a beautiful and wealthy heiress, overlooking the fact that she was half-African. But his attempt to live in Africa was defeated by an essential listlessness or idleness. Even after swindling money from his wife's family and returning to Portugal, he merely lived, doing nothing. He is meant to represent a type of Willie and his father. Ana was fooled into thinking Willie was fundamentally different from her father by the creativity of his book, not knowing he rejected that aspect of himself as soon as it manifested itself.

Ana's Mother

Ana's mother was able to make a favorable marriage in Portugal thanks to her father's wealth, despite her racially mixed background.

Ana's Stepfather

Ana's stepfather attempted to molest her when she was a teenager, which factors into her decision to study in Europe.

Percy Cato

Percy is a fellow student who becomes friends with Willie in London. He comes from Jamaica and is of a racially mixed heritage, including an East Indian grandmother. He has had the confidence to work his way into the same position Willie was given as a gift and utilizes his talents to the greatest possible extent. He grew up in Panama so the shared Anglo-Imperial culture is foreign to him (he knows nothing about cricket, for instance), and is a dandy in his dress and manners. In 1989, Willie learns that Percy has become a communist guerrilla fighting for the revolution in Cuba, where he came to the idea that the logical answer to imperialism is to kill every imperialist in a colonized country. He later took up running a bar in Jamaica.

Chandran

Chandran (whose given name is never mentioned in the novel) is the father of Willie Chandran. His story is told in the novel's first chapter. He drifts through life, attempting to find ways to reinterpret his personal failing as publics successes. Intended for great things by his father (a minor civil servant in an unnamed princely state in British colonial India), he is sent to university. But he finds his course of studies uninspiring and incomprehensible. When Chandran first reads the English Romantic poets (Shelley, Keats, and Wordsworth) at university, he says, "But this is just a pack of lies. No one feels like this." What he means is that he can't imagine anyone feeling anything different from what he feels. So far from possessing great spiritual insight, Chandran is unable, or just cannot be bothered, to exercise even ordinary human insight and realize that other people are different than him. When, during the struggle for Indian independence, Gandhi calls for students to boycott universities, Chandran burns his textbooks, but no one notices. Years later, after he too works as a bureaucrat and is about to be arrested for improprieties, he flees to a Hindu temple, takes a vow of silence to live as a holy man, and spends the rest of his life in that fashion. But he is not a true ascetic; he simply dislikes indulgence in the same measure as he lacks ambition. Here he has more success though,

and impresses the British novelist Somerset Maugham, whose writings make Chandran a minor tourist attraction. Chandran eventually gets a scholarship to England for his son Willie, not, as he claims, because education will help the boy became something greater than his father, but because he fears that otherwise Willie will become a social agitator or a Christian missionary. He sends his son away to preserve his own comfortable life.

Grandfather Chandran

The grandfather sets the story in motion by leaving his impoverished temple and moving to the city. He is an allegorical figure, whose journey recapitulates the whole history of Indian asceticism. His compromise, leaving the dignity of his priestly station for comparatively menial work as a letter writer and then petty bureaucrat, presages his son and grandson's social and economic paralysis.

Mrs. Chandran

The wife of the elder Chandran and the mother of Willie and Sarojini, her given name is never mentioned in the text. She comes from a low caste (a class contemptuously called "backwards" by other Indians), and is looked down upon because of her dark skin. The prejudice against her class is so strong that she had to attend a school run by Christian missionaries since even the servants employed by Indian schools would have nothing to do with her. She is sent to university on a scholarship by the maharajah, who is pursuing a liberal policy of trying to elevate his low-caste subjects. When the elder Chandran meets her, he is repulsed by her physically, morally, and spiritually. He therefore determines to marry her as a means of self-sacrifice. Because of the increased status such a marriage will bring her, she is happy to go along with her abduction and eventual de facto marriage. She educates herself in European manners to help entertain her husband's international visitors. Although she does become accomplished in such manners, Chandran refuses to recognize her achievement because of his own ignorance.

Sarojini Chandran

Sarojini resembles her mother, especially in having dark skin. This repels her father, who early forms the opinion that, since no Indian would marry such a girl, she must seek an international marriage. She eventually marries a German documentary filmmaker, and when Willie finally goes to her in Berlin, he is forced to admit that she is more competent and mature than he is, as she always was despite his racist denials of the possibility.

William Somerset Chandran

Willie is a source of shame to his own father because the boy reminds him of his mother's low caste. In such a circumstance, Willie naturally comes to despise his father by the age of ten. Nevertheless, Willie has inherited his father's principal characteristic of squandering his talents (which the younger possesses in greater abundance than the elder Chandran) and instead acting to sabotage himself. From an early age, Willie cultivates the art of pretending to be sharp and observant but taking in nothing of substance that goes on around him, actively dampening the observational talent that he used to express his family circumstances in elaborate allegorical fairy tales in his early school exercises.

Once he is at university in London, Willie sees, as an outsider, that the institution is a sham, a make-believe Oxford or Cambridge. This gives him the inspiration to fabricate a new past for himself, to escape his true past, of which he is deeply ashamed. He manifests his father's lack of perceptiveness. When he meets his friend Percy, he observes details about him, but either immediately makes false interpretations or denies the interpretations Percy offers. For instance, Percy tells Willie that his family moved to Panama to work on the canal and that his father served as a clerk. Willie actually investigates the claim and discovers that many Jamaicans worked on the canal as laborers, and assumes Percy is lying because his father was a laborer. This projects Willie's own failed strategies onto Percy, and tends to elevate Willie above his friend, since his own family were clerks. In fact, Willie denies every new fact that he learns that does not please him. When his writing becomes better because he turns to introspection and an analysis of his relationship with his family, it overwhelms him: "The writing then began to lead him to difficult things he couldn't face, and he stopped." Ultimately his inability to cope cuts off his promising careers as a writer and a reporter. He cannot offer the excuse of self-sacrifice that his father used; he simply refuses to use his talents and potential. His relationship with Ana and his move to Africa are merely last, grand ways to avoid taking action or responsibility for himself.

College Principal

Willie's father was supposed to marry the daughter of the college principal, an important figure in the administration of the maharajah of the state where the Chandrans live. He has the task of acting as tour guide to Somerset Maugham and, rather than reveal the whole story of his relationship with Chandran, concocts a lie which becomes the basis of Chandran's fame and success (such as they are).

Jacinto Correias

Correias is one of the Mozambique planters in Ana and Willie's social circle. For years, he has been obsessed with the looming disaster of the end of colonialism and kept what money he had stashed away in banks all around the world. As political conditions deteriorate, he uses his contacts in the Portuguese government to become a wealthy importer of Western goods. But Correias, who is not pure Portuguese, has been chosen by his patron in the government to take the fall for the inevitable exposure of his own corruption, so his efforts at self-advancement prove illusory.

The Firebrand

The uncle of the wife of the elder Chandran who is never named is repeatedly referred to as the firebrand because of his inflammatory rhetoric and politics. He is an important union leader in the maharajah's territory. It is hinted that he is a communist, but he does not dare express such a view in public for fear of arrest.

June

June is Percy Cato's girlfriend, an English girl who works at the perfume counter in an up-scale department store. Willie is overcome by desire for her, and she initiates him into sex. She is attracted to the young men of the immigrant community precisely because she fears them.

The Maharajah

In subservience to the British, he rules the small state where the Chandran family originally lived with limited autonomy. The Chandran family rises by entering his service as bureaucrats, while he sends the elder Chandran's wife to college on a scholarship. Like most of the characters in India, he is never named, nor does he appear, but his actions form the framework within which the events in India unfold.

Somerset Maugham

Maugham (1874–1965) was a prominent British novelist and author in the first half of the twentieth century. He traveled extensively in the British Empire in India and the Far East during and after World War I and frequently used this experience as the basis of his writing. In his lifetime, he was widely appreciated as a chronicler of the end of the empire. His visit to an Indian ascetic in the 1930s was the starting point in the real world for Naipaul's fiction in *Half a Life*.

Roger

Roger is a producer at the BBC who meets Willie at a party in Notting Hill and starts employing him as a reporter for the BBC overseas service. Like Willie, he considers his job to just be marking time until something better presents itself. He eagerly gets Willie's stories published through his contacts in the book industry.

Wolf

Sarojini marries Wolf, a German documentary film maker, who is also a socialist.

THEMES

Asceticism

At the beginning of the novel, Naipaul presents a history of the Brahmins, the priestly caste of India. In antiquity, the Brahmins were supported by the revenues of temples, but these declined because of the foreign conquests of India, first by Muslim invaders in the Middle Ages, and later by the British. In fact, the poverty of the priests brought them near to starvation. One day in the 1890s, one priest, the grandfather of the elder Chandran, decided to leave the temple and go to the nearest city to try to find some way to live. These privations forced the creation of asceticism on him. He found that people took pity on him and gave him alms. His incapacity to deal with his experiences left him out of touch with reality so that he no longer noticed anything of the outside world and could manage nothing but introspection, even as he rode the railway for the first time. Naipaul emphasizes this burlesque of the inner vision of the holy man many times in *Half a Life*.

Obviously, Naipaul does not imagine that asceticism was invented in India in the 1890s, nor does he expect his reader to entertain any such idea. Men who were accounted holy and godlike

TOPICS FOR FURTHER STUDY

- Naipaul's latest travel book is *The Masque of Africa: Glimpses of African Belief* (2010). It chronicles his personal discoveries about obscure as well as well-known aspects of religion in Africa. Find some episode in the book that interests you and use it as the basis of a short story written in the style of *Half a Life*.

- Research Mohandas Gandhi in any of the large number of young-adult books about him, including Betsy Kuhn's *The Force Born of Truth: Mohandas Gandhi and the Salt March, India, 1930* (2010), which focuses on the event that impressed the elder Chandran in *Half a Life*. How do Gandhi's actions compare with those of his supposed follower Chandran? Write an essay that compares the two figures.

- Read Somerset Maugham's *The Razor's Edge* and write an essay that compares the meeting with the Hindu holy man in that novel to the version given in *Half a Life*.

- Prepare a multimedia presentation for your class on the role of the holy man (*sadhu*) in contemporary India. Use traditional and online research resources to compile information. Include news reports, audio, and video media to illustrate your interpretation of the role.

because they renounced the world (that is, everything that people ordinarily do, such as talking, sleeping, eating, wearing clothes, and having sex) have always been a prominent feature of Indian cultural life. Indeed, one of the first things noticed by the scholars in the retinue of the ancient conqueror Alexander the Great was that India was crowded with what they called Gymnosophists (naked wise men) who were considered holy because of their self-mortification (i.e., living as if they were dead rather than alive). A comment from Megasthenes' *Indika* (quoted

Willie and Ana move to Mozambique and live a colonial lifestyle. *(EcoPrint | Shutterstock.com)*

at Diodorus Siculus II.40) shows a remarkable continuity between the ascetics of that time and Naipaul's Chandra: "The philosopher who errs in his predictions incurs no other penalty than obloquy, and he then observes silence for the rest of his life."

What Naipaul is trying to imagine is the role of asceticism in modern India, where it is still a powerful force in popular religion. Indian television is full of ascetic holy men who claim miraculous powers and a special mediation between their followers and the divine. To Naipaul, the idea that the spiritual strength of India is to be invested in such men, who are often transparent charlatans, seems a very dull and spiritless belief. So he makes his own archetypal holy men who embrace asceticism as a way of actually starving to death from poverty and, in the case of Chandra, take a vow of silence as a means of not having to answer criminal charges. Willie's story about the Brahmins who end up sacrificing their own children is an allegory about his own family, but it is also an allegory about the decay of traditional Indian culture in the face of commercial popular culture.

Education

Half a Life is not a *bildungsroman*, or novel that takes its plot from the main character's transformation from childhood through adulthood, possibly through education. If anything, the main characters rather resist the possibility of education and personal growth. Nevertheless, a good deal of the text concerns attempts at education. The elder Chandran receives a failed education at college—he is taught English literature by an antiquated and useless process of rote memorization—and he succeeds in failing at it. Even his failure goes unnoticed, and he is not led to any other alternative form of improvement by his experience. Willie Chandran is miseducated in a much grander fashion, receiving a scholarship to an English university where he learns nothing. So far from changing by the experience, Willie's main accomplishment is to learn to lie about his past. Even his short-lived career as a writer seems to be the extinguishing or using up of some natural talent rather than the cultivation of any fruit of growth and learning.

STYLE

Postmodernism

Modern literature generally encompasses the period from around 1850 to 1950. After that, many of the most sophisticated authors and critics judged themselves to be post-modern. This terminology, then, refers to a period of the past as modern, which seems paradoxical, since in everyday usage, *modern* means the world today. But postmodernism takes modern to be instead an attitude about the world that typified that industrial century. Modern authors believed in progress and order and looked to the future with optimism; they understood the tremendous rise in the standard of living, scientific knowledge, medicine, and almost every aspect of life experienced in Western Europe, the United States, and Japan as a result of the industrial revolution to be a sign that all the basic problems of human life were on their way to being solved. Literature was supposed to mirror reality and perfect traditional forms. But by the end of the modern period, the terrible political, social, and economic upheavals of the two world wars, the Great Depression, the failure of imperialism, the realization that the industrial economy could not go on indefinitely exploiting fossil resources, and the terrible threat to human life itself by nuclear weapons had made it clear that the industrial revolution had not brought about a utopia. A late modern author like T. S. Eliot saw the world as a place of lamentation amid the ruins of civilization. The postmodernists, such as Jorge Luis Borges, Joseph Heller, Kurt Vonnegut, and Thomas Pynchon, also recognize that the modern world has broken apart so that meaning and rational understanding are impossible, but they look on the same landscape as a playground.

Naipaul picks up and examines the broken pieces of tradition in order to see that, isolated and defective as they now are, they no longer play their former roles in culture. The novel begins with an autobiographical reminiscence by Willie's father. This is how the narrative voice introduces the story: "The story changed as Willie grew up. Things were added." While it is true that stories told over and again in a family evolve over time, in part because, to a large degree, the teller recalls the last telling more clearly than the original events and because the rhetoric and structure of the story can be improved, the author is clearly stating that his own text cannot be relied upon. It has always been true of fiction that it is fiction, something the author has made up, but the postmodern attitude is to call attention to this fact, working against the reader's suspension of his own knowledge that the fictional world is false so he can enter into the author's creation. Naipaul can be remarkably blunt about this. For example, the title of chapter 2 of the book is "The First Chapter." More importantly, the story examines one of the broken fragments of traditional culture, the religious figure of the Indian ascetic mystic, and constructs a story that explains, not its history or its meaning but rather why the meaning it has in the contemporary world is false and deceptive; it explains, in other words, its lack of meaningful context, rendering it as something to be exploited (by Maugham, who used the fiction of its traditional authority as a commercial device to sell books, as much as by Chandran). Naipaul applies postmodern playfulness and comedy to the same idea. When Maugham asks Chandran if his ascetic life has made him happy, he replies, "Within my silence I feel quite free. That is happiness." But this is a punch line to a joke, since the reader knows he means freedom from prosecution.

Autobiography

Authors must inevitably draw on their own experience. But in many cases, it is possible to see closer ties between some elements of an author's life and work. The London sojourn of Willie Chandran in *Half a Life* has more than a little to do with Naipaul's early days there in his real life. J. M. Coetzee, in his review of *Half a Life* in *Inner Workings: Literary Essays 2000–2005*, observes that "Naipaul has often in the past mined his own life story for his fiction. In certain respects, the apprentice writer W. S. Chandran is based on the apprentice writer V. S. Naipaul." Coetzee mentions that both found early inspiration in Hollywood films. Patrick French, in *The World Is What It Is: The Authorized Biography of V. S. Naipaul*, fleshes out the observation with more points of contact. He finds echoes of Naipaul's first explorations of London in Willie's. A friend's letter warning Naipaul he will never succeed in a job interview while wearing a particularly outlandish sports jacket he favored finds its way into Naipaul's criticism of Willie's attempt at business dress. Nevertheless, Naipaul and Willie both find jobs writing for the BBC. But like many of Naipaul's characters who begin as writers, Willie soon veers off the path Naipaul took, leaving behind no more than a flirtation with autobiography. Willie is terrified of success and backs away from his career as a writer. Naipaul embraced it.

COMPARE & CONTRAST

- **1950s:** Immigration from the British Commonwealth, especially from the Caribbean region to Great Britain, is virtually unlimited, resulting in severe stress on the social safety net provided to immigrants by the British government and in social tensions and even violence, such as the Notting Hill race riots in 1958.

  Today: Immigration to Britain is largely stopped after the Immigration Act of 1972 and other legislation. Social tensions around immigration today revolve around the community of Muslim immigrants from the Indian subcontinent who actively resist assimilation to British culture. In 1959, the Notting Hill Carnival was instituted as a gesture of racial unity. It has grown to be the largest street festival in Europe, though it is marred by relatively minor violence in 2009.

- **1950s:** Mozambique and Angola are still under Portuguese colonial rule.

  Today: The former Portuguese colonies in Africa are independent countries with a history of civil wars in the aftermath of decolonization.

- **1950s:** Writers of non-British ancestry are just coming to be recognized by the British literary establishment.

  Today: The most prominent British novelists today (Naipaul and Salman Rushdie) were born in the former colonial empire and are not of British ancestry.

HISTORICAL CONTEXT

Somerset Maugham

Half a Life begins with the story of the Chandra family, and particularly of the elder Chandra, a story that the narrative voice of the novel admits is highly fictionalized: the English novelist Somerset Maugham visits Chandran, is impressed by his ascetic vow of silence, and makes him famous by writing up a version of the encounter in his novel *The Razor's Edge*. According to J. M. Coetzee's review of *Half a Life* in *Inner Workings: Literary Essays 2000–2005*, this premise is based on a fictionalized version of a historical fact. While Somerset Maugham was a rising author in the 1930s, he visited an Indian Maharshi (holy man), Venkataraman, noted for his asceticism:

> While waiting for his audience, Maugham fainted, perhaps because of the heat. When he came to, he found he could not speak (it must be mentioned that Maugham was a lifelong stammerer). The Maharshi comforted him by pronouncing that 'Silence is also conversation.'

According to Maugham's account in *A Writer's Notebook* (1949) this story was widely circulated in India and acquired the addition of his having a mystical experience during his blackout. Just as Naipaul did, Maugham used the event, transformed into fiction, in his 1944 novel, *The Razor's Edge*. Naipaul seizes on this event, or rather the false reports of the event, as the point of departure for *Half a Life*, supplying a new character and a new outcome. Coetzee insightfully relates this to the postmodern trend of drawing minor characters from literary classics out of their original context to make them the protagonists of modern works of literature, for example Hamlet's two friends from university in Tom Stoppard's play *Rosencrantz and Guildenstern are Dead* or the first Mrs. Rochester from *Jane Eyre* in Jean Rhys's *Wide Sargasso Sea*.

Caste System

The caste system plays a central role in *Half a Life*. The caste system can be traced back to the Indo-European division of society into priests, warriors, and farmers (compare the priests, nobles, and peasants of the European Middle Ages). In India, caste became both more rigid and more elaborated into larger numbers of hierarchical groups than in other Indo-European areas like Iran or Europe. The caste system was described by the Greek historian Megasthenes as early as the third century BCE. As caste evolved in India, each occupation, but also each tribal or ethnic group, became a separate caste. These castes are collectively called *Jati* in Hindi. The Brahmin ideology that relates the castes to each in a hierarchy is called *Varna*.

Caste was determined by one's family background, and higher castes were considered ethically, morally, and spiritually superior to lower castes (again, compare nobles and peasants). Members of a high caste, like the Brahmins or priests, were not even allowed to touch a member of a low caste. The lowest castes are called *backwards*. Although Naipaul presents this term as a slur, it is still the official term used by the Indian government to designate a group of low castes (it is probably an example of Indian English holding on to old-fashioned British terms, but Naipaul clearly considers it an indictment against the Indian government). Caste is not purely racial, but it has a racial component: between 3,000 and 4,000 years ago, India was conquered by lighter-skinned Indo-Europeans, who ruled over darker-skinned indigenous peoples, and the higher castes were originally tied to Indo-European ancestry.

Gandhi denounced caste as a social evil that should be done away with. Wishing to put Gandhi's words into practice, Chandran senior decides to marry a scholarship girl of the lowest caste attending his university. While Gandhi might have approved of a marriage between a Brahmin like Chandran and a "backward" if it were done to reject the caste system, Chandran has no such idea. He agrees with caste ideology that his wife is inferior and despicable and considers that marrying her is a kind of ascetic mortification that he imagines is ennobling for himself. While he insists that he is physically repulsed by her just as were his priestly ancestors, who would not have allowed a person of her caste into a temple, he is still able to father two children with her.

Willie is equally hypocritical, blaming his half-caste status and particular his partial inheritance of his mother's supposed inferiority for his own failures. More importantly, however, wherever he goes, Willie finds analogs of caste. In 1950s Britain, he finds a society driven by

Willie's father followed Mahatma Gandhi and turned his back on his inheritance, a theme that follows Willie in the book. (*Arvind Balaraman / Shutterstock.com*)

racial hatred and discrimination, as well as the favored and disfavored groups mixing sexually. He must hide from the violence of the Notting Hill race riots in 1958, just as he did from the caste riots in India. In Africa, he finds an elaborate social structure based on race. At the top are white Portuguese born in Portugal. Under them are *creoles* like his wife Ana, who is white (one black grandparent is allowed) but born in Africa. Next come *mestizos*, of mixed parentage, and at the bottom, native Africans with no European ancestry. Caste, then, is shown to be analogous to racism in Naipaul's view and has nothing to do with Western imperialism.

CRITICAL OVERVIEW

The seminal work on Naipaul's *Half a Life* is the review by fellow Nobel laureate J. M. Coetzee that appeared in the *New York Review of Books* in 2001 and is reprinted in his *Inner Workings*. Coetzee established the reading of *Half a Life* as a postmodern interrogation of the role of asceticism in Indian life, which Naipaul takes to be a symptom in modern India of the failure to establish a postcolonial identity. Coetzee sees Naipaul's hero, Willie Chandran, as propelled into assuming the role of colonizer himself, first in England and ultimately in Africa. Writing a double review, Coetzee cannot help but provide an extended comparison between *Half a Life* and Anita Desai's 2000 postcolonial novel, *Fasting, Feasting*. Rather ambitiously for a review, Coetzee also researched and documented the episodes from Somerset Maugham's life and writing that sparked *Half a Life*.

Bruce King, in *V. S. Naipaul*, offers the most sustained and extensive treatment of *Half a Life*, one equal in importance to Coetzee's within the context of a general survey of Naipaul's whole literary career. It also balances Coetzee's essay by focusing on the later, African part of the novel, and on the theme of postcolonialism, though he also evaluates the novel in full. King is more extensive than Coetzee in analyzing *Half a Life* in terms of Naipaul's own biography as well as in relation to his other writings. King agrees on the sterility and pointlessness of Willie Chandran's life found by other critics, but observes that inner desolation contrasts with an outer life spent in the invigorating environment of world events. He lived through Indian independence and personally witnessed the violent end of European colonialism in Africa. He was in London during the Suez crisis and in Berlin in 1989 for the fall of the Berlin wall. He was at the center of the transformation of British society by immigration from the empire in the 1950s. Yet these are all events that Willie hides from or flees.

Gillian Dooley, in *V. S. Naipaul, Man and Writer*, analyzes *Half a Life* in terms of Naipaul's youthful work. Dooley finds it unenlivened by Naipaul's earlier humor; his former joyfulness has become joylessness. Dooley speculates at length about the meaning of the title *Half a Life*. The most obvious, and perhaps least interesting, possible significance is that the book ends when its main character, Willie Chandran, is forty-one years old, with half of his life over. Another possibility is that all of the main characters are half one thing and half another, half caste or racially mixed. Dooley finds most satisfying, however (without dismissing the other

possibilities since the title gains in depth as it takes on more than one meaning), the idea that Chandran father and son lead half lives because of their unsatisfying, fruitless existence.

Unsurprisingly, Naipaul's biographer Patrick French, in *The World Is What It Is: The Authorized Biography of V. S. Naipaul*, limits his comments on *Half A Life* to pointing out similarities between Naipaul's own early days in London and those of Willie Chandran in *Half a Life*.

CRITICISM

Bradley A. Skeen

Skeen is a classicist. In the following essay, he analyzes Naipaul's approach to the third world in Half a Life *in light of Edward Said's theory of Orientalism.*

Naipaul's whole literary output is concerned with the intellectual and cultural encounter of the third world with the West in the wake of the break-up of the imperialist system. Accordingly, he is categorized as a postcolonialist writer. Naipaul's own identify as a Trinidadian of Indian descent educated and living in Britain predisposed him to take on this vast subject. In *Half a Life*, Naipaul tackles postcolonialism head on through his main character, Willie Chandran, who is present at the breakdown of the British Raj in India, the Portuguese empire in Africa, the fall of the Soviet Empire in Eastern Europe, and the beginning of the migration of the formerly colonized peoples to Europe. But the entire burden of Naipaul's writings, and nowhere more than in Half a Life, works against a more widely held post-colonial mindset that is common to many other writers who take up the same themes as Naipaul, and which has been crystallized in the work of the literary critic Edward Said.

Said's magisterial work on colonialism is his *Orientalism*. He argued that, as Western European countries conquered the Americas, Africa, and southern Asia for the purposes of economic exploitation, they also attacked the cultural identity of their new subjects with the concept of Orientalism. Westerners created a false image of their subject peoples as weak, effeminate, decadent, scheming, and self-serving, everything that Westerners, in this view, insisted they themselves were not. Paradoxically, even the academic discipline of Orientalism (devoted to the

WHAT DO I READ NEXT?

- In 2004, Naipaul published *Magic Seeds* as a sequel to *Half a Life*. Willie Chandran returns to India at the behest of his sister and becomes a communist guerilla before being arrested and imprisoned by the Indian government. However, he is released when his book of short stories is republished, and he becomes a literary celebrity. Willie returns to England and moves into the London suburbs, again paralleling Naipaul's life.

- Naipaul's most famous public friendship, and most public feud, has been with the travel writer Paul Theroux. The early part of their relationship is reflected in Theroux's *V. S. Naipaul: An Introduction to His Work* (1972).

- Mia Couto is widely considered the most important writer from contemporary Mozambique. His first novel, *Sleepwalking Land* (1992; published in an English translation by David Brookshaw in 2006), concerns the period of the nationalist revolution in his country that also forms the background of the latter part of Naipaul's *Half a Life*.

- In *Reading & Writing: A Personal Account* (2000), Naipaul writes about his passive and active literary experiences, particularly about his identity as an Indian writer, as well as the position of literature in India.

- Jeff Hay's 2005 *Hinduism* offers an introduction for young people to the religion of India through essays focusing on various aspects of Hinduism.

- *In a Free State* won the 1971 Booker Prize for Naipaul. It consists of three parallel stories exploring the themes of autonomy and control in Asian immigrant communities in the United States, the East Indies, Great Britain, and Africa.

- *Born Confused*, a 2003 young-adult novel by Tanuja Desai Hidier, tells the story of a teenage girl who immigrates with her family to India and feels trapped between two cultures.

language and culture of Asia) was part of the Orientalist fantasy in so far as it insisted that Westerners, not Asians themselves, were fit to study Asia. The purpose of Orientalism, Said believed, was to further the racism that supported imperialist ideology: Europeans justified their conquests by propagating the falsehood that their subjects were not fit to rule themselves. While the brute political aspect of imperialism has long since ceased with nearly all colonized countries again becoming independent, the cultural imperialism of Orientalism continues. Said believed that all Western literature about the Orient serves the purpose of justifying imperialism. Even a book like Joseph Conrad's *Heart of Darkness*, which appears to criticize imperialism, Said believed, only denounced the worst imperialist excesses, thereby acting as a defense of its more moderate forms. The purpose of postcolonial literature, therefore, becomes the exposure of Orientalism and the attempt to find an authentic non-Western voice.

Naipaul has been fiercely attacked by Said. In an address given at Skidmore College (published in two parts in the Skidmore literary magazine *Salmagundi* in 1986), Said describes Naipaul as a sheep in wolf's clothing who seems to be a witness for the third world on account of his ancestry, but who actually testifies against the colonized peoples because he has completely internalized Western culture and accepts the Orientalist position. Any criticism Naipaul might offer of the Orientalist interpretation of Western literature and Western culture is motivated by racism paradoxically directed against his own race. The same charge is made against Naipaul by the Nobel Laureate poet Derek Walcott (from the Caribbean Island of St. Lucia) in his poem "Mongoose" (never published, but transcribed in an article by Daniel Trilling in the London *Observer*), particularly in respect to *Half a Life* and its sequel, *Magic Beans*. Said further interprets Naipaul as blaming the colonized peoples for their own difficulties instead of attributing them to the colonizers. Naipaul's true subject matter and audience, Said claims, is not the third world and its peoples but people like Naipaul himself (as well as like Said and Walcott), intellectuals from the third world who have moved to the West and received Western educations and who (unlike Said and Walcott) have internalized Orientalism. Said offers as proof of his case against Naipaul the observation that Naipaul's travel writing and memoirs are based on his own

> **THE ELDER CHANDRAN SETS OUT TO IMITATE GANDHI, BUT DOES SO IN A COMPLETELY USELESS FASHION AND ENDS UP AS A SHAM HOLY MAN, A TRANSFORMATION INDIA AND THE ORIENTALIZING SOMERSET MAUGHAM COUNT AS BECOMING A GREAT SUCCESS, FOR ALL THAT HE IS REALLY A FAILURE."**

observations, impressions, and memories, rather than on sociological scholarship on the regions he describes, and maintains that Naipaul's account is therefore thoroughly Orientalist and racist.

However, it is possible to offer a reading of Naipaul's work, particularly of *Half a Life*, that suggests a different interpretation of the author's thought and motives. The Chandran family is plagued by surrender to fate, passivity in the face of adversity, and refusal to take any initiative to change things for the better. No doubt Naipaul sees these characteristics in modern India, if not in the modern third world. It is also clear that he sees them as caused by colonialism. The Chandrans start their downward spiral as a result of the loss of Indian independence and the marginalization of the Brahmin caste in the face of conquest by foreigners. So far he might seem to agree with Said. But Naipaul differs in this: he blames the Islamic invaders of India in the Middle Ages as well as the European invaders of the eighteenth and nineteenth centuries. That imperialism could be practiced by one non-European people against another is not part of Said's program, yet Naipaul is reminding the reader that it happened nevertheless. The point of Willie's final trip to Berlin is much the same (the sequel *Magic Beans* makes it clear that the scene takes place shortly before the fall of the Berlin Wall). There, Willie is in the midst of the Soviet empire in Eastern Europe, where Europeans have colonized other Europeans, another provocation to Said. According to Said's theory, it ought not to be possible for Europeans to colonize each other, or for non-Europeans to colonize other non-Euroepans, but Naipaul is demonstrating that those very things have happened.

Another point of contention is Mohandas Gandhi. Gandhi was a civil rights activist in India and perhaps the man most responsible for the liberation of India from British rule. He would seem a natural hero of anticolonialism, but Said and almost all other postcolonialist critics have condemned Gandhi with a deafening silence. The reason for this is not hard to find. Gandhi was a Western-educated liberal who wanted, besides ending British rule, to make India a modern liberal country. In Said's terms, this would be to go on colonizing it. But it is impossible to criticize so popular and acclaimed a figure. In his 1964 travel book, *An Area of Darkness*, Naipaul did not, indeed, criticize Gandhi but rather criticized India in respect to Gandhi. Gandhi was received in India as a traditional holy man, a reception that makes it possible for Indians to subvert and deny the radical transformation of Indian society that Gandhi called for. This looks remarkably like the mirror image of Said's Orientalism, a reflection that it should not be casting. But it does, Naipaul insists. He revisits the idea in *Half a Life*. The elder Chandran sets out to imitate Gandhi, but does so in a completely useless fashion and ends up as a sham holy man, a transformation India and the Orientalizing Somerset Maugham count as becoming a great success, for all that he is really a failure.

In *Half a Life*, Naipaul reminds critics of the West that there is no limit to the corrective criticism that could be applied against the West. When Willie visits his sister Sarojini in Berlin, she tells him that his old college friend Percy Cato, a black Jamaican who fought with Che Guevara for the communist revolution in Cuba, has been driven out of his guerrilla band for being too radical. Percy told his comrades, who were of mostly Spanish descent, that "he thought the Spaniards had raped and looted the continent in the most savage way, and no good could come out of the place until all the Spaniards or part-Spaniards were killed." This seems like a *reductio ad absurdum*, an exaggeration to the point of comedy, of anticolonialism. Willie's sister approves of the idea as the logical conclusion of revolutionary logic: "It is a difficult idea, but actually it's interesting, and liberation movements will have to take it on board some day." Taken to its extreme, this proposition would require the death not only of millions of South Americans but also of almost everyone living in the United

States. The irony is furthered by the idea's speaker. His ancestors were brought to the New World as part of the imperialist program, albeit as slaves, so is he not part of the colonial menace that would have to be expunged? The same is true of Naipaul's family in Trinidad. And what of non-European immigrants in Europe like Willie and his sister, and like Naipaul himself? The whole thing is ridiculous because it calls for the murder of people based on their ethnic background. It is not a way to fight racism but the most horrible kind of racism. It is easy to read this as Naipaul's satire against Said and radical anticolonialism as it exists in the postcolonial world. Or it would be, except for the fact that Naipaul gives this idea a name, "the Pol Pot Position." Naipaul does not let his readers ignore the fact that what he is proposing as satire was actually carried out in the killing fields of Cambodia under the Khmer Rouge dictator Pol Pot, resulting in the deaths of more than 1.5 million people for imperialist crimes like speaking French or wearing reading glasses. Naipaul is pointing out that revenge and genocide are the logical consequence of the reaction against Imperialism. If Said denies any such thing, Naipaul can point to history for his evidence. Naipaul sees this as an argument in favor of his position, which is for the colonized and colonizing nations to work together to build a future.

For Said, Naipaul was a self-loathing black (in the British sense of anyone not white who had entirely bought into Western racism and its Orientalizing fantasy). But the Naipaul of *Half a Life* does not very closely resemble the straw man Said built up. Rather he is a careful critic of Said and the architect of a counter narrative to Orientalism. It may be, Naipaul suggests, that India and the third world bear some responsibility for themselves, and it may also be that, in a world dominated and supported by Western civilization through the spread of Western institutions like science and liberal democracy, attacking and destroying Western culture might not even be in the best interests of the colonized peoples themselves. Naipaul believes that the way forward for everyone, colonized and colonizer alike, is as part of an increasingly connected world civilization that cannot help but be based on the West.

Source: Bradley A. Skeen, Critical Essay on *Half a Life*, in *Novels for Students*, Gale, Cengage Learning, 2012.

Bruce King

In the following review, King provides a favorable assessment of Half a Life.

V. S. Naipaul's new novel, *Half a Life*, tells of someone like the author but his opposite, someone who does not know what he wants to do, who wastes his opportunities, who drifts, never takes root, never builds a house, never becomes morally or financially independent. He does many of the things Naipaul has done, such as go to England for further education, write for the BBC, write a book of short stories, travel to Africa, but each parallel ends with flight revealing lack of purpose. Having fled from Africa, Willie Chandran laments, "I am forty-one, in middle life . . . I have risked nothing. And now the best part of my life is over"; at the conclusion, before leaving for Berlin, Willie tells his wife, "The best part of my life has gone, and I done nothing."

Is Willie right? He has traveled from India to England, Africa, and Germany. By the standards of most people, he has had a remarkably full life by the age of forty-one, but is a life of action good? Throughout the novel the value of political action and of political gestures are called into doubt. Ideas of revolutionary justice, liberation, and egalitarianism seem inevitably to lead to "the Pol Pot position" of massive killing to cleanse society and culture of aliens, hybridity, and their influence. Nevertheless, everyone is hybrid.

Although the novel has an epic sweep of allusion, ranging in time from India before the Islamic conquest to the present, with Indians in contemporary Berlin supporting the Tamil struggle in Sri Lanka, its main events cover about a century, starting with a great-grandfather in the 1890s. *Half a Life* is a version of the multigenerational family story within a colonial setting and tells of a foolish father, his bad marriage, and his relationship to his son, who will eventually go to England for further education, become a writer, and tell the reader the story that comprises the novel. *Half a Life* might be regarded as a version of that autobiographical novel which continues to exist at a deep level of the imagination behind much of Naipaul's fiction.

Major themes are conquest, colonialism, its establishment by force, its history, its nature, the social and racial orders it produces, and the problems of what replaces it. The novel suggests that life has always been a series of diasporas of translations from one place to another, and what seems settled is actually undergoing a process of change. Behind the concern with imperialism is the more significant theme that life consists of people desiring more and trying to satisfy and advance themselves by conquering or tricking others. Although we create stories to give order to and to make sense of our lives, history repeats itself as a cycle of themes and variations.

Characteristic of *Half a Life* is the reliance on dialogue and the telling of the histories of characters through compressed anecdotes. The fiction is influenced by Naipaul's nonfictional reportage, in which the author has largely disappeared to be replaced by voices; or, the author has become one of the characters, explaining his perspective on events in relationship to his own experiences. Because the main character lacks in passion, the tone is flat, but the story is filled with social life economically presented, and Naipaul's technique is brilliant.

Source: Bruce King, "Review of *Half a Life* by V. S. Naipaul," in *World Literature Today*, Vol. 77, No. 1, April/June 2003, p. 90.

Patrick Marnham

In the following review, Marnham describes Half a Life *as a novel but also a topical book on contemporary political and cultural issues.*

Willie Chandran, from a family of temple priests, grows up in a maharajah's state in the last days of the Raj. Mocked at school because his middle name is 'Somerset', he discovers that he was named after a great English writer who had a stammer and who once visited his father while travelling to gather material for a book about spirituality. His father had quarreled with his own family by marrying Willie's mother, an ill-favoured and sarcastic woman of low caste. Subsequently this father abandoned all chance of a future as an engineer or doctor; he 'gave up education and unfitted himself for life'. Instead he became a holy man, taking a vow of silence and living by begging in an ashram.

Willie Chandran's childhood is spent in genteel poverty on the fringe of the maharajah's court. But he has hopes of future distinction since he is raised in the shade of the revered Mr Maugham. As Gandhi's 'civil disobedience' spreads through the Raj, Willie's childhood world becomes increasingly confused, his father's certainties dissolve and British rule collapses. Willie's view of India becomes misty and uncertain, like that of a foreigner. And his personal confusion is complicated by the enveloping chaos of Indian independence; this is the familiar world of Naipaul, where ordinary lives are swamped by political turmoil.

Half a Life is entirely set in the recent past and follows Chandran's life, or 'half life', from India to literary failure in London and finally to a Portuguese colony in Africa. These three periods in Chandran's progress act as a sort of background to destinies first glimpsed in *The Mimic Men, Guerrillas* and *A Bend in the River*. But *Half a Life* is more than a reprise; it is an unexpectedly topical book since it links Europe and Asia in a bitter political struggle and depicts some of the consequences of political decline, loss of control, post-colonial weakness, personal confusion and self-hatred, the melancholy litany of themes that support the life of Naipaul's silhouetted characters.

The interlude on the fringes of Fifties literary-political London, Fitzrovia and the slums of pre-gentrified Notting Hill is accomplished in barely 50 pages. Willie knows of Speakers' Corner as an international symbol of freedom, but when he gets there for the first time he is struck by the thought that 'the families of these men might have been glad to get them out of the house in the afternoon'. Later he is taken to lunch at Chez Victor with its little notice 'le Patron mange ici' and a glimpse of V. S. Pritchett across the room—pointed out to Willie as the main reviewer in the *New Statesman*, a paper he had seen in the college library 'full of mystery [and] English issues he didn't understand'.

This is the world of left-wing parties to which a boorish and tedious poet can be invited to recreate Proust's 'nosegay effect', like a little bit of dead fern setting the whole thing off. It is also the world of 'bedroom Marxists', so-called after the room on which their Marxism is centred, and where it stops. One of them, Percy Cato, works for a violent slum landlord who makes an incognito cameo appearance at one such party, bearing champagne. The landlord, surely a portrait of the late Peter Rachman, has 'an extraordinarily soft voice ... an accent that was not the accent of a professional man' and eyes that were 'cold and still'. He explains to Willie that as a property developer his work consists of helping elderly protected tenants in the big houses 'to move out to the leafy suburbs or a nice little country cottage'. Naipaul's jokes are as usual deadly and understated, and if anything darker. Marcus, the West African Marxist, training for presidential power, is dedicated to, or rather insatiable about, interracial sex, but his real ambition is to be the first black man to open an account at Coutts.

Willie, in contrast to his London friends, and in contrast to many of Naipaul's earlier heroes, remains an innocent. When his attempts to contact the great Somerset Maugham meet with a meaningless and senile response he abandons his hopes of becoming a successful writer in London, falls in love with Ana and sets off for Africa in a final bid to make sense of his life. In the past Naipaul has used Africa as a metaphor for disintegration and despair; but Willie Chandran discovers a different continent redolent of strength and fertility. From the sea he first observes the rivers of the northern province, very wide rivers, quiet and empty, whose frightening mouths have barred any possible road or land route. Ana had 'broken out of' Portuguese when she first came to England, regarding her native tongue as an intellectual prison. Now in this obscure corner of the colony, Willie has to learn Portuguese. His youthful unease with archaic Victorian literature develops into something more alarming; he begins to fear that he may be losing his powers of self-expression. Having first abandoned his native tongue and then the English language of his writing, he worries that he will lose the gift of speech itself. For Willie, leaving England means severing the last link with the identity of his childhood and the cultural birthright that would have been his under the Raj, if Gandhi and Nehru had not prevailed.

But in Africa he finds that he is at last able to add an important new dimension to his life with the discovery of sexual passion. As he is overwhelmed by this new happiness his thoughts turn in unexpected directions—he thinks of 'his poor father and mother who had known nothing like this moment'. As passion develops, 'the brutality of sexual life' leads to helpless obsession and then 'sexual madness', and Willie begins to feel some 'respect for the religious outlawing of sexual extremes'. When the affair ends, Africa continues, the broken-down machinery and the broken-down people, the sham grandeur of the last estate managers, an imprisoned snake in a green bottle that time will inevitably release, the abandoned shops and military barracks, the insurgents creeping past the command post and investing the town centre, the constant battle to 'squeeze comfort out of the hard land, like blood out of a stone', and 'the encroaching darkness that covers the mind'.

In *Half a Life* Naipaul remains constant to himself, awkward and uncompromising, succeeding where few novelists venture to go, steadily refusing in his own words 'to tell his readers what they already know', and once again demonstrating his ability to raise the failed lives of his characters to the tragic dimension by reference to public issues and universal truths.

Source: Patrick Marnham, "An Innocent, but Not at Home," in *Spectator*, Vol. 287, No. 9035, October 6, 2001, pp. 69–70.

James Wood

In the following review, Wood applauds Half a Life, *finding it intelligent and complex.*

It is a delight, after the spilt "fury" of Salman Rushdie's latest assemblage, to savour the furious control of V S Naipaul's new novel. Here, anger is measured in sips, and compassion, of which there is more than might be expected in one of Naipaul's late works, is subtly rationed. *Half a Life* confirms Naipaul's stature as the greatest living analyst of the colonial and postcolonial dilemma; and those who have never approved of that analysis, and have objected over the years to what they see as Naipaul's fatalism, snobbery or even racism, may find in this book the surprise of a submerged radicalism, a willingness to see things from the eyes of the disadvantaged. At times, the lion does indeed consent to lie down with the underdog.

In the simplest possible prose, in sentences dried down to pure duty, this novel unfolds its compelling story. One day, young Willie Chandran asks his father about his curious middle name. In the course of providing an explanation, the father tells Willie his life story. The son of a successful clerk and proud Brahmin, Willie's father deliberately ruined his chances of betterment by deciding, in the spirit of Gandhi (it was the 1930s), that he should abandon his college degree and submit to a political sacrifice. The sacrifice involved choosing a wife from a low caste, a "backward". Willie's father had no love

> **THIS IS HOW NAIPAUL'S INTELLIGENT NOVEL WORKS, TOO: ON THE ONE HAND, IT REMORSELESSLY EXPOSES CASTE AND RACE DISTINCTIONS AS NOTHING MORE THAN ACCIDENTS, CHOICES AND FAKE RULES; ON THE OTHER HAND, ITS RELENTLESS ATTENTION TO THOSE VERY DISTINCTIONS MAKES THEM SEEM PATHOLOGICALLY IMMOVEABLE."**

for this woman, was indeed repelled by her "backwardness". But he married her anyway. When their son, Willie, was born, his father anxiously scrutinised him to see "how much of the backward could be read in his features . . . Anyone seeing me bend over the infant would have thought I was looking at the little creature with pride." So Willie, in turn, grows up despising his cruel and cold father, and is eager to leave India. It is 1957. Willie enrolls at a college of education in London, and begins a new life there as a "colonial".

The novel is 50 pages old at this point. The story of this "sacrifice", both cruel and masochistic, is tremendously compulsive; it has the compulsion of illogical logic. Like Stavrogin's similarly masochistic marriage to a low-born woman in Dostoevsky's *The Possessed*, it is a gesture that has the veneer of principle but is in fact pathological; and like Stavrogin's act, it is so abnormal that we read on simply in order to find a solving normality. There is none, as Willie suspects—it is why he so hates his father. Its logic is simply that, having been embarked on, it must be continued to the end—a logic curiously analogous to the reading experience (which explains the deep compulsion of Dostoevsky and, in this case, of Naipaul).

Willie's father makes his sacrifice because of apparently radical, or at least progressive, impulses. But the vileness of his act, its unredeemed quality, lies in the paradox that he is not remotely "progressive" in his treatment of his low-caste wife. He is, if anything, more disdainful of his wife's disadvantage, more obsessed by caste distinctions, than he would have been if he had never married her. It is a paradox that runs like a fault line through the entire novel and provides its special richness of political

complexity. Behind the arras of the apparently political, suggests Naipaul, lies the messy corpse of our actual motives; and our actual motives may have nothing at all to do with the political.

The best example of this is found in Willie's somewhat doomed life. As an Indian student in 1950s London, suffering the usual humiliations, he finds that he is less willing to criticise his father. And as he sees how much of late-imperial Britain is actually the invention of the recent past, he also feels that the old rules of India—the caste traditions, and so on—no longer hold him: "he was free to present himself as he wished. He could, as it were, write his own revolution."

Up to a point, Willie remakes himself. He gets on in the immigrant-bohemian society of Notting Hill; he writes radio pieces for the BBC; he has a brief affair with an Englishwoman who works at the perfume counter in Debenhams; he writes a book of stories that is rather condescendingly accepted and published—here Naipaul revisits the primal scene of his own "humiliation" as a young Indian writer from Trinidad trying to "find the centre", a scenario he has repeatedly described, fictively and autobiographically.

But Willie is ultimately unable to escape his father's negative obsession with caste. He has inherited it. And in imperial or colonial societies, where Willie now lives, an obsession with caste must become an obsession with race. In London, for instance, Willie befriends Percy Cato, a Jamaican of "mixed parentage", "more brown than black". Willie likes Percy, but can't help feeling, because of Percy's blackness, that "he stood a rung or two or many rungs above Percy". Race has become caste. He meets Ana, a Portuguese African from Mozambique (she had a Portuguese grandfather), marries her, and goes to live with her on her family estate in Mozambique. There, Willie and his wife's friends are higher up the ladder than the Africans, but they are not pure Portuguese, either. Slowly Willie realises "that the world I had entered was only a half-and-half world, that many of the people who were our friends considered themselves, deep down, people of the second rank".

So the son of a Brahmin father and a "backward" mother has made it all the way up—to "the second rank". In the last third of the novel, with terse economy and unsparing acuteness, Naipaul uncovers this second-rank world, a world of braggarts, reactionaries and fakers, people who are very big in a wilderness, but who would be very small in an oasis, and who secretly know it. Nothing is finer than the portrait of the local "big shots", Jacinto and Carla Correia. Jacinto, of mixed Portuguese-African descent, has money, and has had his children educated in Lisbon—where he anxiously tells them "always to use taxis. People must never think of them as colonial nobodies."

As if it were not clear enough to Willie that this world is built on false foundations, one day, visiting a restaurant with his friends, he sees the pure-Portuguese owner abusing a black worker, "a big light-eyed mulatto man". Willie says nothing, but tells us that whenever he remembered "the big sweating man with the abused light eyes, carrying the shame of his birth on his face like a brand", he would think: "Who will rescue that man? Who will avenge him?"

Willie spends 18 years in Mozambique, and the novel ends at the moment of his decision to leave. He is in his forties. Thus the novel has covered, literally, "half a life". But Naipaul means his title more darkly, too. Willie has lived only half a life because, of mixed parentage himself, he is only "half-and-half". And Willie chose to spend most of his life in colonial Mozambique, a "half-and-half" society. More deeply, Willie is half a man because his father's baleful shadow has cut across his life, scything it in two. Notionally free to make himself anew, Willie finds that, in truth, he is doomed to repeat the sacrificial frigidity of his father's life; notionally free of the artifice of caste and race, he is in fact as imprisoned by it as his father—with the difference that at least his father chose to imprison himself, whereas Willie never asked for his own imprisonment. The repellent "sacrifice" of Willie's father has the peculiar effect of both undermining caste and inscribing it more deeply in the fabric of life. By turning caste into a decision, a choice, its bases are exposed as artificial; but by making it a curse, to be handed on from father to son, it has been fatalised, turned into a pathology.

This is how Naipaul's intelligent novel works, too: on the one hand, it remorselessly exposes caste and race distinctions as nothing more than accidents, choices and fake rules; on the other hand, its relentless attention to those very distinctions makes them seem pathologically immoveable. It is this paradoxical movement, between sympathy and coldness, between a potentially radical awareness of the disease of race and an apparently more conservative determination to insist on the permanence of that disease, that produces the novel's powerful, shifting complexity.

Those who are suspicious of Naipaul's politics will surely trace the book's ambivalence to its author and accuse him of political pessimism, even fatalism; those more disposed to Naipaul will find power in that pessimism, as well as the seeds of a cold compassion: because what Willie thinks about the abused restaurant worker might also be said, in pity, of poor trapped Willie, and even perhaps of Naipaul: "Who will rescue that man? Who will avenge him?"

Source: James Wood, "Saving Vidia," in *New Statesman*, October 1, 2001, pp. 79–80.

SOURCES

Coetzee, J. M., "V. S. Naipaul: *Half a Life*," in *Inner Workings: Literary Essays 2000–2005*, Viking, 2007, pp. 272–91.

Dooley, Gillian, *V. S. Naipaul, Man and Writer*, University of South Carolina Press, 2006, pp. 121–34.

French, Patrick, *The World Is What It Is: The Authorized Biography of V. S. Naipaul*, Alfred A. Knopf, 2008, pp. 130–43.

King, Bruce, *V. S. Naipaul*, 2nd ed., Palgrave Macmillan, 2003, pp. 180–93.

Maugham, Somerset, *A Writer's Notebook*, reprint ed., Vintage, 2009, pp. 296–305.

Megasthenes and Arrian, *Ancient India as Described by Megasthenes and Arrian: Being a Translation of the "Indika" of Magasthenes Collected by Dr. Schwabeck, and of the First Part of the "Indika" of Arrian*, translated by John Watson McCrindle, Calcutta, 1877, pp. 30–45.

Naipaul, V. S., *An Area of Darkness*, Andre Deutsch, 1964, p. 77.

———, *Half a Life*, Alfred A. Knopf, 2001.

Said, Edward, "Intellectuals in the Post-Colonial World," in *Salmagundi*, Vol. 70–71, 1986, pp. 44–64.

———, *Orientalism*, Vintage, 1979, pp. 1–112.

———, O'Brien, Conor Cruise, and John Luckacs, "The Post-Colonial Intellectual: A Discussion," in *Salmagundi*, Vol. 70–71, 1986, pp. 65–81.

Trilling, Daniel, "Rhyme and Punishment for Naipaul," in *Observer* (London, England), June 1, 2008, http://www.guardian.co.uk/books/2008/jun/01/poetry.news (accessed July 10, 2011).

FURTHER READING

Naipaul, V. S., *A House for Mr. Biswas*, Andre Deutsch, 1961.

The first of Naipaul's novels to attract international attention, *A House for Mr. Biswas* is set among the Indian immigrant community in Trinidad in which Naipaul grew up.

———, *India: A Wounded Civilization*, Alfred A. Knopf, 1977.

This is the first volume of Naipaul's Indian trilogy, three nonfiction books in which he attempts to explain India's relationship with the West and its place in the modern world.

———, *Literary Occasions: Essays*, Alfred A. Knopf, 2003.

This series of essays, from the years leading up to *Half a Life*, especially those on India and on Conrad, throw light on the novel.

Theroux, Paul, *Sir Vidia's Shadow: A Friendship across Five Continents*, Houghton Mifflin, 1998.

In this work, Theroux chronicles his long and deferential friendship with Naipaul, but includes criticism that, in places, amounts to a public attack or effort at revenge.

SUGGESTED SEARCH TERMS

V. S. Naipaul

V. S. Naipaul AND Half a Life

postmodernism AND V. S. Naipaul

sadhu

orientalism

Somerset Maugham AND V. S. Naipaul

Gandhi

Mozambique

Notting Hill Riots

immigrant literature

The Help

KATHRYN STOCKETT
2009

Set in Mississippi in 1962, Kathryn Stockett's debut novel, *The Help*, explores the discrimination and violent repression endured by African Americans during the early years of the 1960s. The novel focuses on three women, and is told from each of their points of view, as Stockett shifts the novel's first-person narration from character to character. Aibileen and Minny are both African American maids, working for powerful, and sometimes racist, white women. Skeeter is a young, rich, white woman who defies the Southern conventions of the time by utilizing her college experience to gain a degree, rather than to seek out the husband her parents expect her to find. Exposed to the racist views of her friends, Skeeter is forced to confront the deep inequities of her society. She attempts to use her own position as an aspiring writer to help Aibileen, Minny, and other African American women tell their stories and expose the truths about the way "the help" is treated by wealthy, white, southern families. Stockett's historical novel explores various aspects of the civil rights movement, and includes the death of civil rights activist Medgar Evers as a plot point. Additionally, the struggles faced by working women are examined through the character of Skeeter, who is driven to pursue a career rather than start a family. Stockett also tackles issues related to Southern notions of social class in her depiction of Celia Foote, a poor, white young woman who has married a wealthy, upper class southern

Kathryn Stockett (© *Allstar Picture Library* | *Alamy*)

gentleman, Johnny Foote. Celia is shunned by Skeeter's social circle for her perceived attempts to infiltrate the ranks of the upper class through her relationship with Johnny.

The Help quickly became a national best seller and earned critical acclaim upon its 2009 publication by Amy Einhorn Books/Putnam. It was also adapted as a film in 2011.

AUTHOR BIOGRAPHY

Born in Jackson, Mississippi, in 1969, Stockett is one of five children. She attended the University of Alabama and earned a degree in English literature and creative writing. She later worked in New York in the magazine marketing and publishing industry for nine years.

The Help was published in 2009 and is Stockett's first novel. At the end of the book, Stockett includes a section titled "Too Little, Too Late," in which she recounts her relationship with

her family's maid, Demetrie. After her parents divorced when Stockett was six years old, she states, her relationship with Demetrie became even more significant than it already was. In "Too Little, Too Late," she describes the way Demetrie comforted her during her mother's frequent absences and when her older siblings seemed to have outgrown her. In many ways, Stockett's relationship with Demetrie inspired her novel. In a 2009 biographical article for the London *Daily Mail*, Stockett writes that Demetrie began working for her grandmother in 1955 and remained with her family for thirty-two years. She describes the South of the 1970s, in which Demetrie was allowed access to white establishments only when wearing her white maid's uniform. "Even though this was the 70s and the segregation laws had changed, the 'rules' had not," Stockett notes. Although she describes her relationship with Demetrie as being extremely close, Stockett also states, with irony, that "as much as we loved Demetrie, she had a separate bathroom located on the outside of the house."

As of 2011, Stockett lived in Atlanta, Georgia, with her husband and daughter.

PLOT SUMMARY

Chapters 1–5

The Help opens with a chapter written in the first person (the narrating character refers to herself as *I*), from the point of view of an African American maid named Aibileen. The date is August of 1962, and Aibileen describes her relationship with her employers, a white family, the Leefolts. Mae Mobley, the Leefolts' two-year-old daughter, adores Aibileen. Silently critical of the unloving way Elizabeth rears Mae Mobley, Aibileen reflects on the tragic loss her own son, Treelore, when he was twenty-four years old. Stockett introduces other primary characters in the novel as they arrive at Elizabeth's home for their weekly bridge game. Skeeter pleasantly greets Aibileen, while Hilly, who arrives with her mother, Mrs. Walters, ignores the maid. Talk at the bridge game turns from Hilly's shunning of Celia Foote, a young woman trying to break into Hilly's social circle, to Mrs. Walter's maid Minny, who is Aibileen's good friend. The conversation is then steered toward Hilly's pet project, the Home Help Sanitation Initiative. Hilly hopes to insure that all white homes have a separate bathroom for their

MEDIA ADAPTATIONS

- *The Help* was adapted for film from Stockett's novel by screenwriter Tate Taylor, who also directed it. The film, which stars Emma Stone, Viola Davis, and Octavia Spenser, was produced by DreamWorks and released in 2011.
- *The Help* is available as an unabridged audio CD (fifteen CDs) published by Penguin Audio in 2009. The book is read by four actors: Jenna Lamia, Cassandra Campbell, Bahni Turpin, and Octavia Spenser. This version is also available as an MP3 file.

African American *help* to use, and she begins by pushing this idea on Elizabeth. The opening chapter makes clear that Hilly is at the helm of the white, upper-class social circle, and that her racist efforts will be a major source of conflict in the novel. Skeeter has asked Aibileen how she feels about the way she has been treated, and questions Aibileen about her own family's maid, Constantine, who departed under mysterious circumstances. The second chapter is also from Aibileen's point of view and shows her transitioning from her work in the world of whites to the black neighborhood where she lives. Back at the Leefolts', Aibileen witnesses Elizabeth attempting to convince her husband that they need to install a separate bathroom for Aibileen. Minny reports to Aibileen that Hilly is sending Mrs. Walters to a nursing home, and that Minny will be out of a job. When Celia Foote calls, asking for Elizabeth and mentioning that she is looking for a maid, Aibileen suggests she call Minny. Celia hesitates, but Aibileen, who knows that Hilly has been spreading lies about Minny, assures Celia that Elizabeth recommends Minny.

Minny's point of view is introduced in the third chapter, as she narrates her encounter with Celia. Minny finds Celia to be somewhat lower class than other white women she works for, and perceives her to be somewhat dimwitted as well,

but Celia appears to have no knowledge that Hilly has been telling everyone that Minny is a thief. Celia hires her. Minny hints at something horrible she has done to Hilly, and relates that Celia does not want her husband Johnny to know that she has hired a maid. In the fourth chapter, Minny begins to teach Celia how to cook.

Skeeter Phelan narrates the fifth chapter, in which Skeeter describes her childhood friendships with Hilly and Elizabeth, which endured through college but have begun to change as Hilly and Elizabeth have not only married but have started families as well. Skeeter is regarded as peculiar in her desire to find employment. Unlike her friends, Skeeter did not drop out of college, but graduated, unmarried. Skeeter, whose real name is Eugenia, is constantly pestered by her mother Charlotte to find opportunities to meet respectable, eligible men. Hilly has been trying to set Skeeter up with the son of a state senator. Her aims are not entirely altruistic; Hilly has hopes that her husband William will be able to win the senator's state seat when the senator runs for national office. Skeeter recalls her youth, and the way she was raised by her family's maid, Constantine.

Chapters 6–10

Skeeter receives a letter from an editor in New York, Elaine Stein, to whom Skeeter has written asking about editorial positions. Ms. Stein advises Skeeter to get a job at a local paper, which Skeeter promptly does. She finds that the *Jackson Journal*'s advice column on cleaning and housekeeping has recently lost its writer, and she is asked to fill the position vacated by the pseudonymous Ms. Myrna. Skeeter approaches Aibileen, asking if she will help her come up with the answers to the Ms. Myrna letters. Aibileen agrees, somewhat reluctantly, but refuses to offer Skeeter any information on what happened to Constantine. Skeeter confronts her mother about Constantine, but she too remains silent, saying only that she fired the maid. Continuing to talk to Aibileen about the Ms. Myrna column, Skeeter confides in Aibileen about the advice and encouragement Ms. Stein has given her, and about her dreams of becoming a writer. Aibileen reveals a little about her son, and his own dreams to write a book about what it was like to work for a white boss. Skeeter later hints that Treelore's book idea sparks one of her own.

Aibileen constantly comforts Mae Mobley against Elizabeth's neglect, verbal abuse, and sometime even the rough slap on the child's bare leg. Elizabeth hits Mae Mobley for using the bathroom Elizabeth had built so that Aibileen would not have to use the same one the family uses. Elizabeth has repeatedly parroted Hilly's belief that African Americans carry diseases that whites do not. Scolding Mae Mobley, Elizabeth yells, "This is dirty out here, Mae Mobley. You'll catch diseases! No no no!"

Aibileen simultaneously copes with the anniversary of her son's death, prepares the Leefolts' Thanksgiving dinner, and learns that her son's friend Robert was beaten and blinded by two white men because Robert accidentally used a white bathroom. Just as these events are unfolding, Skeeter asks Aibileen if she will help her with a book about what it is like to work as an African American maid for rich white women. Aibileen feels it is too dangerous. Skeeter is encouraged by Ms. Stein, the New York editor, to pursue her idea. On her date with Stuart Whitworth, Skeeter is dismayed to discover how rude Stuart is. Later, Skeeter receives a phone call from Aibileen, who tells Skeeter she will help her with the book.

At Celia Foote's home, as Christmas nears, Minny is counting down to the agreed upon day that Celia will inform her husband that Minny is working for them. After Aibileen gently attempts to convince Minny to help Skeeter with the book, Minny begins to contemplate the idea. Minny observes Celia's suspicious behavior, the way she remains so still all day, or, alternatively, the times she sneaks away to the upstairs rooms or locks herself in her bathroom. One morning, Johnny is home unexpectedly, and he happens upon Minny, who is terrified of what he will do. Yet Johnny is not surprised to discover a maid in his home, and he encourages Minny to keep letting Celia think that he does not know about Minny.

Chapters 11–15
Skeeter begins interviewing Aibileen for the book, but the situation is so tense, Aibileen vomits. Aibileen decides to write down her own story and read it to Skeeter, a process which goes much more smoothly for them both. Skeeter sends the partial manuscript to Ms. Stein for approval to continue with the project. Meanwhile, Elizabeth announces that she is pregnant. After a phone call from Ms. Stein, Skeeter presses Aibileen to convince more maids to come forward, as Ms. Stein has asked for there to be about twelve women represented in the book. Minny finally decides to help with the project. Although Skeeter is still angry with Stuart for

the way he treated her, when he seeks her out and apologizes, she relents, and the two begin seeing each other. Later, Skeeter finds and removes from the library a pamphlet itemizing the details of Jim Crow segregation laws. She is dismayed to discover that she has left her bag, containing all the notes for the book she is writing (concealed in a pocket), along with the Jim Crow laws right on top, at a Jackson Junior League (a women's group that focuses on charitable works and social activities) meeting, where Hilly found the bag. Skeeter soon realizes that Hilly has seen something that angered her in the bag, but she does not know how far Hilly has delved. Aibileen, Minny, and Skeeter continue to work on the book, worrying about what Hilly has found. The maids and their friends and families express their sorrow and fear at the shooting death of activist Medgar Evers, while Minny and Aibileen wonder what might be done to them if their own activities are discovered. At a scene at Hilly's country club, Aibileen watches an encounter between Hilly, Elizabeth, and Skeeter, and discovers that, in all likelihood, Hilly has only seen the Jim Crow law pamphlet Skeeter had, not the notes for the book. Skeeter makes an effort at covering up her beliefs.

Chapters 16–20
Aibileen continues to try to convince other maids to help with the project, and Hilly's maid, Yule May, expresses an interest in possibly telling her story. Minny's life at home is depicted, including her relationship with her abusive, alcoholic husband, Leroy. At the Footes', Minny discovers bottles that suggest that Celia has a drinking problem. Minny confronts Celia, and Celia fires her. Aibileen convinces Minny to apologize and ask for her job back. When Minny returns, she discovers Celia in the bathroom. She was pregnant and has miscarried. Minny calls Celia's doctor, and Celia explains that the bottles contained a Native American remedy intended to prevent miscarriage. Minny also reveals that Johnny knows about her.

As Skeeter's chapter opens, she indicates that the date is now 1963. She is becoming increasingly aware of the danger of her activities, which she must hide from everyone. Stuart invites Skeeter and her family to dinner at his parents' home. Initially elated to hear that Yule May will help with the book, Skeeter soon gets a letter from her. Yule May briefly explains how she has diligently saved her money so that her twin boys could both attend college. She was short only a small portion of the tuition, and confesses stealing a ring from

Hilly. Writing from the state penitentiary, Yule May apologizes for not being able to help Skeeter. At Aibileen's, eleven other maids, who have gathered to pray for Yule May and to discuss how they could raise money to send her boys to school, tell Skeeter they will help her. Skeeter soon begins the interviews and is surprised to learn there are some positive stories about the relationships between white employers and black staff that she is exploring. At Senator Whitworth's house, Stuart introduces Skeeter and her parents to his own mother and father. Stuart's former fianceé is repeatedly brought up, and Skeeter learns that the relationship ended badly, when the fianceé cheated on Stuart with a civil rights activist. When Skeeter asks Stuart if he still has feelings for his former girlfriend Patricia, he breaks up with Skeeter.

Chapters 21–25

Skeeter busies herself with the remaining interviews for the book. Hilly has been pressuring Skeeter to print the information about her Home Help Sanitation Initiative in the newsletter for the league, for which Hilly serves as president. Hilly threatens to expose Skeeter as some sort of activist for carrying around the Jim Crow pamphlet, and Skeeter subsequently types the initiative into the newsletter, but with her own twist. On Mae Mobley's birthday, the now three-year-old child insists that Aibileen, not Elizabeth, is her real mother. Later, after the newsletter has come out, it is revealed that Skeeter, who has written about Hilly's coat drive and her sanitation initiative, indicated that old toilets, rather than old coats, were to be dropped off at Hilly's front door. Hilly calls Elizabeth in a panic after finding dozens of old toilets deposited on her front lawn. Between finding the Jim Crow laws in Skeeter's bag and Skeeter's toilet prank, Hilly ascertains that Skeeter is "up to something" and convinces Elizabeth to cut Skeeter out of their social circle, as Hilly is in the process of doing. Aibileen is forbidden by Elizabeth's husband Raleigh from talking to Skeeter about the Ms. Myrna cleaning letters or about anything else. Having witnessed the way Elizabeth either ignores, slaps, or belittles her daughter, Aibileen attempts to bolster the child's self esteem. She additionally begins telling her stories in which she emphasizes the insignificance of skin color, so that Mae Mobley does not grow up to be as racist as her mother. Celia arrives unannounced at the Leefolts', asking for a chance to help out

with the Children's Benefit gala the league is planning. Elizabeth and Hilly have repeatedly refused Celia's efforts, frowning upon Celia's lower-class upbringing. Hilly harbors a particular grudge against Celia, as Celia is now married to Hilly's old boyfriend. When Celia mentions that Minny is her maid, Hilly becomes determined to figure out how Celia has hired Minny based on a recommendation that Elizabeth is credited with but that she did not give. At work at Celia's, Minny's battered face is tended to by Celia. A naked intruder is seen prowling the grounds, and Minny attempts to fight him off, but is injured. Celia remains calm and beats the man with a fireplace poker. Celia plans on attending the league's charity benefit, and Minny previews her low-cut, hot pink dress choices. Celia asks Minny why Elizabeth and Hilly despise her, and Minny underscores the significance of the fact that Celia and Johnny started dating directly after Johnny and Hilly broke up.

Chapter 25 focuses on the benefit, and unlike the other chapters in the novel, it is told in the third person and skips among a number of people for its point-of-view perspective. At the benefit, Skeeter arrives alone and is shunned by her friends. Hilly relishes her role as the league president and hostess of the event. Minny is nervous that Hilly will get her fired by telling Celia about the awful thing Minny did, something that Minny has only alluded to throughout the course of the novel. A tipsy, nervous Celia arrives in her skimpy pink dress, accompanied by Johnny. She is lusted after by every man in the room, and frowned on by every woman. As Hilly reads out the winners of the silent auction prizes, she is horrified to learn that she has won one of Minny's pies. At this moment, Celia, who has been getting increasingly more drunk as the evening progresses, approaches Hilly, and congratulates her on the pie. Angry, Hilly tries to shake off Celia, who is now gripping her arm, and assumes that Celia has arranged for Hilly to win the pie. As Hilly struggles, furiously accusing Minny of putting Celia up to something, Celia accidentally tears the cuff of Hilly's dress, then blurts loudly that she got pregnant after Hilly and Johnny broke up. After Celia vomits, Johnny takes her home. At the end of the evening, Hilly's mother, Mrs. Walters, admits that she signed Hilly up for the pie.

Chapters 26–30

Back at work at Celia's house, Minny tries to convince a despondent Celia to get out of bed.

Humiliated and rejected, Celia will not budge. Finally, Minny tells Celia the story of Hilly and the pie. She recounts the way that Hilly maliciously spread lies about Minny after Mrs. Walters was sent to the nursing home, leaving Minny jobless. She was unable to find employment, and had refused Hilly's offer to hire her, knowing how mean-spirited and manipulative Hilly was. Hilly viciously told Minny what she had done, and how Minny would never find work in Jackson again, and that she may as well work for Hilly for free at this point. Minny then told Hilly that Hilly could eat her feces (Minny uses an expletive). Later, she brought Hilly a chocolate pie, ostensibly as a peace offering. After Hilly had eaten two slices, Hilly's mother asked for some, but Minny explained that the pie was made especially for Hilly, and then she told Hilly what exactly was in the pie. Celia thanks Minny for telling her, and then uses the information to get back at Hilly, noting on the check that she writes to Hilly to cover the cost of the torn dress that the check is for "Two-Slice Hilly." Meanwhile, Skeeter is told she must send a completed manuscript to Ms. Stein six weeks earlier than the original deadline. Skeeter and the remaining maids work long hours to finish in time. Skeeter's mother, thin and ill throughout much of the novel, is getting worse. Stuart attempts to repair his relationship with Skeeter. Aibileen finally agrees to tell Skeeter Constantine's story, as Ms. Stein feels that Skeeter's relationship with her own maid should also be documented in the book. Skeeter learns that Constantine, who had a white father, gave birth out of wedlock to a very pale daughter, one who could pass for white. Knowing the double discrimination the daughter would experience from both whites and blacks due to her mixed heritage, Constantine decided it is best if to send her daughter to an orphanage in Chicago. She almost immediately regretted her decision, but it was too late. The daughter returned as a young woman a number of years later, seeking to rebuild a relationship with her mother. Here, Aibileen stops and hands Skeeter an envelope containing the rest of the story. Skeeter returns home, reads it, and confronts her mother. Skeeter learns that Constantine's grown daughter, Lulabelle, entered the Phelan home through the front door, passing as a white, and attempted to infiltrate Charlotte Phelan's DAR (Daughters of the American Revolution) meeting. Lulabelle confronted Charlotte and spat in her face. Charlotte was furious, and forbade Constantine from having any contact with the daughter. Constantine and

Lulabelle subsequently returned to Chicago, where Constantine died soon after. Skeeter completes her story and mails the manuscript, not certain it will reach Ms. Stein in time.

After learning that her mother is dying of cancer and perhaps only has a few months to live, Skeeter begins spending more time at home. After a few weeks, her mother appears to go into remission. Skeeter, who has gradually let Stuart back into her life, begins to see him more regularly. Stuart proposes, but before she accepts, Skeeter explains as generally as she can, without implicating anyone, what she has been working on over the past year. Stuart is shocked and states that he feels as if he no longer even knows Skeeter. He takes back his ring and departs, the proposal retracted. By mid-January, Skeeter learns that Harper and Row has decided to publish the book. When the early editions of the book arrive, Skeeter shares them with Aibileen, who distributes them to the other maids. Minny, who has revealed that she is pregnant, suspects that her husband has gleaned that she is involved in something. She fears his response.

Chapters 31–34

As Hilly begins to read the book, she suspects the maids are all those employed by women she knows. She guesses at identities and encourages her friends to fire their help. Minny waits anxiously to hear that Hilly has finished the book, which ends with a chapter narrated by Minny and describing the pie incident. Minny felt strongly about including it, thinking that Hilly would not want anyone to know about the pie and would convince everyone that the book with the fictionalized setting is not actually about Jackson. Minny, Skeeter, and Aibileen agreed that this would, in part, protect the maids from Hilly's likely revenge. Skeeter begins to hear positive stories arising from the publication of the book. Later, Hilly confronts Skeeter, indicating both her certainty that the book is about Jackson and her desperation to spread the misinformation that the maids in the book are not from Jackson. Skeeter is offered a job as a copy editor's assistant in New York, which Minny and Aibileen encourage her to take.

In the final chapter, Skeeter tells Aibileen that the editor of the *Jackson Journal* is willing to let Aibileen take over the Ms. Myrna column. Aibileen gets a call from a terrified Minny, who has been beaten, while pregnant, by Leroy. With Aibileen's encouragement, Minny decides to finally leave Leroy. At the Leefolt residence the next morning, Aibileen enters a quiet house. Hilly, with a silent but submissive Elizabeth at her side, fires Aibileen on Elizabeth's behalf. Hilly has figured out that a chapter in the book pertains to Elizabeth and her relationship with Aibileen, and she accuses Aibileen of stealing some of the silverware that Hilly has lent to Elizabeth. Aibileen denies this. Hilly threatens to press charges against Aibileen, but Aibileen reminds Hilly that she knows a secret about her. Mae Mobley and the new baby, Mae Mobley's brother Ross, now nearly a year old, are despondent after Elizabeth tells them Aibileen must leave. Aibileen sets on a new course, contemplating a possible career as a writer.

"Too Little, Too Late"

This section at the end of Stockett's book recounts the author's own experiences as a young white child being raised by an African American maid in the South in the 1970s.

CHARACTERS

Constantine Bates

Constantine appears in the novel only through recollection. She was the Phelan family maid and seemed like a mother to Skeeter. After having a baby who appeared white due to her own racial mix, Constantine attempts to raise the child, but quickly learns firsthand the way the child is and will be discriminated against by both the black and white communities. Constantine gives her daughter up for adoption. Briefly reunited with her daughter after the child is grown, Constantine moves to Chicago with her but dies three weeks later.

Lulabelle Bates

Lulabelle is Constantine's daughter. Like Constantine, she is not a player in the action of the novel but is recalled in Skeeter's efforts to discover why Constantine left. She is given Constantine's address by her adoptive family as a young woman and returns to Jackson to both reunite with her mother and to attack Charlotte Phelan for her hypocrisy. Entering the Phelan home for a (white) social event, Lulabelle reveals her identity and points out to a furious Charlotte how differently she treated her when she thought she was

white. Lulabelle spits in Charlotte's face, an act that ultimately results in Constantine's dismissal.

Louvenia Brown

Louvenia is one of the maids whose story is included in Skeeter's book. She works for Lou Anne Templeton and discusses the positive aspects of her experience. Louvenia cares for her grandson after he is beaten and blinded.

Robert Brown

Robert is a young man who accidentally used a toilet meant for white people and was beaten by two white men with a tire iron. Barely surviving the attack, Robert was blinded. His grandmother Louvenia cares for him after he returns home from the hospital.

Aibileen Clark

Aibileen is one of the novel's protagonists. She works as a maid for the Leefolt family and prefers to work for families with young children. Tending to little ones is her specialty, but as the children grow older and begin to take on their parents' views that blacks are inferior to whites, Aibileen moves on. Mae Mobley Leefolt is very attached to Aibileen, and Aibileen dedicates herself to changing the child's view that she is a bad girl, an impression Mae Mobley has gotten from her mother's verbal abuse. Mae Mobley's mother often scolds or neglects, and sometimes hits, her daughter, and Aibileen sees the effects of this treatment on Mae Mobley. After Hilly attempts to completely thwart Aibileen's friend Minny's chances of finding work, Aibileen agrees to help Skeeter with the book she proposed. Finding that it is easier to write her own story rather than be interviewed by Skeeter, Aibileen crafts prose that impresses and moves Skeeter. Aibileen gently convinces first Minny and then a number of other maids to work with Skeeter on the anonymous collection of personal histories. Aibileen is cautious in the actions she takes, in working with Skeeter and with telling Mae Mobley "secret stories" about the green-skinned "Martin Luther King," but she is determined to make a difference in her own way. She is depicted as wise and loving, a trusted confidant to friends like Minny, and an effective co-conspirator with Skeeter. Skeeter offers Aibileen the housekeeping advice column after she decides to take the New York position she was offered, and Aibileen begins to envision a new life for herself. After she says goodbye to Mae Mobley and Ross Lee-folt, Aibileen re-imagines her future as a writer.

Treelore Clark

Treelore was Aibileen's son. He was killed in a work-related accident when he was twenty-four.

Yule May Crookle

Yule May is Hilly Holbrook's maid. Attempting to send her twin boys to college, Yule May is short on the tuition payment and asks Hilly for a small loan, which Hilly refuses to give her. Yule May steals a ring from Hilly, is subsequently discovered, and is sent to jail. Hilly's connections insure the incarceration is for a much longer period than the crime would normally have elicited. Yule May's fate inspires a number of other maids to come forward and tell their stories to Skeeter for her book.

Celia Foote

Celia Foote is Johnny's wife. She comes from a poor family and desperately seeks to be included in Hilly's social circle. Perceived as white trash, Celia is repeatedly refused access to Hilly and Elizabeth, who insist that there is nothing Celia can help with for the Children's Benefit gala. In addition to the disappointments Celia deals with on the social front, she has also suffered through four miscarriages. Johnny was only informed about the first, and since then, Celia has taken increasingly drastic measures to remain pregnant. This is the primary reason she has hired Minny, so that she can lie still, thinking that if she does not exert herself, she will not miscarry. Celia, as Minny points out, does not see the lines that separate blacks and whites, and upper and lower class whites in Jackson. Minny is unprepared for her white lady to eat lunch with her, ask her to teach her how to cook, and to rely on her as a friend. Celia defends Minny, protecting her from the naked intruder, further forcing Minny to question her own views about Celia, and about her perspectives regarding white people.

Johnny Foote

Johnny Foote is a wealthy Southern gentleman who used to date Hilly. He is now married to Celia and is tolerant of her quirky ways. Johnny is depicted as fair and good-natured, particularly in his treatment of Minny when he discovers she has been secretly hired by Celia.

Mrs. Fredericks

Mrs. Fredericks is Elizabeth's mother. She is portrayed as a wealthy, cold woman who displays little affection toward her daughter and even less to her granddaughter, Mae Mobley.

Hilly Holbrook

Hilly Holbrook, along with Elizabeth Leefolt, are childhood friends of Skeeter Phelan. Together, the young women attended the University of Mississippi, although Skeeter was the only one to graduate. Like Elizabeth, Hilly met her husband at college, and she has two young children when the novel opens. Hilly is instantly recognizable as the head of Jackson's white, upper-class social circle. She is president of the Jackson chapter of the Junior League, a women's organization that raises money for charity but also serves as the center of social life for the women in Jackson. From the onset of the novel, Hilly pushes a segregationist agenda, pursuing her Home Help Sanitation Initiative, designed to insure that all white homes have a separate bathroom for their black help to use. She also expresses her belief that blacks carry diseases that whites do not, that they are dirty, and that they should not be taught at the same schools as whites. Hilly manipulates the women in her social circle to help pursue her aims, and she effectively bans Skeeter from the group when she expresses her distaste for Hilly's agenda. After Hilly attempts to manipulate and blackmail Minny into working for her, she is the object of Minny's own revenge, when she eats a pie Minny has made for her, a pie that contains Minny's own excrement. Horrified and humiliated, Hilly is determined to keep the incident a secret. Minny writes about the pie, anonymously, in Skeeter's book. Although she sought to have every maid associated with the book fired or jailed, Hilly back pedals after reading the last chapter. She is forced to convince her friends that the book is not about Jackson after all. At the same time, a jealous Hilly seeks to humiliate Celia Foote by excluding her as much as possible from her social circle. Hilly is furious to discover that Celia has hired Minny and suspects that Celia knows about the pie. She is effectively silenced when Celia confirms her knowledge by referring to Hilly as "Two-Slice Hilly."

William Holbrook

William Holbrook is Hilly's husband. He possesses Hilly-inspired aspirations to run for the state Senate seat vacated by Senator Whitworth, who is seeking election to the United States Senate. William loses his bid for the seat.

Leroy Jackson

Leroy is Minny's husband. He has a history of alcoholism and domestic abuse. Minny insists to Aibileen that he does not hit her when she is pregnant, and that he has never harmed the children. Near the close of the novel, Leroy does strike the pregnant Minny, and she finally takes steps toward leaving him.

Minny Jackson

Minny plays a primary role in the novel and speaks in the first person in a number of chapters throughout the novel. She is Aibileen's best friend. Minny prides herself on her ability to stand up for herself, but she knows that being perceived as sassy has lost her some of her jobs as well. She is alternately proud of her strength and ashamed that her husband beats her. As the novel opens, Minny is working as the maid of Mrs. Walters, Hilly's mother. When Hilly puts her mother in a nursing home, Minny finds herself out of work. After refusing Hilly's job offer, Minny finds it difficult to get hired by anyone else, because the vindictive Hilly has told everyone that Minny is a thief. With Aibileen's help, though, Minny is hired by Celia Foote, whom she repeatedly describes as crazy. Minny carries a secret with her, which she describes as the "Terrible Awful Thing" she did. Near the novel's conclusion, she reveals the details of the secret to Celia, explaining that after Hilly so self-righteously insisted that Minny had no choice but to work for Hilly now that Hilly had ruined her reputation, Minny tells Hilly that she can eat her excrement, although Minny's choice of words is a bit more vivid. Later, Minny allows Hilly to think that she wants to apologize. When she brings Hilly a chocolate pie, Hilly, gloating about her certainty that Minny would change her mind, devours two slices of the pie. She exclaims how delicious it is and asks Minny what is in it. Minny tells her. A horrified Hilly attempts to keep this event, witnessed by her mother, Mrs. Walters, a secret. Minny uses this to her advantage, knowing that if she lets Skeeter use this story in the book, they will all be protected from Hilly's wrath and vengeance, because she will not allow anyone to know that the pie story is about her. Proving herself to be clever, funny, and strong, Minny at last finds the strength to take her children and leave her abusive husband at the end of the novel.

Elizabeth Leefolt

Elizabeth is a childhood friend of Skeeter and Hilly. Like Hilly, she left the University of Mississippi before graduating after snagging a husband. Wife of Raleigh and mother of Mae Mobley, and later, Ross, Elizabeth is characterized as an unloving mother. She is utterly devoted to Hilly, and her position in Jackson's social elite is of primary importance. When Hilly presses her to have a bathroom built for Aibileen, Elizabeth insures that the request is fulfilled. She expresses moments of overt racism, as when she spanks her daughter for using Aibileen's toilet, telling her daughter how dirty it is and that she could catch diseases. When Mae Mobley plays with Aibileen's comb, Elizabeth asks Aibileen to bathe the child early that day. Extremely self-conscious about the fact that she and Raleigh are not as wealthy as Hilly or others in their social circle, Elizabeth knows that to retain her social standing, she must do so through her fealty to Hilly. Hilly's censure of Skeeter puts Elizabeth in an awkward position. She seems reluctant to shun her friend but does so anyway. She refuses to defend Skeeter when Hilly verbally accosts her at the country club, and she turns away at the women's league meetings when she realizes Hilly is watching them. Elizabeth seems unaware that one of the stories in *Help*, Skeeter's anonymously compiled book, was written about her by Aibileen. Hilly is certain of it though, and she convinces Elizabeth to fire Aibileen on the pretext that Aibileen stole silverware from the set Elizabeth has borrowed from Hilly. Elizabeth cannot voice the words, and Hilly fires Aibileen on Elizabeth's behalf, while Elizabeth stares meekly at the L-shaped crack in her dining room table, perhaps finally making the connection between that crack and the one described by the maid in the book.

Mae Mobley Leefolt

Mae Mobley is the two-year-old daughter of Raleigh and Elizabeth Leefolt. Caring for Mae Mobley is a large portion of Aibileen's job. Mae Mobley is often harshly criticized by her mother, and she turns to Aibileen for comfort, even insisting at one point that Aibileen is her real mother. Aibileen attempts to strengthen the child's opinion of herself by repeating to her how good and kind she is. Aibileen additionally tries to inculcate in Mae Mobley an understanding of black and white that differs from what she observes in the world around her.

Raleigh Leefolt

Raleigh Leefolt is Elizabeth's husband. He works as an accountant and is not as professionally successful as Elizabeth hoped he would be. Raleigh disagrees with Elizabeth's insistence that they build a separate bathroom for Aibileen, as it will be expensive, but Elizabeth wins the fight.

Ross Leefolt

Ross Leefolt is the infant son of Elizabeth and Raleigh. Aibileen observes that Elizabeth is far more affectionate and loving with Ross than with Mae Mobley.

Pascagoula

Pascagoula is the Phelans' maid, hired after Constantine's departure.

Carlton Phelan

Carlton Phelan is Charlotte's husband and Skeeter's father. Although his estate, Longleaf, is a former plantation, Carlton is now essentially a cotton farmer with several African Americans in his employ. He surprises Skeeter with the liberal views he expresses to Senator Whitworth.

Carlton Phelan, Jr.

The younger Carlton Phelan is Skeeter's older brother. Carlton's relationship with Skeeter is affectionate, although their time together is limited, as Carlton is studying law. Skeeter perceives Carlton to be her parents' favorite.

Charlotte Phelan

Charlotte Phelan is the wife of Carlton Phelan and mother to Carlton, Jr., and Skeeter Phelan. Charlotte has long despaired that Skeeter will never find a husband. She fears her daughter is too tall, too frizzy-haired, and too unconventional in her desire to pursue a career. Initially eager for Skeeter to pursue a relationship with Stuart Whitworth, after the couple breaks up, Charlotte remains cool toward Stuart, even after he begins to show interest in Skeeter once again. Thin and ill throughout the novel, Charlotte is diagnosed with cancer. Eventually she reveals to Skeeter the truth about Constantine's departure, and her own role in it. Although she is often perceived by Skeeter to have racist views and to have been overly critical of Skeeter throughout her entire childhood and young adulthood, Charlotte's softer side is exposed through her illness. Skeeter begins to perceive her mother's strengths and the ferocity of Charlotte's desire to

protect her children. At the novel's end, Charlotte's cancer is in remission.

Eugenia "Skeeter" Phelan

Eugenia Phelan, nicknamed Skeeter as an infant by her brother, who thought his skinny, long-limbed baby sister looked like a mosquito, is as critical of her own appearance as her mother is. From the onset of the novel, in her disparaging remarks to Hilly about Hilly's views on separate bathrooms for whites and blacks, Skeeter's liberal ideas are exposed. Unlike her childhood friends Hilly and Elizabeth, Skeeter did not find her husband in college. Instead, she graduated from the University of Mississippi and began looking for work. After receiving advice from New York editor Elaine Stein, Skeeter approaches the *Jackson Journal* about a job, and she is immediately hired to write the housekeeping advice column penned by the pseudonymous Ms. Myrna. She enlists Aibileen's help, as she knows nothing about cleaning or keeping house. Observant of Aibileen's treatment by Elizabeth and Hilly, Skeeter asks Aibileen if she wishes she could change the way things are. Aibileen thinks Skeeter is horribly naïve to even ask this question. Eventually, though, Skeeter develops the idea of a book concerned with the experiences of African American maids working in the homes of Jackson's white, elite women, and convinces Aibileen to help her. Stumbling through the rise and fall of her brief romance with Stuart, Skeeter doggedly works on the book while attempting to keep her activities secret from Hilly, Elizabeth, and her own family. Hilly suspects that Skeeter is involved in activist activities. Skeeter's prank with the league newsletter, in which she instructs people to leave old toilets on Hilly's lawn, and the pamphlet of Jim Crow laws that Hilly finds in Skeeter's bag convince Hilly that Skeeter needs to be cut out of her circle of friends. Skeeter is upset but undaunted and sees the book through to publication. Throughout the course of the novel, Skeeter evolves from a naïve, privileged, idealistic young woman into an individual with a deeper understanding of those outside her immediate society of friends and family. She experiences the fear of the African American maids who have agreed to help her, as they face very real dangers in choosing to come forward, and she begins to see her peers in a new light as well. While she regards Hilly with bitterness and contempt and pities Elizabeth as Hilly's unwitting pawn, she comprehends that she played her own role in cutting people out of her life, just as Hilly did. She completely disregarded

Lou Anne Templeton, for example, as another of Hilly's sycophants, but later revises her view after Lou Anne confides in her. As the novel closes, Skeeter's book has been widely read and the maids who contributed to it have indeed been protected by Minny and her inclusion of the pie story. Skeeter accepts a job in New York and prepares for her new life.

Elaine Stein

Ms. Stein is an editor at Harper and Row, the publishing company Skeeter originally contacts seeking work. Ms. Stein advises Skeeter throughout the novel, encouraging her to get a job, to flesh out ideas for something to write about, and to keep working and writing. Near the novel's conclusion, after the publication of Skeeter's book, Ms. Stein secures an editorial position (as an assistant to a copy editor) for Skeeter at another publisher in New York.

Lou Anne Templeton

Lou Anne is a young woman whom Hilly selects to replace Skeeter in the weekly bridge game she and her friends play. Skeeter has been ousted after the toilet prank. Lou Anne perpetually wears long sleeves, even in the heat of summer, and attributes this to eczema (a skin condition). Lou Anne later confides to Skeeter that the sleeves hid scars from her suicide attempts. She tells Skeeter that Hilly wanted her to fire her maid after the book's publication, but that talking with Louvenia, her maid, is the only thing that keeps her going some days. Reading about Louvenia's positive assessment of her in the book has strengthened Lou Anne.

Patricia van Devender

Patricia does not appear in the novel but is referred to with some regularity by Stuart Whitworth. Patricia is Stuart's former fiancée. She had an affair with a civil rights activist and, subsequently, her engagement to Stuart was terminated.

Mrs. Walters

Mrs. Walters is Hilly's elderly mother. Minny works as her maid until Hilly decides to put Mrs. Walters in a nursing home. Critical of her daughter, Mrs. Walters finds Minny's prank hilarious. At the Children's Benefit, she signs Hilly up to win Minny's chocolate pie in the silent auction and delights in her daughter's horrified response.

Francine Whitworth

Mrs. Whitworth is the senator's wife and Stuart's mother. She discourages the senator from bringing up Stuart's ex-fiancée during the dinner with the Phelans.

Senator "Stooley" Whitworth

Senator Whitworth is Stuart's father. During the Whitworth-Phelan dinner, the senator expresses views on civil rights that are far more liberal than the public stances he has taken, sharing similar opinions with Skeeter's father. The senator drinks heavily and confides to Skeeter that Stuart was deeply wounded by the end of his previous relationship. The senator wins his bid in the election for the U.S. Senate seat.

Stuart Whitworth

Stuart is the son of Senator and Mrs. Whitworth. Hilly makes repeated attempts to set Stuart up with Skeeter. On their first date, he is extremely rude to her. He later reveals that he was not ready to begin dating again, and as the novel progresses, Stuart reveals that not only did his former fiancée cheat on him but she did so with a civil rights activist. He implies that this was a betrayal to his family, as it could have jeopardized his father's career. Later, when Skeeter gives Stuart an overview of her own activities, Stuart is dumbfounded and takes back the ring, and the proposal, which he has just presented to Skeeter. He is stunned that she would even care about such things as the relationship between blacks and whites in Jackson.

THEMES

Civil Rights

The burgeoning civil rights movement is a primary focus in *The Help*. Stockett uses historical events to draw attention to the racial conflicts prevalent in the South in the 1960s. In the novel, civil rights activists are regarded as troublemakers by many white Southerners, including Skeeter's one-time boyfriend Stuart Whitworth. Liberalism and activism are also firmly associated with those from the North, with Yankees. Describing the way he was cheated on, Stuart is angered not only that his fiancée was unfaithful but by the fact that the man was a civil rights activist. He feared the incident could have destroyed his father's career. He states, "If it ever got out who he was, that Senator

TOPICS FOR FURTHER STUDY

- The civil rights movement serves as a backdrop in Stockett's novel. Select one of the civil rights activists Stockett mentions, such as Medgar Evers, Rosa Parks, or Martin Luther King, Jr. Write a biographical essay in which you discuss the significance of the individual to the civil rights movement. Your essay should include facts about the individual's youth and upbringing, his or her role in the movement, and the circumstances surrounding his or her death. Be sure to cite all of your sources.

- Stockett touches very briefly on negative stereotypes of Native Americans in *The Help*, enough to underscore that they were as much victims of the racism of the 1960s as African Americans were. Using sources such as the young-adult resource *Red Power: The Native American Civil Rights Movement* (2007) by Troy Johnson, research this movement in American history. Write a report in which you chronicle the discrimination faced by Native Americans and their process of organizing to protest against racist beliefs and laws. Share your findings with the class by creating a visual presentation (a PowerPoint presentation, a collage featuring newspaper headlines and photos, or a detailed time line) that summarizes your written report.

- The bombing of a church and the marches in Birmingham, Alabama, that followed are mentioned by Stockett in her novel. Christopher Paul Curtis's prize-winning novel, *The Watsons Go to Birmingham—1963*, features an African American family living in Michigan who journey to Birmingham in 1963. The novel, published in 1995, begins

as a humorous story about the Watsons. As they prepare for their trip to Birmingham, their decisions are shaped by the culture of discrimination of the time. In Birmingham, the family witnesses the 16th Street Baptist Church bombing. With a book group, read Curtis's novel and compare its treatment of racial conflict and discrimination with Stockett's. How do the authors use humor in their works? In what ways are the characters in the novel exposed to or become victims of racism? Create an online discussion of the book with your group as a blog, and discuss these topics and your personal responses to the novels.

- In *The Help*, Stockett mentions the ongoing conflict in Vietnam, which will soon evolve into a full-scale war between Communist North Vietnam and South Vietnam, aided by U.S. advisors and eventually troops. Vietnamese poet Nguyen Thi Vinh's poem "Thoughts of Hanoi" offers a Vietnamese perspective on the war. Read the poem (available at http://www.globaled.org/vietnamandcambodia/lessons/v_lesson_04_reading.php). Contemplate the poet's depiction of pre-war childhood experiences and how these are contrasted with the violence of the war. Write an essay in which you analyze the poem's themes, imagery, style, and structure. Using the knowledge you have gained from your study of the poem, perform a dramatic reading of it for your class. Alternatively, make your essay available to your class by creating a Web page with a link to the text of the poem.

Whitworth's daughter-in-law got in bed with a Yankee goddamn activist, it would ruin him." When Skeeter is stopped by the police on her way to the black part of town to see Aibileen, she asks the officer if something has happened.

He responds, "Some Yankee trash stirring up trouble. We'll catch em, ma'am."

Not long after, Medgar Evers, a local NAACP (National Association for the Advancement of Colored People) activist is shot and

The novel takes place in the racially segregated south. *(William Lovelace / Shutterstock.com)*

Minny and Aibileen discuss what might happen to them if their activities are discovered. Thinking about the armed whites that attack blacks, Aibileen notes, "Ain't no colored policemans." Aibileen and Minny agree that if they are caught, the results would be disastrous. Still, Aibileen attempts to reassure her friend, telling her, "We ain't doing civil rights here. We just telling stories like they really happen," attempting to distance herself and Minny from anything that could be described as activist in nature. Still, they pray for the Evers family. Aware of planned sit-ins at the Woolworth's lunch counter, events organized and attended by their church members, Minny and Aibileen opt not to participate, not because they do not believe in the aims of the civil rights movement but because they question the methods. Minny expresses disdain for the idea of sitting down and not fighting back.

While Minny and Aibileen are keenly aware of the activities of and punishments doled out by whites to civil rights activists, Skeeter is almost completely out of touch with the civil rights movement taking hold in other parts of the country. She is informed about Martin Luther King's March on Washington by her New York editor, Ms. Stein. Skeeter watches a young black man being escorted into the University of Mississippi, but she is asked to turn off the television and to not watch such things with their maid; Skeeter does not protest, nor does she discuss the issue further. Her ambivalence is obvious: "I am neither thrilled nor disappointed by the news that they might let a colored man into Ole Miss, just surprised." As the novel progress, Skeeter begins to become more knowledgeable about the danger into which Minny, Aibileen, and the other maids are knowingly stepping, yet she is not aroused to pursue the cause of civil rights. She is aware that the young black man who was beaten with a tire iron and blinded, after accidentally using a white restroom, was someone Aibileen knew personally. She reads about the incident in the *Jackson Journal* without much of a reaction. When Skeeter interviews Louvenia and hears about the incident directly, what moves her is that Louvenia's boss gave Louvenia time off and sat with Louvenia while the injured grandson was in surgery.

To some degree, the racism prevalent in the Southern culture of the 1960s gradually becomes increasingly apparent to Skeeter. Helping the maids to tell their stories is Skeeter's way of acknowledging the presence of such racism. In this way, she is made more knowledgeable by the novel's end. Yet the aims and significance of the civil rights movement remain largely uncontemplated by Skeeter. Furthermore, the movement is firmly condemned by whites like Hilly and Stuart.

Women's Rights

Skeeter is acutely aware that as a wealthy young woman in the South in the 1960s, she is expected to marry, and marry well. Her mother expects this, as do her friends, but Skeeter is determined to graduate from college and find a job. Skeeter is aware of how unconventional, and unpopular, her aims are. She states, "What I needed to do was find an apartment in town, the kind of building where single, plain girls lived, spinsters, secretaries, teachers." She realizes that where she sees independence, others, such as her mother, see loneliness and failure. Skeeter's mother even asks Skeeter if she might be gay. Comparing the help-wanted ads in the local paper, Skeeter notes discrepancies. There are few companies seeking female employees. Of the three listings, two focus on the female applicant's physical appearance. "Poise, manners & a smile" are required for a sales position, while the secretary job offering indicates that the applicant must be "trim, young" and will not be required to type. In the "Help Wanted: Male" section of the paper, there are four columns of job listings, and the pay is better. Ms. Stein, the New York editor, advises Skeeter to seek a job at the local paper and to be expected to make copies and fix her boss's coffee. The discrepancies in opportunities and wages between men and women at this time are the focus of a nascent women's rights movement. Skeeter remains unaware of the movement, yet she is nevertheless attuned to the challenges she faces in the workplace.

STYLE

First-Person Multiple Narration

In *The Help*, Stockett employs multiple point-of-view characters. Three characters—Aibileen, Minny, and Skeeter—narrate the action of the story from their own perspectives. Their stories are told in the first person, meaning they refer to themselves as *I*. In this way, Stockett provides intimate details about the lives of these three very different women. The use of first-person narration allows the reader access to each woman's thoughts, but it also provides the reader with knowledge of the discrepancies that often exist between what a person says and what she is thinking. Minny and Aibileen live in two distinctly different worlds. Their daily lives are filled with responses of "Yes ma'am" to orders given by their employers. They observe an array of events and activities within their employers' homes that they cannot speak of inside that home, for their viewpoint is seldom requested. To speak their thoughts outside the home is risky as well, for speaking against one's employing family could lead to dismissal. Like Aibileen and Minny, Skeeter's thoughts do not often mirror what she says aloud. She must obfuscate, attempting to deflect attention away from her dissenting opinions and actions that could be construed as troublemaking. The first-person thoughts provided by the three women offer an array of insights that could not be offered to the reader if the novel was presented through third-person narration (in which the point of view character is referred to by a narrator as *he* or *she*), or by a single narrator. In addition, each of the narrators has a stylistic difference in their narrative voice, which reflects their position in society. Skeeter's grammar is correct, and her vocabulary is educated, while Aibileen and Minny, who have not had the advantage of a college education, write the way they would speak in conversation.

Historical Realism

Stockett employs historical realism in *The Help*. Historical realism is a mode of writing in which the author represents a particular time period in a manner designed to portray for the reader a true sense of that era's culture and social atmosphere. Stockett's novel focuses on the early 1960s. She incorporates actual historical events into her narration. In addition to mentioning events such as the assassination of civil rights activist Medgar Evers, Stockett also mentions, in passing, other factual moments in history. The characters observe details pertaining to Martin Luther King, Jr.'s March on Washington, the Vietnam War, and the assassination of President Kennedy. The space program is mentioned, as are the development of the birth control pill and Valium. The feel of the time period is also evoked in conversations between the characters, as when Elizabeth discusses with her friends a trip taken to California. She mentions the new trends in home decor, the sleek, modern looking furnishings. In another scene, Skeeter listens to a Bob Dylan song on the radio. Such details underscore the sense that the story is unfolding in a distinctly different time period, one in which the metal tab to open a beer can is a new invention and some women wear short dresses, well above the knee. By incorporating these elements into the fabric of the story, Stockett establishes for the reader the historic, cultural framework within which the events of the story may be better understood.

HISTORICAL CONTEXT

Jim Crow Laws

In *The Help*, Skeeter finds a pamphlet outlining legislation that has become known as the Jim Crow laws. *Jim Crow* was a term used to refer to the institutionalized racism that prevailed in the South, and elsewhere in the country, from the post-Reconstruction era through the mid-1960s. The term originated from a song performed by a white actor who wore blackface makeup and created an exaggerated, stereotypical black character. The Jim Crow character became a stock figure in traveling shows and gradually came into popular usage as a racial epithet for African Americans.

The legislation and culture of the Jim Crow era emphasized a number of core beliefs, including the notion that whites were inherently superior to blacks, and that sexual relationships between the races would produce an inferior mixed race. Many laws were therefore designed to keep the races separated so that such unions would not occur. It was believed that, if blacks were treated equally, relationships between the races would become more likely. Jim Crow laws also advocated violence when necessary in order to keep blacks separate from whites. Beatings and lynchings were common. The legalized separation of the races was enforced based on the 1896 Supreme Court case, *Plessy v. Ferguson*, in which it was deemed that separation was legal and legitimate, provided that equal services were provided to both races. The case is famous for the phrase "separate but equal."

Despite apparent legal equalities in terms of voting rights, for example, blacks were discriminated against by the existence of laws that had not been repealed. Poll taxes were levied against poor blacks; if one could not pay the tax at the polling place, one could not vote. Literacy tests were similarly discriminatory. Blacks who used white facilities or who were perceived to be interacting with whites in an inappropriate manner were subject to punishment by lynch laws, which sanctioned violence and murder of blacks. Lynchings were not only hangings. Blacks were often shot, burned at the stake, beaten to death, or dismembered. Even after various laws were gradually repealed, the notion of Jim Crow etiquette and the culture of fear it inspired remained for many years after.

The Civil Rights Movement in the 1960s

The civil rights movement was spurred by the 1954 Supreme Court decision in the case *Brown v. Board of Education*, in which it was ruled that the racial segregation of public schools was in fact unconstitutional. This decision essentially overturned the "separate but equal" notion engendered by the *Plessy v. Ferguson* decision of 1896. However, many Southern states fought this decision, believing it was up to institutions and states to decide for themselves what was appropriate. Sit-ins and other protests became common in the early 1960s, as blacks asserted, peacefully, their right to equal service at lunch counters, and equal access to public education.

Just prior to John F. Kennedy's election in 1960, Kennedy was pivotal in obtaining a release from jail for Martin Luther King, Jr., the rising star of the civil rights movement, who had been arrested as he led a protest in Georgia. Kennedy became actively involved in civil rights activities following his election as well. In an event covered by Stockett in *The Help*, Kennedy urged the governor of Mississippi to enforce the law and allow African American student James Meredith admission to the University of Mississippi. After sending federal marshals to escort Meredith to campus, rioting broke out, resulting in two deaths and dozens of injuries. Kennedy then mobilized the National Guard, sent federal troops to the University of Mississippi's campus, and insured that Meredith was able to register for classes.

Medgar Evers, an organizer for the NAACP (National Association for the Advancement of Colored People), aided Meredith in his efforts to attend the University of Mississippi. Evers was assassinated outside his home in Jackson,

The story looks at the lives of African American maids in Mississippi in the1960s. (michaeljung / Shutterstock.com)

Mississippi, in 1963. That same year, King organized massive protests in Birmingham, Alabama, seeking an end to the segregation there. King was arrested, but his supporters organized more marches. Police dogs and high-pressure fire hoses were used to subdue the protestors, and more than one thousand people were arrested. King organized another march in 1963, his historic March on Washington, in which more than 200,000 Americans, representing all races, celebrated the anniversary of the Emancipation Proclamation. During this event, King delivered his famous "I Have a Dream" speech.

The civil rights movement was instrumental in the development of civil rights legislation that was entering Congress in 1963. Kennedy was assassinated before the bill was passed. Full legal equality for all races was finally achieved in 1964 with the passage of the Civil Rights Act under President Lyndon B. Johnson, yet the discrimination African Americans endured for

many years after. The Civil Rights Act does, however, insure that a legal basis exists for fighting such instances of discrimination. The following year, 1965, the Voting Rights Act was passed to end voting discrimination in the United States.

CRITICAL OVERVIEW

The Help quickly became popular with the book club set following its 2009 publication. The novel pursues the serious theme of racial conflict in an accessible manner.

In a *New York Times* review, Janet Maslin offers a mixed assessment, praising Stockett's well-rounded characterizations of Aibileen and Minny, but questioning the fact that a southern, white debut novelist "renders black maids' voices in thick, dated dialect." Maslin finds that the world Stockett creates remains "harsh yet still comfortable" and "reader-friendly."

Sybil Steinberg's review in the *Washington Post* was a favorable one, in which she applauds the novel's "authenticity" and further describes it as "a page-turner that brings new resonance to the moral issues involved."

Other reviewers went further in praising the novel. Jessie Kornbluth of the *Huffington Post* compares Stockett's book to Harper Lee's 1960 *To Kill a Mockingbird*. Kornbluth regards as wise Stockett's decision to not focus on the violence of the era. "Smartest of all," Kornbluth states, "Stockett has downplayed the horror that was Mississippi in 1962."

Despite the acclaim and popular success of the novel, in 2011, the book became the target of litigation. As Holbrook Mohr reported in the *Washington Times*, Stockett is being sued by an African American maid named Ablene Cooper, who worked for Stockett's brother and his wife and claimed that Stockett used Cooper's likeness without permission. *New York Times* writer Campbell Robertson maintains that Cooper still works for Stockett's brother, and that Cooper's employers have offered their support of Ablene in her legal complaint. On August 16, 2011, the case was thrown out, because it was filed outside the one-year statute of limitations between when Cooper first received the book from Stockett and when Cooper filed her suit. Cooper's lawyer stated that they were considering an appeal.

CRITICISM

Catherine Dominic

Dominic is a novelist and a freelance writer and editor. In the following essay, she explores Stockett's treatment of class conflict in The Help, *maintaining that notions of social class form the basis of exclusion from a sense of community, and that as sensitive to such exclusions as the character of Skeeter becomes in terms of race, she remains oblivious to the way she herself perpetuates class distinctions.*

One of the most compelling figures in Stockett's *The Help* is Celia Foote, a woman from a poor white background who wants desperately to be welcomed into the white upper-class world into which she married through Southern gentleman Johnny Foote. Yet Celia remains on the outskirts of this circle, never embraced by Hilly or her friends. She is also looked down upon, at least initially, by Minny, who has never before worked for a white woman not born into a world of wealth and privilege. In many ways, Celia's experience as an outsider is reflected in Skeeter's life after she has been excluded from her previous social circle by Hilly, who vehemently disapproves of Skeeter's stance on racial issues. Both Skeeter and Celia are excluded by the same social communities, black and white alike. Yet although Celia reaches out to Skeeter, Skeeter treats Celia with indifference. While Skeeter appears to evolve from a state of ignorance to one of greater experience regarding the racism endured by African Americans in Jackson, she fails to address the other barrier that shapes the city, that of social class.

Skeeter seems to have an understanding that her upbringing has been a privileged one. The irony of her writing a column about cleaning and housekeeping is not lost on her. When she does express an awareness of having more than others, it is an understanding colored by race, not class. In the novel's opening chapter, the disdain Hilly and Elizabeth bear toward Celia is revealed. Skeeter does not question the attitude, only that Hilly lets her intense dislike of Celia prevent her from accepting Celia's offer of help with the Children's Benefit—help Hilly apparently needs. Hilly comments that, upon running into Celia at the beauty parlor, Celia asked if she could help with the benefit. Hilly's tone suggests that it was audacious of Celia to even ask. Skeeter replies that the help is needed,

WHAT DO I READ NEXT?

- *Freedom's Children: Young Civil Rights Activists Tell Their Own Stories*, by Ellen S. Levin, gathers the accounts of children and teenagers who were active in the civil rights movement. The young-adult work was published in 2000.

- Gwendolyn Brooks's *Selected Poems* was published in 1963 and reissued in 2006. Her poetry captures the everyday lives and struggles of African Americans.

- *Deep in Our Hearts: Nine White Women in the Freedom Movement*, published in 2002, provides essays by nine women, from a variety of cultural, philosophical, and social backgrounds, all of whom were active in the civil rights movement in the 1960s. The authors include Constance Curry, Joan C. Browning, Dorothy Dawson Burlage, Penny Patch, Theresa del Pozzo, Sue Thrashner, Elaine DeLott Baker, Emmie Schrader Adams, and Casey Hayden.

- *Invisible Man* by Ralph Ellison is referenced in *The Help*. It was originally published in 1952 and was reissued in 1995. The nameless African American narrator recounts his experiences of exclusion, discrimination, and search for identity.

- Set in the South (in Georgia) in the 1950s, Cyntha Kadohata's young-adult novel *Kira-Kira* describes the struggles of a poor Japanese American family and the cultural isolation they endure. The Newbery Award—winning novel was published in 2004.

- *Stuck Rubber Baby* by Howard Cruse is a graphic novel published in 2000. Set in the South during the 1960s, the story explores racism and homophobia prevalent during that time period.

- Theresa Nelson's young-adult novel *And One for All*, published in 1989, takes places in the 1960s and explores the way the Vietnam War shaped the lives of American families, depicting the war from the perspectives of a young soldier and a peace activist.

> **WHILE SKEETER APPEARS TO EVOLVE FROM
> A STATE OF IGNORANCE TO ONE OF GREATER
> EXPERIENCE REGARDING THE RACISM ENDURED
> BY AFRICAN AMERICANS IN JACKSON, SHE FAILS TO
> ADDRESS THE OTHER BARRIER THAT SHAPES THE
> CITY, THAT OF SOCIAL CLASS."**

but Hilly responds that she lied to Celia, telling her she needed to be a member of the Jackson Junior League to participate. "What does she think the Jackson League is?" Hilly asks. "Open rush?" Hilly refers to a college sorority's practice of allowing anyone a chance to pledge the organization after a more formal procedure has already been implemented. Hilly's disdainful comment demonstrates her elitist notions; she clearly thinks she is superior to Celia. Skeeter questions this, observing that, to her knowledge, the League is allowing nonmembers to help with the benefit since the event has gotten so large. Hilly responds affirmatively, that this is indeed the procedure this year, "But I wasn't about to tell *her* that," she emphasizes. Elizabeth chimes in, "I can't believe Johnny married a girl so tacky like she is." Hilly nods, and Skeeter lets the matter drop. It is significant that Skeeter, educated at the same college as Hilly and Elizabeth, does not object to the elitism inherent in Hilly's comment about "open rush." Her portion of the conversation essentially amounts to her mild surprise that Hilly does not allow Celia to participate.

When Celia is first presented to the reader, it is through Minny's perspective. Minny hones in on Celia's "tacky pink pantsuit." Further evaluating Celia, Minny thinks, "I can tell right off, she's from *way* out in the country. I look down and see the fool doesn't have any shoes on, like some kind of white trash. Nice white ladies don't go around barefoot." As Celia shows her around the house, Minny asks where Celia's family is from. Celia's reply is telling. Minny is aware that Sugar Ditch, Celia's home, is a poor, rural area. Minny recalls seeing newspaper photos of tenant shacks and starving white children. Celia later

reveals to Minny one of the reasons she can cook so few things: her family did not have electricity. As the weeks pass, Minny repeatedly overhears Celia making phone calls to Hilly, leaving messages and checking her phone line for a dial tone. Minny pities her, knowing that Hilly will never welcome "white trash" like Celia into her circle of friends.

After Hilly discovers the Jim Crow materials in Skeeter's bag, she begins to gradually grow suspicious of Skeeter's motives, but she has not yet shut Skeeter out of her social circle. Hilly has become distant, however, and Skeeter feels it acutely. Yet after getting a message from Celia, she disregards it. Minny has insisted that Skeeter never return Celia's calls, attempting to prevent anyone from finding out how she and Aibileen deceived Celia so that Minny would get a job as Celia's maid. Obligingly, Skeeter, for the second time, does not spare a second thought for Celia, who she knows has been eager to help with league activities. Skeeter questions, "Why would Johnny Foote's wife be calling me?" and admits that she does not "have the time to wonder" why Minny asked that she not talk to Celia. Celia is viewed by Skeeter only within the context of her relationship with Johnny. To Skeeter, Celia is Johnny Foote's wife, not the woman who wanted to help but was shut down by Hilly. Skeeter fails to recall the earlier conversation she, Elizabeth, and Hilly had about Celia, and once again puts Celia out of her mind, as focused as she is on her own project. Soon however, Hilly grows more vindictive. Skeeter, writing the league newsletter, types in *toilets* instead of *coats*, conflating the Home Help Sanitation Initiative (Hilly's effort to make sure black maids never use their white bosses' toilets again) with Hilly's coat drive. The result—the deposit of dozens of discarded toilets on Hilly's front lawn—cements Hilly's resolve to essentially banish Skeeter. Not long after, Aibileen notes, Skeeter looks thin, "skittish in the eyes. She try to smile like it ain't that hard on her that she ain't got no friends left." Hilly has insured first that Celia has no friends, then Skeeter.

Celia, however, has not given up. She arrives at Elizabeth's house, unannounced, but is not invited in. From the door, Elizabeth greets Celia coolly. Once again, Celia offers to help with the benefit. Hilly informs Celia that they do not need help, but she invites Johnny and Celia to the attend the benefit. Celia smiles gratefully, but Hilly strikes out in her subtle, cruel way and asks Celia if she would like to buy tickets for eight friends as well, saying, "Then you'd have a whole table." Celia and Hilly both know that Celia does not have any friends to invite. She becomes visibly shaken, only buys two tickets, and is forced to write out a check balancing the checkbook on her knee, since she still stands in the doorway. Yet the friendless Celia is undaunted. Arriving home after her shopping trip to find something to wear for the event, she picks up the phone and hangs it up. "The fool's listening for the dial tone again, in case someone tries to call," Minny observes to herself. The same fool protects Minny by using a fire poker to beat the naked intruder prowling the grounds of the Foote home. Impressed with Celia's calm demeanor and the effectiveness of the beating, Minny thinks, "I see the white-trash girl she was ten years ago. She was strong. She didn't take no [expletive] from nobody." Describing the incident later to Aibileen, Minny states, "She just don't see em. The *lines*. Not between her and me, not between her and Hilly." If Celia is aware of such social barriers as race and class, she has chosen, firmly, to ignore them. When Aibileen asserts her belief that the lines Minny speaks of are constructed in the minds of people like Hilly but do not truly exist, she emphasizes that the differences that separate people are perceived differences only. Minny asks Aibileen, "So I ain't crossing no line if I tell Miss Celia the truth, that she ain't good enough for Hilly?" Minny hopes to spare Celia further humiliation, but Minny cannot help but observe the strength of the social barrier of class. She herself has repeatedly thought of Celia as white trash, as tacky, as not good enough for Hilly's high society circle. But, Minny resolves to make another effort to protect Celia. Minny, in fact, realizes that she is the closest thing Celia ever had to a friend, and she vows to extend herself a little, to help Celia.

The community Skeeter has lost includes confidants of her youth (her childhood friends Hilly and Elizabeth), friends to chat with at social gatherings sponsored by the league, her weekly bridge partners, and women to play tennis with at the country club. This is the community Celia is so desperately trying to get into. Throughout the novel, this white community, which prides itself on appearances and censures those who do not live up to traditional ideals, is contrasted with the community of which Aibileen and Minny are a part. These women confide in each other, aid each other through troubled times, advise one another, and love one another. Coming from such a warm

and nurturing circle, Minny is stunned that Celia would continue to try to break into Hilly's frigid world. She tries another avenue with Celia and encourages her to pursue a friendship rather than a social circle. Taking back her earlier reservations, she tells Celia to call Skeeter. Minny recalls asking "Miss Skeeter this favor a few days ago, to try and be nice to Celia, steer her away from those ladies." To Celia, she asserts, "I think you and Miss Skeeter would get along just fine." Celia, however, insists this is a bad idea. She tells Minny about the way the women of the league have turned their back on Skeeter, how they have said that she is an "embarrassment" to Jackson. When Minny asks if Celia has ever met Skeeter, Celia replies that she has not: "But if all those girls don't like her, then she must be...well she...." Celia trails off as she begins to comprehend Minny's point. Minny waits, frustrated that Celia will not get it, worried that she is in fact a hypocrite. Now, Celia begins to see, to understand that, without even knowing her, the league women she idolizes refuse to welcome her. She recalls her visit to Elizabeth's: "They didn't even ask me in the house. They made me stand out on the steps like a vacuum salesman." When Minny, attempting to be kind, explains to Celia that Hilly and her friends do not like Celia because of Hilly's previous relationship with Johnny, Celia clings to the notion that she might still have hope. She decides to explain to Hilly that she was not seeing Johnny while Hilly was still in a relationship with him. Despite Minny's advice, Celia does not pursue Skeeter. Significantly, despite Minny's request to Skeeter, Skeeter continues to ignore Celia. Perhaps Skeeter planned on "being nice" if Celia called her, but she fails again to reach out. Minny has even explained that she is trying to save Celia from Hilly, and still Skeeter, as the wiser woman who has already been shunned by Hilly, who knows all she is capable of, makes no move to aid Celia.

Skeeter's attitude of indifference is further demonstrated at the benefit. Skeeter, arriving alone, rejected by Stuart and by Hilly and Elizabeth, watches Celia's entrance. Effusive Celia in her low-cut pink gown, attempting to assimilate into a world of primly dressed, repressed Junior League women, is observed in an almost scientific manner by Skeeter. At this point in the story, Skeeter has heard her friends insult Celia, knows Celia wants to help with league functions, has been approached by Celia, and has been asked by Minny to look out for Celia. Yet, Skeeter sees Celia walk into the party and eagerly approach

Elizabeth, who quickly abandons her. Skeeter's response, upon watching Elizabeth rush off, upon looking "at Celia Foote rattling after Elizabeth in her awful dress," is to think that the real story of the evening is "not the flower arrangements or how many pleats are around the rear end of Hilly's dress. This year, it's all about The Celia Foote Fashion Catastrophe." It would not be unsurprising to hear the words "Celia Foote Fashion Catastrophe" coming out of Hilly's own mouth. Skeeter has adopted, consciously or not, her former friend Hilly's own condescending, superior, disdainful attitude toward Celia.

By the end of the novel, Celia has written off Hilly and no longer attempts to befriend a group of people who believe they are above her. Skeeter, too, has come to some important realizations. Hearing Lou Anne Templeton's confession that she has tried to kill herself, Skeeter wonders about what she could have done, if she "could've made her days a little bit easier, if I'd tried. If I'd treated her a little nicer. Wasn't that the point of the book? For women to realize, *We are just two people. Not that much separates us. Not nearly as much as I thought.*" With Lou Anne, Celia understands that there is much she did not see, much she did not know. Previously, she had given Lou Anne little thought, had expected her to be as vapid as Hilly and her friends. She realizes that she, Skeeter, was the "one who was missing the point." Yet she fails to realize how much she missed the point with Celia, a woman who, although not suicidal like Lou Anne, was in desperate need of friendship but was rebuffed repeatedly.

Celia and Skeeter have not found the friendship that was possible for them, and they were both denied access to Hilly's social circle. Although the atmosphere of racial tension in Jackson prevents Celia and Skeeter from pursuing true friendships with Minny and Aibileen, they at least are able to form bonds with women who are all too familiar with the notion of barriers. Aibileen and Minny are both aware, though, that Skeeter does not belong in Jackson. Aibileen observes of Skeeter, "Ain't nobody gone tell her they look after her." Minny tells Skeeter directly, when Skeeter expresses uncertainty about moving to New York, "You got nothing left here but enemies in the Junior League.... And you ain't *never* gone get another boyfriend in this town and everybody know it." At the novel's conclusion, Skeeter has resolved to move to New York, and the friendless Celia relishes the fact that she is

about to make Hilly aware that she knows about Hilly's eating two slices of Minny's chocolate/feces pie. Both women gather strength from their experiences of exclusion. Skeeter leaves, however, without acknowledging the way the notion of class is firmly rooted within her. She may have experienced the weakening of the social barrier of race, but she is blind to the fact that she treated Celia as coldly as the rich, upper class, superior Hilly did.

Source: Catherine Dominic, Critical Essay on *The Help*, in *Novels for Students*, Gale, Cengage Learning, 2012.

Melinda Henneberger

In the following review, Henneberger relates that the appeal of the book is also a source of its discomfort to readers.

A NOVEL, A LAWSUIT & AN UNHAPPY LEGACY

Kathryn Stockett's bestselling novel *The Help*, which has been made into a movie scheduled for release this summer, made me intensely uncomfortable with its *Gone with the Wind*-style Southern dialect and depiction of lopsided relationships between a bunch of white women and their black maids in Jackson, Mississippi, circa 1960. Sometimes, of course, discomfort can be a good and even important thing, and Stockett herself suggests that's what she was trying to evoke: "I was taught not to talk about such uncomfortable things," she says in an author's note, "that it was tacky, impolite, they might hear us." So let's do it anyway.

The book's real appeal, it seems to me, is in its invitation to ease into a warm bath of moral superiority over the racist ninnies in the book, who worry about the diseases they might catch if the women who cook their food and raise their children were also to tinkle in their toilets.

But a little self-congratulation goes a long way, in print as in life. When Stockett also shares in the author's note how she once ground her stiletto heel into the foot of a "drunk man from a rich white Metro North-train type of town" who spoke ill of Mississippi at a New York cocktail party, and then "spent the next ten minutes quietly educating him on the where-from-abouts of William Faulkner, Eudora Welty, Tennessee Williams, Elvis Presley, B. B. King, Oprah Winfrey, Jim Henson, Faith Hill, James Earl Jones, and Craig Claiborne, the food editor and critic for the *New York Times*," she cemented my impression of her as awfully smug. And now we have a new window into Stockett's possible motivations—courtesy of the lawsuit filed recently by her brother's maid.

Ablene Cooper, a sixty-year-old Jackson maid who has a gold tooth, a dead son, and a job minding the children of Stockett's brother and sister-in-law, is suing the writer over alleged similarities between her life and likeness and that of a maid in *The Help*—an Aibileen Clark, who has a gold tooth and a dead son, and works for Jackson's biggest jerks. Not only that, but according to Cooper, it was the brother and sister-in-law who encouraged her to file suit.

"Ain't too many Ablenes," she told the *New York Times*. "What she did, they said it was wrong," she added—the "they" in question being the author's brother and sister-in-law. "They came to me and said, 'Ms. Aibee, we love you, we support you,' and they told me to do what I got to do."

It sounds as though Stockett is really being sued for embarrassing her family—another Southern tradition. But while the author's appropriation has all the subtlety of the attack on Fort Sumter, cases like this are almost impossible to win. Whatever happens with the low-yield suit, Cooper is once again in the situation of at least looking like her white employers are the ones calling the shots. And with the damages sought set at only $75,000—just low enough to keep the case out of federal court—the whole exercise seems disrespectful to the longtime maid, who would have been better advised to write her own darn book and cash in on the upcoming movie in a way that would have allowed her to become a former maid.

Cooper has described the parallels between her life and that of the character in *The Help* as plain "embarrassing"—and just wait until Viola Davis, who plays Aibileen in the movie, drags her onto the big screen this August. Now that she's on record as saying that all this talk about the unequal relationship between maid and employer is so humiliating, it will be hard for her to change her mind and be interviewed alongside Davis later, too, won't it? (Good thinking, aggrieved brother and sister-in-law!)

So am I really arguing that Stockett oughtn't to have written the book? No, nor even that I shouldn't have bought it, since some of the discomfort I feel just might have to do with my own identification with the character of the writer—the author of the tell-all book within the tell-all book—who purloins pretty casually from the lives of others. That character is also a Southerner

(my mom's family is from Kentucky) whose confidence in her own moral superiority is perhaps not as appealing as she imagines.

When I think about my own experiences with the African American woman who helped my grandmother raise my younger cousin after his mom died—and with her daughter, who was my first black friend, or so I thought—I am as embarrassed as Ablene Cooper says she is. On her deathbed, my beloved grandmother lifted her head and told the hospital aide bending over her, "Why, you're colored." "Yes, ma'am, I am," the woman said. And until I know better what in the world to do with that, I guess I had best not pass any final judgment on either Stockett or her litigious brother.

Source: Melinda Henneberger, "Southern Discomfort," in *Commonweal*, Vol. 138, No. 6, March 25, 2011, p. 7.

Rebecca Kelm

In the following review, Kelm notes that The Help *is not easy to read but is definitely worth reading.*

Set in Stockett's native Jackson, MS, in the early 1960s, this first novel adopts the complicated theme of blacks and whites living in a segregated South. A century after the Emancipation Proclamation, black maids raised white children and ran households but were paid poorly, often had to use separate toilets from the family, and watched the children they cared for commit bigotry. In Stockett's narrative, Miss Skeeter, a young white woman, is a naive, aspiring writer who wants to create a series of interviews with local black maids. Even if they're published anonymously, the risk is great; still, Aibileen and Minny agree to participate. Tension pervades the novel as its events are told by these three memorable women. Is this an easy book to read? No, but it is surely worth reading. It may even stir things up as readers in Jackson and beyond question their own discrimination and intolerance in the past and present.

Source: Rebecca Kelm, Review of *The Help*, in *Library Journal*, Vol. 134, No. 1, January 1, 2009, p. 83.

Kirkus Reviews

In the following review, a contributor to Kirkus Reviews *examines how the relationships in the novel reflect the racial issues of the time.*

The relationships between white middle-class women and their black maids in Jackson, Miss., circa 1962, reflect larger issues of racial upheaval in Mississippi-native Stockett's ambitious first novel.

Still unmarried, to her mother's dismay, recent Ole Miss graduate Skeeter returns to Jackson longing to be a serious writer. While playing bridge with her friends Hilly and Elizabeth, she asks Elizabeth's seemingly docile maid Aibileen for housekeeping advice to fill the column she's been hired to pen for a local paper. The two women begin what Skeeter considers a semi-friendship, but Aibileen, mourning her son's recent death and devoted to Elizabeth's neglected young daughter, is careful what she shares. Aibileen's good friend Minnie, who works for Hilly's increasingly senile mother, is less adept at playing the subservient game than Aibileen. When Hilly, an aggressively racist social climber, fires and then blackballs her for speaking too freely, Minnie's audacious act of vengeance almost destroys her livelihood. Unlike oblivious Elizabeth and vicious Hilly, Skeeter is at the verge of enlightenment. Encouraged by a New York editor, she decides to write a book about the experience of black maids and enlists Aibileen's help. For Skeeter the book is primarily a chance to prove herself as a writer. The stakes are much higher for the black women who put their lives on the line by telling their true stories. Although the exposé is published anonymously, the town's social fabric is permanently torn. Stockett uses telling details to capture the era and does not shy from showing Skeeter's dangerous naiveté. Skeeter's narration is alive with complexity—her loyalty to her traditional Southern mother remains even after she learns why the beloved black maid who raised her has disappeared. In contrast, Stockett never truly gets inside Aibileen and Minnie's heads (a risk the author acknowledges in her postscript). The scenes written in their voices verge on patronizing.

This genuine page-turner offers a whiff of white liberal self-congratulation that won't hurt its appeal and probably spells big success.

Source: Review of *The Help*, in *Kirkus Reviews*, January 1, 2009.

SOURCES

"About Kathryn Stockett," in *The Help*, Penguin.com, http://us.penguingroup.com/static/packages/us/thehelp/author.php (accessed July 29, 2011).

Belloni, Matthew, "'The Help': Judge Tosses Lawsuit Claiming Character Stolen from Real Life Maid," in *Hollywood Reporter*, http://www.hollywoodreporter.com/thr-esq/judge-tosses-the-help-lawsuit-223783 (accessed August 19, 2011).

"Civil Rights Movement," in *John F. Kennedy Presidential Library and Museum*, http://www.jfklibrary.org/JFK/JFK-in-History/Civil-Rights-Movement.aspx (accessed July 29, 2011).

Kornbluth, Jesse, "Is *The Help* More than a Surprise Bestseller? Is It a New *To Kill a Mockingbird*?" in *Huffington Post*, October 29, 2009, http://www.huffingtonpost.com/jesse-kornbluth/is-the-help-more-than-a-s-b-333448.html (accessed July 29, 2011).

Maslin, Janet, "Racial Insults and Quiet Bravery in 1960s Mississippi," in *New York Times*, February 18, 2009, http://www.nytimes.com/2009/02/19/books/19masl.html (accessed July 29, 2011).

Mohr, Holbrook, "Family Maid Sues Author of Best-Seller *The Help*," in *Washington Times*, February 17, 2011, http://www.washingtontimes.com/news/2011/feb/17/family-maid-sues-author-best-seller-help/ (accessed July 29, 2011).

Patterson, James T., "Striving for Racial Balance in the 1960s," in *Brown v. Board of Education: A Civil Rights Milestone and Its Troubled Legacy*, Oxford University Press, 2001, pp. 118–46.

———, "What Was Jim Crow," in *Jim Crow Museum of Racist Memorabilia*, Ferris State University, 2000, http://www.ferris.edu/jimcrow/what.htm (accessed July 29, 2011).

Pilgrim, David, "Who Was Jim Crow," in *Jim Crow Museum of Racist Memorabilia*, Ferris State University, 2000, http://www.ferris.edu/jimcrow/who.htm (accessed July 29, 2011).

Ribeiro, Myra, "Introduction," and "A Brutal Murder," in *The Assassination of Medgar Evers*, Rosen Publishing, 2002, pp. 5–13.

Robertson, Campbell, "Family Maid Files Suit Against Author of *The Help*," in *New York Times*, February 17, 2011, http://artsbeat.blogs.nytimes.com/2011/02/17/family-maid-files-suit-against-author-of-the-help/ (accessed July 29, 2011).

Steinberg, Sybil, Review of *The Help*, in *Washington Post*, April 1, 2009, http://www.washingtonpost.com/wp-dyn/content/article/2009/03/31/AR2009033103552.html (accessed July 29, 2011).

Stockett, Kathryn, *The Help*, Amy Einhorn Books/Putnam, 2009.

———, "This Life: Kathryn Stockett on Her Childhood in the Deep South," in *Daily Mail* (London, England), July 18, 2009, http://www.dailymail.co.uk/home/you/article-1199603/This-Life-Kathryn-Stockett-childhood-Deep-South.html (accessed July 29, 2011).

FURTHER READING

Evans, Sara, *Personal Politics: The Roots of Women's Liberation in the Civil Rights Movement and the New Left*, Knopf, 1979.

Evans explores the way female civil rights activists, disillusioned by the devaluation of their contributions to the movement by their male colleagues, were moved to fight for true equality for women.

King, Martin Luther, Jr., *A Testament of Hope: The Essential Writings and Speeches of Martin Luther King, Jr.*, edited by James M. Washington, HarperOne, 1990.

Washington's collection of King's writings and speeches encompasses King's work as a philosopher, activist, and theologian, and includes King's famous "I Have a Dream" speech.

Moody, Anne, *Coming of Age in Mississippi*, 1992, reprint, Delta, 2004.

Moody's autobiography recounts her experiences as a young black girl raised by tenant farmers in rural Mississippi. She details the pervasive fear that shadowed her, knowing that she could be killed because of her race. As an honor student who won a basketball scholarship, Moody was able to attend college, during which time she joined the NAACP.

Santoli, Al, *Everything We Had: An Oral History of the Vietnam War*, Ballantine, 1982.

Nominated for an American Book Award in 1983, Santoli's collection, targeted at a young-adult audience, features the stories of thirty-three American soldiers who fought in the Vietnam War.

SUGGESTED SEARCH TERMS

Stockett AND The Help

Stockett AND civil rights movement

Stockett AND African Americans

Stockett AND women's rights

Stockett AND Vietnam War

Stockett AND historical accuracy

Stockett AND 1960s

Stockett AND Mississippi

Stockett AND American South

Stockett AND Medgar Evers

Housekeeping

MARILYNNE ROBINSON
1980

Marilynne Robinson's first novel, *Housekeeping*, was published in 1980. Although both her agent and her publisher loved the book, they were not sure it would sell, since its style is wildly different from most of the minimalist and postmodern fiction that was being published at that time. However, Anatole Broyard gave it an early and enthusiastic review in the *New York Times*, stating that the book "broke through the ordinary human condition with all its dissatisfactions, and achieved a kind of transfiguration." *Housekeeping* was nominated for a Pulitzer prize, and won the PEN/Hemingway prize for first novel.

Housekeeping has become an American classic for a number of reasons, one of which is that Robinson, herself steeped in classic nineteenth-century American works by Emerson, Thoreau, Melville, and Dickinson, deliberately set out to imagine how the core story of American literature, that of the restless individual who cannot fit into society, might work if the protagonist were female. While Melville ships Ishmael off to sea, Twain sends Huck Finn down the river in a raft, and Thoreau himself journeys on foot, Robinson explores the fracturing in family and community life that might result in a girl like Ruth running off with her unmoored aunt Sylvie. Narrated in Ruth's voice, the book dramatizes the choices Ruth and her sister Lucille must make as they leave childhood and embark on adolescence—do they grow out of their familial inwardness and conform to the norms of Fingerbone, or do they choose the inward voice and sever ties forever?

Marilynne Robinson *(Ulf Andersen | Getty Images)*

Although Robinson wrote two collections of essays after *Housekeeping*, it was twenty-four years before her next work of fiction was released. In the first decade of the twenty-first century, she published *Gilead* (2004) and *Home* (2008), two novels in which she continued to explore central themes laid out in *Housekeeping*: the tension between the ties of family and community, and the wild impulses that rule the individual soul.

AUTHOR BIOGRAPHY

Robinson was born on November 26, 1943, in Sandpoint, Idaho. Her father John worked in the timber industry, while her mother Ellen stayed home with Robinson and her older brother David. During her childhood, the family moved often, a situation that caused Robinson to joke in an interview with Anne E. Voss in the *Iowa Review*, "I have travelled widely in Idaho!" The family settled in Coeur d'Alene for Robinson's high school years, after which

she followed her older brother David to Rhode Island for college. He was enrolled at Brown University, and since Brown did not, at that time, enroll women, Robinson enrolled at Pembroke, Brown's sister college (Pembroke merged with Brown in 1971).

Robinson studied American literature, which, she told Sara Fey of the *Paris Review*, "was unusual then. But it meant that I was broadly exposed to nineteenth-century American literature. I became interested in the way that American writers used metaphoric language, starting with Emerson." She also studied with John Hawkes (a postmodern American novelist). Hawkes was a defender of Robinson's style, which includes the long sentences and extended metaphors that still characterize her work. In the same *Iowa Review* interview, Robinson notes that one of the tasks a writer faces is

> to create a syntax that's amenable to your style of thinking.... If your style of thinking tends toward irony or reflection or ambivalence or whatever, then inevitably you push for syntaxes that accommodate it.

It was while working on her Ph.D. thesis on Shakespeare's *Henry VI, Part II*, that Robinson began work on what was to become *Housekeeping*. As she told Fey, during her Ph.D. she had "started writing these metaphors down just to get the feeling of writing in that voice. After I finished my dissertation, I read through the stack of metaphors and they cohered in a way I hadn't expected." She had been writing scenes from her childhood for several years, and when an acquaintance asked to see her work, she sat down and wrote all of the train scene in *Housekeeping* in one sitting. The friend sent the manuscript to his agent, who sent it to Farrar, Straus and Giroux, who later published it. Broyard reviewed *Housekeeping* for the *New York Times*, earning it instant critical recognition, and the book won the Hemingway/PEN foundation award for best first novel.

Robinson, divorced from her husband and the mother of two grown sons, has taught at the prestigious Iowa Writer's Workshop in Iowa City, Iowa, since 1990. She did not publish another work of fiction until 2005 when *Gilead*, for which she won the Pulitzer and the National Book Critics Circle prizes, was released. In 2008, she published *Home*, a companion novel to *Gilead*, for which she won the Orange Prize for fiction. She has also published three works of nonfiction: *Mother Country* (1989), *The Death of Adam* (1998), and *Absence of Mind* (2010).

PLOT SUMMARY

Chapter 1

Housekeeping opens with first-person narrator Ruth Stone's declaration of selfhood, followed by a succinct and brutal single-sentence description of the losses of caretakers she and her sister Lucille suffered over the course of their childhood. Ruth's litany of loss names her grandmother and her great-aunts, ending with her Aunt Sylvie, who eventually comes to stay with the girls. The list is notable for its omission of Ruth's greatest loss, her mother. The opening sentence, with its echoes of Melville's "Call me Ishmael," signals that, although this is a twentieth-century novel, its frame of reference is set firmly among the great nineteenth century American Transcendentalists. Ruth begins her tale with the story of her grandfather Edmund Foster, a man who came west to Fingerbone only to die there in a spectacular and mysterious train accident, from which no survivors or bodies were ever recovered. Fingerbone is located in the Rocky Mountains, on the shores of an enormous lake. It is surrounded by mountains and the lake is bisected by an enormous railroad trestle. Ruth narrates the story of her grandparents' marriage, the childhoods of her mother and aunts, and her early life in Seattle. She recounts how her mother brought Ruth and her sister Lucille back to Fingerbone, set them on the porch with a box of graham crackers, and proceeded to drive a borrowed car off a cliff into the lake, killing herself. Ruth relates how their grandmother cared for them for the next five years as though reliving the years in which she raised her own daughters—Molly, Helen, and the now missing Sylvie—and the orderly manner in which the household was kept during that time. When their grandmother dies, her younger sisters-in-law, Nona and Lily, come from Spokane to look after the girls.

Chapter 2

Lily and Nona arrive to take care of Lucille and Ruth, but "maiden ladies" to the core, they are at a loss about how to proceed. They worry constantly about the snow, for it is a hard winter in Fingerbone and they are used to a life in the safety of a basement apartment in a brick building in

MEDIA ADAPTATIONS

- Bill Forsythe adapted and directed a movie version of *Housekeeping* in 1987. Starring Christine Lahti, Sara Walker, and Andrea Burchill it is available from Sony Pictures on VHS, or as a streaming download from Amazon.com. Of the movie, Vincent Canby of the *New York Times* said, "Miss Robinson's novel has provided him with material in which the mysterious is an essential component of the mundane, and not simply a leavening agent. Though it's full of moments of real sadness, *Housekeeping* is also startlingly funny."

- An unabridged audio recording of *Housekeeping*, narrated by Becket Royce and published by Macmillan Audio in 2005, is available on CD or for download at Audible.com.

Spokane. The girls take to the lake that winter, for it freezes over, and they skate after school and long into the evening, reluctant to go home. They are routinely the last people left out on the lake, skating in the dark. The great-aunts place advertisements in the personal ad sections of newspapers across the west, asking for information about Sylvie's whereabouts, careful not to announce that her mother has died. When a note arrives, the great-aunts reply with a carefully-worded account of the situation in Fingerbone, asking her to come home.

Chapter 3

Sylvie arrives at the end of winter, a person with "a quiet that seemed compounded of gentleness and stealth and self-effacement." She comes in from the cold with wet hair and cold hands, wearing loafers but no socks and a green satin dress beneath her heavy black coat. Although Ruth, who narrates the chapter, does not say it, Sylvie is clearly a hobo, a transient, someone outside the bounds of normal social codes. In the morning, the girls are surprised to find Sylvie sitting in the dark in the kitchen. She makes them breakfast, then leaves. Lucille is convinced she is not coming back, so the girls follow her into town and find her in the railroad station. She claims she is only warming up, then says, "I think I should stay for a while. . . . The aunts are too old."

Chapter 4

The spring thaw brings a flood to Fingerbone, and although the girls' grandmother had claimed that the house never flooded, it does. The kitchen floods four inches deep, and the residents retreat to the second floor, where they wait the waters out playing Monopoly and listening to Sylvie tell stories about women she met in her travels. On the darkest night of the flood, Sylvie goes downstairs and does not return. The last of the matches have burned out, and Ruth cannot find Sylvie in the dark. Fearing she has left again, Ruth gropes through the dark flooded house, finding Sylvie by the window. When Sylvie won't answer her, Ruth punches her, startling Sylvie back into the present. As the flood recedes, townspeople come to check on them, but the Stone girls do not join the communal task of rebuilding.

Chapter 5

After the flood, school begins again for the girls. They experience school as "hours of tedium . . . relieved by occasional minor humiliations," and after Lucille feigns illness for a week, the girls can't bring themselves to give Sylvie's preposterous note to the principal. So they simply do not return to school. They spend their days by the lakeshore, and as their truancy wears on, they cannot conceive of a way to end it. One day they see Sylvie by the lake and think she must be looking for them as a result of their skipping school. When she never sees them, they are annoyed: "Having waited so many days for someone to come for us, we found her obliviousness irksome." They follow Sylvie as she climbs the railroad bridge and walks out over the water. The girls are frightened that she'll fall, or jump, and it is only when Sylvie sees them that she climbs down off the bridge. The girls realize, "Clearly our aunt was not a stable person," and they begin to watch her, wondering if she will abandon them. At the same time, they notice Sylvie's eccentric housekeeping, which seems to consist of opening the house to its maximum capacity to the outdoors. Leaves and scraps of paper accumulate in the corners; Sylvie continually opens all the doors and windows to let in the air, and she prefers to eat supper in the dark,

filling the house with the elements. The girls begin to diverge from one another as Lucille rebels against Sylvie's strangeness, seeking stability over change, resisting the tug of the "millennial present" in which Sylvie exists.

Chapter 6

Ruth begins "to sense that Lucille's loyalties were with the other world," the world of town and normal society. It begins in the spring, when the girls once again become truants. Sylvie writes notes to the school blaming it on the onset of adolescence, although Ruth notes that it is her younger sister who develops first. "While she became a small woman," Ruth notes, "I became a towering child." The girls spend their days in the woods, or at an old quarry, or along the shores of the lake, and Ruth notices Lucille's increasing impatience. One evening, Lucille turns on the kitchen light while Sylvie makes dinner, illuminating the dilapidated state of the room, including the half-burned curtain Sylvie has never bothered to replace. Lucille begins to press Sylvie for details of her marriage and the location of her husband, and to demand a more ordinary set of household rituals. Sylvie is vague about her husband and simply turns the grocery money over to Lucille while wandering outside, snacking on crackers, while the girls eat dinner. As Lucille asserts herself more, making friends with a girl in town, worrying about what people will think when they come across Sylvie sleeping on a park bench one afternoon, Ruth feels herself dissolving: "It was a source of both terror and comfort to me then that I often seemed invisible."

Chapter 7

Lucille continues to pull away from Ruth, and yet they remain inextricably bonded. They begin to disagree, especially about the nature of their mother's character, her love for them, and even whether she had deliberately killed herself. Meanwhile, Ruth realizes that they "were now in Sylvie's dream with her," and that they had never come "to a place where she had not been before us." It is summer, so the girls are no longer truant, but they continue to wander, once going so far afield to fish that they are caught by darkness, forced to spend the night in the woods. They build a makeshift shelter, and even as Ruth feels herself becoming one with the dark night, letting "the darkness in the sky become coextensive with the darkness in my skull and bowels and bones," Lucille fights against this dissolution remaining "never still, never accepting that all our human boundaries were overrun." In the morning, Lucille refuses to speak as the girls make their way home, and it is this event that sends her into a frenzy of self improvement. She buys fabric and a pattern to make an outfit that "will all be coordinated," and keeps a diary that Ruth discovers is filled with lists and etiquette tips. When Lucille returns from a school dance to find Sylvie sleeping on her side of the bed the girls share, she quietly leaves and moves in with Miss Royce, the home economics teacher. She never returns.

Chapter 8

The next day, Ruth skips school because Sylvie wants to show her a special place. Sylvie drags Ruth out of bed before dawn, hurrying her along, handing her an egg sandwich to eat while they walk. After some searching, Sylvie finds the well-hidden rowboat and refuses to acknowledge the boat's owner, who chases after them, throwing rocks. Sylvie tells Ruth there are houses hidden up in the woods, and that sometimes she tries to find them, and capture the children she senses are nearby leaving marshmallows on twigs. The sun comes up while Sylvie rows until she pulls into a narrow glacial valley where they beach the boat. Sylvie leads Ruth uphill to an abandoned homestead in a stunted orchard. When the sun crests the high ridge, the frost that covers the house, lilacs, apple trees, and "grass shone with petal colors, and water drops spilled from all the trees as innumerably as petals." While Ruth is watching the colors, Sylvie disappears. Ruth senses the presence of the children Sylvie mentioned, and while waiting, she begins to dig in the cellar of the collapsed and abandoned house. At first, she intends to build a fire against the cold, but as she digs, she begins to think about loneliness, about how "having a sister or a friend is like sitting at night in a lighted house," and that "when one looks from the darkness into the light, however, one sees all the difference between here and there, this and that." She speculates that this is why "all unsheltered people are angry in their hearts, and would like to break the roof, spine, and ribs and smash the windows." Ruth tells herself there are children trapped in the ruined basement, and that she is digging to set them free, even as she knows this is not true. Finally, spent, she sits, abandoned by Sylvie, and thinks, "Let them come unhouse me of this flesh and pry this house apart. It was no shelter now, it only kept me here alone." She thinks of her mother, long dead at the bottom of

the lake, and realizes "she was a music I no longer heard." Just then, Sylvie returns, bundles Ruth into her enormous black tramp's coat, and then leads her back to the boat. Ruth curls up in the bottom of the boat, and Sylvie rows, one foot on either side of her. Ruth imagines herself as a seed, swelling in the infinitude of the lake's water until she is reborn into a dark oneness with the world. By the time they get back to Fingerbone, it is dark, and Sylvie holds the boat below the bridge, waiting for the train to pass overhead. Suspended between the sunken train in which the body of Edmund Foster rests and the train overhead, the two are shaken by the noise and the energy of the passing train. Ruth tries to take over rowing, but they are washed away from Fingerbone by the currents and wake in the morning on the far side of the lake. Sylvie beaches the boat, and they catch a freight train back into town. They walk back to the house under the watchful eyes of the townspeople, including Lucille, who comes by the house to ask where they have been. Exhausted by their ordeal, Ruth falls asleep before she can tell her, although she senses Lucille, with kindness, trying to convince her to leave Sylvie.

Chapter 9

Concerned that Ruth has been seen riding a freight train with her aunt, a known transient, the sheriff comes to call on them. The townspeople are concerned—a concern that Ruth connects to the shallow roots that tie Fingerbone, a town prone to flooding and violence, to social convention in the first place. The sheriff is known to tolerate transients, but the town will not tolerate letting Ruth slip away without a fight. Neighbor ladies and church women begin dropping by the house, bringing food and mittens, and their outsiders' gaze on the parlor sends Sylvie into a frenzy of housecleaning. The ladies are not unkind, and their good works spring from good hearts and a concern that Ruth is slipping away, that soon she "would be lost to ordinary society. I would be a ghost, and . . . Like a soul released, I would find here only the images and simulacra of the things needed to sustain me." Sylvie and Ruth clean up the house and attempt to live like ordinary people, but it is clear they're just faking it, and Ruth begins to hear rumors that the townspeople want to take her away. Finally, the sheriff comes to call again, this time to tell Sylvie that there will be a hearing to decide on Ruth's fate.

Chapter 10

Sylvie and Ruth continue their efforts to convince the town that they are family, and that families should not be rent asunder. Ruth muses on the story of Cain and Abel, on Biblical stories of families broken. She posits that it is only in one another's continual simple presence that people can be ordinary, for it is the lost who, in the imagination, grow to enormous size—it is the longing for them that renders them always extraordinary. Ruth imagines how it might have been had their mother waited with them on that day, how it might have been had they visited with their grandmother, then gotten back in the car for the long drive to Seattle. She thinks about what it would have been like to have grown up in that apartment, to have had an ordinary mother, one they could have neglected on occasion. "We would have known nothing of the nature and reach of her sorrow if she had come back," Ruth thinks. "But she left us and broke the family and the sorrow was released and we saw its wings and saw it fly a thousand ways into the hills." Although Ruth and Sylvie have little faith that the hearing will go well, they continue to clean out the house, burning the enormous backlog of papers and magazines in a bonfire in the orchard. When Sylvie returns to the dark house after dousing the fire, Ruth inexplicably hides. They play hide and seek in the orchard while Ruth imagines herself "giddily free and eager, as you do in dreams, when you suddenly find that you can fly." Then the sheriff arrives and calls Sylvie's bluff that she doesn't know where Ruth is, so Ruth leaves the orchard and joins Sylvie on the porch. The sheriff tries to convince her to come home with him, that his wife has apple pie, but she won't go. The sheriff leaves, promising to return the next day.

Chapter 11

Sylvie and Ruth flee into the night after burning the house in order to protect the family's privacy. The house is damp though and won't burn thoroughly, so they abandon it and run into the night. Terrified of being tracked and captured, they decide to cross the railroad bridge that spans the lake. No one has ever done it before, and although it's terrifying and difficult, they manage to get to the other side by morning. For the rest of their lives, Sylvie carries a newspaper clipping pinned to her jacket that describes their deaths, for when the townspeople track them to the bridge, they assume the two have died in the

lake. Sylvie and Ruth never settle down, and they never contact Lucille, even though they pass through Fingerbone on the train more than once. Ruth and Sylvie fall into the life of drifters, picking up work when they run out of money, moving on when the tide feels like it is turning. The novel ends with Ruth's two imagined versions of Lucille's life. In one, she still lives in the house in Fingerbone, keeping it pristine, waiting for them to return. In the other, she has escaped to Boston, the city she dreamed about, and Ruth imagines her in a restaurant, a successful woman waiting for a friend, the type of woman who would never see Ruth and Sylvie even if they were right in front of them, the type of woman who "does not watch, does not listen, does not wait, does not hope" for the return of Ruth and Sylvie.

CHARACTERS

Bernice

Bernice is the Stones' downstairs neighbor in Seattle. She is a very old woman with orange hair who draws her eyebrows on, and the girls love her. She babysits when Helen is at work, checking in on the girls throughout the day. She works as a waitress at a truck stop. Helen borrows Bernice's car for the trip to Fingerbone.

Rosette Brown

Rosette Brown is a girl Lucille befriends at school, whose mother begins to instruct Lucille on the social conventions by which ordinary people live.

Charley

Charley is the husband of Bernice.

Sylvie Fisher

Sylvie is the girls' aunt, their mother's youngest sister. Sylvie is a transient who drifts around the Pacific Northwest and Intermountain West. After the girls' grandmother, Sylvia Foster, dies, their great-aunts come to stay. Feeling they are not up to the task of caring for the girls, they place personal ads in papers across the west asking Sylvie to get in touch. Sylvie is an odd person. She keeps house haphazardly, keeping the doors and windows open whenever possible, allowing swirls of leaves to accumulate in the corners, and hoarding old newspapers, tin cans, and magazines. Sylvie also keeps the habits of a transient even when she returns to Fingerbone and to the family house. Ruth notes that "she always slept clothed, at first with her shoes on, and then, after a month or two, with her shoes under her pillow." As she gets odder and odder, Lucille rebels by becoming more conventional while Ruth becomes more like Sylvie. Sylvie spends her days by the lake, or out on the lake in a rowboat she takes without permission. After Lucille leaves, Sylvie takes Ruth to the abandoned homestead in the valley of the ice crystals, where Ruth experiences a life-changing dissolution of her personal boundaries and the boundaries of the natural world. At the novel's end, Sylvie leaves town with Ruth after attempting to burn down the house, and they take to the road, spending the rest of their lives as transients.

Edmund Foster

Edmund Foster is Ruth and Lucille's grandfather, who died in the train wreck. Originally from the Midwest, Edmund came west looking for mountains, and along the way, he obtained a job working for the railroad. He built the house that the girls live in and decorated much of the furniture with his odd but lovely paintings of natural scenes. After his death, his three daughters left home within the year, and the family was fatally fractured.

Lily Foster

Lily Foster is the girls' great aunt, their grandfather's sister. She comes to stay with her sister Nona after the girls' grandmother dies, but the two old ladies are so set in their ways, and so beset by fears, that they return to Spokane as soon as Sylvie arrives to take care of the girls.

Molly Foster

Molly Foster is the girls' aunt, their mother's older sister. She left Fingerbone to join a missionary society and was sent to the Far East. No one in the family ever heard from her again.

Nona Foster

Nona Foster is the girls' great aunt, their grandfather's sister. She comes to stay with her sister Lily after the girls' grandmother dies, but the two old ladies are so set in their ways, and so beset by fears, that they return to Spokane as soon as Sylvie arrives to take care of the girls.

Mrs. Sylvia Foster

Sylvia Foster is the girls' grandmother. She grew up in Fingerbone and stayed after her husband died and her children left. She is a good housekeeper in the conventional sense; under her tenure, the house was clean and well maintained, as were the children under her care.

Mr. French

Mr. French is the principal of the girls' school, who forgives them their truancy on the promise that they will reform themselves.

Miss Royce

Miss Royce is the Home Economics teacher at the girls' school. When Lucille decides to move out of her home on the night after her first school dance, she turns to Miss Royce, whom she wakes up, for shelter. Miss Royce is described as a tense and solitary woman, high-strung, with a rabbity face, who is routinely the victim of pranks. And yet, as the teacher of Home Economics, she offers Lucille a path into respectability. When the girl arrives at her door, Miss Royce gives Lucille the spare room and, in effect, adopts her.

Sheriff

The sheriff is a tall, fat man who comes to check on Ruth after she is seen on the train with Sylvie. He is known for his kindness to hobos and his ability to keep the violence in town to a minimum. Ruth thinks he seems embarrassed to intrude on them, but the town is concerned that Sylvie is making a transient out of Ruth. He comes back several times, including once to notify Sylvie that there will be a custody hearing. He also appears their final night in Fingerbone, when Ruth is hiding in the orchard. He offers to take her to his house, where he promises her apple pie, but Ruth refuses. That night, Ruth and Sylvie attempt to burn the house down and flee across the railroad bridge.

Helen Foster Stone

Helen Foster Stone is the girls' mother, the middle sister of her family. She married Reginald Stone and moved to Seattle, although Ruth has no memory of her father. When Ruth was seven, Helen borrowed a car and returned to Fingerbone. She settled the girls on the front porch with a box of graham crackers and their suitcases. She then drove Bernice's car off the top of Whiskey Rock into the lake, killing herself. Neither her body nor the car was ever found, although her death was witnessed by two boys who helped her get the car out of the mud. When they did, she drove it as fast as she could go off the top of the cliff. As Lucille and Ruth are growing into their adult personalities, they disagree over whether Helen was a good mother or a neglectful one, whether she killed herself deliberately or in an accident.

Lucille Stone

Lucille Stone is one of the two sisters whose story is at the heart of this novel. As small children, Ruth, the narrator feels that she and her younger sister are "almost as a single consciousness," but as they grow older, Lucille pulls away from Ruth and Sylvie in search of a more ordinary life. Lucille is the younger sister, although she develops first, and since she has a more definitive personality, she often takes the lead between them. As Lucille grows up, Ruth notes, "While she became a small woman, I became a towering child." There are two central experiences of merging with nature in this novel. The first is when Lucille and Ruth get caught out late fishing and have to spend the night in the woods. The second is when Sylvie takes Ruth across the lake to the abandoned homestead. It is after the first episode that Lucille begins to break away from Sylvie and Ruth, embarking on a course of self-improvement, learning to sew her own clothes so that she looks more ordinary, and making friends at school for the first time and studying their home lives. Ruth notes that "Lucille hated everything that had to do with transience," and even before her fateful break from Ruth and Sylvie, she pesters Sylvie about her habits, trying to get her to admit that they are odd, that transience is wrong. She studies the habits of other girls at school, and after a disastrous attempt to make an outfit on her own, spends more and more time in the home economics room, learning how to make clothes and cook proper meals and budget for a household. It is after her first school dance, a landmark event in most girls' experience of growing up, that Lucille leaves home, walks to the house of her home economics teacher, and asks to be taken in. Although she tries to take Ruth with her, Ruth cannot imagine a life in the normal world and cannot respond to Lucille's entreaties.

Reginald Stone

Reginald is Helen's husband and the girls' father. They have no memory of him. He and Helen married in Nevada, then came back to Fingerbone to have a wedding there in order to satisfy Sylvia, who felt that an elopement was not a real wedding. Helen moved to Seattle to be with him.

Ruth Stone

Ruth is the protagonist and narrator of this novel. She is the elder of the two sisters, and it is through her eyes that the story comes to us. An observant child, Ruth is also deeply unattached to the norms of social convention. The novel opens with Ruth's declaration of self, and a litany of the losses she and her sister have endured:

> My name is Ruth. I grew up with my younger sister Lucille, under the care of my grandmother, Mrs. Sylvia Foster, and when she died, of her sisters-in-law, Misses Lily and Nona Foster, and when they fled, of her daughter, Mrs. Sylvia Fisher.

It is noteworthy that this litany omits Ruth's most primal loss, her mother. Ruth and Lucille are so bonded to one another that, when Lucille tells her sister, "We've spent too much time together. We need other friends," Ruth sees it as an attempt on Lucille's part to break free from the oddness that characterizes their family. Ruth does not reply to her sister, but thinks, "She knew my side of things as well as I did. She would have considered already the fact that I had never made a friend in my life." Growing into adolescence forces a crisis for the girls because it means they are going to have to decide what sort of adults they will become. Faced with this, Ruth notes, "We had spent our lives watching and listening with the constant sharp attention of children lost in the dark." While Lucille seeks to improve herself, studying fashion magazines and talking up the older girls so that Ruth was "increasingly struck by Lucille's ability to look the way one was supposed to look," Ruth is unable to make this transition. She's relieved when Lucille abandons her in front of the drug store, leaving her "alone, in the gentle afternoon, indifferent to my clothes and comfortable in my skin, unimproved and without the prospect of improvement." Although it is the episode when Sylvie takes Ruth to the abandoned homestead, where Ruth experiences the dissolution of her sense of self into the sensory world, that cements Ruth's inclination to leave Fingerbone and join Sylvie in her transient lifestyle, it is in that moment outside the drugstore that Ruth realizes that, unlike Lucille, she is not going to

> pull myself into some seemly shape and slip across the wide frontiers into that other world, where it seemed to me then I could never wish to go . . . nothing I had lost, or might lose, could be found there.

In the end, Ruth refuses to cross over, and in order to protect the privacy of their family home, she and Sylvie set it on fire. They then escape Fingerbone by crossing over the enormous railroad bridge across the lake, a bridge considered uncrossable on foot. As a result, the townspeople assume that Sylvie and Ruth have, like Ruth's mother and Sylvie's father before them, drowned in the lake. The pair spend the rest of their lives travelling, drifting, picking up jobs when need be, but mostly living in their own world.

THEMES

Domesticity

Even in cultures where most women work outside the home and many couples split the household chores, how one keeps house may still be the standard by which a woman's worth and competence is measured. By naming her novel *Housekeeping*, Robinson foregrounds domesticity as the central trope of the novel, and indeed, throughout the book, the inner lives of the characters are revealed by the ways in which they keep house.

The first housekeeper we are introduced to in the novel is Sylvia, the girls' grandmother, upon whose doorstep they are left by their mother before she kills herself in the lake. Sylvia is described as a woman who kept a stable loving home for her husband and daughters, as a woman whose love for her daughters was "utter and equal, her government of them generous and absolute. She was constant as daylight." Sylvia is a woman who, even in the wake of her grief at losing her husband and three daughters, takes up the task of raising the two small girls left on her doorstep by attending to the small tasks of domesticity: "She whited shoes and braided hair and fried chicken and turned back bedclothes." Under Sylvia's supervision, the house was clean, the children were attended to, and their lives were stable despite their collective bereavement.

When Sylvia dies, two elderly aunts come from Spokane, but they cannot quite manage the tasks of keeping the house and taking care of the girls. Having been used to living in an apartment building, where maintenance is the responsibility of the management, the aunts find the very house itself daunting. They are so terrified that the snow load will collapse the house that they don't object when the girls stay out until late at night, skating in the dark on the frozen lake. It is at this point in the novel, when we see domestic life beginning to fail the girls, that an alternative is posed: one can escape domesticity by taking to the outdoors. Nature, even the cold nature of winter on a frozen lake, can serve as a refuge from a domestic life that lacks warmth and care.

Sylvie's arrival signals a return of affection to the house, but her housekeeping tends toward the erasure of boundaries, especially the boundaries between indoors and out, between domestic and wild, between civilization and nature. She allows the outside in through the windows and doors she leaves open. She refuses to turn on the lights when she is inside. The image of a lighted house is one Robinson returns to several times, most notably during Ruth's abandonment at the ruined homestead, when she notes, "When one looks from darkness into the light, however, one sees all the difference between here and there, this and that." These are the distinctions that Sylvie rejects, seeking to dissolve the boundaries that separate the house from the wider world. In turn, Lucille reaches out for domesticity as though it is a lifeline, eventually leaving Ruth and Sylvie for the domestic comforts of her home economics teacher, the one person whose job it is to teach the conventions and standards and skills of ordinary domestic life.

Female Identity

One of the central struggles any child must face as he or she grows up is how to assimilate to, or rebel against, the normative gender expectations (what people commonly consider normal for one's gender) of one's time. As small children, Ruth and Lucille live in an almost exclusively female world, one in which their only known male relative is the grandfather who died before they were born. Neither of them knew their father, Sylvie's husband has not been seen in years, the aunts are spinsters, and the only other male characters in the book are tangential figures in their lives. As children, Ruth and Lucille exist "almost as a single consciousness." Together they suffer a string of nearly unimaginable losses, including abandonment by both parents and the death of their grandmother. Left under the inept care of a pair of twittery, anxious spinster aunts, they initially welcome Sylvie's presence in their lives, despite their ongoing fear that she'll slip back into her life of transience. As children, Sylvie's unconventional housekeeping seems like an adventure, and her lack of concern for conventional behavior binds her to them as

TOPICS FOR FURTHER STUDY

- In Dave Eggers's novel *What is the What* (2007), Valentino Achak Deng is forced into transience and homelessness, rather than choosing it like Sylvie and Ruth, as one of Sudan's "Lost Boys." Although Eggers has called his book a novel, it is based on over one hundred hours of interviews with the real Deng. Read the novel and write an essay comparing the concepts of abandonment, home, and grief in the two books.

- *Housekeeping* is a novel deeply concerned with inwardness, language, and perception. The novel was made into a movie in 1987. While novels are primarily a linguistic medium, film is primarily visual. Watch the movie version of *Housekeeping* and analyze how the director translated Ruth's interior consciousness to film. Using a program like iMovie, match up scenes from the film with prose from the novel. Create a presentation for your class comparing and contrasting the manner in which the two media handle the same material.

- Gary Paulsen's young-adult novel *The Crossing*, like *Housekeeping*, hinges on a bridge crossing as a means of escape. Where Robinson draws on myths of the Great Depression for her portrait of transience, Paulsen examines the present-day issue of immigration as the reason for transience. Read Paulsen's novel and research historical media presentations of both Depression-era transients and present-day illegal immigrants. Collect images, historical newspaper and magazine articles, and other representations that describe views of transients in both time periods. How are these images like the characters in *Housekeeping* and *The Crossing*? How are they different? Put together a visual presentation, using software like iPhoto, to show how the characters in each book conform to or diverge from historical representations of transients.

- Families have different standards and rules about keeping house. What is and is not allowed in the house? In many families, children are expected to do household chores starting from a young age. Do a genealogical exploration of what your family means by *housekeeping*. Which members are expected to do household chores? Do they vary by gender? Are the expectations your parents have of your role in keeping the house different from the ones their parents had of them? What expectations did your grandparents have of your parents? Build a Web site whose elements include video interviews with your family, visual representations of your family tree, and visual representations of the expectations surrounding housekeeping over the generations and across your maternal and paternal lines.

- Music is important to the three major characters of *Housekeeping*. Go through the text and collect the references to popular songs. Find recordings of these songs on the Internet. Using images that connect the songs to the novel, create a slideshow set to the music of the novel. Present it to your class with an oral explanation about why you feel the images represent both the events of the novel and the images of the songs.

- Many people have thought, even idly, about running away from home. Write a play about what it might be like to run away from home. You must have at least three characters, and although your play need not take more than fifteen minutes to perform, it should have three acts. In the first act, the character leaves home. In the second act, the main character experiences the challenges of being on his or her own. In the third, the character must resolve these problems. With a group, perform your play for your class.

Housekeeping is set in a small Idaho town. (*Lee O'Dell* | *Shutterstock.com*)

though they are not two children and an adult but three children, marooned together in a big house.

It is the onset of puberty that forces the issue of female identity on Ruth and Lucille, as puberty makes it clear that the girls cannot remain children for much longer. It is Lucille who develops first, becoming "a touchy, achy, tearful creature" whose "clothes began to bind and pull, to irk and exasperate her." Even though she is the younger sister, it is Lucille who becomes "a small woman" while Ruth finds herself remaining "a towering child." As puberty strikes, Lucille becomes increasingly hostile toward Sylvie, while idealizing her dead mother. As she struggles to determine how to become a woman, Lucille comes to hate "everything that had to do with transience." She rejects the fanciful clothing Sylvie buys for them, and fed up one evening, she pulls the chain on the kitchen light, revealing the chaos and dirt that have taken over the once-tidy room. Puberty inspires in Lucille a desperate drive to appropriate the conventional female identity that Sylvie shed long ago. She begins a program of self-improvement, learning correct hairstyling and how to sew a proper dress and

the appropriate codes of behavior. She begins to spend more and more time with the home economics teacher at school, the person who was, in those days, specifically tasked with teaching girls how to keep house and cook, budget and sew clothing, and generally become proper women. Meanwhile, Ruth rejects the notion that female identity depends on self-improvement. When Lucille drags her to the drugstore and tries to force upon her an interest in hairstyles and clothing, Ruth resists her sister's efforts to coerce her "across the wide frontiers into that other world, where it seemed to me then I could never wish to go." It is only when she escapes Lucille's grasp that Ruth finds herself "left alone, in the gentle afternoon, indifferent to my clothes and comfortable in my skin, unimproved and without the prospect of improvement."

However, there is no place in Fingerbone for Sylvie and Ruth once they have definitively slipped off the constraints of conventional female identity. Although they mount a last-ditch effort to convince the sheriff, the man tasked with keeping the peace and enforcing the laws of ordinary behavior, that they are keeping house properly, that Ruth is being fed and housed and going to school, it becomes increasingly clear to everyone that they are failing. The price of failure is high: Ruth knows the townspeople will take her away from Sylvie. When the choice comes down to conforming to a female identity that feels alien or losing each other, the two women escape domestic life altogether, attempting to burn down their house and taking to the rails for a life of transient drifting. Female identity, like the demands of housekeeping, becomes a constraining force to which they cannot accommodate themselves, and so they escape it altogether. Whether this escape represents freedom, or exile, is a question the novel never definitively answers.

STYLE

Initiation Narrative

An initiation narrative is one in which a young person is confronted with and must survive some sort of test in order to become an adult and join the society which seeks to initiate him or her. In *Housekeeping*, Ruth faces a choice of initiations, whether to follow Lucille and be initiated into a world of ordinary femininity, complete with hairstyles and fashion and adherence to conventional social codes, or to follow Sylvie and be initiated into a far less conventional worldview, where boundaries between self and nature are fluid and conventional mores (customs) are irrelevant. In *Housekeeping*, Ruth narrates her transition from passive observer of her life to active participant, a change that begins when Sylvie arrives to care for the two sisters. Sylvie's arrival forces both Ruth and Lucille to become active participants in their own fates. Up until this point, they have remained passive, accepting their fates, allowing themselves to be raised by whichever adult relatives were available. The combined unsuitability of the spinster aunts and the attractive qualities of their unconventional Aunt Sylvie, however, spur the girls to action for the first time. They follow Sylvie to the train station and quietly confront her as she seems ready to flee. Life with Sylvie presents the girls with a choice, to embrace a worldview in which the boundaries between the natural and domesticated worlds erode or to choose the conventional worldview of society, in which the point of housekeeping is to keep the two realms separate. It is Lucille's defection to the conventional society of town that inspires Sylvie to take Ruth off to the icebound valley of the abandoned homestead, where Ruth undergoes an initiation experience and is reborn into the state of consciousness that will forever align her with Sylvie. It is this passage to a new state of perception that makes it impossible for Ruth to return to the life she knew before, the sort of life the sheriff offers her, the sort of life that Lucille chooses.

First-Person Point of View

A first-person narrative is one narrated by the central character, speaking in his or her own voice as though addressing the reader directly. The hallmark of a first-person narrative is that the narrator refers to him or herself as *I*. In *Housekeeping*, it is Ruth who tells the story of the life she and Lucille shared from earliest childhood, including the long drive from Seattle to Fingerbone, where they were left on their grandmother's doorstep by the mother who subsequently killed herself. She narrates the experience of surviving their grandmother's death and the inept ministrations of the spinster aunts. Until Sylvie's arrival, Ruth narrates the novel as though her point of view represents both herself and her sister Lucille, and it is only in the second half of the book, when Lucille pulls away from her, that Ruth's narration becomes singular. Although much of the action of the novel concerns inner states of consciousness as Ruth perceives them, the fact that her version of key plot points seems to be corroborated by the other characters in the novel means that she can be considered a reliable narrator. Many initiation novels are told using a first-person narrator, since they usually narrate the passage of a young child to adulthood. Using the first-person voice allows the author to show how that child's perception changes as he or she grows. Ruth narrates the novel not only in the first person but from a retrospective point of view; that is, she narrates the novel from the point of view of her adult self. This lends a quality of inevitability to the novel, since the adult Ruth knows all along how the story is going to turn out.

Metaphoric Language

In an interview with Sarah Fay of the *Paris Review*, Robinson explains how *Housekeeping* grew out of her interest in the ways that nineteenth-century writers used metaphoric language:

I became interested in the way that American writers used metaphoric language, starting with Emerson . . . I started writing these metaphors down just to get the feeling of writing in that voice . . . and they cohered in a way that I hadn't expected. I could see that I had created something that implied much more. So I started writing *Housekeeping*.

Metaphor is the use of figurative language to evoke new ways of thinking, whether that shift is in the way we think about a particular subject or about the nature of language itself. The work of the writer is to expand the ordinary meaning of words and expressions in order to illuminate new ways of thinking or feeling. There are two primary forms of metaphor. Comparative metaphors rely on the formula *A is B*. In substitution metaphors, the poet uses term *A* in place of term *B*. One can take the title of the novel as an extended metaphor, a metaphor that has many parts and occurs continually throughout a narrative or poem, as Robinson uses the characters' diverse attitudes toward the house they have inherited to explore the meaning of terms we accept as ordinary: house, home, self, other, nature, and civilization. In the end, it is Lucille who must leave home in order to keep house in the conventional sense, while Sylvie leads Ruth through the ruins of an abandoned house in order to radically expand her ideas about what constitutes a home. Although students often misunderstand metaphor as a type of puzzle—that an author is saying something other than what he or she means—it is important to remember that, by creating metaphors, the writer is expanding the reader's understanding beyond the boundaries of ordinary thought. That is, by working with language in a metaphoric manner, the writer creates new ways of imagining language and the world.

HISTORICAL CONTEXT

Great Depression

Although the time frame of *Housekeeping* is never made explicit, the clothing and musical references, as well as mentions of war service performed by the missing male characters, narrow the events of the novel to sometime in the 1950s. While popular culture sometimes portrays the 1950s as a period of unfettered optimism and economic prosperity, Robinson's portrait is of a time not far removed from periods of deep economic uncertainty and the sacrifices of wartime. During the decades that directly precede the events of the novel, millions of people, most of them made homeless by the high unemployment of the Great Depression, took to the rails. A subset of those people took to the hobo lifestyle, and like Sylvie, found that once they'd been unmoored from ordinary life, they could not return.

The Great Depression began in 1929 with the crash of the U.S. stock market that wiped out many people's life savings and began a cascade of economic reduction. By 1932, approximately one-fourth of the workforce was unemployed; cities hosted enormous bread lines to try to feed the hungry, and workers took to the roads and railways in the hopes that work lay over the next horizon. Franklin Delano Roosevelt won the presidency from Herbert Hoover in 1932 and began to put in place a series of economic, social, and political reforms that would come to be known as the New Deal. Roosevelt worked quickly to stabilize the banking and investment systems and set in place work relief programs that put the unemployed to work building roads, schools, parks, and trails. It was during the New Deal that the Social Security Act was passed, a system into which workers pay over their lifetimes and are guaranteed a modicum of financial security in their old age. Although each of these efforts helped, the economy did not fully recover until after World War II.

Hobo Culture

The Great Depression brought mass migration of workers as the unemployed took to the roads and rails in search of work. Maggie Galehouse points out, in her article "Their Own Private Idaho: Transience in Marilynne Robinson's *Housekeeping*," that although hobo culture dates from the turn of the century, when industry replaced agriculture as the dominant employer in America, "by the Depression, hoboes had become folk heroes to many, vagrants who refused factory work in favor of seasonal, agricultural jobs." Hobo culture is a term that refers to the set of customs and beliefs that rose among those homeless or unemployed who took to the rails and decided to stay in that lifestyle. It is characterized by a deep sense that one has cast off social responsibilities and possessions, that one is free and unencumbered in ways that people who have regular jobs, houses, and settled lives in communities are not. When Sylvie returns to Fingerbone,

COMPARE
&
CONTRAST

- **1950s:** Women faced pressure to return to the home after World War II, and are now being told that their destinies are keeping house, raising children, and assisting their husbands. While women are not entirely driven from the workplace, especially those working-class women who fill manufacturing and domestic jobs, this conformist decade sees a massive shift in women's roles.

  1980s: The Equal Rights Amendment fails to be ratified by all fifty states. Although the amendment was first proposed in the 1920s, it is not passed by both houses of Congress until 1972. Some analysts attribute this failure to the increasing political participation, beginning in the early 1970s, of the Christian right, including activists like Phyllis Schlafly, who actively campaign against passage.

  Today: According to the 2010 report by the U.S. Congress Joint Economic Committee, "Women comprise half of all U.S. Workers.... Women's educational attainment outstrips that of men, and women's share of union membership is growing rapidly. Families are increasingly dependent on working wives' incomes in order to make ends meet." However, problems remain. The pay gap means that women earn, on average, only eighty cents for every dollar a man earns. Some industries remain closed to women, and women still bump up against the *glass ceiling*, meaning that they do not rise to executive positions at the same rate as men.

- **1950s:** Poets including Alan Ginsberg, Gary Snyder, and Michael McClure rebel against the conformist politics and social mores of the decade as they begin to coalesce into the Beat movement. Characterized by an interest in Buddhism, drug experimentation, and a rejection of materialism, the Beats open up poetry both stylistically and in terms of what subject matter is considered poetic.

  1980s: The decade is dominated by a minimalist style in literary fiction. Led by influential editor Gordon Lish, writers including Ann Beattie, Raymond Carver, Amy Hempel, and Richard Ford experiment with plain sentence structure, deadpan humor, and a near-total absence of authorial direction. These stories leave gaps that the reader is expected to fill in, and express a sense of despair at the conservative backlash against the political and personal experimentation of the 1960s and 1970s.

  Today: Literary fiction in the early decades of the twenty-first century is characterized by writers including David Foster Wallace, Zadie Smith, Jonathan Safran Foer, and Dave Eggers. These writers' use of irony, hyperbole, and fantastical and comic plot devices marks their work as a hyperrealistic postmodernism, or works that depict real life in a striking or strange way in order to challenge modern assumptions.

- **1950s:** The decade is dominated by a fear of nuclear annihilation as the United States and the Soviet Union compete to develop and deploy nuclear warheads as the cold war begins. Schoolchildren are taught to crouch under their desks in case of a nuclear attack, and fallout shelters are built in major cities.

  1980s: With the fall of the Berlin Wall and the introduction of more open economic policies in the Soviet Union, the cold war begins to come to a conclusion by the end of the decade. Across Eastern Europe, communist regimes fall and a period of both openness and chaos begins.

  Today: The conflict between superpowers of the cold war period is replaced by a war on terrorism. Terrorists attack the United States and nations of Western Europe, who are seen as promoting a secular modernism that is anathema to those who would seek to establish fundamentalist religious societies. The United Nations, NATO, and the United States band together to oppose terrorists across the globe.

it is clear to everyone that she is a transient, a hobo. She sleeps in her clothes and, inappropriately, in public. She befriends the hoboes under the bridge. She is not attracted by the comforts of a house and a home but rather spends the novel trying to break down the divisions between inside and outside that characterize and define a house. The Pacific Northwest has always had a large population of transients, whether because of the largely mild weather or because the culture became entrenched there, and cities like Seattle, Portland, and San Francisco still have active communities of people who are often vagrant by choice. They live on the streets or in communal squats, and many of them follow the fruit industry, migrating south and then east, following the ripening fruit, then returning to the Pacific Northwest in the spring to begin again.

Rollback of Women's Rights after World War II

During World War II, women were called into the workforce to take the place of men who had been called up to war. The call was popularized by Rosie the Riveter, a character who appeared on propaganda posters urging women to take up factory, manufacturing, and agricultural jobs in order to keep the economy and the war effort going. This was a period of great liberation for many women, who discovered they liked working outside the home and were excited by the new opportunities opened to them. After the war ended, however, a period of narrowing gender-roles ensued, and a concerted campaign was launched by the government and in the media to convince women to return to the home and abandon the workplace. Nancy Tuana cites the following examples in "Approaches to Feminism." She notes that "Adlai Stevenson's 1955 address to the Smith College graduating class [urged] these educated women not to define themselves by a profession but to participate in politics through the role of wife and mother." She continues that, in 1956, "*Life* magazine published interviews with five male psychiatrists who argued that female ambition was the root of mental illness in wives, emotional upsets in husbands, and homosexuality in boys." It was a deeply conformist period in America's history, a time when violations of dress codes and social convention were not tolerated. In *Housekeeping*, we see this pressure in Lucille's increasingly desperate efforts to improve herself and to conform to the conventions of the town, a program that

Housekeeping means more than doing the laundry in the novel. (Ingrid Balabanova | Shutterstock.com)

eventually leads to her leaving Ruth and Sylvie altogether, in favor of moving in with her home economics teacher, a woman she sees as capable of teaching her the things she needs to know.

CRITICAL OVERVIEW

Despite prepublication concerns by her publisher and by Robinson herself, *Housekeeping* was published to nearly universal acclaim in 1981 and quickly became a classic of American literature. In an interview with Fay in the *Paris Review*, Robinson notes that, although the book found an agent fairly quickly, it was so different from what was being published at the time that

> she said, I'll be happy to represent it but it could be difficult to place. She gave it to an editor at Farrar, Straus and Giroux, who wrote to me and said, We'd be very happy to publish it but it probably won't be reviewed.

The novel won the PEN/Hemingway Award for best first novel, was nominated for a Pulitzer prize, and shortly thereafter, Robinson was hired to teach at the prestigious Iowa Writers' Workshop, where she has remained for the majority of her career.

The novelist Broyard gave the book an early and important review in the *New York Times*, where he claims that it

> sounds as if the author has been treasuring it up all her life, waiting for it to form itself. It's as if, in writing it, she broke through the ordinary human condition with all its dissatisfactions, and achieved a kind of transfiguration.

He concludes his review by stating that Robinson "knocks off the false elevation, the pretentiousness, of our current fiction. Though her ambition is tall, she remains down to earth, where the best novels happen."

Thomas LeClair, reviewed the book shortly after publication for *Contemporary Literature* and notes:

> For Robinson in *Housekeeping,* style is metaphor: the identification of life with and through unusual language. The elegant, measured prose of *Housekeeping* transforms a year in the life of two small-town teenage girls into a profound meditation on loss, transiency, and the shelters we use for protection.... Best of all, though, is a distinctive rhythm—a matter of pace, syntax, and tone—that cannot be described but lingers after Robinson's equally wonderful visual effects wear off.

The novel has also attracted enormous attention from the academic community, where it has become a staple of women's studies and American literature courses. Writing in 2007, Kenneth Millard notes, in *Coming of Age in Contemporary American Fiction*, that "*Housekeeping* is a novel that...has attracted a remarkable amount of excellent academic criticism, especially for an author's first novel." He summarizes the most influential critics who have written about *Housekeeping*, including Martha Ravits, who "has argued that the novel 'brings a new perspective to bear on the dominant American myth about the developing individual freed from social constraints.'" He mentions Maureen Ryan's feeling that Ruth is a "feminist response to R. W. B. Lewis's 'American Adam,'" as well as Nancy Walker's argument that "*Housekeeping* is revolutionary because 'Robinson challenges the authority of the Creation story by recasting its central figures as women and giving Ruth the power to

be its author.'" Some of the other critics he mentions are Susan Rosowski, who claims that "*Housekeeping* is characterized principally by its serious "engagement with epistemological and political questions of the literary West.'" Millard notes that his summary of the criticism is not complete, "but it gives a sense of the quality of attention the novel has received, and of the cultural terms on which it is valued."

In the twenty-four years between the publication of *Housekeeping* and Robinson's second novel, *Gilead* (2004), she wrote several collections of nonfiction and became known as a stringent critic specializing in religious thought of the Puritans, the effects of Calvinism on American literature and philosophy, and the American romantic movement. Because *Housekeeping* was so beloved, the publication of her second novel in 2004 was greeted with great anticipation, and it did not disappoint. *Gilead* won the Pulitzer Prize for Fiction while its companion novel, *Home* (2008), won the Orange Prize for Fiction.

CRITICISM

Charlotte M. Freeman

Freeman is a writer, editor, and former academic living in small-town Montana. In the following essay, she examines how Robinson complicates the central myth of American literature, that of the individual who cannot assimilate to civilization, through her use of female protagonists in Housekeeping.

In interviews, Robinson has said that the inspiration for *Housekeeping* came from the classic texts of nineteenth-century American literature, and what made the book an instant classic is the manner in which she explored how central tropes of American literature might change when the protagonists were female. She told Sarah Fay of the *Paris Review* that *Housekeeping* had it's genesis "in the way that American writers used metaphoric language, starting with Emerson." One of the central tropes of American Romanticism is the struggle between individual experience and the necessary social constraints of civilization, and the heroes of novels as diverse as *Moby Dick* and *The Adventures of Huckleberry Finn* are men or boys who, like Ishmael and Huck, cannot conform themselves to civilized life. One of the central tasks of *Housekeeping* is the re-examination of this central myth from the point of view of a set of

WHAT DO I READ NEXT?

- Gene Luen Yang's prize-winning graphic novel for young adults, *American Born Chinese* (2008), is the story of Jin Wang, a lonely Taiwanese American boy navigating the challenges of middle school in San Francisco. The novel filters Jin Wang's feelings of being born in the wrong body through the story of the Chinese folk hero, the Monkey King, and through the figure of Chin-Kee, an amalgamation of every ugly Chinese American stereotype. This lively and emotionally affecting book was the first graphic novel nominated for the American Book Award.

- Native American poet and novelist Sherman Alexie's first foray into young-adult fiction, *The Absolutely True Diary of a Part-Time Indian* (2007), is, like *Housekeeping*, the story of a misfit adolescent who both resists and longs for assimilation. Arnold Spirit, known as Junior, was born with hydrocephalus (water on the brain). He is very bright and loves to draw, which, along with his geeky looks, makes him the target of bullies. When he transfers from the reservation school to a rich, white school, he expects the worst but finds, to his surprise, that he makes friends and even winds up on the basketball team. A game played against his old school causes Arnold to grapple with the meanings of tribe and community.

- Twenty-four years passed between the publication of *Housekeeping* and the publication of *Gilead* (2004), Robinson's next novel. *Gilead* is the story of John Ames, an elderly minister in small-town Iowa who has become a father late in life. Because he worries he won't live to see his beloved boy grow up, Ames sits down to write him a letter, telling about his own father and grandfather and how they all came to be. Encompassing historical events like the Spanish Flu and John Brown's violent abolitionism, the book is an extended meditation on creation, and especially on the meaning of redemption.

- A mere four years later, Robinson published a companion novel to *Gilead*, *Home* (2008). The story of John Ames's best friend and lifelong companion Robert Boughton, it takes up the other side of a central story in *Gilead*, the story of the return of John Ames Boughton, Robert's prodigal son. Boughton's daughter Glory has also returned home as her father is failing, and someone must take care of him. Like *Housekeeping*, this novel takes on the concept of home: where is home, and is home the place where they must always take one in? Where the central theme of *Gilead* was judgment, the central theme of *Home* is redemption, and while both books stand alone, in concert they resonate with and amplify one another.

- In *Hoboes: Bindlestiffs, Fruit Tramps, and the Harvesting of the West* (2010), Mark Wyman examines the history of itinerant workers in the West. When the railroads opened up great swathes of the American West, workers invariably followed, many of them as stowaways on the very railroads that eventually provided them with work. Wyman's exhaustive study is nonetheless widely readable and gives insight into what is normally an invisible sector of society.

- Henry David Thoreau's *Walden, or Life in the Woods* (1854) is, like *Housekeeping*, concerned with what it means to have and keep a home. Thoreau's experiment in stripping his life down to its essentials remains a central text of American literature because it speaks to something elemental in the American experience.

---

female characters. It is as if Robinson asks, in a world in which women are still identified with domesticity and the home, with motherhood and settlement, what might this myth look like if it is the female characters who cannot accommodate themselves to civilized life?

> IF THE CENTRAL STORY OF AMERICAN LITERATURE IS THE INDIVIDUAL WHO CANNOT ACCOMMODATE TO SOCIETY, HERE ROBINSON HAS COMPLICATED THAT TALE BY ADDING THE PERFORMATIVE ASPECT OF FEMININITY AS ONE OF THE TRAITS OF CIVILIZATION TO WHICH RUTH CANNOT ADJUST."

Housekeeping is a world in which everything is in flux, and in which change signals only loss. Although the novel is narrated by Ruth, the elder of the two sisters, the plot follows both sisters as they attempt to navigate the minefield of loss in which they are raised. The first loss comes before they are even born, with the train wreck that drowned the girls' grandfather, a wreck in which the seemingly inexplicable happened; as the train crossed the bridge, it somehow jumped the tracks and slipped into the lake "like a weasel sliding off a rock." The Foster family found itself irreparably unmoored by this illogical and yet irrefutable event. This sets up a pattern in the novel in which change is equated with bereavement. Within a year of the train wreck, Sylvia Foster, the girls' grandmother, has been abandoned by all three of her children and remains, bereft, in the house in Fingerbone. Change comes again when Helen, the girls' mother, borrows a car on the pretext of bringing them for a visit with their grandmother, only to abandon the two children on her doorstep in order to commit suicide by driving the car off a cliff into the lake. That this abandonment is deliberate is made excruciatingly clear by the story that comes back to the family. Two boys found Helen bogged down in a meadow. They pushed her car out only to have her turn back and gun the engine, driving deliberately off the cliff on her second try. Neither Sylvia nor the girls can deny that Helen deliberately killed herself, although later in the book, while trying to escape, Lucille tells herself that it was an accident. Ruth, however, not only knows it was not but is just enough older than Lucille to remember their mother's indifferent housekeeping and her inattentive mothering. While Sylvia is alive, the children live a fairly stable life in a home where their grandmother "whited shoes and braided hair and fried chicken and turned back bedclothes," but even this appearance of stability is unreliable. Sylvia's grief at her lost husband and lost children cannot be assuaged by the two grandchildren left in her care, and she goes through the motions of keeping house and raising them "as if re-enacting the commonplace would make it merely commonplace again, or as if she could find the chink, the flaw, in her serenely orderly and ordinary life." Even order, in this case, is not what it seems; it is not true order, true serenity, but an imitation order that cannot cover the abiding sorrow Sylvia carries at the changes the world has brought to her life.

When Sylvia dies, the girls are caught up again by the inescapable reality of their world, a world in which change is inevitable, and inevitably erodes what security they once possessed. Cared for indifferently by two flighty and frightened great aunts, the girls escape their oppressive worry by skating late into the night on the frozen surface of the lake in which both their grandfather and their mother lie entombed. It is at this point in the story that the external world begins a series of changes that reflect the inner instability with which the girls live. During the winter of the aunts, the liquid surface of the lake freezes solid, all the way across. It freezes so solidly that the entire town skates, and there are people hired to sweep the snow clear for the skaters. Only Ruth and Lucille, however, stay out so late that they skate by the light of the moon, navigating home by the reflected lights of the houses in town. Spring brings with it the arrival of their aunt Sylvie, a vagrant who has been riding the rails for years and for whom the great aunts had to advertise in papers across the West. Spring also brings a flood that inundates the town, and while it does not float their house off its foundation as it does some others in the town, the floodwaters do rise through the first floor, leaving Sylvie and the girls mostly stranded on the second floor, with occasional forays downstairs to fetch hot bricks from the stove in order to stay warm. The boundaries of the outside and inside worlds are dissolving, and Sylvie, with her tramp's habits, is not temperamentally suited to rebuilding them. In fact, she contributes to this dissolution of boundaries by leaving the doors and windows open, allowing swirls of dry leaves to accumulate in corners, refusing to use the electric lights, and leaving broken windowpanes unrepaired and burned curtains hanging in the kitchen.

As the girls enter adolescence, their reactions to the domestic flux in which they live begin to separate them. Lucille is the younger sister, but she develops first, becoming "a touchy, achy, tearful creature" whose "clothes begin to bind and pull, to irk and exasperate her." Even though she is the younger sister, it is Lucille who becomes "a small woman" while Ruth continues to grow, yet remains simply "a towering child." As womanhood asserts itself on Lucille, she begins to pull away from Sylvie and Ruth, in large part by rebelling against their passive attitude toward flux. Where Sylvie buys the girls cheap sequined shoes and sweaters from the dime store, not to save money but, because, in the moment, they seem festive, Lucille rebels against the inevitable quick decay of such purchases. Ruth notes that while Sylvie lived in the "millennial present," where "the deteriorations of things were always a fresh surprise, a disappointment not to be dwelt on," for Lucille, "Time that had not come yet . . . had the fiercest reality for her." Ruth notes that, as she grows into womanhood, itself a process of irreversible change, "Lucille saw in everything its potential for invidious change. She wanted worsted mittens, brown oxfords, red rubber boots. Ruffles wilted, sequins fell, satin was impossible to clean." Lucille's war against the laxity in housekeeping that characterizes life with Sylvie takes on new urgency after the night she and Ruth spend in the forest. Stranded by darkness after a day of fishing, the two girls build a shelter, and while Ruth gives herself over to the dark wilderness, letting "the sky become coextensive with the darkness in my skull and bowels and bones," Lucille refuses to do so. She sits beside Ruth, but is "never still, never accepting that all our human boundaries were overrun." The next morning, Lucille refuses to speak as they hike back home, and once they get there, she insists on combing Ruth's hair, dragging her down to the dime store to buy "setting gel," bullying her into compliance with conventional norms of appearance. As Lucille hits adolescence, she acquires an "ability to look the way one was supposed to look," she buys cloth to make an outfit that "will all be coordinated," and she eventually leaves home to live instead with the home economics teacher, the person hired by society specifically to teach girls how to be proper women.

Ruth, on the other hand, reacts to change and loss in the opposite way; where Lucille fights against change, Ruth gives in to it. Although Lucille tries to improve her sister, tries setting her hair and interesting her in fashion magazines, she is no match for Ruth's passive resistance, her absolute refusal to participate. When Lucille drags Ruth to the drug store to buy setting gel, Ruth resolutely leaves the store, walking toward home until Lucille gives up on her, leaving her "alone, in the gentle afternoon, indifferent to my clothes and comfortable in my skin, unimproved and without the prospect of improvement." If the central story of American literature is the individual who cannot accommodate to society, here Robinson has complicated that tale by adding the performative aspect of femininity as one of the traits of civilization to which Ruth cannot adjust. Femininity and gender are not merely physical conditions, but are also cultural constructs, and one of the chief tasks and anxieties of adolescence is learning how self-presentation influences what people think. For Lucille, this task is complicated by the ways in which Sylvie still clearly bears the habits and demeanor of a vagrant. She sleeps on park benches or on the lawn; she eats out of cans and keeps her belongings in a cardboard box under the bed. Lucille's rebellion is to try as hard as she can to assimilate, to please townspeople like the mother of her friend Rosette Brown, and to learn the skills of home economics. Ruth's rebellion is to move further toward Sylvie, to move beyond her experience of the dissolution of human boundaries she had in the woods with Lucille to the experience of rebirth she undergoes in the rowboat with Sylvie as they return from the valley of the frostbitten homestead. Where Lucille seeks salvation in normalcy, Ruth finds herself moving increasingly beyond the pale of ordinary citizenship. She feels herself becoming someone who "would feel ill at ease in a cleanly house with glass in its windows—I would be lost to ordinary society." It is telling that it is only after the night when Ruth once again experiences a loss of boundaries between self and nature in the orchard that she and Sylvie decide to burn the house and flee across the bridge. That last evening, Ruth learns that, " if you do not resist the cold, but simply relax and accept it, you no longer feel the cold as discomfort."

And yet, Robinson does not present either sister's choice as the correct one; rather she dramatizes the consequences of both choices. While her decision to give Ruth the narrator's voice necessarily privileges her point of view, the decision Ruth makes to flee with Sylvie and take up a life of drifting is not presented as a triumphant liberation from the conventions of society or femininity. Ruth and Sylvie share a transcendental worldview that makes it impossible for them to live as ordinary people do, but Robinson is careful not to condemn those like Lucille, who resist transience. Instead, Robinson seems to be presenting two incompatible but not competing worldviews, that of those like Sylvie and Ruth who live in the "millennial present" and those like Lucille, for whom "Time that had not come yet... had the fiercest reality." That Ruth chooses one and Lucille the other is the final act of flux and loss in the novel, as each sister loses the other, and in doing so, loses her last ties to family and home. Like the other great American novels of individualism, Ruth is stripped of everything but her individualism, and it is in this stripping that she comes to know the elemental nature of her own self.

Source: Charlotte M. Freeman, Critical Essay on *Housekeeping*, in *Novels for Students*, Gale, Cengage Learning, 2012.

Maureen Ryan

In the following essay, Ryan argues that Housekeeping *subverts the traditional American myth of wandering, offering a feminist revision that reflects the difficulties faced by women who attempt to escape traditional roles in patriarchal society.*

When Huck "lights out for the territory ahead of the rest" at the end of *Adventures of Huckleberry Finn*, he enacts one of the classic myths of American literature. Confronted with the frontier and the illimitable possibilities for self-development and success that open spaces imply, the male American hero, long recognized as the "American Adam," is "an individual emancipated from history, happily bereft of ancestry, untouched and undefiled by the usual inheritances of family and race; an individual standing alone, self-reliant and self-propelling, ready to confront whatever awaited him with the aid of his own inherent and unique resources" (Lewis 5). At the end of *Housekeeping*, Marilynne Robinson's first novel, on a Melvillean "dark and clouded night," Ruth, the young narrator, and her aunt Sylvie set fire to the family home and start off across the long railroad bridge that no one has ever crossed, to return to Sylvie's life of transiency. "'It's not the worst thing, Ruthie, drifting,'" she says, "'You'll see.'"

Housekeeping is the story of Ruth and Lucille, two sisters who, after their mother's suicide, are cared for by a succession of female relatives, finally and most unconventionally by their

> IN HER MANIPULATION OF PLOT—HER LAYERING OF FEMALE EXPERIENCE THROUGH THESE AND OTHER TALES OF NAMELESS WOMEN; HER REJECTION OF A TRADITIONAL, LINEAR NARRATIVE THAT, FOR WOMEN, TYPICALLY BEGINS WITH ADOLESCENCE AND CULMINATES IN MARRIAGE OR DEATH—ROBINSON PRESENTS HER REJECTION OF THE TRADITIONAL FEMALE STORY."

mother's youngest sister, Sylvie, a wanderer who returns home to attend to her nieces with a peculiar notion of housekeeping. Sylvie's unorthodox mothering—fanciful, impractical clothes; late-night suppers in the dark; a house overrun with newspapers, small animals, and leaves—inspires the conventional Lucille to abandon aunt and sister for a more traditional life with the Home Economics teacher and eventually induces the townspeople to attempt to remove Ruthie from her aunt's iconoclastic care. It is the threat of separation that forces the pair across the bridge. "It is a terrible thing to break up a family," Ruthie offers as explanation for their flight from civilization; her statement is as well Robinson's articulation of her deviation from the myth of the unencumbered American hero. Her female hero is very much entangled with history, ancestry, the inheritances of family and race; she is an individual standing, not alone, but together, with an aunt who is also mother and sister, and with whom she affirms the bonds of family.

Housekeeping is a complex, often amorphous novel about appearance and reality, mutability, and memory and the past. It lends itself to—and has yielded—a variety of critical explications, ranging from Thomas Foster's reading of it as a representation of Julia Kristeva's theory of women's time, to Elizabeth Meese's deconstruction of the novel as Robinson's attempt to explore the creation of an individual and communal female self, to Gunilla Florby's consideration of the author's use of the "machine in the garden" theme. In short, *Housekeeping* is not simply Robinson's engagement of one of the central myths of American literature, but her appreciation for American literature, and her critique of it, are an intriguing element of the novel.

In "Is There Life after Art? The Metaphysics of Marilynne Robinson's *Housekeeping*," Joan Kirkby notes the echoes of American literature in Robinson's recommendation in *Housekeeping* of a return to nature. "Inevitably," Kirkby writes, "*Housekeeping* evokes and improvises on recurring motifs and whole structures and patterns of resonance from the works of those earlier American writers also preoccupied with the interaction of nature and art, Dickinson, Thoreau, Hawthorne, Emerson, Poe" (Kirkby 92–93). Indeed, the student of nineteenth-century American literature recognizes allusions to those and other writers throughout *Housekeeping*.

Ruthie describes the lives of her grandmother and her daughters after their father's death by drowning: "When their mother sat down with her mending, they would settle themselves around her on the floor . . . with their heads propped against her knees or her chair, restless as young children." Recall Louisa May Alcott's presentation of the March women when their father and husband is off to war. "They all drew to the fire, mother in the big chair with Beth at her feet, Meg and Amy perched on either arm of the chair, and Jo leaning on the back . . ." (Alcott 9–10). As the sisters enter adolescence and Lucille grows increasingly impatient with their unusual lifestyle, she begins to keep a diary, which, Ruthie is surprised to discover when she reads it, contains not teenager's secrets, but, like the private writing of Jay Gatsby and Benjamin Franklin, exercises and advice on personal improvement. Melville's discourse on the interdependence of human beings in "The Monkey Rope" chapter of *Moby-Dick* is recalled when tethered young men search for the sunken train that opens the novel, and, later, when Ruthie remembers how her mother would tie her young daughters to a doorknob with clothesline so that they could look out at the street from the lofty porch of their city apartment.

In an interview about *Housekeeping*, Marilynne Robinson speaks of the influence of the American writers whose work reverberates throughout her novel. "I'm a great admirer of nineteenth-century American fiction and I've been told that *Moby-Dick*, for example, is a 'man's book'—all of which led me to think that if *I* would write a book with only female characters that men would

read, then I could have *Moby-Dick*!" She continues, proudly: "And, to be honest about it, men have been very nice about *Housekeeping*. Amazing numbers have read it" ("Marilynne Robinson" 122). Marilynne Robinson may well express amazement at the number of men who have read and liked *Housekeeping*, for underlying her appreciation for, and use of, the traditional male American writers and the myth of freedom in wandering is a subversive female narrative that dramatically rewrites a central myth of canonical American literature.

Feminist literary critics have demonstrated how, in a patriarchal culture in which women are defined by, and in opposition to, men, woman is not subject, but both object and Other. "Culture is male. Our literary myths are for heroes, not heroines," Joanna Russ proclaims in "What Can a Heroine Do? Or Why Women Can't Write" (Russ 7). Judith Fetterley and Nina Baym have applied their feminist critique of phallocentric literary culture to American literature to conclude that, as Fetterly writes, "being American is equated with the experience of being male" (Fetterley xii). As Baym argues, whereas the quintessential white male American writer both defines and criticizes archetypal Americanness (remember Melville's "No, in thunder!"), the American female writer embodies the status quo and effectively becomes the enemy. The classic American experience is the rejection of the restrictive forces of civilization, represented by female characters like the termagant Dame Van Winkle, Huck's Aunt Sally, and Tom Wingfield's suffocating mother and sister. The female reader must identify with secondary, limited, and negative characters or be, in Fetterley's words, "co-opted into participation in an experience from which she is explicitly excluded; she is asked to identify with a selfhood that defines itself in opposition to her; she is required to identify against herself" (Fetterley xii). The woman writer who envisions more for her female hero must struggle to transcend readers' expectations about feminine literary behavior. As Sandra M. Gilbert and Susan Gubar assert, "for the female artist the essential process of self-definition is complicated by all those patriarchal definitions that intervene between herself and herself" (Gilbert and Gubar 17). Indeed, what can a woman writer—or her hero—do?

The nineteenth-century woman writer, according to Gilbert and Gubar, often revised male genres surreptitiously and subversively by creating "palimpsestic works whose surface designs conceal or obscure deeper, less accessible (and less socially acceptable) levels of meaning. Thus these authors managed the difficult task of achieving true female literary authority by simultaneously conforming to and subverting patriarchal literary standards" (Gilbert and Gubar 73). Increasingly, women writers have developed strategies to move beyond the traditional possibilities for female characters—negative characterization; marginal status in the text; or, for central characters, the love story. In "Emphasis Added: Plots and Plausibilities in Women's Fiction," Nancy K. Miller discusses women writers' fulfillment of "the demand of the heroine for something else" and "the extravagant wish for a *story* that would turn out differently" by inserting into their texts "modalities of difference" that are often misinterpreted as "implausibilities" (Miller 44, 42). For Joanne S. Frye in *Living Stories, Telling Lives*, her study subtitled *Women and the Novel in Contemporary Experience*, modernist innovations in fiction, particularly the emphasis on process, have resulted in new possibilities for the female narrative: "The refusal of narrative closure and of a determinate past becomes a way for the novel's plotting of events to show women's lives—like all lives—as ongoing process, not passive entrapment in romance or sexual destiny" (Frye 40–41). Rachel Blau DuPlessis demonstrates how women writers "write beyond the [traditional] ending" for female characters by inventing new narrative strategies that explore reformulated families, brother-sister and woman-to-woman bonds, and communal protagonists; in short, choices that "break the sequence" of traditional plots that end, for women, in marriage or death (DuPlessis 4–5). In *Housekeeping* Marilynne Robinson writes beyond the ending of the archetypal story of the American Adam, the hero "liberated from family and social history or bereft of them" (Lewis 127).

The first line of *Housekeeping* is the narrator's declaration, "My name is Ruth." The reference to Melville's narrator's "Call me Ishmael" is unmistakable, yet from the first line of this novel that is so consciously rooted in the American literary tradition, Robinson emphasizes her revision of that tradition. Created typically as object, denied a central presence in canonical male literature and a tradition of female authorship, the woman writer, and her protagonist, cannot claim their identity freely. As Frye asserts, "saying 'I,' as a woman, remains very nearly a contradiction in terms" (Frye 49). Therefore, for the female author, the adoption of the first-person narrator is in itself a

subversive act. "When the protagonist of the novel is made her own narrator, she thus achieves a very immediate kind of agency and a capacity to renew our notion of plot. She is the agent by which events come into being as part of her story: . . . she sets the context for the causal links in her own life. . . . [S]he claims the capacity for new understanding of her life and selfhood" (Frye 56). Having claimed her own voice, become namer instead of named, Ruthie recognizes and examines throughout her story the subjectivity of experience and the implications of existing in a world in which she refuses to be defined by others: "It was a source of both terror and comfort to me then that I often seemed invisible—incompletely and minimally existent, in fact. It seemed to me that I made no impact on the world, and that in exchange I was privileged to watch it unawares." With the subversive capacities of her appropriation of her own voice, Ruthie, with Sylvie as her role model, resists narrative conventions and social restrictions, in effect claims her own difference. As Elizabeth Meese maintains, in *Housekeeping*, "for a fictive moment the 'other' becomes the 'One'" (Meese 61).

Born into a family of women who live in a rakish, homemade house on a hill, isolated from the community, Ruthie and Lucille are from the beginning unusual children. When their mother's suicide alienates them further and their grandmother's death subjects them to the anxious ministrations of their aged, childless great-aunts, as they grow they become increasingly different. During the long northern Idaho winters the girls spend countless hours skating on the lake that has claimed both mother and grandfather. "Only we and the ice sweepers went out so far," Ruthie writes, "and only we stayed." When, just after Sylvie's arrival, the town floods, the three women take refuge on the second floor, whiling away the time with games of Monopoly and Sylvie's stories of the transients she has met on her travels. Although Lucille wants to venture out to find other people, Sylvie and Ruthie are content to wait in the house, and when the waters subside, "the restoration of the town," Ruthie notes, "was an exemplary community effort in which we had no part." The sisters are indifferent students, and when they begin to skip school and spend their days at the lake, no one seems to care; when they do return, they are not punished, for "apparently it had been decided that our circumstances were special." As the girls age, Lucille makes friends, becomes interested in clothes and boys, and grows increasingly impatient with Sylvie's antisocial behavior. "'We have to *improve* ourselves,'" she tells Ruthie urgently. This is the beginning of Lucille's defection to the world of propriety and acceptable female behavior, the world that in *Housekeeping* becomes the Other. "And," Ruthie remarks, "I was left alone . . . indifferent to my clothes and comfortable in my skin, unimproved and without the prospect of improvement. It seemed to me then that Lucille would busy herself forever, nudging, pushing, coaxing, as if she could supply the will I lacked, to pull myself into some seemly shape and slip across the wide frontiers into that other world, where it seemed to me then I could never wish to go." When the school principal recommends a new attention to studies, "a change of attitude," Lucille promises improvement but cautions him about Ruthie, "'You can't really talk to her about practical things. They don't matter to her. . . . She has her own ways.'"

Lucille abandons her tall, gawky sister, whose ways, increasingly, become the ways of Sylvie, who is married but barely remembers her husband—one of Robinson's rejections of the typical female plot is in her indifference to sexuality; who sleeps with her shoes on and with her belongings in a box under the bed; who, in her affirmation of the credibility of the female voice, tells stories of lonely, vagrant women: stories that reject traditional expectations about the female narrative and offer Ruthie different ways of being female. Throughout *Housekeeping* the central narrative is punctuated by fleeting wisps of women's lives—those of women who react against their traditional roles, such as the two women who flee Fingerbone when the mysterious train wreck widows them. The woman "who was so lonely she married an old man with a limp and had four children in five years, and none of it helped at all" affirms, too, that the traditional female role—marriage, motherhood—fails to satisfy all women. More often, Sylvie's stories of women are eccentric, but optimistic: there is Edith, the old woman, who, wearing all that she owned, quite willingly "came to her rest crossing the mountains in a boxcar, in December," and Alma, with whom Sylvie had sat at sunrise one cold Sunday, singing "Irene" and eating hot dogs, and the memory of whom inspires Sylvie to proclaim that, "'When you're traveling, Sundays are the best days.'" The brief stories of Edith and Alma and the one-armed woman who supports six children by giving piano lessons merge with Ruthie's memories of her own mother and grandmother, and with universal women—Noah's wife, and

Lot's, and "our mother Eve," in Ruthie's assumption that one day "there will be a garden where all of us as one child will sleep in our mother Eve, hooped in her ribs and staved by her spine."

In her manipulation of plot—her layering of female experience through these and other tales of nameless women; her rejection of a traditional, linear narrative that, for women, typically begins with adolescence and culminates in marriage or death—Robinson presents her rejection of the traditional female story. And her presentation of new and multiple possibilities for her hero is effected through Ruthie's engagement with the past, the past that the American Adam, in his insistence upon "the sovereignty of the living," typically rejects (Lewis 15). "The past is a malleable substance, which we work into expressive shapes that in turn shape us. We are creator and creature," Marilynne Robinson has written ("Writers and the Nostalgic Fallacy," 34). Throughout *Housekeeping* Ruthie grapples with the claims of memory and the past to discover a life for herself that will allow her to go beyond "that other world." Frye articulates the uses of the past for the female narrator: "As the needs of the present prompt narrative interpretation of the past, the narrator's memory can yield a different 'reality,' a different chronology: a subversion of fixity, a reopening of cultural 'truth'" (Frye 57). "There is remembrance and communion, altogether human and unhallowed," Ruthie writes, "For families will not be broken."

At the end of *Housekeeping*, Ruthie and Sylvie, like the classic male American hero, abandon home and civilization and embark on an unknown journey; like their forefathers, they are forced to flee an oppressive civilization, but in a female variation of the urge to roam, the pair are threatened, finally, not by the forces of acculturation that they have successfully resisted throughout the novel, but by the danger of separation. Their flight from the other world of normalcy is an affirmation of female solidarity. In an ironic comment on the typical denouement for the female hero who refuses to conform, that other world believes that Ruthie and Sylvie are dead—"LAKE CLAIMS TWO" is the headline of the clipping that Sylvie keeps pinned to her lapel—but in an affirmation of the possibility of female autonomy *and* nurturance, Ruthie and Sylvie remain together, indefinitely and unconventionally. The novel's ending rejects closure, as Ruthie wonders about Lucille and her whereabouts, and underscores Robinson's presentation of openness and unlimited potentialities for her, and other, female protagonists.

"When did I become so unlike other people?" an older Ruthie wonders at the end of the novel. "Either it was when I followed Sylvie across the bridge, and the lake claimed us, or it was when my mother left me waiting for her . . . or it was at my conception." In *Housekeeping*, Marilynne Robinson revises the traditional American myth of freedom and transience, endorsing not independence over commitment, autonomy over family, but both; affirming, finally, female difference. In *Housekeeping* Marilynne Robinson writes beyond the ending and presents a new narrative for a new American Eve.

Source: Maureen Ryan, "Marilynne Robinson's *Housekeeping*: The Subversive Narrative and the New American Eve," in *South Atlantic Review*, Vol. 56, No. 1, January 1991, pp. 79–86.

Marcia Aldrich

In the following excerpt, Aldrich defines Robinson's use of place and nature in establishing the role of the women in Housekeeping.

> Yet how could it be otherwise, since the very notion of a self, the very shape of human life stories, has always, from St. Augustine to Freud, been modeled on the man?
>
> Barbara Johnson, "My Monster/My Self"

When we write primarily of women and not in opposition to men, according to Mary Jacobus, we are subverting convention by presenting "a difference of view"—an attempt to inscribe female difference within writing as an alternative to separatism or appropriation. Such subversions aptly characterize Marilynne Robinson's *Housekeeping*, a novel in which narrative view shifts quickly from Edmund Foster, the patriarch of the novel's central family, to the women who survive him: his widow, Sylvia; her three daughters, Sylvie, Molly, and Helen; and Helen's daughters, Lucille and Ruth (who serves as narrator). Husbands and fathers mysteriously disappear in the first chapter of *Housekeeping* before the lives of the women unfold, almost as a prologue to the novel proper. The novel avoids thereby an oedipal narrative of Edmund Foster, a master plot determined by the role of the father, in order to represent those conflicts generated by the figure of the mother. With the novel's opening sentence ("My name is Ruth")

BUT THIS PARADIGM IS PROBLEMATIC FOR WOMEN AND WOMEN WRITERS, WHO IN ANY TRADITIONAL THEMATICS OF GENDER ARE IDENTIFIED WITH NATURE AND MATTER AND WHO ARE THE CARETAKERS, NOT THE BUILDERS, OF HOUSES."

and its allusion to the Old Testament story of loyalty between daughter and mother-in-law, we are turned to a story of feminine escape and love. The allusion recalls for us how Ruth and Naomi, through their bond of devotion, escape the bitter abandonments of the past, and their escape informs Robinson's novel as its primary theme. *Housekeeping* clearly values the mother/daughter relationship, but in allowing the women of the novel to come into their own, Robinson also attempts a new kind of expressivity, inscribing female difference within writing itself. This "difference within," as Barbara Johnson calls it, is enacted through Robinson's poetics of "transience," a specifically female mode of experience and language.

The place of this rewriting is the American pastoral. The impulse of the dominant ideology of this pastoral, brilliantly charted by Annette Kolodny, is to view the landscape as feminine and as victim to the masculine activity of cultivation. But Ruth's narrative in *Housekeeping* does not entail a despoiling of nature or of the mother; it tries to rid itself of the destructive tendencies which led Thoreau to recognize that "his own pen was a weapon that, however much it celebrated the settlement of America, aligned itself unnervingly with the destruction of the New Eden." Ruth's narrative of female transience and unconventional housekeeping suggests that an illusion of ownership and mastery has blinded men to the meaning of a feminine nature. Ruth attempts to embrace feminine nature and the mother, countering the violence of what John Crowe Ransom in the 1930 agrarian manifesto *I'll Take My Stand* called "the masculine form."

Ruth's account of Edmund Foster before he dies follows the line of narratives that link the seekers of the American primitive with the violation of once inviolate land. The father embodies the American spirit of enterprise; his ambitions for "success, recognition, and advancement" are shaped by his youth spent in an eye-level, sod-bound, womb-like house in the Midwest. Foster, like many heroes from fiction by Cooper, Melville, James, and Fitzgerald, must confound the circumscriptions of his original home by appropriating a space fit for his imagination. He therefore flees the sod house, catches a train west, and settles in stupendously mountainous Idaho, in Fingerbone, a town created out of what "once belonged to the lake" and for which the "whole of human history had occurred elsewhere." Foster's settlement in Fingerbone is identified with the railroad's incursion into the wilderness. He rises rapidly to the rank of stationmaster, and we are reminded of Emerson's use of the railroad to represent the domination of men over nature and to represent the individual who stands out above the masses. The paradox at the heart of American pastoral colonization is the paradox of Foster's narrative: as Kolodny puts it, "The success of settlement depended on the ability to master the land, transforming the virgin territories into something else— a farm, a village, a road, a railway." Foster's cultivation is like Thoreau's "penetration of Nature"— a project analogously yoking writing, building, and plowing—which, as Eric Sundquist rightfully observes, has two sides: "On the one hand, it is a rude despoiling, but on the other, it represents a fathering and impregnation, the necessary cultivation entailed by settlement."

Edmund Foster needs to find natural challenges his imagination can humanize, and his settling signifies claims of ownership and authorship. Foster settles on the outskirts of town, on top of a hill, and, knowing nothing of carpentry, nevertheless builds a house notable for its extraordinary trap doors and pulleys, random fenestration, and self-sufficient air. His yearly wildflower hunt, with its booty of flowers that he presses alphabetically into a dictionary, is an example of the way Foster's efforts mutilate and destroy the objects of his exploration and cast nature as the trophy of his knowledge. Foster is not content either to appreciate or simply pick the wildflowers, but lifts them "earth and all" to replant at home, where they will die. Edmund's wife, Sylvia, wishes that he, rather than a man hunting wildflowers attired in necktie and suspenders, were a "dark man with crude stripes painted on his face and sunken belly." Sylvia wishes he would cultivate his own primitiveness rather than domesticate wildflowers—a reversal Sylvie and Ruth will successfully enact.

Because Foster prides himself on mastery, it is ironic that the event propelling the novel into its own female life is the derailment of the train he is riding, the Fireball, and its plunge off the bridge across the lake leading into Fingerbone. Although no one sees the Fireball's disappearance in the middle of a moonless night, it is the town's most widely, even nationally, reported news. The townspeople gather at the shore, and divers search the chilly, opaque waters through the following days, but the only items retrieved from the wreck are fragmentary, transient, literal, and, to the mind of the townspeople, worthless: a suitcase, a seat cushion, a lettuce—"no relics but three, and one of them perishable." The Fireball, representative of civilization's agents and carrying Foster, the stationmaster, paradoxically repenetrates nature by plunging into the feminized landscape, the bottomless lake out of which Fingerbone was created, in an updated version of the "imperialistic eroticism" Kolodny has observed throughout American literature and described in the phrase "the lay of the land." I say bottomless lake because Robinson emphasizes the impossibility of tapping its depths. When the divers search for Foster's train, the lake temporarily and tantalizingly seems to avail itself to their exploration, allowing what might be a glimpse of the actual train, only to seal over by evening.

The train's plunge might indeed be understood as a sublimated return to the Mother. This is no coincidence; for the women of the novel, the absence of husbands and fathers is the prerequisite for their own development. *Housekeeping* centers primarily on the two granddaughters, Ruth and Lucille. At an early age they are deserted inexplicably by their father and then as well by their mother Helen, who commits suicide by driving a car into the same lake her father's train fell into. Like Edmund Foster, Helen is never found. Her death allows a range of female relations to develop, all prompted by the girls' need of a mother. First, the grandmother, Foster's widow Sylvia, raises them, her second chance at mothering father-less daughters. Upon her death, the elderly, reclusive, and unmarried sisters-in-law, Lily and Nona, try their hand, with disastrous results; for they are too cautious and stiff in their ways to cope with the young girls or the natural challenges of life in Fingerbone. Their defeat makes the unthinkable thinkable—to recall home to Fingerbone the transient, wayward, and outcast Sylvie, sister of Helen, to raise Ruth and Lucille, her nieces. Sylvie had left

Fingerbone some years before to marry, but her husband also mysteriously disappeared, and she began a satisfying life of transience, riding the trains, sleeping on the outskirts of towns with an assortment of female transients, whose stories she later tells—a life, in short, without claims of ownership or settlement. Yet she returns to Fingerbone to assume the care of Lucille and Ruth.

This series of examples of woman-centered housekeeping is neither a utopian fantasy of female homogeneity nor a monolithic tribute to female essence. The lake claims Foster, but traces of his power remain, as embodied in the social institutions of Fingerbone—the Methodist Church, the school, and the sheriff's office, which attempt to remove Ruth from Sylvie's care because their transient housekeeping does not conform to the town's standards. Although the novel concerns itself almost exclusively with the relations among women subsequent to Foster's death, the Foster females, isolated on the edge of town, still must respond to the authoritative dictates of Fingerbone, where social institutions insist upon a gender hierarchy and are intolerant of the unconventional, and from the town's masculine perspective, unfeminine behavior of Sylvie and Ruth, specifically their returning to Fingerbone in a freight car.

Foster's patriarchal legacy also resides in the house he has built—a "reliquary" where even lost things abide and haunt—wherein the women who survive him live, for building houses has been, most obviously in Thoreau's *Walden*, a metaphor for the highly valued masculine and figurative rituals of art. One builds houses to possess what nature otherwise possesses. For Thoreau, Hawthorne, and Emerson, writing is an analogy to building and depends upon the symbolic possession of landscape. But this paradigm is problematic for women and women writers, who in any traditional thematics of gender are identified with nature and matter and who are the caretakers, not the builders, of houses. If woman is identified with nature and matter—the objects of male symbolization—women may wish to preserve nature from the effects of symbolization as they may prefer to extend the rapport with their mothers rather than honor the symbolic order of the father. . . .

Source: Marcia Aldrich, "The Poetics of Transience: Marilynne Robinson's *Housekeeping*," in *Essays in Literature*, Vol. 16, No. 1, Spring 1989, pp. 127–40.

SOURCES

Broyard, Anatole, Review of *Housekeeping*, in *New York Times*, January 7, 1981, http://www.nytimes.com/1981/01/07/books/books-of-the-times-books-of-the-times.html (accessed July 28, 2011).

Canby, Vincent, "Film: Forsyth's *Housekeeping*," in *New York Times*, November 25, 1987, http://movies.nytimes.com/movie/review?res=9B0DE4D6103AF936A15752 C1A961948260&scp (accessed July 28, 2011).

Fay, Sarah, "Marilynne Robinson: The Art of Fiction No. 198," in *Paris Review*, Fall 2008, http://www.theparisreview.org/interviews/5863/the-art-of-fiction-no-198-marilynne-robinson (accessed July 28, 2011).

Galehouse, Maggie, "Their Own Private Idaho: Transience in Marilynne Robinson's *Housekeeping*," in *Contemporary Literature*, Vol. 41, No. 1, Spring 2000, pp. 117–37.

LeClair, Thomas, "Fiction Chronicle: January to June, 1981," in *Contemporary Literature*, Vol. 23, No. 1, Winter 1982, pp. 83–91.

Millard, Kenneth, *Coming of Age in Contemporary Fiction*, Edinburgh University Press, 2007, p. 142.

Robinson, Marilynne, *Housekeeping*, Farrar, Straus and Giroux, 1980.

Ryan, Maureen, "Marilynne Robinson's *Housekeeping*: The Subversive Narrative and the New American Eve," in *South Atlantic Review*, Vol. 56, No. 1, January 1991, pp. 79–86.

Tuana, Nancy, "Approaches to Feminism," in *The Stanford Encyclopedia of Philosophy*, Spring 2011, http://plato.stanford.edu/archives/spr2011/entries/feminism-approaches/ (accessed July 27, 20011).

Voss, Anne E., "Portrait of Marilynne Robinson," in *Iowa Review*, Vol. 22, No. 1, Winter 1992, pp. 21–28.

"Women and the Economy 2010: 25 Years of Progress But Challenges Remain," in *U.S. Congress Joint Economic Committee*, August 2010, p. 1.

FURTHER READING

Hungerford, Amy, *Postmodern Belief: American Literature and Religion Since 1960*, Princeton University Press, 2010.
> Hungerford explores the role of religious belief in the works of a number of contemporary writers, including Robinson. She is particularly interested in the ways that fiction writers portray the tension between belief and practice, an examination she extends to Robinson's novels *Housekeeping, Gilead*, and *Home*.

Limerick, Patricia Nelson, *The Legacy of Conquest: The Unbroken Past of the American West*, W. W. Norton, 1987.

> The American frontier is a powerful myth in American history, and Limerick's seminal study debunks that myth by examining the economic forces that drove white settlement of the West. By examining the economic factors that drove Western growth and that influenced the boom-and-bust cycles that characterized the area for decades, Limerick demythologizes the region and the economy in which Robinson's novel *Housekeeping* takes place.

Melville, Herman, *Moby Dick; or, The Whale*, Harper and Brothers, 1851.

> The great adventure tale at the heart of American literature, *Moby Dick* is the story of Ishmael, who sets sail on the whaling ship *Pequod*, captained by the monomaniacal Captain Ahab. Ahab is obsessed with hunting down the white sperm whale that destroyed his previous ship and bit off his leg. Written in a densely metaphoric style, *Moby Dick* uses this quest as a means to explore concepts of good and evil, wilderness and civilization, immanence and transcendence. Robinson was deeply influenced by *Moby Dick* in the writing of *Housekeeping*. The novel is available in a wide variety of current editions.

O'Connell, Nicholas, *At the Field's End: Interviews with Twenty Pacific Northwest Writers*, Madrona, 1987.

> O'Connell's interview with Robinson puts *Housekeeping* in regional context, touching in particular on issues of the natural landscape in which it is set, while the surrounding interviews with writers from the region expand the reader's understanding of how place factored in to Robinson's portrait of the area.

———, *On Sacred Ground: The Spirit of Place in Pacific Northwest Literature*, University of Washington Press, 2003.

> O'Connell takes a historical approach to the question of just what it is that distinguishes the Pacific northwest as a region. Beginning with Native American stories, O'Connell traces the history of storytelling through the journals of exploration, as well as the early romantic and realistic movements that characterized writers of the region. His discussion of Robinson's work takes place in the context of other contemporary writers of the region.

Robinson, Marilynne, *Absence of Mind: The Dispelling of Inwardness from the Modern Myth of the Self*, Yale University Press, 2010.

> In 2009, Robinson was asked to give the Terry series of lectures on religion in the light of science and philosophy at Yale University. Drawn from that lecture series, these essays probe the tension between science and religion, as Robinson demonstrates how the concept of mind determines how human nature and human civilization are valued and understood.

Twain, Mark, *The Adventures of Huckleberry Finn*, Charles L. Webster, 1885.

> Seen by many as expressing a central myth of American life, that of the moral individualist who cannot incorporate himself into society and thus heads out on a great adventure, *The Adventures of Huckleberry Finn* has become a central text in American literature. Seeking freedom from both the "sivilizing" influences of the Widow Douglas and the brutal treatment his father wreaks on him, Huck runs away. He encounters Jim, the runaway slave of the Widow Douglas, and together, they set off downriver where they hope to smuggle Jim to Ohio, a state that protects fugitive slaves. A series of adventures ensues, in which Huck comes to see Jim as a full human being. The novel is available in a wide variety of current editions.

SUGGESTED SEARCH TERMS

Marilynne Robinson

Housekeeping AND Marilynne Robinson

Calvinism AND Marilynne Robinson

Pulitzer Prize AND Marilynne Robinson

Housekeeping AND female narrative

wilderness AND Housekeeping AND Marilynne Robinson

ecocriticism AND Housekeeping AND Marilynne Robinson

feminism AND Housekeeping AND Marilynne Robinson

transcendentalism AND Housekeeping AND Marilynne Robinson

hobo culture

The Human Comedy

WILLIAM SAROYAN

1943

William Saroyan is best remembered for his 1943 war novel, *The Human Comedy*, a coming-of-age story featuring Homer Macauley, a boy who delivers telegrams to help support his family during World War II while his older brother is overseas serving in the military. The mythical setting of Ithaca, California, is modeled after Saroyan's hometown of Fresno, where he grew up in an Armenian community. The story has been criticized as overly sentimental but has remained popular because it affirms life and the American spirit. Such affirmations were appreciated during the Great Depression and World War II, when he was most popular.

Saroyan wrote novels, short stories, plays, screenplays, and plays for television in a lyrical and allegorical style. *The Human Comedy* has been made into a Hollywood film and a Broadway musical. His well-known play *The Time of Your Life* won a Pulitzer Prize in 1940. Interest in his work declined after World War II, although he continued to write prolifically until his death in 1981.

AUTHOR BIOGRAPHY

Saroyan was born on August 31, 1908, in Fresno, California, to Armenak and Takoohi Saroyan, Armenian immigrants from Bitlis. Armenak, an ordained minister, was forced to become a

William Saroyan (The Library of Congress)

California chicken farmer to support the family and died prematurely when William was three. Takoohi had to put her four children into an orphanage in Oakland. William's five years in an orphanage forever stamped his character. The family was reunited in Fresno in the Armenian community, with Takoohi working in a cannery and little William selling newspapers and later delivering telegrams. He was a voracious reader but left high school before graduation. After his mother showed him his father's writings, William decided to become a writer and published his first stories, based on his experience among the Armenian American fruit growers of the San Joaquin Valley, in the Armenian journal *Hairenik* in 1933.

The short story collection *My Name is Aram* (1940), about Armenian immigrants in the United States, became a best seller. Saroyan's first big success, however, was the publication of "The Daring Young Man on the Flying Trapeze" (1934), a short story about a starving artist during the Great Depression. At first, Saroyan was regarded as a budding genius, but he was soon criticized for turning out too much material too quickly without enough editing. In addition, his drinking, gambling, and difficult personality

detracted from his success with publishers and Hollywood studios. Besides publishing collections of short stories and doctoring screenplays, he wrote plays for Broadway. Two of his most popular plays were produced in 1939, *My Heart's in the Highland* and *The Time of Your Life*, with the latter winning the New York Drama Critics Circle Award and the Pulitzer Prize in 1940. Saroyan turned down the Pulitzer, saying that art should not be supported by commerce, but his mark was made.

In 1941, he wrote the screenplay, *The Human Comedy*, for MGM Studios, wanting to direct it himself. While he was an army private during World War II, he married Carol Marcus and published *The Human Comedy* as a book in 1943. MGM made the story into a movie that won an Academy Award for writing but refused to let Saroyan direct it. His son Aram, who also became a writer, was born in 1943, and his daughter, Lucy, an actress, was born in 1946. He divorced his wife Carol in 1949 and then remarried her in 1951.

Saroyan traveled all over the world turning his trips into stories and essays, and became a writer-in-residence at Purdue University in 1961, during which time his plays were produced for television. Although he never stopped writing and published over sixty books of stories, plays, and novels, he lost popularity after World War II because his optimistic themes seemed more suited for the Depression or the patriotic war effort. He died in Fresno on May 18, 1981, of prostate cancer.

PLOT SUMMARY

Chapters 1–3

During World War II, Ulysses Macauley, a four-year-old boy from Santa Clara Avenue in Ithaca, California, enjoys a day of ordinary miracles, watching birds and gophers in his backyard and then the marvel of a freight train going by. He waves to several people on the train, but no one waves back except an African American man singing a song about "the old Kentucky home far away." He shouts to Ulysses that he is going home. The boy is so pleased at this contact that he smiles and skips home. He finds his mother feeding the chickens, and he helps her look for eggs.

MEDIA ADAPTATIONS

- The feature film *The Human Comedy* was released in 1943 by Metro-Goldwyn-Mayer. It was directed by Clarence Brown and adapted by Howard Estabrook based on a screenplay by William Saroyan, who also published it as a novel the same year. The film starred Mickey Rooney as Homer, Frank Morgan as Mr. Grogan, Van Johnson as Marcus, and Donna Reed as Bess.

- The soundtrack of the Broadway musical *The Human Comedy*, composed by Galt MacDermot in the 1980s, was released in 1997 by Original Cast Records as a two-CD set.

Ulysses's older brother, Homer, is meanwhile bicycling down a dirt road delivering a telegraph message in the California evening. As he enjoys the beauty of the countryside, he sings, thinking of his mother's harp and his sister Bess's piano. He remembers his brother Marcus away in the war. He watches a line of army trucks full of soldiers and salutes them. They return his salute.

Homer returns to the telegraph office, where Mr. Spangler, the manager, is composing a telegram for a customer. A young man is wiring his mother for money to come home to Pennsylvania, and Spangler offers to loan him the money until the mother's money comes. He gratefully accepts. Spangler tells Mr. William Grogan, the night telegraph operator, to send the telegram paid and that he will pay for it himself. Spangler asks Homer how he likes being a messenger and wonders if he has time to play sports. He ran the two-twenty low hurdles himself when he was in school. Homer lied about his age to get the job. He is actually only fourteen, but he needs the fifteen dollars a week to help support his mother. Spangler explains to Grogan that Homer is a good boy from a poor, fatherless family with the eldest son in the war. The sister goes to college. Grogan is an old man with many memories. He gets drunk often and tells Homer he

must wake him if he sleeps on the job. Homer takes a message from the War Department to Mrs. Sandoval saying that her son has been killed.

Chapters 4–6

Bess and Mrs. Macauley play music in their house, and the neighbor girl, Mary Arena, comes to join in the singing. Mary is Marcus's girlfriend. Ulysses asks his mother where his brother Marcus is, and she replies he is in the army. He will not come back until the war is over. Ulysses wants to know where his father is, and his mother says he will not come home at all because the father is dead. She tries to explain death to her son as a natural part of life. She says that Homer is working to help buy food and to share with others who have a greater need than theirs. She tells the boy he must always give. After Ulysses goes to bed, Mrs. Macauley sees the spirit of her dead husband, Matthew, who apologizes for leaving her.

Homer delivers the death telegram to Mrs. Sandoval, a Mexican woman, and is anguished to give her news of her son's death. She insists he come in, and she gives him candy, as though he is her own boy. She cries, and Homer feels sick with compassion for her. He imagines her as a young mother with her baby son.

At the telegraph office, Homer wakes up Mr. Grogan as a message comes in over the telegraph. Grogan admits he is afraid of losing his job, because he is old and outdated. They have machines that can replace him, but he would die without his work. Homer sings a song for Mr. Grogan.

Chapters 7–9

When Homer gets home late, his mother is waiting up for him, and he is glad because he is troubled about the death telegram he had to deliver. He tells his mother that, for the first time in his life, he feels lonely. She tells him he is no longer a child; he feels the despair of the world. If she should get a telegram about Marcus, however, she will not believe he is really dead. She tells Homer to love everyone he meets, because the world is full of frightened children.

In the morning, Homer brings out his bodybuilding course, and Ulysses watches him exercise. Homer is training to run the two-twenty low hurdles, the big race of Ithaca. At breakfast, Homer discusses the value of prayer with his sister Bess. Mary comes into the kitchen from next door to ask if there are any letters from

Marcus. Bess and Mary wish they could get jobs to help out during wartime. On his way to school, Homer jumps over a fence to practice for the two-twenty low hurdles.

Chapters 10–12

Coach Byfield is on the athletic track of Ithaca High School coaching four boys for the race that afternoon. The coach tells Hubert Ackley III that he will win the race. The other boys wish they could beat Ackley, who always comes in first. Miss Hicks, the history teacher, waits for class to start in her classroom. Homer stares at Helen Eliot, whom he adores, but she is a snob and speaks only to Hubert Ackley III when he enters. Joe Terranova, Homer's friend, is the class comedian, one of the boys from the slums. Joe makes some wise cracks, and Homer tells him to be quiet so the class can start. Miss Hicks says that ancient history seems dull, but it is important to know about other times. She asks Helen to read aloud about the Assyrians, who conquered Babylon.

Homer interrupts the reading by getting into a fight with Hubert, the upper class boy, who calls Homer a lower-class hoodlum, and Miss Hicks says the two boys will have to stay after class. They ask, what about the track meet? Coach Byfield goes to the principal to ask him to get his best athlete, Hubert, out of detention in Miss Hicks's class. The principal refuses to interfere, but the coach goes to Miss Hicks's room and says he has permission to take Hubert for the track meet. Miss Hicks is irritated at Byfield's lie and his favoring the rich boy. Hubert leaves, and Miss Hicks gives Homer a talk on the meaning of democracy and equality. She wants her students to be good human beings. She lets Homer go to the meet. He competes against Hubert and is winning when Mr. Byfield tackles Homer to keep him out of the race.

Hubert stops running and waits for Homer to get up. Hubert and Homer tie for first place. Byfield tells Homer he may not compete in sports for the rest of the semester, but Miss Hicks stands up for him. The coach is so angry he calls Joe Terranova a wop, and Homer tackles him. When the principal comes out, Miss Hicks says Byfield owes Terranova an apology for an ethnic slur. The coach apologizes, but Homer limps away with a leg injury.

Chapters 13–15

Big Chris the hunter walks into Covington's Sporting Goods Store to buy a bear trap. He is shown a new trap that lifts the animal and holds it in place. Ulysses Macauley is fascinated and gets caught in the trap. The store owner does not know how to release him. A crowd gathers, and Auggie the newsboy runs for Homer to tell him his brother is caught in trouble. Homer tells Auggie to go to the telegraph office and explain why he will be late. He goes to the store, and Ulysses asks first for his father and then Marcus, but it is Big Chris who breaks the trap and frees the boy and then pays for the trap. Homer takes Ulysses to the telegraph office, and Mr. Spangler watches him while Homer delivers telegrams.

Spangler talks to Auggie and promises to hire the nine-year-old when he is older. A rich young woman named Diana Steed comes in a chauffeured car to the telegraph office to see Spangler. Auggie sells her a newspaper. Diana claims she loves Spangler and wants him to come to dinner to meet her parents. He agrees and then hears a call come in from Sunripe Raisin. Because Homer is not there, Spangler takes the call himself, running. He sees a shy and pretty girl on the street waiting for a bus after work. He notices her loneliness and kisses her on the cheek. Spangler gets to Sunripe Raisin before the Western Union boy and gets the telegrams for Postal Telegraph. He leaves happy and remembers the beauty of the girl he saw, and then goes to Corbetts Bar for a drink. The bartender, a former boxer, tells Spangler he lets the soldiers in his bar have free drinks.

Chapters 16–18

Homer is folding telegrams with Ulysses watching when Spangler returns to the office. Spangler tells Homer to take Ulysses home. Homer puts Ulysses on the handlebars of his bicycle, and they ride down the street singing about the old Kentucky home far away. At home, they hear the harp and piano of their mother and sister and the singing of Mary Arena. Homer goes back to work.

As Spangler has dinner with the Steed family, it begins to rain, and Bess Macauley and Mary Arena walk down the street to deliver Homer's lunch box to the telegraph office. Three soldiers named Fat, Texas, and Horse flirt with the girls and ask them to go to the movies on their last day before being shipped out. Bess thinks they are lonely, and the girls agree, but first they must deliver Homer's dinner. At the telegraph office, the soldiers send telegrams to their mothers and sweethearts. At the movie, they see Churchill and Roosevelt giving speeches, and they feel patriotic.

Meanwhile, in North Carolina, Marcus Macauley is with his friend Tobey George and other soldiers in a bar, waiting to be shipped overseas. Marcus plays the piano and sings. He tells Tobey all about his family in Ithaca. Spangler walks into the Ithaca movie theater with Diana Steed, but not liking the film, takes Diana to Corbett's Bar for a drink. She keeps insisting that she knows he really loves her, and he begins to think he does.

Chapters 19–21

Homer is wet as he returns to the telegraph office. He gets his lunch box and offers to share his supper with Mr. Grogan. A telegram comes in, and Homer tells Grogan he wishes he did not have to deliver death messages. Homer asks if these soldiers are dying for nothing. Grogan gets out his bottle and begins to drink and give a little sermon on how their deaths have meaning. He affirms the unity of all humanity. He suddenly asks Homer to go to the drug store for him. He clutches at his heart and asks for water. Homer takes the death telegram and leaves. Homer rides to a house where a party is going on. He feels sick. He has to deliver a message to a mother on her birthday that her son is dead. Homer delivers it and runs off.

After the movie, the soldiers kiss the girls good night and then horse around in the street ecstatically. Homer returns to the office, and Grogan asks him what is wrong with his leg. Homer tells him about the race, about school, and about Helen Eliot. He wants to be a champion for Miss Hicks, the teacher he admires. Grogan tells Homer he has changed and that he is growing up. Homer says he just wants to know things and be the best person he can be. He wants to help make a better world.

Chapters 22–24

Spangler comes into the office and talks to Grogan, reassuring him he does not need to worry about losing his job because he is old. Grogan admits he had a little heart attack and sent Homer for medicine. Spangler sends Grogan to the bar for a drink. The down and out young man who had earlier wired his mother for money comes into the office with a gun to rob Spangler. Spangler gets out the money but says he would give it to the man anyway because he is desperate but no criminal. He tells him to take a train to his home in Pennsylvania. He will not report the theft. The young man threatens to shoot himself. Spangler talks him out of it. The young man feels lost in the

violent world and sick about the corruption of the human race. He feels satisfied that he has found a decent person in Spangler and thanks him. After he leaves, Spangler wires the mother that the son is coming home.

At home, Homer has a nightmare in which he is on a bicycle racing with the messenger of Death to keep him away from Ithaca, but he cannot catch him. As Mrs. Macauley comforts him, she sees the spirit of her dead husband in the room.

Ulysses is up early on Saturday morning and watches a cow being milked. Then he plays with his friend, Lionel Cabot, who is mentally challenged but sweet and loyal. Auggie is the leader of the neighborhood gang of kids, and he organizes a raid on Old Man Henderson's apricot tree, though everyone knows apricots are not ripe. Auggie will not let Ulysses and Lionel join them. Henderson always scares and chases the boys off but is delighted when they come every spring. Ulysses and Lionel tag along to watch. The boys discuss whether it is a sin to steal apricots and decide it is not. Henderson comes out of his house and scares the boys, and they scatter after their great adventure.

Chapters 25–27

Auggie's Secret Society regroups at Ara's Armenian market. Auggie retains his prestige by having scored one green apricot. Mr. Ara's small son John asks for things from his father, and his father, always trying to please him, gives him an apple, an orange, and candy, but whatever he gives, the boy is not happy. A customer comes in to ask for cookies with raisins, which Mr. Ara does not have. Mr. Ara is unhappy because he cannot satisfy anyone. He speaks in Armenian about how the world has gone mad. He is not happy, but he wants his son to be.

Mrs. Macauley waits for Homer to come to breakfast. She knows he is troubled because of the nightmare. He confesses to his mother that he cried after delivering another death telegram. He rode his bicycle all over Ithaca and prayed nothing would happen to the people. He fears that as a grown-up he will only find out bad things about life. His mother tells him each person has to find a way to deal with life, both its beauty and its pain. Each of us has to remake the world as best we can. The evil as well as the good must be forgiven because we are all one human race.

Ulysses and Lionel come into the kitchen. Lionel explains that the other boys do not like him because he is stupid and send him away every time he makes a mistake. Mrs. Macauley tells him he is the nicest boy in the neighborhood, but he should not be angry because the other boys are good too. Mrs. Macauley tells Homer he must not be afraid of life, even its mistakes. He should trust his heart. When Homer leaves, Mrs. Macauley sees the spirit of her dead husband, Matthew, who tells her that their son Marcus is going to join him. She says she knows.

Chapters 28–30
Lionel and Ulysses pass a funeral procession and then go to the public library and stare at the books in respect, although neither can read. They feel as though they have learned something there just by being around the books.

Homer delivers a telegram to a speaker at the Ithaca Parlor Lecture Club. The women await the lecture of the woman who has traveled all over the world having adventures in wars and foreign lands. Homer delivers the telegram she has sent to herself to look important. He thinks she is an old fake, and when she tips him a dime, he gives it to the legless veteran on the street. Next he has to deliver a telegram to the madam of the local brothel. A young girl his sister's age signs for the telegram. The house has a sickening odor. The young woman secretly gives a letter to Homer to mail to her sister with money in it. The madam returns and asks Homer to distribute her cards wherever he leaves telegrams since the soldiers will be needing a room for the night.

Chapters 31–33
At sundown, Lionel and Ulysses are watching Mr. Mechano in a store window. He is a man, acting like a machine, holding up advertising signs. Lionel goes home, but Ulysses is mesmerized and stays to watch Mr. Mechano. The man looks at him, and Ulysses is terrified, suddenly and wordlessly understanding Death. Until then, the world had been good, but now he finds something horrible. He runs into Auggie selling newspapers and Auggie takes him to Homer in the telegraph office. Spangler buys all of Auggie's newspapers, since the boy cannot go home until he gets rid of all of them. The three boys go home on Homer's bicycle. Homer goes into his house, and Mary is happy because she got a letter from Marcus, and he sent one to Homer also. Mary and Bess are looking for jobs, but Homer says the girls should not have to work, because he will support the family.

A train full of American soldiers is on the way to war. Marcus Macauley speaks to his friend Tobey about his family and Ithaca, and Tobey, who is an orphan with no family to go back to, decides to adopt Ithaca as his hometown. They admit they do not want to die, but they are fighting for small American towns, like Ithaca. Marcus tells Tobey to go to Ithaca after the war and marry his sister Bess. The soldiers on the train ask Tobey and Marcus to sing a church hymn, "Leaning on the Everlasting Arms."

At work, Mr. Grogan is drunk, and Homer listens to his wisdom about life. Grogan recognizes Homer as a great man; he should be proud of his goodness. Then Homer reads aloud the letter from his brother Marcus. Marcus gives everything at home to Homer in case he dies and calls him the man of the family now, and though it will not be easy for him, he believes his brother will find a way to keep the family together. Marcus does not believe in war, but he is proud to serve his country. If he dies, Homer should not believe he is gone. Homer is the best of the Macauleys, and he is what Marcus fights for in the war. If his friend Tobey comes to Ithaca, the family should welcome him. Homer tells Mr. Grogan that, if his brother is killed in the war, he will spit on the world, and he will not be good anymore.

Chapters 34–36
Time goes by in Ithaca as the war continues in Europe. Meanwhile, Thomas Spangler and Diana Steed are out for a Sunday drive. They are in love. They see picnics by the river with many different national groups—Italians, Greeks, Armenians, and Russians. They are from many countries but all Americans.

Chapters 37–39
A train stops in Ithaca and soldiers get off. They are welcomed home by the families near Mr. Ara's market. The Macauley family is out for a Sunday walk, and Homer sees Mr. Grogan is at work. A telegraph is coming in, but Grogan is slumped down, and Homer cannot wake him. He tells his family to go home. He runs to Corbett's for coffee. Mr. Grogan wakes enough to get the telegram from the War Department for Mrs. Macauley informing her that Marcus has been killed. Grogan has a heart attack as he reads it and dies. When Homer returns with the coffee, he realizes the old man is dead. He sees the incomplete telegram but knows what it means. Spangler drives up, calls the doctor, and gets the rest of the

telegram. Homer puts the telegram in his pocket and goes for a walk with Spangler. Homer says he does not know whom to hate. Who is the enemy? Spangler says it is not people. The people of the world are like one man. Marcus will survive in his family's memory.

One of the soldiers off the train makes his way to the Macauley home, which he calls his home. When Homer returns at dark, he sees the soldier waiting on the porch. Mrs. Macauley tells Bess to let him in. Tobey George makes himself at home with his new family as Homer brings the telegram.

CHARACTERS

Hubert Ackley III

Hubert is a rich boy in Homer's high school and the one favored by the coach to win the track race. The coach springs Hubert from detention and leaves Homer, whom he considers unimportant. When the coach tackles Homer to prevent him from winning, Hubert does not take advantage and instead waits for Homer to get up before continuing to race.

John Ara

John is a demanding boy who is never satisfied, even though his father tries to make him happy.

Mr. Ara

Mr. Ara is the Armenian grocer who tries to make people, including his little son, happy but is disappointed that no one ever seems satisfied with his efforts.

Mary Arena

Mary Arena is Bess Macauley's best friend, a neighbor who comes over to sing when the Macauleys play music. She goes to college and is engaged to Marcus Macauley, away in the war.

Coach Byfield

Coach Byfield is the bigoted high-school track coach who favors the rich students and calls Joe Terranova a "wop." He tackles Homer as he is about to win the two-twenty low hurdles because he wants Hubert Ackley to win the race.

Lionel Cabot

Lionel Cabot is called the neighborhood half-wit but is a great and sweet-natured soul, a nine-year-old boy who is Ulysses's best friend. The other children will not let Lionel play their games because he makes mistakes.

Big Chris

Big Chris is a hunter from the hills who tries to buy a bear trap at Covington's store and ends up rescuing Ulysses from the trap. Ulysses worships Big Chris as a sort of protective father figure, since his own father is dead.

Helen Eliot

Helen Eliot is the smart and pretty student in Homer's history class that he adores, but she ignores him because he is from the lower class.

Fat

Fat is one of the three soldiers ready to ship out who take Bess and Mary to the movies.

Tobey George

Tobey George, an orphan, is the best friend and army buddy of Marcus Macauley. Marcus invites him to settle in Ithaca after the war as part of his own family. Marcus tries to set up Tobey to marry his sister, Bess.

Auggie Gottlieb

An imaginative and curious boy, Auggie is the nine-year-old neighborhood leader of the gang of kids. He tries to make up adventures like stealing apricots from Old Man Henderson's tree, even when they are not ripe. Auggie sells newspapers to help support his family, and although he is innocent, he is street-wise. He keeps an eye on Ulysses and the other children so they do not get into trouble.

Willie Grogan

Willie Grogan is the kind and wise sixty-seven-year-old man who is the night telegraph operator where Homer works. He is an old-time telegrapher with lots of memories. He is an alcoholic, and Homer must awaken him when he falls asleep on the job. Grogan is afraid of losing his job to the automated teletype machines. He dies of a heart attack when he has to type out the message of Marcus Macauley's death.

Mr. Henderson

Mr. Henderson pretends to be the nasty guard of the apricot tree in his yard but actually gets a kick out of watching the children steal his apricots each year.

Miss Hicks

Miss Hicks is Homer's compassionate high-school history teacher who tries to teach him that it is better to be a good person of high moral value than rich or of high social standing. She has been the teacher of all the Macauley children and stands up for Homer against Coach Byfield.

Horse

Horse is the second of the three soldiers who take Bess and Mary to the movies.

Bess Macauley

Bess Macauley is Homer's seventeen-year-old sister. She plays the piano and goes to college. At the end of the book, it is implied that she will eventually marry Marcus's best friend, Tobey George.

Homer Macauley

Homer is fourteen and the main character of the story. He takes a job as a telegram delivery boy to help support his fatherless family. He goes through a crisis when he has to deliver telegrams from the War Department reporting the deaths of soldiers to their families. He questions evil, war, and death, trying to keep his optimism about life in the face of the terrible loss and sacrifice everyone must make during the war. He is a boy of great sensitivity and integrity who questions the limitations people would impose on him, such as the coach not wanting him to compete in sports. He has great sympathy and kindness for the families he must tell about the death of their loved ones and is well thought of by adults and teachers. Even his rival, Hubert Ackley III, respects him and stops running in the track meet when Homer falls down, waiting for him to get up again. Homer is forced to become the head of the family prematurely by his brother Marcus's death.

Mrs. Katey Macauley

Mrs. Macauley is a widow who tries to keep her family together under difficult circumstances. She is very wise and understanding, teaching her children to be good human beings above all else. Apparently something of a mystic, she converses with the spirit of her dead husband, Matthew.

Marcus Macauley

Marcus Macauley is the oldest Macauley son and a soldier in the war. He is wise and gentle like the rest of the family, not believing in war but wanting to do his duty. He says no man is his enemy.

He writes a final letter to Homer encouraging him to be a great man and says he is fighting in the war for HOmer's chance to have a better life. He sends his friend Tobey to Ithaca after the war to be part of the Macauley family, thus anticipating his own death and replacing their lost son.

Matthew Macauley

The deceased husband of Katey Macauley, Matthew nevertheless is a presence in the story as a spirit who speaks to his wife about their children, warning her that their son Marcus will soon join him in death.

Ulysses Macauley

Ulysses is the youngest Macauley child, four years old, wide-eyed and innocent, who enjoys life and is curious about everything. He misses his dead father and absent soldier brother, becoming attached to Homer as a father substitute. Ulysses is accepting of everyone and pleased with his everyday adventures in the neighborhood.

Mr. Mechano

Mr. Mechano is a man in a store window who pretends to be a machine, flipping advertising signs. Ulysses becomes terrified of him as his first glimpse of evil when the man stares at him in a threatening way.

Rosa Sandoval

Rosa Sandoval is the Mexican mother to whom Homer delivers his first death telegram. She treats Homer as if he is her lost son.

Tom Spangler

Tom Spangler is the generous manager of the telegraph office where Homer works. He helps people in need, such as the young man who comes in to rob him, talking him out of it and giving him the money to get home. He believes in Homer and gives him a job though he is underage. Tom is in love with Diana Steed, and though he is of lower class than her family, he wants to marry her. He is Homer's mentor, and Homer decides to run the two-twenty low hurdles because Mr. Spangler did.

Diana Steed

Diana Steed is the rich young woman who comes in a chauffeured car to see her boyfriend, Tom Spangler, whom she loves and wants to marry.

Joe Terranova

Joe Terranova is a student from the slums who is class clown in Homer's history class. He is a friend of Homer's, and he is defended by Miss Hicks, who tells the principal that Coach Byfield addressed Joe with an ethnic slur on Italians.

Texas

Texas is the third of the three soldiers who take Bess and Mary to the movies.

THEMES

Love

The Macauley family love is a central metaphor for human society and the need for human love. The Macauleys are poor and without social standing. The father is dead, the oldest son away in the army. The mother has to hold the other three children together by the sheer force of her wise love. This situation reflects the home front during World War II, when every family had a loved one in the war and the ones left behind had to stick together. Saroyan suggests the whole of America is an extended family in the crisis. Marcus tells Homer in his last letter that he loves and believes in his little brother so much that he is willing to fight in the war to preserve a free way of life for him and the future.

The family members sacrifice for one another and even share their core love with others, as Bess and Mary go to the movies with the soldiers who are about to be sent overseas, and Marcus sends his orphan friend Tobey to Ithaca to be part of his family after the war. Tom Spangler adopts every child or stranger who comes into the telegraph office, giving money, time, and parental advice. Mr. Grogan, although he's an alcoholic, acts like a grandfather to Homer, helping him to believe in himself. Even little Ulysses is transformed by his friendly contact with the hobo he waves to on the train. Mrs. Macauley tells Homer he must love everyone he meets because the world is full of frightened children.

Coming of Age

Homer is fourteen and working his first job as a telegraph boy to help support the family during the war. With Marcus gone, Homer is the man of the family and feels responsible. He chides Bess and Mary for wanting to get jobs. He should be the one to support them. However, Homer confides to his

TOPICS FOR FURTHER STUDY

- With a group of classmates, create a presentation the focuses on the role of the U.S. military in World War II. Why was U.S. involvement decisive in the outcome? Include the contributions of the U.S. military in both the European and Pacific theaters. Use both print and electronic media research sources that you accumulate on a wiki space to share with the class. Present your findings as a multimedia presentation or a Web site devoted to the topic.

- The incident with Coach Byfield in *The Human Comedy* is indicative of ethnic prejudice against Italians. Write an essay in which you compare the treatment of European immigrants from enemy nations (Germans and Italians) with the treatment of those of Japanese descent during World War II.

- How does Saroyan depict women's roles in *The Human Comedy*? Using a collaborative research annotation tool like Google Notebook, collect relevant Web sites to show how women's roles changed during World War II. Does Saroyan's view of women corroborate the historical data you found? Create a wiki with your conclusions.

- Compare and contrast the experiences of growing up in California in the 1940s in *The Human Comedy* with those depicted in the young-adult novel *The Circuit*, by Francisco Jimenez, about the hardships of a migrant worker family. In your essay, be sure to provide evidence from both novels as support for your main points.

mother, after his first day, that he did not like delivering the death telegrams to families from the War Department. He feels a sudden change, a loneliness and confusion about the world. He wonders what is happening to him.

She tells him that he is lonely because he is no longer a protected child; he is growing up. He has to grow up quickly because of the war. He mentions that a job seems more real than school now. Mrs. Macauley says that schools keep children off the street, implying that school postpones maturity, because young people do not have to face life yet. Eventually they must go on to the streets and learn for themselves the good and the bad of living. She tries to guide her son in this delicate transition, because he has no role model of father or older brother.

For Homer, it is the realization of death that propels him into loneliness. His wrestling with death and what it means is his initiation into life. He must learn how to deal with loss, especially since the story ends with the death of his brother, Marcus. Homer's coming of age is also reflected in his experience at school, as he falls in love with Helen Eliot, an upper class girl out of his reach. He is taunted in his bid for heroism when he runs the two-twenty low hurdles and prevented from winning by the hostility of the coach, who prefers that the rich Hubert Ackley III win. He attempts to understand the unfairness of class prejudice with the help of Miss Hicks, his encouraging history teacher, who tells him to ignore the mockers of the world.

Human Condition

The title, *The Human Comedy*, is a play on Dante's *The Divine Comedy* and implies that Saroyan is showing the range of life from a human perspective. His idealism is manifest in his acceptance of both the good and bad in human experience as part of a providential benevolence ruling the universe. Four-year-old Ulysses symbolizes the innocence of life, the exuberant and ecstatic discovery of ordinary miracles, like birds, gophers, trains, bear traps, and books in the library.

Homer's adolescent discovery that the world also contains sadness, loneliness, death, and evil is the other end of the spectrum. He does not understand what has happened to make the world go mad. His mother is the main purveyor of wisdom to the boy, confirming that, though his father is dead and there is war and hunger, nothing good ever can be defeated. Goodness is eternal. He must learn to share with all others, for though people may look and act differently, they are all human and deserve respect.

This optimism even embraces the evil person who must not be judged, for everyone will be forgiven in the end. Evil is just a temporary disease that must be cured, as the war will be in time. Tom Spangler talks the young man out of robbing him, telling him he is not really a criminal. The young man tells him he believes the human race is corrupt, but Spangler's generosity restores his faith. Saroyan preaches the unity of all humanity in the book, an affirmation in the face of the terrible national conflicts all over the world.

Finally, the human condition is illustrated in the attempt of the Armenian grocer, Mr. Ara, to satisfy his son with candy and fruit. No matter what the boy asks for and the father gives, the boy is dissatisfied, ever seeking something more, illustrating the insatiable drive of the human spirit.

Faith

Homer is taught by his elders—his mother, Miss Hicks, Mr. Grogan, and Marcus—that he must believe in himself and in life, no matter how terrible things might seem at the moment. He is comforted because none of them gloss over the difficulties he faces, yet they speak a wisdom that can help him through dark times. Miss Hicks tries to explain the ethnic and class prejudice he sees in school while, at the same time, affirming the ideal of American democracy and equality. His mother explains death to him as part of life. His father continues to exist in a spiritual sense, she says, and this is made clear to the reader when she is able to see and speak to the father's spirit.

Mrs. Macauley, Bess, and Homer discuss prayer, and the mother tells them that it is faith that makes life meaningful, not things in themselves. Homer feels that every time he blesses his food, he is asking for Paradise for everyone.

Homer asks Mr. Grogan about the soldiers dying in the war, whether they die for nothing. Grogan affirms the unity of life and the meaningfulness of everything that happens. The war just reflects the dual struggle of good and evil that goes on in each person, and everyone is trying to reach grace, trying as best they can. Grogan tells Homer he is already a great human being, even at fourteen, an accomplishment he should protect. Marcus's letter explains that he is fighting out of duty, but he does not see any man as his enemy. He praises Homer as the best of the Macauleys and urges him to continue being the best.

Many of the characters in The Human Comedy *are named after characters in Homer's* Odyssey.
(Dhoxax | Shutterstock.com)

STYLE

Screenplay

The Human Comedy was first written as a treatment and screenplay for MGM film studios, and thus, it has short atmospheric scenes that suggest a connected story rather than developing it fully. Many characters are briefly introduced to give the impression of a small American town. The Macauley family gives the story a focus, with Homer the main character, but the plot is loose and episodic rather than tightly unified around a single event. After MGM refused to let Saroyan direct the film, he quickly wrote it as a novel and published it before the film was released. There are some differences between the film and novel because MGM made the story even more sentimental than Saroyan's novel version. The novel has more characters and scenes and develops thematic material more fully, such as Saroyan's philosophy of war and the human condition.

Saroyan's screenplay won an Academy Award for its moving story.

Hollywood aided the war effort with many patriotic films about American soldiers in World War II battles or about the home front, such as *Happy Land* (1943), *Tender Comrade* (1943), and *Since You Went Away* (1944). *The Human Comedy* was a popular film about the United States home front to inspire Americans with the values they were fighting for abroad, as Marcus expresses in his letter to Homer. The film showed the average American family as loving, generous, decent, and desirous to share good fortune with others. The people of Ithaca are good neighbors rather than trying to use power for wrong purposes as the Hitlers of the world do. Other famous war films of the era include *Casablanca*, Charlie Chaplin's *The Great Dictator*, *Thirty Seconds Over Tokyo*, and *Mrs. Miniver*, a moving story about a family on the English home front.

American Novel

The Human Comedy tries to portray the American way of life and American values to contrast it to the totalitarian regimes trying to dominate the world at that time (Germany, Italy, and Japan). Miss Hicks's history class offers a discussion of civilizations of the past and suggests that American democracy, with its emphasis on equality and fairness, is superior to other forms of government. Spangler's encounter with the Sunday picnics shows many different kinds of people living harmoniously together, a contrast to the persecution of sects and groups in other countries. The American dream is emphasized in the Armenian grocer, Mr. Ara, running a business and being able to give things to his family that he did not have in the old country.

Candidates for the Great American novel that typifies the American way of life include Herman Melville's *Moby-Dick*, Mark Twain's *The Adventures of Huckleberry Finn*, and Harper Lee's *To Kill a Mockingbird*. *The Human Comedy* tries to sell the American dream as something worth fighting for during the dark days of World War II. The American novel typically features a hero who is an ordinary person or even a marginal person having a chance at success. Homer Macauley is poor and disadvantaged but is shown to have extraordinary potential and faith in life, the sort of ideal citizen the country needs for the future. He represents the generation that will lead the country after the war.

COMPARE
&
CONTRAST

- **1940s:** Women enter the work force by taking over jobs vacated by servicemen during the war but lose them when the men come home again.

  Today: Women have their own careers, and jobs are not generally categorized by gender, although women still have not achieved equal pay and have some difficulty reaching the highest positions of management.

- **1940s:** During World War II, patriotism for the war effort is nearly universal, and men volunteer for the military. Efforts to support the war on the home front are highly visible through the promotion of conservation of energy and products, volunteer defense

efforts, films, music, patriotic decorations, and attire.

Today: American involvement in foreign wars is not popular. The military devotes intensive resources to recruiting its fighting forces without resorting to a draft.

- **1940s:** Saroyan makes a special plea for ethnic groups, including Armenians and Italians, to be rightly included in the goals of the American dream.

  Today: The American mainstream is influenced by a multicultural heritage, with art, cuisine, entertainers, and public figures from all races and ethnic groups.

Coming-of-Age Novel

The coming-of-age novel is a narrative form in which the main character matures during the action. The character's development from childhood to adulthood provides an opportunity to examine the social influences on individuality, such as the influence of Victorian England on the boy David Copperfield in Charles Dickens's novel or that of Irish culture on Stephen Dedalus in James Joyce's *A Portrait of the Artist as a Young Man*. The character typically encounters challenges that must be overcome for him or her to find a place in society.

Homer Macauley is coming of age in America during World War II and has a number of handicaps, such as no male role models and no financial support. He must learn wisdom from the adults around him, such as the drunken telegraph operator, Mr. Grogan, and has to negotiate class prejudice in school when Coach Byfield will not let him participate in the race. The coming-of-age novel discusses the various painful transitions of adolescence, such as sexual awakening, class consciousness, and awareness of evil. Even if the hero successfully grows into adulthood, there is a sense of the loss of the innocence

of childhood. The secure world of four-year-old Ulysses is thus contrasted to Homer's uncertainty in having to face his brother's death and then become the man in the family prematurely.

HISTORICAL CONTEXT

Armenian American Immigration

Saroyan's Armenian heritage figures prominently in his writing. Armenians occupied the highlands of Mount Ararat in Turkey for four thousand years. Haik was the legendary founder who led his people to victory over Babylon. At its height, the kingdom extended from the Caucasus to central Turkey, Lebanon, and Iran. The main religion in the area was Iranian Zoroastrianism until it was conquered by the Roman Empire, when Christianity was adopted. The Turks repeatedly invaded Armenia, and Armenian Christians were always a minority culture with Muslim neighbors or conquerors.

The ethnic cleansing of Armenians under the Ottoman Empire in 1894–1896 resulted in the genocide of over a million people and continued with the Armenian genocide by Turks during World War I in 1915 and 1916, using the excuse that the Armenians were allies of Russia. In 1922, Armenia became part of the Soviet Union. In 1991, it became an independent republic. Saroyan's father was part of the great Armenian emigration, or diaspora of Armenians to other countries, during the ethnic cleansing at the end of the nineteenth century. There was a large Armenian community in Fresno, California (depicted as Ithaca in *The Human Comedy*), in the San Joaquin Valley, and at his mother's urging to be among their own people, Armenak Saroyan moved his family there, only to find himself in poverty, forced to become a chicken farmer.

Great Depression

Saroyan became a popular writer during the Great Depression of the 1930s because his themes dealt with the integrity and the hope of the poor, like that exhibited by his own family, struggling to stay together in adverse conditions. The Great Depression was a worldwide economic depression, the longest and most severe depression of the twentieth century. It originated in the United States with the fall of the stock market, especially after Black Tuesday, October 29, 1929. It affected every country in the world, causing individual income and business profits to fall dramatically, resulting in a near stoppage of world trade because of protective tariffs. Unemployment in the United States reached at least 25 percent.

The Depression was complicated by a deflationary monetary spiral and was also fed by droughts and weather conditions, including the Dust Bowl in the plains and floods that destroyed crops and farmland. Laborers had no jobs because construction was halted, farmers could not sell crops for a profit, and mining and logging suffered. There was widespread poverty, hunger, and despair. People fled to places like California to become migrant workers in the fields. Saroyan worked from boyhood selling newspapers to help the family survive. President Franklin D. Roosevelt's New Deal policies to stimulate the economy, as well as the industrial effort needed to supply World War II, are credited with bringing the country back to normal by the early 1940s.

World War II

World War II (1939–1945) was a global war, the most widespread and deadly war in history, involving most countries of the world, and

When Marcus joins the army, Homer is left as the man of the family. (Rachel L. Sellers / Shutterstock.com)

resulting in more than seventy million deaths. The nations were aligned either with the Allied (United States, Britain, France, and Russia) or the Axis (Germany, Italy, and Japan) powers. The deaths that came as a result of the Holocaust of Jewish people and in the atomic bombings of Hiroshima and Nagasaki were unparalleled in world history. The war began on September 1, 1939, with the invasion of Poland by Hitler's Nazi Germany. Campaigns were fought in Europe, the Soviet Union, Africa, Asia, and the Pacific. In 1944, the Allies invaded occupied France to liberate that country from the Nazis.

Germany surrendered on May 8, 1945, and the war in Asia ended when Japan surrendered on August 15, 1945, after atomic weapons destroyed two cities. The war dramatically altered world political boundaries and alignments. The United Nations was established to monitor conflicts to avoid another such disastrous upheaval. The war was so terrible, with so much at stake, that anti-war sentiment was not tolerated. Saroyan's *The Human*

Comedy, which can seem overly patriotic or simplistic to a modern reader, reflected the urgent plea for all Americans to do their part to defeat the evil wave engulfing the world. Saroyan himself did not believe in war but showed characters like Marcus Macauley doing his patriotic duty.

CRITICAL OVERVIEW

In her comprehensive review of Saroyan criticism, Alice K. Barter, in "Introduction: Saroyan and His Critics," traces the rise and fall of Saroyan's critical reputation from the 1930s to the 1990s. Barter notes that the high point of Saroyan's career came between 1934 and 1945 because the "buoyancy of spirit in both the man and his work gave hope and confidence to Americans worn down by the hardships of the Great Depression and the uncertainties of the Second World War." He was the people's voice, a proletarian writer of less than high school education who stood for the American spirit. After the war, however, Saroyan became something of "an anachronism" and was considered a failure by the end of his career.

Saroyan's two most remembered works stem from his early period. His play *The Time of Your Life* (1939) won a Pulitzer Prize, and his screenplay that he turned into a novel, *The Human Comedy*, won an Academy Award for its film story. Barter notes that Edwin B. Burgum, in *Virginia Quarterly Review*, reports that *The Human Comedy*, though a popular book and film, disappointed critics as an escapist view of the war. Barter also points out that Philip Rahv, in *American Mercury*, criticizes *The Human Comedy* as Saroyan's "corniest public role: that of the supremely devoted lover of mankind." In the 1930s and 1940s, Saroyan was forgiven by the public and some enthusiastic critics who saw his freshness and promise but condemned by others who felt he was maudlin.

Barter reports that, by the 1950s, critics, including William Fisher in "Whatever Became of Saroyan," pronounced Saroyan irrelevant. Fisher noted that "[he was] a man baffled at the failure of the Dream but unwilling to give it up." It was felt that, as an artist, he had stopped developing. With the interest in ethnic studies increasing in the 1960s and 1970s, however, Saroyan was reevaluated from another perspective as an Armenian American author. *My Name is Aram*, his book about the Armenian immigrants in Fresno, for instance, is a record of where his

spiritual vitality came from, having nothing to do with academic ideas of writing. *The Human Comedy* specifically addresses the Armenian immigrant in the tragicomic Mr. Ara. Barter quotes Patrick McGilligan's more favorable 1978 review of *The Human Comedy* in "Mr. Saroyan's Thoroughly American Movie," asserting that Saroyan "excels with mood and theme, and soars buoyantly with character sketches."

Saroyan's enduring legacy centers around his ethnic portrayal of Armenian Americans and in his Whitmanesque optimism. A contributor to the January 1989 edition of the *English Journal* recommends *The Human Comedy* as a young-adult novel that teaches readers to "accept life's trials with the fortitude of the Macauley people." In 2010, R. L. Friedman, in "Saroyan at a Hundred and One," concludes that Saroyan understood the hearts of children and the formative moments in life. He notes that, despite criticism, *The Human Comedy* is still in print.

CRITICISM

Susan K. Andersen
Andersen holds a Ph.D. in literature. In the following essay, she considers the transcendental optimism of The Human Comedy.

Dickran Kouymjian, in "Whitman and Saroyan: Singing the Song of America," suggests parallels between America's great poet of the people, Walt Whitman, and William Saroyan, who acknowledged Whitman as one of his models. Kouymjian notes that Saroyan "regarded himself as a direct literary descendent of Whitman." Saroyan felt close to Whitman because he was a genuine and unlettered man, as was he, who spontaneously uttered his celebration of American life. Although *The Human Comedy* offended some readers as glossing over the realistic suffering of war, Saroyan, like Whitman taking on the challenge of the Civil War, puts forth a transcendental philosophy of the unity of life as the only wisdom great enough to explain evil.

The transcendentalist writers of the 1830s and 1840s established the philosophy of the American Dream as a spiritual quest. Ralph Waldo Emerson, Henry David Thoreau, and Walt Whitman taught that spirituality transcends material success. Like them, Saroyan asserts the primacy of spirit over material life. The book opens with Ulysses's ecstatic enjoyment of a summer morning, ending

WHAT DO I READ NEXT?

- *Dandelion Wine* (1957) is Ray Bradbury's story of Douglas Spaulding's twelfth summer in Green Town, Illinois. It is written with the same nostalgic flavor as Saroyan's *The Human Comedy*.

- *Code Talker* by Joseph Bruchac (2005) is a young-adult novel that tells the story of a Navajo boy who joins the Marines in World War II and becomes a code interpreter, inventing a code using Navajo language that the Nazis could not crack.

- Lebanese American artist and poet Kahlil Gibran's *The Prophet* (1923) offers a similar tone of wisdom about the Middle East that compares to *The Human Comedy*. The book was popular with those involved in the 1960s counterculture movement.

- William Saroyan's *My Name is Aram* (1940) is his most famous collection of short stories. The stories offer a picture of Armenian American heritage from the point of view of a boy growing up in Fresno, California.

- Walt Whitman's *Leaves of Grass* (1855) was used as a model by Saroyan, supplying him with his own exuberant pose as the common man who could celebrate and unify America.

- Anzia Yezierska's *The Breadgivers* (1925) tells the story of Jewish Polish immigrants in the slums of the lower east side of Manhattan. Yezierska offers a look at the ethnic heritage of immigrants and their desire for a better life. The character Sara Smolinsky risks everything, including her family's love, to get an education in this story.

- *Forgotten Bread* (2007), edited and with an introduction by David Kherdian, is a collection of the writings of seventeen first-generation Armenian American authors who are all introduced by a second-generation relative. Saroyan is included with six selections.

in his epiphany of the black man waving to him from the train. Ulysses smiles "the gentle, wise, secret smile which said *Yes* to all things." This

ALTHOUGH *THE HUMAN COMEDY* OFFENDED SOME READERS AS GLOSSING OVER THE REALISTIC SUFFERING OF WAR, SAROYAN, LIKE WHITMAN TAKING ON THE CHALLENGE OF THE CIVIL WAR, PUTS FORTH A TRANSCENDENTAL PHILOSOPHY OF THE UNITY OF LIFE AS THE ONLY WISDOM GREAT ENOUGH TO EXPLAIN EVIL."

saying Yes to all things, including death and war, is the theme of the book. Emerson noted in his 1836 essay "Nature" that few adult persons can truly see nature. In the novel, Ulysses is the mystic child in touch with life. To retain this kind of optimism as an adult, however, is only possible with a spiritual perspective.

All of the Macauleys think with the heart and are prone to philosophical or religious discussions. Homer and Bess at breakfast discussing the benefit of prayer is not a believable family scene, but such inspirational passages are what made and still make the book popular. Homer says that the grace he repeats over his food, "Be present at our table, Lord" means "Grant that this world is Paradise and that everybody we ever have food with is somebody." Like Whitman, Saroyan asserts an immanent God present at all times, making the world paradisal and all people worthy of God's love. When Ulysses asks his mother if the black man will be on the train again today, she says "yes," asserting an eternal truth rather than a logical one. The black man who gave Ulysses joy will forever ride that train in his heart.

Another similarity with Whitman is the celebration of individual potential. All people are equal in America, not simply as a legal right but as a spiritual right as well. Whitman was not extraordinary in any way, and yet he proclaimed his own goodness. Kouymjian quotes Saroyan's opinion of Whitman, "He was Anybody become Somebody by saying so, which is the essence and meaning of America." This is the American dream—that one can rise to one's potential. Miss Hicks tells Homer, "In a democratic state . . . every man is free to exert himself to do good or not, to grow nobly or foolishly," making democracy the testing ground of virtue, the way Whitman thought of it in *Demo-cratic Vistas*. This special destiny and purpose of America had to be defended from the Hitlers of the world. Ithaca is shown to have its faults, but the people are free there to be good, and to the disgust of some critics, almost all the characters are good, except Coach Byfield.

Like Whitman's famous catalogs naming all sorts of people and things—slaves, mothers, lovers, mobs, the city, workers, and thieves—Ithaca too is celebrated for its diversity of all types of people, who are accepted as basically good. There are snapshots of the mentally handicapped, the prostitute, the immigrant, the legless veteran, soldiers, the hunchback, the pretentious, the rich, the poor, the ethnic groups, families, children, the drunk, and the generous Spangler. The book does not develop these characters but, like Whitman's poetry, shows a cross-section of people to build a sense of the unity of all humanity. Mr. Grogan says,

> Every man in the world, right or wrong, is trying . . . all of us, every last one of us—shall reach home, shall have grace, shall be immortal, and this wonderful evil world shall be a place of decency and goodness.

This assertion of universal salvation echoes "Song of Myself," which accepts even the murderer and the atrocities of war. Whitman sees God as the "Great Camerado" who forgives all.

Similarly, Whitman's philosophy of death, that it is just as lucky to die as to be born and that even the dead continue to exist, is echoed by Mrs. Macauley: "Nothing good ever ends. . . . Everything alive is part of each of us." She tells Homer she will not believe it if she finds out that Marcus has been killed. After all, she still speaks to the spirit of her dead husband, Matthew.

There are many critics who feel that Saroyan's optimism in the book fails. Thelma Shinn, in "William Saroyan: Romantic Existentialist," points out that Saroyan's philosophy is a recognition of the contradictions of life, and so he cannot be seen as a mere Romantic writer like Whitman. He shows that life is illusory and absurd, but at the same time, he affirms life.

Saroyan's son Aram, in *William Saroyan*, writes of *The Human Comedy* that all the characters are essentially versions of his father and that his usual narrative charm is replaced in this book by "dogged piety" in the constant preaching of morals. He claims that his father's experience in an orphanage made him an onlooker all his life

and that writing was the only way he could unlock his frozen feelings. *The Human Comedy*, though based on autobiography, was the way Saroyan wished his life had been. His writing is full of the exuberance he could not realize.

In *A Daring Young Man: A Biography of William Saroyan*, John Leggett claims that the war destroyed Saroyan as a man and as a writer. Saroyan was oblivious to the true evil of the times he lived in. He was not interested in politics and hated the war. Saroyan had something of a nervous breakdown when he had to serve in the army, an interesting footnote to his selling the necessity for Marcus Macauley to go to war as a patriot in *The Human Comedy*. Leggett quotes a review by James Agee in *Time*, in which he complains that *The Human Comedy* is "chronic ecstasy." However, Saroyan's personal trauma over the war comes out clearly in the way that he wants to preserve a vision of the innocent America about to be destroyed in the world war.

Howard Floan asserts, in *William Saroyan*, that *The Human Comedy* is "nostalgia for the simple life" in a small American town, not presented realistically but "softened and purified." He finds the ending to have an unconvincing resolution and to actually be a denial of death rather than an acceptance of it, because no one is shown to be upset by Marcus's death, except, of course, Mr. Grogan, who dies of shock when he receives the telegraph message. Floan's response is typical of critics, rather than of readers, who are moved by the continuity of life expressed in Tobey's coming to take Marcus's place.

Floan brings up Saroyan's allegorical vision. Saroyan mentioned that everything he wrote was allegorical, and Floan reports that Saroyan said that "in fact all reality to me is allegorical," possibly because the stories of Armenia he heard from childhood were fables with morals attached to them. This kind of storytelling does not pretend to be realistic but is an ancient form of wisdom literature that Saroyan seemed drawn to.

Nona Balakian, in *The World of William Saroyan*, points out that most of the fiction written in the 1930s and early 1940s was brutally realistic in response to the hardships of the time, but she adds, Armenians "are natural utopians." Kouymjian mentions that the academics and new critics did not understand Saroyan's fantastic style of writing, obviously derived from his Armenian background, nor that his themes reflect the fact that he "seeks the experience of being." In "William

Saroyan and Multiculturalism," David Stephen Calonne asserts that Saroyan celebrated differences in creating "an imaginative world which corresponded to his highest vision of human possibility." Saroyan wanted America to be not a melting pot but a land where his own rich Armenian traditions could add to an American culture that was not yet civilized because devoid of spiritual values.

Saroyan's answer to the problem of evil is elaborated in Chapter 34. The pattern of life, he says, appears to be senseless in times like war, but in fact, with the gathering of experience, the pattern has "beauty of form" because people are busy adding what goodness they can to what darkness there is: "The force of brutality had been tempered and sweetened by the greater force of gentility." In fact, he asserts that there is a chance for even greater goodness than before, the idea that suffering purifies humanity. Spangler assures Homer, "Love is immortal. . . . But hate dies every minute." Saroyan's optimism may have been hard to accept in his own day, and certainly, in this day, with the awareness of planetary depletion, but Saroyan seems to affirm, with Whitman, that even in the midst of chaos, there was never more heaven than there is now and there are millions of suns left.

Source: Susan K. Andersen, Critical Essay on *The Human Comedy*, in *Novels for Students*, Gale, Cengage Learning, 2012.

Alex Tavlian

In the following review, Tavlian remarks that The Human Comedy *remains readable for "people of every era and generation."*

For many teens, growing up seems like the biggest hurdle that one can face. William Saroyan proved that point in his first novel. *The Human Comedy*, retelling his own life through the eyes and experiences of brothers Marcus, Homer and Ulysses Macauley.

The Macauley family lives in a California town named Ithaca, patterned after Saroyan's hometown of Fresno. Saroyan explores the life of 14-year-old Homer, who becomes man of the house after his father dies and older brother Marcus leaves for war.

Homer gets a job as a postal telegraph deliverer at night while attending school during the day. He delivers messages across Ithaca, including one to Mrs. Rosa Sandoval of G Street, telling her that her son has died in World War II.

Homer's mother plays the harp as the family keeps it normal routine alive. (Petrenko Andriy / Shutterstock.com)

Saroyan structured the book as a self-portrait, substituting Homer for the author and his older brother, Henry. Both Homer and Saroyan were telegraph messengers who grew up in single-parent homes. Homer's work takes him to many venues familiar to Saroyan, such as the city high school, the Parlor Lecture Club, the Guggenheim and Foley packinghouses, the Owl Drug Store, the Presbyterian church and the public library.

The story explores socioeconomics at the high school level by comparing the lives of the hardworking Homer and his overprivileged rival, a boy named Hubert Ackley III, whose wealthy family tries to corrupt the school system.

While Homer tries to cope with daily life and baby brother Ulysses gets into trouble, Marcus is on an Army troop train, befriending an orphaned teen named Tobey George. Marcus paints a vivid picture of life in Ithaca and encourages Tobey to relocate there once the war ends. Finding the extraordinary in common people and everyday situations, Saroyan weaves an amazing story of life in a small town in the middle of a great global war. He uses Homer and his bicycle as literary devices and takes the reader from mansions to humble wood homes; from orchards, vineyards and rivers to fancy city-block buildings. Saroyan explores the meaning of life as his characters exhibit a range of human emotions, from selfless-ness to selfishness, from love to hate, from wis-dom to foolishness.

The Human Comedy is a very readable volume for people of every era and generation. The story of a teenage messenger boy trying to lead his family will teach unforgettable lessons to readers of all ages.

Source: Alex Tavlian, "*Human Comedy* Examines Life's Meaning," in *Fresno Bee*, January 1, 2009.

William J. Fisher

In the following excerpt, Fisher surveys Saroyan's career, calling him "the representative American of the mid-twentieth-century."

The story of William Saroyan's amazing suc-cess and rapid decline is, in microcosm, a history of American optimism. Saroyan rose in mid-Depression as a bard of the beautiful life, a restorer of faith in man's boundless capacities; he has declined as a troubled pseudo-philosopher, forced to acknowledge man's limitations, yet uncomfortable in the climate of Evil. Indeed, he has come to dwell on Evil in order to deny its reality, reasserting, blatantly and defensively now, the American Dream of Unlimited Possi-bility and Inevitable Progress. As a self- styled prophet of a native resurgence—believing in the virtue of self- reliant individualism, in the innate goodness of man and the rightness of his impulses—he has followed the tradition of American transcendentalism. (One critic has quite seriously called Saroyan the creator of "the new transcendentalism.") But it need hardly be said that Saroyan is no Emerson, either by temperament or by talent. The extent to which his later work has failed reflects, in one sense, the inadequacy of his equipment for the task he set himself. Yet it is also true that Saroyan is the representative American of the mid-twentieth-century, a man baffled at the failure of the Dream but unwilling to give it up; incapable of facing his dilemma frankly or of articulating it meaningfully.

When Saroyan's stories began appearing in the early 1930's, the literature of the day was som-ber with gloom or protest. And though Saroyan's

> SAROYAN HAS PERENNIALLY BOASTED AN AESTHETICS OF NO-EFFORT, DENOUNCING 'INTELLECTUALISM' AND CONTENDING THAT A MAN SHOULD WRITE AS A HEN LAYS EGGS—INSTINCTIVELY, WITHOUT THOUGHT OR PLANNING."

fiction was also born of the Depression, often tell-ing of desperate men, of writers dying in poverty, it nevertheless managed a dreamy affirmation. Polit-ically and economically blind, Saroyan declared himself bent on a one-man crusade in behalf of the "lost imagination in America." In an era of group-consciousness, he was "trying to restore man to his natural dignity and gentleness." "I want to restore man to himself," he said. "I want to send him from the mob to his own body and mind. I want to lift him from the nightmare of history to the calm dream of his own soul."

This concept of restored individuality gov-erned Saroyan's principal attitudes, his impulsive iconoclasm as well as his lyrical optimism. While Saroyan joined the protestants in damning the traditional villains—war, money, the success cult, standardization—he was really attacking the depersonalization which such forces had effected. He was just as much opposed to regimentation in protest literature as in everyday life. ("Everybody in America is organized except E. E. Cummings," he complained.) Writing about foreigners and exiles, the meek and isolated, "the despised and rejected," he celebrated the "kingdom within" each man. The artists in his stories preserved a crucial part of themselves; there was spiritual sur-vival and triumph, let economics fall where it might. And in the glowing stories about men close to the earth of their vineyards, about glad children and fertile, generous women, Saroyan was affirming what he called the "poetry of life" and exalted with capital-letter stress: Love, Humor, Art, Imagination, Hope, Integrity.

In effect, Saroyan was restoring the perspec-tive without which the writers of the thirties had often (for obvious reasons) reduced the individual potential to a materialism of physical survival. When a character in one of his plays insisted that food, lodging, and clothes were the only realities, another responded, "What you say is true. The things you've named are all precious— if you haven't got them. But if you have, or if you can get them, they aren't." However limiting Saroyan's simplifications might prove, they none the less contained important truths which had been lost sight of amidst the earnestness of agitation-propaganda. If Saroyan is given any place in future literary histories, he should be credited with helping to relax ideologically calcified attitudes....

Saroyan [became], for the moment, an important force in the American theatre—a symbol and an inspiration to playwrights, actors, and audiences. He had come to stand not only for personal freedom after the years of economic and emotional austerity, but also for freedom in style and form.

Whereas Saroyan's stories were often reminiscent of Mark Twain, Sherwood Anderson, or John Steinbeck, there was no recognizable literary tradition behind his playwriting. Rather, it was the showmanship and theatricality of the popular entertainers, made euphonious and articulate, that went into these early plays.... He had developed a decided preference for vaudeville over Ibsen, Oscar Wilde, and the other "serious dramatists" because it was "easygoing, natural, and American."

Thus, his best works for the stage gave the impression of a jamboree which was springing to life spontaneously, right before one's eyes. The inhibitions of both stage people and audience were lifted by a mood of gentle intoxication (sometimes alcoholic, sometimes not). The impulse to play and sing and dance was given free rein without concern for plot or didactic point....

Saroyan's element, indeed, was the flexible time of childhood; he was at his best when writing about dreams fulfilled and faith justified. He was a teller of joyful tales and tales of high sentiment, making a revel of life and lyricizing death, hardship, and villainy.

But not long after the peak of his success at the beginning of the forties, Saroyan's writing began to change. Concerned about the onesidedness of his outlook, he set out to justify his unadulterated hopefulness. Instead of the airy, uncontested supremacy of beauty and happiness, there were now, as Saroyan began to see things, misery and ugliness to contend with, imperfection to account for. At the same time that he took cognizance of the dark side of life, he began trying to prove all for the best in the best of all possible worlds, with the

result that his novels and plays became strange battlegrounds where belief struggled with skepticism. To retain his perfectionist version of man's life on earth, yet to get rid of the unpleasant realities he had come to acknowledge—this was Saroyan's new burden....

Among the earliest works to demonstrate that Saroyan was no longer able to dismiss "evil" casually or to proclaim "belief" summarily was his first novel, *The Human Comedy* (which Saroyan wrote originally as a motion picture in 1943). The protagonist was Saroyan's favorite character type—a young dreamer with untainted senses, a rich imagination, and warm sympathies. Instead of following the old blithe Saroyanesque line, however, the book became a study in doubt and faith, tracing prophetically the pattern of Saroyan's own career. The young hero ... is nearing the age of disenchantment and is especially vulnerable because he has been nourished on inflated ideals and has never been allowed to know adversity. His trust in the benevolence of the universe is consequently threatened when his personal idol, an older brother, goes off to war and faces death.

The outcome is abrupt and arbitrary, as Saroyan contrived to dissolve the conflict with a happy ending. The brother is killed in the war, and the boy is about to plunge into despair when, before mourning can get under way, a wounded buddy of the dead soldier—fortuitously an orphan without ties—appears on the scene and quite literally takes the brother's place in the household as if nothing had happened. Saroyan explained this miracle by inflating his idea of brotherliness into a concept of universal oneness which permits live men to be substituted for dead ones. Since "none of us is separate from any other," according to the logic of the novel, and since "each man is the whole world, to make over as he will," the stranger is able to become at once the son, brother, and lover that his friend had been. It is as simple as this because Saroyan is running the show. Death and disaster are ruled out of order, and the boy's illusions are protected.

But Saroyan was paying a high price for the preservation of unlimited possibilities. This novel had lost all but a modicum of the Saroyanesque buoyancy. In the course of thwarting misfortune, the author had to let the boy abandon his pranks and dramas to face the prospect of sorrow. Meanwhile, there was a moral point that had to be reinforced by sermons on virtue. Large doses of speculative talk adulterated the dreamy atmosphere. Always inclined toward sentimentality, Saroyan now landed with both feet deep in mush. By dwelling on the love and goodness he had previously taken with a skip and a holler, Saroyan was suffocating spontaneity....

The fact that [the] concept of the mutual exclusiveness of good and bad, right and wrong, beautiful and ugly has become an underlying assumption in Saroyan's struggle against disbelief is evidence of his "Americanism."...

[*The Adventures of William Saroyan* and a novel (*The Adventures of Wesley Jackson*)] were weighted down with aimless vitriol about the indignities of war and the Army; and in attempting to write seriously about statesmanship, propaganda, and international affairs, Saroyan exposed to full view his lack of intellectual discipline and integrative capacity.

Saroyan has perennially boasted an aesthetics of no-effort, denouncing "intellectualism" and contending that a man should write as a hen lays eggs—instinctively, without thought or planning. Confusing laziness with casualness and spontaneity, he has continued to oversimplify. Part of Saroyan's charm had been the way he had often, in his enthusiasm about everyday things and people, blurred but intensified the lines of his picture with superlatives: "The loveliest looking mess the girl had ever seen"; "nature at its proudest, dryest, loneliest, and loveliest"; "the crazy, absurd, magnificent agreement." But when, in his later work, he applied this indiscriminate approach to questions of morality and metaphysics, the effect became one of pretentiousness. With sweeping generalizations, he now implied that he was solving man's weightiest problems, yet without evidence of any careful or systematic consideration.... The allegorical scheme he concocted for *Jim Dandy* was more ambitious than Thornton Wilder's in *The Skin of Our Teeth*. The assumption of Saroyan's play, as of Wilder's, was that "everybody in it had survived pestilence, famine, ignorance, injustice, inhumanity, torture, crime, and madness." But instead of a cohesive drama about man's survival through history by the skin of his teeth, Saroyan wrote an incoherent hodge-podge in which everything turns out just jim dandy, as if there has never been a serious threat at all....

Saroyan's efforts to provide clarification have often had [a] tendency to eliminate all distinctions, reducing meaning to some amorphous unit—if not to a cipher. In his yearning for a harmony, for an eradication of conflicts and contradictions, Saroyan is the heir of a tradition which, among Americans of a more reflective or mystical temperament, has included Jefferson's ideal of human perfectibility, Emerson's *Oversoul*, Whitman's multitudinous *Self*, Henry Adams' *Lady of Chartres*, and Waldo Franks's *Sense of the Whole*.

In 1949, there appeared a volume of three full-length plays by William Saroyan, his major works for the theatre since the war. None of these plays—*Don't Go Away Mad; Sam Ego's House; A Decent Birth, A Happy Funeral*—has been given a Broadway production. Indeed so vaguely speculative are they that their author found it necessary to explain them in lengthy prefaces summarizing the plots and offering suggestions for deciphering the allegories. The pseudo-philosophical elements of Saroyan's writing had come more than ever to overshadow the vivid and the colorful.

Moreover, the preoccupation with death virtually excludes every other consideration, especially in *A Decent Birth*, *A Happy Funeral* and in *Don't Go Away Mad*. The action of the latter is set in a city hospital ward for cancer victims, and the characters are all "incurables," tortured by pain and by thoughts of their impending doom. While they clutch at prospects of the slightest delay, they brood over the crises and deaths of fellow inmates and talk endlessly about death, life, time, and the details of their physiological decadence. Yet even here, in these plays about death, Saroyan has conjured up endings of joy....

To negate death has thus become for Saroyan the crucial test of man's free will and unlimited powers. Sometimes, instead of whisking it away by plot manipulations, he had tried to exorcise death by comic ritual, to be as airy about morbidity as he had been about little boys turning somersaults. (Many social analysts have noted the uneasy effort in America to euphemize death, glamorize it, sentimentalize it, and generally make it keep its distance.) He changed the title of his most dismal play from "The Incurables" to *Don't Go Away Mad*. He tried to lighten an act-long funeral ceremony by having burlesque comedians conduct the service while they played with yo-yos and rubber balls and blew tin horns. And some years ago he hailed George Bernard Shaw as the first man "to make a complete monkey out of death and of the theory [sic!] of dying in general." But one of Saroyan's own characters declares that "Death begins with helplessness, and it's impossible to joke about." Perhaps Saroyan has begun to suspect that for him, "Death is a lousy idea from which there is no escape."

The latest novel by Saroyan is called *The Laughing Matter* (1953). Set in the California vineyards and dealing with a family of Armenian heritage, the book has on its opening pages an atmosphere of love and warmth which recalls the earliest and best Saroyan. When the boy and girl of the family are the book's concern, their enjoyment of life and their sensitivity to the world around them—the way they savor figs and grapes, drink in the warmth of the sun, wonder about the universe—are a delight. But before long, Saroyan is trying to handle adult problems and the tale bogs down.... The boy, confronted by the tragic situation which is rocking the security of his beautiful family, cries to the skies, "What was the matter? What was it, always? Why couldn't anything be the way it ought to be? Why was everything always strange, mysterious, dangerous, delicate, likely to break to pieces suddenly?" For although his father has taught him the Armenian words, "It is right," and although everybody chants them over and over (one wise member of the family insists, meaning it, "Whatever you do is right. If you hate, it is. If you kill, it is."), nevertheless, everything goes wrong and there is death and disaster, and there is futility in the face of imperfection. And after it all, at the end of the book, still crying like an echo in the wilderness, is the repeated refrain, "It is right!"

Source: William J. Fisher, "What Ever Happened to Saroyan?," in *College English*, Vol. 16, No. 6, March 1955, pp. 336–40.

SOURCES

Balakian, Nona, *The World of William Saroyan*, Bucknell University Press, 1998, pp. 19, 46.

Barter, Alice K., "Introduction: Saroyan and His Critics," in *Critical Essays on William Saroyan*, edited by Harry Keyishian, G. K. Hall, 1995, pp. 5, 8–10, 15.

Calonne, David Stephen, "William Saroyan and Multiculturalism," in *Journal of the Society for Armenian Studies*, Vol. 6, 1992–1993, p. 107.

Emerson, Ralph Waldo, "Nature," in *Emerson: Essays and Lectures*, Library of America, 1983.

Floan, Howard R., *William Saroyan*, Twayne's United States Authors Series, No. 100, Twayne Publishers, 1966, pp. 124, 152.

Friedman, R. L., "Saroyan at a Hundred and One," in *Hopkins Review*, Vol. 3, No. 1, Winter 2010, pp. 133–40.

Kouymjian, Dickran, "Whitman and Saroyan: Singing the Song of America," in *Critical Essays on William Saroyan*, edited by Harry Keyishian, G. K. Hall, 1995, pp. 72, 74, 77.

Leggett, John, *A Daring Young Man: A Biography of William Saroyan*, Knopf, 2002, pp. 68, 140, 161.

Review of *The Human Comedy*, in *English Journal*, Vol. 78, No. 1, January 1989, p. 23.

Saroyan, Aram, *William Saroyan*, Harcourt Brace, 1983, p. 83.

Saroyan, William, *The Human Comedy*, illustrated by Don Freeman, Harcourt, Brace, 1943.

Shinn, Thelma, "William Saroyan: Romantic Existentialist," in *Critical Essays on William Saroyan*, edited by Harry Keyishian, G. K. Hall, 1995, pp. 96–104.

FURTHER READING

Bedrosian, Margaret, "William Saroyan and The Family Matter," in *MELUS*, Vol. 9, No. 4, 1982, pp. 13–24.
 Bedrosian speaks of the darker view of family life in Armenian American culture shown in Saroyan's work, that awareness of belonging to a dying race. She calls his philosophy a street-wise existentialism.

Goodwin, Doris Kearns, *No Ordinary Time: Franklin and Eleanor Roosevelt: The Home Front in World War II*, Simon & Schuster, 1995.
 This biography of the extraordinary Roosevelt couple covers their circle of White House family and staff. It provides extensive background information on the times during which Saroyan wrote.

Hovannisian, Garin K., *Family of Shadows: A Century of Murder, Memory, and the Armenian American Dream*, Harper, 2010.
 This is a memoir of three generations of Armenian Americans. The great-grandfather witnessed the Armenian Genocide in 1915. The American grandfather became a professor of Armenian history at UCLA. The father immigrated to the independent Armenian republic in 1990 and became a politician.

Kouymjian, Dickran, "Saroyan Shoots a Film," in *William Saroyan: The Man and the Writer Remembered*, edited by Leo Hamalian, pp. 77–83.
 Kouymjian provides an account of Saroyan's attempt to get MGM to let him direct the film version of *The Human Comedy*.

Winkler, Allan, *Home Front U.S.A.: America During World War II*, Harlan Davidson, 2000.

This illustrated history has material on the atomic bomb, women, African Americans, American Jews, Japanese Americans, and other topics related to efforts to support the war on the home front.

SUGGESTED SEARCH TERMS

William Saroyan

William Saroyan AND The Human Comedy

The Human Comedy AND novel

The Human Comedy AND film

The Human Comedy AND musical

Armenian American literature

William Saroyan AND novel

William Saroyan AND World War II

William Saroyan AND Academy Award

Armenian genocide

William Saroyan AND Fresno

William Saroyan AND Armenian immigration

Montana 1948

LARRY WATSON

1993

Montana 1948, released in 1993, was Larry Watson's second published novel (the first, *In a Dark Time*, was his doctoral thesis from the University of Utah). The events of the story, which occur when protagonist David Hayden is twelve years old, are narrated by an adult David some forty years later. David's Uncle Frank, a doctor, is discovered to have molested Native American women patients from the nearby reservation. Since David's father (Frank's brother) is the town sheriff, the revelation precipitates a crisis of conscience for him that will eventually tear the Hayden family apart. All these crises occur while David is already struggling with the difficulties of growing into manhood.

In this coming-of-age tale, Watson explores themes of prejudice, moral ambiguity, the abuse of power and privilege, and the struggle to establish one's identity (at any age). The effects of childhood events and relationships on the rest of an individual's life are a motif Watson returns to in later novels, including *Laura* (2000), in which a boy develops a lifelong obsession with his father's mistress, and *Sundown, Yellow Moon* (2007), in which a writer is haunted by a tragedy he witnessed in childhood. Some critics have compared the novel to Harper Lee's 1960 classic *To Kill a Mockingbird*.

AUTHOR BIOGRAPHY

Watson was born in the small town of Rugby, North Dakota, on September 13, 1947. Like Wesley Hayden, the father in *Montana 1948*, Watson's father was a sheriff. When Watson was five, however, his family moved to the larger city of Bismarck, North Dakota, where his father practiced law. Watson grew up in Bismarck and attended the University of North Dakota, intending to study law. In 1967, while still in college, he married his high school girlfriend, Susan Gibbons.

Watson's plan to study law was put aside when, inspired by writing classes and encouragement from his professors, he instead decided to study creative writing and become a teacher. He earned a masters degree from the University of North Dakota, and then a Ph.D. from the University of Utah. The novel he wrote as his thesis, titled *In a Dark Time*, was published by Scribner's, but despite favorable reviews, it was not wildly successful.

In 1978, Watson moved on to the University of Wisconsin at Stevens Point, where he taught literature and writing for the next twenty-five years. He continued to write, publishing short stories and poetry. However, he struggled to find publishers for his novels. Finally, in 1993, unable to find a publisher for his most recent novel, *Montana 1948*, he entered his manuscript as a contender for the Milkweed National Fiction Prize (sponsored by independent publisher Milkweed Press). The novel won and was published by Milkweed Press.

With glowing reviews from many prominent newspapers, including the *Washington Post* and the *Los Angeles Times*, *Montana 1948* became Milkweed Press's best-selling book to date (as of 2011). Still intrigued by the novel's characters, Watson followed with a fiction collection, *Justice*, that served as a prequel, telling the story of the Hayden family leading up to the birth of David Hayden, the protagonist of *Montana 1948*. Watson created new characters for his next novel, *White Crosses* (1997), though he remained in the fictional town of Bentrock, Montana.

His next novel, *Laura* (2000), was a departure for Watson, telling the story of a man's lifelong obsession with his father's mistress. It was the first of Watson's novels to be set outside of North Dakota and Montana and to venture into modern times; though it begins in the 1950s, it covers forty years of the protagonist's life.

In the spring of 2003, Watson retired from the University of Wisconsin at Stevens Point and took a position as a visiting professor at Marquette University. A few months later, his sixth novel, *Orchard*, was published. In *Orchard*, Watson returns to the 1950s, with a tale of two couples whose lives are entangled by jealousy and obsession. His 2007 novel, *Sundown, Yellow Moon* (set in North Dakota), features a writer who spends years coming to terms with a tragedy he witnessed as a boy. Watson's next novel, *American Boy*, was released in 2011.

As of 2011, Watson and his wife of more than forty years lived in Milwaukee, Wisconsin. They have two grown daughters, Elly and Amy.

PLOT SUMMARY

Prologue

In a brief prologue, an adult David Hayden describes images that will occur in the story he is about to tell, and establishes that it is now forty years in the past. He tells us that his mother and father have both passed away, and that now the story is his alone to tell.

Part One

The novel opens with a description of David Hayden's hometown: Bentrock, a small town in the northeastern corner of Montana. David is twelve years old, and his father, Wesley, is the sheriff of Bentrock; much to David's disappointment, however, Bentrock is a peaceful town, and his father's job is not a glamorous one. David's mother works as a secretary, and while she is at work, a Native American woman named Marie Little Soldier takes care of the house and David.

Late in the summer of 1948, Marie becomes ill; she has a severe cough and a fever. David's mother offers to have Dr. Frank Hayden, David's uncle, come to examine her. Frank, Wesley's brother, is the golden boy of the Hayden clan—star athlete, war hero, handsome doctor with a beautiful wife. However, when David's mother suggests that Frank come to the house to examine Marie, Marie immediately becomes distressed and insists that she would rather see her regular doctor, Dr. Snow. When Frank does arrive, Marie asks David's mother to stay in the room with her during the examination.

After Frank leaves, David overhears a conversation between his mother and father that

MEDIA ADAPTATIONS

- An audiobook version of *Montana 1948* was released in 1995, read by actor Beau Bridges. The audiobook is available on both CD (by Recorded Books) and audiocassette (Simon & Schuster).

- The film rights to *Montana 1948* were purchased by Echo Lake Productions in 2002, but as of 2011, no film of the novel had been produced.

explains Marie's distress. According to Marie, Frank has been molesting his female patients at the reservation. David's father suggests that Marie may be lying, or has simply misunderstood the nature of a doctor's examination. David's mother then spells out, in detail, the things Frank has been doing to his patients. David's father, as sheriff, now feels bound to investigate the matter.

David's father questions Marie, and speaks to his deputy, Len Macauley, a man in his sixties who was deputy for David's grandfather when he was sheriff. David's mother speaks to Daisy, Len's wife. Daisy says she has heard rumors that Frank "doesn't do everything on the up-and-up." After their separate investigations, David overhears his parents talking about what they've learned. At the end of their conversation, David's mother asks her husband why he hasn't said he doesn't believe the news about Frank. David's father says nothing, and David realizes his father knows that Frank is guilty.

Part Two

David's father continues his investigation of Uncle Frank; he questions women at the reservation and a respected local rancher, Ollie Young Bear, and he questions Marie again. During the investigation, the family is invited out to David's grandfather's ranch for dinner. David's mother wants to refuse the invitation, because Frank and his wife will be there, but David's father insists on going.

Grandpa Hayden is a prosperous rancher with an enormous lodge-like house outside of Bentrock. A judgmental, overbearing, and often vulgar man who enjoys having power over others, David's grandfather is aware that Frank has had affairs with women from the reservation; David overhears Grandpa say to his father, "You know Frank's always been partial to red meat." David cannot imagine why Uncle Frank would want other women when he is married to his Aunt Gloria, who is the most beautiful woman he has ever seen.

After an uncomfortable dinner, David asks to be excused to ride his horse, Nutty, which is stabled at his grandfather's ranch. Before he leaves, his grandfather gives him a pistol, and tells him if he sees any coyotes, he should shoot them. While on his ride, David does not see any coyotes, but he does enjoy shooting off the entire box of bullets his grandfather gave him. Mostly he shoots at nothing, but at one point, he shoots a magpie off a tree branch. After killing the bird, he feels oddly calm, as though the violent act has released the pent-up emotions he feels about Uncle Frank's crimes.

Riding back to the ranch, David sees his father and Uncle Frank by the side of a creek, arguing. He cannot hear what they are saying, but he knows it must have to do with Uncle Frank and the reservation women. Uncle Frank suddenly moves toward David's father in a threatening manner, and David aims his pistol at Uncle Frank. The pistol is not loaded, but David wonders what he would do if it were. Finally the two men conclude their argument and return to the ranch.

In the car on the way home, David's father tells his mother that he has spoken to Frank, who has promised to "cut it out." David's mother objects that Frank should be punished for what he has done, but his father refuses to turn in his own brother. When they arrive home, they find that Marie's condition has improved; her fever is down and her cough is less intense than before.

However, the next day when David returns home from fishing with friends, he discovers that Marie has died. Everyone is shocked; she had appeared to be improving. David is not only sad about Marie's passing, he is also struggling with something he knows, a secret he knows he should reveal. His parents send him to the Macauleys' house to get him out of the way. There,

David finds Len Macauley acting strangely, as if he, too, knows a secret about Uncle Frank.

That night, unable to sleep, David goes to his parents' room and tells him his secret: he saw Uncle Frank at the house earlier in the day, with his medical bag, when no one else was home. He had stopped to use the Macauleys' outhouse on his way to go fishing and witnessed Uncle Frank leaving the house from there.

Part Three

A few days after Marie's death, David's father brings Uncle Frank to the house, takes him downstairs to the basement, and returns alone. David fears that his father has killed Uncle Frank, but he tells David and his mother that he has arrested Frank, and is keeping him locked up in the basement rather than the town jail, to save him embarrassment. Before leaving to tell Aunt Gloria of Frank's arrest, he tells David to run and get Len Macauley if there is any trouble while he's gone.

Later that evening, David's grandfather and grandmother arrive. Grandpa Hayden is furious over Frank's arrest, and demands that he be released immediately. David's mother, seeing Grandpa's temper, sends David to his room; there, David puts his ear to the heat register in the floor to eavesdrop on the rest of the conversation. David's father explains that Frank has been molesting his female patients. Grandpa Hayden, still angry, implies that the only reason David's father has arrested Frank is that he is jealous of his brother, the war hero (David's father was unable to enlist because of a bad leg). David's father tells Grandpa that the problem is more severe than the sexual abuse, and then mumbles something neither David nor his grandfather can hear. When Grandpa demands that he speak up, David's father shouts, "Murder!" Grandpa Hayden still refuses to believe Frank has done anything wrong, and berates David's father for upsetting Grandma, who is now weeping. Grandpa Hayden storms out of the house with Grandma in tow.

Though his grandparents have left, David is apprehensive about coming downstairs after the volatile scene, but cannot resist the lure of the chocolate cake he knows is in the kitchen. When he comes downstairs, he sees his father on his knees with his head in his mother's lap; she is massaging his neck. David is struck by how old and weakened his father looks, and he can see that he has been crying. When they all go upstairs to bed that evening, David's father tells him that, if his grandfather or grandmother come by when he is not home, he should not open the door to them.

The next day, David's mother sends him into town to pick up some groceries. As he walks the streets of town, David is ashamed, imagining that everyone knows, or will soon know, of his Uncle Frank's crimes. When he sees some women who were Frank's patients, he wonders what Uncle Frank has done to them. Overcome with shame, he runs all the way home from the grocery store.

Later that day, David notices a truck circling their house. One of the men in the truck is the foreman of his grandfather's ranch. His mother tells him to call his father at his office, but when he does, his secretary says he isn't there. After he gets off the phone, he sees the four men walking toward the house. His mother gets a shotgun and begins clumsily loading it with bullets. David tries to help her, but his mother shouts at him to go find his father, or anyone that can help.

He runs to the state attorney's office, but the secretary tells him that his father left there an hour earlier. Upon returning home, he hears a shotgun blast; his mother has fired a harmless warning shot from the window. She is so inept with the rifle that David feels he should wrest it away from her, but before he can do this, Deputy Len Macauley enters the yard with a pistol, aiming it at the four men. David cannot hear what Len says to the men, but they back off, get back into their truck, and leave.

A few minutes later, David's father arrives. David's mother begs him to just let Frank go before anyone gets hurt. Len agrees, pointing out that convicting Frank would be nearly impossible, with Grandpa Hayden's power and influence in the community and the general prejudice against the main witnesses, the reservation women. David's father goes down to the basement to get Frank, but then returns without him, resolved to keep him imprisoned. Frank has admitted to the murder, and as David's father puts it, "He'd show more remorse over a dog."

That night, David is awakened by the sound of glass breaking. Confused and frightened, he runs to his parents' room, but they are not there. He runs downstairs and finds his parents sitting on the couch, awake. They tell him that Uncle Frank is breaking all the canning jars in the root cellar, one by one. His father tries to reassure him by telling him that, the next day, he will be taking Frank to the town jail.

The crashing of jars continues throughout the night; David wakes up early, still listening for the sound. He goes downstairs and meets his father in the kitchen. David's father says he is waiting to hear Frank stir downstairs before he goes down to get him and take him to the jail. He tells David a story from his childhood, about how Frank saved him and some of his friends from some bullies. Then, thinking he hears Frank, he heads downstairs to get his brother. A few moments later, David hears his father scream, *"Oh my God, no!"* David immediately runs downstairs.

There he sees his father with Uncle Frank's head cradled on his chest. Uncle Frank has slit his wrists with the broken glass from the canning jars; the mess from the jars mingles with his blood on the basement floor. David's father tells him to go get Len right away, and before David leaves, he adds, "And David, don't let your mother come down here. *Don't let her!*"

As David leaves the basement, he is convinced that his uncle's suicide has solved all their problems; his father will not have to put his brother in jail or testify against him, the reservation women will no longer be abused, and no one will need to know that Uncle Frank killed Marie. David, in his innocence, feels grateful to Uncle Frank for what he has done.

Epilogue

David innocently believes that Frank's death will allow the Haydens to resume their former lives, but this is not the case. The family first concocts a story about Frank's death to protect his reputation; they tell everyone that Frank fell from a ladder while helping David's father build some shelves. Somehow—since David is just a boy at the time, he never learns the details—the undertaker is persuaded to keep the wounds on Frank's wrists a secret. David's grandparents and Aunt Gloria will no longer speak to David's parents.

David's mother announces that she cannot continue living in Bentrock. David's father agrees, and the Haydens pack up their lives to move to Fargo, North Dakota, where David's father practices law. Len Macauley becomes the new sheriff of Bentrock.

David, now a middle-aged man, sums up what happened to the rest of the characters over the next forty years; Len Macauley's term as sheriff was cut short by a debilitating stroke, and less than a year later, David's grandfather also suffered a stroke, a fatal one. David, disillusioned

with the law, went on to become a history professor. His father lived for thirty more years before dying of cancer. His mother died just two months before David began to tell his tale.

David concludes the novel with two anecdotes. The first is his favorite memory of Marie. He remembers playing football in the yard with Marie and her boyfriend, Ronnie Tall Bear, on a sunny autumn day, and then relaxing afterward with a jug of apple cider. For the first time, David says, "I felt . . . as though I was part of a family, a family that accepted me for myself and not my blood or birthright."

The other story he relates occurs much later, after David is grown and married. He tells his wife, Betsy, the story of Uncle Frank; however, he neglects to warn her that his parents never speak of it. That Thanksgiving, while visiting his parents, Betsy brings up the subject, saying, "That sure was the Wild West, wasn't it?" David's father, immediately angered, slams his hands on the table and shouts, "Don't ever blame Montana!" He then leaves the room.

CHARACTERS

David Hayden

David Hayden is the main character, or protagonist, of the novel. Though he is twelve years old when the incidents in the story occur, the novel is narrated by David in his fifties; both his parents have died, and he realizes that what happened with his Uncle Frank is a tale "that is now only mine to tell." The nature of his Uncle Frank's crime and the crisis it brings about in the Hayden family force young David to mature quickly and painfully. Family members he has previously loved and respected are presented to him in a new, unflattering light.

Twelve-year-old David fluctuates between a desire to be treated as an adult and a boy's wish to deny the painful truths put before him. For example, when David's grandfather arrives at the house, furious with David's father, David is glad that his mother sends him to his room; the situation is uncomfortable for him. However, once in his room, he eavesdrops on the conversation through the heating register. Later, when he returns downstairs, he wants his parents to explain the situation away: "I wanted them to explain it so it wasn't as bad as the facts made it seem."

In addition to the unsettling family crisis David must deal with, he also struggles with the usual difficulties of puberty. He is ashamed that, when he sees his beautiful Aunt Gloria and his beloved caretaker Marie, he sometimes feels the stirrings of sexual desire. This sexual awakening makes Uncle Frank's crimes against the women of the reservation even more unsettling, especially when he overhears his mother, a very conservative woman, use words like "rape" and "breasts." With the revelation of Uncle Frank's misdeeds, David's image of his world and the people in it is turned on its head.

Enid Hayden

David's grandmother Enid is an emotionally fragile woman. The rest of the family does their best to shelter her from unpleasant realities, a task that becomes more difficult after Frank's crimes have been revealed. She is dominated completely by her overbearing husband, David's grandfather.

Frank Hayden

Frank Hayden is David's uncle. He is the golden boy of the Hayden family, and clearly his father's favorite. A handsome star athlete, war hero, and ladies' man, Frank returned from the war to practice medicine in Bentrock. However, as the novel progresses, affable Frank is revealed to be a sexual predator who is molesting his Native American female patients on the nearby reservation. His desire for the reservation women is based, at least in part, on the prejudice handed down to him by his father; because he sees the Native American women as somewhat less than human, he sees nothing wrong with violating them, or in the end, even murdering them. His father has also passed on to Frank a sense of entitlement, a feeling that the Hayden name can excuse all manner of ills.

Gail Hayden

David's mother is a formidable woman, a devout Lutheran with a strong sense of right and wrong. Originally from North Dakota, she describes herself as "a flatlander at heart," preferring the wide open country to the mountains of Montana. In one scene, she tells David that she loves the wind, but that it smells different in Montana than in her home state. Her love of the wind and her name (Gail, or gale) foreshadow the way that David's mother will handle the winds of change that sweep through the Hayden household. She faces the problems head on, repeatedly confronting David's father and reminding him of the values he has sworn to uphold.

Gloria Hayden

Gloria is Frank Hayden's wife, and David's aunt. David thinks she is the most beautiful woman he has ever seen. Gloria is from Minnesota and is a first-grade teacher. Sweet, friendly, and loyal to her husband, she gives no indication that she is aware of Frank's infidelities.

Grandma Hayden

See Enid Hayden

Grandpa Hayden

See Julian Hayden

Julian Hayden

David's grandfather is a prosperous rancher and the former sheriff of Bentrock. A man who enjoys acquiring and wielding power, he expects people (especially his sons) to do what he tells them, and as a general rule, they comply. He has passed on his bigotry toward Native Americans to both his sons. When he speaks of Frank's dalliances with women from the reservation, he does so with amusement, and says casually that there are probably kids on the reservation who bear a strong resemblance to Frank. In fact, Grandpa Hayden even seems proud of Frank's healthy libido, though he is dismayed that Frank and Gloria have not yet been able to give him grandchildren.

Grandpa Hayden is also vulgar, frequently using profanity and speaking about bodily functions in conversation, which does not endear him to David's mother. Despite his obvious flaws, David believes his grandfather to be a fair man who will stand up for what's right, a belief that will be shattered by his grandfather's behavior during the crisis with Uncle Frank.

Wesley Hayden

David's father is the younger of the Hayden sons and has spent his life in the shadow of his more glamorous, accomplished, and charming brother, Frank. At sixteen, Wesley was kicked by a horse, breaking his leg so badly that he still walks with a significant limp. This disability prevented him from enlisting in the service in World War II, during which Frank naturally became a hero.

Both Hayden brothers have inherited a prejudice toward Native Americans; David says his father "believed Indians, with only a few exceptions, were ignorant, lazy, superstitious and irresponsible." Unlike Grandpa and Frank Hayden, however, Wesley Hayden does not use this belief as an excuse to mistreat or abuse Native Americans, and he believes Native Americans deserve the protection of the law. It is this belief that causes the rift between Wesley and his family when Frank's crimes are revealed.

Though he believes in his duty to uphold the law, Wesley is a pragmatic man who believes in hard evidence rather than gut instinct. When he first learns of Frank's crimes, he reluctantly begins his investigation, postponing any judgment. However, the growing evidence and Frank's callous lack of remorse leads him to take a stronger stand against his brother and his father.

Marie Little Soldier

Marie is a tall, pretty Native American woman who keeps house and watches David while his mother works as a secretary. Fun-loving and outgoing, she loves to tell stories and pull pranks on David. At the opening of the novel, Marie falls ill with pneumonia, prompting the Haydens to call on Uncle Frank.

Daisy Macauley

Daisy is the garrulous wife of Len Macauley, Wesley Hayden's deputy. In her sixties, she is a grandmotherly figure, plump and white-haired, who bakes cookies and pies for David. Her love of gossip allows her to provide David's mother with some key information about Uncle Frank.

Len Macauley

Len Macauley, a shy, slender man in his sixties, has been deputy of Bentrock for many years, first with Julian Hayden, and now with his son Wesley. Len and his wife live next door to David and his family. Once a heavy drinker, Len is now sober. However, David notices that he begins drinking again during the situation with Uncle Frank.

Mel Paddock

Mel, the Mercer County state attorney, is a good friend of Wesley Hayden's. During elections, they pool their funds and campaign together.

Ronnie Tall Bear

Ronnie Tall Bear is Marie's boyfriend, a star athlete who fought with the infantry in World War II. Ronnie provides an example of the prejudice against Native Americans: though he excels in several sports, he is not recruited by any colleges because, as David puts it, "College was not for Indians."

Ollie Young Bear

Ollie Young Bear is one of Wesley Hayden's "exceptions," a Native American who has worked hard and become successful; he is a deacon at the church, and an executive at a utilities company. He is married to a white woman. Though he is respected by the white community, the Native Americans feel he has lost touch with his own culture. As Marie describes it, "He won't be happy until he's white." David finds him stern, humorless, and judgmental.

THEMES

Identity

Both David and his father struggle to define themselves as individuals within the context of also being Haydens. One of the reasons David's mother did not want to move to Montana was that she felt her husband could never truly be himself while living in the sphere of his father's influence. In taking a stand against his father and brother over the murder of Marie, Wesley not only defends the law and its principles but he seeks to define himself as a man with values and beliefs very different from his father's. He begins the investigation reluctantly (after his wife tells him of Marie's accusations, he says, "I wish you wouldn't have told the sheriff"), doing just enough to satisfy his conscience, while trying not to rock the Hayden boat. "I don't want this getting back to my father," he tells David's mother.

However, as the case progresses and the magnitude and severity of Frank's crimes becomes clear, Wesley Hayden becomes more resolute in his stand. The investigation reveals not only the true nature of Frank's character but also the character of Julian Hayden; Wesley discovers that the man to whom he has declared "absolute fealty" has almost as little respect for him as he does for the Native American victims of Frank's crimes. What it means to be a Hayden in Bentrock now takes on a darker tone, making it that much more critical for Wesley to establish his own identity, apart from his father and his brother.

David struggles to define his own self-image; one part of the struggle is simply a natural part of growing up, and the other is his discomfort

TOPICS FOR FURTHER STUDY

- In *Montana 1948*, according to David, the character Marie Little Soldier was originally from the Fort Berthold Reservation. Unlike the fictional Fort Warren Reservation in the novel, Fort Berthold is an actual reservation located along the Missouri River in North Dakota. Conduct online and traditional research about the Fort Berthold Reservation. How many square miles does it cover? What are some of its key features (natural and manmade)? Design an informational brochure for the Fort Berthold Reservation using the information you find, including maps and photos.

- Wesley Hayden is faced with a moral dilemma in *Montana 1948*. He must choose between loyalty to family and adherence to the law. Do you think he makes the right decision? Debate the decision with your classmates; have one group present the argument for arresting and imprisoning Uncle Frank, and another argue for letting Frank go. What if Frank has not murdered Marie Little Soldier? Does this change your argument?

- David, in describing Ronnie Tall Bear's military service, says that he was considered "good enough for the Army, but not for college." Japanese Americans were another minority group that fought in World War II while experiencing appalling prejudice at home. While Japanese American soldiers fought overseas, their families were imprisoned in internment camps at home. In the young-adult book *A Fence Away from Freedom*, author Ellen Levine presents the stories of Japanese Americans confined in the camps. Read the book, and then write an essay examining the role of prejudice and racism in World War II.

- Watch a classic old Western film, such as *Red River* (1948) or *The Searchers* (1956). What stereotypes in these films are defied in Watson's novel? How are Native Americans portrayed in these movies? How does the depiction of the law differ between *Montana 1948* and these films? Using a video camera, act out and film a scene of your choice from the novel. How would this scene differ if it were done in "old movie" style? Film a second version in this style. Post both scenes on your Web page and invite classmates to comment on them.

---

with his family's reputation. Even before the incident with his Uncle Frank, David is uncomfortable in town, preferring to spend his time in nature, with his horse. As David puts it, "Out of town I could simply *be*, I could feel my *self*, firm and calm and unmalleable as I could not when I was in school or in any of the usual human communities." Though David does not offer a reason, this discomfort in town likely stems from the expectations and assumptions conjured by the Hayden name. Unable to reconcile his true self with the template laid out for him by his grandfather, father, and uncle, he is more comfortable in nature, where the Hayden name means nothing. Similarly, when he spends time with Marie and Ronnie, who live in their own community separate from his, he feels he is part of a family "that accepted me for myself and not my blood or birthright." When the novel begins, the Hayden name is something to live up to; at the end, it is something to live down. Either way, it is a burden for both David and his father.

Moral Ambiguity

David tells the reader, at the opening of the novel, that his father is nothing like sheriffs in the movies (much to his disappointment). Likewise, the typical Western movie usually concludes with the hero victorious and the villains locked away. The conclusion of *Montana 1948*, however, is not so clear-cut. While one could argue that Uncle Frank (the villain) has been punished, the "good guys" suffer almost as much from the resolution of the story's dilemma. Wesley Hayden and his wife are estranged from the rest of the family, Len Macauley suffers a stroke not long after, and no one ever learns of Uncle Frank's true character. Likewise, no one ever learns the true cause of Marie's death. If Frank had lived and been acquitted for Marie's murder (which Grandpa Hayden probably could have "arranged"), would he have continued his sexual abuse of the reservation women? Given the publicity of a trial, this seems unlikely. If Wesley had simply released Frank, as his wife suggested, would the end result be less tragic? These kinds of questions result from the ambiguous nature of the novel's conclusion and lead to adult David's disillusionment with the law.

Power and Privilege

It is not just prejudice that allows Frank to exploit his women patients. Because the Hayden name carries great weight in Mercer County, Frank has developed a sense of entitlement. Grandpa Hayden encourages the idea that the Haydens are somehow better than the ordinary residents of Bentrock. This sense of entitlement, coupled with the Haydens' stranglehold on the sheriff's office, allows Frank to believe that he is above the law.

Grandpa Hayden, as David describes him, "was a dominating man who drew sustenance and strength from controlling others." Though Frank is more charming than his father, he possesses this same need for dominance. His choice of profession allows him to exercise this power, as it is a doctor's job to dictate his patient's behavior (take this medicine, avoid these foods, and other behaviors). A great deal of trust is placed in the medical profession, especially during this era. Frank exploits this trust, knowing that his female patients on the reservation will do as he says because he is a doctor and a white man.

Similarly, Grandpa Hayden attempts to use his own power to excuse Frank from his crimes. He has already been able to dictate the course of Wesley's life by making him sheriff of Bentrock ("It would never have occurred to my father to refuse"). When he comes to Wesley's home and demands Frank's release, he expects to be obeyed, because Wesley, Frank, and the people of Bentrock have obeyed him all their lives. When Wesley refuses to release Frank, Grandpa Hayden tries two more power tactics—humiliation (he implies that Wesley is jealous of Frank because

Frank is a war hero and Wesley was unable to enlist) and then intimidation (he sends his hired hands to forcibly remove Frank from his prison). Both are unsuccessful. This is especially frustrating for Grandpa Hayden because his motive in offering the sheriff's position to his son was to maintain his power and influence in Mercer County, not to benefit Wesley and his family.

Prejudice

The theme of prejudice against Native Americans runs throughout the novel. If Frank Hayden had been molesting white women, even Grandpa Hayden would disapprove. But because the victims are Native American women, Frank's crimes are considered excusable. Even David's father, the sheriff, resolves not to pursue the investigation against Frank (telling his wife, "He'll have to meet his punishment in the hereafter") until it becomes clear that Frank is guilty of murder as well as sexual assault.

The most flagrant examples of prejudice come from Grandpa Hayden and his sons. After Wesley arrests Frank and locks him up in the basement, Grandpa Hayden demands that he be released. He tells Wesley, "Screwing an Indian. Or feeling her up or whatever. You don't lock a man up for that." David's father considers most Native Americans to be lazy and ignorant, and even forbids his son to wear moccasins, saying that if he starts wearing them, "Soon he'll be as flat-footed and lazy as an Indian." Frank's prejudice allows him to believe he can violate the reservation women without fear of recrimination.

The novel also offers more subtle forms of discrimination. Ronnie Tall Bear, a record-breaking athlete in high school, is never recruited by any college; Ollie Young Bear pitches for the Elks softball team, but David muses that "he probably could not have been admitted to the Elks as a member"; a rumor circulates among David's friends that a local bar owner keeps an old Native American woman in his storeroom, and allows customers to have sex with her for two dollars. Given Wesley Hayden's feelings about the work ethic of Native Americans, David's family probably employs Marie Little Soldier as a babysitter because she demands less pay for her services than a white woman would.

The Native American women experience prejudice against both their race and their sex; women in this era were largely subservient to men, especially in a rugged state like Montana. Even the

The Hayden family lives in the fictional town of Bentrock, Montana. (*Colton Stiffler | Shutterstock.com*)

white women in the novel have little control over their fates. Grandma Hayden follows along in Grandpa Hayden's wake, making weak apologies for his boorish behavior ("He gets so upset"), but never expressing any contrary opinions. Though David's father treats his wife as more of an equal partner than Grandpa does, his desires still dictate the family's lifestyle. For instance, David says his mother did not want to live in Montana, but obviously her wishes were overruled when David's father accepted the position of sheriff in Bentrock. Similarly, when David's mother insists that Marie stay at their house while recovering from pneumonia, David says, "If my mother said it, it was so, yet my father's confirmation was still necessary."

Secrets and Lies

The psychological and even physical stress of keeping secrets is another recurring motif in the novel. David keeps the secret that he saw Uncle Frank leave the house the afternoon Marie died, and though he keeps it for only a day, it causes him a great deal of anguish. He considers telling the secret several times, but can't bring himself to do it. He loses his appetite, and even refuses a

slice of Daisy's blueberry pie. Finally, when he is unable to sleep, he wakes his parents and reveals his secret.

Frank's imprisonment in the basement is symbolic of the stress and anxiety caused by repressing secrets. The family attempts to continue their normal lives even though they know they have a family member (and a murderer) locked in the cellar below them. Just as David could not sleep with the knowledge he repressed about Uncle Frank, the entire family is kept awake by Frank smashing jars in the cellar all night. Tragically, when Wesley Hayden finally makes the decision to reveal the secret and take his brother to jail, it is too late; Frank has killed himself, giving rise to a whole new set of lies and secrets the family must carry with them for the rest of their lives.

Keeping the secret of Frank's crimes, and how he really died, takes its toll on several of the novel's characters. David, as an adult, theorizes that it was the pressure of keeping the secret that led to Len's stroke, his grandfather's stroke, and his father's cancer.

STYLE

Flashbacks

The story is generally told in chronological order, beginning with Marie's illness and her objection to letting Frank Hayden examine her. However, occasionally David describes a scene that happened earlier in his childhood. For instance, when Grandpa Hayden states that Frank "has always been partial to red meat," David says, "It was the second time I had heard my grandfather say something about my uncle and Indian girls." He then proceeds to describe a trip the family took to Minnesota for his uncle's wedding, five or six years earlier; Grandpa commented then that Frank's pretty new wife ought to be enough to "keep him off the reservation."

Foreshadowing

The most obvious use of foreshadowing is the Prologue; older David describes images out of context that will occur later in the novel. Though the reader lacks the context to completely understand the scenes, they foreshadow danger, conflict, and sorrow. For instance, one of the images David describes is his mother pointing a shotgun out the window, fully intending to use it.

Other instances of foreshadowing include Wesley Hayden's warning to his son not to open the door for his grandfather if he is alone at home (the next afternoon Grandpa Hayden sends his ranch workers to the house to forcibly remove Uncle Frank) and David's comment that the situation with Uncle Frank is ruining his father's health (he later endures a long battle with cancer). Likewise, Wesley's drunken jest, "They couldn't arrest us—we *are* the law!" perfectly predicts Frank and Grandpa's attitude toward Frank's crimes against the reservation women. And the ever-present threat of violence—David aiming his empty pistol at Uncle Frank, his mother aiming the shotgun at the ranch workers, Uncle Frank smashing jars in the basement—all culminate in the death of Uncle Frank in the final chapter.

Memoir

Montana 1948 is told by David Hayden in his fifties, looking back at the incidents that occurred when he was twelve years old. This allows the narrator to fill in missing information that was hidden from young David by his parents, and to offer insights into the story that a twelve-year-old boy would not have. The older David realizes the significance of the incident in his life; it is a loss of innocence, the end of childhood for young David. In the Epilogue, older David tells the reader, "After what I observed as a child in Bentrock, I could never believe in the rule of law again." Through the use of memoir, the reader learns that this incident in David's childhood leads to his being disillusioned, not just with his uncle and his grandfather but also with the legal system, the concept of justice, and even history. Later, as a history professor, he says, "For my students I keep a straight face and pretend the text tells the truth, whole and unembellished."

Metaphor

Watson uses metaphors throughout the novel. For instance, Grandpa Hayden's house is a metaphor for his own character. David says his mother "was especially offended by the house's log construction—usually symbolic of simplicity and humility." Like the house, Grandpa puts up the facade of a down-to-earth mountain man, when in reality he is as power hungry and self-important as any big-city politician. The enormous, ostentatious house reflects his need to dominate both the land and the people on it.

Uncle Frank's imprisonment in the basement is a metaphor for the suppression of secrets that occurs throughout the novel. The members of the Hayden family attempt to continue their everyday lives, trying their best to ignore Uncle Frank's presence. Like the secrets they must repress after Frank's death, however, Uncle Frank makes his presence known.

The Montana wind is mentioned frequently and serves as a metaphor for the changes that blow through the Hayden family, sweeping away life as they know it.

HISTORICAL CONTEXT

Aftereffects of World War II

In the first half of the 1940s, America's main concern was World War II. The United States had adopted a policy of non-intervention toward the developing war in Europe in the late 1930s, but despite a strong isolationist presence in Congress, it had become increasingly clear that the United States would eventually go to war. The Japanese attack on Pearl Harbor on December 7, 1941, made this a certainty.

COMPARE & CONTRAST

- **1940s:** The total population of Native Americans in the United States is about 350,000.

  1990s: The total population of Native Americans in the United States is about 2,000,000—nearly six times the population in the 1940s. This far surpasses the growth of the general population, which roughly doubles during the fifty-year period.

  Today: The total population of Native Americans in the United States is still about 2,000,000.

- **1940s:** The Soviet Union and the United States are wary allies in World War II.

  1990s: After more than forty years of the cold war, political unrest and a failing economy lead to the collapse of the Soviet Union.

  Today: The Soviet Union no longer exists. In its place are the independent countries of Armenia, Azerbaijan, Belarus, Estonia, Georgia, Kazakhstan, Kyrgyzstan, Latvia, Lithuania, Moldova, Russia, Tajikistan, Turkmenistan, Ukraine, and Uzbekistan.

- **1940s:** Crooners and Big Bands provide the era's most popular tunes. In the novel, David tells us that Marie Little Soldier's favorite radio station is one that plays Big Band music.

  1990s: Dance music is all the rage, and hip-hop crosses over into the mainstream.

Nirvana's "Smells Like Teen Spirit" and Whitney Houston's "I Will Always Love You" are two mega-hits of the early 1990s.

Today: Dance music is still popular, as demonstrated by popular artists Usher, the Black-Eyed Peas, Beyonce, and Lady Gaga.

- **1940s:** The number of women working outside the home increases by approximately 50 percent during the war; women are encouraged to work at factory jobs to support the war effort. Many other women take more traditional "women's jobs," such as clerical or teaching jobs, to supplement their family's incomes while their husbands are away at war. After the war, a great many women quit their jobs to return home.

  1990s: Nearly 60 percent of women work outside the home. Though some industries are still largely male-dominated (construction and agriculture, for instance), women are no longer confined to jobs in traditionally female fields.

  Today: The percentage of women working outside the home is still about 60 percent. A recent research study found that, in 22 percent of married couples in the United States, women are the primary breadwinners, a phenomena practically unheard of in the 1940s.

Effects of World War II on American society were manifold. First, the war established the United States and the U.S.S.R. as "superpowers," and the use of the atomic bomb on Hiroshima and Nagasaki brought new dimension to just how powerful a superpower could be. Thus, after World War II ended, the era of the cold war and the arms race began. Second, the return of thousands of American soldiers to civilian life, though welcome, required many adjustments by those left behind. For instance, women who had been encouraged to work during the war were now asked to step back and let the men take over. Unemployment and postwar trauma sometimes made readjusting to "normal" life difficult for veterans.

One of the happier effects of the soldiers' return was the beginning of the baby boom. Husbands returning to their wives were eager to start families that had been postponed, or add to the ones they already had. Many single men returning home, more mature than when they had left, were eager to settle down. This boom in births no doubt adds to Grandpa Hayden's frustration with Frank and Gloria's childlessness in the novel, "Just the one? From both of you?" he complains.

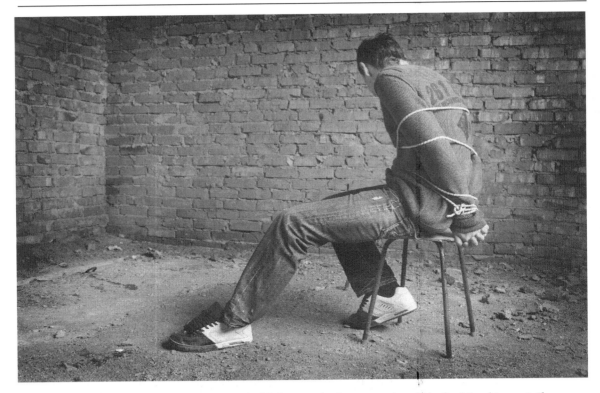

Wes has to arrest his own brother but he holds him in the basement instead of taking him to jail. (*Antonov Roman / Shutterstock.com*)

With industry renewing production of consumer goods, and reunited families eager to buy them, the American economy experienced a postwar boom as well.

Native Americans in Postwar America

Native Americans had a greater per capita participation in World War II than any other group. Of the approximately 350,000 Native Americans living in the United States, 44,000 saw some kind of military service during the war. Included in this group were the celebrated Navajo code talkers. Native American soldiers fashioned a code from the Navajo language that the Japanese were never able to break and used it for secure battlefield communications.

Despite loyal service and the respect of their fellow soldiers earned during the war, Native American soldiers found that their rights at home were still curtailed by prejudice. Though the Indian Citizenship Act of 1924 gave citizenship to all Native Americans, voting rights were still controlled by individual states. For instance, Montana's constitution was amended in 1932 to allow only taxpayers to vote; since Native Americans were not required to pay some local taxes, this amendment was used as an excuse to deny them their voting rights. The last state to finally give Native Americans the right to vote was Utah, in 1956.

However, the GI bill did allow many Native Americans to attend college, an opportunity available to few before the war, despite David Hayden's assertion that "college was not for Indians."

Early 1990s

Montana 1948 was first published in 1993, just two years after the collapse of the Soviet Union. Throughout the 1980s, there was political unrest in the Soviet Union, and its economy was deteriorating. Mikhail Gorbachev, elected general secretary of the Communist Party in the Soviet Union in 1985, attempted to bring more freedoms to the Soviet people, advocating "glasnost" (openness) and "perestroika" (restructuring). The greater openness, however, revealed the extensive corruption and deceit in the government. Later in the 1980s, many Soviet republics began seeking independence. Despite Gorbachev's efforts to hold it together, the Soviet Union finally collapsed in 1991. The collapse officially ended the cold war between the United States and the U.S.S.R., which had its roots in World War II. The U.S.S.R. was divided into fifteen separate countries.

Racial prejudice in the early 1990s was not as widespread as in the 1940s, but racial unrest still existed, as evidenced by the Rodney King incident in 1991. Rodney King was a twenty-five-year-old African American living in Los Angeles. On the night of March 2, 1991, police pulled King over for speeding. When he resisted arrest, four police officers beat him so severely that he suffered broken bones and required several hours of surgery. Unknown to King or the officers, the beating was caught on videotape by a man living nearby. The four officers were put on trial for the beating. On April 29, 1992, three of the officers were acquitted of all charges; the jury was unable to reach a verdict on the fourth. Less than two hours after the verdict was announced, rioting broke out in Los Angeles and continued for days. More than fifty people were killed.

More than one reviewer notes that the novel, because of its brevity and quick pace, would make a good movie. In some cases, however, this was not a compliment. Barbara Finkelstein of the *New York Times* says that "*Montana 1948* reads more like a screenplay than the psychological thriller it purports to be." Finkelstein's review is one of the more negative evaluations of Watson's novel. She writes that "Mr. Watson's coming-of-age novel depends on clichéd characters to lug the story to its conclusion." Though most criticism describes Watson's style as spare and restrained, she criticizes Watson for "purple prose," a phrase used to describe ornate or flowery language.

Even Finkelstein, however, admits that *Montana 1948* is "strong on plot." Richard Francis of the London *Times Literary Supplement*, in a more complimentary review, calls the novel "absorbing," and praises the way Watson takes the usual grand scope of the Western and brings it down to a more human scale. Overall, the book was well liked by both critics and readers; *Montana 1948* is a favorite pick of book clubs, and was called one the best books of 1993 by *Publishers Weekly*.

CRITICAL OVERVIEW

Montana 1948 was a popular success, especially for a small press. It became Milkweed Press's best-selling book to date. In a 1994 review in *Publishers Weekly*, Daisy Maryles called it "Milkweed's Triumph." Reviews were largely positive and often made note of the novel's quick pace and readability. Dave Wood of the *Minneapolis Star Tribune*, for instance, calls it a "page-turner" and exhorts readers to "just go out and buy this book and read it."

Watson's economical, straightforward prose was another element singled out for praise. Annick Smith, in the *Los Angeles Times Book Review*, writes that "the style is so plain you may be tempted to think it is artless. Not so." Likewise, in 1993, a *Publishers Weekly* contributor describes Watson's style as "crisp" and "restrained," and another from *Book* magazine calls it "clean, vivid and uncluttered." Not surprisingly, in an interview with Ronald Kovach for *Writer* magazine, Watson cites Hemingway as an influence on his writing style.

CRITICISM

Laura Beth Pryor

Pryor is a professional writer with more than twenty-five years of experience, with a special interest in fiction. In the following essay, she examines the theme of repression, and especially how it is linked metaphorically to the characters' use of food throughout Montana 1948.

In the Epilogue of Larry Watson's novel *Montana 1948*, the protagonist David Hayden speculates that it was the effort of suppressing the truth of his Uncle Frank's death that caused the deaths of his grandfather and Bentrock's deputy, Len Macauley: "They held it in, the pressure built, like holding your breath, and something had to blow. In their case, the vessels in their brains." This may be the most extreme example of repression in the novel, but there are many subtler forms that recur throughout the story. Nearly everyone in *Montana 1948* keeps secrets and opinions repressed, in the interest of keeping the peace; ironically, it is the keeping of secrets that denies them peace in the end.

WHAT DO I READ NEXT?

- *Justice* (1995) is a fiction collection by Watson that fleshes out the personal history of the adult characters in *Montana 1948*, including Julian (Grandpa) Hayden, Frank Hayden, and David's father, Wesley. The tales go as far back as 1899, when Julian first ventured west to begin a new life on the frontier.

- Sherman Alexie's young-adult novel *The Absolutely True Diary of a Part-Time Indian* (2007) tells the story of fourteen-year-old Arnold Spirit, who lives on a Spokane Indian reservation. Arnold, a bright kid with a love of drawing, is bullied at his reservation school; he expects even worse when he transfers to an affluent white high school, but is pleasantly surprised. However, he still struggles with the question of where, if anywhere, he really fits in.

- *Montana 1948* has been compared by some critics to Harper Lee's classic *To Kill A Mockingbird* (1960). This Pulitzer Prize winner tells the story of Southern lawyer Atticus Finch's defense of a black man charged with rape in the 1930s. Like Wesley Hayden standing up for the rights of Marie Little Soldier, Atticus Finch takes the unpopular stance that a black man has the same right to strong legal representation as a white man does. As in *Montana 1948*, the story is told by a child, Atticus Finch's nine-year-old daughter Scout.

- Novelist Ivan Doig's highly acclaimed 1978 memoir *This House of Sky: Landscapes of a Western Mind* tells of Doig's upbringing in Montana during the 1940s and 1950s. His mother died when he was six, and he was raised by his grandmother and his father, Charlie, who worked as a sheepherder and rancher. Several of Doig's novels are also set in Montana.

- *The Last Best Place: A Montana Anthology* (1992) contains more than 230 writings about Montana, including poems, essays, stories and more from 140 authors. Lewis and Clark, James Audubon, and many others share their impressions of the state, as do a variety of Native American authors. The collection was edited by William Kittredge and Annick Smith.

- Norman MacLean's 1976 novella, *A River Runs through It*, also takes place in Montana and tells the tragic story of two brothers. The narrator reminisces about fly-fishing with his troubled brother, and his efforts to save him from his own self-destructive actions. An audiobook of the novella features Montana author Ivan Doig as the narrator.

- In Watson's *White Crosses* (1997), he returns to the fictional town of Bentrock, but now the sheriff is Jack Nevelson. Like Wesley Hayden, Jack is faced with an ethical dilemma when he discovers two victims of a car accident, a high school girl and an elementary school principal. When he suppresses the truth in favor of a more palatable story, he creates an entirely new set of complications.

David Hayden, at twelve, knows all about secrets. His parents send him from the room whenever a sensitive subject is discussed, and naturally, Uncle Frank's alleged molestation of the reservation women qualifies as sensitive. However, David learns more than his parents could ever imagine by hiding around corners, listening through heating registers, and lurking in bushes. His skulking about gives him his own secret to conceal, just how much he really knows.

Later in the novel, when he witnesses Uncle Frank leaving the Hayden house with his medical bag, David briefly keeps this secret as well.

The Haydens do their best to swallow their secrets and keep them down, which is perhaps why secrets and food seem to be linked throughout the novel. For instance, after learning Marie's secret about Uncle Frank, and having it confirmed by Daisy Macauley, David and his father eat Daisy's rhubarb cake in the kitchen.

> THE HAYDENS DO THEIR BEST TO SWALLOW THEIR SECRETS AND KEEP THEM DOWN, WHICH IS PERHAPS WHY SECRETS AND FOOD SEEM TO BE LINKED THROUGHOUT THE NOVEL."

Wesley stops eating to talk to David's mother when she emerges from Marie's sick room. David's mother asks him, "You never said you didn't believe it. Why is that? Why?" Wesley does not answer. Instead, he picks up his fork and continues to eat cake, swallowing the truth along with it.

Similarly, the adults in David's life use food to keep him from learning the truth. He is repeatedly bribed and distracted with favorite dishes to keep him from getting the real dish on Uncle Frank and his misdeeds. Shortly after Marie's death, as Daisy is comforting David's mother, she commands him to go next door to her house and get some blueberry pie. In a later scene, when David's mother and father want to be alone to discuss something, his mother gives him money to go buy his favorite frankfurters from the butcher shop. David learns this technique as well; at the Macauleys's, just as Len is about to pry from him the secret of Uncle Frank's visit to Marie, David jumps up and exclaims, "I forgot the pie!"

At an uncomfortable dinner at Grandma and Grandpa Haydens's, surrounded by his parents, Uncle Frank, and Aunt Gloria ("How could she not *know*?" he wonders), David finds he is too full of secrets to eat much. Instead, he goes out for a ride on his horse, armed with a pistol (in case of coyotes). He sees no coyotes, but does kill a magpie, an act that he finds strangely cathartic. "The events, the discoveries, the secrets of the past few days...had excited something in me that wasn't released until I shot a magpie out of a piñon pine." Though David finds the experience calming, it is a foreshadowing of his Uncle Frank's greatest crime. The term "magpie," besides being the name of a bird, is also used to describe someone who talks too much. Just as David silences the chattering of the magpie, the next day, Uncle Frank kills Marie Little Soldier, hoping the secret of his crimes will die with her (like the magpie,

Marie is described as a chatterbox, a woman who "loved to laugh and talk"). Ironically, the magpie is also sometimes called a pie—once again, food and repression are linked.

After Marie's death, Uncle Frank is at David's house, filling out a form; his black medical bag is on the kitchen table. David says, "Seeing it there where we ate our meals, I realized how large it was, how if its black mouth opened, it could swallow all the light in the room." Because he saw Frank leaving the house with it earlier, David knows that the truth about Marie's death is contained within the maw of the black bag, a truth that could (and will) darken the lives of his family for years to come. Sitting there at the family table, the bag is like a sinister, unwelcome diner in the Haydens' kitchen.

Though David and his father struggle with what they should reveal or conceal, David's mother is the novel's advocate of truth and openness. She keeps the truth from David to protect him, but she does not otherwise approve of concealment. For example, David says his mother is "suspicious of charm," because she feels its purpose is "to conceal some personal deficit or lack of substance." She prefers wide open land to the mountains, describing herself as a "flatlander at heart." When David's father hedges about what to tell Aunt Gloria regarding the imprisonment of Uncle Frank, she says, "Tell her the truth. She's going to hear it anyway. Don't lie to her." She is not happy about having Frank in the cellar, a measure taken to conceal the truth from the rest of the town, and save Frank embarrassment.

Though the two characters could not be more different, Grandpa Hayden is the only other character who conceals as little as David's mother does. While David's mother is truthful as a matter of principle, his grandfather conceals little as a matter of power. His openness stems from his conviction that he is always right, and from a disregard for the feelings of others. Grandpa Hayden will not repress his opinions, just as he will not withhold his gas; when he greets David and his parents on the front porch before dinner, he says, "I came out here to fart. I had sausage for breakfast and I'm not going to stay in the house any longer and squeeze 'em in. Can't do it." Later in the novel, when Wesley is struggling to tell his father that Frank is a murderer, Grandpa shouts, "Speak up!" While Grandpa Hayden is not against denying the truth (he refuses to believe Frank has done anything wrong) he does not conceal it—until after Frank's death.

The question of what killed Marie, the housekeeper, haunts the Hayden family. (Katrina Brown / Shutterstock.com)

Food and secrets come together again in the climax of the novel, beginning with Uncle Frank's smashing of the canning jars in the root cellar. Concealed in the basement, just as his secret is being concealed by the family, Frank forces everyone in the house to acknowledge his presence. The canned food—carefully sealed away for a later time—is violently released, and David's mother laments, "Who's going to clean up that mess?"

Unknown to David's mother, the "mess" turns out to be Frank's suicide, his slashed wrists, and his blood on their cellar floor. In the figurative sense, the mess is never really cleaned up, but rather covered up, with bribes to the undertaker and lies to the neighbors. The lid goes back on the jar, but eventually the vessel breaks. Grandpa Hayden dies from a stroke, Len Macauley is disabled by one, and cancer eats David's father from the inside. The feat that David first believes his uncle has achieved—the restoration of normalcy—is made even less likely by the secrets and lies they harbor.

In the end, Uncle Frank's reputation is unsullied, but only at a great cost to those he left behind. As Aldous Huxley once said, "Facts do not cease to exist because they are ignored." Or swallowed.

Source: Laura Beth Pryor, Critical Essay on *Montana 1948*, in *Novels for Students*, Gale, Cengage Learning, 2012.

Peter L. Bayers

In the following excerpt, Bayers contends that Montana 1948 *is unique as literature of its period because it calls attention to the problems of revisionist history by Euroamericans.*

"The relation between history and representation . . . is the most crucial subject for critics of the American West to engage." (Handley and Lewis 3)

Evidenced by the success of films such as *Dances with Wolves* and literature such as Barbara Kingsolver's *Pigs in Heaven*, the early '90s saw a rekindling of interest in the Euroamerican popular imagination in the frontier and West, particularly in respect to the U.S.'s colonial relationship with Native Americans. But just what was rekindled remains, at its root, deeply problematic. Works such as *Dances with Wolves* and *Pigs in Heaven* make an overt attempt to redress historical and representational wrongs committed against Native peoples, yet in differing degrees they fall radically short of accomplishing what they set out to do. In fact, despite their efforts, these narratives unwittingly reinscribe what they seek to challenge, which is to say they reinforce white colonial hegemony, either through their method of telling of frontier "history" or representation of Natives or both. One Euroamerican Western novel of this era, *Montana 1948*, by Larry Watson, published in 1993, does not make the mistakes of *Dances with Wolves* and *Pigs in Heaven* in its effort to redress frontier history and represent Native Americans. Like other contemporary films and texts, Watson's *Montana 1948* is preoccupied with the legacy of the U.S. conquest of Native America and the ongoing colonial relationship between the U.S. and Natives. But *Montana 1948* is unique in Euroamerican film and literature of this time period in that it self-consciously calls attention to the problems endemic to Euroamerican efforts to "revision" Euroamerican/Native history. Watson suggests that at best most Euroamericans engage in shallow, self-congratulatory pieties to relieve themselves of guilt in regard to Native America, and that when it comes to telling stories about Euroamerican interaction with Indians, these stories are mired in tired Indian representations that mystify material history and the ongoing colonial status of Natives in the United States. Through his depiction of his flawed narrator, Watson underscores that while the Euroamerican retelling of history and ongoing U.S. colonial relationship with Natives is a morally necessary task, Euroamericans must be more rigorously self-critical as they engage questions of representation and their own deeply held colonial desires when telling that history.

. . . Given the track record of Euroamerican narratives, one has to question whether . . . any non-Native author should even attempt to represent Natives, which is potentially even more problematic given that Natives are more than capable of telling their own histories and representing themselves. Native critic Elizabeth Cook-Lynn laments, "It is unfortunate that, in spite of the burgeoning body of work by Native writers, the greatest body of acceptable telling of the Indian story is still in the hands of non-Natives" (112). But if, as Cook-Lynn writes, "it seems to anyone

> WATSON MAKES IT ABUNDANTLY CLEAR THAT THE 'HISTORY' OF THE AMERICAN WEST IS IN FACT A CONSTRUCTED STORY TOLD FROM THE DOMINANT CULTURE'S PERSPECTIVE IN ORDER TO REPRESS THE TRUTH AND PERPETUATE EUROAMERICAN FANTASIES ABOUT THE WEST AND NATIONAL IDENTITY."

who has been in bookstores lately, at the movies, or privy to the agonized discussions going on in academia about the 'American Canon' that the question of telling Indian stories is still at the heart of what [Euro]America believes to be its narrative of self" (112), one can argue that it is still very much necessary that Euroamericans represent Natives in their stories. To do so, however, Euroamericans must interrogate their "narrative of self," provided they produce narratives that do not mystify the reality that this "self" has traditionally been predicated on representational fantasies that mystify the reality of colonialism.

Watson takes definitive and effective steps in this process of demystification. Watson believes Euroamericans must continue to tell this history—a history in which whites and Natives have a stake—but his depiction of his narrator underscores that Euroamericans must be more critically rigorous in their interrogation of that history. As Watson's novel suggests, if Euroamericans eschew any attempt to (re)tell their narrative of self they risk potentially erasing the reality of U.S. colonial history from the map, at least in respect to Euroamerican imaginings of America. In other words, rather than a story of a North America that was peopled by Natives prior to the arrival of Europeans, the U.S. national narrative would instead resemble Frederick Jackson Turner's now infamous address to the American Historical Association at the Columbian Exposition of 1893, "The Significance of the Frontier in American History," a mythic story of the U.S.'s innocent journey from East to West played out on a supposedly unpeopled "free land," a place where Euroamericans could innocently be reborn in the purity of the frontier wilderness.

The novel is told from the perspective of a middle-aged high school history teacher, David

Hayden, who recalls the summer of 1948, when he was twelve. The effect of this narrative point of view suggests that David's adult imagination is frozen in place, and that his ideas about "Indians" are still framed by his adolescent perceptions. In his recounting of the summer of 1948, David explains that his father Wesley, the locally elected Sheriff, arrested his own brother Frank, a local Doctor and war hero, who murdered the family's Hunkpapa Sioux housemaid, Marie Little Soldier. Marie was ill, and Frank, her doctor, molested her. To protect himself from Marie's accusations, Frank poisoned her. In light of the accusations against him—accusations not brought forward to the public—Uncle Frank committed suicide in the family's basement. His case was never brought to trial, nor was it made openly public. As a result of the crisis, the family's life was shattered, and the Haydens moved away from Bentrock to settle in Minnesota.

To David, the question of justice in regard to Marie and the larger question of justice for Natives are not remotely his concerns as he recounts his past, much in the way that most Euroamericans have historically refused and continue to refuse addressing questions of justice. And the fact that he and his family hide their past is emblematic of how the U.S.'s past is repressed in the national psyche. He explains,

> I did not—do not—believe in the purity and certainty of the study of history over law. Not at all. Quite the opposite. I find history endlessly amusing, knowing, as I do, that the record of any human community might omit stories of sexual abuse, murder, suicide.... Who knows—perhaps the region's most dramatic, most sensational stories were not played out in the public view but were confined to small, private places. A doctor's office, say. A white frame house on a quiet street.... These musings, of course, are for my private enjoyment. For my students I keep a straight face and pretend that the text tells the truth, whole and unembellished.

David wants to imagine that the story remains his and his family's "private" affair, a small, relatively inconsequential history tangential to the grand narrative of history. In his silence about his past, he behaves as if Marie's murder and the events of 1948 in Bentrock never happened, except as they exist in David's private historical memory. As Watson indicates, David's version of the events of 1948 represents a central problem in how the U.S. historical narrative is perpetuated in much of the Euroamerican imagination, particularly with respect to its beliefs

regarding the history of U.S. relations with Native peoples. This story has generally been and continues to be a private story in this version of history, relatively hidden or repressed in the Euroamerican subconscious. David's distinction between history and law obscures the need to link the truthful telling of history and the enactment of justice in respect to the U.S. and its colonial relationship with Native peoples. Ironically, in truth the history of Native America is not an inconsequential history, but has been a major story of conquest and genocide, the reverberations of which resonate throughout Native America today.

Wesley's anxieties about and strategies to cope with the past reflect a long-held Euroamerican anxiety. As Susan Scheckel has written,

> the dispossession of the American Indians has been one of the most troubling episodes in U.S. history. From the beginning, settlement and expansion depended on it, and up to the present it is an act of violence that Americans seem unable to forget. Despite innumerable attempts to rewrite the Indian as the subject of "family" history, the ghost of the Indian as the object of genocidal violence has returned inevitably to haunt the nation and its narratives.

While Marie's murder itself is not an act of genocide, her story is deeply entwined with this history. David's anxieties about the cover-up of Marie's sexual abuse and murder represents the U.S.'s own anxieties about its violent dispossession of and genocide committed against Natives. Marie's subordinate status as a maid is literally predicated on the dispossession of Natives, who became second-class citizens following their conquest, a subordinate reality even today. Yet, David attempts to integrate her into a family history, much in the way the U.S. has historically attempted to integrate Natives into the national family through the distorted lens of myth. He is, however, like the nation, haunted by a violent reality.

On the surface, the story seems to be about the tribulations of the family, and this is certainly how Wesley perceives it as he unravels his past. David explains that at first, following the revelation of Frank's actions, Wesley told his wife Gail, "I think the problem's been taken care of. Frank said he's going to cut it out." Gail responded, "What about what's already been done? What about that, that...*damage?*" His father claimed, "That's passed. That's over and done." David's mother replied, "That's not the way it works.

You know that. Sins—crimes—are not supposed to go unpunished." Afterwards, Wesley tried to address the accusations privately. However, his brother's suspected murder of Marie gave him no choice but to arrest Frank. As he told his son, "David, I believe that in this world people must pay for their crimes. It doesn't matter who you are or who your relations are; if you do wrong, you pay. I believe that. I have to." Here, Wesley suggests that he has been able to put justice ahead of family loyalty, but his conflicted state is evidenced by the fact that rather than incarcerate his brother in the local jail, he locked him in the Haydens' basement root cellar. Although he told David that the next day he would put Frank in the local jail, his action was preempted by Frank's suicide. The suicide relieved Wesley of the burden of shaming his family. As David explains, "it was decided not to reveal any of Frank's crimes. What purpose would it serve?...[T]here was no sense clouding the air with accusations."

Watson sets the story in 1948 to call attention to 1948 legislation under Title 18 of the United States Code: "Crimes and Criminal Procedures." Chapter 53 of that code applies to Indians: for legal purposes "Indian Country" was defined in order to decide Federal or State jurisdiction over crimes committed by Indians or non-Indians in "Indian Country." While tribal courts have a degree of control over minor crimes in "Indian Country," since 1885 with the passage of the "Major Crimes Act," a major blow to Indian sovereignty, Natives have had no jurisdiction on their lands over "murder, manslaughter, rape, assault with intent to kill, arson burglary and larceny" (Prucha 166). While Congress passed this Act in order to address Indian-on-Indian crime, Natives also have no power to prosecute and try non-Natives who have committed crimes in Indian Country, even if the crime is committed against Natives themselves.

The double-standard of these laws is clear and attests to the legacy of *Cherokee Nation v. Georgia* (1831), in which Justice John Marshall defined Indian tribes as "domestic dependent nations"—a vexed and oxymoronic statement, to say the least. Whites have full right to mediate justice in Indian country, but Indians have no power to mediate justice in Euroamerican country. In fact, traditional Native forms of justice, which historically have differed considerably from Euroamerican notions of justice, are rendered moot by this law. Watson has this double-standard in mind in regard to questions of justice toward Natives. Granted, no Native character in David's past made a serious attempt to investigate Marie's murder, but since Wesley, a representative of the U.S. justice system, did not pursue it, Natives had little recourse to pursue it themselves. Wesley's inaction underscores that laws governing U.S./Native relations serve U.S. interests.

Watson makes it abundantly clear that the "history" of the American West is in fact a constructed story told from the dominant culture's perspective in order to repress the truth and perpetuate Euroamerican fantasies about the West and national identity. For instance, David recalls having to repaint the Hayden house, and as he worked Wesley explained to him, "Paint. Fresh paint. That's how you find life and civilization. Women come and they want fresh paint." David recollects, "Then he rapped sharply on the wall, three quick knocks to warn it that Wesley Hayden and his son were coming with scrapers, sandpaper, paintbrushes, and white paint, paint whiter than any bones bleaching out there on the Montana prairie." The fresh white paint represents the insistent reapplication of the triumphant white story of progress and redemption in the West, a story of seeming purity and innocence. Frank's incarceration in the Hayden basement metaphorically underscores that the true history of Euroamerican relations with Natives is hidden from public consciousness. Like the basement supporting the house, but also hidden beneath that structure, Frank's dark personal history metaphorically reveals the "true" foundation of Western history and U.S. national identity.

Implicitly, the foundation of Frank's identity is intimately tied to his family's legacy and its triumph in the context of the story of the West. A war hero, Frank was the favored child of the Hayden family, the quintessential American boy and scion of *the* established family of the community. Frank and Wesley's family lived on the outskirts of town, their house a reflection of the wealth their father acquired as a rancher and power broker. Frank's actions and mores, it is suggested, are a direct legacy of his family history and Western history. At least on the surface, in the vein of the classic literary or filmic Western hero— emblemized by the likes of Cooper's Natty Bumppo, or Wister's Virginian—Frank was brave and courageous, an emblem of the ideal Anglo-America male. Before he went to war, he had a reputation for sexual forays with Native women. David's grandfather recounts to Wesley, "You know Frank's always been partial to red meat. He couldn't have been any older than Davy when Bud caught him down in the stable with that little Indian girl. Bud said to me, 'Mr. Hayden, you better have a talk with that boy. He had that little squaw down on her hands and knees. He's been learnin' from watching the dogs and the horses and the bulls.'" The callously described and derogatory image of a Native woman suggests that she was, as the grandfather indicates, little more than "red meat" to Frank, an object to be controlled and dominated by him. Central to Frank's identity, then, are his exploitative relationships with Native women—he is not what he seems to be. Metaphorically, Frank's perversion mirrors the perversion at the root of national history.

For David, the problem with Frank's actions is not Marie's death, but the loss of David's ability to sustain his utopian fantasies about his own relationship with Marie, a fantasy that mimics long-held Euroamerican fantasies about Indians. Marie's labeling as an "Indian," at least on the surface, seems largely irrelevant to how David perceived her in the past and how he continues to perceive her as he tells the story. As the Haydens' housemaid, she was ostensibly part of the family. After Marie's murder, Wesley says, "I tried to tell Mrs. Little Soldier that this was Marie's home also and that we thought of her as a member of the family." David's sentiments are reinforced later in his narrative. His "happiest memory" of Marie "takes place the autumn before she died." He remembers playing a game of football with Marie and Ronnie (Marie's boyfriend), a game without any rules: "It was a game, yet it had no object and no borders of space or time or regulation." David remarks, "I felt that what we played, more accurately *how* we played, had its origin in Ronnie and Marie's Indian heritage, but I had no way of knowing that with any certainty. All I could be sure of was that I never had more fun playing ball, any kind of ball, in my life." Afterward they share cider, and David believes that "I remembered that incident so fondly not only because I was with Marie and Ronnie, both of whom I loved in my way, but also because I felt, for that brief span, as though I was part of a family, a family that accepted me for myself and not my blood or birth-right." David's fantasy of being accepted by Indians outside the confines of space and time, of imagining his interaction with Indians as one of familial harmony and acceptance, reflects a wider Euroamerican desire in regard to Indians.

As Watson suggests, by imagining Indians as "family"—best exemplified by the holiday of Thanksgiving—Euroamericans mystify the material reality of Anglo/Native history, preserving a peaceful utopian image of white/Indian interaction in the national story. Marie's place as a supposed family member masked the material conditions of her existence—in fact, David knew and still knows little about her. David was and is still much more interested in imagining Marie as a member of *his* family than as someone who has her own desires and history. He does not reflect on the reasons why Marie "chose" to be the Haydens' housemaid. David, in fact, never even hints at the conditions on the reservation that caused Marie to need the job. Moreover, David's ideas about Marie and Ronnie's culture are decidedly trite. Despite Marie and Ronnie's physical proximity to him, David's cultural distance from them is underscored by the fact that he imagines that their ball-game "had its origin in . . . Indian heritage," but that he could not know with "certainty." The ambiguity of his sentiment reflects Watson's awareness of the gap between Euroamerican perception and fantasy about Natives and the reality of their cultures. David's pathetic reflection on his boyhood fantasies of familial harmony between himself and Marie—a fantasy he clearly still cherishes as an adult—represents his frustration with the fact that Frank destroyed his "innocence," an innocence that he wants to restore through the telling of his past . . . .

Source: Peter L. Bayers, "Larry Watson's *Montana 1948* and Euroamerican Representation of Native/Euroamerican History," in *Rocky Mountain Review of Language and Literature*, Vol. 61, No. 1, Spring 2007, pp. 35–50.

Norman Oder

In the following interview, Oder and Watson discuss Watson's background and its effect on his novels.

For 16 years, novelist Larry Watson has taught at the University of Wisconsin at Stevens Point, a tidy town of neighborly folk not unlike his childhood home, Bismarck, N.D. Though Watson likes Wisconsin, it has marked him far less than did North Dakota, with its tight human ties, tough terrain and pre-'60s ethos. And in his middle age, those memories have fostered a hardy fictional landscape, evinced in *Montana 1948*, his surprise 1993 success, and its prequel,

> WATSON SAYS HE'S GROWN TO ENJOY
> BOOKSTORE READINGS—EVEN IN THE FEW CITIES
> WHERE HIS WIFE, SUSAN, OUTNUMBERED
> SPECTATORS. AND HE'S REVISED HIS ATTITUDE
> TOWARD HIS OWN WORK."

Justice, to be published next month by Milkweed Editions. And, most likely, more such taut, literary westerns to come.

Watson, 47, seems a youthful grandpa—a vigorous six-footer, he has a full head of graying hair and the self-discipline that saw him through a 13-year drought between his first novel and *Montana*. Watson speaks softly, his emotions reined, although, as from his spare prose, wry humor does emerge. "I sometimes feel I'm working the dark side of Lake Wobegon," he muses, citing the tension between civic duty and personal loyalty that recurs in his tales. On his first visit ever to New York City, in a hotel room overlooking Central Park, the author reflects further on his work and his world.

The grandson of homesteaders of Scandinavian and English stock, Watson was born in Rugby, a small town in northeastern North Dakota. His dad was sheriff, as was his granddad—details transmuted into *Montana*, in which Sheriff Wesley Hayden, successor to his father Julian, must confront his brother's crimes. "My father was sort of the 'white sheep,'" Watson recalls, and, yes, there were tensions with his brothers. But Watson knew this only indirectly: when he was five, the family moved to the larger Bismarck, and his father—like Wesley Hayden, ultimately—worked as an attorney. Writing *Montana*, Watson grants, may represent an inverse Oedipal drama, a way to reconnect with the lawman heritage he barely knew. Watson senior, a formal type who kept his tie on for dinner, was an older dad, and his son admits some regret at their distance. "We got along tolerably well, even if we didn't play catch in the yard," he recalls.

Athletic but introspective, young Larry was a reader—"comic books crappy novels, good novels"—but an unmotivated student. After junior college, during which he proclaimed himself pre-law and married his highschool sweetheart, Susan, he took the "worn path" to the University of North Dakota. There, he enrolled in a writing course and began writing poems: "I guess it answered something in me."

At UND, he found faculty encouragement and encountered visiting writers like poet James Welch and novelist James Crumley. He says he "latched onto" teaching as a career, writing short stories for an M.A.; he then moved to the University of Utah, lured by the mountains and the flexible Ph.D. program in creative writing. He studied with such teachers as short story-writer and playwright David Kranes, and met itinerant heavyweights like E.L. Doctorow and John Cheever. He discovered Peter Taylor, adding his work to the earlier influences like Hemingway and Salinger.

Most of all, Watson imbibed the daily grind of apprenticeship. For his thesis, he wrote a mystery of sorts, *In A Dark Time*. When he sent part of the manuscript to support a fellowship bid, reader Ned Leavitt called back, saying he would soon be an agent at William Morris, and offered to represent it. "Piece of cake," Watson offers, with a grin. Scribner's editor Laurie Graham bought it; the book gained a few respectful reviews and just earned back its $3000 advance. Watson allows that he might resemble his protagonist, an unemotional teacher calibrating his reactions, and those of his colleagues and community, to murders in their midst. But, he protests, he also put himself in other characters.

After Utah, Watson found a job teaching writing and literature at Stevens Point, a campus best known for environmental studies. He kept at fiction every day, writing longhand, on yellow pads, following instinct rather than plan. "I feel I write pretty close to the bone," he says. He writes slowly; two hours is a maximum stretch: "I tend to tidy up as I go along." On good days, he might add poetry, essays or journal entries.

Success was elusive. Watson gained some grants and published short stories and a chapbook of poetry (his verse, he notes, is much more autobiographical). He wrote some unfinished novels; a new agent unsuccessfully pitched two others. "Yeah, it was frustrating," Watson concedes without rancor, but he learned to find satisfaction in daily craft.

THE PRIMAL SIN

Montana's moral and physical landscape percolated in his mind. If slavery may seem America's most enduring scar, for Watson, a more primal sin was plain: the dispossession of Native Americans. In Bismarck, frontier clashes were history, the local Indians "pretty much beaten down," variably treated with respect and cruelty. At college, Watson began to make sense of this "strange" situation, reading *Bury My Heart at Wounded Knee* and encountering new Native American activism. When he taught a composition class for Native Americans, he read more of their literature.

Later, at Stevens Point, Watson taught a course on Midwestern literature, ranging from Evan Connell to Louise Erdrich. "Perhaps," he proposes, "I began to see the possibilities for fiction in my own region and own ancestry." And when he reached his father's age, Watson, "beginning to feel curmudgeonly," aimed his muse at an earlier era when conflicts between head and heart were more stark. "I think my life and values have been all of a piece, but I find myself somewhat at odds with contemporary society," he says.

A few years ago, Watson conjured up *Montana*'s arresting prologue: narrator David Hayden recalling childhood images of his parents in extremis, and a young Sioux woman near death. He spent the next year crafting the story behind it, centering on Wesley Hayden's pursuit of his brother Frank, a war hero who molested Indian girls. "I'm not writing to convert," he says of his themes. "I want to tell a good story."

For details, not only could Watson rely on memories of town streets and people's tics, he also could draw on nearby objects as he wrote, helping, for instance, his father's sheriff's badge. His eastern Montana setting, he explains, is much like the plains of western North Dakota; however, he recognizes that *Montana* has more of a frontier flavor.

Watson sent the manuscript to a New York publisher, and got nibbles but never a full response. After six months, he asked for his work back. Agentless, he decided to seek Milkweed's annual National Fiction Prize, thinking that a smaller house might give him more attention. Milkweed publisher Emilie Buchwald read *Montana* in one sitting and resolved to publish it even if it didn't win the prize. It did, however, with judge David Huddle calling it "a complete refreshment of a classic American narrative." The advance was again $3000.

HOMESPUN APPROACH

Montana needed little editing, but Buchwald offered a few key boosts. She had the author—

known as Lawrence only for publication—revert to the more homespun "Larry." To Watson's quasi-Orwellian title, *1948*, she added the mythic *Montana*. And she helped find an evocative, elegiac landscape by *Montana* painter Russell Chathamone[, one] of Watson's favorite artists, it turned out—to make a striking cover.

Pre-publication reviews lauded *Montana* (*PW* gave it a star), and Milkweed used a national grant for promotion and a tour. The book earned raves not only from regional papers but also from the *Washington Post* and *Los Angeles Times*. (The one negative review was an "In Brief" disparagement in the *New York Times Book Review*, but that came late.) Most of all, *Montana* became a hand-selling favorite at bookstores, enjoyed by both men and women.

Montana went through six printings; at 32,500 copies, it's Milkweed's best seller ever. Foreign rights have been sold in nine countries. A spirited paperback auction garnered $302,000 from then-editorial director Jane Rosenman of Washington Square Press/Pocket Books, encouraged by the imprint's success with authors Pam Houston and Norman MacLean. The house plans a first printing of 100,000, a 10-city tour and a feature in its reading group newsletter.

For Milkweed, Watson's success has raised its profile among booksellers and authors, and it's allowed the house to add a second editor. And Buchwald, knowing Milkweed authors like Susan Straight earned New York contracts for their next books, savvily signed Watson to a two-book deal. Watson agreed, with no regrets. "I may be naive," he says, "but I'm not that naive. It had been a long time between novels."

And Watson did have another book in mind. He'd found that his characters—unlike those in his previous fiction—wouldn't escape his subconscious, "and in fact started accumulating stories." Thus, he wrote *Justice*, a seven-chapter prequel to *Montana*. For *Justice*, which *PW* called "finely crafted," Watson could spread out, writing in the third person instead of the first, and doing more to sketch character. Though he concedes that it is less plot-driven than *Montana*, Watson feels that *Justice* has closure in the birth of David Hayden, *Montana*'s narrator, at its end.

The writing again came easy, but this book required a bit more shaping. Watson originally ordered the chapters chronologically. Buchwald proposed that he place *Outside the Jurisdiction*, the novella recounting a youthful incident involving Wesley and Frank, as the leadoff. "You can see who these people are going to become." She also suggested the title *Justice* and ordered up another Chatham cover. A Major Investment Milkweed plans a first printing of 25,000, its largest ever. WSP bought paperback rights for $125,000. "We have a major investment in Larry, and we wanted to continue with it," explains associate editor Donna Ng. Milkweed will promote *Justice* by piggybacking on the April paperback tour for *Montana*. Watson says he's grown to enjoy bookstore readings—even in the few cities where his wife, Susan, outnumbered spectators. And he's revised his attitude toward his own work. In *Montana*, Granddad Hoyden says being sheriff means "knowing when to look and when to look away." Watson meant that as criticism; now, he says, he recognizes virtues in such small-town tolerance.

Watson has enjoyed hearing from readers, but hardly courts fame. One encounter in a restaurant was "creepy," he recalls; a fan said she'd watched him eat. Some more fortune, however, may arrive. Agent Sharon Friedman, of New York's John Hawkins & Associates, contacted Watson after reading *Montana* in galleys; she says there's "considerable enthusiasm" in New York for his next book. And a *Montana* movie may appear, as Paramount recently renewed its option on the book.

Watson's success has let him cut his teaching time in half. With one daughter grown and the other in college, he and Susan may leave Stevens Point; they're comfortable in many places, he says, even finding the Big Apple surprisingly unhorrific. And to his fiction, a new home may not matter. Though the Haydens have been put to rest, their landscape remains. Says Watson, "I could see myself tilling that soil for the rest of my writing career."

Source: Norman Oder, "Larry Watson: 'I'm Working the Dark Side of Lake Wobegone,'" in *Publishers Weekly*, Vol. 242, No. 4, January 23, 1995, pp. 48–49.

SOURCES

"Aldous Huxley Quotes," in *1-Famous-Quotes.com*, http://www.1-famous-quotes.com/quote/76974 (accessed August 2, 2011).

"American Indian Voting Rights," in *Native American Netroots*, http://nativeamericannetroots.net/diary/352/american-indian-voting-rights (accessed August 2, 2011).

"American Indians in World War II," in *American Indian Heritage Month*, http://www.defense.gov/specials/nativeamerican01/wwii.html (accessed August 1, 2011).

Brogan, Hugh, "Cold War Abroad and at Home: 1945–61," in *The Penguin History of the USA*, Penguin, 2001, pp. 584–614.

"Fall of the Soviet Union," in *The Cold War Museum*, http://www.coldwar.org/articles/90s/fall_of_the_soviet_union.asp (accessed August 1, 2011).

Finkelstein, Barbara, Review of *Montana 1948*, in *New York Times*, December 12, 1993, p. 22.

Francis, Richard, "Go West, Young Man," Review of *Montana 1948*, in *Times Literary Supplement* (London, England), August 18, 1995, p. 20.

Fullerton, Howard N. Jr., "Labor Force Participation: 75 Years of Change, 1950–1998 and 1998–2025," in *Monthly Labor Review*, December 1999, pp. 3–12.

"Historical National Population Estimates: July 1, 1990–July 1, 1999," in *U.S. Census Bureau*, http://www.census.gov/popest/archives/1990s/popclockest.txt (accessed August 2, 2011).

"The Image and Reality of Women Who Worked During World War II," in *Rosie the Riveter: Women Working During World War II*, http://www.nps.gov/pwro/collection/website/rosie.htm (accessed August 2, 2011).

Kavanaugh, Jim, "Rodney King, 20 Years Later," in *CNN.com*, March 3, 2011, http://articles.cnn.com/2011-03-03/us/rodney.king.20.years.later_1_laurence-powell-theodore-briseno-king-attorney-milton-grimes?_s=PM:US (accessed August 1, 2011).

Kovach, Ronald, "Hearts in Conflict: Larry Watson Weaves Fine Novels from Emotional Tension," in *Writer*, July 2004, p. 20.

Maryles, Daisy, "Behind the Bestsellers," in *Publishers Weekly*, January 3, 1994, p. 33.

Oder, Norman, "Larry Watson: 'I'm Working the Dark Side of Lake Wobegone,'" in *Publishers Weekly*, January 23, 1995, p. 28.

"Picks Recommendations for Book Clubs," Review of *Montana 1948*, in *Book*, September 2001, p. 93.

Parker–Pope, Tara, "She Works. They're Happy," in *New York Times*, January 24, 2010, http://www.nytimes.com/2010/01/24/fashion/24marriage.html (accessed August 2, 2011).

Review of *Montana 1948*, in *Publishers Weekly*, July 12, 1993, p. 69.

Smith, Annick, "Don't Blame It on Montana: *Montana 1948*," in *Los Angeles Times Book Review*, October 10, 1993, http://articles.latimes.com/1993-10-10/books/bk-44053_1_larry-watson (accessed August 1, 2011).

"Total Native Americans (Most Recent) by State," in *Statemaster.com*, http://www.statemaster.com/red/graph/peo_tot_nat_ame-people (accessed August 2, 2011).

Watson, Larry, *Montana 1948*, Milkweed Editions, 2007.

Wood, Dave, "Milkweed '93 Winner Has It All," in *Minneapolis Star Tribune*, September 12, 1993, p. F13.

FURTHER READING

Childers, Thomas, *Soldier from the War Returning: The Greatest Generation's Troubled Homecoming from World War II*, Houghton Mifflin Harcourt, 2009.

Through the stories of three soldiers returning home from World War II (one of them his father), Childers illustrates the difficulties experienced by veterans readjusting to civilian life. Unemployment, feelings of alienation, nightmarish memories of combat, and resentment at the years lost to war all contributed to the struggles of the World War II veteran, despite media images of happy celebrations and reunited families.

Howard, Joseph Kinsey, *Montana: High, Wide and Handsome*, University of Nebraska Press, 2003.

Originally published in 1943, Howard's enthusiastic history of his adopted state (he was born in Iowa and moved to Montana at age 13) is considered a classic. Howard was a journalist with strong views about the value of preserving Montana's cultural heritage and natural wonders. Though a few of Howard's arguments may seem dated today, the book is still considered one of the best histories of the state.

Kristofic, Jim, *Navajos Wear Nikes: A Reservation Life*, University of New Mexico Press, 2011.

This memoir tells of Kristofic's life as a white boy ("bilagaana") who grows up on a Navajo reservation. Kristofic tells of his struggle to fit in, both on the reservation, and later when he moves to a white high school in Utah. He also describes the many hardships of reservation life, including poverty and abuse.

Stegner, Wallace, *Angle of Repose*, Modern Library, 2000.

Stegner is known as the Dean of Western Writers, and this novel, first published in 1971, won him the Pulitzer Prize. It tells the story of a wheelchair-bound professor, coping with a failed marriage, who writes a history of his pioneer grandparents and their more successful union. Stegner weaves the two stories together throughout the novel.

Steinbeck, John, *East of Eden*, Viking, 2003.

Steinbeck's classic retelling of the biblical story of Cain and Abel spans two generations of brothers. First, Adam and Charles Trask clash when Adam marries a treacherous prostitute who betrays him with his own brother. She gives birth to twin brothers Aron and Caleb and then leaves him. Adam raises the twins himself; these two brothers come into conflict as well, both vying for their father's approval.

SUGGESTED SEARCH TERMS

Larry Watson

Montana 1948 AND Larry Watson

Montana 1948

Larry Watson AND western genre

Montana 1948 AND racism

Montana 1948 AND western genre

Montana AND ranching

Native Americans AND 1940s

Native Americans AND racism

Native Americans AND reservations

Native Americans AND World War II

The Moonstone

WILKIE COLLINS

1868

The Moonstone, by British author Wilkie Collins, was first published serially in thirty-two weekly parts in 1868. The magazine in which it ran, *All the Year Round*, was created and run by Collins's famous contemporary, Charles Dickens. In the United States, it was published simultaneously in *Harper's Weekly*. The first book edition of the novel was published that same year, and for nearly a century and a half, *The Moonstone* has remained popular as one of the most gripping novels to come out of the Victorian period in England.

The Moonstone has often been cited as the first true detective story, although some literary historians point to earlier fiction that could make that claim. *The Moonstone*, however, is the most popular of such early detective stories, and it entrenched many of the conventions of the detective genre. These conventions are used in the service of a story about the mysterious disappearance of a magnificent Indian jewel, the "Moonstone," and efforts made to recover it. *The Moonstone* is also noteworthy for its narrative technique. Rather than simply narrating the story in a conventional third-person mode, Collins constructed his story as a series of narratives written by several of the characters, each of whom provides his or her perspective on the events surrounding the Moonstone and clues that lead to the final resolution of the case.

The Moonstone is widely available, including an edition published by Simon and Brown in 2011.

Wilkie Collins (*The Library of Congress*)

A free online version can be found at the Project Gutenberg Web site at http://www.gutenberg.org/ebooks/155.

AUTHOR BIOGRAPHY

Collins was born on January 8, 1824, in London, England, where he lived most of his life. His father, William Collins, was a popular landscape painter and member of the Royal Academy. Collins endured a miserable childhood at boarding school, where he was bullied by the other students, though he later said that he developed his narrative skills by telling stories to one of his tormentors, thus keeping him at bay. His father tried to set him up in the tea trade, but Collins had no interest in commerce. When he was twenty-two years old, he took up the study of law at London's Lincoln's Inn, and he was called to the bar (that is, became a lawyer) in 1851. That year, though, his career took a new direction when he met novelist Charles Dickens. Rather than practicing law, he devoted himself to literature; he had begun writing as early as 1848.

In the years that followed, Collins wrote twenty-five novels. Two are still widely read: *The Woman in White*, published in 1859–1860, and *The Moonstone*, published in 1868. Two other of Collins's novels have also remained relatively popular: *No Name*, published in 1862, and the revenge thriller *Armadale*, published in 1866. Additionally, Collins published dozens of short stories and nonfiction pieces. He also wrote more than a dozen plays, some of them in collaboration with Dickens, who wrote plays for amateur theatrical performances. During the mid-Victorian period, Collins was among the most popular, and highest paid, fiction writers in England. He was almost as popular as his better known friend, Dickens, and his novel *The Woman in White* achieved the status of a best seller.

Marring Collins's literary triumphs was his health. He suffered from gout, a painful condition caused by the buildup of uric acid in the joints, usually the toes. He also suffered from rheumatism. To alleviate the pain, he took laudanum, an opiate, and throughout much of his later life he was addicted to the drug—an addiction reflected in the opium addiction of one of the characters in *The Moonstone*, Ezra Jennings. The pain was so bad while he was writing *The Moonstone* that he dictated portions of the novel from his bed. Because of these health problems, all worsened by his expanding girth, Collins visited spas on the European continent in an effort to obtain relief. Meanwhile, he had a falling-out with Dickens when he signed a contract with a competing publisher. As if all this were not enough, his domestic arrangements were highly unconventional. After 1859, he lived with Caroline Graves (on whom he based the lead character in *The Woman in White*). Caroline got married—Collins even attended her wedding—but she returned to live with Collins. Then in about 1864, Collins met Martha Rudd, and the two had three children together, though they never married. From that point on, Collins maintained two households, often writing feverishly to earn enough money to do so. In an effort to boost sales, he embarked on a reading tour of his works in North American in 1873. In 1877, Collins adapted *The Moonstone* as a stage play.

Early in his life, Collins developed a contempt for conventional society and manners, in part as a reaction against the intense religiosity of his parents. As an adult, he dressed oddly, sported a long beard, and—as his domestic arrangements suggest—spurned the conventions of middle-class morality and respectability. He was well known in England's literary set, for he was friends with not only Dickens but also such literary luminaries as George Eliot and Anthony Trollope.

Collins's health continued to decline during the later years of his life. He died in London on September 23, 1889, from complications of a stroke and bronchitis.

PLOT SUMMARY

Prologue: The Storming of Seringapatam (1799)

The prologue purports to be an extract from family papers. It is written by a cousin of John Herncastle and narrates the events surrounding the storming of the castle at Seringapatam, India, in 1799. Herncastle stole the Yellow Diamond, also called the Moonstone. The Moonstone was originally part of a Hindu shrine to the moon god, who commanded that the diamond be guarded by three Brahmin priests. In the process of the theft, Herncastle killed two Indians.

First Period: The Loss of the Diamond (1848)

CHAPTERS I–III

The First Period is narrated by Gabriel Betteredge, the house steward at Lady Verinder's Yorkshire estate. On May 22, 1850, Lady Verinder's nephew, Franklin Blake, asks Betteredge to write down his account of the disappearance of the Moonstone at Lady Verinder's house in 1848. Betteredge begins by describing Lady Julia Verinder, the youngest of three Herncastle sisters. He describes too his early career as page-boy, then bailiff, for Lady Verinder and her husband, Sir John Verinder (now deceased). Betteredge's daughter, Penelope, lives with him.

Penelope offers Gabriel access to her diary written at the time of the diamond's disappearance. Accordingly, he begins his narrative proper with May 24, 1848, when Lady Verinder announces that Franklin Blake will arrive the next day for her daughter Rachel's birthday celebration; Blake has been absent for many years, studying on the European continent. On the day of Blake's arrival, Gabriel and Penelope encounter three Indians and an English boy in front of the house. Blake assumes that the Indians are in search of the Moonstone.

MEDIA ADAPTATIONS

- In 1934, *The Moonstone* was adapted for film by Adele S. Buffington and released in the United States by Monogram Pictures Corporation. The film was directed by Reginald Barker and starred David Manners, Charles Irwin, and Phyllis Barry. The film was re-released by Synergy Entertainment in 2007.

- On March 11, 1945, *The Moonstone* was episode number sixty-seven of the radio series, *The Weird Circle*, produced by NBC Radio in New York City.

- In 1959, the BBC adapted *The Moonstone* into a seven-episode television serial, starring James Hayter, Annabelle Lee, Barry Letts, and Mary Webster as Rachel Verinder.

- In 1972, *The Moonstone* was filmed in the United Kingdom and shown in the United States on PBS's *Masterpiece Theatre*. The five-part series was released by Acorn Media in 2006. Running time is 221 minutes.

- In 1996, *The Moonstone* was again filmed in the United Kingdom for television by the BBC and Carlton Television in partnership with WGBH of Boston, Massachusetts. It aired in the United States on PBS's *Masterpiece Theatre*. It starred Greg Wise as Franklin Blake and Keeley Hawes as Rachel Verinder. It was released by WGBH Boston Video in 2005. Running time is 120 minutes.

- In 2011, BBC Radio 4 serialized *The Moonstone* in four one-hour episodes in its *Classic Serial* series.

CHAPTERS IV–VI

Rosanna Spearman, a housemaid, is late for dinner. Gabriel offers to find her at her usual hideaway, Shivering Sand, a stretch of quicksand beach. Rosanna had been a thief, but Lady Verinder hired her from a reformatory just a few months ago. Rosanna, a loner, has a deformed shoulder, and Gabriel feels sorry for her. Blake comes across Gabriel and Rosanna as they are conversing; Rosanna blushes and departs quickly, to Blake's puzzlement.

Blake is in possession of the Moonstone, which he shows to Gabriel. Blake explains that, in his will, his uncle had left the diamond to Rachel as a birthday present. Blake's task is to deliver it. Gabriel explains to Blake that Herncastle was dishonorable and shunned by the family. Two years earlier, Lady Verinder had barred Herncastle from the house. Blake wonders whether Herncastle meant to involve Lady Verinder in a conspiracy by leaving the Moonstone to Rachel. Blake reports that, after he had taken the stone from a bank vault in London, he was followed by a man with a dark complexion. Blake fears that the bequest is meant to bring harm to Rachel and her family. Gabriel advises Blake to deposit the diamond in the bank at Frizinghall, a nearby town.

CHAPTERS VII–IX

Rosanna is acting strangely. Penelope suggests to Gabriel that Rosanna felt an instant attraction to Blake. Later, Gabriel learns from the other servants that Blake and Rachel seem to be attracted to each other. That night, Gabriel sees a shadow outside and hears the sound of running feet when he goes to investigate. He suspects that the intruders were the Indians.

Over the following days, Blake and Rachel decorate the door to Rachel's room by painting it. June arrives, and the servants speculate that Blake and Rachel will marry, but Gabriel disagrees, arguing that Rachel will marry her cousin Godfrey Ablewhite, a handsome, respectable philanthropist. Blake, though, continues to try to charm Rachel, though his chances take a blow when he is visited by a foreign man about a business affair and Rachel chastises him about his presumed debts.

The day of Rachel's birthday arrives. Gabriel suggests that, after Blake withdraws the diamond from the bank, he ride back to the house with Ablewhite and his sisters. That afternoon, Blake does just that. Blake meets with Rachel privately until Gabriel hears a scream from the drawing room. He enters to see Rachel holding the diamond. Lady Verinder is reading Herncastle's will. Later, Lady Verinder solicits Gabriel's thoughts about Herncastle's motives in leaving the Moonstone to Rachel. Gabriel later learns from Penelope that Rachel has refused a marriage proposal from Ablewhite.

CHAPTERS X–XI

Among the guests at a dinner party celebrating Rachel's birthday is Thomas Candy, a doctor, and Mr. Murthwaite, an Indian explorer. After dinner, the Indians reappear. Murthwaite speaks to them in their own language and explains to Gabriel and Blake that the Indians are Brahmins (members of the highest caste in India) who have disguised themselves as low-caste jugglers in their efforts to retrieve the Moonstone. He states that the Indians would be willing to kill to retrieve it because of its religious significance.

That night, Rachel places the diamond in a cabinet in her room. The following morning, the diamond is missing. The house is searched, and Blake notifies the police in Frizinghall. The Indians, of course, are suspected, yet they are innocent, for they have spent the night in jail. Superintendent Seegrave questions the servants. He is annoyed that the servants have apparently smeared the new paint on Rachel's door. Blake sends a telegraph to London requesting an investigator.

CHAPTERS XII–XIV

Sergeant Richard Cuff, a well-respected investigator, arrives. As he examines Rachel's room and questions Blake, he concludes that the paint smear on Rachel's door was made overnight. Lady Verinder agrees to allow Cuff to search the entire house, looking for a dress with paint stains on it. Cuff asks for the washing book in an effort to determine whether any articles of clothing are missing. When Rosanna brings the book, Cuff recognizes her as a former thief.

As Gabriel and Cuff walk in the garden, Cuff notices Rosanna lurking about. Cuff accepts Gabriel's explanation that she does so because Blake often walks in the garden. Cuff interviews each of the servants and learns that Rosanna was burning a fire in her room during the night of the theft. Blake wants to tell Lady Verinder about Rosanna's suspicious behavior, but Cuff stops him and indicates that Rachel is still under suspicion.

CHAPTERS XV–XVII

Cuff follows Rosanna's tracks in the Shivering Sand, determining that she walked into the water, perhaps to hide something. He also theorizes that her gown was stained with paint and that she had procured materials to make another. Gabriel takes Cuff to Cobb's Hole, a fishing village, the home of a fisherman named Yolland. Yolland and his wife have a deformed daughter,

Limping Lucy; because of their deformities, Lucy and Rosanna had become friends. Cuff learns from Mrs. Yolland that Rosanna had come to their house earlier that day and written a long letter. She also bought a waterproof tin case and two dog chains from Mrs. Yolland. Cuff suspects that Rosanna hid something in the case, sunk it in the water, and used the chains to secure it. When he and Gabriel return to the house, they learn that Rachel has recently decided to live with Ablewhite's mother in Frizinghall; her decision corresponded with Rosanna's return home. Cuff asks Lady Verinder to delay Rachel's departure. By now, Cuff has concluded that Rachel has stolen her own diamond. The following day, Rosanna overhears a conversation between Blake and Cuff in which Blake says that he has no interest in Rosanna. Later, Gabriel tries to cheer the distraught Rosanna up.

CHAPTERS XVIII–XXI

After a visit to Frizinghall, Cuff determines that the Indians are innocent and that Rosanna has purchased cloth to make a new nightgown. As Rachel leaves the house, Cuff arranges to have one of his men monitor her movements. As she departs, she treats both Cuff and Blake rudely. Blake, discouraged by Rachel's attitude toward him, resolves to leave England. A servant tells Cuff that she last saw Rosanna leaving the house with a letter addressed to Cobb's Hole in her hand. Another servant reports that Rosanna was at Shivering Sand. Cuff follows Rosanna to a rocky ledge called South Spit. Gabriel concludes that Rosanna has killed herself; his conclusion is confirmed by a suicide note found in Rosanna's room. Lady Verinder, blaming Cuff for Rosanna's death, tries to dismiss him and pay him, but he refuses payment, since he has not completed his work.

CHAPTERS XXII–XXIII

Gabriel receives a letter from Rachel, who declares that she does not have the diamond. Lady Verinder instructs Gabriel again to dismiss Cuff and pay him. As he departs for London, Cuff makes three predictions to Gabriel: that the Yollands will contact Gabriel as soon as they receive the letter from Rosanna, that Gabriel will hear about the three Indians again if Rachel goes to London, and that Gabriel will hear about a London moneylender named Septimus Luker, an acquaintance of Rosanna.

Plans are made for Lady Verinder to take Rachel to London. The next day, Limping Lucy appears, looking for Blake, whom she blames for Rosanna's suicide. She has in hand Rosanna's letter and insists that Blake come to Cobb's Hole to get the letter himself. Gabriel, though, learns that Blake has left England. Gabriel also learns that Rachel has been entertaining Godfrey Ablewhite. Gabriel's narrative comes to a close as he receives from Cuff a clipping from a London newspaper reporting that the moneylender was attacked by the three Indians. All of Cuff's predictions have come true.

Second Period: The Discovery of the Truth (1848–1849)

FIRST NARRATIVE: CONTRIBUTED BY MISS CLACK; NIECE OF THE LATE SIR JOHN VERINDER

The First Narrative consists of eight chapters written by Drusilla Clack, Rachel's pious and self-righteous cousin. Blake has asked her to record her observations of Rachel in London after the disappearance of the diamond, which she does in her diary. She reports that, shortly after the Verinders' arrival in London, Godfrey Ablewhite (the leader of the Christian charity to which she belongs) and Septimus Luker were attacked, apparently by the Indians. The attackers took from Luker a receipt for a valuable. The next day, Miss Clack has lunch with the Verinders. After Ablewhite joins them, Rachel questions him about his relationship with Luker. Ablewhite denies any knowledge about the Moonstone but admits that gossip is circulating that he pawned the Moonstone to Luker. Rachel, though, is convinced that Ablewhite is innocent.

Later that day, the reader learns that Lady Verinder is dying; she asks Miss Clack to witness the signing of her will. When Miss Clack later returns to witness the will, Mr. Bruff, Lady Verinder's lawyer, summarizes the case against Ablewhite in connection with the theft of the diamond, but Miss Clack defends him. Bruff concedes her point and begins to suspect Rachel in the theft. Miss Clack tries to pay a visit to Lady Verinder; as she is waiting, she eavesdrops on a conversation between Rachel and Ablewhite. Rachel confesses that she loves another person, but Ablewhite is able to persuade her to agree to marry him. A servant appears to announce that Lady Verinder is dead.

The narrative continues after a month has passed. Rachel has moved to Brighton to live under the care of Ablewhite's father and mother, and of Miss Clack. Rachel tells Miss Clack that she will never marry Godfrey Ablewhite, who confirms that the engagement is broken. The next day, Ablewhite asks her to leave the house, and Mr. Bruff offers to serve as her guardian.

SECOND NARRATIVE: CONTRIBUTED BY MATHEW BRUFF, SOLICITOR, OF GRAY'S INN SQUARE

Bruff's narrative consists of three chapters. As the family lawyer, Bruff drew up the will for the late Sir John Verinder, who left his estate to Lady Verinder. Lady Verinder, in turn, left the estate to Rachel. Bruff learns that Ablewhite viewed Lady Verinder's will at the court. He realizes then that Ablewhite's motive in asking Rachel to marry him was mercenary. At Brighton, he persuades Rachel to break the engagement. He assumes the guardianship of Rachel, in part to shield her from the anger of Ablewhite's father.

Rachel leaves the Bruff household. A week later, Bruff meets with a man with a dark complexion who bears a card from Septimus Luker as introduction. He suspects that the man is one of the three Indians. The man inquires about loans and how long one is customarily given to repay a loan. Bruff learns that Luker had a similar conversation with the Indian. Bruff then meets Mr. Murthwaite at a dinner party. Murthwaite explains that the Indians would try to reclaim the diamond at some point when it was not under lock and key. He believes that the Moonstone is in the possession of Luker and that the Indians would attempt to reclaim it in a year, in June 1849, when the pledge for the diamond could be redeemed in London.

THIRD NARRATIVE: CONTRIBUTED BY FRANKLIN BLAKE

Blake's narrative, consisting of ten chapters, begins when he returns to England in 1849 after the death of his father. He is still in love with Rachel and left England because of her treatment of him. He is determined to solve the mystery of the Moonstone. He meets with Gabriel at the Verinder home, where Gabriel tells him that, if he wants to launch his inquiries, he would do well to start with the letter from Rosanna, still in the hands of Limping Lucy Yolland. The next day, he goes to Cobb's Hole, where Lucy treats him with disdain but gives him the letter, which contains directions to a hiding place at Shivering Sand. There Blake finds the tin box, held in place by the dog chains. Inside he finds a nightgown with a paint smear and a letter. Inside the nightgown is the name of the owner, Franklin Blake.

Blake is astonished. Later, Gabriel reads the letter, in which Rosanna confesses that she loves Blake. It was she who discovered the nightgown with the paint smear on it and concluded that it was evidence of intimacy between Blake and Rachel. She decided to replace the nightgown, but then concluded that Blake was in Rachel's room to steal the diamond. She bore the suspicions that surrounded her to protect Blake. Ezra Jennings, Mr. Candy's assistant, arrives to inform the men that Mr. Candy is ill.

Rosanna's letter continues. She explains that, after she was interrogated by Cuff, she hid the nightgown. The letter ends with her declaration that she will kill herself if Blake continues to be cruel to her. Blake feels remorse about his treatment of Rosanna. In London, Blake shows the letter to Bruff, who agrees that Rachel suspects Blake of having stolen the diamond. Bruff arranges to have Rachel visit his house when Blake will be present to question her. In a letter, Gabriel informs Blake that Mr. Candy wants to see him.

Rachel is shocked to see Blake at Bruff's house. It is clear that she loves him, but she suspects him of the theft of the Moonstone, claiming that she saw him take it. Her intention originally was to loan him money to pay his debts and conceal the theft, but after Blake led the investigation of the crime, she concluded that he was a dishonest man. To prove his innocence, Blake wants to call Cuff out of his retirement, but Cuff is out of the country. He resolves to question all the dinner party guests again, but the only one he is able to learn anything about is Ablewhite, who became engaged to an heiress, but again the engagement was broken off. Blake also learns that Ablewhite inherited a substantial sum of money.

Blake returns to Frizinghall, where he meets with Candy. Candy seems to have something important to tell him, but he cannot remember what it is. Blake then encounters Ezra Jennings, an opium addict. Jennings says to Blake that he can prove that Blake was unconscious of his own actions the night of the theft. It turns out that Blake had been having trouble sleeping because he had given up smoking for Rachel's sake. Candy had given Blake a dose of opium to settle a minor dispute about medicine the two men had. Blake, under the influence of the drug, seized the diamond, believing that, in so doing, he would be keeping Rachel safe. Blake and Jennings agree to recreate the events at the Verinder house the night of the diamond's disappearance, including the use of opium.

FOURTH NARRATIVE: EXTRACTED FROM THE JOURNAL OF EZRA JENNINGS

Ezra Jennings's narrative consists of a number of entries from his journal. Jennings proposes recreating the events on the night of Rachel's birthday dinner. For several days, Blake gives up tobacco, causing him to sleep badly. On the evening of June 25, he goes to bed early, then is administered opium in the form of laudanum. As Jennings predicted, Blake seems to awaken, but in a drug-induced haze, he goes to Rachel's room and seizes a substitute diamond, thus repeating his actions on the night of the Moonstone's disappearance. Rather than leaving, though, he falls asleep on Rachel's couch. The next morning, he awakens. Rachel, along with Gabriel and Bruff, is now convinced of his innocence and the two are reconciled. The question remains, though, as to the present whereabouts of the Moonstone.

FIFTH NARRATIVE: THE STORY RESUMED BY FRANKLIN BLAKE

Blake's narrative resumes after the experiment. Blake and Bruff follow Luker to his bank, waiting for him to emerge from an inner office. Present at the bank is a tall, bearded man who appears to be a sailor. Cuff and his assistant take a cab to the docks at the east end of London, where they discover that the sailor has taken a room. They break into the room and discover that the "sailor" is dead, although after they remove a false beard and makeup, they discover that the sailor is Godfrey Ablewhite in disguise. In the room is a box with a receipt for the Moonstone.

SIXTH NARRATIVE: CONTRIBUTED BY SERGEANT CUFF

The Sixth Narrative is in the form of a letter from Cuff to Blake dated July 30, 1849. He has concluded that the Indians smothered Ablewhite to death to obtain the Moonstone, and then departed London on a steamboat bound for Rotterdam. He reports that Ablewhite led a double life. He appeared to be a philanthropist but he was actually living luxuriously off the proceeds of a trust fund of a child for whom he was the trustee. He needed to replace the money he had stolen. He initially hoped to recoup the money by marrying Rachel. He then participated in the drugging of Blake, who, unconsciously, handed him the Moonstone. When it was clear that Blake did not remember his actions, Ablewhite took the gem. Luker then loaned money to Ablewhite in exchange for the diamond. A year later, Ablewhite tried to redeem the Moonstone, using money that a charity lady had willed to him.

SEVENTH NARRATIVE: IN A LETTER FROM MR. CANDY

The Seventh Narrative reproduces a letter from Mr. Candy to Blake. The letter reports the death of Ezra Jennings, who has left Blake the pages from his diary that concern Blake.

EIGHTH NARRATIVE: CONTRIBUTED BY GABRIEL BETTEREDGE

With the Eighth Narrative, Gabriel again picks up the story. He reports the marriage of Rachel and Blake. Later, Blake tells him that Rachel is pregnant.

Epilogue: The Finding of the Diamond

THE STATEMENT OF SERGEANT CUFF'S MAN (1849)

The first chapter of the epilogue consists of a statement from a colleague of Sergeant Cuff that explains how he tracked the Indians to the steamer bound for Bombay.

THE STATEMENT OF THE CAPTAIN (1849)

The second chapter consists of a statement from the captain of the steamboat *Bewley Castle*, who reports that the steamer has been delayed off the coast of India because of calm weather. The captain then noticed that a small rowboat was missing, as were the Indians, who appeared to have rowed ashore.

THE STATEMENT OF MR. MURTHWAITE (1850) (IN A LETTER TO MR. BRUFF)

The novel concludes with a letter from Murthwaite to Bruff. Murthwaite visited a Hindu shrine in India. There he watched a ceremony honoring the moon god. He spotted the three Indians and learned that they were Brahmins who, in the service of the moon god, had forfeited their high caste. After the Indians departed on a pilgrimage, a curtain opens to reveal the shrine to the moon god, the Moonstone in its forehead.

CHARACTERS

Godfrey Ablewhite

Ablewhite is the villain of the novel. He appears to be a gentlemanly philanthropist, but in reality, he has embezzled funds from a trust account. As the minor for whom he is trustee is approaching the age of majority, Ablewhite has to restore the funds to the account. His original plan is to marry Rachel Verinder and gain control of her inheritance, but she refuses him. Then the Moonstone falls into his hands when Blake takes it from Rachel's room. He borrows money from Septimus Luker, using the diamond as collateral. Later, it is learned that he tried to marry another heiress, but the engagement was broken off. He is eventually murdered by the Indians, who reclaim the Moonstone for their temple.

Gabriel Betteredge

Gabriel is the house steward to Lady Verinder at her estate in Yorkshire. He narrates the longest section of the novel, explaining the events surrounding the arrival of Franklin Blake, the disappearance of the Moonstone, and the investigation of Sergeant Cuff into the affair. He places great reliance on *Robinson Crusoe*, the 1719 novel by Daniel Defoe, often consulting it for prophecy and guidance.

Penelope Betteredge

Penelope is Gabriel's daughter. Her principal purpose is to provide her father with her diary so that he can recreate the events surrounding the Moonstone's disappearance.

Franklin Blake

Blake, Lady Verinder's nephew, is the conventional hero of the novel. He is at the center of most of the events. He is in love with Rachel Verinder and wants to marry her, but she suspects him of the theft of the Moonstone. As it turns out, she is partly right. On the evening of her birthday dinner, Blake gets into a dispute with Mr. Candy, a doctor, about the efficacy of certain medicines. Later that evening, he is given an opiate drug as a demonstration. In a drug-induced haze, he enters Rachel's room and takes the diamond. After leaving the room, he gives the diamond to Godfrey Ablewhite. He has no recollection of doing so, allowing Ablewhite to take the diamond for his own gain. Ultimately, it becomes clear that Blake is innocent of intentional wrongdoing. He and Rachel reconcile, marry, and have a child. Blake functions as editor of the various accounts provided by the other characters.

Mathew Bruff

Bruff is the Verinder family lawyer. He aids in the investigation of the Moonstone's disappearance, and he and his family briefly serve as Rachel's guardians. His function is to serve as a link between the Verinder family and Septimus Luker.

Thomas Candy

Candy is a doctor who practices in the town near the Verinder estate. He is one of the guests at the dinner party for Rachel Verinder's eighteenth birthday. His dispute with Blake about medicine leads to the drugging of Blake, which in turn leads to the disappearance of the Moonstone. Later, Candy becomes ill. It is clear that he wants to explain his involvement in the events on the evening of Rachel's party, but his illness prevents him from doing so.

Captain of the Steamboat

The captain of *Bewley Castle*, a steamboat bound for Bombay, narrates the events of the epilogue's second chapter. He notices the disappearance of the Indians from his boat.

Drusilla Clack

Miss Clack is in many respects a comic character. She is intensely religious, and she is affiliated with Godfrey Ablewhite through shared charitable activities. She is pious and intensely self-righteous. She leaves behind religious tracts after she learns that Lady Verinder is dying.

Sergeant Richard Cuff

Sergeant Cuff is a prototype for the clever detective who is called on the scene to solve a crime. He arrives from London to investigate the disappearance of the Moonstone. He conducts an investigation, initially suspecting Rachel and Rosanna of stealing the diamond. As he pieces together the evidence, though, he arrives at a correct understanding of what actually happened. Cuff is the character who immediately sees the significance of the paint smear on Rachel Verinder's bedroom door.

John Herncastle

Herncastle never appears directly in the novel. In the novel's prologue, the reader learns that he was a participant in the Battle of Seringapatam in 1799 and that he was guilty of the theft of the Moonstone. He is described as a n'er-do-well who was denied admission to the Verinder household. It is suspected that he willed the diamond to Rachel Verinder as a way of bringing trouble to the Verinder family. The reader shares this view because of a statement in the Prologue: "The dying Indian sank to his knees, pointed to the dagger in Herncastle's hand, and said, in his native language:— 'The Moonstone will have its vengeance yet on you and yours!'"

The Indians

Never named in the novel, the three Indians are members of the Brahmin caste who disguise themselves as low-caste jugglers and travel to England, hoping to recover the Moonstone, which is a holy object. Over the course of the novel, they attempt to break into the Verinder household, attack Godfrey Ablewhite and Septimus Luker, and eventually kill Ablewhite in their efforts to retrieve the Moonstone. In the epilogue, the three Indians flee to India aboard a steamboat and are later encountered by Mr. Murthwaite at the Hindu shrine that honors the moon god, where the Moonstone has been restored.

Ezra Jennings

Jennings is Mr. Candy's assistant. He is terminally ill and addicted to opium. Through Jennings, the reader learns what really happened on the night of the Moonstone's disappearance. With the help of Blake and Gabriel, he recreates the events of that night by giving Blake an opiate drug.

Septimus Luker

Luker is a London moneylender. He loans money to Godfrey Ablewhite, taking the Moonstone as a pledge for the loan.

Mr. Murthwaite

Murthwaite is a traveler and adventure. He is able to speak to the Indian jugglers in their own language. He explains the religious significance of the Moonstone, as well as the willingness of the high-caste Indians to forfeit their caste in their efforts to retrieve the diamond. At the end of the novel, he reports to Bruff that the diamond has been restored to the statue of the moon god in India.

Superintendent Seegrave

Seegrave conducts the initial investigation into the disappearance of the Moonstone. He exemplifies the detective-novel convention of the inept local constabulary that is unable to solve the mystery, requiring that a more clever police detective be called in.

Sergeant Cuff's Man

A colleague of Sergeant Cuff narrates the first chapter of the epilogue. He tracks the Indians to a steamer that sails for Bombay.

Rosanna Spearman

Rosanna is an ex-thief whom Lady Verinder hired into the household from a reformatory. She has a deformity, causing Gabriel to feel sorry for her. She falls in love with Franklin Blake, and because of this love—and the impossibility of Blake returning her love—she becomes distraught and emotionally disturbed. She discovers his nightgown with the paint smear on it and hides it. She believes that Blake stole the diamond to repay debts. She is suspected of the crime, but she willingly bears the suspicion as a way of protecting Blake. When Blake rejects her, she commits suicide.

Sir John Verinder

Lady Julia Verinder's husband, and Rachel's father, Sir John Verinder is deceased before the novel begins. He left his entire estate to his wife; his will was drawn up by the family solicitor, Mathew Bruff.

Lady Julia Verinder

Lady Verinder is the head of the household, as her husband, Sir John Verinder, has died. She inherited the estate from her husband and, in turn, willed it to her daughter, Rachel. Later, Lady Verinder becomes ill and dies—another death suggesting that the Moonstone bears a curse.

Rachel Verinder

Rachel is the heroine of the novel. As the novel opens (after the 1799 prologue), she is about to turn eighteen. A party celebrating her birthday is planned. One of the guests is Franklin Blake, who has been charged with delivering the Moonstone to her as a present. Rachel has all the characteristics of a conventional heroine. She is beautiful and spirited, and the reader believes that she and Blake would make a suitable couple. Gabriel Betteredge says this about her: "She was unlike most other girls of her age, in this—that she had ideas of her own, and was stiff-necked enough to set the fashions themselves at defiance, if the fashions didn't suit her views." She is initially suspected of having stolen her own diamond. In fact, she sees Blake take the diamond from the cabinet in her room. She believes, incorrectly, that Blake is in debt, motivating him to steal the diamond. She wants to protect him and use some of her money to pay his debts, but when he leads the investigation of the diamond's disappearance, she concludes that he is dishonest and treats him with disdain. Only after it is proven that Blake is innocent does she relent, and the two marry.

Limping Lucy Yolland

Limping Lucy Yolland is the daughter of the Yollands, who live in the fishing village Cobb's

TOPICS FOR FURTHER STUDY

- The event that begins *The Moonstone* is the storming of Seringapatam in India in 1799. Conduct research into the Battle of Seringapatam. Who were the combatants? What was the source of the conflict? What was its outcome? Present the results of your research in an oral report to your class. Supplement your report with PowerPoint images of the conflict, and of British-controlled India, during this time period.

- *The Moonstone* presents the points of view of various characters, but the reader never hears directly from any of the Indians involved, particularly the mysterious Indian jugglers. Write a new scene for the novel that incorporates the viewpoint of the Indians. Share your composition with your classmates, either orally or on your social networking site, and invite their comments.

- Wilkie Collins is often classified as a writer of Victorian sensation novels. Conduct research, both in print sources and on the Internet, about this class of novels. What were their characteristics? Why did they become so popular during the Victorian Age? What modern writers continue to use the conventions of the sensation novel? Present the results of your research in a written report or by creating a Web site.

- Trace the history of detective fiction written in English, beginning with Collins. Your research might take into account such writers as Arthur Conan Doyle (creator of the famous detective Sherlock Holmes), Agatha Christie (known for her sleuths Miss Marple and Hercule Poirot), Dorothy Sayers, or P. D. James. Make a chart listing the important authors and their major works. Be prepared to explain how each author uses—or changes—the conventions of detective fiction.

- A young-adult novel that turns many of the conventions of detective fiction on their heads is *The Case of the Missing Books* by Ian Sampson (available from HarperCollins in a 2007 edition). The sleuth is a Jewish vegetarian, Israel Armstrong, who has taken a job as a librarian in an Irish town, only to discover that thousands of the library's books are missing. Write a report in which you compare and contrast the bumbling efforts of Armstrong to solve the mystery of the missing books with Sergeant Cuff's efforts to find the missing Moonstone.

- *The Moonstone* is a relatively lengthy novel, yet the 1996 film adaptation by WGBH Boston, released in 2005, runs for just two hours. Watch the film, and then compare it with the book. What did the producers leave out? How did they condense the story? Which version—the book or the film—is most successful? Summarize your views in a Roger Ebert–style review and post your review on your Web site or social networking page. Invite your classmates to agree or disagree with your views.

Hole. Because of a deformity, she forms a bond with Rosanna, who is likewise deformed.

Mr. Yolland

Mr. Yolland is a fisherman and Limping Lucy's father.

Mrs. Yolland

Mrs. Yolland is the wife of a fisherman and mother to Limping Lucy.

THEMES

Experience

The Moonstone explores the relationship between objective and subjective experience. On the one hand, the novel embodies the value of subjective experience. Rachel, for example, continues to love Franklin Blake even though she believes that he stole the Moonstone to get money to settle his debts. Further, the novel, in many respects, turns on her subjective love for Blake, for she buries the evidence of her senses—she actually saw Blake take the Moonstone from her cabinet. Had she been willing to say what she knew to be true, the mystery would have been solved right away. The Indians embody the value of subjective experience, for their interest in the Moonstone is not based on its monetary value but on its religious significance—in contrast to Ablewhite, who sees the diamond strictly in monetary terms and, at one point, refers to the diamond as just a hunk of carbon. Presented against this emphasis on subjectivity is the objectivity of such characters as Sergeant Cuff, Mr. Bruff, and Gabriel Betteredge. In investigating the disappearance of the Moonstone, these characters want objective, physical evidence. They want to be able to prove their points of view. Sergeant Cuff, as a prototypical detective, has his suspicions and theories, but he tends to keep them to himself until he can prove his case. He even refuses payment from Lady Verinder when she tries to dismiss him, for he has not completed his job.

British Imperialism

Collins was personally troubled by the history of British-controlled India. Just a decade before he wrote the novel, the Sepoy Revolt and its bloody aftermath of retribution rocked England. It is thus no surprise that he presents his Indian characters in a sympathetic light. They are immediately suspected of having committed the crime, but the evidence is clear that they did not; all they want to do is reclaim a piece of their religious heritage. The character of John Herncastle stands in direct contrast. In the novel's prologue, Herncastle is presented as a selfish, violent character who is willing to commit murder to obtain the Moonstone. This action is symbolic of, in Collins's view, British exploitation of India. A half century later, Herncastle's crime comes to England and affects the lives of the characters. Thus, *The Moonstone* is at least in part Collins's commentary on British history and expresses his belief that history would in some way catch up with England.

Social Class

The Moonstone depicts members of a range of social classes. At the top of the hierarchy are Lady Verinder and her daughter, Rachel. Just beneath the Verinders are such characters as Franklin Blake and, at least apparently, Godfrey Ablewhite. Numerous members of the middle classes are also portrayed, including the lawyer, Mr. Bruff, and the doctor, Mr. Candy. Farther down the social scale are such characters as Sergeant Cuff and the moneylender, Septimus Luker. The servant class is

Colonel Herncastle originally stole the Moonstone from India during a major battle.
(Pborowka | Shutterstock.com)

represented by such characters as Gabriel Betteredge and Rosanna Spearman. Also among the lower classes are the Yollands. Among the Indians, the jugglers who follow the Moonstone to England are Brahmins, members of the highest level in India's caste system. They are willing to give up their position to become jugglers in order to retrieve the Moonstone. This depiction of the entire range of social classes indicates Collins's sense that the events surrounding the Moonstone and the British colonization of India have affected the entire nation. It also provides the reader with a wide range of points of view in the novel.

STYLE

Genre

The Moonstone is a detective novel, placing it within the tradition of detective fiction that continued with such writers as Sir Arthur Conan Doyle and Agatha Christie. Accordingly, it uses many of the conventions of detective fiction and, in fact, created many of those conventions. Among them are the country house robbery, the concept of an inside job, an eccentric but celebrated police detective (Cuff), an inept local constabulary (represented by Seegrave), false suspects (particularly the Indians and Rosanna

Spearman), a locked-room murder (the murder of Godfrey Ablewhite), a reconstruction of the crime, and a final plot twist. These and similar conventions would continue to be used by writers of detective fiction and are still used today.

Symbolism

The chief symbol in *The Moonstone* is the Moonstone itself. The gem represents the sense of mystery and exoticism of Asia. It seems to glow with its own peculiar light. It is of immense monetary value, but its value to the Indians is religious and cultural rather than monetary; in contrast is the view of Godfrey Ablewhite, who sees only how the diamond can solve his financial problems and keep him out of prison. In this way, the Moonstone becomes a symbol that reinforces the theme of objective versus subjective experience. It is also noteworthy that the Moonstone is associated with the moon god. Conventionally, the moon has been associated with sexual innocence (in contrast to the sun). Franklin Blake's seizure of the Moonstone while in a drug-induced haze can be read as symbolic of his seizure of Rachel's virginal innocence.

Point of View

One of the chief features of *The Moonstone* that has attracted praise from readers is its use of point of view. In a conventional novel, a particular point of view is adopted and maintained throughout the novel. Some writers use a first-person point of view, allowing one character—often a major character, but sometimes a minor character who functions as an observer—to narrate the events. Other writers adopt a third-person point of view, referring to the characters as *he, she,* and *they*. In some novels, the reader is allowed access to the thoughts and perceptions of the characters; in others, the point of view is limited to what can be observed. *The Moonstone* adopts a first-person point of view, but various portions of the novel are narrated by different characters. Gabriel Betteredge records his observations in much of the novel, but other parts are narrated by Franklin Blake, Miss Clack, Ezra Jennings, Sergeant Cuff, Mathew Bruff, and others. Each of these characters has incomplete knowledge. Their narratives then supplement one another, each narrative filling in the gaps that other narratives leave. It is noteworthy that Rachel Verinder never assumes the role of narrator; if she had, the mystery would have been revealed. It is also noteworthy, too, that Blake functions as a kind of editor of the varying accounts. The overall purpose of his efforts to urge others to write down their observations and to collect them is to establish his own innocence.

HISTORICAL CONTEXT

British Imperialism in India

The historical context that surrounds the events of *The Moonstone* involves the British colonization of India. On the last day of the year 1600, the British Crown established the British East India Company, a private enterprise that conducted British governmental and administrative affairs in India and also carried on trade in such commodities as silk, cotton, indigo dye, tea, saltpeter, and opium. British control became more entrenched when, in 1751, British and Indian troops under the command of a young captain, Robert Clive, began the process of driving French colonists out of India. Later, British forces completed the task at the Battle of Plassey in 1757.

In the years that followed, the British East India Company expanded its control over some two-thirds of India. A series of scandals involving corruption, bribery, and excessive use of force prompted Parliament to take steps to rein in the East India Company. Principal among these was the 1784 India Act, which brought the civil, economic, administrative, and military activities of the company under governmental control. Then in 1813 Parliament passed the Charter Act, which ended the East India Company's trade monopoly in India. Nevertheless, discontent with British rule festered until 1857 when the sepoys, or Indian soldiers serving under the British, revolted in what is variously called the Sepoy Mutiny, the Sepoy Rebellion, the Great Mutiny, and, among Indians, the First War of Indian Independence. The revolt erupted on May 10, 1857, near Bengal. In ensuing weeks, sepoy garrisons in several cities mutinied. In time, British forces gained control of the cities where the sepoys had revolted and reasserted the authority of the East India Company. The revolt was finally put down on June 20, 1858. The conflict was bloody, and British forces felt justified in retaliating. Entire villages were wiped out, and mutineers were executed.

COMPARE & CONTRAST

- **1850s:** Great Britain's colony in India is under the control of the British East India Company, a private concern that conducts administrative and government affairs and engages in the trading of various commodities.

  1860s: As a result of the Sepoy Revolt of 1857 and its aftermath, Britain's Queen Victoria removes Indian administration from the control of the East India Company and assures Indians that Britain will respect Indians' religion and culture.

  Today: India is independent from Great Britain, having achieved independence in 1947. The influence of the British continues to be felt, with the English language serving as a common tongue among the nation's hundreds of language groups.

- **1850s:** Under British law, women have no property rights. It is somewhat unusual for a character such as Sir John Verinder to bequeath his estate to Lady Verinder, and for her to will her estate to her daughter.

  1860s: Because of the passage of the 1857 Divorce and Matrimonial Causes Act, some women have more rights over property. Men still enjoy most rights over marital property, and most men continue to bequeath their property to a male heir.

  Today: Men and women enjoy the same property rights, without regard to gender. Considerably less emphasis is given to locating a male heir for property.

- **1850s:** England hosts the Great Exhibition of 1851, a kind of World's Fair. The exhibition is a tribute to England's greatness in military, economic, industrial, and artistic affairs.

  1860s: The British Empire continues to flex its muscles internationally with a military campaign in Abyssinia (encompassing today's Ethiopia and several other nations on its periphery). England is the world's preeminent imperial power, controlling its colonies with the world's most powerful navy.

  Today: Great Britain is no longer a major imperial power. It is a major member of the Commonwealth of Nations, which includes fifty-three nations, many of them former British colonies that cooperate on matters involving trade, human rights, governance, and similar common concerns. It is also a member of the European Union, a partnership of twenty-seven countries, NATO, and the United Nations.

England was torn over how to respond to the revolt and its bloody aftermath. Ultimately, Queen Victoria decided to exercise clemency. In 1858, just a decade before *The Moonstone* was written, Queen Victoria issued a proclamation announcing that England was assuming control of its Indian colonies, removing them from the administration of the British East India Company. She also reassured the people of India that Britain intended to respect and preserve Indian culture, particularly the right of Indians to practice their traditional religions, a concept reflected in the religious significance of the Moonstone in Collins's novel. In the decades that followed, the British established a complex legal and administrative structure referred to as the Raj (a Hindustani word meaning *reign*). The Indian economy would develop rapidly as the British constructed schools, railroads, and ports—an entire economic infrastructure—to the point that the Raj sometimes satirically referred to the licenses, taxes, permits, and red tape that became part of Indian affairs. The English language facilitated communication among India's four hundred or more language groups, and still today, English is spoken by even moderately educated Indians. India gained independence from the British in 1947.

Colonel Herncastle leaves the Moonstone to his niece Rachel in his will. (tankist276 | Shutterstock.com)

CRITICAL OVERVIEW

The Moonstone received a critical boost when poet T. S. Eliot, nearly six decades after the novel's original publication, wrote in his 1927 essay "Wilkie Collins and Dickens" (quoted by Tamar Heller in *Dead Secrets*) that the novel is "the first and greatest of English detective novels." But even in the years immediately following its publication, *The Moonstone* was highly praised by contemporary reviewers.

Writing in an 1868 *Athenaeum* review, Geraldine Jewsbury referred to the "carefully elaborate workmanship, and the wonderful construction of the story; the admirable manner in which every circumstance and incident is fitted together."

A contributor to the London *Times* praises *The Moonstone*, stating that "those who admire the spectacle of ingenuity in the construction of a plot, and of the power of bringing home to the imagination the dreariness and terror of dreary

and terrible scenes, should seek, and will find, it in *The Moonstone.*"

A reviewer in Philadelphia's *Lippincott's* magazine was equally enthusiastic: "The story is singularly original." The reviewer continues, "And how admirably is the story told! Clear, lucid and forcible in style, never straying into the alluring but pernicious paths of description or dissertation, the narrative moves onward in its unbroken and entrancing course."

Not all contemporary reviewers, though, found much of merit in *The Moonstone*. For example, a reviewer for *Spectator*, commenting on the characters, writes, "Such an array of dummies was never got together in any book of Mr. Wilkie Collins's before, or . . . in any book written by a man with the same literary reputation."

In the *Nation*, a contributor concludes, "There is nothing new in Mr. Collins's stories, if the reader has ever read a book of puzzles, and they serve none of the recognized purposes of the novel." The reviewer also notes that the mysteries "reflect neither nature nor human life; the actors whom they introduce are nothing but more or less ingenious pieces of mechanism, and they are all alike."

CRITICISM

Michael J. O'Neal

O'Neal holds a Ph.D. in English. In the following essay, he examines The Moonstone *as an example of the sensation novels popular in the 1860s.*

In the twenty-first century, Wilkie Collins is not exactly a household name. In the 1860s and 1870s, though, his novels and stories were immensely popular, principally because he virtually invented not just one but *two* types of fiction. The first was the detective story, exemplified by *The Moonstone* (although literary historians cite Edgar Allen Poe and others as important in the early development of detective fiction). The other came to be called the *sensation* novel—a term literary critics used, oftentimes disparagingly, to refer to a new type of fiction that relied on suspense, a spooky and threatening atmosphere, and a general sense of terror and mystery. The best example of a sensation novel from Collins's pen is his earlier novel *The Woman in White*, published in 1859–1860. Over the next decade, a number of

WHAT DO I READ NEXT?

- Collins's other famous novel, *The Woman in White*, was published in 1859–1860. The novel traces the aftermath of an encounter between a young drawing master and a mysterious woman, dressed entirely in white, who has escaped from an insane asylum. The novel is available in numerous editions, including one published by Bantam Books in 1985.

- *The Chinese Maze Murders* by Robert van Gulik was published by the University of Chicago Press in 2007. Gulik is a student of Chinese literature, and he created this mystery/detective story based on his earlier translation of an actual eighteenth-century detective novel written in China, one that features historical characters.

- Sir Arthur Conan Doyle's Sherlock Holmes story, "The Adventure of the Blue Carbuncle," was first published in 1892 and is available in *The Adventures of Sherlock Holmes*, published by Tribeca in 2011. In the story, Holmes investigates the mystery surrounding the theft of a jewel from a countess staying at a London hotel.

- James Skinner is the author of *The Recollections of Skinner of Skinner's Horse*. The book's subtitle is *James Skinner and His "Yellow Boys"—Irregular Cavalry in the Wars of India Between the British, Mahratta, Rajput, Mogul, Sikh & Pindarree Forces.* The book was published by Leonaur in 2006. This volume provides a firsthand historical account of the kind of military action that led to the Battle of Seringapatam in 1799 and provides insight into the attitudes of British colonists in India.

- Among the best known young-adult mystery novels are those in the "Hardy Boys" series (written by Franklin W. Dixon) and "Nancy Drew" series (written by various writers under the pen name Carolyn Keene). Dixon's *The Disappearing Floor*, published in 1940, involves a notorious jewel thief. Keen's *The Clue in the Jewel Box*, first published in 1943, involves the priceless heirloom of a former queen.

- The first recognized mystery/detective novel written by an African American is *The Conjure-Man Dies* by Rudolph Fisher, first published in 1932 and available in a 1992 edition by the University of Michigan Press. The book is set in Harlem, New York, during the Harlem Renaissance.

---

writers adopted the conventions of the sensation novel, and their novels became wildly popular.

The sensation novel relied on a number of conventions. It often featured lurid themes involving adultery, incest, bigamy, and illegitimacy—sins that reached out from the past into the present. Letters were often misdirected. People became enmeshed in romantic triangles. Young heroines faced threats, their legacies in danger from greedy relatives and adventurers. People were afflicted with emotional disturbances, often leading to self-destructive behavior and even suicide. Drugs and drug-induced hallucinations were prevalent, as were disguises and mistaken identities. Villains were often aristocratic, hiding their villainy behind a veneer of respectability. Considerable emphasis was placed on the psychology of characters, including their fears and obscure motivations. All of these conventions were enlisted to create harrowing tales intended to make the flesh creep and the hair stand on end.

A number of social developments, as well as developments in publishing, conspired to make sensation novels popular. First, levels of literacy were increasing, expanding the audience for popular fiction. Paper was becoming cheaper, making books cheaper, and the circulation of newspapers and magazines was expanding. Circulating libraries

ARRAYED AGAINST THE FORCES OF
RATIONALITY AND STABILITY IN *THE MOONSTONE* IS
A STEW OF OPPOSING FORCES—EXOTICISM, THEFT,
MURDER, SUSPICION, INTRIGUE, HALLUCINATIONS,
DRUGS, VIOLENCE, SUICIDE—FORCES THAT THREATEN
TO UNDERMINE THE VICTORIAN SOCIAL STRUCTURE.
YET THAT STRUCTURE ENDURES."

made novels more widely available. The founders and editors of new literary magazines (such as Dickens's *All the Year Round*) determined that they could hook readers by publishing novels serially; once a reader was immersed in a story such as *The Moonstone*, that reader would certainly buy the next monthly or weekly issue to find out what happened next, so the cliffhanger became integral to the plotting of fiction. Interestingly, these magazines enjoyed widespread circulation even after they were purchased. It has been estimated that for every one issue of the magazine that was purchased, as many as ten people would read (or have read to them) the latest installment of the current novel the magazine was publishing. It was very common for a head servant (someone like Gabriel Betteredge) to pass evenings reading aloud to the lower servants, many of whom were likely illiterate. These developments gave rise to tabloid-type journalism, with its emphasis on sensationalism, particularly on sensational crimes and the legal proceedings that followed in their wake. People were captivated by the melodramatic and theatrical. They longed for fiction similar to that of eighteenth-century Gothic writers such as Ann Radcliffe. Thus, the sensation novelists, with Collins at their head, found fertile ground for their tales.

The Moonstone has been referred to as a detective novel, and indeed, it conforms to many of the conventions of detective fiction. This, however, does not preclude the novel from adopting, at least in part, other sets of conventions, including those of the sensation novel. To be sure, *The Moonstone* is tame compared with other sensation novels of the 1860s. The novel contains no adultery, incest, or sexual impropriety. There is the merest hint of such impropriety when Rosanna suspects that Franklin Blake smeared his nightgown with paint when he illicitly entered Rachel's room the night of the theft, but this suspicion of a sexual liaison turns out to be without foundation. But Collins had found success with sensation fiction earlier in the decade with *The Woman in White*, so some of those conventions found their way into *The Moonstone*.

First is the character of Rachel Verinder. In common with many of the heroines of sensation fiction, she is young, beautiful, and spirited. Her legal status as a person is explored through her inheritance not only of her father's estate (through her mother) but also of the Moonstone itself. Indeed, wills were a common feature of much Victorian fiction. The will and the inheritance of property were fundamental sources of social stability, ensuring that estates and accumulated wealth were passed down and remained intact in stable family structures. Debt threatened that stability, for debt could lead to the dissipation of an estate, undermining the social structure. So it is no surprise that much of *The Moonstone* hinges on debt (both real and imagined), the borrowing of money (through a moneylender such as Septimus Luker), and the pawning of a valuable object such as the Moonstone. The presence of the sinister Indians and the disappearance of the Moonstone surround Rachel with a vague aura of threat, an aura heightened by other deaths in the novel: Rosanna's (from suicide), her mother's, and later Godfrey Ablewhite's and even Ezra Jennings's. These deaths suggest that the Moonstone carries a power that enables it to determine the outcome of human affairs.

The characters of Rosanna Spearman and Ezra Jennings also draw on the conventions of sensation fiction. Rosanna is an ex-thief, so her background is immediately suspect; her physical deformity (as well as that of Limping Lucy Yolland) adds to the auras of threat and suspicion that surround her, as does her fascination with the aptly named Shivering Sand. She develops a morbid fascination for Franklin Blake, causing her to act irrationally. Ultimately, she commits suicide, but not before recording her thoughts and beliefs in a mysterious letter that remains under wraps, but that becomes crucial to the solution of the mystery. Ezra Jennings is terminally ill and addicted to opium (which during the Victorian period was often taken in the form of

How did the Moonstone get back to the back vault? (*Kirsty Pargeter | Shutterstock.com*)

laudanum, a drug widely prescribed for pain, emotional distress, menstrual discomfort, and a host of other maladies, including teething in infants). The outcome of the novel turns on a major stroke of irrationality: Franklin Blake acts under the influence of the drug and does not know what he has done.

The Moonstone also explores social hypocrisy—the sense that all is not as it should be under the conventions of polite society. Lady Verinder is a perfectly proper Victorian woman from a proper family. Yet lurking in the Verinder past is John Herncastle, a violent criminal whose actions set the plot of the novel in motion. Two years before the events of the novel, Lady Verinder denied Herncastle admittance to her home. Suspicions abound that Herncastle has willed the Moonstone to Rachel as a way of getting back at the family for shunning him, for Herncastle would have known that the Indians would stop at nothing to reclaim the diamond. Then there is the character of Godfrey Able-white (an ironic name, for he is neither "able" nor "white" in the conventional Victorian sense

of innocent, nor is he in any sense "God"-like). When the reader is first introduced to Ablewhite, he appears to be respectable. He is handsome, and he is involved widely in charitable and philanthropic activities. As the novel unfolds, though, it becomes clear that this is all hypocrisy. Ablewhite is a grifter, a con man, who has embezzled money from a trust account and faces prison if he does not restore the money to the account before the child reaches the age of majority. Near the novel's end, he is unmasked, both literally and figuratively.

A different type of hypocrisy is depicted in the character of Drusilla Clack. Collins was brought up in an intensely religious, High Anglican household. As an adult, he rejected the religiosity of his parents and lived a life that was highly unconventional, particularly in his domestic arrangements. It comes as no surprise, then, that he would create a character like Miss Clack: unmarried, obsessed with her narrow vision of Christian charity and salvation, and susceptible to the blandishments of a fraud like Godfrey Ablewhite.

The sensation novels of the 1860s and 1870s were Victorian in the sense that they depicted a world of respectability, moral probity, rationality, and realism—all represented by the rationality of Sergeant Cuff and Mr. Bruff and through the conscientious reportage of Gabriel Betteredge. The novel is built on a solidly Victorian social structure in which each character appears to conform to his or her proper role. Yet all is not as it appears. Arrayed against the forces of rationality and stability in *The Moonstone* is a stew of opposing forces—exoticism, theft, murder, suspicion, intrigue, hallucinations, drugs, violence, suicide—forces that threaten to undermine the Victorian social structure. Yet that structure endures. The Moonstone is restored to its proper place. Hypocrisy is exposed. Franklin Blake and Rachel Verinder marry and have a child. The reader has witnessed events that threaten to undermine the familiar, solidly English world of London and Yorkshire. For now, that world survives.

Source: Michael J. O'Neal, Critical Essay on *The Moonstone*, in *Novels for Students*, Gale, Cengage Learning, 2012.

London Times

In the following excerpt, a contributor to the London Times *examines the story in relation to Collins's preface and analyzes the techniques Collins uses to keep the reader in constant suspense.*

It would be unjust to the memory of Edgar Poe, or perhaps—to look further back still—to Mrs. Radcliffe, to style Mr. Wilkie Collins the founder of the sensational school in novels, but he long ago placed himself at its head. He proved, indeed, at so early a period his skill in the construction of a plot that he has since been his own most formidable rival. His *Basil* displayed a more intense concentration than, perhaps, any of his later tales of tragic interest, of however painful a kind, but about one or two characters only, in *The Woman in White* he evinced that he could preserve the unity and concentration of interest while multiplying his actors and circumstances; and in the present story [*The Moonstone*] he has shown himself a master in the art of amalgamating the most unmalleable and inconsistent of facts—fatalism and Hindoo mysticism and devotion, English squirearchy, detectives, and housemaids—and seems to have taken by choice difficulties for his resources....

Mr. Wilkie Collins explains that the distinction between the present and former tales of his

> MR. WILKIE COLLINS NEVER ONCE QUITS HIS HOLD OF HIS READERS' INTEREST. WHEN ONE PART OF THE MYSTERY IS SOLVED, THE INTEREST IN WHAT REMAINS BECOMES STILL MORE EAGER."

is that the attempt made in this is to "trace the influence of character on circumstances," and to show that the conduct of the several actors directs the course of those portions of the story in which they are concerned.... The character of each of the real actors in the story is the centre of attraction within the orbit of its own circumstances, the actions of each in conformity with such person's character becoming in their turn circumstances on which the characters of the others have to operate. The robbery of the sacred diamond is in conformity with Herncastle's sullen obstinacy and defiance of opinion, combined with his brooding imaginativeness. His sister's somewhat unbending haughtiness predisposed her to find the stigma affecting her daughter's name unbearable. Her daughter's morbid habit of reticence involved her in a maze of doubt and reproach, and postponed a general clearing up of the mystery, to the reader's signal profit, who has thereby gained Miss Clack, but to Rachel's misery, for a whole year. Rosanna's experiences as a thief render her ready to suspect that Franklin Blake is a thief too; her love makes her desire to find him one, that there may not stand between her and him "the dreadful reproach which honest people are in themselves to a woman like her," and it makes her, in the resolution to save him from the discovery of his imagined crime, take a course which wonderfully complicates the difficulties of the plot. Finally, Franklin's own manysidedness of character, which leads him through various phases of controversy till he politely informs his antagonist, a surgeon, that medical men are all impostors, puts him up as a mark for a little medical experiment of very serious consequences to himself.

So much for Mr. Wilkie Collins's theory. His readers, probably far too soon for their retention of the scientific placidity necessary for the due weighing of the principles laid down in his preface, if they ever read it, will be caught in the vortex of his plot. The essence and secret of sensational novel-writing is to keep flashing a metaphorical bullseye up the particular dark archways where the thief is not lurking; to make the circumstances agree with one given explanation, which is not the true one; and to disguise as long as possible the fact that they agree also with a perfectly different conclusion. It is to present a real clue and a pseudo clue, and tempt the reader on to follow the pseudo clue till past the middle of the third volume. The whole school has this habit of laying eggs and hiding them. But Mr. Wilkie Collins has a complex variety of this propensity for secretiveness. He is not satisfied with one false clue, but is perpetually dropping clues, and, like a bird, by his demonstrative employment of various arts to lead his readers elsewhere, away from the spot where he originally induced them to fancy the nest was, only makes them more eagerly bent on keeping the old path. Every character in the book has his or her theory as to the mystery, and each of the theories is partly true. But then it is also partly, and that manifestly, false. So when, as often, a hint of the truth is let fall by one of them, the reader has by this time grown so suspicious that he refuses to accept it. "No one has stolen the Diamond," says Sergeant Cuff, and Sergeant Cuff is a very king among detectives. But, as Sergeant Cuff says also "Your young lady has got a travelling companion, Mr. Betteredge, and the name of it is the Moonstone," in which he is certainty wrong, the reader disbelieves the true part of his theory. The idea at the foundation of the story is the discovery by a young girl, given to act for herself and not fond of sympathy, that her lover is a thief and has robbed herself;—and the question is what her consequent conduct will be. The author's main object throughout seems to be to conceal this. For this purpose the second volume, direct and positive as are the merits of Miss Clack, is interpolated. Almost everything of materiality to the plot is given in the first and third. If all from Rosanna's suicide, and Rachel's departure from home, at the end of the first, to the discovery made by Franklin on the seashore at the end of the second, were omitted, the plot would remain whole and entire. The creation of a rival heroine to Rachel in the person of Rosanna Spearman has the same object. Rosanna and her whole story do not, in fact, advance the action of the novel one inch. It is not any reflection of her suspicion of Franklin's dishonesty, which lowers him in Rachel's eyes. It does not expose him to the suspicions of Cuff. An old intimacy which she is stated to have had with Luker leads to nothing. Her love does not make Rachel jealous. She might have gone on living without the course of this story being slackened or quickened. Franklin himself discovers what it was she had hidden; and the revelations in her posthumous letter are made to him. He uses them to force on an explanation from Rachel of her strange aversion from him. But that must have come on scarcely later of itself. She is made, perhaps, the most interesting personage in the book; and a larger space is devoted to her character and doings than to those of any one else;—and all solely for the sake of throwing the reader out, and seducing him from a too exclusive concentration of attention on the simple facts of Rachel's change of demeanour to her lover.

Mr. Wilkie Collins never once quits his hold of his readers' interest. When one part of the mystery is solved, the interest in what remains becomes still more eager. The true test of writings like this, and one which *The Moonstone* will stand, is whether at each stage and break of the story a negative answer must be returned to the question whether the final denouement be yet seen. When the diamond is first found to be stolen the reader suspects the Indians. By the time that it is clear that it is not they, it becomes apparent that Rachel knows something, but is hiding it to shelter some one, not herself. It seems equally clear that there is knowledge, and probably, but not so certainly, not directly guilty knowledge, in Rosanna. The reader suspects, with the sergeant, that there is collusion between them, though not, as the sergeant fancies, to shield Rachel. When the absence of this is proved at Rosanna's death, there still lurks a doubt as to Rosanna's freedom from innocent connexion with the theft. A suspicion now also arises, and goes on gaining strength continually, that another person has, at all events, the benefit of the theft, and that either Rachel or Rosanna has known this. When Rachel's indignation at the rumour against that person exonerates her from such knowledge, there is still nothing to clear Rosanna of collusion. When the discovery on the sea shore and her letter show this is not so, but it becomes more and more certain who has the diamond, the double difficulty how it has been taken and how the possessor became such, appears no nearer its solution. When the author shows his whole hand, and while he is revealing the procedure by which it was taken by the one and came into the hands of the other, the interest even yet does not flag, and the reader traces each step to the goal which he sees before him in eager suspense and uncertainty, up to the last page, whether the real catastrophe be not still behind. Mr. Wilkie Collins has built his plot like an iron ship with the several compartments combining perfectly, but isolated and all watertight. It is not till every one has been burst open that the plot sinks, and the reader's interest with it;—although it must be confessed that when it does sink it sinks, after the manner of sensational plots, utterly, and can never be weighed up again. Or to explain our meaning by another comparison, the plot of *The Moonstone* has the quality which was fixed as a condition of the competition for the new law courts. One made free of the building will find all the rooms communicating with each other as soon as he gets inside; but the public, coming out of curiosity, can make their way from one court into another only by going outside and entering it by its own special door.

The book has its shortcomings. There are some petty ambiguities and flaws in the plot.... There is, again, a certain pervading high-pressure tone about the characters which is exhausting. The medical men are so very medical; the lawyers are so very legal, and peruse abstracts of title with "breathless excitement;" the politicians are so very political, and are seen "amusing" themselves "at home with the Parliamentary plaything which they call a Private Bill." "Eminent" professional personages outside the action of the book are so extremely pompous and silly, and philanthropists such hypocrites and cheats at bottom. Those who are retained for the narrative are so extremely sagacious, and, if by their special profession trained to be bitter, display for that reason natural tempers so much the more benevolent and kindly. Every character is sure to have his pet theory as to life, and to be exceedingly epigrammatic. There is a superabundance of law; and lastly, and above all, every narrator makes too much a point of giving to his simplest statements the air of depositions taken before a police magistrate.

But some of these faults are very closely allied to the merits of the book. We could not spare one item of Miss Clack's "patience" and "abstinence from judging" others, though all pious ladies are not malignant; Betteredge's frequent stumblings into epigram are none too many; and the legal tediousness and preciseness of the ordinary course of the narrative arises from the same intellectual quality whence come the minute touches (each doing its own work without projecting the smallest shadow in front), which work up the reader's

interest at any important crisis to boiling point. To object again, as some ungrateful readers probably may, that there is no desire to turn back to the first volume when the last is read and con over each separate detail fondly, is to complain that the tale belongs to a class in which in proportion to the intensity of interest in the catastrophe is the suddenness of the descent into acquiescence when that is reached; it is to murmur at Mr. Wilkie Collins because his primary aims are not those of Miss Austen or even Mr. Anthony Trollope. There is one positive and intrinsic defect in Mr. Wilkie Collins as a novelist. It is a want of what Mr. Matthew Arnold has called "sweetness" and "charm." But those who admire the spectacle of ingenuity in the construction of a plot, and of the power of bringing home to the imagination the dreariness and terror of dreary and terrible scenes should seek, and will find, it in *The Moonstone*.

Source: Review of *The Moonstone*, in *London Times*, October 3, 1868, p. 4.

Geraldine Jewsbury

In the following review, Jewsbury suggests that a second reading of The Moonstone *reveals the elaborate workmanship of the novel.*

[When readers of *The Moonstone*] have read to the end, we recommend them to read the book over again from the beginning, and they will see, what on a first perusal they were too engrossed to observe, the carefully elaborate workmanship, and the wonderful construction of the story; the admirable manner in which every circumstance and incident is fitted together, and the skill with which the secret is kept to the last; so that even when all seems to have been discovered there is a final light thrown upon people and things which give them a significance they had not before. The "epilogue" of *The Moonstone* is beautiful. It redeems the somewhat sordid detective element, by a strain of solemn and pathetic human interest. Few will read of the final destiny of *The Moonstone* without feeling the tears rise in their eyes....

The various characters of the romance are secondary to the circumstances. The hero and heroine do not come out very distinctly, though we are quite willing to take them upon testimony. Ezra Jennings, the doctor's assistant, is the one personage who makes himself felt by the reader. The slight sketch of his history, left purposely without details, the beautiful and noble nature developed in spite of calumny, loneliness, and the pain of a deadly malady, is drawn with a firm and masterly hand; it has an aspect of reality which none of the other personages possess. . . .

Source: Geraldine Jewsbury, "New Novels: *The Moonstone*: A Romance," in *Athenaeum*, No. 2126, July 25, 1868, p. 106.

Lippincott's Magazine of Literature, Science and Education

In the following review, a contributor to Lippincott's *praises* The Moonstone *as a "perfect work of art."*

[*The Moonstone* is the best novel] that Mr. Collins has of late years given to the world, and we are inclined to consider it, with the one exception of *The Woman in White*, the best he has ever written. The story is singularly original; and when we remember the force and extent of Hindoo superstition, we can scarcely venture to pronounce it improbable. And how admirably is the story told! Clear, lucid and forcible in style, never straying into the alluring but pernicious paths of description or dissertation, the narrative moves onward in its unbroken and entrancing course. Let the impatient reader, hurrying to reach the dénouement, skip half a dozen pages. Instantly the thread of the story is broken, the tale becomes incomprehensible, the incidents lose their coherence. *The Moonstone* is a perfect work of art, and to remove any portion of the cunningly constructed fabric destroys the completeness and beauty of the whole.

It would be well if some of the New England writers, who look upon a novel as a mere vehicle for the introduction of morbid and unwholesome metaphysical and psychological studies, or long dissertations on Art—well enough in their way perhaps, but strangely out of place in a story—would study the elements of their art from Wilkie Collins. Then would the words "American novel" cease to be synonymous with weariness of spirit and much yawning on the part of the reader, and arguments for amalgamation would be placed before the public in their naked deformity, instead of under the thin disguise of novels possessing little plot and less probability.

Source: Review of *The Moonstone*, in *Lippincott's Magazine of Literature, Science and Education*, Vol. 2, December 1868, pp. 679–80.

The Nation

In the following excerpt, a contributor to the Nation *denigrates Collins's art, particularly censuring his lifeless characters.*

Mr. Wilkie Collins's new book [*The Moonstone*] is very suggestive of a game called "button," which children used to play, and probably play now. A number of little folks being seated in a circle, each with hands placed palm to palm in front of him, one of the party, who holds a button, comes in turn to each of the others, and ostensibly drops it into his closed hands. Of course, but one of the party can receive it, but in each case the same motions are gone through with; and having made his rounds, the principal performer enquires, "Who's got the button?" Each one, including him who has it, but who intentionally misleads the rest, guesses at the puzzle, and he who guesses right carries the button at the next trial. The Moonstone riddle is so like in its essential features to this child's-play, that it might very well have been suggested by it. Mr. Collins's art consists, in this particular case, in converting the button into a yellow diamond, worth thirty thousand pounds; in calling the players Hindoos, detective policemen, reformed thieves, noble ladies, and so on, and in thus more effectually distracting his reader's attention from the puzzle itself, which turns out at last, like most of Mr. Collins's mysteries, to have no vital connection with his characters, considered as human beings, but to be merely an extraneous matter thrown violently into the current of his story. It would perhaps be more correct to say that there is no story at all, and that the characters are mere puppets, grouped with more or less art around the thing the conjurer wishes to conceal until the time comes for displaying it. These books of his are, in their way, curiosities of literature. The word "novel," as applied to them, is an absurd misnomer, however that word is understood. There is nothing new in Mr. Collins's stories, if the reader has ever read a book of puzzles, and they serve none of the recognized purposes of the novel. They reflect neither nature nor human life; the actors whom they introduce are nothing but more or less ingenious pieces of mechanism, and they are all alike—like each other and like nothing else. They teach no moral lessons; they are unsuggestive of thought, and they appeal to no sentiment profounder than the idlest curiosity. They are simply conundrums. It is for this reason that Mr. Collins, wise in his generation, deprecates any attempts on the part of his critics to tell the plot of his stories. One commits, however, no breach of trust in speaking of the theatrical properties which supply, in our author's case, the place of dramatic ability. He cannot create a character, unless the solitary instance of Count Fosco be an exception; he can only dress a lay-figure with more or less of skill.

Take his Moonstone, for instance—which, as far as the real business of the plot is concerned, might as well have been a black bean or a horn button—call it a yellow diamond, stolen, centuries ago, from the forehead of an Indian idol, and make its recovery a part of the religion of three mysterious, lithe, swarthy East Indians in flowing white robes, and there is a chance of awakening, in the most hardened of novel-readers, a curiosity which would assuredly have slept over the possible whereabouts of a button.

But it is hardly worth while to go on. One might say of the book, that it is like a pantomime—the characters appear to speak, but really say nothing, and are merely conventional figures, and not characters at all Mr. Collins ventriloquizes behind each of his puppets, in order to give a sufficient number of misleading sounds. But his art is bad, and he has not art enough—his voice always betrays him, and the reader is never deceived into thinking that it is anybody but Mr. Collins that is talking. We do not know of any books of which it is truer than of Mr. Collins's to make the damaging remark, that nobody reads them twice, and that when the end of the first perusal is reached, everybody thinks his time has been wasted.

Source: Review of *The Moonstone*, in *Nation*, Vol. 7, No. 168, September 17, 1868, p. 235.

Heller, Tamar, *Dead Secrets: Wilkie Collins and the Female Gothic*, Yale University Press, 1992, p. 142.

Jewsbury, Geraldine, Review of *The Moonstone*, in *Wilkie Collins: The Critical Heritage*, edited by Norman Page, Routledge & Kegan Paul, 1974, p. 170; originally published in *Athenaeum*, July 25, 1868, p. 106.

Merriman, C. D., "Wilkie Collins," in *The Literature Network*, http://www.online-literature.com/wilkie-collins/# (accessed June 9, 2011).

Porter, Andrew, and Alaine M. Low, eds., *The Oxford History of the British Empire*, Vol. 3, *The Nineteenth Century*, Oxford University Press, 1999.

Review of *The Moonstone*, in *Wilkie Collins: The Critical Heritage*, edited by Norman Page, Routledge & Kegan Paul, 1974, pp. 179–81; originally published in *Lippincott's Magazine*, December 1868, pp. 679–80.

Review of *The Moonstone*, in *Wilkie Collins: The Critical Heritage*, edited by Norman Page, Routledge & Kegan Paul, 1974, pp. 173–75; originally published in *Nation*, September 17, 1868, pp. vii, 235.

Review of *The Moonstone*, in *Wilkie Collins: The Critical Heritage*, edited by Norman Page, Routledge & Kegan Paul, 1974, pp. 172–73; originally published in *Spectator*, July 25, 1968, pp. 881–82.

Review of *The Moonstone*, in *Wilkie Collins: The Critical Heritage*, edited by Norman Page, Routledge & Kegan Paul, 1974, p. 175–78; originally published in *Times* (London, England), October 3, 1868, p. 4.

Wolpert, Stanley, *A New History of India*, 8th ed., Oxford University Press, 2008.

SOURCES

Allingham, Philip V., "The Victorian Sensation Novel, 1860–1880–'Preaching to the Nerves instead of the Judgment,'" in *The Victorian Web*, http://www.victorianweb.org/genre/sensation.html (accessed June 14, 2011).

———, "Wilkie Collins (1824–89): A Brief Biography," in *The Victorian Web*, http://www.victorianweb.org/authors/collins/bio.html (accessed June 9, 2011).

"Book Clubs/Reading Guides: *The Moonstone*," in *Penguin.com*, http://us.penguingroup.com/static/rguides/us/woman_white_moonstone.html (accessed June 9, 2011).

Brinjikji, Hiam, "Property Rights of Women in Nineteenth-Century England," in *University of Michigan Web site*, http://www.umd.umich.edu/casl/hum/eng/classes/434/geweb/PROPERTY.htm (accessed June 14, 2011).

Collins, Wilkie, *The Moonstone*, edited by Joy Connolly, Barnes and Noble Classics, 2005.

Connolly, Joy, "Introduction," in *The Moonstone*, by Wilkie Collins, Barnes and Noble Classics, 2005, pp. xxi–xxxiii.

FURTHER READING

Pool, Daniel, *What Jane Austen Ate and Charles Dickens Knew: From Fox Hunting to Whist—the Facts of Daily Life in Nineteenth-Century England*, Touchstone, 1994.

Modern readers can sometimes be mystified by the details of Victorian life. What did people eat? What did they wear? How did they behave in polite society? How did they get about from place to place? How did they care for themselves personally? This volume looks at the details of everyday life among the Victorians and would provide readers of *The Moonstone* with a picture of the circumstances in which the novel's characters lived.

Pykett, Lyn, *Wilkie Collins*, Oxford University Press, 2009.

This relatively brief biography of Collins, part of Oxford University Press's "Authors in Context" series, examines Collins's life in the context of the literary marketplace of mid-nineteenth-century England. It also looks at his fiction in the context of social changes taking place in Britain at that time.

Radford, Andrew, *Victorian Sensation Fiction*, Palgrave Macmillan, 2009.

This volume presents literary criticism of the Victorian subgenre called sensation fiction, of which Collins was a practitioner. The volume contains contemporary reviews of sensation novels as well as modern critical analysis.

Steinbach, Susie L., *Understanding the Victorians: Politics, Culture and Society in Nineteenth-Century Britain*, Routledge, 2011.

This volume constitutes a social history of Victorian England. It includes sections on gender, religion, economics, and material culture. Readers will gain a clearer understanding of the environment in which Collins wrote.

Sutherland, John, *The Longman Companion to Victorian Fiction*, 2nd ed., Longman, 2009.

First published in 1988, this volume is a massive compendium of information about Victorian fiction. It includes plot summaries of hundreds of novels, as well as biographical information on the principal authors. Readers can use this volume to trace the impact Collins had on other authors who used his techniques in their own work.

SUGGESTED SEARCH TERMS

Battle of Seringapatam

British India

detective fiction

Hindu caste

nineteenth-century British imperialism

Queen Victoria Proclamation India 1858

sensation fiction

Sepoy Revolt

Wilkie Collins

Wilkie Collins AND Charles Dickens

Wilkie Collins AND Moonstone

sensation fiction AND Wilkie Collins

Number the Stars

LOIS LOWRY
1989

Winner of the 1990 Newbery Award, Lois Lowry's *Number the Stars* is a young-adult historical novel inspired by the Danish resistance movement in World War II. After surrendering to Nazi Germany, the Danish people protected their Jewish population by smuggling Jewish families out of the country and into Sweden. Lowry's book centers on ten-year-old Annemarie Johansen and her best friend Ellen Rosen, who is Jewish. When the Johansen and Rosen families learn, through their contact in the Danish resistance movement, that the Nazis are beginning to "relocate" the Danish Jews, Ellen is sent to live with the Johansens. Meanwhile, Ellen's parents escape, with the aid of resistance members, before the German officers can find them. Annemarie, Ellen, and Annemarie's little sister Kirsti flee with Mrs. Johansen to Annemarie's uncle's house by the sea.

Although the girls enjoy pretending they are sisters, as the dangerous situation requires, the gravity of the situation is not entirely lost on them. Before long, the resistance has delivered Ellen's parents and several other Jews to Uncle Henrik's home. From there, the Jews are escorted by Annemarie's mother to Henrik's fishing boat, where they plan to hide until Henrik takes them to Sweden the next morning. Annemarie waits anxiously for her mother's return. Near dawn, she finds her mother close to home, her ankle broken from her run through the dark woods. Mrs. Johansen is

The family lives in Copenhagen, Denmark, during the Nazi occupation. (Fedor Selivanov / Shutterstock.com)

horrified to discover that an important packet that Ellen's father was to have delivered to Henrik had fallen from his pocket.

Annemarie sees the urgent need to deliver the packet and takes it upon herself to do so. Hiding the mysterious envelope in a basket under the food she ostensibly is delivering to her uncle, Annemarie begins her perilous journey. She is stopped by Nazi soldiers, who remove everything from the basket, even the envelope, which contains a handkerchief. The soldiers release her, and Annemarie completes her journey. Upon her uncle's return later that day, Annmarie learns that her friend and the other Jewish families made it safely to Sweden, and that the handkerchief was treated with a substance that prevented the Nazis' dogs from smelling the people hidden under the boards on the boat. The novel closes with the ending of the war and the Johansens anxiously awaiting the return of their friends, the Rosens.

Number the Stars was published in 1989 by Houghton Mifflin Books for Children.

AUTHOR BIOGRAPHY

Born on March 20, 1937, in Honolulu, to Robert E. Hammersberg and Katharine Landis Hammersberg, Lowry traveled extensively as a child because of her father's career as an army dentist. During World War II, she lived in Pennsylvania, and in the years following the war, her family lived in Japan. Later, she attended a private school in Brooklyn, New York. After completing two years at Brown University, Lowry left college in 1956 to marry Donald Grey Lowry. While her husband completed a law degree at Harvard, Lowry worked part-time and had four children by 1962. After the Lowrys moved to Maine, Lowry was able to complete her college education and earned a bachelor of arts degree from the University of Maine in 1972.

She began writing professionally after her graduation, authoring textbooks, articles, and short fiction. Her first novel, *A Summer to Die*, was published in 1977 and was positively reviewed by critics. The same year, Lowry's twenty-one year marriage ended in divorce. She continued to write many young-adult novels, and became well known for a series of novels, published in the 1980s, featuring the character Anastasia Krupnik. Lowry published her Newbery Award–winning novel *Number the Stars* in 1989 and, in 1994, also won a Newbery Award for her 1993 novel, *The Giver*. In 2010, *The Birthday Ball* was published. As of 2011, Lowry resides in Cambridge, Massachusetts.

PLOT SUMMARY

Chapter 1: Why Are You Running?

Set in Copenhagen, Denmark, in the 1940s, *Number the Stars* opens with Annemarie Johansen and her friend Ellen Rosen racing down the street, trailed by Annemarie's little sister, Kirsti. They are stopped by German soldiers who ask them why they have been running. Annemarie and Ellen are terrified as one of the soldiers prods Annemarie's backpack with his rifle. Kirsti, however, remains unafraid, because she is only five years old, young enough to not remember what her city was like before the German occupation and too young to understand the threat the soldiers pose. She angrily yells at one of the soldiers when he reaches down to touch her hair, as he observes to his companion that she resembles his own daughter. Once back in the Johansen apartment, the girls find Mrs. Rosen "having coffee" with Mrs. Johansen. Annemarie notes that, since the Nazi occupation, of course, there is no coffee; rather, they drink an herbal tea. Such details underscore the changes in everyday life the Danes experience during the war. The girls tell their mothers what happened, and the mothers discuss reports in the illegal newspaper, published by the Danish resistance movement, of the group's bombings of factories that produce war materials.

Chapter 2: Who Is the Man Who Rides Past?

Annemarie tells her little sister stories and recalls the death of her older sister Lise, who was killed when hit by a car just before her wedding to Peter Neilsen, the young man who delivers the resistance newspaper. Annemarie and her parents later discuss King Christian X of Denmark's decision to surrender to Nazi Germany. Mr. Johansen stresses the family's

MEDIA ADAPTATIONS

- *Number the Stars* is available as an unabridged audio CD published by Listening Library in 2004. It is read by Blair Brown.

- An unabridged 1993 audio CD recording of *Number the Stars*, published by Recorded Records, is narrated by Christina Moore.

loyalty to the king and to Denmark, and his willingness to die to protect the king. Annemarie feels compelled to vow that she too would be willing to do so.

Chapter 3: Where Is Mrs. Hirsch?

Annemarie describes the way electricity is rationed, and the way her family must now use a little stove installed into the chimney to cook and for heat. Sent on an errand to buy a button from Mrs. Hirsch's shop, Annemarie reports to her mother that the shop is closed and that a German sign with a swastika, the symbol of Nazi Germany, is on the door. Later that evening, after another dinner of potatoes, Annemarie is awakened by her parents and brought into the living room, where Peter Nielsen waits. Peter, her mother, and her father explain that the Nazis are closing Jewish shops and that they will now have to help take care of their Jewish neighbors.

Chapter 4: It Will Be a Long Night

Annemarie and Ellen play with paper dolls, while details about the Nazi occupation filter through this attempt at normalcy. Mrs. Johansen has purchased a new pair of shoes for Kirsti, but the little girl is disgusted that they have been made out of fish skin, as leather is no longer available. Annemarie also remembers the night of Kirsti's birthday, which happened to be the night that Denmark's king destroyed his own naval fleet to avoid the ships being appropriated by the Germans. Mrs. Johansen had told Kirsti that the explosions were fireworks in honor of her birthday. Annemarie is told that Ellen will be spending several days with them, but she deduces that something is wrong. Her father explains that the Nazis have taken lists of names of Jews from the synagogues and are gathering Jews for arrest and relocation. Mr. Johansen goes on, saying, "We don't know even know what that means. We only know that it is wrong, and it is dangerous, and we must help." Peter has taken Mr. and Mrs. Rosen someplace safe, Mr. Johansen informs them, and Ellen is to stay with the Johansens. The girls are told they must behave like sisters if German soldiers question them.

Chapter 5: Who Is the Dark-Haired One?
Ellen and Annemarie nervously chatter that evening, and Ellen shows Annemarie her Star of David necklace before the girls drift off to sleep. Awakened by a pounding on the door, the girls listen as German soldiers question their parents. Ellen desperately tries to remove her necklace before the soldiers enter the bedroom. The clasp is stuck and Annemarie yanks the chain from her friend's neck, clutching it in her fist just as the soldiers enter. The soldiers are suspicious of Ellen, as she has dark hair, unlike her supposed sisters, the blond Annemarie and Kirsti. Ellen identifies herself as Lise Johansen, using the name of Annemarie's dead sister. Mr. Johansen tears pictures from a family album to show the soldiers. One photo is of a dark-haired baby, Lise. The soldiers depart.

Chapter 6: Is the Weather Good for Fishing?
After the soldiers leave, Mrs. Johansen explains to the girls that Lise was born with dark hair, but that it lightened to blond by the time she was two. Considering their options, Mr. and Mrs. Johansen also try to gently reassure Ellen that she and her parents are safe. Annemarie's parents discuss the need to get the girls to safety, but Mr. Johansen initially disagrees with Mrs. Johansen's idea to take the girls to her brother Henrik's house by the sea on her own, while he, Mr. Johansen, remains in Copenhagen to continue going to work and to keep up the appearance of normalcy. Fearful for his family, Mr. Johansen eventually agrees that his wife's plan is their only choice. Mrs. Johansen and the girls take a train to the seaside town where Henrik lives, and Mrs. Johansen is questioned on the train by a Nazi soldier. Having arrived at Uncle

Henrik's, Annemarie, Kirsti, and Ellen enjoy playing in the new, rural location.

Chapter 7: The House by the Sea
Although the children are allowed to romp outside, Mrs. Johansen cautions them against speaking to anyone. "It is too difficult—maybe even dangerous—to explain who Ellen is," she tells the girls. Ellen expresses her longing for her parents and wonders where they might be.

Chapter 8: There Has Been a Death
Annemarie overhears her mother and uncle talking in a peculiar way. They decide it is good weather for fishing, but Annemarie knows that her uncle fishes in any kind of weather and suspects they may be discussing something more serious. Mrs. Johansen informs her brother that she has cleaned the living room and arranged the furniture, preparing it. Annemarie interrupts, wondering what the room has been prepared for. She is told her Great-aunt Birte has died, and her casket will be brought into the living room, so her family can mourn her before the burial. Confused, Annemarie remains silent, certain that she never had a Great-aunt Birte.

Chapter 9: Why Are You Lying?
Annemarie confronts her uncle. He tells her that at times, it is easier to be brave when you do not know everything about a situation. He then confirms that he and Annemarie's mother did lie to her about there being a great aunt who died, but he tells her it is safer if she does not know anything else. Annemarie decides that she will protect Ellen by not telling her about the nonexistent great aunt. When Annemarie's mother describes the people who begin funneling into the home that evening as friends of the great aunt, she and Annemarie exchange glances. Annemarie is certain that her mother knows that she, Annemarie, knows the truth. Ellen's parents are among those who come to Uncle Henrik's that night, and with them is Peter Neilsen. Henrik departs for his fishing boat.

Chapter 10: Let Us Open the Casket
As the group sits quietly, Nazi soldiers soon begin pounding on the door, questioning Mrs. Johansen about the large number of people that has gathered. Mrs. Johansen begins spinning a tale, telling the soldiers that there has been a death in the family. The soldiers advance on

the coffin, wondering why it is not open, knowing that the Danish people customarily have open-casket viewings of the dead prior to burial.

Thinking quickly, Mrs. Johansen agrees with the soldier, insisting suddenly that he is right. She explains that the doctor has told them to keep the casket closed, because the aunt has died of typhus, "and he said that there was a chance the germs would still be there, would be dangerous." Mrs. Johansen goes on, acting as though she will disregard the views of the doctor and open the casket anyway, as custom dictates. When she moves to open it, the Nazi officer slaps Mrs. Johansen's face. He angrily tells her to open it after they leave.

The soldiers depart, but Mrs. Johansen and Peter know that they are probably still being watched. They settle in while Peter begins to read from the bible. The passage he reads indicates the significance of Lowry's title. "It is he [God]," Peter reads, "who heals the broken in spirit and binds up their wounds, he who numbers the stars one by one." Annemarie reflects on this but is not comforted. After what seems to Annemarie to have been a long time, Peter states that they will open the casket.

Chapter 11: Will We See You Again Soon, Peter?

Inside the casket are piles of warm clothing, coats, and blankets. Mrs. Johansen and Peter help distribute the items, and Peter administers a sedative to an infant. Peter gives a packet to Mr. Rosen, with the instruction to give it to Henrik, who is already waiting on his boat. After dividing the parties into two, Peter says goodbye to Annemarie, then leads the first group away.

Chapter 12: Where Was Mama?

The Rosens say goodbye to Annemarie. Ellen promises to return to her friend one day. They hug, and they too depart, led by Mrs. Johansen. Mr. Rosen stumbles on the loose stair on the way out. Annemarie waits anxiously in the dark house for her mother's return. She dozes fitfully, waking just before dawn, and is alarmed to find that her mother has not yet returned. Looking out at the darkened path behind the house, she sees a figure slumped on the ground and realizes it is her mother.

Chapter 13: Run! As Fast As You Can!

Annemarie discovers that her mother has injured, possibly broken, her ankle. Mrs. Johansen is relieved to think that the Rosens and the others will soon be sailing away to safety. On the grass, Annemarie finds the packet that Mr. Rosen was supposed to have delivered to Henrik. It fell from his pocket when he stumbled. Mrs. Johansen is distressed. "It may all have been for nothing," she states, knowing the importance of the packet and the fact that, with her injured ankle, she can never get the packet to her brother in time. Annemarie volunteers to take it. Her mother instructs her to hide the packet beneath a napkin in a basket they then fill with food. Her mother tells her to behave like a silly girl without a care if she is stopped by soldiers.

Chapter 14: On the Dark Path

Annemarie runs swiftly on the wooded path, imagining the fairy tales she used to tell to Kirsti, thinking of herself as Little Red Riding Hood. In this way, she quells her fears enough to proceed. Almost to the harbor, she is stopped by Nazi soldiers patrolling with two growling dogs.

Chapter 15: My Dogs Smell Meat!

Recalling her mother's instructions, Annemarie remembers the way her little sister fearlessly dealt with the Nazi soldiers, and she attempts to be as much like Kirsti as she can. She greets the soldiers and, when asked, tells the men she is taking her forgetful uncle his lunch. As they continue to question her, Annemarie thinks of Kirsti and how she would respond. Attempting to seem as though she has no reason to fear the soldiers, Annemarie chatters aimlessly. The soldier begins to take the food out of the basket, and Annemarie responds angrily and with some impatience as they continue to detain her.

After the soldiers have emptied the basket of food, the dogs continue to strain at it, as if something delicious remains hidden. They remove the napkin that hides the packet, then ask Annemarie what else is in the basket. She responds in a frustrated tone that she does not know, but she really must continue on her way. As Annemarie grows tearful, the soldiers discover that the packet contains a handkerchief. They tell Annemarie to stop crying and to be on her way. Annemarie then makes her way to her uncle's boat. She hands him the torn envelope and the handkerchief, and he assures her that everything is fine.

Chapter 16: I Will Tell You Just a Little

Uncle Henrik praises Annemarie for her bravery and explains to Annemarie the way the Rosens and the other Jewish families were hidden on his boat when she arrived. Annemarie also deduces that Peter is part of the Danish resistance. She marvels at the way all the hidden people were able to remain quiet for so long in a dark, cramped space, even while the boat was searched by soldiers. Henrik then tells Annemarie of the significance of the handkerchief. He explains that, since the Germans have begun using dogs to sniff out the people hidden on the fishing boats, the resistance worked with scientists to develop a drug. It works by attracting the dogs, who sniff the drug on the handkerchief but then lose their sense of smell. Henrik assures Annemarie that everyone made it safely to Sweden.

Chapter 17: All This Long Time

Two years later, the war ends. Annemarie observes the way she and other Danish families have kept up the deserted homes of their Jewish friends, hoping one day they would return safely. She also describes the way her family heard that Peter had died. He was shot after having been captured by the Nazis. Annemarie has also learned the truth about her sister Lise's death, that she too was part of the Danish resistance. After retrieving Ellen's Star of David necklace, Annemarie asks her father to repair it and vows to wear it until her friend returns home.

Afterword

Lowry explains the factual basis for the novel, discussing the historical facts she incorporated into her novel. She reviews the circumstances surrounding King Christian's surrender and notes that he did destroy his own navy. Lowry informs the reader that nearly seven thousand Danish Jews were smuggled to Sweden, nearly the whole Jewish population of Denmark. The use of the drug-laced handkerchief by the resistance and their supporters is also historically accurate, Lowry points out, explaining that the substance was a mixture of powdered rabbit's blood (to attract the dogs) and cocaine (to temporarily destroy the dogs' sense of smell).

CHARACTERS

Henrik

Henrik, also called Uncle Henrik, is Inge Johansen's brother and Annemarie's uncle. He plays a major role in the Danish resistance. As a fisherman, he has a boat large enough to hide and transport Danish Jews across an inlet of the Baltic Sea to Sweden. Inge jokes often with her brother about his untidiness and how he needs a wife. Once Annemarie, her sister Ellen, and her mother come to stay with Henrik, he talks to Annemarie about bravery and helps her understand the need for secrecy and the seriousness of the Nazi efforts to capture the Jews. After he opens his home to the escaping Danish Jews, including the Rosens, and helps secure their freedom, Henrik provides Annemarie with more information on how their operation was accomplished and praises her for her courage. In the absence of Annemarie's father, who has remained in Copenhagen, Henrik serves as a father figure to Annemarie, offering her guidance and protection.

Mrs. Hirsch

Mrs. Hirsh, a Jewish shopkeeper, does not appear in the story, but Annemarie is instructed to go to her shop, where she sells sewing notions, to buy a button. Annemarie finds the shop closed, with a German sign on the door. Later, Peter informs Annemarie and her family that the Nazis have ordered that Jewish shops be closed. This incident inspires Annemarie to declare that "all of Denmark must be bodyguard for the Jews."

Annemarie Johansen

Annemarie Johansen is the protagonist of the story; the novel is told in the third person from her perspective. A bright ten-year-old girl, Annemarie seeks increasingly greater inclusion in the world of her parents. She questions them about the war, the army and the aims of Nazi Germany, and the politics of her own country's response to the war. Annemarie fears for her friend Ellen after Ellen's parents go into hiding and Ellen is left with the Johansens. She watches with both trepidation and pride her parents' efforts to aid and protect their Jewish friends.

Annemarie exhibits her courage at various points throughout the novel, although she fears being called upon to be brave. She clutches

Ellen's Star of David in her hand while being questioned by Nazi soldiers. The biggest test of her courage comes when she must deliver the packet Peter has instructed Mr. Rosen to give to Henrik. Unbeknownst to him, Mr. Rosen dropped the packet before leaving Henrik's house. Annemarie discovers it after helping her injured mother back to the house. She offers to take the packet to her uncle. Knowing that lives depend upon Annemarie's success, her mother allows Annemarie to go.

On her journey through the dark woods, Annemarie uses her imagination to overcome her fears, stepping into the role of Little Red Riding Hood as she might have told the tale to Kirsti. Knowing that the only way she will fool the Nazi soldiers is by acting silly and unafraid, Annemarie attempts to behave the way Kirsti would have and manages to talk her way through the encounter with the soldiers and their snarling dogs and make it to her uncle's boat before it is searched. The novel ends with Annemarie awaiting the return of her friend Ellen Rosen after the war's end.

Inge Johansen

Inge Johnson, also referred to in the story as Mrs. Johansen or Mama, is the mother of Annemarie, Kirsti, and the deceased Lise. She is the wife of Mr. Johansen. Throughout the novel she strives to teach her children about loyalty to one's friends and neighbors, yet she also seeks to protect her children from danger and knowledge about the evils the Nazis are perpetrating against the Jews. At great risk to her own family, she and her husband take in the daughter of their Jewish friends, the Rosens, treat her as their own, and deliver her to the relative safety of the seaside village where Inge's brother lives. From there, Inge becomes instrumental in helping the Rosens and other Jewish families escape to Sweden. She demonstrates her quick intelligence and bravery in responding to the questioning of Nazi soldiers. After injuring her ankle on her return trip to her brother's house from the fishing boat where she has delivered the Rosens, Inge must rely on her daughter to deliver the packet that will mean the difference between life and death for the escaping Jews.

Kirsten (Kirsti) Johansen

Kirsten Johansen, known affectionately as Kirsti, is the five-year-old daughter of Mr. and Mrs. Johansen. Kirsti has no fear of the Nazi soldiers. Not only has she lived with their presence in her city for most of her life, she has no understanding, at her young age, of the danger they represent. She speaks defiantly to them when two soldiers confront her sister and Ellen on the street and, in doing so, provides Annemarie with a model for dealing with the soldiers later in the novel.

Lise Johansen

Lise Johansen does not appear in the story. She was Annemarie and Kirsti's older sister. She was eighteen and engaged to be married to Peter Nielsen. Annemarie was always told that Lise was struck accidentally by a car and killed but later discovers that, like Peter, Lise was part of the Danish resistance and was, in fact, killed by Nazis.

Mr. Johansen

Mr. Johansen is Inge's husband and father to Annemarie and Kirsti (and the deceased Lise). He credits Annemarie with having the maturity to handle information about the war, the Nazis, and what he knows about their intentions toward the Jews. He seeks to teach his daughter loyalty toward the country, the king, and their Jewish neighbors.

Nazi Soldiers

Several groups of Nazi soldiers appear in the novel. Unknown individually to Annemarie, except for the soldier she has nicknamed "Giraffe" for his long neck, the men represent a collective enemy to the Danish population. Annemarie, Kirsti, and Ellen encounter a pair of soldiers who question them in the street. Another group of soldiers bursts into the Johansen home after the family has taken in Ellen. Mrs. Johansen is questioned on the train by another pair of soldiers. At Henrik's house, a group of soldiers enters and interrogates Mrs. Johansen about the casket in the living room and the reason for the gathering of people; one of the soldiers strikes Mrs. Johansen. The final confrontation between a Danish character and Nazi soldiers occurs when Annemarie is stopped by soldiers with dogs on her way to deliver the important packet containing the drug-laced handkerchief to her uncle Henrik. This incident is perhaps the most tense of all such similar confrontations in the novel, because Annemarie faces the men alone.

Peter Nielsen

Peter Nielsen was the fiancé of Lise Johansen before her death. He plays an important role in the Danish resistance, an organization dedicated to thwarting the aims of the Nazis. He treats Annemarie kindly, joking with her the way he would have done had he actually been able to become her brother-in-law. Peter is instrumental in keeping Mr. and Mrs. Rosen safe, in reuniting them with Ellen, and in securing the Rosen family's escape on board Henrik's fishing boat. He is also credited with working with the Danish scientists in developing the powder applied to the handkerchiefs; the substance temporarily destroys the dogs' sense of smell and hence their ability to locate the Jews hiding on board fishing vessels. Peter is captured by the Nazis and shot before the war's end. Before his execution, Peter writes to the Johansens, in hopes that they can have him buried next to Lise, but they are unable to fulfill that request.

Ellen Rosen

Ellen Rosen is the daughter of Sophy and Mr. Rosen and the best friend of Annemarie Johansen. After being left in the Johansens' care, Ellen attempts to quell her fears and enjoy her time with Annemarie, yet she understands the danger she is in. She shows Annemarie her Star of David necklace and is later unable to remove it when the Nazi soldiers enter the Johansen home. Annemarie snatches it from Ellen's neck just in time and subsequently hides it. Accompanying Mrs. Johansen and her daughters to the seaside village where Henrik leaves, Ellen experiences a way of life previously unknown to her, as she has never before left the city. She enjoys time with her friend, running outside, wading in the sea, and exploring. At the same time, she and Annemarie are cautioned against speaking to anyone, reminding them that, even here, they are in danger of exposing themselves to the Nazis. Ellen is reunited with her parents one night when Peter brings them to Henrik's home in preparation for their escape. Before departing, Ellen promises Annemarie she will one day return.

Mr. Rosen

Mr. Rosen is Ellen's father and Sophy Rosen's husband. He flees with his wife under the protection of the Danish resistance and is reunited with his daughter at Henrik's home.

From there, they escape together in Henrik's boat and are delivered to freedom in Sweden. Mr. Rosen is entrusted with a valuable packet Peter has instructed him to deliver to Henrik, but Mr. Rosen places it in his coat pocket, and when he stumbles, the packet falls out, and he unknowingly leaves it behind.

Sophy Rosen

Sophy Rosen is Ellen's mother and Mr. Rosen's wife. She is also Inge Johansen's close friend, and the women meet often and discuss the war, among other topics. Sophy invites the Johansens to celebrate the Jewish New Year with her family, but the plan is thwarted when the Rosens learn that the Nazis are arresting Danish Jews and taking them away to an unknown fate. Leaving Ellen with the Johansens where they hope she will be safe, Sophy and her husband go into hiding with the help of Peter and the Danish resistance. She is later reunited with her daughter, and the family escapes to Sweden together.

THEMES

Courage

A number of acts of great courage are depicted in *Number the Stars*, and the notion of courage is something Annemarie contemplates often. When Annemarie learns about Mrs. Hirsch's shop closing and that the Nazis plan to close many Jewish stores, Annemarie worries about what will happen to her Jewish neighbors. Her mother answers by telling her, "Friends will take care of them. . . . That's what friends do." This prompts Annemarie's declaration that the citizens of Denmark must protect the Jews. That night, Annemarie considers whether or not she is fully prepared to make the sacrifices she spoke of.

Still living in a world of childhood stories, Annemarie thinks, "It was only in the fairy tales that people were called upon to be so brave, to die for one another. Not in real-life Denmark." Allowing that soldiers and people in the resistance movement must be brave and sometimes die, Annemarie still insists to herself such acts are not those that "ordinary people," would be required to make and thinks how glad she is to be such an ordinary person, one "who would never be called upon for courage." However,

TOPICS FOR FURTHER STUDY

- A 1998 television movie, *Miracle at Midnight* features a Danish family who aids the resistance movement against Nazi Germany during World War II. A DVD of the film was released by Walt Disney Video in 2004. Based on a true story of the Koster family, the film visually dramatizes events similar to those that Lowry covers in her novel. With a small group, watch the film and compare it to Lowry's novel. How does the movie treat the violence of the war, a topic Lowry largely skirts? What is the overall tone of the film? Does it focus on the rescue of the Jews and hope for the future? Or is it a bleaker approach to the topic? Create an online blog in which you and your classmates discuss these issues and your personal responses to both the film and Lowry's novel.

- Targeted at the same young-adult audience as *Number the Stars*, Yoshiko Uchida's 2004 novel, *Journey to Topaz*, is similarly set during World War II. Uchida's novel, however, focuses on an eleven-year-old Japanese American girl who, along with her family, is sent to live in a Japanese internment camp in Utah after the Japanese army bombed Pearl Harbor in 1941. Read *Journey to Topaz* and consider the experiences of Yuki before and after her relocation to the camp. Write an essay in which you either analyze the plot, character, structure, themes, and style of Uchida's book or compare these elements with those in Lowry's novel. Consider in particular the way Yuki, or Yuki and Annemarie, both of similar ages, respond to the war and the tragedy that surrounds them.

- Using print and online resources, research the history of the Danish resistance movement in Denmark during World War II. Who were some of the key figures of the resistance movement? How did German officers and officials react to the movement? Detail the ways in which the resistance members helped the Danish Jews escape, and discuss the other activities of the movement, before and after the rescue of the Jewish population. Write a research paper in which you include a bibliography of your sources.

- Offering an alternative perspective to that provided by Lowry's novel, Christa Blum Mercer's young-adult memoir, *German War Child: Growing Up in World War II*, published in 2004, chronicles the author's life as a German youth during the war. Similarly, Wolfgang W. E. Samuel collects the stories of dozens of individuals who, like him, were children in Germany during the war. His 2002 collection, *The War of Our Childhood: Memories of World War II*, details the experiences of fear and suffering that Germans endured during the war years and immediately after. Select one of these works and consider the way the individual or individuals' views on Hitler were reshaped as the war progressed. How were the lives of these children and their families affected by the war? Create a Web page in which you display a time line of the major events and battles of World War II, and present an essay discussing the way Mercer or the children in Samuel's work responded to Hitler and his war effort in the early months of the conflict, during the war years, and after. Consider the knowledge the children had about Hitler's treatment of European Jews and how the children and their families were viewed and treated by the Allied forces occupying Germany after the war.

The Johansen family tries to save a Jewish girl, Ellen, pretending that Ellen is Annemarie's older sister.
(Zurijeta | Shutterstock.com)

Annemarie must be increasingly brave in order to help protect her friend Ellen and Ellen's family. When Ellen comes to stay with the Johansens, Annemarie bravely clutches the Star of David necklace she has ripped from Ellen's neck at the last minute, when Ellen could not undo the clasp. Indeed, it was Annemarie who realized that the necklace would have to be removed in the first place.

Later, Annemarie's Uncle Henrik discusses bravery with her, when she asks about the lie he and her mother have told about the dead great aunt who does not exist. Her uncle asks her how brave she considers herself to be. Annemarie grows uncomfortable: "It was a question she did not want to be asked. When she asked it of herself, she didn't like her own answer." Such thoughts prompt Annemarie to admit that she does not consider herself to be very brave at all. Henrik disagrees and compares Annemarie favorably with her parents and himself, describing them all as "frightened, but determined." He is certain that, if Annemarie needs to be brave, she will rise to the occasion.

After Annemarie volunteers to deliver the packet to Henrik and is confronted by the Nazi soldiers and their dogs, her uncle praises her as being brave and acknowledges that she risked her life. Annemarie describes how frightened she was and tells her uncle that she did not even think about the danger she herself faced. Henrik replies, "That's all that *brave* means—not thinking about the dangers. Just thinking about what you must do." Annemarie was thinking about her friends and the obvious importance of the packet, even though she knew not what it contained. Henrik goes on to explain the importance of the handkerchief that she successfully delivered, and Annemarie thinks about what would have happened if she had not spotted the packet on the ground or made it through the woods and passed the soldiers.

She begs her uncle for reassurance that her friends are now safe in Sweden. "You're sure?" she asks. Annemarie thinks of Ellen, and whether she will ever see her again, and as the book ends, she puts on Ellen's necklace to wait for her friend's return, after the war has ended.

Throughout the novel, Lowry explores the relationship between friendship and courage and demonstrates, through the Rosens and the Johansens, that friendship inspires courage.

Coming of Age

Number the Stars is, in many ways, about Annemarie's journey from childhood toward adulthood, from innocence to experience. Such a journey is often referred to as "coming of age." As Annemarie's knowledge of the Nazi plans for the Jews develops, Annemarie grows increasingly fearful of what lies ahead, for Denmark, for her Jewish friends, and for her own family. She wonders whether she is truly prepared to die to protect Denmark's Jews. Depicting Annemarie's struggle, Lowry writes, "Annemarie was honest enough to admit, there in the darkness, to herself, that she wasn't sure." Later, when Annemarie becomes complicit in her mother's lie about the death of the fictional Great-aunt Birte, Annemarie supposes that because her mother has acknowledged with a glance Annemarie's understanding of the lie and its importance, "in that moment, with that look, they became equals."

Annemarie's journey toward maturity is just beginning. Even so, she comprehends that Peter has evolved from the freckle-faced boy who was to marry her sister into a man. When Peter calls Annemarie's mother by her first name, Inge, Annemarie is startled. The act forces her to see Peter in a new light. "It was as if he had moved beyond his own youth and had taken his place in the world of adults." Although Annemarie has no knowledge of Peter's experiences, she understands, as her mother "waited for his instructions," that Mrs. Johansen now regarded Peter as an equal. Through Annemarie's act of bravery, by facing the Nazi soldiers on her own and delivering the mysterious packet to her uncle, Annemarie becomes a part of the resistance and takes another step in the journey away from childhood and toward independence and adulthood.

STYLE

Symbolism

In *Number the Stars*, Lowry incorporates the use of the Star of David as a symbol associated with Judaism as well as the biblical reference to stars in the passage read by Peter. According to Joyce Eisenberg and Ellen Scolnic in *The JPS Dictionary of Jewish Words*, the Star of David, a six-pointed star that appears as two overlapping triangles, became the official seal of the Jews in the Middle Ages. During World War II, the Nazis forced Jewish people to wear a yellow Star of David so that they could be easily identified.

Ellen wears a Star of David necklace, marking her as a Jew. Notably, this pendant was given to her by her father, Ellen tells Annemarie. She has not been forced to wear it as an outward sign of her faith and heritage, as Jews in Germany and elsewhere have been. The yellow emblem the Nazis forced Jews to wear led to their persecution. Ellen, however, wears hers as a source of pride, but Annemarie is aware of how dangerous the symbol has become, and she tears it from Ellen's neck before the Nazi soldiers see it. Annemarie later wears the necklace herself as a symbol of friendship and loyalty, as she waits for Ellen to return after the war.

The symbol of the star is invoked once again when Peter reads a passage from the Bible, in Psalms 147. "It is he," Peter reads, referring to God, "who heals the broken in spirit and binds up their wounds, he who numbers the stars one by one." Annemarie contemplates this idea, thinking that there were too many stars for anyone to count, and that the sky that held them was too large. She recalls something Ellen said, that her mother feared the ocean because it "was too cold and too big." Annemarie feels the same way about the sky, and in her fear, this idea becomes amplified. "The whole *world* was: too cold, too big. And too cruel," she thinks.

Far from being reassured by the passage, by the notion of a God who knows each star individually, Annemarie does not regard the stars as a symbol for people, as the anonymous author of the Psalm was perhaps implying. She does not derive peace from thinking of a God who knows each person individually and is perhaps watching over them. In her thoughts, Annemarie has linked the notion of a star-filled sky with that of the sea, regarding both entities as vast, cold, and cruel. Later, however, the sea is the path to salvation and freedom for the Danish Jews, for they are transported by the sea to Sweden. The sea and the stars, symbols with previously negative connotations for Annemarie, transform into symbols of hope.

Historical Realism

Lowry's novel combines fictional characters with historical events. The comments on the accuracy of these historical features in the afterword section of the novel explain which features of the story were purely from her imagination and which were rooted in historical fact. Into the fictional Annemarie's story, Lowry incorporates the facts of Denmark's 1940 surrender to Germany, the Danish destruction of its own navy, and the warning Danish Jews received from their rabbis to flee before they were arrested by the Germans. Lowry states that a high-ranking German official, at much personal risk, informed the Danish government of the German plan to arrest Jews based on lists maintained by synagogues. The smuggling of the majority of the Danish Jewish population across the sea and into Sweden is also a historically accurate feature of the novel. Similarly, Lowry explains, the Danish resistance movement did use handkerchiefs laced with rabbit's blood and cocaine to prevent the German dogs from discovering the Jews hidden on board ships. The use of real historical facts in the novel solidifies its authenticity and provides readers with an accurate sense of the time period covered by the novel.

Third-Person Limited Point of View

Number the Stars is told from Annemarie's point of view and is recounted in the third person. This means that Annemarie does not refer to herself as "I," as she would if the story were told in the first person. Rather, an unidentified narrator, who is not a character in the novel, relates the events and refers to Annemarie and the other characters in the novel by their names or through such pronouns as "she" and "he." However, the narrator's storytelling is restricted to Annemarie's perspective. This type of narrative technique is referred to as limited point of view. By contrast, some third-person novels employ an omniscient point of view, in which the novel's narrator can take the perspective of any number of characters and share a variety of thoughts and points of view with the reader. By limiting the narration of the story to Annemarie's viewpoint, Lowry emphasizes Annemarie's youth and innocence and allows young adult readers a perspective to which they can relate.

HISTORICAL CONTEXT

World War II and the Occupation of Denmark

In 1939, Germany, under the leadership of Adolf Hitler, began World War II through its invasion of Poland on September 1. In response, Great Britain and France declared war on Germany on September 3. Weeks later, Poland was defeated, by both the Germans and the Soviets, with whom Germany had a mutual non-aggression pact. Within months, on April 9, 1940, Germany invaded Norway and Denmark. The Danish government surrendered quickly to Hitler's forces, hoping to avoid massive casualties in open warfare. Initially, despite the presence of German soldiers, life in occupied Denmark was not drastically different from pre-occupation times. By 1942, the deprivations of the war began to be felt by Danish citizens. Fuel was scarce, food was rationed. German soldiers became increasingly less tolerant of any signs of opposition. Germany had taken control of the Danish government by 1943.

Meanwhile, Italy had joined the war as an ally of Germany in 1940. Also that year, the Nazis engaged in an air war over England, known as the Battle of Britain, and occupied northern France after France and Germany signed an armistice treaty. Violating their pact with the Soviets, the Germans invaded the Soviet Union in 1941. The United States entered the war in 1941 after Japan, also allied with Germany, bombed Pearl Harbor, in Hawaii. In 1942 and 1943, the Allied forces (Great Britain, the United States, and France) assaulted German forces in Germany and Northern Africa. At the same time, the Germans maintained their offensive against the Soviet Union, but the Soviets ultimately prevailed in the Soviet city of Stalingrad.

With Italy supporting Germany as well, Italy became the target of attack by the Allied forces, led by U.S. troops in 1943. Although Hitler's ally, Italian Prime Minister Benito Mussolini, surrendered to British and American forces, German troops continued to maintain control of northern Italy. In 1944, Allied forces liberated France and began to invade Germany from the west. On the eastern front, Soviets invaded German as well. Western Poland was liberated by the Soviets in 1945, and Hungary, a German ally, surrendered. Allied forces continued to assault the Germany army, and in

COMPARE
&
CONTRAST

- **1940s:** King Christian X is the ruler of Denmark at the time of its invasion by the German army. Under pressure from the Germans, the Danish government (including the prime minister and cabinet members) and King Christian resign. The Germans institute a military regime. After the war, the government returns to power and King Christian rules until his death in 1947.

  1980s: Queen Margrethe II has ruled Denmark since 1972, when she ascended to the monarchy following the death of her father Frederick IX, who was the son of King Christian X.

  Today: The Danish government, a constitutional monarchy, continues to be ruled by Queen Margrethe II. Although the role of the queen is largely ceremonial, her government's legislation still requires her signature before it is made law. The governing body in Denmark consists of a single-chamber parliament known as the Folketing, led by Prime Minister Lars Loekke Rasmussen.

- **1940s:** In German-occupied Denmark, schools remain open and Danish children, Christian and Jewish alike, continue to attend, although under the watchful eyes of German soldiers. In 1943, when the Germans begin seeking out Jews for arrest and deportation, Jewish children are no longer able to attend Danish schools.

  1980s: The Danish government extends educational funding to rural education and higher education, and a corresponding increase in university enrollment occurs. Children are required to attend school from age seven through fourteen. The government additionally provides limited support to specialized private schools.

  Today: Public education in Denmark is required from age seven through sixteen. Education is free in Denmark through the university level.

- **1940s:** About 7,500 Danish Jews reside in Denmark prior to the German occupation in 1940. They are smuggled out of Denmark to Sweden by their countrymen when the Nazis begin searching for Jews. About 120 Danish Jews die during the Holocaust, and most Danish Jews return to their home after the war.

  1980s: Jews entering Denmark in the 1980s are immune from the nationalism felt by some Danes during this time and are welcomed as fellow Danes. It is estimated that there are between 6,000 and 7,000 Jews living in Denmark.

  Today: There are an estimated 8,000 Jews living in Denmark. Most reside in the city of Copenhagen.

1945, Hitler committed suicide. Shortly after, the German army surrendered to the Allied forces. Japan surrendered later that year after the United States dropped two atomic bombs on the Japanese cities of Hiroshima and Nagasaki. Only after that final horrific act did the war come to an end.

Danish Resistance Movement

When the Germans invaded Denmark, approximately 7,500 Jews lived there. The Danish government and the Danish Lutheran Church had, to this time, insured a peaceful existence for Jews due to policies instituting social equality and religious tolerance. At the onset of the German occupation, the Jews were largely ignored by the German soldiers. In 1943, the Danish government resigned after the German army demanded that German military courts be used to try individuals attempting to sabotage the German war effort. Such saboteurs were in fact members of the Danish resistance

The Star of David, a major Jewish symbol, is on Ellen's necklace. *(Odelia Cohen / Shutterstock.com)*

movement and were involved in civil resistance through an illegal newspaper. Resistance acts also included bombings of German facilities, labor strikes, and railway sabotage.

Martial law (rule by the military) was declared in Denmark immediately after the resignation of the Danish government. Efforts then ensued to use the newly established military government to begin deporting Danish Jews. German General Werner Best, who had initially proposed the deportation effort, began to question the political wisdom of the deportation of the Jews. Unable to halt Hitler's agenda where the Jews were concerned, General Best informed German naval attaché Ferdinand Duckwitz about the impending arrests and deportation of Jews. Duckwitz and other German officials got word, through non-Jewish Danes, to the Danish Jewish community about the horror that was about to ensue. A massive effort by resistance members and their supporters was then initiated to move Jews into hiding and then transport them to the coast, where they were ferried by Danish fisherman to the neutral country of Sweden. The vast majority of Danish Jews were

rescued from Nazi arrest in this fashion through the heroic efforts of the Danish resistance movement and its supporters throughout Denmark.

CRITICAL OVERVIEW

Despite an initially negative assessment, *Number the Stars* is counted among the works that helped solidify Lowry's critical reputation. In a 1993 review of one of Lowry's later works, Karen Ray notes that it is Lowry's "haunting and unpredictable serious novels," including *Number the Stars*, "that help make her work so rewarding." However, upon the publication of *Number the Stars* in 1989, *New York Times Book Review* critic Edith Milton harshly scorned the book's failure "to offer . . . any sense of the horror that is the alternative if the Johansens' efforts to save Ellen and her family fail." She goes on to note that Annemarie's "innocent viewpoint keeps us at too great a distance to see clearly either the scale of the evil or the magnitude of the courage from which the story springs."

After Lowry received the 1990 Newbery Award for the novel, it quickly became incorporated into school curricula and used as a teaching tool, a springboard for historical discussions on the Holocaust and World War II. June Cummins observes, in a review article in *MELUS*, that *Number the Stars* and Jane Yolen's Holocaust novel, *The Devil's Arithmetic*, "have achieved canonical status."

Other critics have assessed *Number the Stars* within the context of young-adult Holocaust literature. Elizabeth Goodenough and Andrea Immel, editors of *Under Fire: Childhood in the Shadow of War*, state in their introduction to their work that

> while Lowry deals more indirectly with the Holocaust than novels set in German or Polish concentration camps, she avoids privatizing the public sphere through the banalization of trauma and asserts the importance of collective memory and will.

In an essay in *Under Fire: Childhood in the Shadow of War*, Maria Tatar examines Lowry's use of fairy tale motifs in *Number the Stars*, stating that, in this novel, as in some other Holocaust novels, "it is a fairy-tale heroine who is invoked as a model of courageous action and shrewd behavior." Tatar goes on to discuss the way Annemarie imagines herself both as Little Red Writing Hood and as her sillier, younger sister, asserting that Annemarie's tale "shows how children can...draw on the wisdom of fairy tales to inspire confidence and lay claim to real agency in a situation that leaves even adults powerless."

CRITICISM

Catherine Dominic

Dominic is a novelist and freelance writer and editor. In the following essay, she explores Lowry's treatment of loss and sacrifice, particularly as endured by parents, in the novel Number the Stars.

In Lowry's *Number the Stars*, the notion of suffering, sacrifice, and loss plays a prominent role. The reader sees the daily examples of deprivations suffered by the Danish citizens during the war, but as the novel progresses, Lowry depicts the much graver sacrifices parents make in the story. Written as a young-adult novel, Lowry is careful to omit the details concerning

> ALTHOUGH THE EXISTENCE OF DANGER IS UNDERSCORED, THE DETAILS THEMSELVES ARE PURPOSEFULLY UNCLEAR. HOWEVER, IN SUBTLE WAYS, LOWRY MAKES PLAIN THE DEVASTATION AND SORROW OF THE WAR, USING THE CHARACTER OF INGE JOHANSEN TO EMBODY A NOTION OF SACRIFICE THAT ONLY MORE MATURE READERS ARE LIKELY TO FULLY COMPREHEND."

the fate of many Jews during World War II. Although the existence of danger is underscored, the details themselves are purposefully unclear. However, in subtle ways, Lowry makes plain the devastation and sorrow of the war, using the character of Inge Johansen to embody a notion of sacrifice that only more mature readers are likely to fully comprehend.

As the novel opens, the presence of Nazi soldiers on the streets of Copenhagen immediately thrusts the reader into a time and place where danger lingers at every corner. Innocently racing through the streets of their city, Annemarie and Ellen are stopped and questioned by the soldiers. One prods his rifle at Annemarie's backpack and then strokes Kirsti's hair. All three girls understand these actions to be violations, and they all are aware of the curtailing of their personal freedom. Other wartime deprivations are depicted once the girls return to the Johansens' apartment. Their mothers, who in the past have enjoyed the ritual of having coffee together, still cling to the idea of coffee-drinking as a therapeutic social activity, yet the women now only have hot water mixed with herbs to drink.

Later, Annemarie is frustrated by yet another meal consisting only of potatoes. Kirsti longs for cupcakes with pink frosting, while her mother points out that sugar and butter belong to another time, to pre-occupation Denmark. Furthermore, the apartment is cold, and dark. Electricity is rationed; heat is distributed only by the small stove placed Mr. Johansen has placed in the chimney. The children keep warm at night by snuggling together, and Annemarie says that

WHAT DO I READ NEXT?

- Lowry is well known for her collection of dystopian fantasy novels, including *The Giver* (1993), *Gathering Blue* (2000), and *The Messenger* (2004). *The Giver* is counted among Lowry's best works, and like *Number the Stars*, it won a Newbery Medal. The three books were published as a boxed collection in 2006.

- Ellen Levine's *Darkness Over Denmark: The Danish Resistance and the Rescue of the Jews* (2000) is a young-adult nonfiction resource that provides detailed historical information on the German occupation of Denmark and the Danish resistance movement.

- *Girl with the White Flag*, by Tomiko Higa, is a memoir of Higa's experience as a child during World War II. When she was seven years old, Higa witnessed the death of her brother and was separated from her sisters. She subsequently wandered through war-ravaged Okinawa for seven weeks until she was eventually taken under the care of an elderly, handicapped couple. The young-adult work was published in 1992.

- In Jane Yolen's young-adult novel *The Devil's Arithmetic* (1990), a twelve-year-old girl is transported back in time to a Polish village during World War II, where she witnesses the horrors of the war and the Holocaust that her elderly family members repeatedly recount.

- Originally published in 1982 and republished in 2001, Yehuda Bauer's *A History of the Holocaust* is a resource aimed at older or more mature students. The author provides a history of Jewish persecution before discussing the experience of Jews in World War II.

- *Home Front U.S.A.: America during World War II*, by Allan Winkler, was published in 1986 and republished in 2000. Winkler offers an overview of the changes in American life that evolved during the course of the war years and specifically explores the experiences of Jewish Americans, African Americans, and Japanese Americans during this time.

- The Holocaust classic, *The Diary of Anne Frank*, was published in a revised, critical edition in 2003. In addition to the original story, this edition contains a comparison of the three versions of the diary that have been used throughout the years. Biographical information on the family is provided to help understand Anne's perspectives, and a summary of the critical events that took place surrounding the arrest helps add to understanding of this tragic story.

---

her friend Ellen has no sister to help keep her warm at night. Annemarie is also aware that members of the Danish resistance sometimes die in their attempts to sabotage the German army, but she does not associate such deaths with the lives of "ordinary people."

However, the notion of sacrifice soon comes to take on increased significance. Although Annemarie is initially told that Mr. and Mrs. Rosen must go stay with relatives, despite the fact that the Rosens and the Johansens had plans to celebrate the Jewish New Year together, she soon learns the truth: the Nazis have plans to arrest all the Danish Jews and take them away. Mr. Johansen does not offer details, stating only that no one knows where the Jews will be taken or why they are being taken. He emphasizes, however, "that it is wrong, and it is dangerous." Ellen sobs while Annemarie asks about Ellen's parents. Mr. Johansen informs his daughter that they are only able to hide Ellen and that Peter has taken Mr. and Mrs. Rosen to safety. Mr. Johansen tries to reassure Ellen that her parents are safe, but her distress is apparent, as is Annemarie's. As the girls prepare to go to bed, they talk of death, Annemarie's sister Lise's death, and Ellen guesses at the danger her family is in: "I wouldn't want the Germans to take my family away—to make us live someplace else. But still, it wouldn't be as bad as being dead."

Here, the notion of a parent's sacrifice, although not fully understood by Annemarie, is touched on. Although guided by Peter and the resistance, and their views on how best to keep the entire Rosen family safe, Mr. and Mrs. Rosen have been forced to decide that leaving their daughter in the care of another family is best. They must consider the fact that they might never see her again and are forced to be prepared to sacrifice their relationship with her. Their actions suggest their willingness to sacrifice their own lives to keep their daughter safe. Had they all gone into hiding together, they likely would have been in greater danger. As Mr. Johansen states, "We couldn't take all three of them. If the Germans came to search our apartment, it would be clear that the Rosens were here. One person we can hide. Not three." For the Rosens to decide to separate from their daughter at such a time must have been an excruciatingly difficult sacrifice to make.

Soon, the Johansens are forced to make their own difficult decisions. Like the Rosens, they too must separate. Mrs. Johansen must take the children away from Copenhagen to the relative safety of the fishing village in which her brother lives. Mr. Johansen must stay behind. Traveling together, they would arouse suspicion, something they cannot afford when entrusted with the care of Ellen. When Mrs. Johansen states that she will take the children by herself, Mr. Johansen is surprised and fearful: "Stay here and let you go alone? Of course not. I wouldn't send you on a dangerous trip alone." As a husband and father, his instinct is to be with his family, to protect them. Mrs. Johansen points out that they will be safer if separated. Annemarie is acutely aware, as she watches her father, that, however right her mother may be, her father agonizes over the decision to let them go without him. Knowing the dangers his wife will face, Mr. Johansen must sacrifice his need to protect his family, must cut himself off from the family, however temporarily, in order to help ensure their survival. As the girls and Mrs. Johansen journey to Henrik's village, Ellen's dark hair once again brings the family under scrutiny, as it did the night the soldiers entered their home. Mrs. Johansen is

subsequently questioned on the train by Nazi soldiers, and these events underscore the danger the family faces.

Once Mrs. Johansen and the girls arrive at Henrik's, she, her brother, and the resistance members begin to make plans to smuggle the Rosens and other Jews to Sweden via Henrik's fishing boat. Annemarie becomes involved when Henrik confides a little of the truth to her: the dead great-aunt is a fiction. Sitting with the Rosens and the other so-called mourners who have gathered around the casket, Annemarie begins to see the way her relationship with Ellen is being sacrificed. She understands that, although "the bond of their friendship had not broken," something had shifted, "as if Ellen had moved now into a different world, the world of her own family and whatever lay ahead for them." Soon, Nazis arrive but find nothing suspicious upon which they can act, because of Mrs. Johansen's quick thinking. Although her efforts earn her a blow from one of the soldiers, she prevents them from opening the casket. Annemarie witnesses another loss, that of her mother's personal safety. The night is filled with loss for Annemarie, as she says goodbye to her friend and to her almost-brother, Peter.

When Mrs. Johansen stumbles home in the dark after escorting the Rosens to Henrik's boat, she realizes she must make an agonizing decision. Annemarie finds the packet that Mr. Rosen has dropped. Peter had stressed that it was vitally important to deliver the packet to Henrik. Mrs. Johansen's ankle is likely broken, and it is nearly dawn. Her mother's dismay at seeing the undelivered packet is distressing to Annemarie, who volunteers to take the packet herself. Mrs. Johansen, without hesitation, urgently instructs her daughter on how to hide the packet in a basket under some food. She will pretend she is taking her uncle his lunch. "Annemarie," her mother implores, "you understand how dangerous this is." The exchange happens quickly. Before the reader can pause to consider and assess Mrs. Johansen's position, Annemarie is running through the woods, and the reader embarks on this frightening journey with her.

Mrs. Johansen, however, possesses knowledge that has not yet been divulged to Annemarie, or to the reader for that matter. Lise, Mrs. Johansen's eldest daughter, did not die by being hit accidentally by a car, as Annemarie has been told. In truth, the car was

Psalms 147 comments that God has numbered all the stars in the sky. (*Viktar Malyshchyts | Shutterstock.com*)

driven by Nazis. Lise was killed by the Nazis for her involvement in the Danish resistance movement. The reader will later learn that Peter divulged this information to Mr. and Mrs. Johansen after Lise's death. In the space between Annemarie's volunteering to deliver the packet and Mrs. Johansen's response, Mrs. Johansen must be considering the fact that she has already lost one daughter to the resistance. Now, she may be knowingly making that same sacrifice, that ultimate, horrific sacrifice once again.

Mrs. Johansen, as an adult who reads the resistance newspaper, who has greater knowledge of the war and what the Nazis are capable of than her daughter, has just sent her daughter Annemarie into a situation that could possibly end in her daughter's death. If Mrs. Johansen knows what is in the packet, perhaps she supposes that the Nazis will do Annemarie no harm for carrying a handkerchief and a basket of food. However, given the fact that she instructs Annemarie on how to carefully hide the packet and on how to act like a "silly, empty-headed little girl," it seems likely that Mrs. Johansen is

aware of what the packet contains, particularly when Henrik has repeatedly emphasized the importance of knowing as little as possible when involved in such activities. In the event that the packet held documents that alluded to the activities of the resistance, Annemarie could have been taken away for questioning, or worse. She could even have been killed on the spot. Knowing these risks, Mrs. Johansen only tells her daughter to pretend to know nothing and to hurry.

Only Mrs. Johansen's comment upon Annemarie's discovery of the packet alludes to the only possibly reason she would have sent her daughter into such obvious danger. "My God," she states. "It may all have been for nothing." Her words suggest that the Rosens and the other Jews that have escaped to Henrik's boat may in fact be in mortal peril themselves unless the packet is delivered. As the story progresses, the reader learns that this is in fact the case. If Henrik did not have the handkerchief, the Nazi dogs that searched his boat would have undoubtedly sniffed out the hiding Rosen family and the others. The Nazi soldiers would undoubtedly have arrested them, and their fate would likely have mirrored that of the countless other Jews that the Nazis relocated to concentration camps. To save the lives of the Rosens and the other Jewish families, Mrs. Johansen is willing to sacrifice a second daughter.

The action of the story propels the reader beyond this event, beyond the moment of a mother's split-second decision, and many readers will not dwell on this, as they are swept along with Annemarie to her encounter with the Nazi soldiers and beyond, to her successful delivery of the packet. Such pacing is consistent with Lowry's treatment of the darker aspects of war in the novel: Lowry does not dwell on loss and suffering in this work, although she does not shy away from the sorrows and sacrifices of the war. Rather, she emphasizes for her young readers the notions of hope and friendship, the importance of bravery and a sense of community. When the decisions made by the parents in the story are analyzed, however, the reader is made aware of the deep grief and loss suffered by families during the war. In the end, separations, sacrifices, and deaths haunt *Number the Stars* but do not dominate the story.

Source: Catherine Dominic, Critical Essay on *Number the Stars*, in *Novels for Students*, Gale, Cengage Learning, 2012.

Don Latham

In the following excerpt, Latham examines the blurred boundaries between childhood and adulthood in Number the Stars.

. . . It is the Romantic, sentimental view of childhood that Lois Lowry both invokes and critiques in her Newbery Award-winning novels, *Number the Stars* and *The Giver*. In both books, Lowry blurs the distinctions between her child protagonists and the adults around them. Both protagonists are on the verge of adolescence, a time when the pressures of growing up cause the distinctions to blur for most children. But in these two books additional pressure is brought to bear by the unique situations in which the protagonists find themselves. *Number the Stars* is set in Denmark in 1943 during the German occupation, while *The Giver* is set in a dystopian community in which free will and individualism have been sacrificed for security, isolation, and, to use Lowry's word, "sameness." Under such circumstances as we see in these two novels, the distinction between childhood and adulthood

> THE PRESSURE OF THE WAR AND THE NAZI OCCUPATION DO NOT FORCE ANNEMARIE TO GROW UP MORE QUICKLY, BUT INSTEAD SERVE TO THROW THE VARIOUS DIMENSIONS OF HER COMPLEX, MULTIFACETED CHARACTER INTO RELIEF."

becomes even fuzzier—hence my title, "Childhood Under Siege." But Lowry's point, I would argue, is not merely that tough times force children to grow up faster, although no doubt that is part of her theme. More important is Lowry's implied idea that the usual distinctions we make between children and adults in "ordinary" times may not really be valid after all. In forcing readers, both children and adult readers, to recognize this, Lowry herself is laying siege to the Romantic view of childhood that so pervades our society.

Number the Stars is the story of Annemarie Johansen, a ten-year-old Danish girl, who along with her parents and uncle helps a Jewish family to escape Nazi persecution during World War II. The story, as Lowry explains in the Afterword, is fiction, but it is based on fact, for during the war, the Danish people helped thousands of Jewish citizens escape to Sweden. In the book Annemarie displays many characteristics that are typically associated with children, but also others considered adult, thus calling into question the traditional notions of childhood and adulthood and blurring the distinctions between the two.

The environment in occupied Denmark changes the traditional roles of the children and adults who inhabit it. No doubt, the constant presence of menacing soldiers puts everyone on guard, even the very young. In the opening scene of the book, Annemarie, her sister Kirsti, and her Jewish friend Ellen are racing home from school when they are stopped and questioned by two Nazi soldiers. Suddenly, the carefree fun of a childhood activity is interrupted by the intrusion of hostile adult authority. As David Russell has noted, "In the typical Holocaust story, we find young children reaching maturity before their time, the extenuating circumstances demanding it. And so it is with Annemarie" (270). By the same token, adults are treated like children, as is the case in most totalitarian societies. Because of the omnipresent soldiers, who represent a constant threat of searches and arrest, the adults have lost their autonomy. Ironically, their closely circumscribed lives, with their lack of freedom, resemble those of many children, who are rarely granted much autonomy or latitude by adults.

More significantly, though, the soldiers represent the atrocities committed by the Nazis against the weak and the innocent, including children. The litany of abuses is familiar but no less deplorable: local Jewish citizens, like Mrs. Hirsch, the owner of a button shop, are arrested and their businesses are closed; vicious dogs are used to track down Jewish refugees; Annemarie's mother is slapped by a soldier; Annamarie's older sister Lise is killed as is her fiancé, Peter. Throughout the book, Lowry incorporates images of the soldiers' glossy black boots. They are the first things Annemarie notices when she is stopped on the way home from school. They also figure prominently in the scene in which soldiers search the Johansens' apartment, looking for their neighbors, the Rosens. Mr. Johansen saves Ellen, who is staying with the Johansens, by pretending that she is his (now deceased) daughter Lise. To lend credence to his claim, he takes out a photograph of Lise when she was a baby. Annoyed at having to accept the story, "[t]he officer tore the photograph in half and dropped the pieces on the floor. Then he turned, the heels of his shiny boots grinding into the pictures, and left the apartment." In her Newbery Award acceptance speech, Lowry noted that her editor had asked her to reduce the numerous references to black boots. Upon reflection, Lowry refused, saying, "... those high shiny boots had trampled on several million childhoods and I was sorry I hadn't had several million more pages on which to mention that" (420).

Such an environment tends to blur the distinctions between children and adults, showing that both groups, in spite of being victimized, can prove to be resourceful, capable, and courageous. The Danes, for instance, destroyed their own navy as the Germans were approaching to take over the ships. Mr. Johansen displays both courage and cleverness when he passes Ellen off as his own daughter Lise. Mrs. Johansen

displays those same qualities later in her brother's farmhouse. She keeps the soldier from looking into a casket filled with blankets for Jewish refugees by claiming that her Aunt Birte had died of typhus and that the doctor had warned that the casket should remain closed because germs might still be present. The greatest testament to the Danes' resourcefulness, courage, and compassion is the fact that during the war they helped nearly 7,000 Jews escape to Sweden (*Number the Stars*).

The adults in the novel also go to great lengths to protect one another, and especially the children, from dangerous knowledge. Mr. Johansen, for example, regrets having to inform his older daughter about the necessity of the Rosens' flight: "'I wish that I could protect you children from this knowledge,' he said quietly. 'Ellen, you already know. Now we must tell Annemarie.'" Similarly, Uncle Henrik does not explain to Annemarie the significance of the handkerchief used to frustrate the dogs' sense of smell. As he explains, not even adults know everything: "'... it is much *easier* to be brave if you do not know everything. And so your mama does not know everything. Neither do I. We know only what we need to know.'" The very real danger posed by knowing too much in wartime Denmark stands in marked contrast to the dangers adults often perceive as constituting threats to children.

Annemarie, though a child, also proves to be as resourceful, capable, and courageous as any adult. The opening scene introduces the theme of childhood versus adulthood and illustrates Annemarie's resourcefulness in being able to move between the two. The book begins with a typical childhood activity, a footrace home from school between Annemarie and her friend Ellen, that is suddenly interrupted by the stern voice of a Nazi soldier, who orders them to halt. When the soldier asks Annemarie why she is running, she responds by playing the role of a child. She says, "I was racing with my friend .... We have races at school every Friday, and I want to do well, so I—," and her voice trails off. At the same time, she plays a more adult role, consciously monitoring her actions and words: "'Don't talk so much,' she told herself. 'Just answer them, that's all.'" She takes a similar attitude toward her five-year-old sister: "'Stand still, Kirsti,' Annemarie ordered silently, praying that somehow [her sister] would receive the message."

The climactic scene of the book, another encounter with soldiers, reinforces the blurring of the distinction between childhood and adulthood. In this scene, Annemarie must take a packet to her Uncle Henrik, who is waiting on his boat to take Jewish refugees to Sweden. Although she does not know exactly what the packet contains, she understands that her mission is crucial to her uncle's success in getting his passengers across the water. Before she leaves, her mother tells her, "'Annemarie, you understand how dangerous this is. If any soldiers see you, if they stop you, you must pretend to be nothing more than a little girl. A silly, empty-headed little girl....'" However, Annemarie does not really need her mother's advice here, for early on, she has learned that in order to survive her encounters with soldiers, she must play the role of a "little girl." When she is stopped by four soldiers with dogs, she pretends to be nothing more than a child. Ironically, Annemarie must pretend not to recognize the danger of the situation. Throughout her encounter, she thinks of her little sister and how she reacted to the soldiers earlier: "Kirsti hadn't been frightened. Kirsti had been—well, nothing more than a silly little girl.... She had known nothing of the danger, and the soldier had been amused by her." Annemarie adopts this role for herself, chattering away and getting upset when one of the soldiers takes the basket she is carrying. The soldiers are fooled and Annemarie is allowed to continue on her mission. Because of her, the Jewish refugees are transported safely to Sweden.

In addition to being resourceful, Annemarie also plays the role of protector, a role typically associated with adults, especially parents. After her initial encounter with the soldiers, she decides not to tell her mother because she doesn't want to worry her. Again, Annemarie engages in a bit of role playing as she ascends the stairs to her apartment. The narrator describes her as "practicing in her mind a cheerful greeting for her mother: a smile, a description of today's spelling test." When Kirsti spills the beans about the encounter, Annemarie reassures her mother, "'She's exaggerating, as she always does.'" In the final part of this opening scene, Annemarie again plays the role of a child, pretending "to be absorbed in unpacking her schoolbooks" while actually listening to her mother and Mrs. Rosen talk about the fact that the soldiers are on edge after the latest incidents involving the Resistance movement. Later, Annemarie protects her friend Ellen by lying to her about the "death" of her fictional Great-aunt Birte:

> She understood that she was protecting Ellen the way her mother had protected her. Although she didn't understand what was happening, or why the casket was there—or who, in truth, was in it—she knew that it was better, *safer*, for Ellen to believe in Great-aunt Birte. So she said nothing.

Suddenly, in playing the role of protector, Annemarie recognizes her connection to her mother: "Annemarie knew that Mama was lying again, and she could see that Mama understood that she knew. They looked at each other for a long time and said nothing. In that moment, with that look, they became equals."

Annemarie also plays the role of the adult in her use of stories. Several critics have pointed out the importance of stories, especially fairy tales, in this book. Virginia Walter, for example, says that Annemarie finds in stories both a metaphor for frightening events and a mantra that gives her courage. I would add that Annemarie's use of stories also illustrates her fluid movement between the worlds of childhood and adulthood. Fairy tales are typically associated with children, although they were originally folktales intended for both adults and children. Annemarie often assumes the role of storyteller with her younger sister, playing the role of the adult, telling Kirsti stories at night to help her fall asleep. During her trip through the woods, Annemarie tells herself the story of "Little Red Riding-Hood" to comfort herself and to shore up her courage. In this scene, she plays the role of both child and adult, telling herself a story in order to help herself face the dangers of the forest. Or, to put it another way, we may say that the child Annemarie calls on the resources of her "inner parent." But Annemarie, in spite of her physical resemblance to Little Red Riding Hood, is actually much different—acutely aware of the danger but capable of thwarting it by pretending to be unaware. As Virginia Walter notes, "Unlike Little Red Riding Hood, Annemarie neither trusts the wolf's intentions nor requires the hunter's protection. She is not seduced by the Nazi soldiers. She succeeds, however, by *appearing* to take the German soldiers at face value and by appealing to them to accept her at face value as well."

Finally, Annemarie displays an innate desire for connectedness to people beyond her immediate family. In recalling the story of King Christian, the Danish king who could ride every morning alone on his horse because all of Denmark was his bodyguard, Annemarie says to her father, "'. . . now I think that all of Denmark must be bodyguard for the Jews, as well.'" When the soldiers come in the middle of the night looking for the Rosens, Annemarie rips Ellen's Star of David necklace off her friend so as to conceal her true identity. Throughout the terrifying incident, Annemarie clutches the necklace in her fist. Once the soldiers are gone, Annemarie unclenches her fist and realizes that the Star of David has been imprinted into her palm. The imprint symbolizes Annemarie's intimate connection with Ellen, for in that moment she has become one with her friend.

It is tempting, because of Annemarie's age and the circumstances, to see this novel as merely a coming-of-age story. However, the facts suggest that Annemarie has been an adult all along—or more properly, she always has been able to function successfully in the worlds of both children and adults all along. The pressure of the war and the Nazi occupation do not force Annemarie to grow up more quickly, but instead serve to throw the various dimensions of her complex, multifaceted character into relief. . . .

Source: Don Latham, "Childhood Under Siege: Lois Lowry's *Number the Stars* and *The Giver*," in *Lion and the Unicorn*, Vol. 26, No. 1, January 2002, pp. 1–15.

Shirley Haley-James

In the following essay, Haley-James explains that Lowry takes readers both into and beyond themselves in her novels.

Pine logs snap and crackle in the fireplace of a cabin in the North Georgia mountains as four adults sit reading. There is no other noise. It is a tradition that when it rains during their annual October weekend amid the fall foliage of the Appalachian foothills everyone reads on Saturday afternoon, undisturbed. One of the readers breaks the silence by giggling—at first a little, then a lot. A moment later she guffaws. This goes on until she looks up from her book to see six annoyed eyebrows questioning her. Saying, "You've got to hear this," she begins to read from *Anastasia Again!* (Houghton). Now all four laugh, and three ask to hear more. The afternoon flies by as they all enjoy the remainder of the story. In books such as those in the Anastasia series, Lois Lowry takes people—the young and the not-so-young—out of themselves by tickling their funny bones.

Lowry takes readers into themselves as well. With "it was a long time ago," she begins her story set on Autumn Street. It is specific to a particular time and place, but it causes both young and more experienced readers to remember, and to reflect about the meaning of, their own "times of hollow places that ache with memory and with fear." Because they read about Autumn Street, both their self-understanding and their compassion for others grow.

But, most significantly, Lowry takes readers beyond themselves. In none of her books does she succeed in this to a greater extent than in *Number the Stars* (Houghton), a story in which she makes the abstract concepts of love, commitment, and courage visible and real. Through the decisions of Annemarie Johansen and her family, we are made to wonder, "Would I have it in me to do what they did to save others?" And we realize that, through this book, a new generation will be informed of a time in the history of the world that humankind dares not forget.

Books that ring as true as Lois Lowry's virtually always emerge from honest exploration of experience and from an inner ear finely tuned to what is going on both within and around the writer's life. There is integrity as well as consistency in who the writer is, what she studies, and what she writes. This is true in the case of Lowry's work. She can tickle funny bones with her books because she sees and appreciates the humorous and the ridiculous in the things she, and all of us, say and do. She can touch the pain in our lives because she has lived through her own and because she is not afraid either to relive it when that serves a purpose or to enter ours when she can be of help. She can write about the devastation of the Holocaust as well as about the courage and humility of people who risked their lives to save others, because her conscience requires that she speak of the unspeakable as well as honor that which is good.

Integrity and consistency also characterize her daily life and her relationships. I have heard her speak to parents, librarians, teachers, and children. Each time, she has tailored her presentation to fit the audience. I have watched her interact with family, friends, and strangers over a span of a dozen years, and, without exception, all have been treated straightforwardly, respectfully, and fairly. It's easy to understand why even people who have just met her feel that she is their friend—or at least that she would be, if they needed one.

Beneath the integrity and consistency that characterize Lowry's work and her daily life and relationships, there is a woman of strength who has worked for and achieved a peace with herself. She can speak of her goals and of her mistakes, of times she has been treated unfairly, and of what she feels proud of without self-pity and without smugness. She knows who she is. She works on polishing what she views as her rough edges.

On this bedrock Lois Lowry creates. She is a photographer whose pictures arrest the eye and compel the viewer. She is a nonfiction writer for adults who has published articles in numerous well-known magazines. She is an author of fiction for young adults and children whose legions of faithful readers finish her most recent book and begin anticipating the next. She is a booster of morale, an instiller of confidence, and a picker-upper of those around her when they are down. Beyond all of this, she tells funny stories, and she loves to laugh.

It is not just Lowry's writing skills that account for her ability to take readers out of themselves, into themselves, and beyond themselves. It is also the person she is and the way she has chosen to live her life. It is the sum of all her parts that could create such a sterling book as *Number the Stars*. And that is why we rejoice that it has received the prestigious Newbery Medal.

Source: Shirley Haley-James, "Lois Lowry," in *Horn Book*, Vol. 66, No. 4, 1990, p. 422.

Lois Lowry

In the following essay, Lowry relates how she conceived of the idea for the book and the experiences she underwent in preparation for writing it.

A chilly week in Bermuda with an old friend was the starting-off place for my book *Number the Stars*. If it had been hot, Annelise and I would have spent the week swimming. If we had been rich, we might have spent it shopping. But we were chilly and scrimping, and so we talked. We talked about everything. She and I have so much in common: our marriages (and divorces), our work, our children. I suppose we even talked about our knitting, since she and I

> IT IS SO GRATIFYING TO HEAR FROM THEM NOT ONLY THAT THEY ENJOY THE EXCITEMENT OF THE STORY, BUT THAT ON A DEEPER LEVEL THEY RESPOND AS WELL TO THE COURAGE AND INTEGRITY OF THE DANES IN THOSE YEARS."

both tend to click away with knitting needles while we relax. (I suppose it takes our minds off the fact that we'd rather be smoking—she and I have *that* in common, too.) And we talked about our childhoods.

Our childhoods were so different. I grew up in a small Pennsylvania town during World War II, flattening tin cans for the weekly drive at school, buying war stamps, and helping my mother color the tasteless white butter-substitute yellow; and I have a vague memory of the ration stamps we used for things like meat and gas and shoes.

But Annelise grew up in Denmark—in Copenhagen, during the years that her country was occupied by the Nazis. She talked about being cold—there was never any fuel for heat, and she wore mittens, she said, to bed. She talked about being scared—the armed Nazi soldiers stood on every street corner in Copenhagen, and controlled every aspect of the lives of Danish citizens.

And she talked about being proud of her people, and what they had done to save their Jews.

I suppose I had heard the story before, of the way the Danes smuggled their Jewish population to Sweden in 1943. But I had never heard it before in such a riveting, personal way.

Finally, by the end of that talk-filled week in the spring of 1988, I was convinced that it could be told, and told for children, in a fictional way that would put the reader right there with a frightened, brave, proud little Danish girl. I asked Annelise's permission to do so, and she gave me the gift of her childhood and her willingness to have me shape it into a story for young readers.

Early summer was very hot in Boston that year, and I spent some of it in the non-air-conditioned basement of The Boston Atheneum, wondering if I might have made a bad choice, not in the content of the book, but in the timing. But the story by then consumed me. And so I went through those dusty, long-unread books in that oppressive heat, searching out the facts and details of that historic time. Now and again I even shivered, not in response to the temperature, which stayed mercilessly in the 90s, but because I was so moved by the unwavering integrity and courage of an entire population.

Once I wept. It was when I looked at a photograph of a young man named Kim. He looked so very much like my own sons: light-haired and handsome, outdoorsy and athletic. Yet at that very moment, as I held his photograph in my hands, my own two sons were doing the things that tan, happy, agile young men do: one was enjoying some spring skiing in France; the other was joyfully preparing for his wedding 3 weeks away. I had recently received funny Mother's Day cards from each of them. Yet this boy, this Kim who looked at me from the photograph, had died at 21: tied to a wooden post, shot by the Nazis in retaliation for his work in the Danish Resistance. He, too, had written to his mom (later, in Copenhagen, I would see the actual letter). He did so the night before he was to die. He told her, in his letter, that he was not afraid.

I mourned for him and his unfulfilled dreams. He spoke in his letter of "a world of human decency," and that world seemed so far away, still. But thinking of him renewed my feeling that it is young people like him, like my own children, like the kids I write for, whose hopes and needs will change the future.

By late June I felt that I *knew* enough and could turn next to my imagination. It was in my (air-conditioned) apartment on Boston's Beacon Hill that I created the child whom I named Annemarie: the child who mourned a lost older sister (as the real Annelise did; and as I did too, years ago). I created her family, and their apartment (seeing in my mind Annelise's Copenhagen apartment, which I had visited) and again and again I called my friend to ask her for the ordinary details of her long-ago life. What did she wear to school? What games did she play? What might a Danish dog be named?

And I created Peter, keeping the image of the young man named Kim in my mind as I did so.

Usually I write a book quickly. It's the *thinking* that precedes writing that takes most of my time. And this book, like others, moved along at a rapid pace after my thinking was complete.

But quite suddenly—toward the end—I became aware of something that I had not anticipated. I had thought the book was almost complete, and now I realized that it wasn't at all. I realized that I had to go back to Denmark.

I had the facts—they were all there, in the books in the Atheneum basement. And I had the characters, and the plot—they were all there, in my imagination at first, and by now on the pages that I'd written and rewritten. I had the details that Annelise had provided.

But I hadn't been to Denmark in several years; and I could no longer *feel* Denmark.

My calendar was very full, I groaned when I looked at it and realized that I had promised to be on the staff of a weeklong conference in late July, and was committed to speak at another event in Los Angeles in August. The book by now was under contract to the publisher and was due at the publishing company in September, after which I was due to leave on an extended tour of Australia and New Zealand. So time was in short supply.

I called my travel agent and made reservations to go to Denmark for 4 days. Even he—accustomed as he is to my frequent traveling—was startled. I could hear him gulp before he quoted me the undiscounted airfare. "If you could wait 30 days—" he suggested. "Or maybe if you could just stay at least a week—"

But I couldn't, and didn't.

I made up a private itinerary for myself, and I chuckled, wondering what a stranger would make of a schedule that included instructions like: "Stand on the coast north of Copenhagen and smell the ocean."

But it was what I needed to do, and what I did. From Copenhagen I took the train north, stood on the coast, looked across to Sweden, and smelled the air and sea.

I stood on the balcony of a kind stranger's apartment—because Annelise was now living in the United States—and looked down into the street, picturing the celebration of the war's end in 1945 while a woman whom I had never met before described the church bells ringing and the people singing and dancing below, that May night so many years ago.

I went to the place in Copenhagen where the Resistance fighters had been executed. When I saw that the Danes still place flowers there each day, after close to 50 years, it reinforced my admiration for them and my need to tell their story.

One afternoon as I sat in an outdoor cafe, wearily drinking a cup of coffee, a flustered-looking man approached me apologetically and said, "Excuse me, I'm American, and I'm lost; do you understand English?"

He was the only American I spoke to for those 4 days and I realized that I had begun to feel, briefly, quite Danish myself. Apparently I had begun to *look* Danish as well.

Finally, at the end of those 4 exhausting days, I came home and rewrote the entire book. Same characters; same plot. But now it had the real Denmark in it.

Enough time has elapsed now since the publication of *Number the Stars* that the letters are coming from kids who have read it. It is so gratifying to hear from them not only that they enjoy the excitement of the story, but that on a deeper level they respond as well to the courage and integrity of the Danes in those years.

Many write to ask, "What happened afterward? After the war? Did Ellen and her family come home?"

A little girl in Texas answered that for herself. She wrote a sequel to *Number the Stars* and sent it to me. "After the war ended," she wrote, "Annemarie decided to look for Ellen. So she took a boat to Sweden. When she got to Sweden she got off the boat and went to a restaurant. There was Ellen, at the salad bar!"

Well, I'll leave it to the teachers out there to take up the cultural history of the salad bar in their classrooms. My satisfaction comes from hearing that kids *care* what happened afterward.

There are a lot of Ellens out there, still: grown up now, the age I am, and the age of my friend Annelise. There is a woman living in Chicago who was 10 years old when she was smuggled to Sweden in a fishing boat, as Ellen was. There are other Ellens in Israel, or in their original homes in Denmark, or who stayed to make a home in Sweden.

I hope their grandchildren will one day read *Number the Stars* and learn how the Danish people changed the history of the world.

Source: Lois Lowry, "*Number the Stars*: Lois Lowry's Journey to the Newbery Award," in *Reading Teacher*, Vol. 44, No. 2, October 1990, pp. 98–101.

SOURCES

"Background Note: Denmark," in *Diplomacy in Action*, U.S. Department of State, March 1, 2011, http://www.state.gov/r/pa/ei/bgn/3167.htm (accessed August 1, 2011).

"Biography," in *LoisLowry.com*, http://www.loislowry.com/bio.html (accessed August 1, 2011).

Cummins, June, "Rivka's Way," in *MELUS*, Vol. 27, No. 2, 2002, pp. 237–45.

"Denmark," in *CIA World Factbook*, https://www.cia.gov/library/publications/the-world-factbook/geos/da.html (accessed August 1, 2011).

"Denmark," in *Holocaust Encyclopedia*, United States Holocaust Memorial Museum, http://www.ushmm.org/wlc/en/article.php?ModuleId = 10005209 (accessed August 1, 2011).

"Denmark: Education," in *Denmark Education Guide*, http://www.denmarkeducationguide.com/ (accessed August 1, 2011).

Eisenberg, Joyce, and Ellen Scolnic, "Star of David," in *The JPS Dictionary of Jewish Words*, Jewish Publication Society, 2006, p. 155.

Goodenough, Elizabeth, and Andrea Immel, eds., "Introduction," in *Under Fire: Childhood in the Shadow of War*, Wayne State University Press, 2008, pp. 1–18.

Goodman, Myrna, "Foundations of Resistance in German-Occupied Denmark," in *Resisting the Holocaust*, edited by Ruby Rohrlich, Berg Publishers, 1998, pp. 213–38.

"HM The Queen of Denmark," in *The Danish Monarchy*, http://www.kongehuset.dk/publish.php?dogtag = k_en_fam_oue (accessed August 1, 2011).

"The Jewish Community in Denmark," in *Mosaiske.dk*, 2011, http://www.mosaiske.dk/english/jewish-community-denmark (accessed August 1, 2011).

Karesh, Sara E., and Mitchel M. Hurvitz, "Denmark," in *Encyclopedia of Judaism*, Facts on File, 2006, pp. 111–13.

Lowry, Lois, *Number the Stars*, Houghton Mifflin Books for Children, 1989.

Milton, Edith, "Escape from Copenhagen," in *New York Times Book Review*, May 21, 1989, p. 32.

Ray, Karen, Review of *The Giver*, in *New York Times*, October 31, 1993, http://www.nytimes.com/1993/10/31/books/children-s-books-335293.html?scp = 12&sq = %22number + the + stars%22 + lowry&st = nyt (accessed August 1, 2011).

Shields, Jacqueline, "Denmark," in *The Virtual Jewish History Tour*, American-Israeli Cooperative Enterprise/ Jewish Virtual Library, http://www.jewishvirtuallibrary. org/jsource/vjw/Denmark.html (accessed August 1, 2011).

Tatar, Maria, "'Appointed Journeys': Growing Up with War Stories," in *Under Fire: Childhood in the Shadow of War*, edited by Elizabeth Goodenough and Andrea Immel, Wayne State University Press, 2008, pp. 237–50.

"World War II in Europe," in *Holocaust Encyclopedia*, United States Holocaust Memorial Museum, http:// www.ushmm.org/wlc/en/article.php?ModuleId = 10005137 (accessed August 1, 2011).

FURTHER READING

Jespersen, Knud, J. V., *A History of Denmark*, Palgrave Macmillan, 2004.

> Jespersen details the history of Denmark from the Reformation through the twenty-first century and develops a notion of Danish national and cultural identity throughout the work.

Pudnik, Herbert, *In Denmark It Could Not Happen: The Flight of the Jews to Sweden in 1943*, translated by Anette Mester, Gefen, 1998.

> Pudnik's narrative is based on his own rescue story as a Danish Jew smuggled out of Denmark by his friends.

Purdue, A. W., *The Second World War*, St. Martin's Press, 1999.

> Purdue's analysis of World War II provides an overview of the political and philosophical issues informing the war. The author cautions against the view that the war was only a war waged against the fascist regimes of Germany, Italy, and Japan and explores contemporary attitudes toward the war.

Zusak, Markus, *The Book Thief*, Knopf Books for Young Readers, 2006.

> Zusak's acclaimed young-adult novel tells the story of the German people's experiences during World War II from a unique perspective, that of Death. The novel focuses on a nine-year-old girl sent to live with a foster family in a working-class neighborhood of Molching, Germany. She witnesses the tragedies of the war from the perspective of her foster family, who secretly oppose Hitler and aid in the escape of a Jewish friend.

SUGGESTED SEARCH TERMS

Lois Lowry AND Number the Stars

Lois Lowry AND biography

Lois Lowry AND Danish resistance

Lois Lowry AND Holocaust

Lois Lowry AND Danish Jews

Lois Lowry AND World War II

Lois Lowry AND King Christian X of Denmark

Lois Lowry AND historical fiction

Lois Lowry AND Star of David

Lois Lowry AND Newbery Award

Olive Kitteridge

ELIZABETH STROUT

2008

Small-town life as experienced by the more or less wizened residents of Crosby, Maine, is vividly portrayed in Elizabeth Strout's award-winning novel in stories *Olive Kitteridge* (2008). Strout herself was raised in small towns in Maine and New Hampshire, and in her first two novels, she availed herself of her native knowledge of the small-town milieu to wide critical praise. For her third major work, she elected to employ a fairly unconventional formula. *Olive Kitteridge* consists of thirteen independent short stories, some of which focus on the title character and her closest relatives, others that include Olive only indirectly while focusing on other towns-people and families in the Crosby area. The thought-provoking result is a fictional collage that reproduces the fragmented understanding people in small communities develop toward one another in sharing certain experiences while allowing others to remain secret. The profound and unbiased empathy demonstrated by this novel in stories inspired its most glowing reviews, and the volume was awarded the 2009 Pulitzer Prize for Fiction.

AUTHOR BIOGRAPHY

Strout was born in Portland, Maine, on January 6, 1956, and grew up partly in the coastal town of Harpswell and partly in neighboring New

Elizabeth Strout (© *MARKA* | *Alamy*)

Hampshire, where her father was on the animal sciences faculty at the state university in Durham. Interests in keen observation of the world around her and the accurate recording of experience were instilled in her by her mother, who played games with her daughter imagining the lives of strangers around town. Her mother gave her notebooks to fill with her perceptions of real-life episodes, and Strout was inspired to become a writer at such a young age that she cannot remember ever truly wanting to be anything else. This solitary dream was perhaps also encouraged by the relative strictness of her fairly puritanical parents, who did not allow Strout and her brother the passing distractions of television and newspapers or the social pleasures of dates and parties. Strout thus became enamored with the physical world, from toads to turtles, creeks to coastlines, and pine needles to periwinkles.

Strout found high school inimical and so left early to attend Bates College, where the English chair encouraged her quiet development as a writer. After graduating, she proceeded to England's Oxford University for a year and then to

law school at Syracuse University, earning a law degree as well as a certificate in gerontology (the study of aging) from an adjoining school in 1982. In law school, she met her future husband, with whom she would have one daughter, Zarina. After living together in New York City, the couple eventually divorced. Finding herself disinclined to pursue an adversarial career in law, Strout enjoyed a wide variety of occupational experiences before earning the life of a successful writer. In the course of her early life, she found employment as a house cleaner, ice-cream server, secretary, department-store clerk, law-office clerk, waitress, and piano player. She even took a stand-up comedy class, which left her mining her Maine roots for material and thus realizing how integral her home state was to her identity and worldview.

Accordingly, Strout set her first two novels—*Amy and Isabelle* (1998), which took her the better part of a decade to write surreptitiously, and *Abide with Me* (2006)—in Maine, making the small-town environments play critical roles in the plot and in character development. Pursuing the Maine-small-town angle further with *Olive Kitteridge* (2008), Strout proved her mastery of her material by earning the 2009 Pulitzer Prize. Retaining a faculty post in the low-residency writing program of Queens University in Charlotte, North Carolina, as of 2011, Strout continued to reside and write in New York City.

PLOT SUMMARY

Pharmacy

In his pharmacy one town away from home, the middle-aged Henry Kitteridge has recently found his days brightened by the new clerk, Denise Thibodeau, an effusively nice college graduate who is married to a virile young plumber also named Henry. Though his wife, Olive, deplores the idea, Henry Kitteridge invites the couple over for a pleasant dinner. At work, Denise bolsters the esteem of the chubby young deliveryman, Jerry McCarthy, whom she encourages to enroll in college classes. Flashing forward twenty years, the pharmacy is gone, and Henry Kitteridge gets annual friendly letters from Denise describing her obese son and athletic twin daughters. The story then returns to the earlier timeframe. One day, Henry Thibodeau goes hunting and is accidentally killed by his friend. Henry Kitteridge lends Denise emotional support

MEDIA ADAPTATIONS

- An audiobook version of *Olive Kitteridge* was produced by Brilliance in 2008, and is read by Sandra Burr, who Nola Theiss reported in a *Kliatt* review to have "the authoritative and flinty edge needed to characterize Olive's character and the Maine setting."

and comes close to seeking a connection with her— but only cares for her paternally. Meanwhile, Henry and Olive grow distant from each other. Years later in church, Henry recalls how a pregnant Denise and her self-improved husband Jerry, along with their son, stopped by for a visit.

Incoming Tide

Kevin Coulson has been sitting in his car near the marina, in view of a diner, for some time, gazing around, having not returned to his childhood hometown since he was thirteen. In the diner, Patty Howe notices Kevin and remembers the somewhat strange boy from school. Kevin is planning on returning to his home to kill himself and recalls snippets of conversations with a psychiatrist. Olive, his old math teacher, knocks on the window, invites herself into his car, and obliges him to converse—even about his mother's suicide. Patty Howe goes out near the water to clip some flowers, and when Olive sees that she has slipped in, Kevin races out, jumps in the water, and supports Patty until more help arrives.

The Piano Player

Angela O'Meara has been playing the cocktail lounge piano at the Warehouse Bar and Grill for many years and is showing her age despite her (overly) youthful style. She thinks about Malcolm Moody, a selectman whom she has loved, and gets a request from an old flame, Simon. Taking a break, which she never does, Angie calls Malcolm, who is at home, presumably with his wife, and tells him she cannot see him anymore. Saying hello as Angie plays, Simon tells her about his wife and kids, and she tells him she has to run when she gets

off work. He makes a lewd reference to her mother, who was a prostitute. When she reaches home later, Angie is called a crazy drunk by the waiting Malcolm.

A Little Burst

In the afternoon of her son Christopher's wedding day, Olive is worn out and wishes everyone would leave. She and Henry had that house built especially for their son. As Olive lies in the bedroom, one of the bride's little nieces enters and makes insulting comments about her appearance. Later she overhears the bride, Suzanne, tell another woman how ridiculous Olive's dress is. Before leaving for doughnuts with Henry, Olive marks one of Suzanne's sweaters and steals a bra and a shoe.

Starving

At the marina outside the diner, Harmon is somehow uplifted by a cute, hip young couple— someone's cousin from New Hampshire and his girlfriend. On his way home, Harmon brings the widowed Daisy Foster a doughnut, and they retreat to the bedroom. Harmon then proceeds home to his wife, Bonnie, who, after their son Derrick went to college, proclaimed herself finished with physical intimacy. At his hardware store, Harmon suspects the cousin of stealing something. In the paper at home, he reads about how the young couple, Timothy Burnham and Nina White, were arrested on marijuana-related charges. Bonnie mentions that Nina is anorexic. In the fall, Harmon visits Daisy—just a friend now— to find that Nina is staying there, having run away from the hospital. Olive happens by seeking Red Cross donations, chats with Nina, and breaks down in tears. After a sullen holiday season, with his sons too emotionally distant, Harmon notices Olive's car at Daisy's place and enters to hear that Nina has died of a heart attack. Harmon begins renting the place vacated by the young couple and prepares to leave Bonnie for Daisy.

A Different Road

A year after a traumatic event, the people of Crosby concede that the seventy-year-old Kitteridges have changed. The night in question started with a huge dinner out with the Newtons. On the ride home, Olive needs to use a restroom immediately, so she forces Henry to stop at the hospital emergency room. Afterward, the nurse mentions that a woman last night had been allergic to crabmeat and went into shock, so she obliges Olive to get checked. The kindly young doctor asks her to don a hospital gown, and then a man in a blue ski mask barges in, as does a rifle-bearing man in a pig mask. They force Olive into the bathroom with the nurse, doctor, and Henry, whose comments of concern elicit threats from Blue-Mask and harsh retorts from Olive, even when her robe leaves her exposed. Olive feels deep sympathy when Blue-Mask reveals himself to be an exceedingly nervous young man who has shaved off his red hair. Finding his accomplice with his mask off, Pig-Face castigates Blue-Mask. After more bitter words from Olive to Henry, the police arrive and free everyone.

Winter Concert

The elderly Bob and Jane Houlton, happily married, drive past houses decked with Christmas lights before going to a seasonal concert at a church. On the street, they pass by Alan and Donna Granger, parents of a friend of their daughter's, reminding Jane, a retired school nurse, about Lydia Granger's abortion in high school. At the concert, when the Houltons chat with the Grangers, Donna gives Jane the impression that her husband is hiding something about a trip to Miami. He denies it at first but eventually admits that, some years ago, he visited an old flame there and spent the night. Jane is stricken, but they will stick together.

Tulips

Olive recalls how long ago the Larkins holed themselves up after some tragedy, as well as how Christopher moved out to California with Suzanne four months after their wedding—they soon divorced, but he stayed there. Henry is adapting to retirement, which Olive has grown accustomed to. During a trip to the grocery store, he has a sudden stroke and is left in a vegetative state. Christopher visits but cuts his stay short. Getting a note from Louise Larkin, Olive visits, but the thin, suave woman—whose son long ago stabbed a young woman many times—turns nasty, evidently seeking to enjoy Olive's suffering. Olive slowly recovers and reminisces about her family.

Basket of Trips

The middle-aged Marlene Bonney's deceased husband Ed is being buried, and Olive joins Molly Collins to prepare the Bonney house for the reception. Olive refrains from telling Molly about Christopher's divorce. Kerry Monroe, a cousin of Marlene's who has been staying there,

gets drunk and needs Marlene's help getting to bed. When Olive finds her there, Marlene tells Olive she is thinking of killing Kerry, who told Eddie Junior that she had an affair with his dad. Olive advises against it. Marlene asks Olive to take away a basket filled with brochures for trips that she and Ed, during his fatal illness, talked about taking someday.

Ship in a Bottle

Julie Harwood is being counseled by her mother, Anita, about how to cope with her fiancé recently breaking their engagement on their wedding day; Bruce wants to live with Julie but not marry, which Anita considers disgraceful. Jim, father to Winnie (biologically) and Julie (adoptively), is building a ship in the basement that may never be removed intact. Julie tells her little sister Winnie that their home—with, for example, a shower stall and curtain-obscured toilet each directly off the hallway—is abnormal. When Bruce drives up to visit Julie, Anita fires a rifle in his direction. One Sunday, Julie skips church to catch a bus from Moody's store to find Bruce in Boston. Upon returning, Winnie finds a secretive note, and later her uncle calls; he only just saw her when the bus pulled away.

Security

Christopher is in Brooklyn now, with a new wife, Ann, and he has finally called to invite his mother back into his life; Olive visits to help out during Ann's pregnancy with her third child (with a third father). Olive is uplifted by the flight but thrown into confusion upon arrival, getting lost in the airport and baffled by her son's talkativeness. The apartment is slovenly, the yard miniscule, and the wife taller than Olive and somehow overly friendly—and she furtively smokes and drinks a bit each night. A Christian parrot upstairs squawks blessings every time someone curses. Olive stays in the basement, from where she phones Henry now and again. She remembers being in love with her fellow teacher Jim O'Casey and thinking about running away with him. A married man, Jim drove Olive and Christopher to school daily, but one day, driving by himself and likely drunk, crashed into a tree and died. Olive has no rapport with Ann's preschool boy and is little help with her baby girl but can at least take the dog for walks. But at the park, the upstairs neighbor offends her with intrusive questions. Talking with Ann and Christopher, Olive grows convinced that their therapist—whom they moved to New York to follow—has helped them formulate blame of her and find prescriptive ways to deal with her. Announcing that she is leaving early, Olive argues aggressively with Christopher, who resigns and bids her farewell. At the airport, a careless comment earns Olive a security escort out of the line of passengers.

Criminal

Rebecca Brown steals a magazine from the doctor's office to finish a story, and she orders her boyfriend, David, an advertised shirt by phone, chatting amiably with the southern agent. When Rebecca's mother fled to California (later becoming a Scientologist), Rebecca was left with her stoic minister father, who has recently died, leaving Rebecca with dirty thoughts and arsonous impulses. Between comments on the violent television shows he watches, David commiserates with Rebecca about her inability to find a job she can hold. The shirt would have been better for her old boyfriend, who broke up with her for some blonde. At the doctor's, Rebecca is told she is only imagining a serious stomach illness. At home, Rebecca gathers fire-lighting equipment, planning to walk to the doctor's office and expecting to get arrested.

River

Jack Kennison is perceived by Olive as an arrogant man, not a real Mainer but just a transplanted retiree. One morning during her six-mile walk, the widowed Olive finds Jack Kennison lying on the ground near a bench, and she cares for him and accompanies him to the doctor. His wife has recently died. They talk on the phone; she asks him to lunch, but he would rather have dinner. They start going on dates and even kiss. Talking with Bunny and the distant Christopher on the phone leaves Olive annoyed. Jack cannot accept his daughter's being a lesbian, and Olive grows irritated with his Republican leanings. After a conciliatory e-mail exchange, Olive visits Jack and lies down with him, accepting what company she can.

CHARACTERS

Ann

Ann has found in Christopher a third father for her third child; pregnancy fails to prevent her from smoking and drinking. Her firstborn, Theodore, strikes Olive as a burgeoning brat, while

Annabelle is just getting on her feet. Ann has voyaged through therapy with Christopher and subtly allies with him against Olive, who has evidently been blamed for much in his life.

Suzanne Bernstein

Christopher's first wife, Suzanne, is a modern doctor who seems, in her commentary on Olive's wedding wear and in her patronizing flower talk, to scoff at Olive's very existence. She and Christopher move to California, breaking the elder Kitteridges' hearts, but soon divorce.

Blue-Mask

An accomplice of Pig-Face in the hostage-taking at the hospital, the man in the blue mask reveals himself to the doctor, nurse, and Kitteridges to be an edgy young redhead, shaved nearly bald and thoroughly strung out, evoking profound sympathy in Olive.

Marlene Bonney

After the death of her grocer husband, Ed, Marlene finds out from her drunk cousin Kerry that she and Ed have been illicitly intimate. When Kerry is passed out, Marlene feels ready to kill Kerry, but Olive happens in and helps dissipate Marlene's agitation.

Bonnie

Inspired by her own empty-nest independence, Harmon's wife withdraws not only from their physical intimacy but also from their spiritual connection, leaving Harmon to find comfort, and ultimately love, elsewhere.

Rebecca Brown

A ne'er-do-well whose minister father has (finally) died and whose mother has disappeared into the cult of Scientology, Rebecca proves to have kleptomaniacal and arsonous impulses.

Timothy Burnham

A cousin of a local girl, the pothead Timothy hangs around town with his girlfriend Nina White until he cheats on her with a mutual friend, Victoria.

Molly Collins

A retired home-economics teacher from Olive's school, Molly helps prepare the Bonney household for the funeral reception.

Kevin Coulson

Haunted by his mother's suicide and a recent tumultuous relationship and unable, despite his own psychiatric training and the help of Dr. Goldstein, to find peace in his life, Kevin has returned to Maine with the intent of killing himself behind his family's old house. But something about Olive's voice stirs the desire to live within him, and rescuing Patty Howe from drowning in the tide leaves him overwhelmed by the sight of this same desire in her.

David

Rebecca Brown's body-building, violent television-watching boyfriend is basically clueless.

Daisy Foster

Childless and widowed by her aged police-officer husband, Daisy carries on an affair with Harmon, who finds true friendship with her. She is hospitable toward the distressed Nina White.

Alan Granger

Alan is Donna Granger's amiable husband.

Donna Granger

At the winter concert with her husband, Alan, Donna (dubbed "Mrs. Lydia," after their daughter) subtly communicates to Jane Houlton (who despises the smug Donna) that Bob is hiding something from her.

Harmon

Owner of the local hardware store, Harmon, whose beloved sons (including Derrick and Kevin) have all left the nest and whose wife, Bonnie, has declared an end to their sexual relationship, finds first physical love and then platonic friendship with Daisy Foster. He grows to love her and plans to leave his wife for her.

Anita Harwood

Julie's off-center mother runs her household with misguided vigor, refusing to allow her daughter to live in sin with Bruce after he declines to marry her. Anita fires a rifle when Bruce gets too near the house.

Jim Harwood

Father to Winnie and Julie, Jim is a school janitor who builds, in the Harwood basement, a ship that may never see daylight.

Julie Harwood

To escape her mother's influence and stay with Bruce after he proves unwilling to marry her, Julie runs away.

Winnie Harwood

Enamored of her older sister, Winnie learns from Julie that life at the Harwood household is abnormal and worth leaving behind.

Bob Houlton

Bob spent a night with an old flame a number of years ago. When his wife finds out, she is despondent at first but chooses not to let it ruin their marriage.

Jane Houlton

Retired from her post as nurse at Olive's school, Jane knows much about other people's daughters but is chilled by the thought of others knowing secrets about her own children. She is greatly upset by news of her husband's infidelity but does not want to let it sabotage their relationship.

Patty Howe

Saddened by her repeated miscarriages, Patty takes solace in simple things like bouquets of wildflowers. Upon seeing Kevin Coulson while waitressing, she remembers him from school. When picking lilies, she slips into the roiling surf, and Kevin rescues her.

Jack Kennison

A retired professor whom the widowed Olive helps in a time of need, the widower Jack becomes an acquaintance of hers. He gets under Olive's skin but may be her last shot at shared intimacy and love.

Christopher Kitteridge

Olive is such an overbearing mother—having been abusive physically toward Christopher and verbally toward Henry—that Christopher flees the house his parents had built for him in order to move to California with his first wife (whose wardrobe Olive sabotaged). He effectively excludes his mother from his life, even after his father's stroke, until he needs help with his pregnant second wife, Ann, and adoptive kids in Brooklyn. He surprises his mother with his talkativeness, but she eventually feels his interactions to be stage-managed by their therapist, Arthur, and lashes out at him. They later reconcile at least enough to chat on the phone from time to time as Olive dates Jack and Christopher's son starts growing up.

Henry Kitteridge

A man ever inclined to see people's troubles resolved, as befits a pharmacist, Henry proves a decent match for the aggressive, unapologetic Olive. But their differences lead Henry to find a new happiness in his friendship with Denise Thibodeau, which he nonetheless declines to allow to lead to anything more intimate. Everyone seems to appreciate his good-natured warmth. When he is rendered semiconscious by a stroke, Olive realizes how essential he has been to her contentment.

Olive Kitteridge

The title character of Strout's volume is the ornery, judgmental, self-righteous, and somehow ultimately charming and likable Olive Kitteridge, retired seventh-grade math teacher. The stories collectively show many interesting sides of Olive—how she fosters an interest in someone else's spouse while her husband does likewise, how she instinctively gives a suicidal young man a critical interpersonal boost, how she truly feels about her husband's mother, how she responds when her husband suffers a stroke, how she copes with the alternate reality of her son's second marriage; and how she may still be ready to fall in love in her seventies, among other circumstances. Perhaps not surprisingly, given her profession, she seems to connect best with, or have the best effects on, younger people unrelated to her. Sometimes people just need a sympathetic ear and a few insightful thoughts, and she offers as much to Kevin Coulson, Marlene Bonney, and even Nina White. Rebecca Brown, on the other hand, felt too anxious to allow Mrs. Kitteridge to befriend her, and, perhaps not coincidentally, she is greatly lacking in direction. With regard to her family, however, Olive perhaps allows too much of the unapologetic authority that served her well in the classroom to be absent-mindedly wielded over her husband and son, both of whom seem subjugated by her. In the end, the reader understands Olive to be a character whose various flaws do not quite obscure her driving concern that others, like herself (and unlike her suicide father), manage to shrug off the occasional harshnesses of life and forge ahead.

Louise Larkin

A disturbingly composed woman who has been living in hiding, along with her estranged husband Roger, ever since her son Doyle murdered a woman and was sent to prison, Louise seems to extend sympathy to Olive after Henry's stroke. But Louise's prying comments about suicidal thoughts leave Olive to realize that Louise is only seeking to bask in Olive's misery.

Jerry McCarthy

Somewhat slovenly in his habits after graduating from high school and working as a deliveryman, McCarthy finds inspiration in the kindly Denise, and he ends up marrying her.

Kerry Monroe

A cousin of Marlene Bonney's who has been staying with Marlene's family, Kerry drunkenly confesses to the stone-skipping Eddie Jr., at Ed's funeral, to adulterous indiscretion with his father.

Malcolm Moody

A married town selectman, Malcolm has been entertaining a decades-long affair with Angie O'Meara. When she calls him at his home to end it, he drops by in order to curse at her.

Bunny Newton

Bunny and her husband, Bill, are good old friends of the Kitteridges but live two hours away. The Kitteridges tell only the Newtons, who have their own familial trials with their daughter Karen, about Christopher's divorce. After Henry's death, Bunny seems to be Olive's only confidante.

Jim O'Casey

A fellow schoolteacher whose gruff personality aligned well with Olive's, Jim drove her to and from school and caught her fancy—but died by crashing his car into a tree.

Sean O'Casey

A leather jacket-wearing, dog-walking, parrot-training Christian, Christopher's upstairs tenant in New York is probably not related to Jim O'Casey.

Angela O'Meara

The longtime cocktail-lounge piano player at a local restaurant, Angie O'Meara still needs to drink—and get emotional boosts from the bartender Joe and the (gay) barstool fixture Walter Dalton—to overcome her stage fright. After she finally gathers enough self-regard to end her infatuation and ongoing affair with Malcolm Moody, she declines to entertain the idea of an evening with Simon. While these arrogant men see fit to insult her, she at least still has her beloved music.

Pig-Face

The man in the pig-face mask is the leader of the hospital heist.

Simon

A piano-playing inspiration and old flame of Angie O'Meara's who is now a married lawyer, Simon makes a pass at her. When she deflects his overtures, he suggests that he was intimate with her mother, in apparent vengeance.

Denise Thibodeau

The mousy, simple Denise brings a permanent aura of joy to Henry Kitteridge's workaday life in the pharmacy. When her husband dies, she gets mired in grief, with Henry providing crucial emotional support and nearly more—but romantically she ends up with Jerry McCarthy.

Henry Thibodeau

Denise's husband is amiable and admired by Henry Kitteridge, but his accidental death upends Denise's life.

Nina White

A girl whose fresh youthfulness gives Harmon a lift, Nina's fatigue is symptomatic of her actually suffering from anorexia. After her break-up, she happens to find refuge at Daisy Foster's house, but the kindness she is shown there by Harmon and Olive cannot save her from the heart attack that soon claims her life.

THEMES

Loneliness

Perhaps the most prominent theme in *Olive Kitteridge* is that of loneliness, a sorrowful state that afflicts characters and motivates their most critical actions in nearly every story. Loneliness within marriage is experienced by both Kitteridges and also by Harmon, leading all three to drift toward extramarital friendships. Denise Thibodeau and Marlene Bonney are left lonely by their spouses' deaths, as, ultimately, are Olive and Jack Kennison. And loneliness is an implicit factor in the planned suicide of Kevin Coulson, who seems never to have recovered from one

TOPICS FOR FURTHER STUDY

- Read five or more stories from Sherwood Anderson's *Winesburg, Ohio* (1919) and write a paper comparing and contrasting the approaches to small-town life executed by Anderson and by Strout in *Olive Kitteridge*.

- Compose a short story providing yet another perspective on Olive Kitteridge, addressing either circumstances alluded to in Strout's novel—like her teaching or her raising the young Christopher—or circumstances entirely of your own invention.

- Collect images of Maine, including samples from major works of art, monographs, encyclopedias, tourist brochures, advertisements, magazines, and any other relevant print or online media. Present the images as a series in an online gallery, assigning captions that lend some degree of narrative arc to the series. To accompany the gallery, write a brief essay comparing the collective effect of your gallery to the collective effect of Strout's novel in stories. If completed digitally, post to your Web page and invite comments from classmates.

- Choose three stories from *The Color of Absence: 12 Stories about Loss and Hope* (2001), a young-adult collection edited by James Howe, featuring situations reminiscent of those found in *Olive Kitteridge*. Compose an essay comparing and contrasting how the respective authors approach the traumatic circumstances described. Consider such factors as the nature of depictions of trauma or death, the extent of explorations of grief, and how the authors identify new relationships as offering respite to those suffering from loss.

- Write a research paper on the modern relevance of the field of gerontology—the study of aging and its psychological, physical, and social effects—making reference to current population trends, consequences of advances in medical care, the state of Social Security and Medicare, the nursing-home industry, and so forth. Be sure to use scholarly journals for some of your information.

manic girlfriend, and in the criminality of Rebecca Brown, whose parents have disappeared from her life and whose boyfriend's priorities seem to be his physique and the television.

Olive Kitteridge herself is by far the novel's most revealing case study in loneliness, in spite of the reliable companionship of her marriage and her working relationship with her son. As she muses in considering what will become of Christopher's first marriage, "They think they're finished with loneliness.... Loneliness can kill people—in different ways can actually make you die." That she and Henry had built their son a house nearby in the clearly stated hope that he would marry and spend his life there— with no suggestion made that Christopher himself requested this—reflects the profound dependence they have developed on the constant nearness of their only child. Olive feels "positively squeezed to death by an unendurable sense of loneliness" in his total absence following his move to California, and Henry, too, is said to be heartbroken. In turn, Olive is thrown into turmoil by Henry's debilitating stroke, even if within the confines of her marriage she had at times "felt a loneliness so deep" that even the dentist's touch left her aching for intimacy. Ultimately, Olive is compelled to cure her loneliness not in a self-destructive way but in pairing with Jack Kennison, which mercifully allows her "to close her eyes to the gaping loneliness of this sunlit world."

Life and Death

Not a few of Strout's chapters or stories deal with characters' passing from, or nearly passing from, life to death. Some characters, like the husbands of Denise and Marlene, meet tragic ends that upend their surviving spouses' lives. Patty Howe nearly drowns, Kevin Coulson nearly kills himself, and Nina White effectively does kill herself in succumbing to anorexia. Olive and Henry's lives are threatened when they are taken hostage at the hospital, and Bruce's life is endangered when he gets too near Julie's unstable mother, Anita. Through these various circumstances, Strout seems to seek to highlight, on the one hand, the myriad ways that major tragic events can intrude on people's lives and fundamentally change them and, on the other hand, the small but significant events—the "little bursts," in Olive's words—that can prove to be critical swing factors in people's survival or recovery.

Befitting Olive's status as title character, she is often the one to either provide or try to provide such little bursts to people in need. She succeeds with Kevin Coulson and Marlene Bonney, averting potential suicide and murder, respectively, while Nina White and Rebecca Brown might be said to represent her failures. Her comments to Nina White about how everyone is starving, so to speak, may offer insight into the constant human need for love and affection, but they evidently failed to breach the psychological defenses of Nina, who offers a sardonic rejoinder, "Heavy," that indicates her utter indifference to this self-centered old woman's cosmic perspective. Nina's death follows soon after. Rebecca Brown, rather than finding any inspiration in the quirky Mrs. Kitteridge and her occasionally piercing gaze, was merely made to feel anxious. Perhaps Rebecca would have been more receptive to Olive's invitation to chat if the math teacher had been a little more warmly personable. Regardless, in the absence of her parents, Rebecca surely could have used some conscientious guidance, which might have prevented her from evolving into a criminal. Of course, some people simply connect more—or less—naturally with other people; no person can wield a life-saving or death-defying influence over everyone they meet.

While not all Strout's characters survive or persevere in virtue, the moments when they cling to life or find renewed value in it offer the novel's most shining passages. The contented Jane Houlton muses at Christmastime, "No matter what people's lives might hold...still and all, people were compelled to celebrate because they knew somehow, in their different ways, that life was a thing to celebrate." In reconnecting with her son, Olive "remembered what hope was": "that inner churning that moves you forward, plows you through life the way the boats below plowed the shiny water, the way the plane was plowing forward to a place new, and where she was needed." Perhaps most dramatically among such moments, Kevin Coulson has a sort of epiphany when he experiences Patty Howe "holding him with a fierceness that matched the power of the ocean— oh, insane, ludicrous, unknowable world! Look how she wanted to live, look how she wanted to hold on."

Small-Town America

Intertwined with the connected themes of loneliness and life and death is the particular setting

Olive Kitteridge *is set in a coastal town in Strout's home state of Maine.* *(Natalia Bratslavsky | Shutterstock.com)*

of Strout's novel, a cozy Maine town that could be generalized as representing small-town America. Strout furthermore focuses on the sorts of middle-class folks who have steady ordinary jobs, are married or have been married, have a child or a few, and are generally habituated within the confines of traditional American society. That is to say, her characters include no professional or amateur artists, actors, or athletes; no business executives or nonprofit crusaders' and no modern spiritual gurus or followers, as well as few seriously impoverished people or blue-collar laborers of any sort (with one janitor portrayed condescendingly, one plumber dying prematurely, and fishermen given only throwaway lines). The characters are—by implication in light of the setting and names—nearly all white, and only one minor character is described (but not acutely portrayed) as homosexual. In sum, Strout's characters lead lives devoid of modern and/or urban existential dilemmas or contexts, for example, with respect to ethnicity or nationality, circumstances that might give those afflicted some compelling external guide, motivation, or vision to

their lives. There are no movements or revolutions taking place among these characters. Rather, they live day by day; they try to fulfill their needs—primarily for companionship and love—with the help of those around them; and they wake up the next day and do everything again. Some are lonelier than others; some are confronted by death or have a chance to reaffirm life. Nearly all try to live in as straightforward, honest, and peaceable a fashion as they are able.

STYLE

Novel in Stories

Regarding the fictional status of Strout's volume—"Is it a novel or a short-story collection?" one might easily ask—efforts were made to present the book as a "novel in stories," an increasingly popular classification of modern works of fiction. Some early reviews cite the full title of the book as *Olive Kitteridge: A Novel in Stories*, while the 2008 Random House Reader's Circle edition cover includes a blurb specifically classing it as such. On the other hand, another 2008 Random House cover calls it simply "fiction," while the 2011 Simon & Schuster edition includes a blurb calling it simply a "novel." The format is relatively unique: a set of stories nominally revolving around the title character but, given the divergence of several stories from her life, more technically centering on the town of Crosby, Maine. In this sense, Strout is recognized as following the pattern of Sherwood Anderson's *Winesburg, Ohio* (1919), which focuses on the title town but centralizes one character in using a townsperson as the narrator of the stories and tracing the trajectory of his life there.

Strout's approach imposes a sort of postmodern formula on Anderson's precedent. The reader's introduction to Olive Kitteridge is oblique, with Olive appearing as a background presence in the first story, a supporting character in the second, and a mere walk-on in the third. From there, Olive serves as the main protagonist in half of the remaining stories. But even these stories—which indeed cannot really be called chapters, given their functioning within the typical boundaries of the short story, such as being defined by a single day, episode, or relationship—allow the reader only limited insight into Olive's character. In fact, Olive is thereby encountered primarily in extraordinary or highly stressful circumstances—the afternoon of her son's wedding, a hostage crisis, the aftermath of her husband's stroke, a trip to visit her practically estranged son in a strange city, and the lead-up to her first relationship as a widow. The reader is thus given only a fragmentary perspective on Olive that is confined to her post-retirement years, with the events that shaped her life beforehand merely mentioned or alluded to. And yet, by virtue of both the authentic behavior elicited by the intense pressure of the circumstances described and the striking originality of Olive's habitual dialogue, the reader is likely to come away from the novel with a definitive conception of Olive as a person. Given the sketchy, composite nature of her portrayal, one reader's conception of her may not entirely coincide with that of the next—but such is the reality of everyday life: depending on the precise nature of shared circumstances, any given person is likely to be perceived slightly differently by everyone he or she has met. Strout's novel in stories successfully evokes this aspect of reality with respect to Olive Kitteridge.

Key Images

Most of the stories in this collection can ultimately be said to revolve around or be symbolically concentrated in a single key image or metaphor, typically as suggested by the title—a hallmark of many short stories. In general, these motifs are confined within the individual stories rather than carrying over from one to another. The title "Pharmacy" is interesting in that the exclusion of the article *the*, which one might expect there, elevates the pharmacy to the level of, say, a church (since one would likely say "I'm going to church" rather than "I'm going to the church"), signifying the veritable sacredness of the place for Henry Kitteridge. "Incoming Tide" begins with the image of the ocean swelling as the tide comes in, and by the end, the reader may link this with the flood of love for life that infuses Kevin Coulson when he jumps in that very water to save Patty Howe. The governing image of "A Different Road" highlights not the hostage crisis itself but the way in which the crisis redirects the Kitteridges' shared fate, leading them along a different road than was expected. In "Tulips," in the absence of her stricken husband and distant son, Olive's relationship with her flowers becomes paramount to her existence. "Ship in a Bottle" suggests the impossibility of a person fully developing—sailing the open waters, in sea-vessel terms—within a home or family structure whose very design restricts growth and escape. The suspense as to what exactly is meant by the "Basket of Trips" is sustained until near the story's end, when the image is explained as embodying the hopes that one nurtures just to get through the days, even if one knows in one's heart that those unfulfillable hopes will someday bring nothing but heartbreak—at which time one may need a friend to carry that basket away. Each of the collection's key images and metaphors serves to direct the reader's attention to a certain aspect of the story at hand and suggest where the greatest symbolic or sentimental relevance is to be found.

HISTORICAL CONTEXT

Contemporary America

Although several stories or scenes in Strout's 2008 novel stretch back through the last decades of the twentieth century, a number of incidental comments and clues firmly situate the majority of the action in the early twenty-first century. While a few of these scattered clues evoke a potpourri of contemporary concerns such as attention deficit disorder and the cult/religion of Scientology, the more prominent references evoke the politics of and opinions about the terrorist attacks of September 11, 2001; the ensuing war in Iraq, and more generally the administration of George W. Bush. On that date in 2001, nineteen Muslims now known to have been ultimately directed by Osama bin Laden, the Afghanistan-based leader of the terrorist group al Qaeda, in an act of *jihad* (or holy war) hijacked four American passenger planes and crashed them into the two towers of the World Trade Center, the Pentagon, and (thwarted by passengers) a field in Pennsylvania. The American response to these acts included a declaration of a "war on terror" and an invasion of Iraq under the premise that Iraqi president Saddam Hussein was suspected of possessing weapons of mass destruction, which could be used either by him or by terrorist allies. Strout did not foreground this historical context, however. The story "Ship in a Bottle" mentions "the hooded prisoners overseas," alluding to a scandal at the Iraqi prison Abu Ghraib in which American military jailers humiliated captives, and "River" mentions America's "cowboy for a president," but these allusions, while revealing particular facets of characters like Anita Harwood and Jack Kennison, respectively, bear minor relevance to the stories' plots. No firemen or policeman appear in Strout's novel—emergency personnel being the class whose ranks were most decimated by the collapse of the World Trade Center towers—and the mention of the yellow ribbon decal adorning a stock character's truck is the closest any actual soldier comes to being involved.

"Security," set primarily in New York City, represents Strout's most ambitious level of engagement with modern historical reality. The story's first paragraph relates Olive's own personal reaction to the attacks of September 11, 2001, specifically to the sight of people jumping from the burning towers. Aside from her sympathy for the victims and the city itself, Olive imagines the "dark-haired hijackers" as having been "silently thrilled with their self-righteousness"—a terse description verging on caricature, suggesting not religious followers solemnly engaged in what they perceive as a holy war but rather simple men excited to be carrying out a murderous plan. Indeed, many Americans developed such a simplified view of the aggressors. When conversation between Olive and Christopher veers toward the possibility of more attacks, Christopher reveals his

Olive Kitteridge is a testy old woman. *(Elena Ray / Shutterstock.com)*

own bias against any Arab/potential terrorist in claiming that he could tell that a local Pakistani store owner was a bad guy, so to speak, just from the look in his eyes when they spoke—a spurious claim at best. Strout offers few post-9/11 reflections beyond these, in sum suggesting a marked distance, a dimensional gap, between the political drama of the so-called war on terror and the lives of average small-town Americans, who may feel little connection with cities in general, including New York, and likely feel little fear that their own small town will be affected by a subsequent attack.

CRITICAL OVERVIEW

Olive Kitteridge earned especially warm reviews that prefigured the novel's formal critical recognition with the Pulitzer Prize. An *Atlantic* reviewer calls the volume "superb" and "poignant and hopeful" and recognizes Strout as "adept at showing the complex coincidence of tenderness and fury, appreciation and disappointment that exists between those who are closely tied." A contributor to the *New Yorker* remarks that "Strout makes us experience not only the terrors of change but also the terrifying hope that change can bring: she plunges us into these churning waters and we come up gasping for air." In the *New York Times Book Review*, Louisa Thomas reflects on the virtues of the novel-in-stories form, which combines "the sustained, messy investigation of the novel with the flashing insight of the short story"— though the stories in which the title character is marginalized are considered "the two weakest," as without Olive, "the book goes adrift, as if it has lost its anchor." Thomas concludes that the pleasure of reading Strout's volume "comes from an intense identification with complicated, not always admirable, characters," which leads to "the honest recognition that we need to try to understand people, even if we can't stand them."

A perceptive review from a popular viewpoint was offered by Trudy Bush, writing in *Christian Century* after the book won the Pulitzer. She observes, "There are lots of epiphanies but not much cheer in these stories." After noting how readily an older person can identify with Strout's characters, Bush posits that, "as we go through the pains and losses that aging brings, we may need something other than stories that make us feel them more keenly. We may need stories that convey the value and beauty of life—stories that give us a sense of transcendence." In *Olive Kitteridge*, "Characters talk about their souls, but usually about how those souls are hurting or wearing out." While this may seem on the surface to be a merely sentimental criticism, it amounts to an objection to the amorality of many postmodern tales, in which acknowledgment of the validity of all perspectives means the prioritization of none. Without any greater overarching moral direction to this fictional work, Bush concludes, "Excellent though Strout's stories are, they leave me sad and earthbound, and tell me little that I don't already know."

CRITICISM

Michael Allen Holmes

Holmes is a writer and editor. In the following essay, he reflects on what may be missing from Strout's portrayal of Olive Kitteridge via a novel-in-stories technique.

WHAT DO I READ NEXT?

- Strout's debut novel was *Amy and Isabelle* (1998), which depicts the tumultuous relationship between a mother and her wayward sixteen-year-old daughter in a small town in Maine.

- Among the most famous works of the nineteenth-century poet Henry Wadsworth Longfellow—like Strout a native of Portland, Maine—is *Evangeline, a Tale of Acadie* (1847), an epic poem treating a woman's search for her lost love in a time of upheaval in the Maine region in the eighteenth century.

- Strout has expressed, in an interview, a particular fondness for the work of the Pulitzer Prize–winner Oscar Hijuelos, who is Hispanic. In *Empress of the Splendid Season* (1999), Hijuelos uses the story of a once-prosperous Cuban émigrée reduced to the position of a cleaning woman in New York as a portal into the lives of the various people she works for.

- The Chilean author Isabel Allende, whose works are often characterized as magical realist, offers a collection of well-spun tales about the unique and romantic lives of ordinary and extraordinary people alike in *The Stories of Eva Luna* (1989).

- The accomplishments of the Maine native Dorothea Dix, a nineteenth-century advocate for people suffering from mental illness— whose sympathy for troubled souls might be said to prefigure Strout's—are detailed in Thomas J. Brown's *Dorothea Dix: New England Reformer* (1998).

- Melissa Walker's young-adult novel *Small Town Sinners* (2011) traces the maturation of a sixteen-year-old daughter of an evangelical pastor in a small town in the South, offering an in-depth exploration of the role of religion in young people's lives.

With *Olive Kitteridge*, Elizabeth Strout earned particular critical praise for her insightful portrayal of all manner of small-town characters and the ways in which their lives intersect. Most commentators have highlighted the author's presentation of the unique title character, whose idiosyncratic, often unpredictable manner enlivens every scene in which she appears. In the *New York Times Book Review*, Louisa Thomas declares that Olive functions "like a planetary body, exerting a strong gravitational pull." Regarding the novel-in-stories format, Strout noted in an interview with Robert Birnbaum for the online *Morning News* that she elected to approach Olive from multiple angles "to give people a break from the full-front effect of her" and because it helps the reader "understand that we're all more complicated than we appear. There are different aspects of Olive, and these different ways to look at her ... help to bring that out." And yet, arguably, Strout sacrificed a fair degree of insight into her title character in presenting her through this particular assembly of stories.

Over the course of Olive's numerous scenes in the volume, the reader is eventually given a fairly specific conception of her physical appearance. Through "Pharmacy," this conception remains quite vague, as Olive offers intriguing dialogue, but as far as physical details are concerned, the reader is told only that she has "dark hair" and "full breasts." When she appears, to Kevin Coulson's surprise, in "Incoming Tide," only a few clauses' worth of physical details are added, with reference to "that forthright, high-cheekboned expression" and to her as "a big woman, taking up the whole bucket seat, her knees close to the dashboard." With her passing cameo in "The Piano Player," the reader learns only of her "loud voice." Such glancing descriptions are what a reader is likely to expect from a short story, in which the author's imperative is to communicate only what is essential to the focus of the story. Often, a full physical description of a short-story character is not only extraneous but perhaps

disadvantageous, since it pigeonholes the reader's image of the character without necessarily fleshing the character out in a way that justifies or legitimizes that image. That is, in approaching a story, the reader may benefit more from his or her own instinctively conceived image of a character, as derived from the immediate dialogue and action, than from a specific image provided by the author. But of course, here, Strout's stories are intended not to stand alone but to constitute a novel.

In the fourth story, "A Little Burst," the reader is finally given a more substantial account of Olive's physicality, largely from her own point of view:

> she has always been tall and frequently felt clumsy, but the business of being *big* showed up with age; her ankles puffed out, her shoulders rolled up behind her neck, and her wrists and hands seemed to become the size of a man's.

After Olive's ruminations on being overweight, the description is sealed in comedic fashion, in that, lying on a bed, "she probably looks like a fat, dozing seal wrapped in some kind of gauze bandage." The reader is thus provided with a summary image that is reducible to a convenient, and unflattering, metaphor and which is thereby restricted by that metaphor. In other words, just as exposure to racial stereotypes may limit one's ability to fully conceive of the humanity of a member of a given race, exposure to this caricatured description limits the reader's conception of Olive; the five words that open the above descriptive passage seem to say everything the reader needs to know: "Olive is a big person."

At this point, it may be instructive to compare the presentation of this Olive to the presentation of one of her few literary namesakes, Olive Chancellor, of Henry James's *The Bostonians*. A renowned fictional master, James first presented *The Bostonians* (1886) to the public through serial publication in *Century* magazine over the course of a year—a fictional format that has all but disappeared in the modern era, owing presumably to a lack of the requisite long-term attention span among consumers of periodicals. Olive Chancellor's first appearance at the end of the first chapter elicits a number of telling physical details. She is said to have "a smile of exceeding faintness ... just perceptible enough to light up the native gravity of her face." Aurally, "Her voice was low and agreeable—a cultivated voice." In greeting Basil Ransom, a cousin, she extends "a slender white hand" that "was at once cold and limp." In the second chapter, James immediately allows Basil the opportunity to contemplate her appearance and demeanor, noting first "that she was agitated and trying to conceal it." The narrator proceeds to remark that she "was subject to fits of tragic shyness, during which she was unable to meet even her own eyes in the mirror," with such a fit seizing her just then. From Basil's point of view, Olive's status as one of "the people who take things hard . . . was written so intensely in her delicate face that he felt an unformulated pity for her before they had exchanged twenty words." In sum, James provides a series of acute physical details that are directly relevant to Olive's personality. The narrator actually asserts that Olive's character traits "were not present to [Basil] as definitely as I have written them here; they were summed up in the vague compassion which his cousin's figure excited in his mind, . . . obvious as it was that with such a face as that she must be remarkable." Thus, James has so thoroughly conceived this character that he is able to describe her behavior in these particular circumstances with exacting insight as well as to connect her physiognomy with her disposition. All of these details are provided within the first several minutes of Olive Chancellor's appearance on the scene. Throughout the novel, James further fleshes out this major character with descriptions of precisely how she stands, how she sits, how she walks, and so forth.

In contrast, in *Olive Kitteridge*, the reader is often told what actions the title character performs but is largely left to imagine independently how, exactly, she performs them. Indeed, the reader may not get far beyond imagining that Olive acts however "a big person" generally acts. When she appears in "Starving," Olive "stood in the doorway to the dining room, almost filling the space up." The physical description ends there. When the sight of Nina's frailty leads Olive to weep, the reader is offered a variation on what is becoming a stock description: "There she sat, *large and big-wristed*, her mouth quivering, tears coming from her eyes" (emphasis added). In the ensuing paragraphs, Olive is said in passing to have a "large hand," a "big lap," and a "big body." This reductive mode of description is continued in the ensuing stories. In "A Different Road," standing alongside a short woman, "Olive, *big, solidly built*, towered over her" (emphasis added). In "Winter Concert" at the church, Olive "walked in, *tall and broad-shouldered* in a navy blue coat" (emphasis added). As introduced in "Basket of Trips," she "is *big-boned and taller by a head* than Molly"

(emphasis added). Toward the volume's end, the Olive-centric stories "Tulips," "Security," and "River," in presenting the events from Olive's perspective, forgo descriptions of her physicality almost entirely. A passage in "Security" describing the middle-aged, rather than elderly, Olive seems intended to differentiate her appearance back then but does so only to the slightest degree: "She was *tall*, and the weight that came with menopause had only begun its foreshadowing, so at forty-four she had been a *tall, full-figured* woman" (emphasis added). As it happens, many readers in this politically correct age may read "full-figured" as no more than a euphemism for "big."

By the end of *Olive Kitteridge*, the reader may not even realize how little has been said about Olive's physical presence—an outcome that attests to the power of Strout's stories. They indeed bring her characters to life regardless of the degree of physical detail provided. And one cannot deny that this markedly cursory style of description is suited to the narrowed scope of the short-story format; within the context of each individual story, Olive, like the other characters, is amply personified for that story's purposes. But Strout wishes this work to be considered as elevated above the status of short-story collection. She remarked in her interview with Birnbaum, "I think of this book as a novel, really, because it has the heft of a novel, it has the arc of a novel: This woman's life is being addressed." Yet while Olive's life is centrally addressed, and while a certain span of years is covered, the arc of the work does not encompass any transformation on Olive's part. She undergoes dramatic changes in her life—the movement of her son out of and back into her life, the incapacitation and death of her husband, and the discovery of a new companion—but personality-wise, she is remarkably static. The Olive whom the reader meets in the earliest stories does not appear any different from the Olive of the later stories, regardless of age. A central protagonist who fails to evolve is not a feature of a great number of novels. In this respect, one may be inclined to second-guess the composition of the volume; had the work been (derivatively) titled *Crosby, Maine*, the slate of stories would have been perfectly agreeable, but for a work titled *Olive Kitteridge*, Strout could have surely offered a more powerful volume had she left out the stories in which Olive is most distant—like "Winter Concert," "Ship in a Bottle," and "Criminal," all of which were originally published in

Olive's husband, Henry, is gentle and kindly. *(Lauren Rinder | Shutterstock.com)*

periodicals back in the 1990s—and composed entirely new stories portraying Olive in earlier circumstances in her life. Strout might have thus presented Olive in her classroom, the environment that perhaps reveals more about a teacher than any other; raising Christopher, perhaps to illustrate the contention that she physically abused him and more fully account for the nature of their ongoing relationship; and/or coping with her father's suicide, perhaps the one event that did accomplish a transformation in her. But Strout elected to directly approach none of these scenes, which admittedly would have been challenging to write. Perhaps unintentionally, then, the post-modern, minimalist character sketch of Olive Kitteridge found in Strout's collection of stories—a sketch that ultimately allows the reader to witness but not understand Olive's character—illustrates another comment of hers from the interview with Birnbaum: "I'm so interested in the fact that we really don't know anybody. We think we know the people close to us, but we don't, we really don't."

Source: Michael Allen Holmes, Critical Essay on *Olive Kitteridge*, in *Novels for Students*, Gale, Cengage Learning, 2012.

Mary Ellen Quinn

In the following review, Quinn notes the human and sympathetic qualities that Strout brings to the characters in the novel.

Hell. We're always alone. Born alone. Die alone," says Olive Kitteridge, redoubtable seventh-grade math teacher in Crosby, Maine. Anyone who gets in Olive's way had better watch out, for she crashes unapologetically through life like an emotional storm trooper. She forces her husband, Henry, the town pharmacist, into tactical retreat; and she drives her beloved son, Christopher, across the country and into therapy. But appalling though Olive can be, Strout manages to make her deeply human and even sympathetic, as are all of the characters in this "novel in stories." Covering a period of 30-odd years, most of the stories (several of which were previously published in the *New Yorker* and other magazines) feature Olive as their focus, but in some she is bit player or even a footnote while other characters take center stage to sort through their own fears and insecurities. Though loneliness and loss haunt these pages, Strout also supplies gentle humor and a nourishing dose of hope. People are sustained by the rhythms of ordinary life and the natural wonders of coastal Maine, and even Olive is sometimes caught off guard by life's baffling beauty. Strout is also the author of the well-received *Amy and Isabelle* (1999) and *Abide with Me* (2006).

Source: Mary Ellen Quinn, Review of *Olive Kitteridge: A Novel in Stories*, in *Booklist*, Vol. 104, No. 9, January 1, 2008, p. 46.

Beth E. Andersen

In the following review, Andersen lauds the link that Olive provides for the thirteen short stories that make up the novel.

In her third novel, *New York Times* best-selling author Strout (*Abide with Me*) tracks Olive Kitteridge's adult life through 13 linked stories. Olive—a wife, mother, and retired teacher—lives in the small coastal town of Crosby, ME. A large, hulking woman with a relentlessly unpleasant personality, Olive intimidates generations of community members with her quick, cruel condemnations of those around her—including her gentle, optimistic, and devoted husband, Henry, and her son, Christopher, who, as an adult, flees the suffocating vortex of his mother's displeasure. Strout offers a fair amount of relief from Olive's mean cloud in her treatment of the lives of the other townsfolk. With the deft, piercing shorthand that is her short story-telling trademark, she takes readers below the surface of deceptive small-town ordinariness to expose the human condition in all its suffering and sadness. Even when Olive is kept in the background of some of the tales, her influence is apparent. Readers will have to decide for themselves whether it's worth the ride to the last few pages to witness Olive's slide into something resembling insight. . . .

Source: Beth E. Andersen, Review of *Olive Kitteridge: A Novel in Stories*, in *Library Journal*, Vol. 133, No. 2, February 1, 2008, p. 65.

Kirkus Reviews

In the following review, a contributor to Kirkus Reviews *describes the novel as "a perfectly balanced portrait."*

The abrasive, vulnerable title character sometimes stands center stage, sometimes plays a supporting role in these 13 sharply observed dramas of small-town life from Strout (*Abide with Me*, 2006, etc.).

Olive Kitteridge certainly makes a formidable contrast with her gentle, quietly cheerful husband Henry from the moment we meet them both in "Pharmacy," which introduces us to several other denizens of Crosby, Maine. Though she was a math teacher before she and Henry retired, she's not exactly patient with shy young people—or anyone else. Yet she brusquely comforts suicidal Kevin Coulson in "Incoming Tide" with the news that her father, like Kevin's mother, killed himself. And she does her best to help anorexic Nina in "Starving," though Olive knows that the troubled girl is not the only person in Crosby hungry for love. Children disappoint, spouses are unfaithful and almost everyone is lonely at least some of the time in Strout's rueful tales. The Kitteridges' son Christopher marries, moves to California and divorces, but he doesn't come home to the house his parents built for him, causing deep resentments to fester around the borders of Olive's carefully tended garden. Tensions simmer in all the families here; even the genuinely loving couple in "Winter Concert" has a painful betrayal in its past. References to Iraq and 9/11 provide a somber context, but the real dangers here are personal: aging, the loss of love, the imminence of death. Nonetheless, Strout's sensitive insights and luminous prose affirm life's pleasures, as elderly, widowed Olive thinks, "It baffled her, the world. She did not want to leave it yet."

A perfectly balanced portrait of the human condition, encompassing plenty of anger, cruelty and loss without ever losing sight of the equally powerful presences of tenderness, shared pursuits and lifelong loyalty.

Source: Review of *Olive Kitteridge*, in *Kirkus Reviews*, February 1, 2008.

Audrey Larson

In the following review, Larson explains how the book is about relationships, written with great insights into people.

Each chapter in the book is a short story of different people and families living in a Maine community. Olive Kitteridge is a retired math teacher who knows, and/or has contact with, the people in the stories.

Olive Kitteridge is a female curmudgeon. She is harsh, opinionated, judgmental, quite unlikeable, and manages to offend someone every time she opens her mouth. Most of us know a woman or women similar to Olive Kitteridge, who are abrasive, irritating and cause stress everywhere they go. Often, they don't even know, understand or care how badly they affect others. Olive's own son told her she was the most feared teacher in the school. Olive alienates her son with her harsh language and ways, even though she loves him. And people are always wondering why her husband puts up with her. Her husband, Henry Kitteridge, is just the opposite of Olive. He is happier, more easy-going, pleasant, positive, helpful and accepting of others. Henry is a very likeable person, where Olive is not.

This book is about relationships, family dynamics, every-day, ordinary people with their troubles, problems, tragedies, mistakes, and learning experiences throughout their lives. There seems to be very little happiness, peace or humor in any of the characters' lives. Certainly, Olive Kitteridge is too negative in all her thinking, and seems to lack a sense of humor. She takes herself way too seriously.

Olive Kitteridge is a senior citizen who keeps right on analyzing, learning and doing a bit of growing right to the end of the book. But describing her is a bit like "we grow too soon old and too late smart."

This 270-page book is well written, and the author has good insights into people's personalities, flaws, weaknesses and human nature. There is almost no humor in the book, except for a funny parrot. "Olive Kitteridge" would be far better with more humor, because even with all the characters' troubles and unhappiness, very few people really live totally humorless lives. But it is an interesting read. I give it three stars.

Source: Audrey Larson, Review of *Olive Kitteridge*, in *MBR Bookwatch*, March 2008.

SOURCES

Andersen, Beth E., Review of *Olive Kitteridge*, in *Library Journal*, Vol. 133, No. 2, February 1, 2008, p. 65.

Birnbaum, Robert, "Elizabeth Strout," in *Morning News*, August 26, 2008, http://www.themorningnews.org/ article/elizabeth-strout (accessed August 2, 2011).

Bush, Trudy, Review of *Olive Kitteridge*, in *Christian Century*, Vol. 126, No. 21, October 20, 2009, pp. 54–55.

Dargan, Michele, "Pulitzer Winner Says Curiosity Drives Writing," in *Palm Beach Daily News*, January 15, 2010, p. 1A.

James, Henry, *The Bostonians*, Barnes & Noble Classics, 2005, pp. 7–10.

Quinn, Mary Ellen, Review of *Olive Kitteridge*, in *Booklist*, Vol. 104, Nos. 9–10, January 1, 2008, p. 46.

Randolph, Ladette, "Elizabeth Strout: A Profile," in *Ploughshares*, Vol. 36, No. 1, Spring 2010, pp. 174–79.

Review of *Olive Kitteridge*, in *Atlantic*, Vol. 302, No. 1, July/August 2008, p. 140.

Review of *Olive Kitteridge*, in *Kirkus Reviews*, February 1, 2008.

Review of *Olive Kitteridge*, in *New Yorker*, Vol. 84, No. 12, May 5, 2008, p. 77.

Review of *Olive Kitteridge*, in *Publishers Weekly*, Vol. 254, No. 49, December 10, 2007, p. 31.

Strout, Elizabeth, *Olive Kitteridge*, Random House, 2008.

———, *Olive Kitteridge*, Simon & Schuster, 2011.

Teicher, Craig Morgan, "Maine Idea," in *Publishers Weekly*, Vol. 255, No. 5, February 4, 2008, p. 32.

Theiss, Nola, Review of *Olive Kitteridge*, in *Kliatt*, Vol. 42, No. 5, September 2008, pp. 50–51.

Thomas, Louisa, Review of *Olive Kitteridge*, in *New York Times Book Review*, April 20, 2008, p. 13.

FURTHER READING

Bryson, Bill, *The Lost Continent: Travels in Small-Town America*, Harper & Row, 1989.

> Known for his pleasantly humorous travelogues, the Iowa native Bryson relates his search through America's heartland for the perfect small town.

Devlin, Keith J., *Mathematics, the Science of Patterns: The Search for Order in Life, Mind, and the Universe*, Scientific American Library, 1994.

> Perhaps a greater understanding of Olive Kitteridge could be gleaned through a greater understanding of the focus of her professional life: mathematics. This volume considers mathematics as not merely the language of numbers but a means of understanding patterns in all aspects of the universe.

Olson, Laura Katz, ed., *Age through Ethnic Lenses: Caring for the Elderly in a Multicultural Society*, Rowman & Littlefield, 2001.

> In light of modern political dilemmas regarding how to allot/secure funding for such programs as Social Security and Medicare, Olson's text examines the circumstances faced by elders among various ethnic groups in the United States.

Wood, Monica, and Patrick Quinlan, eds., *The Way Life Should Be: Stories by Contemporary Maine Writers*, Warren Machine, 2005.

In this collection, seventeen different Maine authors provide stories revolving around the particular ways of life practiced in their home state.

SUGGESTED SEARCH TERMS

Elizabeth Strout AND Olive Kitteridge

Elizabeth Strout AND Portland, Maine

Elizabeth Strout AND New York City

Olive Kitteridge AND novel in stories

Olive Kitteridge AND Pulitzer Prize

Maine AND fiction OR history

Maine AND best small town

small town AND America OR life

Elizabeth Strout AND Abide with Me OR Amy and Isabelle

Oryx and Crake

MARGARET ATWOOD

2003

Canadian writer Margaret Atwood's 2003 novel *Oryx and Crake* paints a terrifying picture of a not-so-distant future in which genetic engineering runs amok and all of human civilization lies in ruins, the victim of a deadly viral plague. Although some classify the novel as science fiction, Atwood prefers the term *speculative fiction*, as this term suggests that the story is rooted in ideas, concepts, and events already present in contemporary society. Indeed, the advances in bioengineering in years since the novel's publication eerily parallel some of the events in the story.

Atwood reveals, in an essay she wrote for *PMLA*, that she began the novel while on a trip to Australia, "the land of dreamtime." She continues, "I 'saw' the book as I was looking over a balcony at a rare red-headed crake, during a birding expedition."

Like many of Atwood's earlier novels, *Oryx and Crake* has been popular with both critics and general readers. It was shortlisted for the Man Booker Prize in 2003 and was also named a *New York Times* Notable Book.

Oryx and Crake is not a book for children; readers should be aware that there are many troubling scenes depicting violence, drug use, pornography, and sex. In addition, the postapocalyptic setting is frightening. For the more mature reader, however, *Oryx and Crake* offers not only a look toward a horrifying future but

Margaret Atwood *(Francois Guillot | AFP | Getty Images)*

also a biting satire of contemporary society, a heartbreaking romance, and an exciting quest story.

AUTHOR BIOGRAPHY

Atwood was born on November 18, 1939, in Ottawa, Ontario, Canada, to Margaret and Carl Atwood. Her father was an entomologist who conducted research in the bush country of northern Ontario and Quebec. Consequently, Atwood and her brother spent every summer camping in the far north, returning to Toronto each year for the school year. (Her younger sister was not born until 1951.) During this time, she accompanied her father in the field, but she also spent a great deal of time reading.

Atwood began writing seriously when she was sixteen. She attended Victoria College of the University of Toronto beginning in 1957; there, she earned an arts degree with honors in English. She published her first book of poetry, *Double Persephone*, in 1961, the year she graduated.

Next, she attended Radcliffe College, which is associated with Harvard University, on a graduate fellowship and completed a master of arts degree in English. She began Ph.D. studies at Harvard but did not complete the degree and returned to Canada. She spent the next ten years teaching English at a variety of Canadian universities. In 1967, she married James Polk, an American. However, the marriage did not last, and the couple separated in 1972 and divorced in 1977. Atwood established a long-term relationship with the Canadian novelist Graeme Gibson in 1972, and the couple remains together. They have one daughter.

The 1970s were good years for Atwood creatively; she published three novels (including *Surfacing* in 1972), a book of short stories, and five volumes of poetry. She also wrote the benchmark critical survey of Canadian literature, *Survival: A Thematic Guide to Canadian Literature*, in 1972. In 1980, Atwood and her family moved to Toronto, where they have remained ever since.

Throughout the next decades, Atwood proved herself to be an amazingly prolific writer, producing many well-received critical works, including novels, volumes of short stories, books of poetry, children's books, and essays. Atwood's Web site lists seventeen volumes of poetry, seven collections of short stories, thirteen novels, seven children's books, and nine book-length collections of criticism. She has also edited six books, written a play, and published a number of special editions for small presses.

Although Atwood has been well known as a writer since the 1970s, her 1985 novel *The Handmaid's Tale* was her breakout success, winning her global readership. The novel was shortlisted for the Booker Prize, and it won the Arthur C. Clarke award in 1987 for best science fiction novel and the *Los Angeles Times* fiction award. In addition, the book was wildly popular with readers, appearing on the *New York Times* best-seller list for fifteen weeks in the hardcover edition. In 1987, when the novel was released in paperback, it again appeared on the *New York Times* list, this time for eight weeks. When the movie version of the novel appeared in 1990, the novel once more hit the best-seller lists. In 2000, the novel *Blind Assassin* won the Booker Prize.

In 2003, Atwood returned to speculative fiction with the publication of *Oryx and Crake*, a dystopic novel that describes a near-future global catastrophe. In 2009, Atwood published *Year of the Flood*. The setting of this novel is contemporary with *Oryx and Crake*, and some of the same characters appear in both.

Atwood's work has been translated into more than forty languages, according to her Web site. She is far and away the most honored and recognized writer in Canada. Moreover, she is acknowledged internationally as one of the most important writers of the twentieth and twenty-first centuries.

MEDIA ADAPTATIONS

- In 2003, Random House produced *Oryx and Crake* as an unabridged, downloadable audiobook, narrated by Campbell Scott.

PLOT SUMMARY

Oryx and Crake is narrated by a character called Snowman who tells the story both in the present and in flashback, when, as a child and young man, he was known as Jimmy. The book opens in a strange and forbidding setting, and the reader must piece together both the past and the present to make sense of the story. In this summary, the name "Snowman" is used to indicate the present time in the novel, while the name "Jimmy" refers to events in flashback.

Chapter 1

The first chapter introduces Snowman as he awakens, somewhere near a seacoast. There are reefs made of destroyed cars and buildings; as the scene unfolds, it becomes clear that the setting is postapocalyptic and that the story is told in some unspecified future time after a huge catastrophe. Even on the first page, the tone is grim: Snowman is terrified, he is covered in bites and scabs, there is little food, and his only clothing is a dirty bed sheet and a Red Sox baseball hat.

In the next scene, Snowman watches some children on the beach. These children and their parents are the Children of Crake, also called Crakers—beautiful, genetically engineered to withstand the sun's dangerous ultraviolet light and viral diseases. Snowman appears to be the only human being who has survived the catastrophe, and he is barely surviving. The Children of Crake treat Snowman as if he is a god or an oracle, someone who can teach them about the world. Although the names Crake and Oryx are referenced, little is revealed, other than that Snowman seems to blame Crake for the current situation, and he hears Oryx's voice in his mind.

Chapter 2

The second chapter is a flashback to Snowman's childhood, to when he was a boy named Jimmy. In the flashback, Jimmy's father works as a genographer, or someone who maps genes, at OrganInc Farms, a place where scientists genetically engineer animals to serve as hosts for organs that can be transplanted into humans. Pigoons, for example, are pig derivatives that have been developed to grow five or six kidneys.

One of Jimmy's earliest memories is watching a huge bonfire of cows, sheep, and pigs that were infected by disease; there is some indication that humans caused the animals to become infected. The incident foreshadows later events in the novel.

Jimmy, his mother, and his father live at the OrganInc compound, a sealed community. Jimmy attends OrganInc School. Outside the compound are the pleeblands, inhabited by violent and unpredictable poor people. Jimmy's mother and father are growing increasingly estranged. Once a microbiologist for OrganInc, she now stays at home all day, growing ever more depressed.

Chapter 3

The story returns to the present. Snowman has problems with the heat, humidity, and intense sun. Severe storms occur as well, and although the setting is vaguely on the eastern coast of North America, the daily afternoon thunderstorms suggest a tropical climate. The implication is that these are the products of global warming. There are references to Snowman's early days in this strange new world and information about the other creatures that share the world with Snowman. The pigoons have become feral and dangerous. Wolvogs, a genetically engineered cross between a wolf and a dog, also roam in packs.

Chapter 4

In a flashback, Snowman recalls his tenth birthday, when his father gives him a rakunk. The rakunk is a cross between a skunk and a raccoon, developed as part of a "Create an Animal" game played among the geneticists. Jimmy calls him Killer.

Jimmy's father gets a new job at HelthWyzer, and the family moves to a new compound where the security is even stricter than at OrganInc. Jimmy's mother grows more and more despondent and says she feels like a prisoner. She is opposed to the research Jimmy's father is doing. Meanwhile, fanatics storm the HelthWyzer gates with spray bottles of highly dangerous infectious diseases.

Jimmy's mother finally leaves the family. She destroys her computer and her husband's computer before she leaves. It is unclear whether she does this in revenge or as a security precaution. She also takes Jimmy's pet rakunk with her; in a note to Jimmy, she says that she will "liberate" the creature. Jimmy is bereft and angry. Jimmy and his father are questioned by men from CorpSeCorps, or corporate security corps, a quasi-police agency that wields tremendous power.

Meanwhile, Jimmy has met a student named Glenn, who later assumes the name of Crake. Jimmy's teacher asks him to show Crake around the school. Crake is brilliant and quickly moves to the top of the class. He and Jimmy become close friends and spend all of their time outside of school together, usually playing computer simulation games. Their favorite is Extinctathon, a game in which the player has to identify bioforms that have gone extinct within the previous fifty years.

The two boys also surf the Internet, visiting pornography sites by using a password belonging to Crake's mother's boyfriend. They also smoke his marijuana while they play on the computer. It is while they are surfing the Internet that they run across a child porn site and are both entranced by a small girl. In the flashback, Snowman refers to the girl as Oryx, although it is unclear whether the child they see on the porn site is really the same person as the woman they later know as Oryx.

At the end of the chapter, Snowman flashes back to a time after Jimmy's childhood and adolescence, a time when, as adults, Jimmy and Oryx become lovers.

Chapter 5

In a return to the present, Snowman recalls how he began teaching the Crakers in the days immediately after the catastrophe. He tells them that Crake created them and Oryx continues to provide for them. One of the "laws" he hands down to them is that the genetically engineered rabbits that dot the countryside are sacred to Oryx and must not be eaten. He also specifies that the Crakers must catch and grill a fish once a week and bring it to him to eat.

In this chapter, readers learn more about the Crakers: they are vegetarian, their skin tones range from very white to black, they have green eyes, and they are all beautiful. They ask Snowman to explain the things they find on the beach, the remains of a human civilization that has gone extinct. Snowman finds himself making up answers for them, and it seems that the Crakers are developing a religion that centers around Oryx and Crake.

Snowman gives into his desolation and searches out a bottle of Scotch whiskey he has been saving. He drinks it all and howls at the moon. Soon, wolvogs surround the base of the tree where he sleeps. He tosses the bottle at them and they scatter, but he knows it is only a matter of time before they hunt and kill him. His mind returns to Oryx; he seems to miss her presence more than anything else.

Chapter 6

Snowman recounts the story of Oryx, as she told it to him when they were lovers. As a child living in a developing nation, Oryx was a member of large and desperately poor family living in a remote village. A man called Uncle En periodically visited villages like this one, offering to buy children and take them to the city, where they could earn money. Oryx and her brother were sold.

They were taken to a tiny room in a city inhabited by many children. Oryx was instructed to sell flowers in the street until a man asked her to come up to his room. Once there, he told her to take off her dress. Uncle En burst into the room and extorted money from the man.

Later, another man took charge of the children, and Oryx learned that Uncle En had been murdered. Her new job was to act in pornographic movies like the one that Crake and Jimmy watched on their computer. As Oryx tells Jimmy about her life, he becomes very angry and protective of her. Oryx, on the other hand, is very matter-of-fact about what has happened to her.

Chapter 7

Snowman awakens from his drinking binge on the platform in the tree where he lives. He knows that he must find some food. Retrieving his remaining food from a hiding place, he realizes that he does not have enough to sustain himself in the long run. If he can kill a pigoon, he thinks, he will have plenty of food. But the pigoons are very smart and violent, and he has no weapons. He decides he must travel to the RejoovenEsense Compound to gather supplies and guns. The RejoovenEsense Compound is where he lived with Crake and Oryx before the catastrophe. Crake built a bubble dome called Paradice where the Crakers were created.

Snowman goes to the Crakers' village to tell them he will be gone for a few days. He finds the men performing their morning ritual of urinating around the perimeter of their settlement. Crake has genetically engineered them to give off chemicals in their urine that act as a repellent to creatures such as wolvogs, bobkittens, pigoons, and rakunks.

He also observes the women engaging in purring, a practice that involves sound waves in healing. One of the children has been attacked by a bobkitten, and the women purr over him. He also notes that the Crakers grow very quickly, reaching adolescence by four years old. At age thirty, they die.

Snowman tells the Crakers he is going to see Crake. They want to come along, but he forbids it. Snowman starts out on the long journey.

Chapter 8

While walking toward the compound, Snowman flashes back to the day when he and Crake graduated from HelthWyzer High. Crake finished at the top of his class and was invited to attend Watson-Crick Institute, while Jimmy was accepted only at the very low ranking Martha Graham Academy. At their graduation party, Crake tells Jimmy that his mother has died, the victim of a horrible virus that dissolved her flesh. Crake's father died some time before, the result of falling off a highway overpass.

Soon after, large numbers of people begin protesting the Happicuppa coffee bean, devised by HelthWyzer. This bean could be harvested with machines. While watching the protests on television, Jimmy sees his mother as part of a shouting crowd rushing CorpSeCorps men. He fears for her safety.

Later, the boys go their separate ways. The Martha Graham Academy is an underfunded, deteriorating institution. Once a school where students studied fine arts, most students at Martha Graham now studied graphics arts and writing designed for advertising, marketing, and propaganda. As a Martha Graham student, Jimmy is not challenged intellectually, and he spends most of his time chasing girls.

Crake, on the other hand, is at the prestigious Watson-Crick Institute, where students study mathematics and science. He invites Jimmy to visit him over Thanksgiving, and Jimmy accepts. Once there, Jimmy is again interrogated by CorpSeCorps men concerning his mother.

Crake takes Jimmy on a tour of the campus and shows him the new products that students are working on, including something called "ChickieNobs." These are genetically engineered chickens that have no beaks, brains, or eyes, but they have extra legs, thighs, and breasts. The chickens are headed for the fast-food industry.

Crake also confides in Jimmy that his father's death was not an accident. He suspects that CorpSeCorps had him murdered because he knew that HelthWyzer was not only creating cures for disease but also creating diseases so that they could sell the cures.

Later, Crake reveals that he has become a grandmaster in Extinctathon and that "playrooms" on the site are filled with leaked documents from CorpSeCorps. It becomes clear that the inner workings of Extinctathon are being run by anti-corporation activists known collectively as MaddAddam.

Chapter 9

This chapter flashes to the present, with Snowman walking through the pleeblands. He finally reaches the RejoovenEsense Compound and tries to find food in a house. The inhabitants of the house are dead; the husband's body is still in the bathtub, and the wife's body is in the bedroom. There is a child's room and pictures of the family, but the child is not in the house. Snowman steals some supplies and then leaves the house, only to find a group of pigoons watching him. Snowman is able to scare them off, but just barely. He knows they will return.

Suddenly, a huge storm approaches. He slips into one of the gatehouses next to the security building. The lights come on, and he sees dead bodies in biosuits. He moves to the interior of the building, sits, and starts to drink the alcohol he found in the house.

Chapter 10

Snowman flashes back to his graduation from Martha Graham. He moves in with his girlfriend and her roommates, who are all artists. However, the relationship sours and ends when Jimmy takes a job with AnooYoo, a minor corporate compound.

Jimmy moves to AnooYoo and cuts off all communication with his father and his second wife. He receives a promotion and begins buying electronics and other consumer goods. In addition, he has a series of affairs with married women who are only looking for a little excitement. Neither Jimmy nor the women want commitment of any sort.

Meanwhile, Crake is working at Rejooven-Esense, one of the top compounds. He and Jimmy have some communication, and Crake tells Jimmy that his mother's boyfriend has died suddenly, with a virus. The implication is that Crake has maneuvered to make this happen.

While watching the news, Jimmy becomes aware of a wave of young girls found locked in garages. The girls have been forced to engage in the sex trade and pornography. One young woman is interviewed on the television, and Jimmy recognizes her as the child he and Crake saw on the Internet some ten years earlier. It is the woman he will come to know as Oryx.

The CorpSeCorps men begin interrogating him about his mother again. They show him a blindfolded prisoner about to be executed for treason. Just before she is shot, she says, "Goodbye. Remember Killer. I love you. Don't let me down." He realizes that she is his mother. After this encounter, he enters a deep depression and realizes that the work he has been doing at AnooYoo is meaningless. What he wants is revenge.

Chapter 11

Snowman, hiding in the gatehouse, is awakened from a dream by the sound of a land crab digging through the wall. As he leaves the gatehouse, he sees a group of pigoons charging him. He runs back to the gatehouse, but the pigoons follow him in. He runs upstairs, since pigoons have not yet learned to climb. However, he knows it is only a matter of time until they learn how to manage the stairs.

Trapped upstairs, he looks through the supplies that are left in the guardhouse. He finds a radio and hears another human voice speaking in a foreign language. He tries to reply but is unsuccessful.

Earlier, he cut his foot, and now he tends to the cut. There are many viruses and bacteria loose, and he could develop a fatal infection. When night falls, he finds a bed in the gatehouse. He has a troubled night's sleep filled with dreams of his mother.

In the morning, he resupplies himself and makes a plan to escape the guardhouse through the air vents. He is still intent on making it to Paradice.

Once outside, he sees smoke rising from the general direction of the Crakers' encampment. Not knowing what he is facing, he feels an even greater need to acquire weapons from Paradice.

Chapter 12

Snowman pushes on, the heat and his throbbing foot slowing him down. He flashes back to his last days at AnooYoo. Unexpectedly, Crake shows up and offers him a job at Rejooven-Esense. Jimmy accepts and finds himself living in great luxury. Crake tells him about a pill called BlyssPluss. The pill will wipe out all sexually transmitted diseases, improve sexual performance, and prolong youth. Jimmy's job will be to handle the advertising campaign.

Jimmy soon gets his first glimpse of Paradice. It is a dome in the RejoovenEsense Compound. It is highly guarded, and only Crake and those he vouches for are allowed to enter. The dome has airlocks so that it can be completely sealed off in the event of terrorism or unexpected plague. Jimmy discovers that the people working on gene splicing in Paradice were all members of MaddAddam. Although they are anti-Compound, Crake has coerced them into coming to work for him.

Crake then shows Jimmy his life's work, the Crakers. Later, when Jimmy looks through the one-way glass into the place where the Crakers live, he sees Oryx. Crake explains that Oryx is their teacher. Crake has found her through a service that provides prostitutes to students at Watson-Crick. He is in love with her.

However, Jimmy is in love with her too. He begins an affair with her and tries to convince her to run away with him. Both Crake and Oryx, at different times, ask Jimmy to take care of the Crakers if anything should happen to them.

One evening, Oryx runs out for a pizza, and while she is gone, an epidemic of a fatal virus breaks out in Brazil. Because Crake is away from the compound and Jimmy is next in charge, he monitors the outbreak. Suddenly, the outbreaks are everywhere throughout the world. He is racked with anxiety over Oryx's location. Finally she calls, crying. She tells him that the virus was in the BlyssPluss pills she has been taking all over the world.

By midnight, it is clear that this is a major catastrophe. The next morning, Oryx and Crake return, and stand at the airlock waiting for Jimmy to let them in. Jimmy refuses, but Crake tells him that he has immunized Jimmy against the virus.

Jimmy opens the airlocks, and Crake staggers in with Oryx, who has passed out. He looks at Jimmy, and says, "I'm counting on you." Then Crake slits Oryx's throat. Jimmy shoots him.

Chapter 13

Snowman walks around Paradice, his foot throbbing. He finds some antibiotics and injects himself. Then, he flashes back to the days immediately after the catastrophe and Oryx and Crake's deaths. He spends hours watching the Crakers, finally introducing himself to them as Snowman. He tells them that Oryx and Crake have left, and that Snowman must take them to a new place. Jimmy leads them out of Paradice, stepping over the bodies of Oryx and Crake. He shoots any infected humans who try to approach them.

Chapter 14

Snowman makes it back to the beach, the infection in his foot growing worse. The Crakers are singing his name in an attempt to lead him back to them. They tell him that they have been visited by two men and a woman while he was gone and that they had guns. Snowman promises to visit the people the next day.

Chapter 15

Snowman wakes early, before sunrise. He is frightened by the thought of confronting the other humans. He does not know whether to try to talk to them or kill them. He fears that if he does not kill them, they will kill him and then kill the Crakers. Yet he does not want to do so. The last words of the book are ambiguous: "From habit he lifts his watch; it shows him its blank face. Zero hour, Snowman thinks. Time to go."

CHARACTERS

Crake

Crake is the name assumed by a green-eyed boy originally known as Glenn. He takes this name when he and his friend Jimmy play the Web-based computer game Extinctathon. The red-necked crake is a bird found in New Guinea and Australia. A secretive bird, it is rarely seen by observers. Likewise, throughout the novel, Crake is a secretive character who reveals little about himself.

Crake (then called Glenn) arrives at the HelthWyzer school after his father dies and while his mother is living with her boyfriend, a man Crake calls Uncle Pete. Their teacher asks Jimmy to show Glenn around the school, and the two become fast friends, spending most of their out-of-school time together smoking Uncle Pete's dope and surfing the Internet. They use Uncle Pete's password to access seedy pornography sites. Crake is very adept at hacking into sites and creating computer labyrinths to hide their viewing history and the use of the password. At one point, Crake and Jimmy stumble into a child porn site and see a girl they come to know as Oryx.

Crake is particularly taken with the game Extinctathon, a game that requires an impressive knowledge of extinct creatures. The webmaster of the site is an entity known as MaddAddam. Years after they leave high school, Crake reveals to Jimmy that he has become a grandmaster at the game, and in so doing, has entered the world of MaddAddam, a disruptive, anti-Compound collective of computer hackers and scientists.

While still in high school, Crake proves himself to be a particularly brilliant but cynical young man. He is recruited to attend the Watson-Crick Institute, an elite and powerful university. At Watson-Crick, he lives a life of luxury and begins his studies of gene splicing. Unbeknownst to Jimmy, Crake has Student Services secure for him a young female prostitute while he is in college; he feels sure that she is the girl they saw years before on the Internet. He names her Oryx. After graduation, Crake receives a job at RejoovenEsense, one of the most powerful of all the compounds, taking Oryx with him.

At RejoovenEsense, Crake works on a product known as BlyssPluss, a pill that will increase sexual prowess, eliminate sexually transmitted diseases, and lengthen life span. He hires Jimmy to manage the ad campaign.

Crake's success with this project gives him a great deal of power. As always, he is very secretive about a project of his own design in a dome he calls Paradice. He coerces the top minds of MaddAddam to join his project. (It is implied that he has eliminated the other scientists working in MaddAddam, a clue to his ruthless, secretive nature.)

The project is to genetically engineer a race of humanoids who have all the qualities Crake believes are important for their survival. They are immune to disease, their reproduction is carefully controlled, and they mature early and die upon turning thirty. In creating these beings, Crake reveals his own hubris (pride): all of the creatures have his green eyes, though they have many different colors of skin. In addition, Crake's hubris persuades him that he knows what qualities make up a "perfect" life form.

When Crake shows the project to Jimmy, he reveals that he has Oryx working with the Crakers, as the creatures are called. He also implies that he is in love with her.

As secretive as he is, there are clues to the vengeful nature of Crake's personality. He reveals that his father's death was not an accident but rather the work of the CorpSeCorps men, who did not want his father to reveal that HelthWyzer not only produces diseases as well as their cures. Crake's ultimate vengeance on the human race may be a punishment for his father's death. Likewise, although it is not stated explicitly, there are hints that the disease that kills his mother and Uncle Pete was his creation, a trial run of the disease he would use to destroy the entire human race. Again, this punishment may have been revenge for what he viewed as his mother's betrayal of his father. Finally, Crake kills Oryx in front of Jimmy, an act that could be considered punishment for their affair.

Crake's Father

Crake's father is dead before Jimmy and Crake meet, the supposed victim of an accident in which he fell off a bridge. Crake, however, knows that he was murdered. Crake's father knew that the HelthWyzer Compound produced both cures for diseases and the diseases themselves, in order to turn a profit. That knowledge cost him his life.

Crake's Mother

Crake's mother is a shadowy figure who ends up dissolving because of a terrible disease. Clues in the story suggest that she knew that her husband knew about HelthWyzer Compound's creation of diseases and informs on him to the CorpSeCorps. She and Crake move in with her boyfriend shortly after her husband's death.

Glenn

See Crake

Jimmy

See Snowman

Jimmy's Father

Jimmy's father is a genographer, a scientist who maps gene sequences. He is very good at his job and is hired by an important biogenetic firm known as HelthWyzer. Although he believes that the work he does is for the benefit of humanity, there are times when he seems to know that he has morally sold out in order to obtain a good lifestyle.

After his wife leaves, Jimmy's father begins an affair with his laboratory assistant, who eventually moves into the house. He seems oblivious to the needs of his child, Jimmy.

Jimmy's Mother

Jimmy's mother is a bioscientist who previously worked for the OrganFarm Compound. After Jimmy is born, she spends more time at home, eventually not working at all. She is despondent about her condition and grows increasingly agitated by the work her husband is doing. She believes that the genetic work he is doing is against nature and is morally wrong. Eventually, she escapes from the compound, destroying her and her husband's computers as she leaves. She also takes Jimmy's rakunk with her, leaving a note that tells Jimmy that she will "liberate" the animal.

She continues to send unsigned postcards to Jimmy throughout the story. Jimmy sees her participating in a protest against a HelthWyzer product, and later sees a video of her execution as a traitor.

Jimmy's mother may have followed her moral compass in leaving the HelthWyzer Compound, but in so doing, she left her son to fend for himself. She emerges as an essentially selfish person, despite her willingness to fight for what she believes in. Her absence and her choice to put protest before motherhood mark Jimmy deeply.

Oryx

Oryx is a young woman originally from a developing country. Her family, desperately poor, has sold her to a man who wants her to sell flowers in the city at first, but who really wants to engage her in the child sex trade. Later, she is sold to another man who has her act in pornographic movies. Finally, she meets Crake when she comes to him as a prostitute. He is in love with her, and he hires her as part of a special project.

Of the three main characters in *Oryx and Crake*, Oryx is the greatest mystery. She tells the details of her life to Jimmy in a very matter-of-fact manner and never dwells on the terrible conditions under which she has had to live. She seems to understand her own sexuality, even as a child, as a commodity to be bought and sold.

While Jimmy agonizes over her past, Oryx wants to leave it behind. She suggests that the conditions working in the child pornography studio were much better than the conditions in her home village. There is a moment, however, when it is clear that, as a small child, she desperately missed her mother. In the flashback sequences to Oryx's childhood, it is clear that she misses her mother dreadfully.

Like Jimmy, Oryx has been deserted and betrayed by her mother. Like Jimmy, she does not seem to form close personal bonds. Although she is intimate with both Crake and Jimmy, she shares very little of herself or her emotional life with either of them.

Snowman

Snowman is the narrator of the story, so all its events and characters are filtered through his consciousness. His age is not specified, but through the course of the story, readers learn that he is probably in his thirties. He may be slightly mad; he hears the voice of a woman he loves in his head. He appears to be the sole survivor of a catastrophe that has destroyed the entire human race. He lives in a tree to protect himself from the carnivores that inhabit the landscape. His primary responsibility is to care for the Children of Crake, a genetically engineered race of hominids.

Over the course of the book, Snowman recalls his life as Jimmy (his given name) in flashbacks, ranging from the time he was five years old until the apocalyptic moment when everyone is dying of a viral infection and he shoots Crake.

Jimmy is a lover and collector of archaic words. Just as Crake is fascinated with extinct bioforms, Jimmy is entranced by extinct and dying words.

As a boy, Jimmy is intelligent but underachieving. He is deeply sensitive to his parents' marital problems, and he alternately loves and hates both his mother and his father. As a child, he seems to have had no friends. The only thing he truly loves is the rakunk, a genetically engineered animal that his father gives him for his tenth birthday. The gift, however, causes another rift in his parents' marriage.

When Jimmy's mother ultimate leaves her family, Jimmy feels angry, grief-stricken, and betrayed. Not only has his mother deserted him, she has taken his rakunk with her, leaving him without love. Moreover, when his father begins bringing home his lab assistant, Jimmy feels once more betrayed and unloved.

In high school, Jimmy meets Crake (then called Glenn), and Crake becomes his one true friend. The two spend all of their time together, mostly surfing the Internet. Jimmy is deeply touched when they see a girl on a pornography site, and her image stays with him the rest of his life.

Jimmy is not a good student. Although it seems clear that he is intelligent, he does not apply himself. In addition, his intellectual strength is words, not mathematics or science. Because the arts are so devalued in this society, he finds himself at a run-down, dilapidated university while Crack goes off to the most elite university.

Jimmy does not apply himself in college either and is unable to form lasting relationships with women, although he always has a girlfriend. It is likely that his mother's desertion and the general tone of the society he lives in have made it impossible for him to emotionally commit to anyone.

When he ultimately comes to work with Crake at RejoovenEsense, he discovers Oryx there, and knows that Crake is in love with her. Despite this, he has an affair with Oryx; he is deeply in love with her. This love, however, causes him pain because he is betraying Crake, his one friend.

After Crake kills Oryx in front of Jimmy during the early hours of the massive viral epidemic, Jimmy, without even thinking, shoots Crake and kills him. It is difficult to know whether this is yet another betrayal of Crake, whether it is a crime of passion, or whether Jimmy does this to protect the world from the monster Crake has become.

As Snowman, he reveals himself as a morally ambiguous man. He is a person of great sadness, yet he shoulders the responsibility put on him by both his mother and Crake. He will protect the Crakers, even with his own life.

Uncle En

Uncle En is the man who comes to Oryx's village to persuade the poor people to sell their children. He does not treat the children unkindly, according to Oryx, but he does initiate them into the child sex trade.

Uncle Pete

Uncle Pete is Crake's mother's boyfriend, who lives with her and Crake after Crake's father dies. He has a stash of skunkweed, another name for marijuana, and he also has passwords for pornographic Web sites. He dies of a virulent disease, and the implication is that Crake has killed him.

THEMES

Motherhood

While it might seem strange to think about motherhood as a theme in *Oryx and Crake* in that the mothers are largely absent, their very absence forms a thematic thread. Indeed, this thread continues back to Atwood's 1985 novel *The Handmaid's Tale*. In this novel, the narrator Offred's mother is an environmental activist who initially appears only in Offred's memory; her mother has disappeared. Later, Offred discovers that her mother has been arrested and shipped off to the interior part of the country to clean up

toxic wastes. She finds this out when she sees her mother in a newsreel film.

In *Oryx and Crake*, Jimmy's mother seems absent even before she finally leaves the family. Her unhappiness with her marriage and with the corporation for which she and her husband work leads her to feeling trapped and powerless. She grows distant from both her husband and her son. When she finally decides to leave, it becomes clear that she really *was* trapped. She must fake a visit to a dentist for a root canal in order to leave the compound.

While her commitment to her beliefs might be seen as admirable in other circumstances, in *Oryx and Crake*, her decision to leave comes across as selfish and destructive to her son. As Shuli Barzilai notes in an article appearing in *Critique*, "She does not love him enough to put him before her own needs and desires. She abandons Jimmy for a cause...that she ardently embraces." Worse, she takes away Jimmy's rakunk, a decision she makes on the basis of her own firmly held beliefs rather than Jimmy's feelings.

In the years that follow, she sends postcards to Jimmy, unsigned and sent from unknown locations. Rather than establishing a motherly presence, however, the postcards merely underscore her absence.

Crake's mother is also a shadowy figure. There are not many references to her in the story, only the comment that she likes Jimmy and that she began living with Uncle Pete, her boyfriend, after Crake's father died. Much later in the story, Crake reveals that his father died not from simply falling off a bridge but because he was pushed. Although not explicitly stated, the implication is that Crake's mother had some part in the assassination; she either plotted against him or did nothing to save him. When she dies a particularly gruesome death, the victim of a virus that dissolves her, there is the additional implication that Crake may have orchestrated her death. In any event, the nature of the virus causes her to literally disappear, again pointing to her absence as a mother figure.

Finally, Oryx's mother, in desperate circumstances, chooses to sell her children. Although she may believe that she is ensuring their survival, in reality, she has condemned them to lives devoid of love and nurturance. Indeed, this mother turns her own children into a commodity, using them as a means of exchange.

TOPICS FOR FURTHER STUDY

- In *Oryx and Crake*, Atwood sets her story in a time in the near future, when global warming has changed the climate significantly. Using recent, credible sources on the Internet and in your library, research global warming. What do scientists predict will happen within the next twenty years? Within the next century? Locate specific references to the weather in *Oryx and Crake*. Does her book seem to follow scientific predictions? Write a researched-based essay reporting your findings about the possibility of the events Atwood imagines actually happening. Be sure to cite your sources.

- South African writer Lauren Beukes's *Moxyland* (2008) is set in Cape Town, South Africa, in the near future. Corporations are powerful, disease epidemics run rampant, and terrorist attacks are always a threat. Read *Moxyland* with a group of your peers. How is Beukes's vision of the future similar to or different from Atwood's? With your small group, prepare an imaginary newscast originating either in the world of *Oryx and Crake* or in Moxyland, reporting on a major news event. Record your newscast and post it to YouTube for your classmates to view and critique.

- Create an online, interactive poster using Glogster (http://www.glogster.com) that captures the essence of *Oryx and Crake*. To effectively complete the task, you should address the themes, characters, and contexts of the book. Upload your poster to your Web page.

- *Oryx and Crake* comments at length on genetic engineering. Research the topic of genetic engineering by consulting reputable Web sites, books, and journal articles. What are the limits of genetic engineering at present? What kinds of gene splicing are scientists currently undertaking? Do you think genetic engineering will help people or harm people? With a group of your classmates, prepare a debate on the topic, arguing for or against unlimited genetic research and engineering.

- Language is an important theme for Atwood in all of her novels. In *Oryx and Crake*, she creates Jimmy as someone who loves language and who collects words that are nearing extinction. Make a list of these words and look up their definitions. Choose ten words and do a ten-minute free writing session on each. Using Wordle (http://www.wordle.net), paste in your list of words and your free writing and make a word cloud. Experiment with color, font, size, and orientation. Print and post your word cloud in your classroom.

- Like *Oryx and Crake*, M. T. Anderson's young-adult novel *Feed* (2004) satirizes consumerism and the intrusion of corporations into the lives of its characters. Read *Feed* and *Oryx and Crake* and identify specific examples from contemporary culture that Anderson and Atwood satirize. With a group of your peers, create a television commercial that satirizes some aspect of contemporary culture. Record the commercial and upload it to YouTube for viewing by your classmates. Write a short essay explaining why you chose the example you did and how your commercial satisfies the definition of satire.

In these instances, Atwood has created mothers who behave badly and who do not nurture their offspring. Lorrie Moore, writing in the *New Yorker*, suggests one remaining mother thematically underpinning the novel: "The ur-mother in *Oryx and Crake* is, of course, Mother Nature herself—captured, tortured, and mocked, in classic gothic fashion, but elusive and indestructible, in her way." Atwood's Mother Nature is not a nurturing, loving force, providing sustenance for her children, but rather a tortured, vengeful, violent force that must be reckoned with.

Science

Science is an important thematic concern, and it is evident reading the acknowledgment page that Atwood spent significant time researching the current state of knowledge in bioengineering. Moreover, Atwood grew up in a household of scientists. As Earl G. Ingersoll writes in an article appearing in *Extrapolation*, she was obliged to "'read up on' the popularized science of Stephen Jay Gould and others to have some background for dinner-table conversation." For *Oryx and Crake*, Atwood did not have to invent anything new for the science represented in the novel. Rather, Atwood maintains that "the science in *Oryx and Crake* represents a mere extension of present knowledge in genetic engineering," according to Ingersoll. Thus, both her research and her background have led her to speculate about what happens when the implications of new scientific discoveries are pushed to extremes.

For Atwood, this sometimes involves satire, such as her description of ChickieNobs, the chickens grown with multiple legs or breasts for use in the fast food industry. As disgusting as the sight of these creatures is for Jimmy, later in the book he eats ChickieNobs. In this case, Atwood highlights how humans will use the products of science while conveniently ignoring the means through which those products have been attained.

Atwood also satirizes genetic scientists at OrganInc Farms. This group engages in a competition called "Create a Species" for no other reason than the competition. In this instance, the scientists have lost reverence for life; they essentially are joking around with the building blocks of life, the DNA sequencing of various species. They do it simply because they can. Ironically, the creatures the scientists create in jest become feral and dangerous when they escape the confines of the laboratory.

Atwood thematically attacks the unholy marriage of science and profit. It does not take much digging to find examples of this in the real world. For example, food giant Nestlé acquired Jenny Craig, a weight loss company, in 2006,

Jimmy, aka Snowman, becomes an ad copy writer after attending the Martha Graham Academy. (pashOK | Shutterstock.com)

according to Andrew Ross Sorkin, writing in the *New York Times*. The company also owns the Lean Cuisine product line. At the same time, Nestlé also manufactures Digiorno Pizza, Hot Pockets, a wide assortment of candy lines, and Häagen-Dazs ice cream. Thus, in the pursuit of profit, Nestlé produces products that increase obesity, as well as products that supposedly combat obesity. Consumers who purchase and consume too much candy and ice cream can then purchase and consume diet products. The cycle ensures that the company that produces both will always turn a profit. The world of *Oryx and Crake* pushes this cycle to the extreme, with science-driven food and pharmaceutical companies interested only in the bottom line.

While it is possible to view some of the scientific work in *Oryx and Crake* as rooted in a sincere desire to help humankind by providing medicine and organs for transplant, the novel also shows the dark underbelly of the pharmaceutical industry. With the BlyssPluss pill, the industry not only creates a product for profit that sells like wildfire but it also creates the conditions for the destruction of all humankind.

Although science in *Oryx and Crake* is often shown in a negative light, Atwood herself does not see science as bad in and of itself. In an interview with Atwood appearing on the Random House *Oryx and Crake* Web site, Atwood states,

> Please don't make the mistake of thinking that *Oryx and Crake* is anti-science. Science is a way of knowing, and a tool. Like all ways of knowing and tools, it can be turned to bad uses. But it is not in itself bad. Like electricity, it's neutral.

The message of *Oryx and Crake*, then, is this: science divorced from ethics and morality is a dangerous tool, one that can lead to places no human ever wants to go.

STYLE

Bildungsroman

A *bildungsroman* is a type of story that traces the moral and psychological growth of a central character from childhood to adulthood. In English, the form is often referred to as a coming-of-age-story. The word *bildung* means formation, and throughout a bildungsroman, the protagonist faces challenges and finds teachers who help form his or her character. *Star Wars* offers a familiar example: young Luke Skywalker grows from a young man who knows nothing of the outside world to become a Jedi knight, as a result of difficult challenges and circumstances. Along the way, his mentor Obi-Wan Kenobi and his teacher Yoda help him. Viewers watch as Luke undergoes the process of spiritual, psychological, physical, and emotional formation and grows into a man worthy of respect.

Although not as obviously, *Oryx and Crake* also functions as an example of the genre. As Barzilai points out, the fractured chronology of the story and the constant shifting from present to past hide the straightforward story of growth one expects to find in a bildungsroman. However, when the parts of the story are reordered sequentially, according to Barzilai, "what emerges is the story of the constitution of a twenty-first century (male) subject whose

primary caretakers and educators include the electronic media: the Internet, video games, and television."

The picture of young Jimmy that first emerges is that of a child who does not understand the world nor himself. He hungers for the attention of his parents, but they are so wrapped up in their own problems that they ignore him. This neglect contributes to the adult Jimmy becomes, someone who is unable to establish intimate relationships. When Jimmy's mother leaves, he feels deserted. From this point on, he finds it difficult to trust anyone.

Later, readers discover that Jimmy has little ambition and does not apply himself to his studies. Although he is older, he has not grown much. He still takes the easy way and prefers to immerse himself in video games rather than educate himself about the world. Still later, when he meets Oryx and falls in love with her, he betrays his best friend by having an affair with her. This would not appear to be growth; however, his relationship with Oryx is formative. Through his love for her and through her simple acceptance of life, he begins to stop seeing himself as a victim.

Jimmy is a late bloomer. Little that has happened during the course of the novel suggests that he will have the strength of character to be completely responsible for the Crakers. Yet when civilization ends, Jimmy does as Crake has asked him: he does not let the Crakers down. He steps into a role he does not want and performs it to the best of his ability. By the end of the story, it appears that he is willing to risk his life to protect the Crakers.

Menippean Satire

A Menippean satire is a long prose work that attacks social structures and attitudes. Named after the Greek cynic Menippus, the form has a long literary history that includes works such as Jonathan Swift's *Gulliver's Travels*, Voltaire's *Candide*, and Lewis Carroll's *Alice in Wonderland*. Chris Baldick, writing in *The Oxford Dictionary of Literary Terms*, notes that Menippean satire often includes "miscellaneous contents" and "displays of curious erudition."

Oryx and Crake is clearly satire when considered in these terms. In the first place, Atwood chooses a wide variety of content to satirize in her book: climate change and global warming, bioengineering, commercialization of life, the loss of government and the rise of corporations, security fears, terrorism, the commodification of sex, and the extinction of many life forms, among others. As she ranges among these topics, Atwood displays erudition (that is, educated mastery of a topic) beyond what a reader might expect in a novel. Her erudition gives her the authority to satirize. In each of these topics, Atwood starts with what is already present in contemporary life and then extrapolates what might happen in these areas in the future. For example, scientists warn that global warming will cause serious climate change and unsettling weather conditions in the future if humans do not stop burning fossil fuels. Atwood guesses the humans will neither limit their consumption of gas nor cease to burn coal, and so when she projects the global warming trend into the future, she sees a world where the East Coast of the United States is under water, the Midwest and West are dry and drought-stricken, and storms rage through temperate latitudes every afternoon. Likewise, she knows that scientists have concerns about the destruction of the ozone layer (the atmospheric layer that protects the Earth from dangerous radiation) due to the use of fluorocarbons. She guesses that the trend will continue, and so she creates a future where radiation from the sun is deadly to humans, although not to Crakers.

Further, Brian Lee, in *The Routledge Dictionary of Literary Terms*, quotes literary critic Northrup Frye on satire: "Satire demands at least a token fantasy, a content which the reader recognizes as grotesque, and at least an implicit moral standard." *Oryx and Crake* fulfills this requirement. The entire book is fantasy. Although it is possible to see Atwood's future firmly rooted in the present, she pushes the implication of those roots to their extreme, in order to shock and amuse her readers. For example, in present-day society, the fast food industry utilizes vast quantities of chicken meat. Bioengineering has already created poultry with huge breasts in order to increase the amount of white meat (such as the Honeysuckle White brand of turkey). Atwood pushes this trend into the future and posits the bioengineering of chickens that have no heads, beaks, or eyes. These chickens grow multiple breasts or drumsticks. The product will find its way into the fast food industry as ChickieNobs. Although Jimmy is disgusted, later in the book, ChickieNobs has become part of everyday life, and Jimmy himself eats them.

ChickieNobs also show Atwood's implicit moral standard regarding food and the humane treatment of animals. By portraying fast food and bioengineering at their most grotesque, she implies that both are morally wrong when they create inferior products that require the inhumane treatment of animals.

HISTORICAL CONTEXT

Bioterrorism

The plot of *Oryx and Crake* revolves around an event that is not explained or made clear until late in the book, yet every other thing that happens in the novel pushes the plot toward the dreadful moment when Crake, in an unthinkable example of bioterrorism, unleashes a terrible plague on the world, a plague that destroys human civilization.

It is perhaps not a surprise the bioterrorism would be at the core of Atwood's novel; in her speculative fiction, Atwood often appears to be prophetic. She began writing *Oryx and Crake* in about 2001, after having "dreamed" the book while visiting Australia. Suddenly, it was September 11, 2001: two planes flew into the World Trade Center in New York, another hit the Pentagon in Washington, DC, and a fourth plane, headed to Washington, crashed in rural Pennsylvania when passengers overpowered the terrorists who had killed the flight crew.

Then, within weeks, letters and packages containing a deadly weaponized form of the anthrax bacterium were sent through the United States mail. In a 2008 briefing, the Federal Bureau of Investigation called the anthrax scare "the worst case of bioterrorism in U.S. history." Although only five people died and seventeen were sickened, according to the FBI, the scare caused panic and mayhem in a nation already demoralized by the September 11 attacks. Further, the anthrax investigation cost the country millions of dollars and worker-hours over the next decade.

In the 2008 briefing, the FBI and Department of Justice attributed the anthrax attacks to one man, Dr. Bruce Ivins, who committed suicide before charges could be leveled against him. According to National Public Radio's David Kestenbaum, Ivins worked as a microbiologist for over thirty years at the Army's

Crake becomes a prominent bioengineer and develops a deadly virus. *(Kurhan | Shutterstock.com)*

biodefense laboratory at Fort Detrick, in Maryland.

In an interview appearing on Random House's *Oryx and Crake* Web page, Atwood said that she did not change the plot after the events of September and October 2001, but she almost gave up writing the book. "Real life was getting creepily too close to my inventions—not so much the Twin Towers as the anthrax scare.... The main object of these kinds of actions is to sow panic and dismay."

SARS

While the anthrax scare was a terrorist attack, its scope was limited. Potentially more dangerous was the 2002–2003 outbreak of a virus causing severe acute respiratory syndrome (SARS). This was a naturally occurring outbreak, not bioterrorism. However, the rapidity with which the disease spread and the high rate of infection associated with the disease struck fear into both the medical community and the general population. Worldwide, according to the U.S. Centers for Disease Control (CDC), 8,098 people became ill with SARS, and 774 people died between November 2002 and July 2003. Like the epidemic in *Oryx and Crake*, SARS broke out around the world almost simultaneously. The CDC reports that there were cases in more than two dozen countries.

Forty-four people died in Toronto, Ontario, Canada, of SARS during this period, and the city was in virtual lockdown. The Canadian Broadcasting Corporation (CBC), in an April 22, 2004 news story on *CBC News Online*, reported that Ontario Justice Archie Campbell "observed that Ontario's health system had been unable to manage the crisis.... The province's medical infrastructure was pushed to its limits and the region's hospitality industry was also paralyzed by the outbreak."

SARS brought to light the serious social disruption that takes place in an epidemic, even a small one. Thus, it does not take a very great stretch of the imagination to imagine a worldwide epidemic or plague bringing down all of human civilization.

Global Warming

Throughout *Oryx and Crake*, readers see evidence that the Earth's climate is in real trouble, even before the day the Crake unleashes the virus. In creating her setting, Atwood drew on scientific information regarding global warming and climate change available in the early 2000s. She imagined that all of the scientists' predictions were accurate, and accordingly created an environment that would reflect those predictions.

The statistics available to Atwood during the writing of *Oryx and Crake* regarding global warming were frightening. Moreover, those predictions have remained largely the same since the turn of the twenty-first century.

Holli Riebeek, writing in NASA's *Earth Observatory*, summarizes the effects, stating, "For most places, global warming will result in more frequent hot days and fewer cool days.... Longer, more intense heat waves will become more common. Storms, floods, and droughts will generally be more severe." This, in turn, will lead to changes in agriculture and food production.

In addition, global warming will cause sea levels to rise, potentially inundating coastal areas. In *Oryx and Crake*, this has already happened along the East Coast of the United States. As sea levels rise, not only will farmlands be flooded but they will be flooded with salty seawater that kills any crops and prevents further farming of the land. Again, food shortages could result.

Scientists also predict that infectious diseases will increase. For example, mosquitoes that carry malaria are already moving northward from tropical areas. It is possible that malaria will become a serious health risk in the southern United States in decades to come.

These changes will have a serious impact on all life on earth. Because all life is intertwined, a change in one ecosystem necessarily has an impact on others. Atwood's vision of the future grows directly out of present-day scientific research.

CRITICAL OVERVIEW

With *Oryx and Crake*, Atwood returned to the genre of speculative fiction she first explored in *The Handmaid's Tale*. The novel was reviewed widely, provoking discussion and debate and gaining the book a wide readership. A critical success, the novel was shortlisted for the Booker Prize in 2003.

Contemporary reviews were generally very favorable. For example, in a review appearing in *Américas*, critic Barbara Mujica writes, "Replete with dark humor, Margaret Atwood's brilliantly crafted new novel is magnificently entertaining." Likewise, short story author Moore, writing in the *New Yorker*, calls *Oryx and Crake* a "towering and intrepid" novel.

Some critics view *Oryx and Crake* as a novel that should be noted for its ideas, rather than for its plot or action. Tom Wilhelmus, writing in *Hudson Review*, argues that what is "most interesting" about the novel "is not the rather obvious machinery of the plot but rather the archaeological insight Atwood brings to life today as she looks back on it from the future." In contrast, well-known literary scholar Elaine Showalter sees the novel as one of action and suspense. Writing in the *London Review of Books*, Showalter calls *Oryx and Crake* "a highly cinematic adventure story of daring and survival." Further, she contrasts the novel to Atwood's earlier works in which the writer "never emphasised action."

Not all contemporary reviewers were as positive about *Oryx and Crake*. Hugo Barnacle, for example, writing in *New Statesman*, suggests that Atwood's plot repeats that of a Tom Clancy novel, and although Atwood's version is "just as readable, and more elegantly written" than Clancy's novel, *Oryx and Crake* nonetheless "contrives to be at once sillier and less funny."

In the years since the publication of the novel, literary scholars have analyzed *Oryx and Crake* in a variety of ways. In an article in *Science Fiction Studies* comparing *Oryx and Crake* with William Gibson's *Pattern Recognition* and Greg Egan's *Schild's Ladder*, Veronica Hollinger reads *Oryx and Crake* as "a satire about the catastrophic potential of increasingly commodified technoscience." She argues, "Of these three novels, Atwood's is the most concerned to encourage something like conventional political action on the part of its readers."

Shari Evans, writing in *Femspec*, agrees: "The desire to warn contemporary society seems to be the impetus behind each of Atwood's speculative forays, *The Handmaid's Tale* and *Oryx and Crake*." She also believes that Atwood's novel offers a small measure of hope. Through individual action, the slide toward dystopia can be stopped:

> Atwood's novel... offers a glimpse of redemption through individual practice. This utopic hope—that individual human decisions can begin to reverse the tide of dystopic disintegration—suggests that something as slight as an individual's ethical decision can alter the overwhelming cultural forces that inundate our lives.

The novel's conclusion, she contends, offers Snowman the chance to make an ethical decision, to not kill the other humans. Although this is an unsafe option, it is also "the right thing to do."

Ingersoll, writing in *Extrapolation*, on the other hand, focuses on the theme of survival in *Oryx and Crake*. He also offers a clear study of the contexts in which Atwood wrote the novel, showing that the novel should be read in connection not only to *The Handmaid's Tale* but also to other works of fiction, including *Frankenstein, 1984*, and *Brave New World*, among others. Similarly, in her book *Margaret Atwood*, Coral Ann Howells comments on the wide range of genres that Atwood uses in her novel: "dystopia, satire, wilderness survival narrative and castaway narrative, tragic romance triangle, and the quest to the Underworld."

Finally, many scholars use ecocriticism, the study of literature and the environment, to discuss *Oryx and Crake*. Heidi Slettedahl Macpherson, writing in *The Cambridge Introduction to Margaret Atwood*, notes that "the environmental concerns Atwood raised in *The Handmaid's Tale* are writ large in *Oryx and Crake*.... She creates a world that valorizes science and lets scientists play God." From Macpherson's perspective, Atwood's concern with the environment comes down to ethical choices; scientists must be held accountable. She argues, "[The novel] is based on present-day practices and the potential of scientists to deny the ethics of their acts. Atwood casts an artist's eye over this power, and asks us, the readers, to do the same."

CRITICISM

Diane Andrews Henningfeld

Henningfeld is a professor of English at Adrian College who writes widely on literature and current events for educational publishers. In the following essay, she discusses the intertextual elements of Oryx and Crake, *concluding that it is the intertextual nature of all literature that connects readers to the past, present, and future.*

A word used frequently by contemporary literary theorists is *intertextuality*. The term is both simple and complicated. On the one hand, it simply points to the implicit and explicit relationships between texts. For example, the English dramatist Tom Stoppard wrote a play in the 1960s called *Rosencrantz and Guildenstern Are Dead*. In the play, Stoppard retells the story of William Shakespeare's *Hamlet* from the point of view of two minor characters. The dialogue of the characters other than Rosencrantz and Guildenstern is directly from Shakespeare. On this level, the play is overtly intertextual.

At a deeper level, the term intertextuality suggests that *all* texts are combinations of other texts, either through influence or through language. Nothing is original. Even the most experimental texts draw on shared language: allusions to other works, events, ideas, and people from the past and present; common themes; and recognizable styles. Richard Posner, in a review of *Oryx and Crake*, cites Margaret Atwood's teacher Northrop Frye, who said famously, "Poetry can only be made out of other poems, novels out of other novels." Frye's comment suggests that there are no totally original works and that the role of the author is to put together the bits and pieces of previous literature to create something new. Indeed, as Posner argues, "Atwood's literary debts are numerous."

Oryx and Crake is an unabashedly intertextual work, a work that is influenced thematically and structurally by some of the great novels of the English language and by the language and innovations of science and technology. A reader unfamiliar with the texts that underlie *Oryx and Crake* misses out on the full depth of the novel. Thus, an exploration of some of Atwood's intertextual borrowings should allow a better understanding of the novel.

In her book *Margaret Atwood*, Coral Ann Howells reviews the various genres Atwood employs in *Oryx and Crake*, "In characteristic

WHAT
DO I READ
NEXT?

- Nancy Farmer's young-adult novel *The House of the Scorpion* (2002) is a futuristic story set in a country called Opium, a land that was once Mexico. The protagonist, Matteo Alacrán, is a boy cloned from the DNA of El Patrón. Conceived in a Petri dish and incubated in a cow's womb, Matteo faces sinister characters and his own struggle to understand himself. The book won the 2002 National Book Award for Young People's Literature and was a 2003 Newberry Honor Book.

- In *The Year of the Flood* (2009), Atwood returns to the same setting as *Oryx and Crake*, in the days immediately before and after the catastrophe. Many of the same characters populate both novels.

- Nathalie Cooke's *Margaret Atwood: A Biography* (1998) remains the standard Atwood biography. Cooke's later book, *Margaret Atwood: A Critical Companion* (2004), provides not only biographical detail but also a critical overview of all Atwood's major works through *The Blind Assassin*.

- *Brave New World*, written by Aldous Huxley in 1931 and published in 1932, is often noted as an influence on Atwood's *Oryx and Crake*. Like Atwood, Huxley provides a frightening and satiric vision of the future that addresses many of the pressing issues of his own time.

- *Opposing Viewpoints: Genetic Engineering*, edited by David M. Haugen in 2009, is a collection of articles debating the pros and cons of genetic engineering for a young-adult audience.

- Susan Beth Pfeffer's *Life As We Knew It* (2008) is a coming-of-age story featuring high school student Miranda, who must contend with the after-effects of a huge meteor hitting the moon, pushing it off its axis, and causing earthquakes and tsunamis on Earth.

- Atwood chooses lines from Jonathan Swift's *Gulliver's Travels* as an epigraph to *Oryx and Crake*, and many critics have cited the influence of this book on Atwood's speculative fiction. Although written in 1726, *Gulliver's Travels* remains a classic of social satire.

- Climate scientists Michael E. Mann and Lee R. Klump collaborated on the 2008 book *Dire Predictions: Understanding Global Warming*, which explains the findings of the Intergovernmental Panel on Climate Change in lucid prose designed for the lay reader. The book contains many photos, charts, illustrations, and artwork.

---

fashion Atwood splices together a variety of generic forms: dystopia, satire, wilderness survival narrative and castaway narrative, tragic romance triangle, and the quest to the Underworld." In Howells's view, Atwood borrows the structure and themes of well-known stories and novels that exist in contemporary culture. She continues, "This transgeneric construction highlights the fabricated quality of her narrative."

Part of this fabrication includes conventions common to anti-utopias, also known as dystopias. Many critics (and Atwood herself) have drawn connections between *Oryx and Crake* and other important twentieth-century dystopias, most notably those in the work of Aldous Huxley and George Orwell. Huxley's most famous novel is *Brave New World*, published in 1932. The title, taken from Shakespeare's play *The Tempest*, is ironic. The setting of Huxley's novel is some hundred years in the future, at a time when human beings are hatched, not born. Scientists manipulate the conditions in each embryo's pod, thereby creating classes of people for particular roles in society. Some babies are deprived of oxygen, and thus become part of a

ORYX AND CRAKE IS AN UNABASHEDLY
INTERTEXTUAL WORK, A WORK THAT IS INFLUENCED
THEMATICALLY AND STRUCTURALLY BY SOME OF THE
GREAT NOVELS OF THE ENGLISH LANGUAGE AND BY
THE LANGUAGE AND INNOVATIONS OF SCIENCE AND
TECHNOLOGY."

class who must undertake the menial jobs of the society. *Oryx and Crake* builds on some of these ideas, particularly in the areas of technology and class structure. Scientists hold a central role in both novels. Crake is singled out to attend an elite college based on his performance in high school, while Jimmy attends a much less impressive school. Even further down the chain of classes are the pleebs, who live outside of the compounds. Like the setting of *Brave New World*, the world of *Oryx and Crake* is a highly stratified society. Atwood also nods to Orwell's *1984* and *Animal Farm*. Posner notes that Atwood's "'pleebs' are Orwell's 'proles.'" In addition, Posner draws the connection between the "sinister intelligence" of the pigoons with that of the pigs in *Animal Farm*. Likewise, the sequestered existence of party members in *1984* is similar to that of the scientists and their families who live within compounds.

Atwood also signals that her work is at least partially satire, in the mode of Jonathan Swift. She does so by including a line from Swift's *Gulliver's Travels* as an epigraph (an introductory quotation) to the novel:

> I could perhaps like others have astonished you with strange improbable tales; but I rather chose to relate plain matter of fact in the simplest manner and style; because my principal design was to inform you, and not to amuse you.

Like Swift, Atwood creates an alternate reality that, in its exaggeration, casts a sharp light on the problems in contemporary society. Although Swift's traveler Gulliver overtly confronts giants and tiny people, Swift is subversively making comments about eighteenth-century England. Likewise, Atwood creates an alternate reality designed to inform readers, not

amuse them (although there is no doubt that, at times, *Oryx and Crake* is wickedly funny in its send-up of contemporary society).

Earl G. Ingersoll, writing in *Extrapolation*, notes that *Oryx and Crake* can also be compared to Mary Shelley's *Frankenstein*. Crake bears remarkable resemblance to Shelley's Dr. Frankenstein with his conviction that he can create perfect life. Atwood perhaps owes another debt to Mary Shelley. A number of critics have noted a similarity in theme and plot between *Oryx and Crake* and Shelley's *The Last Man*. In Shelley's novel, set in 2100, one man survives a worldwide plague.

Similarly, critics such as Shuli Barzilai suggest that "*Oryx and Crake* may also be read as a reworking of Daniel Defoe's *Robinson Crusoe* (1719) and other survivor stories." Ingersoll agrees, noting that "Atwood's own work ... has been virtually from the beginning preoccupied with the theme of Survival." As Posner, Barzilai, and Ingersoll all note, the last chapter of *Oryx and Crake* is titled "Footprints," a clear nod to *Robinson Crusoe*. In Defoe's novel, Crusoe finds footprints in the sand, letting him know that he is not alone on the island. Likewise, when Snowman discovers footprints in the sand, he knows he is not alone, either.

Atwood also borrows one of the most enduring of all narrative structures in *Oryx and Crake*, a structure that can be traced all the way back to Greek mythology and *The Epic of Gilgamesh*. Indeed, there are those who would argue that there is only one kind of story, the quest or journey tale. The quest story usually involves a hero accepting a challenge, undertaking an arduous journey, finding challengers and helpers along the way, locating a treasure, and returning with the treasure to tell the tale. *The Odyssey*, *The Iliad*, *Beowulf*, and *Lord of the Rings* are all examples of tales that inform and underpin Western culture. For Atwood, however, there is a striking difference in the articulation of the quest story in Canadian literature, bound up with its preoccupation with survival. In Atwood's first major work of criticism, *Survival: A Thematic Guide to Canadian Literature*, she writes about two kinds of stories: the frontier quest and the island survival stories, and how these differ in Canadian literature from the prevalent conventions found in Western literature. She argues,

Margaret Atwood was inspired to write the novel after observing the ruddy crake. (phdwhite / Shutterstock.com)

Our central idea is one which generates, not the excitement and sense of adventure or danger which The Frontier holds out, not the smugness and/or sense of security, of everything in its place, which The Island can offer, but an almost intolerable anxiety. Our stories are likely to be tales not of those who made it but of those who made it back from the awful experience—the North, the snowstorm, the sinking ship—that killed everyone else.

Surely, Snowman's journey to Paradice demonstrates Atwood's Canadian-ness in her handling of the quest motif. Snowman is not motivated by a sense of adventure or the quest for treasure. He must undertake a journey he does not want to take in order to simply survive. He is frightened and anxious. Clad in a dirty bed sheet and a baseball cap, he stands in stark contrast to heroes such as King Arthur or Beowulf. He is chased by pig-creatures, not the more noble lions, or tigers, or bears. Although he faces many dangers, the one that seems most likely to kill him is a simple cut on his foot.

Moreover, Atwood's choice of name for his destination, Paradice, is ironic for several reasons. In the first place, it is now quite clearly *not*

a paradise. Rather it is the site of death and destruction, of Snowman's most painful memory. Subtler, perhaps, is the pun made apparent by the spelling, leading the reader to think of the throw of dice. Indeed, a pair of dice indicates a game of chance. Unlike conventional quest-heroes in Western literature, Snowman's success or failure in his undertaking has little to do with his own courage or preparation; instead, it depends on the random toss of a pair of cosmic dice.

In the classic stories of quest, the hero returns in triumph to tell his story. Usually, he brings with him some form of treasure, either real treasure of monetary value or the treasure of wisdom and lessons learned. In Canadian literature, Atwood argues, "The survivor has no triumph or victory but the fact of his survival; he has little after his ordeal that he did not have before, except gratitude for having escaped with his life." Snowman illustrates this well: although he has snagged a few supplies and a gun from Paradice, he does not return in triumph. Indeed, his return is fraught with anxiety. There is no one other than the Crakers left to greet him, and he knows they will not understand the story of his journey. He also knows that he will have to face other survivors and decide what to do. He is no wiser after his journey, and it seems just as likely that he will die from the cut on his foot as from an encounter with fellow humans.

Atwood draws on many other novels, ideas, essays, and historical events in her construction of *Oryx and Crake*. However, the examples given here are sufficient to illustrate an important point: well-known novels, stories, ideas, and conventions can be pulled apart and reassembled to form a work that is at once highly original and at the same time completely intertextual. The world of *Oryx and Crake* is one that will continue to live in the canon of dystopian literature, and it will itself be disassembled for parts by later writers, just as Atwood did herself in her later novel, *The Year of the Flood*. It is the intertextual nature of literature that connects readers to the past, to the present, and to the future.

Source: Diane Andrews Henningfeld, Critical Essay on *Oryx and Crake*, in *Novels for Students*, Gale, Cengage Learning, 2012.

Danette DiMarco

In the following excerpt, DiMarco focuses on Crake's compulsion to recreate the world at the expense of humanity.

Margaret Atwood's novel *Oryx and Crake* (2003) critiques modernity's commitment to *homo faber*—he who labors to use every instrument as a means to achieve a particular end in building a world, even when the fabrication of that world necessarily demands a repeated violation of its materiality, including its people. Atwood propels her novel through the memories of the main character, Snowman, a survivor of a deadly viral pathogen created and unleashed by his best friend, Crake. Too much a product of a profit-driven world who mirrors its economy of self-interest, Crake emerges as the quintessential *homo faber*, making it unlikely that any kind of positive social change will happen directly through him.

Instead, Atwood's character Snowman serves as a potential site for change. He faces the challenge of either taking deliberative and participatory action in the creation of a yet-to-be imagined inviolate world, or imitating *homo faber*. Atwood marks this tension from the outset of the novel, symbolizing it in Jimmy's name change to Snowman, which evokes The

> EDUCATION IN THE UTILITARIAN TRADITION MUST ULTIMATELY FIND A WAY TO SEPARATE THE WHEAT FROM THE CHAFF, EVEN IN CASES WHEN THOSE BEING DIVIDED ARE ALREADY AMONG THE PRIVILEGED."

Abominable Snowman—"existing and not existing, flickering at the edges of blizzards [. . .] known only through rumours and through its backward-pointing footprints." These mythic and multi-directional footprints (they point backward as they move forward) represent Snowman's liminal position and potential power—to repeat a past cycle of aggression against nature in the name of personal profit, or to re-imagine a way for future living grounded in a genuine concern for others. Snowman's narrative about his past is concomitant of his ability to cross boundaries on several levels and to challenge existing structures all while working within them. At novel's end, when the possibility for again belonging to a community is revealed to him, he must choose: to retreat from, attack, or engage humanely the strangers with whom he is confronted. If he chooses the third option, it is possible that he will help to build a world unlike that which *homo faber* has produced.

Undergirding the development of *homo faber* is a basic, instrumental philosophy that has contributed to an elision of violence against material goods, including human instruments. This instrumentalism has naturalized the division of labor under capitalism and led to an increased decentralization in governing communities and alienation among individuals. *Homo faber*'s instrumental worldview—grounded in separation and enclosure—acts as the cohesive agent that assures Jimmy a leading role in Crake's "Paradice" project. Of course, it is this same instrumental perspective that separates the two men as well. On one hand, Crake's scientific intelligence, evident through his work in Paradice where he creates the BryssPluss pill and the genetically-spliced Crakers, positions him as a member of an elite class that values instrumental production only as it is linked with personal gain. On the other hand, Jimmy's humanistic tendencies socially marginalize him. Even as he is part of the privileged, scientific community because of his family background, he moves forever closer to membership in the "uncivilized" Pleebland culture that literally sits beyond the walls of his world.

Belonging and not belonging to his community is a marker that Snowman/Jimmy is Atwood's vehicle for showing that potential social change may be enacted. The supposed "good" life that *homo faber* has fabricated, and that has been reified in modernity, finds itself in question in this novel. Though it is plausible that readers, through Snowman, might concede the possibility for re-making a world in imitation of its predecessor, they might also be able to imagine a potential watershed moment in his decision—where future-life will be motivated less by personal gain and grounded more in a genuine care and respect for others. Since the novel concludes before that decision is made, however, choice and accountability are left in the minds of the readers, although Atwood does guide readers to contemplate seriously the ethical implications of particular choices. . . .

THE MEANS TO "PARADICE"

An analysis of the social epistemology that informs Crake's and Jimmy's childhood and teenage years demonstrates how the creation of "Paradice," the dome where Crake completes his work, is inevitable. Crake's two-fold project—to create the BlyssPluss pill and the Crakers—is symptomatic of his life-work as modern *homo faber*. Both Jimmy and Crake grow up in highly privileged, private communities with family members who engage in, more or less, experimental scientific research. It is expected that the boys will engage in similar work. This section examines how the boys' lifestyles and educations are embedded in a systemic acceptance of separation and enclosure from communities and people not engaging in similar work—which provides them both the means for getting to Paradice.

A division of communities and labor is at the crux of Atwood's construction of the boys' early development. That they grow up naturalized to the idea of separation is symbolized by the very real walls that enclose their communities. As part of an elite community involved in scientific research and mind work, the boys are protected from the Sodom and Gomorrah-like visceral nature of the society beyond the walls. Robert Reich calls this process of enclosure "secession" (269), a pulling out of larger society by richer, more elite workers who inevitably, in their acquisition of private living, withhold not just their money and knowledge but their participation. As Barber stresses, the "restructuring of the global economy to meet the demands of the new age information/entertainment sector further reinforces the boundaries between the privileged and the rest" (271). In Barber's view, Reich's "symbolic analysts," who live within the walled communities and who are the fabricators of new technologies and markets, generally ensure an endemic division of labor and social inequality. In *Oryx and Crake*, the expansive areas beyond the walls are called the "pleeblands," and they conjure pejorative yet mythological ambivalence. According to those living in the compounds, the inhabitants of the pleeblands are "mental deficients." And the mythological nature of place becomes evident through Jimmy, who never actually visits the alien territory until he is an adult, although he does physically get pushed to the margins of the compound when he becomes a writer and not a scientist.

Power through enclosure is certainly not a new idea. More recently in literary and cultural studies, discussions of identity formation under colonial ideology have focused on the symbolic domestication or enclosure of the "wild" landscape. Civility continues to be linked with the metropolitan (and vice versa), and cutting-edge "work" takes place in these inner-sanctums. Using DeFoe's *Robinson Crusoe* as a centerpiece for discussion—the same text that Atwood alludes to in her last chapter titled "Footprint"—Robert P. Marzec identifies the human desire to stand above nature until it is successfully contained as "the Crusoe syndrome" (131). He stresses how novels in the English tradition have dealt repeatedly with this topic. Whatever nomadic desires to cross real physical boundaries Jimmy and Crake may have—especially as teenage boys—they are curbed through their community's domestication of them. Even when the boys demonstrate the potential for unbridled energy, it is in a cyber environment, and it generally can not occur without their breaking through some kind of already-made enclosure. Their forays into the HottTotts site and Crake's hacking into his uncle's computer are just two examples. Jimmy's father explains,

Long ago, in the days of knights and dragons, the kings and dukes had lived in castles, with high walls and drawbridges and slots on the ramparts so you could pour hot pitch on your enemies [. . .] and the Compounds were the same idea. Castles were for keeping you and your buddies nice and safe inside, and for keeping everybody else outside.

Much later in the novel, Crake builds the Paradice dome within the already walled-in RejoovenEsence community, eschewing the public domain even more. The entire fabrication of Paradice demands that Crake don a metaphysical, Crusoe-like attitude, and his early socialization into such a way of knowing has, no doubt, validated this vision.

Educational utilitarianism serves as a critical enclosure in both boys' lives as well. Reminiscent of the Dickensian portrait of education in his *Hard Times*, Snowman recalls that his junior high Life Skills class tried to provide students only with directly useful information. As the class motto ran, "We are not here to play, to dream, to drift. We are here to practice Life Skills." In this class students practiced

> Double-entry on-screen bookkeeping, banking by fingertip, using a microwave without nuking your egg, filling out housing applications for this or that Module and job applications for this or that Compound, family heredity research, negotiating your own marriage-and-divorce contracts, wise genetic match-mating, the proper use of condoms to avoid sexually transmitted bioforms.

While some of the skills seem to focus innocently on the quotidian aspects of living (using a microwave, for example), others more obviously reflect educational efforts to perpetuate the style of living—an elitist one at best—that is expected to occur within the Compounds (e.g., wise genetic match-mating). There is no analysis of *why* such skills are important in life, or *who* claims such skills are crucial in good living, let alone the ethical dimensions integral to such a process. Later, Jimmy enrolls in a public college, Martha Graham, where he discovers that the school's original Latin motto *Ars Longa Vita Brevis* had been given an addendum: "Our Students Graduate With Employable Skills." Chances are the English translation bears the real weight of the work that is to be accomplished at Martha Graham, especially since "the enthusiasm of the dedicated artsy money had waned" and "the curricular emphasis had switched to other arenas." Martha Graham had

become a school whose main area of content was "no longer central to anything," interesting but tangential to "real" life, like "Latin, or bookbinding." Even the once popular visual arts had been lost to technological advances; "[a]nyone with a computer could splice together whatever they wanted, or digitally alter old material, or create new animation." In a search to regain an identity, Martha Graham made "everything" have "utilitarian aims." Compound life's tendency to provide a less-than-liberal approach to education in Life Skills class merely plays itself out at a higher level in college.

Education in the utilitarian tradition must ultimately find a way to separate the wheat from the chaff, even in cases when those being divided are already among the privileged. Favored over Jimmy because of his strengths in science and math, Crake is courted by several prestigious and private institutions of higher education. Deciding finally upon Watson Crick, a highly protected "palace" when compared with the falling apart, unprotected Martha Graham that sits adjacent to the sprawling and wild Pleeblands, Crake more fully becomes inculcated into the lessons of *homo faber*. Jimmy, meanwhile, although still within the system, becomes alienated from the values of Compound life as he furthers his education:

> After a humiliating wait while the brainiacs were tussled over by the best Edu-Compounds and the transcripts of the mediocre were fingered and skimmed and had coffee spilled on them and got dropped on the floor by mistake, Jimmy was knocked down at last to the Martha Graham Academy.

The brainiac's merit—that is the compunction to engage in scientific research to "better" the world—marginalizes Jimmy further. He gets a single room at the Academy, he doesn't successfully keep a love interest for very long, and he thinks of Crake as his only friend. Jimmy's admission into the once-liberal-arts Academy, and Crake's into Watson Crick, is just one example of how the division of labor—and unproductive versus productive labor—is supported. More than once Crake asserts the dictum of this division. Once, while visiting Crake at Watson Crick, Jimmy inquires whether Crake has a girlfriend. Crake's response is "Easy for you to say [. . .]. You're the grasshopper, I'm the ant. I can't waste time in *unproductive* random scanning" (my emphasis). Even Jimmy has internalized outward social expectations of him. He is all too aware that "his wordserfjob [with AnooYoo] was surely one that Crake would despise.". . .

Source: Danette DiMarco, "Paradice Lost, Paradise Regained: *homo faber* and the Makings of a New Beginning in *Oryx and Crake*," in *Papers on Language & Literature*, Vol. 41, No. 2, Spring 2005, pp. 170–95.

Hugo Barnacle

In the following review, Barnacle argues that Oryx and Crake *satirizes the corporate world while demonstrating a "scant understanding of, or interest in, the way big business works."*

The basic plot of Margaret Atwood's dystopian blockbuster [*Oryx and Crake*]—a leading biochemist is secretly an eco-warrior with a master plan to save the planet by wiping out the human race—has already been used, arguably to better effect, by Tom Clancy in *Rainbow Six*. Atwood's version is just as readable, and more elegantly written, but nevertheless it contrives to be at once sillier and less funny.

Jimmy, a former advertising copywriter, finds himself living up a tree somewhere on the US East Coast, about half a century from now. As a result of the viral catastrophe engineered by his brilliant, if misguided, boyhood friend Crake, Jimmy is the last man left alive on earth, or at any rate the fast man on this bit of seaboard, apart from the "Crakers", a small group of placid, genetically-modified humans that Crake has developed to repopulate the world in a sustainable manner.

Jimmy's survival is not an accident. Crake surreptitiously dosed him with a vaccine against the super-Ebola GM virus, making him as immune as the Crakers themselves. The Crakers can't stay in the bubble-dome of artificial forest at Crake's corporate HQ, because the power supply has shut down along with the rest of civilisation-as-we-know-it. Someone has to help them adjust to life on the outside. Crake, it seems, was not prepared to face the consequences of his actions, and bequeathed the responsibility to Jimmy.

As Jimmy is not modified to exist on grass and leaves like the Crakers, he is at constant risk of starvation. He decides, not for the first time, to make the dangerous trek back through the nearby city to the Crake complex and raid the place for more supplies. The danger arises from all the GM animals on the loose. The pigs,

developed as organ donors, can be just as fearsome as the attack dogs, developed for corporate security purposes. The Crakers have pheromones that ward off predators, but Jimmy is not so blessed. Worse, he has no more "virtual bullets" for his "spraygun" and he's never managed to find an old-fashioned, lead-bullet gun lying around either.

As he goes along, we are told Jimmy's story in flashback. He and Crake both grew up in the "Compounds", the sealed-off luxury enclaves for the technocratic elite, as opposed to the "pleeblands" (presumably a comical distortion of "pleblands"), the seamy cities where everyone else made do. (Your standard science-fiction shtick.) This is a society with no books and little culture to speak of, just porn and cheap thrills, such as "deathrowlive.com" (executions on webcam), and bastardised science; luminous green rabbits, the product of some idiotic GM enterprise, have been a common sight ever since Jimmy was little.

Not being specially bright by Compound standards, Jimmy ended up at a run-down college for the liberal arts, which "was like studying Latin or book-binding: pleasant to contemplate in its way, but no longer central to anything", whereas Crake went to the cutting-edge Watson-Crick institute, the top academy for mad scientists.

On a visit to Watson-Crick, Jimmy recalls seeing one of the students' experiments: "a large bulblike object that seemed to be covered with stippled whitish-yellow skin. Out of it came twenty thick fleshy tubes, and at the end of each tube another bulb was growing."

This is the ChickieNob, a kind of GM chicken on "the sea-anemone body plan", which produces only breast meat. Jimmy "couldn't see eating a ChickieNob. It would be like eating a large wart." A few years later, however, he was ordering ChickieNob Nubbins takeaways without a thought.

The ChickieNob is a memorably nightmarish image, somewhat undercut by Atwood's quaint notion that research scientists would be involved in marketing. "They've already got the takeout franchise operation in place," Crake explains. Much of the book is a satire on the excesses of big business, but it shows scant understanding of, or interest in, the way big business works. As with all the material about climate change, designer babies, the decline of literacy, the gulf between the haves and have-nots, the obsession with youth and so on, it merely reflects the general anxiety that many people get from paying too much attention to what they read in the papers. It doesn't offer any genuinely original perceptions.

Sorry? Who's Oryx? Oh, Oryx is Jimmy's lost love. She's already dead at the start of the book, so there isn't a great deal of scope for development there. In the flashbacks, however, she appears as a charming, enigmatic personality: the only character, apart from Jimmy's troubled mother, to exhibit more depth than this simplistic fable strictly requires.

Source: Hugo Barnacle, "The End is Nigh," in *New Statesman*, Vol. 132, No. 4638, May 19, 2003, p. 50.

Philip Hensher

In the following review, Hensher lauds Atwood's powerful vision in Oryx and Crake *despite the weakness of the subplot involving the character Oryx.*

It's quite unusual for a novelist to write two entirely separate and different dystopic visions of the future. I suppose it runs the risk of suggesting that the novelist doesn't quite mean one or both of them. It's impressive of Margaret Atwood to have turned away from her habitual commitment to the rich, realist documents of contemporary lives for a second time, and given us another terrifying fantasy [*Oryx and Crake*] about the future to sit next to *The Handmaid's Tale*. That novel, published in 1985, has grown steadily in plausibility and authority; and it would seem perverse of Atwood to risk undermining it by writing so entirely different a projection as *Oryx and Crake*.

Most dystopias are really satirical versions of contemporary society, and not ideas of the future at all. *The Time Machine* is about Edwardian class anxiety; *Nineteen Eighty-Four* is about the regimentation and deprivations of Attlee's England. *The Handmaid's Tale* is very unusual in that it really does seem like an attempt to imagine the future of America, and an increasingly plausible one. It suggests a fundamentalist revolution will take place, after which racial and social minorities will be expelled or executed. Women will be prevented from working or from owning property, and the whole state will sink into a giant theocracy. It seemed, in 1985, like a wild fantasy, but there are aspects of it

which are now quite plausible. The excuse for the suspension of civil liberties in the book are atrocities supposedly committed by Islamic fundamentalists: that was a brilliant insight 20 years ago. And the whole premise appears much less fantastic now: it is unnerving to observe how contemporary America fulfils almost every one of the classic features of pre-revolutionary France or Russia. It's not remotely unlikely that at some time in the next 20 years a violent revolution might take place there, and its face, as Atwood saw, would be a religious one.

Oryx and Crake is an entirely different idea of the future, although it begins from an image at the end of *The Handmaid's Tale*, a throwaway line about an artificial virus causing sterility inserted in jars of caviar. It is almost as impressive and just as terrifying, but the focus here is on technology raised to the point of godlike capacities. It is the story of Snowman, who for most of the book seems to be the last human being alive. The novel is the account of the assumption of divine powers of creation which the last men achieved, and, in its shadow, the catastrophe which wiped out the human race.

It's characteristic of Atwood that, returning to the start of the story, she takes care to make it almost humdrum, a recognisable account of two adolescent boys, Snowman and Crake. Although their circumstances are not like ours—they live in closely guarded compounds, islands of professional life, with a wild sea of lawlessness unseen outside the gates—their interests are deliberately banal. Crake is dazzlingly brilliant, and Snowman does his best to keep up; they want to go to a good school, to get good jobs in one of the vast corporations, and they enjoy watching scenes of death and sex over the internet. Atwood insists on this, and somehow she makes us accept that this interest is at once typical and unremarkable in adolescent boys, and at the root of the monstrosities Crake will come to perpetrate.

Snowman and Crake's aspirations and pleasures are familiar ones, but they are exercised in a harsh and unfamiliar society. The vast corporations dominate the landscape, and sinister corps of private militia patrol the many internal borders in the name of security. It is brilliantly plausible; everyone has seen how even quite small companies these days require their lobbies and borders to be patrolled and secured, and how quickly the minor operatives of the security industry start exercising what power they have. Science has reached a point of effortless virtuosity and can achieve more or less anything. Crake joins the intellectual aristocracy, and goes into bio-engineering; Snowman is condemned to labour in the lower reaches of the vast self-help industry.

Bio-engineering is what the novel is about, and the reader is asked to envisage a world in which science can create any kind of animal it chooses. Atwood's creatures are not, for the most part, Hieronymus Bosch grotesques, but pigs with spare organs for transplants, a dog which looks affectionate but will bite your hand off without warning, a chicken with multiple breasts to supply the fast-food industry. Crake goes into this industry, and devotes his energies to two grand tasks; the first is to create a new and improved race of human-like beings; the second we do not discover until near the end of the book, and it explains why Snowman is left alone, the last of the humans, watching the new beings carry out acts of worship of their creator, Crake. Atwood loves the description of sinister rituals, and the lives of the post-humans consist of little else.

It's a powerful and exuberantly imagined book, and it's characteristic of its author that she exerts her imagination not in creating scientific monsters but in delineating the human world. The adolescent games of Crake and Snowman are meticulously and intricately done, and the whole atmosphere of arrogant irresponsibility within the institutes is a real tour-de-force, summed up by impenetrable jokes on T-shirts and fridge magnets. Brilliantly done, too, is the world after the apocalypse, encapsulated in a conversation in which Snowman tries to explain 'toast' to Crake's grass-eating creations, and quickly finds that they don't understand 'flour', 'electricity', 'butter' or 'bread' either.

The weakness lies in another substantial story, of the girl Oryx; her odyssey, from a poor village in the developing world through the child-pornography industry to being ultimately summoned by Crake to play a role in his project, is extravagant and often powerful, but somehow not in the right book; it doesn't amplify the main concerns of the novel, and Oryx, despite Atwood's best efforts and admirable ambition to portray an individual and not a case-study of abuse, never interests us. The rest of the book has such intellectual life that we only unwillingly go back to quite an ordinary love-story of the *Jules et Jim* variety.

Nevertheless, this is a powerful and impressive fable, more fantastic and less imminent than *The Handmaid's Tale*—you have to accept a most unlikely premise about science's capabilities—but much less optimistic. The society in that earlier book, the epilogue suggests, collapsed like any other; at the end of *Oryx and Crake* humanity is done for.

Source: Philip Hensher, "Back to the Future," in *Spectator*, Vol. 291, No. 9116, April 26, 2003, p. 35.

SOURCES

"Anthrax Investigation: Closing a Chapter," in *Federal Bureau of Investigation*, August 6, 2008, http://www.fbi.gov/news/stories/2008/august/amerithrax080608a (accessed July 15, 2011).

Atwood, Margaret, "*The Handmaid's Tale* and *Oryx and Crake* in Context," in *PMLA*, Vol. 119, No. 3, May 2004, pp. 513–17.

———, *Oryx and Crake*, Doubleday, 2003.

———, *Survival: A Thematic Guide to Canadian Literature*, 3rd ed., McClellan & Stewart, 2004, p. 42.

"Author Q & A," Random House Web site, http://www.randomhouse.com/acmart/catalog/display.pperl?isbn=9780739304082&view=qa (accessed July 15, 2011).

Baldick, Chris, "Menippean Satire," in *The Oxford Dictionary of Literary Terms*, 3rd ed., Oxford University Press, 2008, p. 202.

Barnacle, Hugo, "The End Is Nigh," in *New Statesman*, Vol. 132, No. 4638, May 19, 2003, p. 50.

Barzilai, Shuli, "'Tell My Story': Remembrance and Revenge in Atwood's *Oryx and Crake* and Shakespeare's *Hamlet*," in *Critique*, Vol. 50, No. 1, Fall 2008, pp. 87–110.

"Biography," in *Margaret Atwood Home Page*, http://www.margaretatwood.ca/bio.php (accessed July 5, 2011).

Evans, Shari, "'Not Unmarked': From Themed Space to a Feminist Ethics of Engagement in Atwood's *Oryx and Crake*," in *Femspec*, Vol. 10, No. 2, 2010, pp. 35–58.

"Fact Sheet: Basic Information about SARS," in *Severe Acute Respiratory Syndrome*, Centers for Disease Control and Prevention, May 3, 2005, http://www.cdc.gov/ncidod/sars/factsheet.htm (accessed July 15, 2011).

Hollinger, Veronica, "Stories about the Future: From Patterns of Expectation to Pattern Recognition," in

Science Fiction Studies, Vol. 33, No. 3, November 2006, pp. 452–72.

Howells, Coral Ann, *Margaret Atwood*, 2nd ed., Palgrave McMillan, 2005, pp. 1–19, 170–91.

Ingersoll, Earl G., "Survival in Margaret Atwood's Novel *Oryx and Crake*," in *Extrapolation*, Vol. 45, No. 2, June 22, 2004, pp. 162–75.

Kestenbaum, David, "Who Was Bruce Ivins?" in *All Things Considered*, National Public Radio, August 1, 2008, http://www.npr.org/templates/story/story.php?story Id = 93194941 (accessed July 15, 2011).

Lee, Brian, "Satire," in *The Routledge Dictionary of Literary Terms*, edited by Peter Childs and Roger Fowler, Routledge, 2006, p. 211.

Macpherson, Heidi Slettedahl, *The Cambridge Introduction to Margaret Atwood*, Cambridge University Press, 2010, pp. 1–10, 78–82.

Moore, Lorrie, "Bioperversity," in *New Yorker*, Vol. 79, No. 12, May 19, 2003, p. 88.

Mujica, Barbara, "Of Fantastic Futures and Imagined Pasts," in *Américas*, Vol. 55, No. 5, September/October 2003, p. 55.

Posner, Richard, "The End Is Near," in *New Republic*, Vol. 229, No. 12, September 22, 2003, pp. 31–36.

Riebeek, Holli, "Global Warming," in *Earth Observatory*, National Aeronautic and Space Administration, June 3, 2010, http://earthobservatory.nasa.gov/Features/GlobalWarming/page6.php (accessed July 24, 2011).

"Severe Acute Respiratory Syndrome," in *CBC News Online*, April 22, 2004, http://www.cbc.ca/news/background/sars (accessed July 15, 2011).

Showalter, Elaine, "The Snowman Cometh," in *London Review of Books*, Vol. 25, No. 14, July 24, 2003, p. 35.

Sorkin, Andrew Ross, "Nestlé to Buy Jenny Craig, Betting Diets Are on Rise," in *New York Times*, June 19, 2006, http://www.nytimes.com/2006/06/19/business/worldbusiness/19deal.html (accessed July 20, 2011).

Thompson, Lee Briscoe, "Margaret Atwood," in *Dictionary of Literary Biography*, Vol. 251, *Canadian Fantasy and Science Fiction Writers*, edited by Douglas Ivison, The Gale Group, 2002, pp. 11–21.

Wilhelmus, Tom, "Next," in *Hudson Review*, Vol. 57, No. 1, Spring 2004, pp. 133–40.

FURTHER READING

Berger, James Hank, *After the End: Representations of Post-Apocalypse*, University of Minnesota Press, 1999.
    Berger examines artistic, literary, and cinematic works that portray postapocalyptic Earth. He notes the features of contemporary culture that influence these works, as well as the way that postapocalyptic representation affects culture.

Ingersoll, Earl G., ed., *Waltzing Again: New and Selected Conversations with Margaret Atwood*, Ontario Review Press, 2006.
    Ingersoll presents twenty-one interviews with Atwood, held from 1972 to 2006, including a 1972 interview with Atwood's partner Graeme Gibson. Atwood's intelligence and wit are clearly evident throughout.

Sullivan, Rosemary, *The Red Shoes: Margaret Atwood Starting Out*, HarperCollins, 1998.
    Sullivan's biography provides details about Atwood's early years in the 1940s, 1950s, and 1960s, concluding in the early 1970s.

Wilson, E. O., *The Future of Life*, Knopf, 2002.
    Atwood suggests in an interview on the *Oryx and Crake* page at the Random House Web site that if readers were to read just one additional book, it should be this one by famed Harvard biologist E. O. Wilson. The book summarizes the condition of the earth at present, as well as the chances for survival of the human race.

Wynn-Davies, Marion, *Margaret Atwood*, Writers and Their Work series, Northcote House Publishers, 2010.
    Wynn-Davies presents a critical study of Atwood, examining the connections among Atwood's work and feminism, multiculturalism, terrorism, ecology, and global warming.

SUGGESTED SEARCH TERMS

Margaret Atwood

Oryx and Crake

Margaret Atwood AND Oryx and Crake

The Handmaid's Tale AND Atwood

Year of the Flood AND Atwood

postapocalypse

speculative fiction

genetic engineering

science fiction AND Margaret Atwood

Menippean satire

quest story

survival

Canadian writers

The Remains of the Day

1993   When the film adaptation of Kazuo Ishiguro's novel *The Remains of the Day* was released in 1993, audiences had every reason to expect a quality cinematic experience. The novel that served as the basis for the film had been an international success when it was published in 1989, winning the coveted Mann Booker Prize for Fiction. The film was adapted by producer Ismail Merchant and director James Ivory, who had produced a string of adaptations of literary works, including Henry James's *The Europeans* and *The Bostonians*, Jean Rhys's *Quartet*, Carson McCuller's *The Ballad of the Sad Café*, and three novels by E. M. Forster—*A Room with a View*, *Maurice*, and *Howard's End*. The film's screenplay was written by frequent collaborator Ruth Prawer Jhabvala, who had written scripts for more than fifteen of their movies, including their first, an adaptation of Jhabvala's own novel *The Householder* in 1963. A Merchant Ivory production was expected to be a quality period piece that captured the tone of some of the most refined literature of the nineteenth and twentieth centuries, and *The Remains of the Day* was no exception.

The story it tells centers around James Stevens, who has served as the head butler in a British manor house for decades. Near the end of his life, when he realizes that he has watched life slip away as he struggled to perfect his professional performance, the story follows Stevens on a journey across England to reunite with the

woman who may have been the great love of his life. His trip takes him through a series of flashbacks, during which viewers see the decline of the British Empire between the two World Wars play out among the aristocracy passing through Darlington Hall, the house over which Stevens presides. Actor Anthony Hopkins was hailed by critics worldwide as the very embodiment of Ishiguro's fastidious butler, and Emma Thompson was lauded as his equal as the former housekeeper whose memory haunts him. *The Remains of the Day* was nominated for eight Academy Awards in 1993, but, competing in a particularly strong field that year, it failed to capture any.

PLOT SUMMARY

The opening credits of this film play over a shot of cars driving up the long drive leading to Darlington Hall. A voiceover plays the narration of the letter that Mrs. Benn, formerly Miss Kenton, has sent to Mr. Stevens, the head butler at Darlington Hall. She discusses having read in the newspaper that Darlington Hall was to be sold after the death of Lord Darlington. As she discusses the fact that an American millionaire named Jack Lewis (a Mr. Farraday in Ishiguro's novel) bought the hall, the auction for many of the home's treasures is shown. Her letter speculates whether this Lewis might be the same American congressman who attended the conference in 1936, introducing this important event into the film.

Her recollection of her years at Darlington as the happiest in her life leads to images of Stevens and the footmen and under-butlers he commanded in the years when the house was fully staffed. She says she has left her husband for good and is staying in Kingston, at a friend's boarding house.

The credits end, and the story begins with Stevens serving Mr. Lewis, who is blithe and sarcastic in a way that the butler does not understand. Stevens mentions Lewis's previous suggestion that he take a vacation. He plans to visit Mrs. Benn, to see if she might want to work at Darlington Hall again. When he speaks her name he pauses, which Lewis notices.

Stevens starts his journey in the Daimler, a grand old car, while his voice on the soundtrack narrates a letter to Mrs. Benn telling her of his

plans. His letter recalls her first arrival at Darlington Hall, which the film then shows, indicating the bygone, more wealthy time with a fox hunt that begins as Miss Kenton arrives by bicycle.

At their first interview, Stevens lays out his displeasure about household staff forming personal relationships, which could lead to running off and leaving the house understaffed, as a former maid and under-butler have just done. Miss Kenton agrees. To replace the under-butler, Stevens later suggests to Lord Darlington that they hire his own father. Darlington meets William Stevens, the father, and hires him immediately.

Miss Kenton picks some flowers in the garden and brings them to Stevens to decorate his office. He thanks her but asks her to not bring more, as flowers can be "a distraction." Then he criticizes her for referring to her father as "William," though she explains that she has always called under-butlers by their first names. She leaves, offended, but when she is gone, Stevens chuckles to himself.

The novel's ongoing discussion about what it takes to be a great butler is concentrated in the film into a discussion at the large table where the butlers and maids eat together. William Stevens immediately offers an answer to the question, proposing that it is "dignity" that makes a butler great. He tells a story that he has told often about a butler in India who found a tiger in the dining room of the house where he worked, went to his employer to ask permission to shoot the tiger, and, after killing it, still managed to serve dinner on time.

William Stevens suffers a dizzy spell while sweeping the stairs and puts his broom down on a step before wandering away. Miss Kenton finds the broom. She goes to Stevens and tells him that he has been negligent, leaving his things around; when Stevens goes to see what she is talking about, he realizes that his father is becoming forgetful.

Lord Darlington and his friends are planning the upcoming conference on international politics. While William Stevens is serving them, a drop of sweat falls from his nose. The men do not notice, but Stevens, who is also serving them at the time, does, and he discreetly hands his father a handkerchief. Later, Miss Kenton comes to Stevens to point out that a statue that his father has dusted has been returned to the wrong place. Stevens says he is too busy to talk

FILM TECHNIQUE

- A cinematic mask, also referred to as a blackout lens, is a technique in which part of the frame is covered up, creating an effect of looking at the action through a shape. Some common examples are a rounded frame that implies looking through a telescope and the double circles that indicate looking through binoculars. In *The Remains of the Day*, Ivory uses this technique after Miss Kenton has asked Stevens to go with her to see the Chinese statues that have been put in the wrong places. Stevens stays in the room to defy her, but he cannot leave because she is outside the door, so the film uses a keyhole-shaped mask to show that he is peering through the keyhole.

- As the important international conference is about to begin, Stevens gives a speech to the staff at Darlington Hall. His words on the soundtrack play over a series of shots of the workers going about their preparations. A sequence of visual images presented in a film to establish a pattern is called a montage. Ivory uses shots of workers polishing silverware, sharpening knives, scrubbing floors, trimming hedges, and making beds to give viewers a sense of the massive effort that goes into preparing for a conference. The quickness of the shots in a montage, just a few seconds each, implies that there is much more going on than is shown in the film. The montage ends with fresh food and drink being delivered, which shows that the conference is ready to begin, and then the story returns to the normal pace of storytelling with the arrival of the first guest.

Another montage shows the preparations for the last dinner of the conference, minutes later in the film, indicating that Stevens's diligence over the staff has been consistent over the days.

- Ivory frequently makes use of the voiceover technique, with the soundtrack for the film playing the voice of someone who is not part of the scene being shown. This is used repeatedly with the letters exchanged back and forth between Stevens and Mrs. Benn: the sender's voice reads the letter aloud, while the camera shows the events being described in the letter. A voiceover is also used during Stevens's speech to the staff; the camera leaves the table where they are all assembled to show viewers scenes of the kind of preparation he is talking about.

- When Miss Kenton informs Stevens of the death of his father, the scene is lit from behind. Viewers see the blue wall of the stairway in the background, but in the foreground they only see black silhouettes of Emma Thompson and Anthony Hopkins, instead of seeing the actors' features. Removing their individuality in this way draws attention to the general situation, that of one person telling another person devastating personal news. Viewers can expect Stevens to act as any ordinary person would, with grief, but the film quickly reminds them that Stevens is not an ordinary person. Instead of responding to the news he has been given, Stevens remains in character and insists on returning to his duty.

to her, and he watches the hall through the door's keyhole, seeing she is not leaving. Ishiguro's novel plays this scene for minor humor, as Stevens considers leaving through the window to avoid her, but the film is very serious: as he tries to leave the room, Miss Kenton stops him and uses the misplaced Chinese statue to bring up

other things his father has been doing wrong. She insists that William Stevens should be relieved of his duties.

William Stevens trips on a step in the garden as he is bringing tea to Lord Darlington and two associates. The silver tea service flies from his hand with a clatter, as the men run to comfort

© *AF archive | Alamy*

him. Darlington calls Stevens to his study that night to suggest that his father be given fewer duties while the upcoming conference is going on, since an error might make the conference go badly. Still, he does not ask that William Stevens be fired, just relieved of strenuous duty.

After he has talked to his father about his new duty assignment, which disappoints William Stevens greatly, Stevens and Miss Kenton watch from an upstairs window as William Stevens, pretending that he is carrying a heavy tray, walks over the area where he fell again and again, to convince himself that he can do it safely. They share a look of pity between them.

Soon before the conference, Lord Darlington asks Stevens to have a talk with his godson, Reginald Cardinal. Reginald is engaged to be married, and since his father is dead, it is Darlington's responsibility to tell him about sex, a responsibility he passes to Stevens. Stevens takes the common expression "the birds and the bees" literally, and approaches Reginald in the garden to illustrate his sex talk by awkwardly mentioning the sexual behaviors of ducks and insects, but Reginald does not understand what he is hinting

at and agrees to come back to Darlington Hall in the spring to go fishing.

The French delegate, Dupont D'Ivry, is expected to oppose Lord Darlington's plan to relieve Germany of some of its postwar debt. Almost immediately after he arrives, D'Ivry is approached by the United States delegate, Congressman Jack Lewis. Lewis tells D'Ivry that he has overheard other members of the conference plotting against France's hard-line position. Later, when the conference is under way, Stevens shows D'Ivry and Lewis to a private room where they can talk. As he helps D'Ivry remove his shoes, a footman comes to the door to call Stevens away because his father has taken ill. Stevens finds William Stevens hunched over his cart of cleaning supplies, immobilized. The scene alternates between the pampered D'Ivry grimacing as he soaks his sore feet and the deathly ill servant carried to his bed.

In between serving the conference attendees, Stevens stops in at his father's bedside. William Stevens confesses to his son (whom he calls, for once, "Jim") that he lost the ability to love at some point in his life. He insists that Stevens go back to serving at the conference, as he falls asleep.

D'Ivry, whose support for Germany was doubted, gives a speech saying that he will try to have his country ease the rules that keep Germany weak. Congressman Lewis gives a speech about the dangers of noblemen dabbling in politics, which insults many of the attendees. As Lord Darlington rises to speak, Stevens is called out into the hall, where Miss Kenton tells him his father has died. Stevens returns to his duties, explaining to her that his father would have wanted it that way.

The film returns to Stevens on his cross-country trip in the 1950s, more than twenty years after the conference at Darlington Hall. He stops at a grocery store in a town along the way, where he has arranged for Mrs. Benn to write to him. As they chat, he tells the grocer that he comes from Darlington Hall in Oxfordshire. The grocer remembers reading about Lord Darlington as a Nazi sympathizer, but Stevens lies and tells him that he had no acquaintance with that man. His letter from Mrs. Benn tells him that she would be glad to meet him at a tea shop to talk over old times, and the film returns to the past, when she was Miss Kenton.

Miss Kenton ushers two young women, Elsa and Irma, who are refugees from Germany, into the study to meet Lord Darlington. He welcomes them and tells them that Miss Kenton will look after them.

Darlington welcomes several carloads of black-shirted Nazis to Darlington Hall. At dinner, they discuss the way that the Nazis on the rise in Germany are keeping order by putting Jews and people of color in concentration camps. Meanwhile, Stevens has brandy and cigars with Thomas Benn, himself a butler who once worked with Miss Kenton. Benn warns Stevens about the Nazis upstairs, but Stevens says that he does not listen to the people he serves. When Miss Kenton passes through, Benn comments on her good looks. Stevens says he would be lost without her, hastening to mention that he is referring to the importance of a good housekeeper.

Lord Darlington approaches Stevens and tells him that he must fire Elsa and Irma because they are Jewish, and he is concerned for the well-being of his guests. Stevens mildly objects. When he tells Miss Kenton, she threatens to leave if they are fired. When they leave, though, she does not go, explaining later to Stevens that she is a coward and afraid of facing the world alone. Stevens tells her how important she is to the house, but he averts his eyes before the situation becomes emotional.

On his car trip in the 1950s, Stevens runs out of gas. In a nearby inn, his talk with the locals turns to politics. They are impressed by the fact that he has been involved in international affairs and has met important people, and he leads them to believe that he is a powerful person himself, not a butler. The room given to Stevens for the night has a picture of the innkeeper's son, who was killed in World War II, and the son's clothes hanging in it, which makes Stevens reflect on his support for Lord Darlington's pro-German policies.

He recalls serving at Lord Darlington's house when one of Darlington's acquaintances, Mr. Spencer, calls Stevens over to ask him some complex questions about international policy. Spencer's point is to ask questions beyond his comprehension, to show that democracy, which relies on giving equal power to every citizen, is no longer relevant for the complex modern age. As each question is asked, Stevens, increasingly humiliated, politely apologizes for being unable to help.

The next morning, Dr. Carlisle, a physician, drives Stevens back to his car. He asks if Stevens is not really a manservant, and Stevens admits that he is. While discussing Darlington Hall, Carlisle recalls Lord Darlington, who was involved in trying to make a deal with Hitler before the war, and who lost a famous libel case against a newspaper. Stevens, uncomfortable, denies knowing Lord Darlington again. Later, as they are saying goodbye, Stevens admits that he did know Lord Darlington. Carlisle asks if he shared his opinions, and Stevens explains that it was his place as his butler to accept whatever Lord Darlington said. When he asks if Stevens would not rather have made his own mistakes in life, Stevens explains that he is on his way to correct a great mistake.

He remembers Lord Darlington asking if he could find the two maids, Elsa and Irma, nearly a year after they had been fired. Darlington feels bad about firing them for being Jewish and wants to do something to make up to them. When Stevens tells this to Miss Kenton, he also mentions that he felt bad about their dismissal, too. She is outraged that he did not show his feelings at the time.

One night, Miss Kenton goes to Stevens's study and catches him reading a book. She playfully asks to see what book it is, and when he refuses to show it, she jokes that he must be reading something sexy. In fact, it is a romance novel. As she pries the book from his hand they become close and almost intimate, but Stevens offends her by reacting coldly, complaining that his privacy has been invaded.

A young couple on the staff leaves to marry. Miss Kenton finds herself upset and distracted. Stevens is surprised to see her leaving to take her appointed day off. The film, unlike the novel, shows her courtship with Mr. Benn when they sit talking at a tavern. He makes fun of Stevens's rigidity and discusses his plans to open a shop in the west. He suggests that she marry him.

On a rainy night, Reginald Cardinal stops by Darlington Hall unexpectedly, explaining that his car has broken down nearby, and that he hopes to be able to stay in his godfather's home. Stevens tells him that would be fine, though they are going to have visitors. He goes to Miss Kenton to ask her to prepare a room for Reginald, and she admits that Mr. Benn has asked her to marry him. Stevens shows no emotion, wishing her a pleasant evening.

The visitors that night are the British prime minister and the German foreign minister Ribbentrop, an emissary from Adolf Hitler. Security for the evening is high, so that, when Miss Kenton returns to Darlington Hall that night, Stevens is called to the door to vouch for her identity. He gives little response when she says that she has accepted Mr. Benn's proposal, so she tells him that she and Mr. Benn often laugh at him.

In his room, Reginald explains that he did not come to the house that night by accident but to try to stop Lord Darlington from making a big mistake. The meeting is about getting the prime minister to enter into a pact with the Nazi German government.

As he passes her room, Miss Kenton steps out to apologize for being so harsh, but Stevens pretends that he did not listen to what she said earlier. Later, returning from the wine cellar with a bottle for the meeting, he hears her crying in her room. He enters, but as she dries her tears, he talks about business, about an alcove that needs dusting.

In the 1950s, Stevens arrives at the town of Little Compton. As Mrs. Benn prepares to see him, she is stopped by Mr. Benn in the lobby of her boarding house. He tells her that their daughter is pregnant and proposes that they go together to see her.

Stevens and Mrs. Benn meet at a busy tea room. They discuss how the libel suit devastated Lord Darlington, leaving him depressed and friendless until his death.

After tea, they take a walk along the shore, and Mrs. Benn explains that she is going to stay with her husband, help her daughter raise the baby, and therefore will not return to Darlington Hall. They watch the lights come on along the pier; in the novel, Stevens does this alone, the day after their meeting.

It is raining when he drives her to the bus stop and waits with her. As she boards the bus, they shake hands to say goodbye, and the bus pulling away is what separates their hands from each other's.

In the last scene, Stevens is back at Darlington Hall. As he and Jack Lewis talk, a bird flies into the ballroom through the fireplace. Stevens and Lewis work together to catch the bird and release it, signifying the kind of friendship and mutual respect that is going to grow between the new master of Darlington Hall and his butler.

CHARACTERS

Mrs. Benn
See Miss Sally Kenton

Thomas Benn
Benn is the man Miss Kenton marries. In the novel (where he does not appear directly), he seems to be a cruel and possibly violent man; Miss Kenton leaves him several times, and the letter that has Stevens driving across the country to see her indicates that she has broken up from Benn for good. He is a former butler. The film shows Benn having a conversation with Stevens when he is still a butler, before he has begun to court Miss Kenton. They marry after a brief, hidden relationship and go back to his hometown, where he leaves domestic service and goes into business for himself. The film goes further toward showing that he is not necessarily a bad man by showing the scene in which he reconciles with his wife, which occurs moments before her meeting with Stevens.

Reginald Cardinal
Reginald Cardinal is a young man, Lord Darlington's godson. He is played by Hugh Grant. In the film, he attends the conference at Darlington Hall

as Darlington's secretary, and his father, David, is dead. In the book, though, his father is still alive, and they attend the conference together. The distinction is that, in the book, his father has given Darlington the task of talking to Reginald about sex because he is engaged to be married, and Darlington uncomfortably passes the task off to Stevens. Stevens approaches the task so awkwardly that Reginald does not understand what he is talking about, thinking that their conversation is about fishing.

Later, as World War II approaches, Reginald is older and works as a newspaper writer. He comes to Darlington Hall because he now understands the international situation better than Lord Darlington, and he hopes to prevent Darlington from being used as a pawn by the Nazis. Instead, he stays in his room while the Nazis are meeting with Lord Darlington.

Doctor Richard Carlisle

When Stevens stops in the town of Moscombe, the common country people treat him like he is royalty, but Dr. Carlisle understands enough to figure out that he is a butler. He is polite to Stevens about the misunderstanding and, hearing that Stevens worked for Lord Darlington, is curious about the man whom he has seen reviled in the newspapers, but he is not judgmental.

Charlie

Charlie is the head footman at Darlington Hall. He has the potential to rise in the ranks as an under-butler and then a head butler, but he falls in love with the new maid, Lizzie. They throw away their careers to run off and be married.

Lord Darlington

Lord Darlington, the nobleman whom Stevens served for most of his career, is played by British actor James Fox, whose film career spans more than half a century. Darlington is a well-meaning man who is not content to simply inherit wealth. He is trying to use his title, and the social power that comes with it, to promote peace in the world. His early friendship with a German, Karl-Heinz Bremann, taught Darlington to respect people from a country with which his own country might be at war.

Darlington's interest in helping the world is shown in two parallel situations, with opposing results. The conference at Darlington Hall does what he wants it to do, with people coming together from all over the world in an informal atmosphere to discuss their political differences. In the second instance, however, he brings British and German diplomats together, hoping to avoid war, and instead he is used by Germany's underhanded Nazi regime to help keep England from defending the weaker countries that Germany is invading.

In the novel and in the film, Darlington's openness to Germany while the Nazis are rising to power creates a change in his moral values. The novel specifically mentions a brief affair that he has with a Mrs. Carolyn Barnet, whose influence leads him to fire any Jewish workers on his staff. In the film, Mrs. Barnet is not mentioned, but he takes the same drastic step. Lord Darlington eventually recovers his senses and asks Stevens to find the fired workers, so that he can repay them.

Lord Darlington ends up being ridiculed in the press. He sues one newspaper for libel, but his loss in court seems to confirm that he is the Nazi sympathizer that they said he was. Throughout World War II and after it, he is shunned from British society, and he dies alone and bitter.

Dupont D'Ivry

D'Ivry is the delegate from France. The conference attendees fear that he will take a hard line against softening Germany's punishment for World War I. Congressman Lewis meets privately with him to tell him to stay tough against the German position, but D'Ivry ends up supporting the Germans.

Elsa

Elsa is one of the two Jewish girls who are brought to work at Darlington Hall as refugees from Germany as the Nazis come to power. They are fired because Lord Darlington is convinced that having Jewish people on his staff will mean trouble.

Irma

Irma is one of the two Jewish girls who are brought to work at Darlington Hall as refugees from Germany as the Nazis come to power. They are fired because Lord Darlington is convinced that having Jewish people on his staff will mean trouble.

Miss Sally Kenton

Emma Thompson was nominated for an Oscar for her portrayal of Miss Kenton, the head of the housekeeping staff at Darlington Hall in the 1930s. She is the female counterpart of Mr. Stevens: she is in charge of the household's female workers. She is like Stevens in her rigid, formal temperament, though Miss Kenton is more open to human emotion than Stevens allows himself to be. She jokes with Stevens, and in her jokes, she sends him signals that she is romantically interested in him. For instance, she jokes about his reluctance to take Lizzie on as a new maid because, she says, he might be afraid to have a pretty girl around, distracting him. The way Thompson delivers the lines shows that she is trying to find out whether Stevens really does take an interest in pretty girls, but he remains aloof. When Miss Kenton takes his novel from him and is touched to find that he is reading a romance novel, she shows him clearly that she is impressed by his capacity to understand love, and she is hurt by his abrupt retreat from the subject.

Miss Kenton's romantic frustration is pushed further when Lizzie announces that she and Charlie are running off to marry. Lizzie dismisses her advice to be financially sensible and instead talks about how her love is more important than financial security, which starts Miss Kenton thinking. Soon after, she accepts a proposal of marriage from Mr. Benn, fearing that her chance at love will simply melt away if she continues waiting for Stevens to show some emotion. She does not show the same attraction to Mr. Benn that she has for Stevens.

Her relationship with Mr. Benn is a difficult one. Her letter to Stevens says that she has left him for good. In the novel, she tells Stevens, at their meeting, that she has decided to return to Benn because they have a history together, but the film, unlike the novel, includes the actual scene of her and Mr. Benn reconciling.

The relationship between Miss Kenton and Mr. Stevens is summarized in their last scene together. Their handshake lingers, as if they were lovers holding hands, but the real-world circumstances of Miss Kenton's life pull her away from him as her bus pulls away from the curb.

Jack Lewis

Jack Lewis is an American congressman, played by American actor Christopher Reeve. Lewis has become wealthy as a manufacturer of cosmetics and is a powerful member of the Foreign Affairs Committee of the House of Representatives. He is one of the international guests at the conference at Darlington Hall. When he enters,

he is cheerful and supportive of Lord Darlington's plan to have the financial burden on Germany lowered or suspended. Later, though, Stevens overhears him talking with the French delegate, Dupont D'Ivry, who is the strongest opponent of forgiving Germany's debts. In private, Congressman Lewis tells D'Ivry that Germany should continue to pay, though that is not the position he takes publicly.

When D'Ivry surprises the conference by announcing his support for lowering Germany's debt, Congressman Lewis stands up and gives a speech that denounces the entire conference, explaining that modern politics are too complex to be handled by amateurish, well-meaning noblemen. Though he seems to be an angry hard-liner who has stabbed Lord Darlington in the back, his position is later proved correct by Reginald Cardinal, who tells Stevens that Lewis is right: Darlington's involvement in international affairs will be dangerous to England because it encourages acceptance of the Nazi party in Germany.

In Ishiguro's novel, Darlington Hall is bought by an American named Faraday after Lord Darlington's death. Jhabvala's screenplay eliminates Mr. Faraday completely and brings Jack Lewis back to England in the 1950s, to be the house's new owner and Stevens's new employer.

Lizzie

Lizzie is the maid who replaces the Jewish maids Lord Darlington dismisses. She is not very experienced, but Miss Kenton insists that she be hired because she is angry about how Lizzie's predecessors were fired. Eventually, Lizzie shows promise as a housekeeper, but then she throws her career away to run off with Charlie, the under-butler. Miss Kenton warns her that this is a bad choice, but Lizzie believes more in love than in security.

Harry Smith

Harry Smith is the town know-it-all in Moscombe. All of the people in this small town gather to see Stevens when he is stranded there, and Harry Smith is the loudest of them all, trying to engage the new man in talk about politics. When Stevens asks Dr. Carlisle whether Harry Smith is considered a humorous figure, Carlisle says that the people's feelings about him are more complicated than that.

Spencer

An acquaintance of Lord Darlington, Mr. Spencer calls Stevens over and asks him complex questions to prove a point about common people such as butlers being incapable of understanding international politics. He represents the members of the upper class who look down on common people for reasons that they think are scientific.

James Stevens

Stevens is played by Anthony Hopkins in an Academy Award–nominated performance. His given name, James, is given only once in the film, when he picks up his mail, though his father does, near the end of his life, address Stevens as Jimmy.

He is a man who has little understanding of other people, who is entirely immersed in his quest to be a great butler. His dedication to his job is illustrated by the fact that, when his father falls ill as the Darlington Hall conference is beginning, Stevens chooses to remain at his post, serving the conference attendees instead of staying by his father's bedside. He explains that his father, who was a butler himself, would have wanted it that way.

Stevens never openly acknowledges his hopes for a romantic relationship with Miss Kenton. When they work together, he backs away when any possibility of intimacy arises. Hopkins shows Stevens's wariness about physical contact most clearly in the scene in his study, when Miss Kenton tries to take the book he is reading to see its cover: their close proximity seems to imply romance, but Stevens shrinks back from her touch. Throughout the film, he deflects her friendliness and concern with a mask of professional stoicism. He does eventually admit to Dr. Carlisle that he is undertaking his trip to correct a great mistake he made in his life, an admission that is more direct than anything Stevens acknowledges in the novel.

Politically, Stevens's devotion to Lord Darlington drives him to support positions that he could never support on his own. He is against the firing of the two Jewish maids, but he never voices his opposition, even privately to Miss Kenton. His conscience bothers him when Reginald Cardinal tells him that the meeting between the prime minister and German minister Ribbentrop will leave England at the mercy of the rising Nazi government. Hopkins allows viewers to see how this idea distresses Stevens, but Stevens never speaks a word against Lord Darlington's plans, out of loyalty to his employer. Still, later in his life, he twice denies having known Lord Darlington while on his road trip, insulting the memory of his former employer.

In the end, Stevens seems to have found peace in his life, not by reuniting with Miss Kenton, which he believed throughout the film would be the solution to his discontentment, but by changing his rigid expectations of what a butler should be and coming to an understanding with his new employer, Jack Lewis.

William Stevens

William Stevens, the father of the film's protagonist, was once a head butler himself. Stevens convinces Lord Darlington to hire him soon after Miss Kenton is hired, to replace a maid and under-butler who ran off together. William Stevens takes his duties as seriously as his son does. His favorite story is about a butler in India who finds a tiger under the dining room table and deals with it before serving dinner, a story he tells to show the ideal poise a butler should have. As he ages, however, he becomes weaker and more forgetful. With the big international conference coming, his son is required to limit William's duties, which shames him greatly.

On his deathbed, William confesses to his son that he lost his ability to love. His regret is a warning to Stevens, who has pushed away all attempts at friendship from Miss Kenton so that he can be the best butler imaginable, the way his father was.

THEMES

Parent-child Relationships

The introduction of William Stevens into the serving staff at Darlington Hall is significant to the story of the protagonist, James Stevens, because it shows the son what he can expect his future to hold. In famed British character actor Peter Vaughan in the role of William Stevens, Merchant and Ivory have even found a performer who bears a strong physical resemblance to Anthony Hopkins. In the story, William Stevens is a former head butler himself; he once held the position that his son now holds. The decline in his social standing and in his physical state foretell what will happen to James Stevens, who is at the height of his career in the early years of

READ, WATCH, WRITE

- Watch *Batman Begins* (2005) or *The Dark Knight* (2008), the first films in Christopher Nolan's reboot of the "Batman" series, with an eye on Michael Caine's portrayal of Alfred Pennyworth, Bruce Wayne's butler. Rate Alfred as a butler as you think Stevens would, making a list of things that you think Stevens would find honorable or dishonorable about Alfred's professionalism. Complete your list by giving Alfred the overall grade you think Stevens would give him. Post your grade to your Web page and invite comments from others who view the films.

- Read *Roberts' Guide for Butlers and Other Household Staff—the House Servant's Directory*, an 1827 guidebook written by Robert Roberts and reprinted by several publishers (Applewood Books in 1993, Pomona Press in 2008, and Kessinger Publishing in 2010). Choose an actor to play Roberts, the narrator, and make a video that adapts one of the sections of the book for would-be domestic servants.

- Read Jerzy Kosinski's 1971 novella *Being There*, a fantasy about a domestic servant, a gardener, who leaves the sheltered household he has lived in all his life. Kosinski's protagonist Chance has no clue about how to act in the world at large and ends up, because of how other people view his simplicity and eagerness to help, as a possible presidential candidate. Write an essay that uses examples from Kosinski's book and from *The Remains of the Day* to support your theory about whether political figures should be complex or simple in the way they view the world.

- With the death of the British Empire after World War II, the use of domestic staff in Western countries dwindled, but developing countries, particularly in the Middle East, still use domestic workers regularly. Research the life of a domestic worker in Hong Kong, Singapore, Malaysia, or Saudi Arabia, and write a report about how the life you researched differs from the life of a butler in Britain after World War I.

- Stevens specifically tries to avoid aesthetic (artistic) judgment, as he shows by rejecting the flowers Miss Kenton brings on several occasions. Create a painting or drawing that you think Stevens would create if he had artistic talent. Explain to your class in detail why he would choose that subject and why he would depict it in that style.

- Hanif Kureishi, like Ishiguro, is a British writer of Asian descent who looks at his country's attitudes with a multicultural perspective. He is most famous in America for having written *My Beautiful Laundrette*, a play adapted by director Stephen Frears as a 1985 film of the same name. Set in London in the 1980s, it tells the story of life for an immigrant Pakistani family, incorporating the realities of modern life including drug use, alcoholism, racial tensions, and gay relations. The film, released on DVD in 2003, stars Saeed Jaffrey, Roshan Seth, Daniel Day-Lewis, and Gordon Warnecke. Watch the film and, in an essay, compare its multicultural perspective with *The Remains of the Day*, considering whether servant and master being from the same culture changes the dynamics of the relationship.

---

this story and is facing his own humbling decline near the end.

In the film, father and son show no overt affection for one another, as indicated by having Stevens call William Stevens "Father." The respect Stevens has is shown indirectly, in the way that Stevens insists that Miss Kenton is not allowed to refer to his father as "William," because that would draw attention to the fact that he is not a head butler anymore. Stevens does not want his father embarrassed, but he also clearly does not want to believe that his

© *Moviestore Collection Ltd | Alamy*

father is not a great man anymore. When forced to relieve his father of his duties, Stevens delivers the news with a cool, unemotional tone, but Hopkins allows his sorrow to show.

On his deathbed, William Stevens breaks down the wall of formality between them a little by calling his son "Jimmy": Stevens is never called by his given name by any other characters. He apologizes to Stevens because he fell out of love with his mother, and he explains that by noting that he lost the capacity to love. Though Stevens is in the exact same position as his father and is aware of growing feelings between himself and Miss Kenton, he does not realize that his father's apology is actually a warning of what his own life could hold.

Love

The relationship between Stevens and Miss Kenton grows toward love, but it never actually arrives there. The basis of their relationship is in their social equality: he is the head of the butlers and she is the head of the maids, and they meet regularly in the evenings to discuss the staff. Most of the time, she matches him in

having a cold, professional outlook toward life, though sometimes she shows more emotion, as in the firing of Elsa and Irma, the two Jewish maids.

As their relationship develops, Miss Kenton teases Stevens. She points out that he never hires good-looking women and suggests that he is afraid that they might distract him. Clearly, she is curious to see his reaction, but he does not react. When she wants to see the novel he is reading, she is playful about taking it from his hand, unpeeling his fingers from it in the same motion that he used to remove his stricken father from the cleaning cart when he fell. She is moved to see this unemotional man reading a romance, but he quickly explains that he is reading it to study human behavior. These scenes and others indicate that Miss Kenton might have been flirting with him, though Stevens does not realize it until decades later.

When Lizzie announces her intention to run away with Charlie, Miss Kenton tries to talk her out of it as an impractical career move. Lizzie announces that she does not care about her career, because she is in love. Miss Kenton realizes what she is missing in waiting for Stevens, and soon she accepts Mr. Benn's marriage proposal.

Her marriage to Benn is not a good one. She leaves him several times. In the end, though, she explains to Stevens that she learned to fall in love with her husband over the course of years. They did not run off in a moment of romantic enthusiasm, as Lizzie and Charlie did, but they have a lasting love that is more secure and true. It is the kind of relationship she might have had with Stevens, if he had shown interest.

Responsibility

Stevens, like his father, represses his personal life because he feels that his responsibility to his employer is more important than his own humanity. The film introduces this humorously, showing his bafflement and discomfort when given the task of educating Reginald Cardinal about sex. Later, while his father lies dying, Stevens is driven to attend to the people at the international conference. His father even tells him in the middle of this section of the film that he lost the ability to love, but Stevens cannot see any other course than staying true to his duty. He tends to the sore feet of the French minister while his father is on his deathbed, leaving Miss Kenton with the very personal task of closing William Stevens's eyes when he has passed away.

Stevens is so intent on projecting an air of dignity, as a good butler should, that he does not see the signs that Miss Kenton might care for him until years later, when it is too late to do anything about it. Even when he does think that he might have a chance at rekindling their relationship, he does not admit his feelings to himself or to Mr. Lewis, but instead disguises his trip to see her as part of his responsibility to make sure Darlington Hall is staffed properly. Years of service have taught Stevens to put aside his own wishes for the wishes of the man he serves, so that when his new, American employer tries to talk to him as a friend, he is uncomfortable.

STYLE

Epistolary Format

An epistolary novel is one that is told as if it were a collection of letters between two people. Ishiguro's novel is not an epistolary novel, though it does contain excerpts from letters written by Mrs. Benn and Stevens. It is told in the first person, with Mr. Stevens talking to his audience, sometimes even addressing the reader as "you" to make a point. Although a film could never be made to look like the contents of a letter, Ivory does capture some of the narrative voice of the novel by inserting voiceovers that narrate the letters that Stevens and Mrs. Benn send to one another. The film sometimes combines the voiceover with visuals of action that the letter is describing, as when the film shows Miss Kenton arriving at Darlington Hall just as Stevens says that he remembers that day. The film also uses the letters for contrast, as when Mrs. Benn talks about how she misses Darlington Hall in a letter that leads Stevens into a flashback of the day Elsa and Irma were dismissed, a day she hated.

Quest Structure

This story is about many things, from love and duty to European history between the two world wars. In order to present these elements to audiences, Ishiguro structured the tale of James Stevens into a quest narrative, a structure that propels the story forward.

Quest narratives have been used in fiction and mythology for centuries. They generally tell the tale of a hero who is sent out into the world, out of the small zone in which he has lived comfortably for years. The quest usually entails obtaining some significant object and returning home with it. According to tradition, the hero will fulfill the quest and will mature in the process of fulfilling it, helped and hindered by important people he meets along the way.

It is not an object that Stevens sets out after in *The Remains of the Day*, but rather a person, Mrs. Benn. The film makes it clear that he has not been away from Darlington Hall in decades, and the encounters he has along the way help him put his life in perspective. He learns that he is ashamed of Lord Darlington when he finds himself telling people that he never knew him, and he finds that he has a large amount of vanity when he allows the people at the inn to believe that it was he, not his employer, who was an important person in international affairs. These revelations allow him to put past events into perspective, so that when he does not return home with Mrs. Benn, he is nonetheless a better person for having undertaken his quest.

Set Design

The Remains of the Day, like many of the films that Merchant and Ivory adapted from nineteenth- and twentieth-century literary works, takes place among the wealthy. The exterior shots of Darlington Hall were filmed at Dyrham Park, a mansion in Gloucestershire, England, that dates back to the seventeenth century and has been used in many films. The grounds are photographed to show the wide acreage that has, according to the story, been in the Darlington family for generations. Every interior shot serves to show the immensity of the place and therefore to convey the wealth that Lord Darlington must control. Viewers are shown libraries with bookshelves rising fifteen feet high and kitchens busy with dozens of cooks. The props of wealth extend to the study where Stevens spends his quiet time alone, drinking fine whiskey and smoking expensive cigars, indicating that he is enjoying Lord Darlington's wealth by association.

Stevens takes some of that wealth on the road with him in the form of the Daimler, a gigantic, dated automobile that conveys wealth and extravagance. The film uses the car and the suit he wears to mark him as an outsider in the small villages of rural England that he visits. Although these items serve to establish that he is very different from the people he encounters, the film remains consistent in photographing the towns he visits in the same earth tones and with the same attention to detail that are used to show the wealth of Darlington Hall. Stevens does not encounter a loud, bright world outside the place he leaves, but instead one that is consistent with the world of serene wealth that is common to most Merchant Ivory productions.

CULTURAL CONTEXT

The Treaty of Versailles

Although the armed combat of World War I ended with the signing of the armistice on November 11, 1918, the war did not officially end until 1919. The nations that had been involved in the war spent more than seven months following the war in negotiations, to determine what limitations would be put on the countries that had been defeated to ensure that they would not rise up in arms again and to assign reparations, money that the defeated countries would pay to make up for the damage caused by the war.

There were several treaties signed between the victorious Allied Powers and the defeated Central Powers of Germany, Austria-Hungary, Bulgaria, and the Ottoman Empire. The most significant of these was the Treaty of Versailles. Signed on June 28, 1919, exactly five years after the assassination of Austrian Archduke Franz Ferdinand, which started the chain of events that led to war in the first place, the Treaty of Versailles was the agreement with which Germany formally accepted peace.

The treaty's ratification was delayed because parties on both sides had differing opinions about how best to ensure peace. American president Woodrow Wilson was greatly concerned with making this war the last war the world would ever know. Wilson's primary concern was the establishment of the League of Nations, a precursor to the modern United Nations, as a body that could arbitrate international disputes. The United States took a position of treating Germany gently, and it withheld its assent to the passage of the treaty and never signed. Britain and France, on the other hand, had suffered directly during the war and were inclined toward making Germany weaker and receiving compensation for the losses they had suffered. Russia had been overthrown by revolution in the middle of fighting the war, and the newly formed Soviet Union was not a participant in the treaty process.

There were 402 articles, or items, in the Treaty of Versailles. Limitations were put on the size of the German military. Many of the articles concerned the new borders that would identify Germany, taking away the countries that had been annexed during the war, which Germany had claimed as its rightful, historical legacy. The most controversial articles, though, were those that dealt with reparations. Article 231 directly put the blame for the war on Germany, and the following articles laid out a program that would require Germany to pay France and England billions of Reischmarks (Germany's unit of currency) over the coming decades.

The strictness of the reparations required of Germany made it difficult for the country to become economically independent after the war. For many in the Allied powers, this was exactly the point of imposing a heavy toll. The crushing debt was seen to cause rampant inflation, though, leading to massive suffering for the German people. In the 1930s, Adolf Hitler rose to political power by speaking out against the

© *Moviestore Collection Ltd | Alamy*

oppression of the Germans at the hands of merciless foreign powers.

Appeasement

By 1935, Hitler was taking actions in violation of the provisions of the Treaty of Versailles. He reinstated the country's air force and, later, the navy, claiming that a strong military was necessary for the protection of the country. He started a compulsory draft for German citizens. He then began invading forbidden territories.

Although the military build-up was illegal, England continued its policy, as shown in *The Remains of the Day*, of appeasing (attempting to satisfy or calm) Germany. Ishiguro's novel even mentions one prominent politician, David Lloyd George, who was on record as supporting weakening the sanctions imposed by the treaty. Joachim von Ribbentrop, who would become the minister of foreign affairs of Germany as World War II drew near, was sent on a series of meetings with influential British citizens in an effort to win British support despite the opposition of those in the government, including Winston Churchill and Joseph Austen Chamberlain, who supported maintaining the hard line.

When Germany attacked Czechoslovakia in 1938, to restore German territory that had been given up in 1919, Hitler met with British prime minister Neville Chamberlain, along with French prime minister Édouard Daladier and Italian premier Benito Mussolini, to ensure that there would be no war with those powerful nations. Chamberlain and Hitler signed an accord that was supposed to limit German aggression and promote peace. In August of 1939, Chamberlain signed a treaty with Poland, assuring the Poles that Britain would support them if they were attacked. The German invasion of Poland on September 1, 1939, forced Britain to declare war on Germany, after years of allowing Hitler to build a formidable military structure.

CRITICAL OVERVIEW

By the time *The Remains of the Day* was released, Ismail Merchant, who produced it along with Mike Nichols and John Callay, had been working with director James Ivory for three decades. Audiences had come to expect a certain kind of formal rigidness in a Merchant Ivory film. Their works were associated with British masters of the social novel, including E. M. Forster and Henry James, who had each been adapted several times by the Merchant Ivory production team. Although written recently by a relatively young novelist, the subject matter of *The Remains of the Day* fit the Merchant Ivory style perfectly. As Mike Wilmington put it in his review of the film for the *Chicago Tribune*, the film "is another small wonder of moviemaking intelligence, taste and tact from the producer-director-writer team of Ismail Merchant, James Ivory and Ruth Prawer Jhabvala." Comparing it to the team's adaptations of Forster's novels, Wilmington noted that "*Remains* is admirably economical and high-style, beautifully pitched and polished, full of glitteringly arch, yet thrillingly expert, performances." Vincent Canby, writing in the *New York Times*, was even more supportive of the film, commenting that "nothing that Mr. Merchant, Mr. Ivory and Ms. Jhabvala have done before...has the psychological and political scope and the spare authority of this enchantingly realized film." Canby was so impressed with that film that he predicted, incorrectly, that it "could become a quite unlikely smash." It was, in fact, only ranked number sixty-six in box office ticket sales for 1993, according to the Box Office Mojo Web site.

While the film was almost universally praised, there were critics, even among its supporters, who compared the film unfavorably to the novel and to other Merchant Ivory productions. In *Variety*, which is a publication geared at the business and not necessarily the artistic side of movies, Todd McCarthy expressed the concern that its "appeal may not be as deep or long-lasting as that of *Howard's End*," the Merchant Ivory film starring Anthony Hopkins and Emma Thompson that had been released the year before. "But if it doesn't quite reach the brass ring," McCarthy went on to explain, "[the] film still possesses plenty of riches to beguile the discriminating viewer." Jack Kroll, writing in *Newsweek*, saw a crucial problem in adapting Ishiguro's first-person novel to the screen. Ishiguro was able to control the "ironic nuances" of Stevens's story in a way that a film could not. As he explained it, "The novel is a writer's tour de force, but the film...sets the characters in the light of reality, and it may arouse more impatience than empathy." Though the film was

nominated for eight Academy Awards in 1993, including nominations for best picture, best director, and best adapted screenplay and acting nominations for Thompson and Hopkins, it won none, with Steven Spielberg's *Schindler's List* sweeping the awards that year.

CRITICISM

David Kelly

Kelly is an instructor of literature and creative writing. In the following essay, he examines The Remains of the Day *as an example of an excellent film that still could not surpass the novel on which it was based.*

The 1993 film adaptation of Kazuo Ishiguro's novel *The Remains of the Day* stands out as an excellent example of why people often say, as they are walking out of a theater, "The book was better." The film is, on its own, a fine, stately presentation, skillfully directed by James Ivory and presented with cool intelligence via Ruth Prawer Jhabvala's script. Anthony Hopkins and Emma Thompson were nominated for Oscars for the lead roles, and they are supported with just the right drollness by Edward Fox, Christopher Reeve, and the rest of the supporting cast. Like practically anything out of the Merchant Ivory production stable, it is a bit humorless, especially when compared with the novel's wit, but the loss of humor is a fair trade-off for letting audiences walk away with the sense that they have participated in high art. What really makes the difference between the film and book of *The Remains of the Day* is that the visual language that film uses is simply not as fluid as words can be in the hands of a master like Ishiguro.

There are changes that a screenwriter makes when adapting a novel to film that alter the facts but that make no major difference to the overall story. The most notable of these happens in the film's opening moments, as audiences find out that Mr. Faraday, the American who bought Darlington Hall after Lord Darlington's death, is replaced by Jack Lewis, the book's other American character. It is a fair substitution. Mr. Faraday's function in the book is to make Stevens, his butler and the story's protagonist, uncomfortable with his overly familiar American manners, and for that function, one American is as good as the next. At the end of the film, this

WHAT DO I SEE NEXT?

- The 1971 miniseries *Upstairs Downstairs* was the most popular British series ever shown on American television, and it won multiple Emmy awards. It concerns the intertwined lives of an aristocratic London family and its servants before and after World War I. The entire twenty-five-hour series is available in a new fortieth-anniversary deluxe set.

- The same year that *The Remains of the Day* was released, Martin Scorsese, who is generally considered an action director, released a moody and richly detailed adaptation of Edith Wharton's novel *The Age of Innocence*, starring Daniel Day-Lewis, Michelle Pfeiffer, and Winona Ryder. It tells the story of repressed love in upper-class New York society in the 1870s, a time period that made many reviewers compare it to a Merchant Ivory film.

- *The Remains of the Day* explores the attitudes that wealthy British people felt about the rise of Hitler and the Third Reich in Germany in the 1930s. The result of the Nazis' success is seen most starkly in another film from 1993, Steven Spielberg's *Schindler's List*. Spielberg's film shows the systematic removal of the rights of Jewish people in Nazi-ruled Poland, from work camps to death camps, and tells the story of one man who gave up his wealth to save as many lives as he could. It was the winner of seven Academy Awards that year and was nominated for another five.

- *The Remains of the Day* represents a reunion for the key figures who made it. In 1992, a year before this film was released, Emma Thompson won the Academy Award for Best Actress when she starred with Anthony Hopkins in *Howard's End*, a Merchant Ivory production film about social class in Britain at the turn of the twentieth century. Ruth Prawer Jhabvala won the Oscar for Best Adapted Screenplay for her script, based on a novel by E. M. Forster.

- In 2001, director Robert Altman used the backdrop of an English estate where the rich intermingle with their servants for his murder mystery *Gosford Park*. Starring Maggie Smith, Ryan Phillippe, and Kristin Scott Thomas, the story unravels in Altman's unique style, with intercut conversations implying the complexity of the social situation.

- Many young adults have learned history from the British Broadcasting Corporation's "Blackadder" series, a comedy starring Rowan Atkinson (best known as Mr. Bean) as a character who appears in different historical circumstances each season. In *Blackadder the Third*, the title character is a butler during the British Regency period of the early nineteenth century, working for a very foolish Prince of Wales, played by Hugh Laurie. The six-episode season, which originally ran in 1987, was released in a remastered edition in 2009.

---

same kind of compression of characters helps emphasize the prospective love affair. Ishiguro's novel has Stevens sitting on the pier at Weymouth watching the colored lights come on and talking to a stranger who happens to occupy a bench with him. In the film, that moment is shared with his old acquaintance and would-be lover, Miss Kenton (now Mrs. Benn). Keeping the focus on the two lead actors makes more sense to viewers than introducing new characters in the film's final

scenes, and anything that keeps a superb actor such as Emma Thompson in the picture for a few more minutes must be considered a smart decision by the film's producer.

What the film is unable to capture on-screen is the richness of the narrative voice that Ishiguro has given Stevens. He lacks self-awareness, but at the same time he is bound up by self-consciousness. His most human desires for love and respect manifest themselves in his actions,

"BECAUSE IT CAN PRESENT STEVENS FROM INSIDE HIS HEAD AND CONTRAST THOSE THOUGHTS, MOMENT BY MOMENT, WITH HIS EXPERIENCES OF THE WORLD AROUND HIM, HIS AWARENESS OF SOCIAL SITUATIONS IS ALWAYS RELEVANT TO THE BOOK. THE FILM SIMPLY CANNOT KEEP UP."

even while his ongoing interior monologue pretends that no such desires exist. Because it can present Stevens from inside his head and contrast those thoughts, moment by moment, with his experiences of the world around him, his awareness of social situations is always relevant to the book. The film simply cannot keep up.

The film does what it can to show Stevens's thoughts. In one scene, for example, he tries to exert authority over Miss Kenton by refusing to go and look at some Chinese figurines she says have been put out of place. It is an error that, had Stevens noticed it, would have been marked as a major blunder, but he feels he would be giving up power if he acknowledged that she was right, so he tells her he is too busy to leave the billiard room to look. She waits for him in the hall, though. Stevens is a victim of his pride, a prisoner. The novel plays the irony of his stubbornness keenly: "Resolved not to waste further time on account of this childish affair," he explains, "I contemplated departure via the french windows." The film's way of showing his contradiction, without the benefit of Stevens's voice, is showing him bent down, peeking through the keyhole to see whether she has gone. It captures the point by being more obvious. A similar addition occurs later, when Stevens is in the room of a man who has been killed in the war. His guilt over supporting his employer's actions, which probably helped bring about World War II, is made visible in the way Hopkins looks over the dead man's clothes, but the scene, good as it is for film, has a hard time conveying more than one simple emotion.

One eternal quandary that defines Stevens's character is the question of what makes a truly great butler. In the novel, it nags at him persistently. He dwells on the characteristics of butlers who are universally acknowledged as great, men named Mr. Marshall and Mr. Kane, and discusses a trade organization for butlers, the Hayes Society, as well as their newsletter, *A Quarterly for the Gentleman's Gentleman*. The film, unfortunately, cannot capture Stevens's obsession with greatness in his profession. It does not take readers into his mind, and the very nature of his character is that he is isolated and has no one to talk with about his interests. What the book presents as an ongoing concern, the film reduces to just one scene, in which Stevens raises the question of what makes a great butler at dinner, while talking to an under-butler who might be interested in rising in the profession. By giving him a reason for bringing the subject up, the film dilutes even the little bit of obsession that this one scene could imply.

The greatest shortcoming of the film version is in its handling of the romantic potential between Stevens and Miss Kenton. In some respects, this relationship is ideal for presenting on film, because it is all about the external clues that can be observed by anyone watching. When Miss Kenton brings Stevens flowers, for instance, or when he rocks back and forth on his feet while teasing her about her threat to quit, there is clearly flirting going on. A scene such as the one in which he explains to Mr. Lewis that he is going to drive cross-country to hire a former maid shows his transparency, as Lewis teasingly asks if the woman he is speaking of is his "girlfriend." Audiences do not need access to Stevens's thoughts in cases like this because his thoughts are written on his face.

However, the film simplifies the complexity of the love story, grinding it down to a basic, generic sense of longing. The closest Stevens and Miss Kenton ever come to intimacy, for instance, is in a scene in his study in which she tries to see what book he is reading. She backs him into a corner and touches him. The scene is shot with low, romantic lighting from the desk beneath them, and the music swells as their faces draw nearer before his professional haughtiness kicks in once more to destroy the mood. By contrast, Stevens the narrator of the novel describes the situation this way:

> There she was standing before me, and suddenly the atmosphere underwent a peculiar change—almost as though the two of us had been suddenly thrust on to some other plane of being altogether. I am afraid it is not easy to describe clearly what I mean here. All I can say is that everything around us suddenly became very still; it was my impression that Miss Kenton's manner also underwent a sudden change; there was a strange seriousness in her expression, and it struck me she seemed almost frightened.

© *Moviestore Collection Ltd | Alamy*

Not only is the passion touched on and denied, as it is in the film, but the subtlety of language and the first-person narration makes it possible for Ishiguro to show how Stevens blocks out the obvious even while he is telling readers about it.

As usual, the book is "better," better at conveying the complexity of the emotions it covers and better at letting readers know the issues involved. The economic reality of the situation, though, is that books, even when they are winners of prestigious awards, just do not reach the audience that films do. If there had been no Merchant Ivory film of *The Remains of the Day*, many people would never have heard of the story, and those people would never have heard of Kazuo Ishiguro. Film might be restrained by the methods of storytelling it has available, but it is a great publicity machine, opening doors for authors who deserve widespread audiences.

Source: David Kelly, Critical Essay on *The Remains of the Day*, in *Novels for Students*, Gale, Cengage Learning, 2012.

Earl G. Ingersoll

In the following excerpt, Ingersoll examines the use of the male gaze in the filming of The Remains of the Day.

. . . The framework of this discussion of Kazuo Ishiguro's novel *The Remains of the Day* and the Merchant/Ivory film adaptation will be provided by a group of film theorists based in post-Freudian, and more specifically Lacanian, psychoanalysis. These theorists—pre-eminently the feminists Laura Mulvey, Kaja Silverman, and Teresa de Lauretis—acknowledge their debt to Christian Metz, whose seminal work *The Imaginary Signifier* opens up Lacan's register of the Imaginary as a fertile field for film theorizing.

According to Mulvey, film engenders subjects as either "masculine" through the scopic drive, making them voyeurs in line with their dominant role in our culture, or as "feminine," as objects of scopophilia, making them exhibitionists who passively invite the male gaze. The technology of film aligns the look of the actor(s) in the text with the look of the viewer and most important the "look" of the camera itself. Thus, the look of the actor stands in for, or covers over, the look of the camera, as it stands in for the look of the viewer. Connoting what Mulvey calls "to-be-looked-at-ness," the female subject in this structure of looks plays a crucial role in a masquerade of femininity by representing "lack," the absence of power or privilege, experienced by both men and women. Her body, then, represents the "lack" which makes possible the illusion of mastery in the male subject, involved in a kind of masquerade of masculinity.

. . . The opening of the film *Remains of the Day* clearly indicates that we are in a cinematic rather than a novelistic world. In the novel, *Ishiguro* decided to make Stevens (Anthony Hopkins) the first-person narrator, one who exposes the world of stately houses to which he has an entree as a servant. The "present" of the novel—1956—marks an England experiencing a decline from a past—the '20s and '30s—when stately homes like Darlington Hall guaranteed the luxury of privacy to the rich and powerful. The film's "present" is also the '50s; however, the audience can be counted on in part to have swollen the ranks of tourists who have helped in recent years to keep these "mausoleums" in existence by exposing their private world to the "public." Thus, the film screens Darlington Hall for a new audience of "lookers"—tourists hungry to see what would have been veiled from the view of all but Lord Darlington's guests and servants. The camera takes the audience through the park to the house, down a roadway so narrow that it will one day need to be widened to accommodate the parade of tour busses. We are offered literal "scenic" shots, accompanied by a voice-over of Mrs. Benn (Emma Thompson) reading her letter into the film text, followed by Stevens's purported response.

From the outset, the film powerfully authorizes the technology of cinema (the camera, tape-recorder, and all the equipment supporting them) as the "one presumed to know." We are a long distance from the novel's opening sentence in which Stevens tentatively asserts the probability that he will set out on the journey westward to Cornwall, a notion which triggers all the memories comprising the bulk of the narrative: "It seems increasingly likely that I really will undertake the expedition that has been preoccupying my imagination now for some days." That tentativeness in the novel is enhanced, it might be said in passing, by its structuring as a journal in which Stevens is purportedly recording the present, day by day, thus robbing the narrative of any foregone conclusion. If, as Peter Brooks has argued in *Reading for the Plot*, the ending, or at least the end of the action, conventionally precedes the beginning of storytelling, this is a story being told by a character who does not yet know its outcome. Thus, the mode of storytelling opens a space in which his desire may yet be fulfilled. This is, of course, the very kind of space that narrative film always opens because it usually lacks an overt "teller" for whom in fiction the action has already been completed.

The decision of the film makers to allow Mrs. Benn and then Stevens to read their letters into its text as voice-overs has consequences for the delicate ambiguity of the novel. The film seems almost to approximate the first-person of the novel, but with a tremendous difference: in the novel the reader comes to doubt the accuracy of Stevens's reading of Mrs. Benn's letter, as Stevens himself does, despite his persistent rereading of her text. In the novel we get his quotations from the letter, but not the whole text, and thus it functions as a kind of "purloined letter," a signifier whose signified is unrepresented even though it has a great impact upon Stevens. Here is Stevens in the novel, just before his meeting with Mrs. Benn:

> [I]t will be my responsibility to determine whether or not Miss Kenton has any interest, now that her marriage, sadly, appears to have broken down and she is without a home, in returning to her old post at Darlington Hall. I may as well say here that having reread her letter again tonight, I am inclined to believe I may well have read more into certain of her lines than perhaps was wise. But I would still maintain there is more than a hint of nostalgic longing in certain parts of her letter, particularly when she writes such things as: "I was so fond of that view from the second-floor bedrooms overlooking the lawn with the downs visible in the distance."

In the film this indeterminacy gives way to the technological "ear" that hears for us a certainty in the voice of Mrs. Benn reading her letter aloud. Here the "cinematic apparatus," to borrow the term from de Lauretis and Heath's title, has a powerful authority to allow viewers of the film a much higher level of certainty about the truth of Mrs. Benn's situation, for example, than the general uncertainly Ishiguro crafts in his text through his choice of the limited and unreliable narrator, Stevens.

The film's first scene of Stevens serving breakfast to the new owner of Darlington Hall sets in motion the plot as energized by desire. Stevens will travel west to ascertain Mrs. Benn's interest in returning to Darlington. "My, my, Stevens. A lady-friend. And at your age," quips the novel's Farraday, or "An old girl friend?" teases the film's Lewis. Interestingly, the film moves very quickly into its characteristic mode of representation—the male gaze. The world of film as a complex system of looks announces itself as Stevens in the present looks through that marvelous circular window in the door, which closes off the servants' quarters from a corridor in the house itself, to see the image of the young Miss Kenton walking toward him from the early days of her stay at Darlington, which "dissolves" as she comes near. It provides a brilliant transition from the present to the past, motivating the rekindling of Stevens's desire for Miss Kenton, as she continues to be named, despite her long before having become Mrs. Benn. The scene is beautifully anticipated by the introductory scene, accompanied by the voice-over of Mrs. Benn's letter, in which the reception area of Darlington Hall from her days is crowded with under-butlers and footmen whose images fade as Stevens walks into the present.

For Stevens, Miss Kenton as the Mrs. Benn of the present is essentially "feminine" once again in her vulnerability. Just as she was without a "position" and vulnerable when, despite her youth and inexperience, he hired her as housekeeper, she is once again without a "position" and therefore vulnerable now that her "marriage is finally over" and she is "without a home." In a patriarchal structure such as Darlington Hall—owned and managed by men—to be without a "position" is to be positioned as vulnerable, and therefore "feminine." What Stevens reads, of course, as her vulnerability is his own "lack," for as the novel makes inescapably clear at the outset he is in danger of losing his position since he is beginning to "slip." Like his father, who came as under-butler when Kenton became housekeeper, he has been remiss in keeping the silver polished, one of the hallmarks of a superior butler, always in control of details. It is this increasing awareness of lost authority which is forcing Stevens to acknowledge what is essentially the illusion of mastery. Thus, it is imperative that he recover a Miss Kenton, or some other woman, to play her part in the masquerade of femininity so that he can cover his own "lack." Reading his desire for her return into her letter which he reads over and over, but not into the text in its entirety, Stevens says: "if Miss Kenton were indeed to return to Darlington Hall, such little slips, I am sure, would become a thing of the past." What Stevens cannot acknowledge is that the "slips" in his behavior are ultimately less important than the

slips or gaps in his "speaking" which expose his desire, allowing the reader/listener to hear it speaking him with the discourse of the Other.

Other examples of the male gaze in the film are rare because of the essentially homosocial nature of the household with its bachelor master and its butler circumscribing heterosexual desire in its servants—albeit in vain, it would seem. Desire disrupts the orderly functioning of the household, from Stevens's point of view, and, obviously enough, he was forced to expend precious energy and attention in interviewing applicants for the position vacated by Kenton's predecessor who deserted "Darlington" for another man. Thus, in his interview of Kenton and later Lizzie, Stevens tells each woman she must abide by the rules of the household: "Rule #1: no gentlemen callers." Tellingly, he never seems to get around to listing the remaining rules.

In addition, all the expressions of the male gaze have little or no basis in the novel. Perhaps the most important is in the scene preparing the spectator for Miss Kenton's first intrusion upon Stevens in his inner sanctum. We look through an upstairs window—and also through the gaze of Stevens—at Kenton cutting flowers in the garden below. Although the scene quickly gives way to the shot of her back as she walks into his room with them, this gaze clearly inscribes his desire as a male and her femininity as the object of that gaze. Indeed, even Kenton herself seems aware of a gaze while she stoops to cut the flowers. Although garbed in a dark, rather matronly dress, Kenton is not wearing the sort of housekeeper's uniform we might expect from her countless counterparts in manor-house scenes, like the ominous housekeeper of Rebecca. Especially in the scenes near her arrival at Darlington, Kenton appears rather girlish, as she is, in fact, in the novel where she begins work in 1922, rather than in the film's 1932. In fact, the film makers may have advanced the date of her arrival and the international conference at Darlington into the '30s not only to implicate its master more naively in Nazism but to keep Mrs. Benn from being too advanced in years in the final scenes where Stevens must still find her physically attractive.

In this decision, the film makers seem to be bent on "clarifying" a critical precinct of male desire in Darlington. In the novel, Ishiguro subtly explores the background of Darlington's support for what in the film is already becoming the Third Reich. Ishiguro emphasizes Darlington's desire first to minister to the widow of his friend Karl-Heinz Bremann, who survived the "Great War" but not the cruel peace of the Versailles treaty, and, when she cannot be traced, all the widows in the nation of his martyred friend. Drawing on the mythos of the First War's occasional moments of mortal enemies becoming bloodbrothers, immortalized in Erich Maria Remarque's masterful Christmas scene of German and Allied soldiers singing "Silent Night" together, Ishiguro posits a "higher love" between Darlington and his German friend which Ivory and Merchant introduce but leave underdeveloped in their desire to rush Darlington into becoming a fascist dupe.

That role for Darlington—and the other conferees, it might be added—foregrounds itself in another scene which the film interpolates. True to its form, the film depends on the male gaze, and Merchant/Ivory dramatize the banquet scene from the 1923 conference of the novel as though it were taking place in 1932. Because of its obviously pictorial nature, the film reminds the spectator—as the novel may not reveal to its reader—how exclusively male the world of Darlington Hall is. Lord Darlington is unaccountably unmarried, a surprising situation for an aristocrat who might be expected to produce a male heir to inherit the estate. Darlington's asexuality is not so noticeable in the novel because the discourse is in the control of Stevens who is equally self-repressed sexually. (At the same time, it might be noted that both novel and film include the humorous episode of Stevens struggling to tell young Cardinal the "facts of life," following his master's request.) The film attempts to minister to the lack of women by foregrounding the German representative to the novel's 1923 conference, a countess, who happens to be traveling together from Germany with "the formidable Eleanor Austin." This countess addresses the conference in the novel; however, Stevens says "I was at this point, for some reason I do not recollect, obliged to leave the drawing room for an extended period." The film repairs this gap by allowing her to speak and to sing, like a Lorelei, luring the other representatives, with the exception of the American Lewis, into her trap in what seems an allegory of international politics. Focusing the gaze of Darlington on the German countess seems the film's way of implicating His Lordship in the masquerade of masculinity, perhaps as a means of avoiding the novel's clear indication of the priority of the bond between Darlington and Bremann. . . .

> OBSERVE, FOR EXAMPLE, HOW HE HANDLES THE POSTWAR SCENES IN WHICH HIS LOYALTY TO LORD D. BEGINS TO EMBARRASS EVEN HIM: YOU GET A SENSE OF PAINED PERPLEXITY SUCH AS FEW COULD MAKE SO ELOQUENT."

Source: Earl G. Ingersoll, "Desire, the Gaze, and Suture in the Novel and the Film: *The Remains of the Day*," in *Studies in the Humanities*, June/December 2001, pp. 31–47.

John Simon

In the following review, Simon considers the three main levels of the film and the success of each.

I have not read Kazuo Ishiguro's *The Remains of the Day*, but seeing the Merchant–Ivory movie version makes me want to do so, which is a good sign. Had I begun by seeing the inept *Howards End*, nothing about it would have induced me to read Forster's masterpiece. *The Remains of the Day*, on screen, has a restraint, an elegant spareness, an invitation to thought: it is rather like a Japanese rock garden, and also a poignant portrait of the English class system up to World War II. The samurai credo joins the gentleman's gentleman mentality, the twain meeting in a coupling that puts Kipling to rest.

Stevens, the butler hero, is a superlative practitioner of the craft of service, near-indentured to his master, Lord Darlington, an aristocratic twit secretly working on appeasement with Hitler as he convokes international meetings at his stately manor, Darlington Hall. Stevens stands by his master through the thick of political intrigue and the thin of postwar disgrace. Finally, Darlington Hall is bought by a millionaire American (the movie, I gather, conflates two characters here, somewhat awkwardly), and the new master, Mr. Lewis, lends Stevens a Daimler (a Ford in the novel, but the Merchant–Ivory appetite for luxury must be indulged) for a trip from Oxfordshire to the West Country. Most of the story is told in flashbacks as Stevens journeys and remembers.

He is off to meet Miss Kenton, the meticulously dedicated ex-housekeeper of Darlington Hall, who slowly fell in love with him but could not deflect him from his emotionally repressed, intellectually blinkered robotism into becoming a man. She eventually left to get married west of the mooning she did over Stevens, but the marriage ultimately failed, and she is, twenty years later, seeking employment. Stevens sets out to get her back—as housekeeper and keeper of his heart. But alas for the best-laid plans of butlers and men!

The film operates on three levels. The overplot concerns Lord Darlington's political machinations; the plot, the relationship (or nonrelationship) of Stevens and Miss Kenton; the underplot, the below-stairs activities and permutations. There is, perhaps, even a fourth, quasi-documentary, level about how a great manor is run, from butler and housekeeper down to the last footman and scullery maid. Every aspect of service, from dusting to decanting, is scanned by the camera; from setting a table to setting an example to those lower in the hierarchy—the hierarchy of service, that is, which ceremoniously reflects that of the Empire. Both, we can sense, are headed for extinction.

There is an interesting coincidence in that just as Kazuo Ishiguro was born Japanese and bred English, Ruth Prawer Jhabvala, the screenwriter, was born in Germany but is domiciled in India. So East and West meet in both novelist and scenarist. And the class system was equally marked in England and India, Japan and Germany (if, like Mrs. J., you were of Eastern European Jewish origin). *The Remains of the Day* views this strict social order with mingled admiration and distaste. Thus Stevens, who permits himself no political opinions of his own, is questioned by a sadistic guest at Darlington Hall about political matters, and emits no more than a ceremonially formulaic, perfectly noncommittal answer. The inquisitor then turns this into proof that the lower orders are incapable of thought.

It is to Mrs. Jhabvala's credit that she has managed to objectify and animate what in the novel is mostly internalized, point-of-view reflection. And, for once, that basically amateurish director, James Ivory, rouses himself to greater professionalism. His chief flaw has been the inability to hit on the right tempos: compartmentalizing scenes into languid talkiness or hectic action, and not finding musical ways for the orchestration and interpenetration of the two. Here, because the nature of the material calls for small, spasmodic outbursts within an overwhelming stasis, Ivory's idiosyncrasy can feel right at home.

Thus in the earlier sequences of the film, the tone is set by Miss Kenton's shocked observing of the fate of Stevens's father: himself a fine former butler, he is now hired by his son as underbutler, but old-age failings reduce him to something even lower on the scale, until he sickens and dies—all this without a single moment of filial emotion from the son. In later sequences, as Miss Kenton falls deeper and deeper in love, Stevens's nonresponse elicits similarly intensifying shock on the woman's part. Her weapon becomes raillery; his, impassivity.

The best scenes are those where Stevens almost breaks through his self-imposed carapace; either humorously, as when he is commanded to disburse sexual enlightenment to Lord Darlington's ward, or desperately, when Miss Kenton comes upon him in his private quarters reading a Victorian novel of feelings, and his shame is equal to having been caught masturbating. Such scenes, of course, are bound to stand out from the surrounding flatness, which, in turn, derives pathetic significance from them.

The real pathos is kept carefully in abeyance till the end, when it gathers intensity until, at the very last, it makes the film almost unendurably moving. Here both Anthony Hopkins and Emma Thompson crown their excellent work with a bravura duet that skewers the heart. Throughout, Miss Thompson manages to be both wry and tremulous, her Miss Kenton a double-bottomed creature, aglow under her surface propriety or acerbity. That great, equinely English face of hers, pitched somewhere between Virginia Woolf and Joyce Grenfell, represses as much as it expresses.

But at this game, owing to his bigger part, she is surpassed by the amazing Mr. Hopkins. He does not even get the privilege of a rich, contradictory inner life until the very end, yet he must somehow make credible that this self-castrated character can arouse a woman to love. Perhaps only Ralph Richardson could have pulled this off, but Mr. Hopkins, lacking Sir Ralph's wonderful eccentricity, nevertheless comes close. Observe, for example, how he handles the postwar scenes in which his loyalty to Lord D. begins to embarrass even him: you get a sense of pained perplexity such as few could make so eloquent.

Everyone in the cast is very good, notably James Fox as the vapid and vainglorious Darlington, with one exception: the Lewis of Christopher

Reeve, who should never be allowed to play a character not based on a comic strip. Even though Lewis is far from a demanding role, Mr. Reeve, whose head looks to me always screwed on upside down, turns him into a boob the equal of Darlington. We are told that he made his fortune in dry-goods; all the more reason not to seem perennially wet behind the ears.

There is highly accomplished cinematography from Tony Pierce-Roberts; the fox hunters foregathering on the front lawn of Darlington Hall couldn't look better in the finest British sporting prints; the cutlery and crystal on the Darlington dinner table glisten brightly enough for gods, never mind quislings. Equally fine are the costumes by Jenny Beavan and John Bright; Richard Robbins's music is entirely adequate. But the accomplishment above all others is the production design of Luciana Arrighi, who, with the help of the architectural historian Joe Friedman, assembled four separate English country houses seamlessly into Darlington Hall, making it stupendously palatial above-stairs, and wondrously warren-like below.

Despite minor directorial flaws (I can't imagine Stevens, or the camera representing his point of view, spying through a peephole), *The Remains of the Day* will long remain in your memory as a portrait of heroic futility, heartbreaking fatuity, and purblind doggedness, as they become the downfall of a society, an empire, and, worst of all, a single human soul....

Source: John Simon, "'Remains' To Be Seen," in *National Review*, Vol. 45, No. 24, December 13, 1993, p. 61.

Jack Kroll

In the following review, Kroll examines the character Stevens's role in the film.

When P.G. Wodehouse was creating jeeves, his immortal English manservant, he hired a butler and took notes on his behavior. "Useful chap to have around," remarked a friend, "but a bit on the somber side." He should have met Stevens, the butler in *The Remains of the Day*. Somber would be a fun mood for the magisterially morose Stevens (Anthony Hopkins), who has buttled for Lord Darlington (James Fox) for 35 years. The vapid Lord D., a Nazi sympathizer before World War II, receives German bigwigs at his stately home, Darlington Hall. During these sessions, butlerian protocol calls for Stevens to keep his eye on the truffles and off the treachery. When the housekeeper, Miss

Kenton (Emma Thompson), is upset at the sacking of two Jewish maids, Stevens explains that Lord D. and his ilk understand "many things that you and I don't." When his father (who's serving as a subbutler under him) dies of a stroke during a big dinner party, Stevens goes on dispensing the port and cigars. And he chickens out in his one chance at emotional fulfillment, with the vibrant Miss Kenton.

Stevens is meant as a tragicomic figure, which is easier to accept in the prize-winning original novel by the Japanese-English writer Kazuo Ishiguro. There the story is told by Stevens himself, with Ishiguro controlling all the ironic nuances of a narrative that moves from complacent self-deception to chagrined realization of a wasted life. The novel is a writer's tour de force, but the film, scripted by Ruth Prawer Jhabvala, sets the characters in the light of reality, and it may arouse more impatience than empathy. "Come off it, Stevens, you stiff upper drip," we may think as the butler performs his ballet of elegant obsequiousness, a very Baryshnikov of bowing and scraping.

The film reunites the team that made the deservingly honored *Howards End*, producer Ismail Merchant, director James Ivory, writer Jhabvala and the two stars. Hopkins and Thompson are superb actors, but they (and Ivory) can't shake the sense that Stevens and Miss Kenton are less fully fleshed characters than embodiments of a thesis about the English class system. The genius of jeeves was that he was a subversive parody of that system; the butler was smarter than the asses he worked for. The most painful scene in the film occurs when a guest of Lord D.'s, to prove that democracy doesn't work, quizzes Stevens about arcane political issues. "I'm unable to be of assistance," says the butler. Jeeves would have replied with dazzling doubletalk, throwing the snobs into confusion. *The Remains of the Day* is stately but depressing. Satire is the best revenge.

Source: Jack Kroll, "I Say, Stevens, Bit of a Wasted Life, What?," in *Newsweek*, Vol. 122, No. 19, November 8, 1993, p. 78.

SOURCES

Bloch, Charles, "Great Britain, German Rearmament, and the Naval Agreement of 1935," in *European Diplomacy Between Two Wars, 1919–1939*, edited by Hams W. Gatzke, Quadrangle Books, 1972, pp. 126–49.

Canby, Vincent, "*Remains of the Day*: Blind Dignity; A Butler's Story," in *New York Times*, November 5, 1993, http://movies.nytimes.com/movie/review?res=9F0CE1D 9153CF936A35752C1A965958260&partner=Rotten% 20Tomatoes (accessed August 3, 2011).

Ishiguro, Kazuo, *The Remains of the Day*, Vintage International, 1993, pp. 58, 166–67.

Kroll, Jack, "I Say, Stevens, Bit of a Wasted Life, What?," in *Newsweek*, November 8, 1993, p. 78.

Lederer, Ivo J., *The Versailles Settlement: Was it Foredoomed to Failure?*, D. C. Heath, 1960, pp. vii–x.

McCarthy, Todd, Review of *The Remains of the Day*, in *Variety*, September 23, 1993, http://www.variety.com/review/VE1117901314?refcatid=31 (accessed August 3, 2011).

"*The Remains of the Day*," in *Box Office Mojo*, http://boxofficemojo.com/movies/?id=remainsoftheday.htm (accessed August 3, 2011).

The Remains of the Day, DVD, Columbia Pictures, 2001.

"Treaty of Versailles, 1919," in *Holocaust Encyclopedia*, United States Holocaust Memorial Museum, January 6, 2011, http://www.ushmm.org/wlc/en/article.php?Modu leId=10005425 (accessed August 7, 2011).

Wilmington, Mike, "The Great Repression: Hopkins is the Perfect Butler in *The Remains of the Day*," in *Chicago Tribune*, November 5, 1993, p. A.

FURTHER READING

Gale, Steven H., *Sharp Cut: Harold Pinter's Screenplays and the Artistic Process*, University of Kentucky Press, 2003.

Pinter, acknowledged as one of the greatest playwrights of his generation, bought the screen rights for *The Remains of the Day* before the novel was even published and wrote the first draft of the screenplay, but he had his name removed from the final film. In this study, Gale gives the background of Pinter's involvement in the film, as well as some samples of his version of the story.

Long, Robert Emmett, *The Films of Merchant Ivory*, updated ed., Harry N. Abrams, 1997.

Long gives production background of the partners' films, including *The Remains of the Day*, telling the story of how James Merchant came to be involved with the creation of the film and how he and Ismail Ivory joined forces with Mike Nichols, the producer originally on the project, in order to create the film that exists today.

Long, Robert Emmett, *James Ivory in Conversation: How Merchant Ivory Makes Its Movies*, University of California Press, 2005.

While being interviewed by an author who is well versed with his works, Ivory reveals much about the process of bringing the novel to screen and about his long working relationship with the screenwriter and the principal actors.

Matthews, Sean, "'I'm Sorry I Can't Say More': An Interview with Kazuo Ishiguro," in *Kazuo Ishiguro: Contemporary Critical Perspectives*, edited by Sean Matthews and Sebastian Groes, Continuum International Publishing, 2009, pp. 114–25.

In this interview, Ishiguro gives some insight into his way of working, though he is not a very talkative subject. He does discuss his opinion of Anthony Hopkins as Stevens and of the film in general.

Petry, Mike, "A Butler's Life-Long Illusion: *The Remains of the Day*," in *Narratives of Memory and Identity: The Novels of Kazuo Ishiguro*, Peter Lang, 1999, pp. 89–126.

This extensive analysis of the novel's narrative voice shows the contrast with the film version, which lacks that voice.

Sim, Wai-chew, "Film Adaptation," in *Kazuo Ishiguro*, Routledge, 2010, pp. 157–64.

This analysis of the adaptation of this novel includes Ishiguro's personal responses to the film and insights from other reviewers about the change of style required for the film and the historical background as seen in both versions.

Trimm, Ryan S., "Inside Job: Professionalism and Postimperial Communities in *The Remains of the Day*," in *Literature Interpretation Theory*, Vol. 16, 2005, pp. 135–61.

This academic study examines the ways in which both the novel and the film view the service profession in which Stevens works and how his devotion to his job reflects the dissolution of the British colonial system.

SUGGESTED SEARCH TERMS

Kazuo Ishiguro

Ishiguro AND Harold Pinter

Kazuo Ishiguro AND Remains of the Day

Remains of the Day AND film

Merchant Ivory AND Remains of the Day

Merchant Ivory AND historical drama

Hopkins AND Merchant Ivory

Anthony Hopkins AND Emma Thompson

domestic servants AND postwar England

appeasement of Hitler

Ribbentrop AND non-aggression

Glossary of Literary Terms

A

Abstract: As an adjective applied to writing or literary works, abstract refers to words or phrases that name things not knowable through the five senses.

Aestheticism: A literary and artistic movement of the nineteenth century. Followers of the movement believed that art should not be mixed with social, political, or moral teaching. The statement "art for art's sake" is a good summary of aestheticism. The movement had its roots in France, but it gained widespread importance in England in the last half of the nineteenth century, where it helped change the Victorian practice of including moral lessons in literature.

Allegory: A narrative technique in which characters representing things or abstract ideas are used to convey a message or teach a lesson. Allegory is typically used to teach moral, ethical, or religious lessons but is sometimes used for satiric or political purposes.

Allusion: A reference to a familiar literary or historical person or event, used to make an idea more easily understood.

Analogy: A comparison of two things made to explain something unfamiliar through its similarities to something familiar, or to prove one point based on the acceptedness of another. Similes and metaphors are types of analogies.

Antagonist: The major character in a narrative or drama who works against the hero or protagonist.

Anthropomorphism: The presentation of animals or objects in human shape or with human characteristics. The term is derived from the Greek word for "human form."

Anti-hero: A central character in a work of literature who lacks traditional heroic qualities such as courage, physical prowess, and fortitude. Anti-heroes typically distrust conventional values and are unable to commit themselves to any ideals. They generally feel helpless in a world over which they have no control. Anti-heroes usually accept, and often celebrate, their positions as social outcasts.

Apprenticeship Novel: See *Bildungsroman*

Archetype: The word archetype is commonly used to describe an original pattern or model from which all other things of the same kind are made. This term was introduced to literary criticism from the psychology of Carl Jung. It expresses Jung's theory that behind every person's "unconscious," or repressed memories of the past, lies the "collective unconscious" of the human race: memories of the countless typical experiences of our ancestors. These memories are said to prompt illogical associations that trigger powerful emotions in the reader. Often, the emotional process is primitive, even primordial. Archetypes are the literary images that grow out of the "collective unconscious." They appear in literature as incidents and plots that repeat basic patterns of life. They may also appear as stereotyped characters.

Avant-garde: French term meaning "vanguard." It is used in literary criticism to describe new writing that rejects traditional approaches to literature in favor of innovations in style or content.

B

Beat Movement: A period featuring a group of American poets and novelists of the 1950s and 1960s—including Jack Kerouac, Allen Ginsberg, Gregory Corso, William S. Burroughs, and Lawrence Ferlinghetti—who rejected established social and literary values. Using such techniques as stream of consciousness writing and jazz-influenced free verse and focusing on unusual or abnormal states of mind—generated by religious ecstasy or the use of drugs—the Beat writers aimed to create works that were unconventional in both form and subject matter.

Bildungsroman: A German word meaning "novel of development." The *bildungsroman* is a study of the maturation of a youthful character, typically brought about through a series of social or sexual encounters that lead to self-awareness. *Bildungsroman* is used interchangeably with *erziehungsroman,* a novel of initiation and education. When a *bildungsroman* is concerned with the development of an artist (as in James Joyce's *A Portrait of the Artist as a Young Man*), it is often termed a *kunstlerroman.*

Black Aesthetic Movement: A period of artistic and literary development among African Americans in the 1960s and early 1970s. This was the first major African-American artistic movement since the Harlem Renaissance and was closely paralleled by the civil rights and black power movements. The black aesthetic writers attempted to produce works of art that would be meaningful to the black masses. Key figures in black aesthetics included one of its founders, poet and playwright Amiri Baraka, formerly known as LeRoi Jones; poet and essayist Haki R. Madhubuti, formerly Don L. Lee; poet and playwright Sonia Sanchez; and dramatist Ed Bullins.

Black Humor: Writing that places grotesque elements side by side with humorous ones in an attempt to shock the reader, forcing him or her to laugh at the horrifying reality of a disordered world.

Burlesque: Any literary work that uses exaggeration to make its subject appear ridiculous, either by treating a trivial subject with profound seriousness or by treating a dignified subject frivolously. The word "burlesque" may also be used as an adjective, as in "burlesque show," to mean "striptease act."

C

Character: Broadly speaking, a person in a literary work. The actions of characters are what constitute the plot of a story, novel, or poem. There are numerous types of characters, ranging from simple, stereotypical figures to intricate, multifaceted ones. In the techniques of anthropomorphism and personification, animals—and even places or things—can assume aspects of character. "Characterization" is the process by which an author creates vivid, believable characters in a work of art. This may be done in a variety of ways, including (1) direct description of the character by the narrator; (2) the direct presentation of the speech, thoughts, or actions of the character; and (3) the responses of other characters to the character. The term "character" also refers to a form originated by the ancient Greek writer Theophrastus that later became popular in the seventeenth and eighteenth centuries. It is a short essay or sketch of a person who prominently displays a specific attribute or quality, such as miserliness or ambition.

Climax: The turning point in a narrative, the moment when the conflict is at its most intense. Typically, the structure of stories, novels, and plays is one of rising action, in which tension builds to the climax, followed by falling action, in which tension lessens as the story moves to its conclusion.

Colloquialism: A word, phrase, or form of pronunciation that is acceptable in casual conversation but not in formal, written communication. It is considered more acceptable than slang.

Coming of Age Novel: See *Bildungsroman*

Concrete: Concrete is the opposite of abstract, and refers to a thing that actually exists or a description that allows the reader to experience an object or concept with the senses.

Connotation: The impression that a word gives beyond its defined meaning. Connotations may be universally understood or may be significant only to a certain group.

Convention: Any widely accepted literary device, style, or form.

D

Denotation: The definition of a word, apart from the impressions or feelings it creates (connotations) in the reader.

Denouement: A French word meaning "the unknotting." In literary criticism, it denotes the resolution of conflict in fiction or drama. The *denouement* follows the climax and provides an outcome to the primary plot situation as well as an explanation of secondary plot complications. The *denouement* often involves a character's recognition of his or her state of mind or moral condition.

Description: Descriptive writing is intended to allow a reader to picture the scene or setting in which the action of a story takes place. The form this description takes often evokes an intended emotional response—a dark, spooky graveyard will evoke fear, and a peaceful, sunny meadow will evoke calmness.

Dialogue: In its widest sense, dialogue is simply conversation between people in a literary work; in its most restricted sense, it refers specifically to the speech of characters in a drama. As a specific literary genre, a "dialogue" is a composition in which characters debate an issue or idea.

Diction: The selection and arrangement of words in a literary work. Either or both may vary depending on the desired effect. There are four general types of diction: "formal," used in scholarly or lofty writing; "informal," used in relaxed but educated conversation; "colloquial," used in everyday speech; and "slang," containing newly coined words and other terms not accepted in formal usage.

Didactic: A term used to describe works of literature that aim to teach some moral, religious, political, or practical lesson. Although didactic elements are often found in artistically pleasing works, the term "didactic" usually refers to literature in which the message is more important than the form. The term may also be used to criticize a work that the critic finds "overly didactic," that is, heavy-handed in its delivery of a lesson.

Doppelganger: A literary technique by which a character is duplicated (usually in the form of an alter ego, though sometimes as a ghostly counterpart) or divided into two distinct, usually opposite personalities. The use of this character device is widespread in nineteenth- and twentieth-century literature, and indicates a growing awareness among authors that the "self" is really a composite of many "selves."

Double Entendre: A corruption of a French phrase meaning "double meaning." The term is used to indicate a word or phrase that is deliberately ambiguous, especially when one of the meanings is risqué or improper.

Dramatic Irony: Occurs when the audience of a play or the reader of a work of literature knows something that a character in the work itself does not know. The irony is in the contrast between the intended meaning of the statements or actions of a character and the additional information understood by the audience.

Dystopia: An imaginary place in a work of fiction where the characters lead dehumanized, fearful lives.

E

Edwardian: Describes cultural conventions identified with the period of the reign of Edward VII of England (1901-1910). Writers of the Edwardian Age typically displayed a strong reaction against the propriety and conservatism of the Victorian Age. Their work often exhibits distrust of authority in religion, politics, and art and expresses strong doubts about the soundness of conventional values.

Empathy: A sense of shared experience, including emotional and physical feelings, with someone or something other than oneself. Empathy is often used to describe the response of a reader to a literary character.

Enlightenment, The: An eighteenth-century philosophical movement. It began in France but had a wide impact throughout Europe and America. Thinkers of the Enlightenment valued reason and believed that both the individual and society could achieve a state of perfection. Corresponding to this essentially humanist vision was a resistance to religious authority.

Epigram: A saying that makes the speaker's point quickly and concisely. Often used to preface a novel.

Epilogue: A concluding statement or section of a literary work. In dramas, particularly those of the seventeenth and eighteenth centuries, the epilogue is a closing speech, often in verse, delivered by an actor at the end of a play and spoken directly to the audience.

Epiphany: A sudden revelation of truth inspired by a seemingly trivial incident.

Episode: An incident that forms part of a story and is significantly related to it. Episodes may be either self-contained narratives or events that depend on a larger context for their sense and importance.

Epistolary Novel: A novel in the form of letters. The form was particularly popular in the eighteenth century.

Epithet: A word or phrase, often disparaging or abusive, that expresses a character trait of someone or something.

Existentialism: A predominantly twentieth-century philosophy concerned with the nature and perception of human existence. There are two major strains of existentialist thought: atheistic and Christian. Followers of atheistic existentialism believe that the individual is alone in a godless universe and that the basic human condition is one of suffering and loneliness. Nevertheless, because there are no fixed values, individuals can create their own characters—indeed, they can shape themselves—through the exercise of free will. The atheistic strain culminates in and is popularly associated with the works of Jean-Paul Sartre. The Christian existentialists, on the other hand, believe that only in God may people find freedom from life's anguish. The two strains hold certain beliefs in common: that existence cannot be fully understood or described through empirical effort; that anguish is a universal element of life; that individuals must bear responsibility for their actions; and that there is no common standard of behavior or perception for religious and ethical matters.

Expatriates: See *Expatriatism*

Expatriatism: The practice of leaving one's country to live for an extended period in another country.

Exposition: Writing intended to explain the nature of an idea, thing, or theme. Expository writing is often combined with description, narration, or argument. In dramatic writing, the exposition is the introductory material which presents the characters, setting, and tone of the play.

Expressionism: An indistinct literary term, originally used to describe an early twentieth-century school of German painting. The term applies to almost any mode of unconventional, highly subjective writing that distorts reality in some way.

F

Fable: A prose or verse narrative intended to convey a moral. Animals or inanimate objects with human characteristics often serve as characters in fables.

Falling Action: See *Denouement*

Fantasy: A literary form related to mythology and folklore. Fantasy literature is typically set in non-existent realms and features supernatural beings.

Farce: A type of comedy characterized by broad humor, outlandish incidents, and often vulgar subject matter.

Femme fatale: A French phrase with the literal translation "fatal woman." A *femme fatale* is a sensuous, alluring woman who often leads men into danger or trouble.

Fiction: Any story that is the product of imagination rather than a documentation of fact. characters and events in such narratives may be based in real life but their ultimate form and configuration is a creation of the author.

Figurative Language: A technique in writing in which the author temporarily interrupts the order, construction, or meaning of the writing for a particular effect. This interruption takes the form of one or more figures of speech such as hyperbole, irony, or simile. Figurative language is the opposite of literal language, in which every word is truthful, accurate, and free of exaggeration or embellishment.

Figures of Speech: Writing that differs from customary conventions for construction, meaning, order, or significance for the purpose of a special meaning or effect. There are two major types of figures of speech: rhetorical figures, which do not make changes in the meaning of the words, and tropes, which do.

Fin de siecle: A French term meaning "end of the century." The term is used to denote the last decade of the nineteenth century, a transition period when writers and other artists abandoned old conventions and looked for new techniques and objectives.

First Person: See *Point of View*

Flashback: A device used in literature to present action that occurred before the beginning of the story. Flashbacks are often introduced as the dreams or recollections of one or more characters.

Foil: A character in a work of literature whose physical or psychological qualities contrast strongly with, and therefore highlight, the corresponding qualities of another character.

Folklore: Traditions and myths preserved in a culture or group of people. Typically, these are passed on by word of mouth in various forms—such as legends, songs, and proverbs—or preserved in customs and ceremonies. This term was first used by W. J. Thoms in 1846.

Folktale: A story originating in oral tradition. Folktales fall into a variety of categories, including legends, ghost stories, fairy tales, fables, and anecdotes based on historical figures and events.

Foreshadowing: A device used in literature to create expectation or to set up an explanation of later developments.

Form: The pattern or construction of a work which identifies its genre and distinguishes it from other genres.

G

Genre: A category of literary work. In critical theory, genre may refer to both the content of a given work—tragedy, comedy, pastoral— and to its form, such as poetry, novel, or drama.

Gilded Age: A period in American history during the 1870s characterized by political corruption and materialism. A number of important novels of social and political criticism were written during this time.

Gothicism: In literary criticism, works characterized by a taste for the medieval or morbidly attractive. A gothic novel prominently fea-

tures elements of horror, the supernatural, gloom, and violence: clanking chains, terror, charnel houses, ghosts, medieval castles, and mysteriously slamming doors. The term "gothic novel" is also applied to novels that lack elements of the traditional Gothic setting but that create a similar atmosphere of terror or dread.

Grotesque: In literary criticism, the subject matter of a work or a style of expression characterized by exaggeration, deformity, freakishness, and disorder. The grotesque often includes an element of comic absurdity.

H

Harlem Renaissance: The Harlem Renaissance of the 1920s is generally considered the first significant movement of black writers and artists in the United States. During this period, new and established black writers published more fiction and poetry than ever before, the first influential black literary journals were established, and black authors and artists received their first widespread recognition and serious critical appraisal. Among the major writers associated with this period are Claude McKay, Jean Toomer, Countee Cullen, Langston Hughes, Arna Bontemps, Nella Larsen, and Zora Neale Hurston.

Hero/Heroine: The principal sympathetic character (male or female) in a literary work. Heroes and heroines typically exhibit admirable traits: idealism, courage, and integrity, for example.

Holocaust Literature: Literature influenced by or written about the Holocaust of World War II. Such literature includes true stories of survival in concentration camps, escape, and life after the war, as well as fictional works and poetry.

Humanism: A philosophy that places faith in the dignity of humankind and rejects the medieval perception of the individual as a weak, fallen creature. "Humanists" typically believe in the perfectibility of human nature and view reason and education as the means to that end.

Hyperbole: In literary criticism, deliberate exaggeration used to achieve an effect.

I

Idiom: A word construction or verbal expression closely associated with a given language.

Image: A concrete representation of an object or sensory experience. Typically, such a representation helps evoke the feelings associated with the object or experience itself. Images are either "literal" or "figurative." Literal images are especially concrete and involve little or no extension of the obvious meaning of the words used to express them. Figurative images do not follow the literal meaning of the words exactly. Images in literature are usually visual, but the term "image" can also refer to the representation of any sensory experience.

Imagery: The array of images in a literary work. Also, figurative language.

In medias res: A Latin term meaning "in the middle of things." It refers to the technique of beginning a story at its midpoint and then using various flashback devices to reveal previous action.

Interior Monologue: A narrative technique in which characters' thoughts are revealed in a way that appears to be uncontrolled by the author. The interior monologue typically aims to reveal the inner self of a character. It portrays emotional experiences as they occur at both a conscious and unconscious level. images are often used to represent sensations or emotions.

Irony: In literary criticism, the effect of language in which the intended meaning is the opposite of what is stated.

J

Jargon: Language that is used or understood only by a select group of people. Jargon may refer to terminology used in a certain profession, such as computer jargon, or it may refer to any nonsensical language that is not understood by most people.

L

Leitmotiv: See *Motif*

Literal Language: An author uses literal language when he or she writes without exaggerating or embellishing the subject matter and without any tools of figurative language.

Lost Generation: A term first used by Gertrude Stein to describe the post-World War I generation of American writers: men and women haunted by a sense of betrayal and emptiness brought about by the destructiveness of the war.

M

Mannerism: Exaggerated, artificial adherence to a literary manner or style. Also, a popular style of the visual arts of late sixteenth-century Europe that was marked by elongation of the human form and by intentional spatial distortion. Literary works that are self-consciously high-toned and artistic are often said to be "mannered."

Metaphor: A figure of speech that expresses an idea through the image of another object. Metaphors suggest the essence of the first object by identifying it with certain qualities of the second object.

Modernism: Modern literary practices. Also, the principles of a literary school that lasted from roughly the beginning of the twentieth century until the end of World War II. Modernism is defined by its rejection of the literary conventions of the nineteenth century and by its opposition to conventional morality, taste, traditions, and economic values.

Mood: The prevailing emotions of a work or of the author in his or her creation of the work. The mood of a work is not always what might be expected based on its subject matter.

Motif: A theme, character type, image, metaphor, or other verbal element that recurs throughout a single work of literature or occurs in a number of different works over a period of time.

Myth: An anonymous tale emerging from the traditional beliefs of a culture or social unit. Myths use supernatural explanations for natural phenomena. They may also explain cosmic issues like creation and death. Collections of myths, known as mythologies, are common to all cultures and nations, but the best-known myths belong to the Norse, Roman, and Greek mythologies.

N

Narration: The telling of a series of events, real or invented. A narration may be either a simple narrative, in which the events are recounted chronologically, or a narrative with a plot, in which the account is given in a style reflecting the author's artistic concept of the story. Narration is sometimes used as a synonym for "storyline."

Narrative: A verse or prose accounting of an event or sequence of events, real or invented. The term is also used as an adjective in the sense "method of narration." For example, in literary criticism, the expression "narrative technique" usually refers to the way the author structures and presents his or her story.

Narrator: The teller of a story. The narrator may be the author or a character in the story through whom the author speaks.

Naturalism: A literary movement of the late nineteenth and early twentieth centuries. The movement's major theorist, French novelist Emile Zola, envisioned a type of fiction that would examine human life with the objectivity of scientific inquiry. The Naturalists typically viewed human beings as either the products of "biological determinism," ruled by hereditary instincts and engaged in an endless struggle for survival, or as the products of "socioeconomic determinism," ruled by social and economic forces beyond their control. In their works, the Naturalists generally ignored the highest levels of society and focused on degradation: poverty, alcoholism, prostitution, insanity, and disease.

Noble Savage: The idea that primitive man is noble and good but becomes evil and corrupted as he becomes civilized. The concept of the noble savage originated in the Renaissance period but is more closely identified with such later writers as Jean-Jacques Rousseau and Aphra Behn.

Novel: A long fictional narrative written in prose, which developed from the novella and other early forms of narrative. A novel is usually organized under a plot or theme with a focus on character development and action.

Novel of Ideas: A novel in which the examination of intellectual issues and concepts takes precedence over characterization or a traditional storyline.

Novel of Manners: A novel that examines the customs and mores of a cultural group.

Novella: An Italian term meaning "story." This term has been especially used to describe fourteenth-century Italian tales, but it also refers to modern short novels.

O

Objective Correlative: An outward set of objects, a situation, or a chain of events corresponding to an inward experience and evoking this experience in the reader. The term frequently appears in modern criticism in discussions of authors' intended effects on the emotional responses of readers.

Objectivity: A quality in writing characterized by the absence of the author's opinion or feeling about the subject matter. Objectivity is an important factor in criticism.

Oedipus Complex: A son's amorous obsession with his mother. The phrase is derived from the story of the ancient Theban hero Oedipus, who unknowingly killed his father and married his mother.

Omniscience: See *Point of View*

Onomatopoeia: The use of words whose sounds express or suggest their meaning. In its simplest sense, onomatopoeia may be represented by words that mimic the sounds they denote such as "hiss" or "meow." At a more subtle level, the pattern and rhythm of sounds and rhymes of a line or poem may be onomatopoeic.

Oxymoron: A phrase combining two contradictory terms. Oxymorons may be intentional or unintentional.

P

Parable: A story intended to teach a moral lesson or answer an ethical question.

Paradox: A statement that appears illogical or contradictory at first, but may actually point to an underlying truth.

Parallelism: A method of comparison of two ideas in which each is developed in the same grammatical structure.

Parody: In literary criticism, this term refers to an imitation of a serious literary work or the signature style of a particular author in a ridiculous manner. A typical parody adopts the style of the original and applies it to an inappropriate subject for humorous effect. Parody is a form of satire and could be considered the literary equivalent of a caricature or cartoon.

Pastoral: A term derived from the Latin word "pastor," meaning shepherd. A pastoral is a literary composition on a rural theme. The conventions of the pastoral were originated by the third-century Greek poet Theocritus, who wrote about the experiences, love affairs, and pastimes of Sicilian shepherds. In a pastoral, characters and language of a courtly nature are often placed in a simple setting. The term pastoral is also used to classify dramas, elegies, and lyrics that exhibit the use of country settings and shepherd characters.

Pen Name: See *Pseudonym*

Persona: A Latin term meaning "mask." *Personae* are the characters in a fictional work of literature. The *persona* generally functions as a mask through which the author tells a story in a voice other than his or her own. A *persona* is usually either a character in a story who acts as a narrator or an "implied author," a voice created by the author to act as the narrator for himself or herself.

Personification: A figure of speech that gives human qualities to abstract ideas, animals, and inanimate objects.

Picaresque Novel: Episodic fiction depicting the adventures of a roguish central character ("picaro" is Spanish for "rogue"). The picaresque hero is commonly a low-born but clever individual who wanders into and out of various affairs of love, danger, and farcical intrigue. These involvements may take place at all social levels and typically present a humorous and wide-ranging satire of a given society.

Plagiarism: Claiming another person's written material as one's own. Plagiarism can take the form of direct, word-for-word copying or the theft of the substance or idea of the work.

Plot: In literary criticism, this term refers to the pattern of events in a narrative or drama. In its simplest sense, the plot guides the author in composing the work and helps the reader follow the work. Typically, plots exhibit causality and unity and have a beginning, a middle, and an end. Sometimes, however, a plot may consist of a series of disconnected events, in which case it is known as an "episodic plot."

Poetic Justice: An outcome in a literary work, not necessarily a poem, in which the good are rewarded and the evil are punished, especially in ways that particularly fit their virtues or crimes.

Poetic License: Distortions of fact and literary convention made by a writer—not always a poet—for the sake of the effect gained. Poetic license is closely related to the concept of "artistic freedom."

Poetics: This term has two closely related meanings. It denotes (1) an aesthetic theory in literary criticism about the essence of poetry or (2) rules prescribing the proper methods, content, style, or diction of poetry. The term poetics may also refer to theories about literature in general, not just poetry.

Point of View: The narrative perspective from which a literary work is presented to the reader. There are four traditional points of view. The "third person omniscient" gives the reader a "godlike" perspective, unrestricted by time or place, from which to see actions and look into the minds of characters. This allows the author to comment openly on characters and events in the work. The "third person" point of view presents the events of the story from outside of any single character's perception, much like the omniscient point of view, but the reader must understand the action as it takes place and without any special insight into characters' minds or motivations. The "first person" or "personal" point of view relates events as they are perceived by a single character. The main character "tells" the story and may offer opinions about the action and characters which differ from those of the author. Much less common than omniscient, third person, and first person is the "second person" point of view, wherein the author tells the story as if it is happening to the reader.

Polemic: A work in which the author takes a stand on a controversial subject, such as abortion or religion. Such works are often extremely argumentative or provocative.

Pornography: Writing intended to provoke feelings of lust in the reader. Such works are often condemned by critics and teachers, but those which can be shown to have literary value are viewed less harshly.

Post-Aesthetic Movement: An artistic response made by African Americans to the black aesthetic movement of the 1960s and early '70s. Writers since that time have adopted a somewhat different tone in their work, with less emphasis placed on the disparity between black and white in the United States. In the words of post-aesthetic authors such as Toni Morrison, John Edgar Wideman, and Kristin Hunter, African Americans are portrayed as looking inward for answers to their own questions, rather than always looking to the outside world.

Postmodernism: Writing from the 1960s forward characterized by experimentation and continuing to apply some of the fundamentals of modernism, which included existentialism and alienation. Postmodernists have gone a step further in the rejection of tradition begun with the modernists by also rejecting traditional forms, preferring the anti-novel over the novel and the anti-hero over the hero.

Primitivism: The belief that primitive peoples were nobler and less flawed than civilized peoples because they had not been subjected to the tainting influence of society.

Prologue: An introductory section of a literary work. It often contains information establishing the situation of the characters or presents information about the setting, time period, or action. In drama, the prologue is spoken by a chorus or by one of the principal characters.

Prose: A literary medium that attempts to mirror the language of everyday speech. It is distinguished from poetry by its use of unmetered, unrhymed language consisting of logically related sentences. Prose is usually grouped into paragraphs that form a cohesive whole such as an essay or a novel.

Prosopopoeia: See *Personification*

Protagonist: The central character of a story who serves as a focus for its themes and incidents and as the principal rationale for its development. The protagonist is sometimes referred to in discussions of modern literature as the hero or anti-hero.

Protest Fiction: Protest fiction has as its primary purpose the protesting of some social injustice, such as racism or discrimination.

Proverb: A brief, sage saying that expresses a truth about life in a striking manner.

Pseudonym: A name assumed by a writer, most often intended to prevent his or her identification as the author of a work. Two or more authors may work together under one pseudonym, or an author may use a different name for each genre he or she publishes in. Some publishing companies maintain "house pseudonyms," under which any number of authors may write installations in a series. Some authors also choose a pseudonym over their real names the way an actor may use a stage name.

Pun: A play on words that have similar sounds but different meanings.

R

Realism: A nineteenth-century European literary movement that sought to portray familiar characters, situations, and settings in a realistic manner. This was done primarily by using an objective narrative point of view and through the buildup of accurate detail. The standard for success of any realistic work depends on how faithfully it transfers common experience into fictional forms. The realistic method may be altered or extended, as in stream of consciousness writing, to record highly subjective experience.

Repartee: Conversation featuring snappy retorts and witticisms.

Resolution: The portion of a story following the climax, in which the conflict is resolved.

Rhetoric: In literary criticism, this term denotes the art of ethical persuasion. In its strictest sense, rhetoric adheres to various principles developed since classical times for arranging facts and ideas in a clear, persuasive, appealing manner. The term is also used to refer to effective prose in general and theories of or methods for composing effective prose.

Rhetorical Question: A question intended to provoke thought, but not an expressed answer, in the reader. It is most commonly used in oratory and other persuasive genres.

Rising Action: The part of a drama where the plot becomes increasingly complicated. Rising action leads up to the climax, or turning point, of a drama.

Roman à clef: A French phrase meaning "novel with a key." It refers to a narrative in which real persons are portrayed under fictitious names.

Romance: A broad term, usually denoting a narrative with exotic, exaggerated, often idealized characters, scenes, and themes.

Romanticism: This term has two widely accepted meanings. In historical criticism, it refers to a European intellectual and artistic movement of the late eighteenth and early nineteenth centuries that sought greater freedom of personal expression than that allowed by the strict rules of literary form and logic of the eighteenth-century neoclassicists. The Romantics preferred emotional and imaginative expression to rational analysis. They considered the individual to be at the center of all experience and so placed him or her at the center of their art. The Romantics believed that the creative imagination reveals nobler truths—unique feelings and attitudes—than those that could be discovered by logic or by scientific examination. Both the natural world and the state of childhood were important sources for revelations of "eternal truths." "Romanticism" is also used as a general term to refer to a type of sensibility found in all periods of literary history and usually considered to be in opposition to the principles of classicism. In this sense, Romanticism signifies any work or philosophy in which the exotic or dreamlike figure strongly, or that is devoted to individualistic expression, self-analysis, or a pursuit of a higher realm of knowledge than can be discovered by human reason.

Romantics: See *Romanticism*

S

Satire: A work that uses ridicule, humor, and wit to criticize and provoke change in human nature and institutions. There are two major types of satire: "formal" or "direct" satire speaks directly to the reader or to a character in the work; "indirect" satire relies upon the ridiculous behavior of its characters to make its point. Formal satire is further divided into two manners: the "Horatian," which ridicules gently, and the "Juvenalian," which derides its subjects harshly and bitterly.

Science Fiction: A type of narrative about or based upon real or imagined scientific theories and technology. Science fiction is often peopled with alien creatures and set on other planets or in different dimensions.

Second Person: See *Point of View*

Setting: The time, place, and culture in which the action of a narrative takes place. The elements of setting may include geographic location, characters' physical and mental environments, prevailing cultural attitudes, or the historical time in which the action takes place.

Simile: A comparison, usually using "like" or "as," of two essentially dissimilar things, as in "coffee as cold as ice" or "He sounded like a broken record."

Slang: A type of informal verbal communication that is generally unacceptable for formal writing. Slang words and phrases are often colorful exaggerations used to emphasize the speaker's point; they may also be shortened versions of an often-used word or phrase.

Slave Narrative: Autobiographical accounts of American slave life as told by escaped slaves. These works first appeared during the abolition movement of the 1830s through the 1850s.

Socialist Realism: The Socialist Realism school of literary theory was proposed by Maxim Gorky and established as a dogma by the first Soviet Congress of Writers. It demanded adherence to a communist worldview in works of literature. Its doctrines required an objective viewpoint comprehensible to the working classes and themes of social struggle featuring strong proletarian heroes.

Stereotype: A stereotype was originally the name for a duplication made during the printing process; this led to its modern definition as a person or thing that is (or is assumed to be) the same as all others of its type.

Stream of Consciousness: A narrative technique for rendering the inward experience of a character. This technique is designed to give the impression of an ever-changing series of thoughts, emotions, images, and memories in the spontaneous and seemingly illogical order that they occur in life.

Structure: The form taken by a piece of literature. The structure may be made obvious for ease of understanding, as in nonfiction works, or may obscured for artistic purposes, as in some poetry or seemingly "unstructured" prose.

Sturm und Drang: A German term meaning "storm and stress." It refers to a German literary movement of the 1770s and 1780s that reacted against the order and rationalism of the enlightenment, focusing instead on the intense experience of extraordinary individuals.

Style: A writer's distinctive manner of arranging words to suit his or her ideas and purpose in writing. The unique imprint of the author's personality upon his or her writing, style is the product of an author's way of arranging ideas and his or her use of diction, different sentence structures, rhythm, figures of speech, rhetorical principles, and other elements of composition.

Subjectivity: Writing that expresses the author's personal feelings about his subject, and which may or may not include factual information about the subject.

Subplot: A secondary story in a narrative. A subplot may serve as a motivating or complicating force for the main plot of the work, or it may provide emphasis for, or relief from, the main plot.

Surrealism: A term introduced to criticism by Guillaume Apollinaire and later adopted by Andre Breton. It refers to a French literary and artistic movement founded in the 1920s. The Surrealists sought to express unconscious thoughts and feelings in their works. The best-known technique used for achieving this aim was automatic writing— transcriptions of spontaneous outpourings from the unconscious. The Surrealists proposed to unify the contrary levels of conscious and unconscious, dream and reality, objectivity and subjectivity into a new level of "super-realism."

Suspense: A literary device in which the author maintains the audience's attention through the buildup of events, the outcome of which will soon be revealed.

Symbol: Something that suggests or stands for something else without losing its original identity. In literature, symbols combine their literal meaning with the suggestion of an abstract concept. Literary symbols are of two types: those that carry complex associations of meaning no matter what their contexts, and those that derive their suggestive meaning from their functions in specific literary works.

Symbolism: This term has two widely accepted meanings. In historical criticism, it denotes an early modernist literary movement initiated in France during the nineteenth century that reacted against the prevailing standards of realism. Writers in this movement aimed to evoke, indirectly and symbolically, an order of being beyond the material world of the five senses. Poetic expression of personal emotion figured strongly in the movement, typically by means of a private set of symbols uniquely identifiable with the individual poet. The principal aim of the Symbolists was to express in words the highly complex feelings that grew out of everyday contact with the world. In a broader sense, the term "symbolism" refers to the use of one object to represent another.

T

Tall Tale: A humorous tale told in a straightforward, credible tone but relating absolutely impossible events or feats of the characters. Such tales were commonly told of frontier adventures during the settlement of the west in the United States.

Theme: The main point of a work of literature. The term is used interchangeably with thesis.

Thesis: A thesis is both an essay and the point argued in the essay. Thesis novels and thesis plays share the quality of containing a thesis which is supported through the action of the story.

Third Person: See *Point of View*

Tone: The author's attitude toward his or her audience may be deduced from the tone of the work. A formal tone may create distance or convey politeness, while an informal tone may encourage a friendly, intimate, or intrusive feeling in the reader. The author's attitude toward his or her subject matter may also be deduced from the tone of the words he or she uses in discussing it.

Transcendentalism: An American philosophical and religious movement, based in New England from around 1835 until the Civil War. Transcendentalism was a form of American romanticism that had its roots abroad in the works of Thomas Carlyle, Samuel Coleridge, and Johann Wolfgang von Goethe. The Transcendentalists stressed the importance of intuition and subjective experience in communication with God. They rejected religious dogma and texts in favor of mysticism and scientific naturalism. They pursued truths that lie beyond the "colorless" realms perceived by reason and the senses and were active social reformers in public education, women's rights, and the abolition of slavery.

U

Urban Realism: A branch of realist writing that attempts to accurately reflect the often harsh facts of modern urban existence.

Utopia: A fictional perfect place, such as "paradise" or "heaven."

V

Verisimilitude: Literally, the appearance of truth. In literary criticism, the term refers to aspects of a work of literature that seem true to the reader.

Victorian: Refers broadly to the reign of Queen Victoria of England (1837-1901) and to anything with qualities typical of that era. For example, the qualities of smug narrow-mindedness, bourgeois materialism, faith in social progress, and priggish morality are often considered Victorian. This stereotype is contradicted by such dramatic intellectual developments as the theories of Charles Darwin, Karl Marx, and Sigmund Freud (which stirred strong debates in England) and the critical attitudes of serious Victorian writers like Charles Dickens and George Eliot. In literature, the Victorian Period was the great age of the English novel, and the latter part of the era saw the rise of movements such as decadence and symbolism.

W

Weltanschauung: A German term referring to a person's worldview or philosophy.

Weltschmerz: A German term meaning "world pain." It describes a sense of anguish about the nature of existence, usually associated with a melancholy, pessimistic attitude.

Z

Zeitgeist: A German term meaning "spirit of the time." It refers to the moral and intellectual trends of a given era.

Cumulative Author/Title Index

Cumulative Nationality/Ethnicity Index

Cumulative Nationality/Ethnicity Index

Guyanese

Braithwaite, E. R.
To Sir, With Love: V30

Haitian

Danticat, Edwidge
Breath, Eyes, Memory: V37
The Dew Breaker: V28

Hispanic American

Allende, Isabel
Daughter of Fortune: V18
Eva Luna: V29
The House of the Spirits: V6
Benitez, Sandra
A Place Where the Sea
Remembers: V32
Cisneros, Sandra
The House on Mango Street: V2
García, Cristina
Dreaming in Cuban: V38
Hijuelos, Oscar
The Mambo Kings Play Songs of
Love: V17

Hungarian

Koestler, Arthur
Darkness at Noon: V19
Orczy, Emmuska
The Scarlet Pimpernel: V31

Indian

Desai, Kiran
Hullabaloo in the Guava Orchard:
V28
Divakaruni, Chitra Banerjee
Sister of My Heart: V38
Markandaya, Kamala
Nectar in a Sieve: V13
Mukherjee, Bharati
Jasmine: V37
Naipaul, V. S.
A Bend in the River: V37
Half a Life: V39
Roy, Arundhati
The God of Small Things: V22
Rushdie, Salman
Midnight's Children: V23
The Satanic Verses: V22

Irish

Bowen, Elizabeth Dorothea Cole
The Death of the Heart: V13
Joyce, James
A Portrait of the Artist as a Young
Man: V7
Ulysses: V26
Murdoch, Iris
Under the Net: V18

Stoker, Bram
Dracula: V18
Wilde, Oscar
The Picture of Dorian Gray: V20

Italian

Eco, Umberto
The Name of the Rose: V22
Machiavelli, Niccolo
The Prince: V9

Japanese

Abe, Kobo
The Woman in the Dunes: V22
Ishiguro, Kazuo
Never Let Me Go: V35
The Remains of the Day: V13
The Remains of the Day (Motion
picture): V39
Mori, Kyoko
Shizuko's Daughter: V15
Watkins, Yoko Kawashima
So Far from the Bamboo Grove: V28
Yoshimoto, Banana
Kitchen: V7

Jewish

Asimov, Isaac
I, Robot: V29
Bellow, Saul
The Adventures of Augie March:
V33
Herzog: V14
Humboldt's Gift: V26
Seize the Day: V4
Foer, Jonathan Safran
Extremely Loud & Incredibly
Close: V36
Kafka, Franz
The Castle: V34
The Trial: V7
Kertész, Imre
Kaddish for a Child Not Born:
V23
Malamud, Bernard
The Assistant: V27
The Fixer: V9
The Natural: V4
The Natural (Motion picture):
V34
Potok, Chaim
The Chosen: V4
Davita's Harp: V34
Roth, Philip
American Pastoral: V25
Salinger, J. D.
The Catcher in the Rye: V1
Franny and Zooey: V30
Spiegelman, Art
Maus: A Survivor's Tale: V35

West, Nathanael
The Day of the Locust: V16
Wiesel, Eliezer
Night: V4
Yezierska, Anzia
Bread Givers: V29
Yolen, Jane
Briar Rose: V30

Korean

Choi, Sook Nyul
Year of Impossible Goodbyes: V29

Mexican

Esquivel, Laura
Like Water for Chocolate: V5
Fuentes, Carlos
The Old Gringo: V8

Native American

Alexie, Sherman
The Absolutely True Diary of a
Part-Time Indian: V38
The Lone Ranger and Tonto
Fistfight in Heaven: V17
Reservation Blues: V31
Dorris, Michael
A Yellow Raft in Blue Water: V3
Erdrich, Louise
The Beet Queen: V37
Love Medicine: V5
Momaday, N. Scott
House Made of Dawn: V10
Silko, Leslie Marmon
Ceremony: V4
Welch, James
Winter in the Blood: V23

New Zealander

Hulme, Keri
The Bone People: V24

Nigerian

Abani, Chris
GraceLand: V35
Achebe, Chinua
No Longer at Ease: V33
Things Fall Apart: V3
Emecheta, Buchi
The Bride Price: V12
The Wrestling Match: V14

Norwegian

Rölvaag, O. E.
Giants in the Earth: V5

Polish

Conrad, Joseph
Heart of Darkness: V2
Lord Jim: V16

Subject/Theme Index

Passion
  Half a Life: 106
  The Remains of the Day: 319
Pathos
  The Remains of the Day: 323
Patriarchy
  The Grapes of Wrath: 86
  Housekeeping: 152–153
Peace
  The Remains of the Day: 308
Persecution
  Number the Stars: 240
Pessimism
  Half a Life: 108
Point of view (Literature)
  The Cruel Sea: 51–52, 57
  The Moonstone: 218
  Number the Stars: 241
Politics
  The Grapes of Wrath: 62, 75
  Half a Life: 105, 107
  The Remains of the Day: 309, 323
Popular culture
  American Born Chinese: 6, 19
Postcolonialism
  Half a Life: 101, 105, 106
Postmodernism
  Half a Life: 98
  Olive Kitteridge: 266, 271
Postwar society
  Housekeeping: 147
  Montana 1948: 192–194
Poverty
  The Grapes of Wrath: 66, 70–72,
    78, 83
Power (Philosophy)
  Housekeeping: 158
  Montana 1948: 182, 187, 190, 192,
    197
  Oryx and Crake: 282
  The Remains of the Day: 308
Prejudice
  American Born Chinese: 3, 8, 15, 22
  Half a Life: 94, 100
  The Human Comedy: 169
  Montana 1948: 182, 185, 187–188,
    190–191, 195
Pride
  The Remains of the Day: 318
Privilege
  Montana 1948: 190
Prostitution
  Oryx and Crake: 280
Punishment
  Montana 1948: 200–201
  Oryx and Crake: 282

Q

Questing
  The Grapes of Wrath: 87
  Oryx and Crake: 276, 291, 293–295
  The Remains of the Day: 313

R

Race relations
  The Help: 130–131
  Montana 1948: 198–202
Racism
  American Born Chinese: 17–18,
    21, 22
  Half a Life: 100, 102–104
  The Help: 110, 112, 114, 116,
    120–124, 128, 131
  Montana 1948: 190–191, 195
Rationality
  The Moonstone: 224
Reality
  The Cruel Sea: 57
  Number the Stars: 241
  Olive Kitteridge: 266
Rebellion
  Housekeeping: 151
Regret
  The Help: 115
Rejection
  American Born Chinese: 2, 14, 15
Religion
  Housekeeping: 158
  The Moonstone: 223
Repression
  The Help: 110
  Montana 1948: 191, 195–198,
    200
  The Remains of the Day: 322
Resilience
  The Grapes of Wrath: 85
Resistance
  American Born Chinese: 21
  Number the Stars: 230, 241, 247,
    253–254
Resourcefulness
  Number the Stars: 249, 250
Respect
  The Remains of the Day: 307, 317
Responsibility
  The Remains of the Day: 313
Revenge
  The Help: 117, 131
  Oryx and Crake: 280, 282,
    285–286
Right and wrong
  Montana 1948: 187
Romantic love
  *Balzac and the Little Chinese
    Seamstress:* 25, 28, 29, 32
  Oryx and Crake: 276, 280, 281,
    287, 291, 292
  The Remains of the Day: 309,
    318
Romanticism
  The Grapes of Wrath: 86
Rural life
  *Balzac and the Little Chinese
    Seamstress:* 25, 29, 37, 38–39
  The Grapes of Wrath: 82

S

Sacrifice
  Half a Life: 94, 107, 108
  The Human Comedy: 167, 168
  Number the Stars: 237, 244, 245,
    247
Sadness
  The Human Comedy: 169
  Olive Kitteridge: 272
Salvation
  The Human Comedy: 175
  *Number the Stars:*Friendship 240
Satire
  Half a Life: 104
  Oryx and Crake: 276, 286,
    287–288, 290, 291, 293, 299
Science
  Oryx and Crake: 286–287, 290, 300
Science fiction
  Oryx and Crake: 275, 276–277
Seafaring
  The Cruel Sea: 45–48, 50
Secrecy
  Montana 1948: 191, 192, 195–198
  The Moonstone: 225
  Number the Stars: 235
Self consciousness
  The Remains of the Day: 317
Self deception
  The Remains of the Day: 324
Self destruction
  Half a Life: 95
Self doubt
  Half a Life: 92, 106
Self hatred
  American Born Chinese: 16, 19
  Half a Life: 105
Self identity
  American Born Chinese: 1, 4, 5,
    7–9, 13–15, 19, 21
  Half a Life: 106
  Montana 1948: 188–189
Self image
  The Help: 118
  Montana 1948: 188–189
Selfishness
  American Born Chinese: 8
  The Moonstone: 217
  Oryx and Crake: 283, 286
Selflessness
  American Born Chinese: 13
Sensation novels
  The Moonstone: 220–225
Sentimentality
  The Cruel Sea: 54
  The Human Comedy: 160
Separation (Psychology)
  Oryx and Crake: 296
Setting (Literature)
  The Grapes of Wrath: 73
  The Remains of the Day: 314

5/17/12